HENRY KAPLAN AND THE
STORY OF HODGKIN'S DISEASE

HENRY KAPLAN
and the STORY *of*
HODGKIN'S DISEASE

Charlotte DeCroes Jacobs

STANFORD GENERAL BOOKS

An Imprint of Stanford University Press
Stanford, California

This book has been published with the assistance of the
Drs. Ben and A. Jess Shenson Professorship.

Stanford University Press
Stanford, California

Library of Congress Cataloging-in-Publication Data

Jacobs, Charlotte DeCroes.
    Henry Kaplan and the story of Hodgkin's disease / Charlotte DeCroes Jacobs.
        p. cm.
    Includes bibliographical references and index.
    ISBN 978-0-8047-6866-5 (cloth : alk. paper)
    1. Kaplan, Henry S., 1918–1984. 2. Radiologists—United States—Biography.
3. Oncologists—United States—Biography. 4. Hodgkin's disease—
Radiotherapy—United States—History. 5. Cancer—Treatment—United
States—History. I. Title.
    R154.K235J33   2010
    362.196'994460092—dc22
    [B]

                                                              2009040649

Printed in the United States of America on acid-free, archival-quality paper.
Typeset at Stanford University Press in 10/13 Minion.

FOR EHUD

Contents

Acknowledgments   ix

Prologue   1

1   Morbid Appearances   11

2   Arrogant Ancestors   20

3   Diagnosing Hodgkin's Disease   23

4   Growing Up Brilliant   28

5   Roentgen's Rays   42

6   A Spartan Existence   49

7   The Courtship of Leah Lebeson   58

8   Headway with Hodgkin's Disease   66

9   The Fledgling Investigator   71

10 The Unlikely Aftermath of Mustard Gas   80

11 The Stanford Wooing   86

12 The Outsider   92

13 Vera Peters: Daring to Cure Hodgkin's Disease   103

14 The Cancer-Killing Cannon   111

15 Moving to the Farm   122

16 Saul Rosenberg: A Promising Young Oncologist   137

17 The L-1 Protocol: Christine Pendleton and
    Douglas Eads   145

18 The L-2 Protocol: Petra Ekstrand and   151
    Joey Radicchi

19 International Cooperation   159

20 A Famous Father   168

Contents

21	The Single-Minded Focus of Vince DeVita	179
22	A Walking Textbook of Radiation Morbidity	191
23	Living Autopsies	196
24	Protégés	205
25	Intellectual Playmates	211
26	Peace Now!	222
27	Mary Lasker's Moon Shot for Cancer	228
28	A Cancer-Causing Virus	238
29	The Ann Arbor Conference	248
30	Bookends	257
31	The Cancer Center Debacle	261
32	Deadly Complications	274
33	High-Dose DeVita	280
34	The S-5 Protocol: Chris Jenkins	284
35	Inconsolable	294
36	Without a Spleen	299
37	Kaplan's Moby Dick	308
38	The Elusive Human Tumor Virus	314
39	The Quiet Conviction	326
40	The Boy in the Bubble	347
41	The C-1 Protocol: Wendy Podwalny	354
42	The Quest for the Magic Bullet	364
43	The Death of a Difficult Woman	371
44	Felled	376
45	Dying Adagio	385
	Epilogue	397
	Source Notes	399
	Bibliography	421
	Index	431

Photographs follow pages 130 and 338.

Acknowledgments

How fortunate I have been to study writing for over a decade with a master—Ehud Havazelet. He taught me the craft of and instilled into me a passion for writing, which has enriched my life. It is to him that I dedicate this book.

I am grateful to the late Leah Kaplan, who agreed to a biography of her husband, but only if I would portray the man as he was, not a saint. She spent hours with me, relating his life with honesty and humor. She opened her home, her personal files, and her heart. Paul Kaplan recounted family stories with candor and the exquisite detail of an artist. Ann Kaplan Spears, Richard Kaplan, and the rest of the Kaplan family provided thoughtful reminiscences.

When I sought my first literary agent, I started at the top, writing to Robert Lescher. Mickey Choate, formerly at Lescher & Lescher, Ltd., initially embraced my work and brought it to Robert's attention. To my amazement and delight, Robert Lescher accepted my biography with an enthusiasm that has never waned. I will be forever grateful for his wisdom, confidence, and friendship.

The late Dr. Ben Shenson and Dr. A. Jess Shenson gave me one of the greatest gifts—that of academic freedom—when they endowed the Stanford University professorship I am privileged to hold. I appreciate how Ronald Levy, chief of Medical Oncology, never questioned the project's time or value. The Vermont Studio Center and the Virginia Center for the Creative Arts provided the solitude and creative atmosphere for writing. John Feneron, Norris Pope, and the publishing team at Stanford University Press guided the book to its completion. Peter Dreyer, the copy editor, smoothed the rough edges and taught me how to use the delete button.

My thanks to all those who spent hours sharing their memories of Henry Kaplan. Each story, each letter gave me insight into this multifaceted man. I am especially appreciative of Vincent DeVita, Saul Rosenberg, Norman Coleman, and the late Vera Peters, for whom many of these memories were bittersweet. Spyros Andreopoulos kindly gave me a copy of his interview with Kaplan just prior to his death. My thanks to Todd Wasserman, who interviewed Sir David

Smithers and provided photographs and encouragement. Several people read sections of the manuscript for accuracy: Jacob Haimson helped me understand the history and physics of linear accelerators, and Ron Levy examined the description of monoclonal antibodies. Margaret Wootton and my husband, Rod Young, read the entire manuscript from the lay perspective, making valuable suggestions.

I am grateful to the patients and families who welcomed me into their homes and their lives, especially Chris Jenkins and Tran Tuyet, Mary Murray Vidal, Wendy Podwalny, Douglas Eads, Christine Pendleton, and Annuziata Radicchi. And my eternal gratitude goes to the hundreds of patients with Hodgkin's disease who participated in clinical trials and who, through that courageous choice, are responsible for the high cure rate today.

Many friends sustained me through the years of research and writing, including Lucy Berman, Linda Ara, and Ellen King. Writers Mary Dilg, Ruth Roach Pierson, and Emilie and John Osborn lent their moral support. And I owe special thanks to Sarah Donaldson, whose exuberance has persisted at the highest level. Finally, I turn to my family. My love and gratitude goes to my sons, Ben and Adam Elkin, who remained supportive and patient through the years. And I am blessed with a caring, selfless husband, Rod, the proverbial wind beneath my wings.

HENRY KAPLAN AND THE STORY OF HODGKIN'S DISEASE

Prologue

HODGKIN'S DISEASE SURVIVORS GATHER AT STANFORD
TO CELEBRATE GOOD HEALTH

At 38, Doug Eads is the picture of health. He is Fremont's city clerk—an active, articulate man who loves to romp with his two young children, jog, ski the Sierras and race around on a racquetball court. If Eads had been born five years sooner, he wouldn't be around to enjoy all that. He'd be dead. In 1965, Eads noticed a small lump in his groin. A doctor told him it was Hodgkin's disease, a cancer of the lymphatic system that would kill him in three to five years. But at the Stanford University Medical Center . . . scientists were trying some new treatments involving irradiation and drugs. Eads became a patient in the Stanford clinical trials. . . . They worked, and Eads has been free of the disease for the last 17 years. Today he and 400 other Hodgkin's patients who were treated—and cured—in the trials at Stanford in the last 20 years will gather at the university to celebrate their health and the success of the program. The patients meet once more with Henry S. Kaplan and Saul Rosenberg, the two doctors who directed the bold treatment and research effort.
—*San Jose Mercury News*, May 8, 1982

The fountains in front of Stanford University Medical Center had just been switched on, and a family of ducks glided across the reflecting pool. Sunlight, filtering through the lattice trim, gave the hospital a lacy façade. Asparagus ferns dangled from hanging baskets; a medical student rode by on his bicycle. As Maureen O'Hara walked toward Fairchild Auditorium, she felt out of place in her silky dress and heels; it was the first time in years that she hadn't worn a nurse's uniform to the hospital. Her face looked freshly scrubbed, with soft freckles scattered across her cheeks. Her loose brown hair bounced as she walked. Maureen didn't know what to expect. When she had received an invitation to "Twenty Years of Research and Progress in the Treatment of Hodgkin's Disease," she had thought it would be wonderful to see some of her former patients. She hadn't anticipated the scene she was about to encounter.

Over four hundred people filled the auditorium—women straight from their hairdressers, men and children in their Sunday best. The atmosphere felt

1

festive. Spirited conversations were punctuated by noisy outbursts, resembling a high school reunion, a wedding, a graduation. Smiles and handshakes gave way to cheers and hugs. A woman in a cashmere sweater rushed forward and threw her arms around Maureen. It took a few seconds for Maureen to recognize her. Eight years earlier, she had lain in a hospital bed, her body limp from repeated vomiting, while Maureen held her hand. Now she hugged Maureen with great strength.

A lanky man with long blond hair and a familiar face approached Maureen—Chris Jenkins. "Maureen, this is my daughter, Melinh," he said. Maureen recalled the baby lying in a basket at Chris's bedside while he recovered from surgery. Melinh had just started to talk when her father contracted meningitis. The month he was hospitalized in an isolation unit, he could only look at his wife and daughter through a small window. All the ugliness of disease, however, had not erased Chris's smile. Maureen fumbled in her purse for a tissue.

Jan DiJulio, the charge nurse on the cancer ward, was searching for a familiar face. "The patients looked so different," she said, "no hospital gowns, and hair." A man in a checkered jacket approached Jan and introduced his wife and daughter. "I was treated in 1965," he said, "and I wouldn't be here if it weren't for Dr. Kaplan and Dr. Rosenberg." A woman lined up three teenagers in front of Jan. "Remember me?" she asked. "I'm Nancy from Fresno." Jan looked puzzled. "I had that lung mass," she said. "These are my children. It's wonderful that I can now make long-term plans with them." Jan rushed to call her husband. "You've got to come to this event," she said. "Something really exciting is happening here."

When Sarah Donaldson entered the auditorium, the reaction overwhelmed her. Trained by Henry Kaplan, Donaldson was now a Stanford professor, internationally known for her work on pediatric Hodgkin's disease. Behind her youthful ebullience was a shrewd, intelligent woman. Donaldson stood looking at the crowd and smiling so broadly her cheeks began to hurt. A teenager introduced himself. Sarah thought back to the distraught parents who had brought their four-year-old to her with the most advanced stage of Hodgkin's disease.

A new round of cheers arose when renowned radiation oncologists Eli Glatstein and Norman Coleman entered the auditorium. They had been two of Henry Kaplan's favorite trainees. What a pair they made: Eli, baby-faced and rotund, was known as "Mr. Wonderful." Norm, gangly with a mass of unruly black curls, a scraggly beard, and a large nose he made fun of himself, stood a head taller. A woman from Modesto with an Italian name he couldn't remember spoke to Eli. He was pleased to find her still alive; she had relapsed numerous times. A San Francisco psychiatrist smiled and shook his hand. Eli had no trouble remembering him. He had complained to Glatstein almost daily throughout treatment. "He didn't think I was so great then," Eli said.

Before the formal program began, the patients mixed with the social workers, nurses, and physicians. "There was such a high in that auditorium," Maureen recalled. "It was marvelous. People that you treated years ago were there—the survivors."

⌒

Stanford University's president, Donald Kennedy, approached the podium to open "Twenty Years of Progress in Research on Hodgkin's Disease," an event proposed by Saul Rosenberg and Henry Kaplan as a tribute to the patients who had taken part in their clinical trials. "Every cancer patient needs courage," Kennedy said. "Those who are willing to participate in previously untried treatments draw upon additional courage." Chris looked at his wife, Tuyet. Their life in Vietnam during the war had required enormous fortitude. They had had to dig deep into their reserve of willpower again when he developed Hodgkin's disease. "It is 1982," Kennedy said, "150 years since Thomas Hodgkin, an English physician, first recognized the disease . . . twenty years after the Kaplan-Rosenberg trials began." He spoke of their multidisciplinary approach—Kaplan the radiation oncologist and Rosenberg the medical oncologist bringing together a team of specialists from several fields to attack one disease—an unheard of concept at the time. "Above all," Kennedy said, "they have provided excellent care." A cannery worker from Gilroy clapped until his thick hands stung. Five years earlier he had come to Kaplan with an undiagnosed fever, wasted and unable to work. He didn't know how to express his thanks. So he just clapped harder.

President Kennedy adjusted his glasses. "I guess you all know Henry Kaplan." In the third row, Glatstein and Coleman chuckled; they still considered themselves "Kaplan boys." Christine Pendleton, a trim Palo Alto housewife, took a deep breath and looked at her husband, Red. Fifteen years ago, her physician had told him that she would be dead in two months. That was before she met Dr. Kaplan. A murmur rippled through the auditorium. "It was like a ground swell," Jan DiJulio said.

Henry Kaplan walked to the podium, and the audience fell silent. A large, balding man in his early sixties, over six feet tall, Kaplan wore a white coat and a bow tie. His stature imparted an air of confidence. "HSK had a commanding presence," Glatstein said. "When he entered the room, you sat up straighter." He had an overbite and rarely smiled, making him look austere. And his eyes were piercing, watchful; he didn't miss anything. The look that intimidated some associates seemed kind and warm to patients. Kaplan held the side of the lectern, the two giant fingers of his right hand in full view. He didn't hide the deformity that had tormented his mother.

Everyone knew the man behind the podium had developed the first medical linear accelerator, which delivered radiation with such accuracy and potency that it changed the outcome for cancer patients. Everyone knew of his innovative therapies for Hodgkin's disease and other lymphomas. What they didn't know about were his family struggles, his ill-fated love affair with Stanford University, the humanitarian efforts that had imperiled him. Most perceived only a few facets of the hundreds that constituted the mosaic of this enigmatic man, called a "saint" by some, a "malignant son of a bitch" by others.

Patients saw only the loving side of Dr. Kaplan. But several of his closest associates, his brother, and his own son couldn't reconcile the man who touched patients with such tenderness with the man who devastated them with his sharp words. Cancer researchers appreciated another aspect—the exhilaration he felt solving problems. A gifted scientist, Kaplan had discovered a virus that causes leukemia in mice and believed he was close to finding a cancer-causing virus in man. At the same time, he was developing monoclonal antibodies to treat cancer. Intoxicated by science, he loved his work. He called his laboratory his golf course; his wife, Leah, called it his mistress.

Although seemingly self-sufficient, Kaplan had the capacity for intense friendships. Intimate with him were a handful of brilliant, creative men. They traveled together, corresponded regularly, shared art, music, witticisms—and vulnerabilities.

As an associate, Kaplan could be the most collegial of collaborators or the most formidable opponent. Some wondered how he could be a gracious host, welcoming them into his home, charming them with clever conversation, yet be abrupt, even caustic in debate. Although he stimulated trainees and young faculty, encouraging them to explore their own ideas, he had high expectations and no use for those he viewed as inept. Perfection and loyalty—he expected them, demanded them. He bruised colleagues with his intolerance, but he bore the scars of betrayal. Love, hate, devotion, jealousy: Kaplan generated the extremes of emotions. Much of his success resulted from his remarkable self-confidence, bordering on a sense of his own infallibility. Rarely diplomatic, he seemed dictatorial to many. And he had the annoying habit of having the last word.

At the core of Henry Kaplan's being lay a passion—a passion to cure cancer. That drive dominated his life and his relationships. It pushed him to persist despite failures. It helped him weather the storm of criticisms that followed in the wake of almost every one of his innovations. His passion had extracted a high price, however, leaving several casualties along the way. Seemingly oblivious to his devastating impact on others, he kept his eyes on the enemy, and the enemy was cancer. He called it his "Moby Dick," and Hodgkin's disease was one malignancy he had set out to annihilate.

Now Kaplan planned to unfold the story of this cancer. Before he could speak, however, the entire audience rose to a standing ovation. Somewhat embarrassed—after all, this was supposed to be a tribute to the patients—Kaplan raised his hand to quiet them. This only heightened the response. He glanced over at Saul Rosenberg and nodded, his only acknowledgement that this idea of Rosenberg's had been a good one. "For all their supposed difficulties," Coleman said, "I detected a tremendous affection between the two that day." The year before, Rosenberg had reminded Kaplan that 1982 marked the twentieth anniversary of their work together at Stanford. He proposed a program that would demonstrate to the public what cure of this cancer meant in terms of individuals and their families. Kaplan liked the idea of celebrating the courage of patients who had participated in a treatment for which the outcome was unknown. This time they had agreed.

Kaplan cleared his throat and began. When he had entered the field of radiation therapy in the early 1950s, he said, just one patient in twenty with Hodgkin's disease survived. Treatment planning was haphazard, radiotherapy equipment rudimentary. They needed a way to generate high voltage to kill cancers more effectively while minimizing damage to normal tissues. When he began to hear cocktail party talk of a new atom smasher being built by Edward Ginzton on the Stanford campus, he invited him to lunch. Their subsequent collaboration led to development of the first medical linear accelerator in the Western Hemisphere. They had never anticipated that their first patient would be a seven-month-old with bilateral retinoblastomas, cancers that were treated by surgical removal of both eyes. Instead, Kaplan had irradiated him using the new linear accelerator, and now that baby had become a man who could appreciate the beauty of a sunny day such as this one.

Armed with a more powerful means of delivering radiation, the Stanford group began its trials for patients with Hodgkin's disease. All they knew at the time was that the illness involved lymph nodes in the neck and chest and later spread to lymph tissue in the spleen, liver, and bone marrow. They didn't know its cause, but they did know it had a predilection for young adults and eventually killed most patients. Although they could arrest disease in the neck or chest with irradiation, it recurred in the abdomen in a significant number of patients. In order to design curative therapies, they needed to determine how the disease spread.

Kaplan and Rosenberg set out to find the answer, performing a series of tests in newly diagnosed patients to detect all sites of disease—a process called "staging." They began to subject patients to a surgical procedure—staging laparotomy—in which the surgeon sampled intra-abdominal nodes, biopsied the liver, and removed the spleen. Cancer specialists criticized the Stanford team for this; one publicly denounced them for performing "living autopsies." Nevertheless, they frequently demonstrated unsuspected disease in the abdomen, which had to be detected if patients were to be cured. They had been able to make these crucial observations because hundreds of patients had agreed to undergo staging laparotomy. "Without the patients," Kaplan said, "we could not have made the advances."

In the early 1960s, most specialists treated Hodgkin's disease with low doses of radiation to small fields. "Radiotherapists had an almost superstitious fear of treating people [both] above and below the diaphragm with large doses of radiation," Kaplan said. But he knew that was the only way to cure patients with widespread disease. The Stanford team had withstood censure when they implemented total lymphoid irradiation—delivery of radiation to all lymph node groups in the body. A prominent radiotherapist accused them of "burning bodies." But they persisted. "Today" he said, "about 40 percent of patients treated twenty years ago with so-called 'radical, high-dose radiation' are still alive." Kaplan ended his talk by saying, "Many of the most productive insights came from observations of particular patients. They taught us new lessons, which gave us the new ideas."

Then he introduced the next speaker, Vincent T. DeVita, director of the National Cancer Institute. This handsome middle-aged man with thick, dark hair in a pinstriped suit and tailored white shirt set the national agenda for cancer research. Polished and congenial, he showed no trace of the duck-tailed gang member who had grown up in the Bronx. Although he was seventeen years junior to Kaplan, they had a longtime friendship, rooted in mutual admiration, shared confidences, and a commitment to eradicating cancer.

DeVita regularly informed the public of progress in cancer research, but this event—the gathering of cured cancer patients—was unique, even to him. Moved by the idea of such a celebration, he compared it to a reunion of veterans—"survivors of trench warfare, coming together to bring each other up to date, [to] compare notes on our common enemy." Research physicians, too, he went on to say, had participated in "trench warfare," for the early experimental trials had been a perpetual battle. Since most physicians considered Hodgkin's disease fatal, "it was as if doing something other than comforting the patient during his or her final illness were an act of deliberate cruelty," DeVita said. He reflected upon the struggle to defy the prevailing norm. One need only look at Henry Kaplan—the deep creases in his forehead—to know that to be true. In ending, DeVita said, "We have recognized the courage and commitment of the patient's family and friends as a limitless trust fund of the human spirit. You have faced the tempest with fortitude."

Next Kaplan introduced Saul Rosenberg, his colleague of twenty years. In his praise, one couldn't detect the years of conflict between the two, an initial admiration that had evolved into intermittent open hostility, followed by an uneasy truce. Rosenberg was nine years younger than Kaplan, shorter and of a slighter build, with soft, smooth hands, and immaculately dressed. Having struggled for his white coat, rebuffed at every step, he projected an image of self-confidence and humility.

The audience again rose to applaud. Many patients, especially those who had received chemotherapy, considered Rosenberg their savior. "He was different from any physician I'd ever met," Dan Shapiro recalled. "The first time we met, he strode into the room and immediately came to where I was sitting and put his hand on my shoulder. His hand felt large and heavy for such a small man." After examining him, Rosenberg said: "I don't think I can cure you, but I'm going to try."

Now Rosenberg lowered his chin, looked over the top of his reading glasses at hundreds of such patients, and shook his head. He was pleased. "Twenty years ago," he began, "the field of chemotherapy and medical oncology didn't exist at Stanford and in most places in the world." As a case in point, his own oncology division had grown from one faculty member in 1965 to almost seventy people. Progress in treating Hodgkin's disease had been a team effort. Rosenberg's first slide listed those responsible for the work at Stanford. When Jan DiJulio's name appeared, her husband squeezed her hand.

Reviewing the treatment of Hodgkin's disease with chemotherapy, Rosenberg called DeVita's development of MOPP a landmark. This four-drug combination had cured half of the patients with advanced disease. But it required endurance: severe vomiting, constipation, numbness, infection, and sterility accompanied MOPP. And with the high cure rate emerged an unexpected toxicity—acute leukemia. Rosenberg went on to explain how he had designed an alternative chemotherapy regimen to lessen the acute side effects, and, later, another combination to eliminate unacceptable long-term complications, in particular sterility and second malignancies. He didn't tell the audience how DeVita had publicly censured those regimens, calling them "awful." The incident had almost destroyed DeVita's friendship with Kaplan. Rosenberg predicted that future therapy would have even fewer adverse effects. "It's a measure of our success that in a disease that was once invariably fatal," he said, "we now have the luxury of looking into the quality of life."

As Rosenberg returned to his seat, he gently touched the shoulder of Mary Murray-Vidal, one of two patients asked to speak that day. A thirty-five-year-old art historian, Mary had survived against all odds. The audience watched this elegant, fragile-appearing woman move to the podium. She seemed unblemished with her upturned nose and silken hair, but at a closer look, one could see her one visible scar—a blue dot on her upper chest—the tattoo from her radiation port.

"I am happy and very fortunate," she said, "to be able to join in this celebration of a medical victory and . . . of life." Fourteen years earlier, Mary had been diagnosed with Hodgkin's disease. "At twenty-one, I was barely past being a girl," she recalled, "just becoming a woman with a future to plan, and yet any future for me was suddenly and seriously in question." While in college, she had developed severe fatigue, night sweats, and a lump in her armpit. Her physician thought she had mononucleosis, but when she hadn't improved after two months, he ordered a biopsy. Hodgkin's disease, she was told. "His words did not shock me," Mary recalled. "I had never heard of this disease of the lymph system. Perhaps out of kindness or caution the doctor did not tell me that it was cancer or that it was fatal."

Mary had no health insurance, and Stanford's lymphoma team offered to take over her care. "From the very beginning," she said, "I felt confidence in my treatment and in my doctors. . . . I never felt I was a guinea pig, but rather someone very special." Eli Glatstein smiled; he had been one of her doctors. Tests completed, she was determined to have stage IIIB disease, involving lymph nodes in the neck, chest, and abdomen, and was assigned to an experimental program of irradiation and chemotherapy. "I don't recall at this point having a constant or overwhelming feeling that I was facing death," she said. She stopped; something caught in her throat. "What I feared most, as a young woman," she continued, "was the threat to my ability to bear children." Chris Jenkins put his arm around Melinh. Fortunately, she had been conceived before treatment left him sterile.

After starting radiotherapy, Mary began to feel better almost immediately. Two months later, she began MOPP. "My first chemotherapy treatment was overwhelming," she recalled. "With the injections came tremendous nausea. . . . The chemotherapy made me very weak and at one point caused serious intestinal problems. These were the months when I truly felt I was struggling against the disease, and this was when I learned the meaning of willpower." The man in the checkered jacket nodded; he remembered that ordeal. Mary completed the therapy only to find the next few years almost more difficult, at least psychologically, because of the ever-present fear of a recurrence. One day, however, she reached the five-year mark. "Then I truly felt cured," she said. Sarah Donaldson had to blink fast to keep tears from welling up in her eyes. Several patients wept. She was telling their story. A hush enveloped the auditorium for a moment, followed by a surge of applause. When it died down, Kaplan introduced a second patient, Douglas Eads.

This slight man with a brush mustache and tinted glasses appeared uncomfortable as he adjusted the microphone. He started with an apology. "I'm not sure I really earned my stripes," he said. Also a college student when diagnosed, Eads had been told he would die. Then he came to Stanford. The team performed a staging laparotomy and found disease confined to the groin and pelvic lymph nodes—early stage. A short course of radiation cured him, although he never quite believed it until five years had passed. "I'm willing to bet," Eads said, "that there are among us today a fair number who, when they learned they had Hodgkin's disease . . . promised to themselves or to the Almighty that if they were spared, they would dedicate themselves to a life of unselfish service to their fellow man." The man in the checkered jacket whispered to his wife—it was true. "I'm equally sure," Eads continued, "that . . . those promises were plea-bargained down to something like a promise to be kind to animals. But I think we can be forgiven; after all, we are mere imperfect mortals . . . all, that is, except Drs. Kaplan and Rosenberg. As we all know, they are saints." Rosenberg lowered his head; Kaplan shifted in his seat. They did not look at each other. With enthusiastic applause, the formal program came to an end.

⌒

Attendees gathered in Grant Courtyard for a champagne reception. A string quartet played Vivaldi, and although hors d'oeuvres were served, most people were too excited to eat. "That reception was the most moving, unforgettable part of the affair," Rosenberg said. "It was a time for patients, nurses, and physicians to embrace and take pictures. People came up to me with children, people who were teenagers themselves when treated." Maureen watched Kaplan move among the crowd, touching patients, patting them. "It was like he had all the time in the world for every single person," she said.

A small party gathered around Kaplan's wife, Leah. A tall, striking woman in her early sixties, she had thick auburn hair, full red lips, and a spirited laugh. "I'm a survivor of ten years," a patient said, shaking her hand. "I'm a survivor of fifteen years," another told her. "They treated me like royalty," Leah said.

One young woman Sarah Donaldson had treated showed her a snapshot of her twin sons. She had given them special middle names—Henry and Saul. A young nurse stood with Maureen while three former patients talked about their careers and children. When they parted, Maureen asked the nurse, "Do you know what those three people have in common?" She watched them mingle, laughing, drinking champagne. "They were all in the intensive care unit on respirators," Maureen said.

In the late afternoon, as shadows crossed the courtyard, a few lingering people exchanged addresses and quietly drifted away. As Kaplan stared at the departing figures, the delight faded from his expression. "Twenty-five years ago we knew that there was nothing we could do," he told a reporter. "We could accept that. Today it is much harder on me emotionally to realize that there are patients we can't help. Perhaps that's the reason we make progress. We have not felt satisfied; we feel an obligation to push forward." So, as these cured patients returned to their homes and their lives, he mourned for those who were not with them. "It never left him completely," Leah said, "that you didn't win them all."

A great deal had been said that day about courage and success, about Henry Kaplan and Saul Rosenberg, about Hodgkin's disease, about the patients; nothing had been said about failure, enmity, and despair. But there was much more to this story, which spanned several continents and decades. These powerful men were only two among a large cast of players whose drama culminated that day in 1982.

The story began in an English village in 1798.

1   Morbid Appearances

Thomas Hodgkin was born on August 17, 1798, in Pentonville, just north of London. He was the first child of Elizabeth and John Hodgkin to survive infancy. John, a scholar and renowned master of calligraphy, made his living tutoring ladies from wealthy families. Elizabeth ran a strict Quaker household. The Society of Friends had a strong sense of community, strengthened by the public ridicule they suffered, such as being called "Quakers," because of the belief that members of the sect worked themselves into such a frenzy that they quaked. They lived by a rigid set of principles, "The Rules of Discipline," which included humble speech, plain dress, refusal to bear arms, and rejection of worldly pleasures. These Quaker beliefs, engrained in Thomas Hodgkin, along with the restrictions of the English middle class, shaped his future.

As a youth, Thomas was described as "sweetly docile" by some relatives and as "extremely volatile" by others. All agreed that he had an inquisitive mind. An avid student, he became fluent in five languages and excelled in the sciences. Young Thomas observed the Quaker dress code. In early nineteenth-century England, when fashionable young men donned velvet waistcoats, lacy shirts, and stovepipe hats, Thomas wore a black suit without a lapel and a flat, round hat with a wide brim. This Quaker attire, designed to be inconspicuous, had the opposite effect; outside the Society, he appeared peculiar. His clothing accentuated his pale face, thick eyebrows, deep-set eyes, and dour expression. In talking, he customarily used "thou" and "thine." His Quaker teachers had instilled rigorous standards of thought into him and sharpened his keen sense of observation, both of which contributed to his later achievements in medicine. They also fostered intolerance for imperfection and a righteous temperament.

When time came to select a career, Thomas favored medicine. But Quakers were prohibited from attending English universities. Besides, most physicians came from the upper class and had degrees from Cambridge or Oxford, which meant restriction to members of the Church of England. As an alternative, Thomas could become an apothecary. Tradesmen, mostly from the middle class, apothecaries were licensed to prescribe medicine following an apprenticeship and hospital experience. In his late teens, Thomas became apprenticed to John Glaisyer, a distinguished member of the Society of Friends. After working twelve-hour days in the apothecary's shop, Thomas read until the early morning hours. On his day of rest, he explored the countryside, often accompanied by his cousin, Sarah Godlee, a bright and amiable young woman. They traded books on botany and studied the geography of the local area. His family became alarmed at this budding romance, because the Society forbade marriage between first cousins.

In 1819, Hodgkin began his clinical experience on the wards of Guy's Hospital in London. At the time he enrolled as a twelve-month pupil, the ports of Great Britain were being guarded against entry of the plague. Outbreaks of scarlet fever and diphtheria decimated neighborhoods; four out of every ten children died before age five. Apothecaries treated syphilis with mercury and considered a theriac, a mixture of up to sixty ingredients, the remedy for most ailments. Surgeons performed operations without anesthesia, using nerve clamps and alcohol to dull pain. Unaware of the association between bacteria and infection, they operated in open amphitheaters while students in their street clothes gathered around to watch. Patients commonly died of postoperative infections. "At the beginning of the nineteenth century," one historian wrote, "medical knowledge consisted of nurses' gossip, sick men's fancies, and the crude compilations of a blundering empiricism." This was the medical environment in which Thomas Hodgkin, intolerant of the imperfect, began his medical studies.

Guy's Hospital was considered one of the finest medical establishments in England. "Guy's alone of all the schools in London," said an account of the times, "conducted organized teaching of Medicine and of the sciences on which it rests, and it was at Guy's that the scientific interests of the time were congregated." Much of this reputation was attributable to two men: its star surgeon, Sir Astley Cooper, and its treasurer, Benjamin Harrison, who assured the hospital's prosperity. "King Harrison," as he was called, ruled over Guy's for fifty years; no one dared contradict his decisions.

Hodgkin attended lectures for five hours daily. He soon discovered that empiricism and ignorance underlay most clinical practice, and the cause of death remained unknown in many cases. Only two or three autopsies were performed monthly at Guy's. Hodgkin thought that physicians would have to learn to discern the cause of disease before they could hope to design effective therapies. He became dissatisfied with his career choice; apothecaries could dispense drugs but not examine patients or participate in medical discovery. To change the status quo, Hodgkin needed to be a physician, but for a middle-class

Englishman, this required a circuitous route. He had to leave England to earn an MD degree and, on return, pass a test administered by the Royal College of Physicians to obtain licensure. Even then, he didn't know how or if the medical profession would receive a Quaker.

Hodgkin enrolled at the University of Edinburgh, the foremost medical school in Great Britain. Given his academic inclinations, his professors encouraged him to spend time in Paris, where research was beginning to revolutionize the practice of medicine. There he studied at the Hôpital Necker in Paris with an eminent physician, René Laennec, who impressed upon Thomas his conviction that to unravel the mystery of disease, one must correlate physical examination with pathologic findings. At the bedside, Laennec used a novel instrument, the stethoscope, which consisted of an earpiece connected by a nine-inch wooden tube to a flat disc. When he held the disc on a patient's chest, Hodgkin could distinguish breath sounds of different maladies and hear heart murmurs clearly for the first time. He promptly wrote a paper for the Physical Society of Guy's Hospital introducing the stethoscope into England, but the medical community discounted the observations of the young Quaker student.

In 1823, Hodgkin received his MD degree from Edinburgh University and was commended on his thesis, *De absorbendi functione,* written in perfect Latin, which contained unique observations on the function of blood and lymph. With a stethoscope in his bag and a passion to understand disease in his soul, he then returned home. He easily passed his oral examination to qualify as a licentiate of the Royal College of Physicians. To pursue an academic career, however, he needed to secure a staff position at one of the teaching hospitals. Coveted for their prestige and financial reward, such posts were limited in number. "In the 1820's," one historian wrote, "appointments to hospitals were obtainable only by family or money influence." Having neither, Hodgkin feared that he might have to abandon his aspirations and establish a medical practice. But in 1825, dissension at Guy's Hospital proved advantageous.

Guy's and the adjacent St. Thomas's Hospital had been united for teaching purposes for forty-five years. When Guy's chief surgeon, Sir Astley Cooper, retired, he chose as his successor his nephew, Bransbury Cooper. St. Thomas's staff found the latter unacceptable, however, and a quarrel followed, resulting in dissolution of their association. The Museum of Pathology remained at St. Thomas's, so Guy's needed to establish its own. Hodgkin applied for the new post—inspector of the dead and curator of the Museum. Known to be a brilliant, recent graduate of Edinburgh University, he was offered the position.

Hodgkin found his early years at Guy's Hospital stimulating. Young researchers were beginning to approach disease in a scientific manner, challenging popular doctrines such as the pythogenic theory, which postulated an atmospheric source of fever, and accepted practices such as bloodletting. Hodgkin joined a notable group committed to the study of clinical medicine through postmortem examinations. "With the arrival upon the scene of that great triumvirate, Richard Bright, Thomas Addison, and Thomas Hodgkin," an account of the times said, "we seem to emerge from the remote past to the present." Addison was a talented researcher who first described adrenal insufficiency and pernicious anemia. Richard Bright, later known as the "father of nephrology," made significant contributions to the understanding of kidney diseases. Both felt hampered in their research by the difficulty of obtaining autopsies. "To connect accurate and faithful observation after death with symptoms displayed during life," Bright said, "must . . . forward the objects of our noble art."

In their new curator, they found the solution to their dilemma. Thomas Hodgkin undertook his job with zeal, and in four years, he assembled one of the best collections of pathologic material in England. He arranged 1,677 specimens with clinical histories to demonstrate the effects of specific diseases on different organs. He published papers on the classification of malignancies, as well as some of the earliest descriptions of appendicitis and aortic insufficiency (an abnormality of a major heart valve). He encouraged physicians to use the stethoscope and the laryngoscope, a novel instrument that allowed examination of the throat and vocal cords. He co-authored a paper with Joseph Lister on a new microscope that provided greater magnification and better detail than any to date. And he taught one of the first courses in anatomic pathology. Had he been content building his museum and investigating disease, he probably would have been rewarded with promotions and honors. But he was not.

Thomas Hodgkin had a strong reformist inclination. "I quickly perceived," he said, "that to cure or alleviate actual sickness was not all that was necessary . . . I saw that there were many causes constantly operating to disturb, ruin, and destroy [health]." To improve public health, he gave a series of community lectures on disease prevention. His superiors considered educating the masses unbefitting for an esteemed member of Guy's medical staff. In addition, Hodgkin disparaged contemporary medical education. He thought it absurd that after only six months of lectures at a medical school, physicians could begin to practice. He raised his voice for reform. Medical education was the province of senior physicians, however, and senior Guy's staff viewed him as a self-righteous agitator.

Meanwhile, Hodgkin continued to enjoy the company of his cousin, Sarah Godlee, against his parents' wishes. He hoped to persuade the Society of Friends to change its rule forbidding first-cousin marriages. But Sarah moved to Edinburgh to assist a distant relative, eighteen years her senior, who had recently been widowed, with two small children. A giving, selfless woman, Sarah eventually married him. Thomas, in his grief, turned to his work.

On September 24, 1828, Richard Bright asked Hodgkin to conduct an autopsy on a ten-year-old boy named Ellenborough King, who had been admitted to Bright's care a month earlier. The child had been in good health when he suddenly developed enlargement of his glands and spleen. By the time he was brought to Guy's, the glands in his neck had become massive in size, and his abdomen was distended with fluid. A sizable ulcer on the abdominal wall marked multiple attempts to drain the fluid. Perplexed by this constellation of physical findings, Bright had not been able to save the boy. Now he was asking Hodgkin to elucidate the underlying cause of his death.

When Hodgkin opened the chest, he found inflammation in the lungs and large lymph glands, which he described as "equalling in size a pigeon's egg," surrounding the bronchial tubes. As he cut into the abdomen, a thick, purulent material spilled onto the table. The abdominal lymph glands were similarly enlarged, hard in consistency, and streaked with black material. The spleen was four times its usual size and covered with dark spots. The case reminded Hodgkin of a nine-year-old boy on whom he had carried out an autopsy two years earlier. That boy, too, had had enlarged lymph nodes and a spleen of unusual character. Here again were the same curious findings.

Fifteen months later, Thomas Addison asked Hodgkin to perform an autopsy on Thomas Westcott, a fifty-year-old carpenter who had recently died on the clinical ward. The patient had been transferred to Addison in a wasted state, blind in his left eye, confused, with enlarged lymph glands and a swollen abdomen. Before Addison could examine him, the patient was found dead in bed. At postmortem, Hodgkin recorded a "rose-red lump" in the right side of the brain, occupying a space about the size of a "crown piece." Throughout the body he found enlarged lymph glands, which he described as having the texture of a "testicle." The spleen had "an infinite number of small, white, nearly opaque spots which were seen pervading its substance."

Then, six months later, Hodgkin conducted an autopsy on Thomas Black, a fifty-year-old who had been admitted to Guy's with intermittent fevers and a swelling on the side of his neck. He, too, died before a diagnosis could be made. Hodgkin recorded numerous tumors in his chest and abdomen, varying in size "from that of a horse-bean to that of a hen's egg," which he noted to be of "semi-cartilaginous hardness." He realized he was observing a disease not previously described and informed his colleagues: "All these cases agree in the remarkable enlargement of the absorbant glands [which] appears to be a primitive affection of these bodies." At a time when the public regarded autopsies with suspicion, when politics and superstition dictated medical science, Thomas Hodgkin had detected a new disease.

On January 10, 1832, his paper, "On Some Morbid Appearances of the Absorbant Glands and Spleen," was submitted to the Medical and Chirurgical Society (which later became the Royal Society of Medicine). Inasmuch as he was not a member of the society himself, Hodgkin was prohibited from presenting his work in person. Instead, the society secretary read his manuscript. "The morbid alterations of structure which I am about to describe," the paper began, "are probably familiar to many practical morbid anatomists." His own six cases and others sent to him had similar pathologic findings: massive, firm lymph glands, unusual in their uniformity and absence of inflammation, and an enlarged spleen, "thickly pervaded with defined bodies of various sizes, in structure resembling that of the diseased glands." These abnormalities of lymph nodes and spleen had not previously been noted. Hodgkin thought they suggested a malignancy. "A pathological paper may perhaps be thought of little value," he went on to say, "if unaccompanied by suggestions designed to assist in the treatment, either curative or palliative. On this head, however, I must confess that I have nothing to offer." He did not advocate dosing with a theriac or bloodletting. Hodgkin didn't know the source of this malady, nor could he recommend therapy, but he had taken the first key step—recognition of a new disease and careful description of its presentation and progression.

Members of the Medical and Chirurgical Society received Hodgkin's presentation with indifference, and his manuscript lay forgotten in the volumes of *Medico-Chirurgical Transactions*. Unaware of the significance of the disease he had described, Hodgkin did not even give this "affection," later known as Hodgkin's disease, a name. He never knew how much his observations would aid mankind or that they would secure his place in medical history.

⌐

Had Thomas Hodgkin focused his energy on research and teaching, he likely would have contributed even more to medical science. But with his Quaker upbringing, he felt compelled to bring about social reform. He spoke out against the medical establishment and its methods of selecting and remunerating physicians for attending the poor. Accusing many medical officers of negligence, he proposed that the post of medical officer be awarded through competitive examinations. An active member of the Anti-Slavery Society, he published several pamphlets such as *On Negro Emancipation and American Colonization*. He worked to relocate freed slaves to West Africa. He welcomed them into his home and rode with them in his open carriage through the streets of London, to the dismay of fellow lecturers at Guy's.

But of all Hodgkin's causes, the one that proved his downfall was his allegation of mistreatment of Native Americans, which brought him into direct conflict with King Harrison. A founder of the Aborigines' Protection Society, Hodgkin denounced methods employed to "civilize" Indians, and he reported to the House of Commons regarding abuse in the British colonies. In doing so, he revealed egregious practices by the Hudson Bay Company, including use of alcohol to domesticate Canadian Indians. Harrison served as a member of the Committee of the Hudson Bay Company. Hodgkin wrote to apprise him of the problems, stating that he knew Harrison would be concerned, since he had devoted his life to an institution whose sole purpose was the relief of suffering. He went so far as to suggest changes in company policy that would improve the Indians' situation.

Hodgkin developed a friendship with Chief Hesh-ton-a-quet, a Chippewa chief who had been invited to England with his wife and four other Indians, presumably as guests of the king of England. Upon arriving, their sponsor had put them on public display. Three died, and the chief was accused of child molestation. Hodgkin provided his bail, and in a highly publicized trial, the chief was acquitted. Following this, Hodgkin drove into the hospital square with an Indian many thought to be Chief Hesh-ton-a-quet in full costume beside him. He stopped in front of King Harrison's quarters. So angered was Harrison, the events that followed should not have been surprising.

In 1837, upon the death of a Guy's staff physician, the post of assistant physician became available. Such a position would allow Hodgkin to do more than teach and conduct autopsies; he would be able to admit patients to the hospital and help determine Guy's policies. Hodgkin felt confident that Harrison would grant him the post; after all, he had served as curator of the Museum and lecturer at Guy's Medical School for twelve years. Instead, Harrison appointed a clinician whose father had been on the staff at Guy's. Despite an outcry from students and staff physicians, King Harrison prevailed.

The *Lancet*, which Hodgkin had helped to convict in a slander suit, recognized the injustice, writing:

> To those who are acquainted with the management of affairs at Guy's Hospital . . . little surprise will be created by the . . . displacement of Dr. Hodgkin. Many years of severe duty at Guy's, as curator of the Museum, as lecturer on pathology, as demonstrator of anatomy with the most profuse adulation . . . would seem to present strong claims in favor of Dr. Hodgkin, but King Harrison thinks otherwise. It seems that Dr. Hodgkin is a Dissenter—that he is supposed, under the rose, to be liberal in politics.

With bitterness, Hodgkin resigned from Guy's Hospital at the age of thirty-nine leaving behind him one of the greatest collections of pathologic material in England. Years later, Guy's *Hospital Gazette* observed, "This resignation was an immense disaster to the cause of scientific medicine."

The year following his resignation, Hodgkin suffered from an attack of epilepsy, recurrent headaches, and depression. Sarah Godlee Rickman, now a widow with two children, returned from Edinburgh and nursed him back to health. Thomas, still very much in love with his cousin, petitioned the Society of Friends for permission to marry her. He published a pamphlet entitled *On the Rule of the Society of Friends Which Forbids the Marriage of First Cousins*, which emphasized the lack of scientific data to support this restriction. He pointed out that the Scripture did not sanction the elders' authority in this matter. In desperation, he revealed a number of such intermarriages within the society. Still the elders denied his request. He threatened to withdraw from the society, but, in the end, Hodgkin remained devoted to his faith, and he and Sarah parted forever.

His academic career over, Hodgkin opened a small medical practice. He could not, however, equate medicine and business and regarded collection of fees as distasteful. A failure in his academic career, in his attempts to marry Sarah, and in medical practice, he focused on his humanitarian efforts. But he was lonely. He wrote to his brother John that he was resigned to a life of celibacy, calling his situation "pitiful." Then at the age of fifty-one, Thomas suddenly announced plans to marry Sarah Frances Scaife, a large, simple woman, former wife of a tradesman. Friends described them as a devoted, loving couple.

Hodgkin's dedication to the relief of human suffering still burned brightly, and in his zeal to aid the oppressed, he found a kindred spirit in Sir Moses Montefiore. They had met when Hodgkin attended his brother, who was suffering from tuberculosis. Some wondered at the intimacy between these two men of such diverse backgrounds. As a Sephardic Jew, Montefiore had been barred from a university education in England. But he was intelligent and shrewd, and after an apprenticeship, entered the Stock Exchange as one of a dozen Jewish brokers licensed in London. He amassed a fortune and became highly influential in the financial and political spheres, knighted by Queen Victoria after serving as sheriff of London. This Orthodox Jew and Quaker, both outspoken humanitarians of independent spirit, stood out in nineteenth-century England. Friends for forty years, Montefiore and Hodgkin traveled together in Europe, Asia, and Africa to protest slavery and anti-Semitism.

Montefiore first took Hodgkin to Palestine in 1857 with plans to build a hospital. On their second trip, two years later, they stopped in Rome to try to rescue a Jewish child abducted by the papal police. On another occasion, they traveled to Morocco, where a Jew had been falsely accused of murder. These trips exhausted Hodgkin; the discomforts of the primitive Middle Eastern conditions taxed his health. In 1866, when drought and cholera devastated Palestine, Montefiore gathered a large benefit fund and set off with Hodgkin to the Holy Land. When they reached Alexandria, Hodgkin became acutely ill with severe abdominal pain and diarrhea. Diagnosing himself with cholera and knowing that he would likely die, he wrote a farewell letter to his wife and gave the poor all his possessions, which included six pairs of spectacles and a pair of scissors.

Thomas Hodgkin died in Jaffa on April 5, 1866, and was buried there in an English cemetery. Deeply affected by the death of his dear friend, Montefiore wrote in the *Jewish Chronicle*: "To one so guileless, so pious . . . and so desirous to assist with all his heart in the amelioration of the condition of the human race, death could not have had any terror."

When Montefiore returned to Palestine several years later, he found Hodgkin's grave overgrown with brush. Hodgkin's manuscript, "Some Morbid Appearances of the Absorbant Glands and Spleen," remained buried in the archives, and his important observations on this new disease entity were, like his grave, soon forgotten.

2   Arrogant Ancestors

Sarah Brilliant Kaplan was born on January 15, 1895, in the Ukrainian city of Kiev. Her father, Henry, had established a successful mushroom business and was comparatively wealthy, especially for a Jew. The Brilliant family had survived the Kiev pogrom that followed the assassination of Tsar Alexander II of Russia in March 1881, as well as the subsequent economic sanctions targeting Jews under Alexander III. Regarded as members of the intelligentsia, they frequented the ballet and opera. The Brilliant children attended schools that enforced a strict *numerus clausus*, admitting only select Jews of high intelligence and social position. When Sarah and her sisters left for school in their uniforms decorated with brass buttons, they knew they were among the elite. Relatives thought this privileged status imparted an arrogance to the family.

Although life in the Brilliant household was stimulating, it was at the same time oppressive. Called the "redheaded *frimayeh*" or "redheaded fanatic" because of his religious zeal, Henry Brilliant was stern and unyielding. He towered almost two feet over his wife, Clara. A sweet woman, she was said to have a "mental strain," later manifested in other family members. Clara bore five children—Abraham, Anuta, Florence, Sarah, and a son who died of measles at a young age. Henry knew his children's future depended on their education. He demanded perfection; it was key to their survival.

Anuta, the oldest daughter, became a registered nurse with a degree in dentistry. The second daughter, Florence, was feminine and shy. She performed poorly in school and faced expulsion, which would threaten the family's position in the Gentile community and jeopardize their security. Young Sarah watched her father beat Florence whenever she failed at her lessons. She tried to tutor her older sister and protect her from their father's wrath. Years later, Florence's learning difficulties were attributed to nearsightedness. At a young age, Sarah learned a lesson from her father: they must be flawless in intellect, physique, and behavior, or they could be stripped of their position and wealth and relegated to life in a shtetl like the majority of Russian Jews.

The entire family had to submit to Henry's directives. The children weren't allowed to express their thoughts. When Anuta fell in love with a young man, and they sought permission to marry, Henry refused. He considered the boy inferior socially and intellectually and arranged a more suitable marriage to a pharmacist, Benjamin Kalom. Years later, Anuta attempted suicide and was institutionalized with the family "mental strain." Her severe depression was attributed to her grandfather's tyranny. But Henry didn't scare his youngest daughter, Sarah. Dark-haired, short for her age, and square in build, she bore no physical likeness to her father. But of all the children, Sarah resembled him most in character. She was strong, quick to learn, eager to excel. And she wanted to be perfect.

The Brilliants may have been prosperous; they may have been among the intellectual elite, but they were still Jews, and underneath their superiority lay vulnerability. Sarah watched Gentile youths throw stones at Jewish children and yell "Zyid! Zyid! Zyid!" Cossacks rode through her neighborhood regularly, screaming obscenities. She knew what could happen. A gang of Russian peasants walked down the street singing a song. At its completion, they raided the house in front of which they stood, stealing anything they wanted, beating and molesting the family. Even barred inside, they weren't safe. "Spontaneous" fires destroyed whole neighborhoods. Fifty years later, Sarah told her granddaughter that she could close her eyes and still smell flames and hear the sounds of hoof beats, Cossacks singing, bottles breaking, people screaming. When Kiev came under strict police surveillance, and more young Jewish men were conscripted into the army, Henry sent his son Abe to America.

Fear pervaded the Jewish community. "Russian youngsters got drunk and pillaged our homes," Sarah's cousin Max recounted. "My brother Barney and I sat up all night to repel attacks by these hoodlums." Max was only eight years old. He recalled one particularly unsettling time when he had traveled with his parents to a town six miles away to shop. His brothers and sisters remained at home. "We returned late at night," he said, "and we could see the house from the distance. Our blood froze in our veins when we saw our house was dark." They had heard too many stories of raided homes with furniture toppled, dishes broken, the family butchered. Max's father slowly opened the door to find the house intact, the children gone. Warned of a possible attack, they had hidden in a neighbor's barn. The only harm inflicted was a deepening fear—fear of a raid, of a pogrom—a fear that never left them. "We were always insecure," Max said.

Under the last tsar, Nicholas II, pogroms grew more frequent, more violent. Every day brought news of some new atrocity. After the body of a mutilated Christian boy was found near Kishinev, local Jews were accused of ritual murder, even though the boy's uncle confessed to the crime. On April 6–7, 1903, rioters fell upon Kishinev at Passover, looting stores, burning homes, and stalking Jews like wild animals. An eyewitness report described "people torn in two ... bellies split open, tongues cut out, women with breasts cut off, men castrated, blinded, hanged, hacked to death."

"There was always danger," Max recalled. "We had dogs to defend the household, and my father slept with a spear beside his bed. There was no security; you just had to leave." One thought was on everyone's mind—emigration. When Abe Brilliant wrote to his father about the freedom and opportunities in Chicago, Henry knew the decision he had to make.

In 1905, the Brilliant family left Russia for the New World. With Henry and Clara were Anuta and her husband, the shy, almost mute Florence, clinging to Clara, and ten-year-old Sarah. Her square jaw set, her chin tilted up, and her voice strong, she likely impressed the immigration officer. Her childhood had been marred by mistrust and fear, and she brought with her to America a paranoia she would never completely lose. "Throughout her life, she looked over her shoulder," Leah Kaplan said. But she also brought the Brilliant attitude of superiority and a determination to succeed.

3   Diagnosing Hodgkin's Disease

Thomas Hodgkin's "On Some Morbid Appearances of the Absorbant Glands and Spleen" might have been relegated to obscurity, and his name never associated with the disease, had it not been for the intellectual honesty of another Guy's Hospital pathologist, Samuel Wilks.

By the time Wilks joined Guy's staff, Hodgkin's work on lymph glands had already been forgotten. Wilks was studying lardaceous diseases, so-called because the affected organs resembled lard. In 1856, he published a series of cases in which the major features included enlargement of the lymphatic glands and spleen. Unbeknown to Wilks, four of his illustrative cases from the Museum of Pathology had already been reported by Thomas Hodgkin twenty-four years earlier. Believing he had made an original observation, Wilks must have been surprised when reading Richard Bright's discourse on abdominal tumors to find reference to Hodgkin's paper. Bright wrote that Hodgkin had described patients who had "extensive disease of the absorbent glands" and spleens "completely infiltrated . . . with a white matter of almost the appearance of suet." This led Wilks to the seventeenth volume of *Medico-Chirurgical Transactions*, which contained Hodgkin's work. He appended an apology to his manuscript: "One or two of the cases extracted from our museum have already been published. . . . Had I known this earlier I should have altered many expressions which I have used with respect to any originality of observation on my part."

By 1865, Wilks had collected fifteen cases of this disorder. As it was customary for a physician to attach his own name to a newly described illness, Wilks could have called it "Wilks's disease." Instead, he assured Thomas Hodgkin a place in the annals of medicine when he published his classic paper "Cases of Enlargement of the Lymphatic Glands and Spleen, (Or, Hodgkin's Disease) with Remarks." Traveling at the time toward his death in Palestine, Hodgkin never knew of this distinction.

Wilks posed several important questions regarding the nature of the illness: Did Hodgkin's disease arise in one lymph node and spread to other areas, or did it originate in multiple sites simultaneously? Did it affect only lymphoid tissue or other tissues in the body as well? Was it an infection or a cancer? "It must take its place in the rank of malignant disease," Wilks concluded, yet he thought several of its characteristics—fever, enlarged neck nodes, deposits in the lung—resembled tuberculosis. What was the true nature of this disease? It would be almost forty years before a young Johns Hopkins pathologist, Dorothy Reed, took the next major step in answering these questions.

⬅

Born in 1874 to a shoe manufacturer and socialite, Dorothy Reed defied convention when she chose a medical career. Johns Hopkins was one of the few medical schools open to women at the time. Even so, Reed had to withstand repeated acts of male chauvinism and discrimination during her training. But she persisted, and after internship, she was offered a fellowship in pathology at Johns Hopkins.

An autopsy on a nine-year-old boy who had died from Hodgkin's disease piqued Reed's interest in this relatively rare illness. He had been a healthy child, so his mother hadn't worried about the enlarged glands in his neck that persisted following his recovery from whooping cough. Two years later, they began to grow. The family physician described multiple lymph nodes in the boy's left neck, varying in size from "a chestnut to a hen's egg," and deep in each armpit, a lump "the size of a hickory nut." A test for tuberculosis was negative. A surgeon excised a four-centimeter mass from the child's left neck. Under the microscope, the lymph node appeared to be almost completely replaced by fibrous bands, interspersed with large, atypical cells. The diagnosis—Hodgkin's disease. The boy was treated with Fowler's solution, an arsenic-based concoction. He did well until the summer, when he developed a persistent cough and fever. By the start of the next school year, he was bedridden. The child was admitted to Johns Hopkins Hospital in severe pain, his legs and abdomen grossly swollen. He died soon thereafter.

Dorothy Reed reviewed everything she could find on Hodgkin's disease. "It is seventy years since Hodgkin called the attention of the medical world to the peculiar enlargement of the lymphatic glands," she wrote. Understanding of the disease, however, had not greatly increased in the interval. Progress had been hampered, in part, because almost every scientist investigating the disorder had concentrated on a single clinical feature and reported it as a new disease. Pieter Klaases Pel and Wilhelm Ebstein had described patients with cyclical bouts of fever (later known as picket-fence fever, because its graphic representation resembled a picket fence). Emphasizing this aspect, they called the disease chronic relapsing fever. Others referred to it as lymphosarcoma, pseudoleukemia, or adenie. "We have almost as many synonyms for Hodgkin's disease as we have important publications," Reed observed.

Most pathologists believed Hodgkin's disease to be a form of tuberculosis. Reed didn't agree, and in trying to disprove this theory, she challenged some of the most eminent pathologists of the day. Like Hodgkin, Reed performed her research by correlating autopsy findings and clinical history. A careful investigator, she meticulously recorded every detail of her cases—precise measurements of tumor size, blood counts, skin tests for tuberculosis—relating them to the gross appearance of the disease in affected tissues and to the microscopic findings. In addition, she inoculated rabbits and guinea pigs with fragments of lymph nodes from patients, searching for evidence of infection.

Reed wrote an elegant description of the clinical characteristics and typical course of Hodgkin's disease. She concluded that half of the cases occurred in children and young adults, with a male predominance. Most had previously been in good health and had no known exposure to tuberculosis. The disease usually began in the neck and spread to adjacent lymph nodes, then to lymph tissue throughout the body. She described three stages: "During the first stage of disease, which may be prolonged over months, the general physical condition is apparently normal, even while the glands are increasing rapidly." After a year or two, the patient entered the second stage of disease, characterized by marked debility, anemia, and fever. In the last stage, the disease affected numerous lymph nodes, the spleen, and the liver. Enlarging masses gradually compressed vital organs. Most patients survived only one to four years, often dying from a secondary infection, such as tuberculosis.

After outlining the clinical presentation and pattern of spread, Reed entered the debate over the cause of Hodgkin's disease: Was it a malignancy or an infection? Most pathologists believed it to be a form of tuberculosis. The eminent Austrian pathologist Carl Sternberg demonstrated tubercular lesions in the organs of over half his cases and concluded that the disease was "a peculiar type of tuberculosis of the lymphatic apparatus." And under the microscope, Hodgkin's disease resembled tuberculosis. To prove an infectious cause, Sternberg inoculated guinea pigs with minced glands from patients with Hodgkin's disease. All the animals contracted tuberculosis. Dogmatic about his viewpoint, Sternberg convinced others, and patients diagnosed with Hodgkin's disease were prescribed anti-tuberculosis treatment, including bed rest, open-air therapy, and pneumothorax—a procedure in which air was injected into the chest to collapse the lung and restrict its exertion.

Reed openly criticized Sternberg's work. "The clinical histories are meagre," she wrote. "[I] cannot understand his conception . . . of the tubercle bacillus, which he suggests is the cause of such a growth." She maintained that tuberculosis was a secondary infection afflicting these debilitated patients. And Reed said she couldn't comprehend how one could confuse Hodgkin's disease and tuberculosis under the microscope. "The glands may appear alike to the casual observer," she commented, especially "in poorly prepared or carelessly studied specimens," but she had "little difficulty in distinguishing the two processes." Furthermore, her inoculation experiments demonstrated no spread of a tuberculosis-like disease from patient to animal.

If not an infection, what caused the disorder? Hodgkin and Wilks had suggested its malignant potential, but Reed pointed out that Hodgkin's disease did not spread through the bloodstream and invade other organs in the same manner as cancer. She favored an inflammatory process. Regarding treatment, she wrote, "No therapeutic measure has been discovered which influences, either constantly or permanently, the course of the disease. . . . This disease is apparently uniformly fatal."

While studying the relationship between tuberculosis and Hodgkin's disease, Reed made an important observation. It concerned the status of the immune system. She applied tuberculosis skin tests to patients and found all to be nonreactive. Even those expected to be positive—patients with active tuberculosis—had negative tests. This was the first observation of what would later be termed "immunologic incompetence" in these patients. Their immune systems failed to respond normally to an infection. Thus they were susceptible to tuberculosis *because* they had Hodgkin's disease.

Reed's major contribution, however, was to establish criteria for the diagnosis of Hodgkin's disease microscopically. Much of the confusion about this illness had resulted from making a diagnosis on clinical grounds. The symptoms of lymph node enlargement and fever characterized several diseases. Pathologists had no diagnostic test or specific histologic criteria to guide them. Hodgkin's and Wilks's reports lacked detailed pathologic description because of the rudimentary state of microscopes at the time.

In every case Reed examined, she found the same abnormal cell, one not previously observed in any other disease. "The large giant cells are the most striking feature of these specimens," she wrote. "They vary in size of two or three red blood corpuscles to cells twenty times this size." She noted that the nucleus, or center of the cell, was quite unusual. It occupied a larger proportion of the entire cell; instead of being round, it was indented or bean-shaped; instead of a single nucleus, each cell contained multiple nuclei. These bizarre cells appeared specific for Hodgkin's disease, and Reed concluded: "These giant cells, so far as our observation reaches, are peculiar to this growth, and are of great assistance in diagnosis." Sternberg described the same cell, which he said gave the tissue "a peculiarly characteristic appearance." Reed and Sternberg published their findings independently, and years later, this pathognomonic cell was named the Reed-Sternberg cell, joining the names of these two adversaries forever.

In 1902, Reed's elegant work was published in the *Johns Hopkins Hospital Report*. At twenty-eight, she had established the criteria for diagnosing Hodgkin's disease and effectively challenged the theory that it was a form of tuberculosis. She had done all this in just one year. How much more she could have accomplished, given the opportunity. But when she asked about a faculty position at Johns Hopkins, the dean told her that there would be "great opposition" to the appointment of a woman. She could, however, stay on as a postdoctoral fellow. Disheartened and incensed, Reed walked away from the laboratory, never to return. "May 30, the very day I left Baltimore," she wrote in her autobiography, "was the lowest point of my life. . . . On that day I turned my back on all I wanted most and started to make a new life for myself. My house had come down on my head."

Dorothy Reed is credited in medical history with describing the diagnostic cell in Hodgkin's disease. And her insightful observations on the clinical characteristics and pattern of spread proved to be accurate. Praising Reed's work decades later, Henry Kaplan noted: "Virtually all of the principal clinical features of Hodgkin's disease had been described by the end of the nineteenth century."

4   Growing Up Brilliant

In 1905, the Brilliant family settled in Chicago. Along with thousands of other Jewish immigrants, they moved into a ghetto about a mile square on the West Side, with Maxwell Street at its center. The brick tenements lining the muddy streets were dark and poorly ventilated. Several families shared one apartment and one toilet. "Life in Chicago was pretty primitive," Sarah's cousin, Max Crocker, recalled. "My father had a Jewish market, and we lived and slept in it, behind a partition." For most this was better than Russia, where home had consisted of a wooden shack with a privy in the backyard. For the Brilliants, however, these conditions were insufferable.

Chicago's West Side was crowded with two-wheeled pushcarts and horse-drawn trolleys. Wooden sidewalks served as open markets, displaying kosher meats and trinkets from the Old Country. From outside her window, Sarah heard the incessant babel of gossip and haggling in Yiddish, Russian, and Polish. She smelled challah baking and onions frying, along with rotting garbage. The odors intensified in the stagnant summer air; only the chilling autumn wind from Lake Michigan could dissipate them. The familiar sights, sounds, and smells of their homeland might have comforted some immigrants, but they reminded Sarah of life in a shtetl, and she was used to better.

Work was scarce. Many took jobs in sweatshops, where long hours, poor sanitation, and overbearing foremen were reminiscent of Russia. "In my family," Max said, "the girls worked in a factory ten hours a day, sixty hours a week, for five dollars. They brought home things to sew at night to make extra. I used to clean the sidewalks for twenty-five cents." Everyone had to start over. Max's father had been a businessman with a full staff. "He'd never even hitched a horse," Max said. Now he rode to the stockyards at dawn, bargained with butchers, and loaded a side of beef his own size onto his cart. But he never despaired. "This is a wonderful country," he used to say. "When I go to sleep and hear noises outside, I don't worry. I know there aren't any Guards coming to get me."

The Brilliants, too, had to readjust. In Kiev, Henry Brilliant had been known as the "king of mushrooms." He had left behind a successful business, a fine home, private schools, and a circle of learned friends, trading all this for security. But there would be no sweatshops for Henry's daughters. Sarah attended school and later apprenticed in her brother-in-law's pharmacy. With education, hard work, and the right husband, she could attain the lifestyle she deserved.

Sarah watched her sisters marry men of promise. Anuta's husband, Benjamin Kalom, owned a drugstore on Fourteenth Street, and when it prospered, they moved to a spacious apartment in a fashionable neighborhood and sent their five children to private schools. Florence's husband owned a farm in Seattle—a source of great pride for the Brilliants, since Jews were forbidden to own land in Russia. The key to a woman's success was the right marriage, choosing a mate not necessarily for love but for his potential. And Sarah had many beaux from whom to choose. Although not a beauty, she had intellect and an intensity that set her apart. A formal photograph taken in her teens shows her standing in a trim silk gown, her long black hair piled high on her head and a set to her mouth that suggests she might smile. What is striking is the lift of her chin, which makes her appear taller than she is and leaves the impression of a headstrong young woman. A number of admirers courted Sarah, but none suited her. She had plans—plans to get out of the ghetto, to have the things her sisters had, and more.

In her late teens, Sarah met the man with whom she thought she could achieve her rightful station in life. Nathan Morris Kaplan, a dental student, had also emigrated from Kiev. "Nathan was a sweet guy," relatives said, even-tempered and fun-loving. Five-and-a-half feet tall, he had wavy black hair, a brush mustache, and splendid dark eyes. Everyone liked him—"always a smile, always a joke," a cousin said. He was usually surrounded by friends—riding in the country, picnicking at the beach. He had a pleasing voice, and at parties, friends begged him to sing.

Although from the same world, the Kaplans were nothing like the Brilliants. Nathan's father, Motell, had been a pharmacist in Kiev. Though moderately prosperous, he was not a member of the intelligentsia. In Chicago, he ran a small grocery, although he preferred to spend his time singing at the synagogue. The Kaplans were a handsome family: Nathan's mother, Jeannette, wore tiny ringlets, and Motell's patrician features were accentuated by his long white beard. Friends described them as gentle, humble people.

Sarah was different from the other girls Nathan knew. She had opinions about classical music and politics; she was studying to be a pharmacist and was not afraid of hard work. She didn't try to flatter him, and he never heard her giggle. When spoken to, she didn't avert her eyes demurely but looked straight at him. What Nathan hadn't noticed yet was the way she always had to have the last word. Relatives all agreed that he would have his hands full; Sarah acted as if she were still a member of Kiev's Jewish elite.

Why did Sarah accept Nathan's proposal? Dentistry was a fine profession; he would be a good breadwinner. He wasn't scholarly, but he was smart enough; he wasn't sophisticated, but he could learn. He would clearly not seek to control the household the way her father had; theirs would be a marriage of equals. Nathan did have one serious deficiency that Sarah wouldn't recognize for years—he didn't have the Brilliant drive.

In 1916, they married. Relatives observed that it was not a marriage of like souls. Sarah enjoyed a good intellectual debate; Nathan preferred a good joke. She always stood erect, her shoulders square; he slouched. Sarah pursed her lips; Nathan smiled with his entire face. She was rigid; he was malleable. Perhaps she had thought she could change him once they were married; maybe he had thought he could tame her.

The first years of their marriage appeared to be happy ones. Nathan was an affectionate man, and letters to Sarah reveal his ardor; he called her "sweetheart" and "my darling wife." Sarah worked at the Mount Sinai Hospital pharmacy while Nathan built his practice. Their small apartment behind his dental office contained only a few remnants of the Brilliants' life in Russia—the ornate samovar on the buffet and Sarah's demure mother, waiting to be served tea. Sarah's discontent soon began to surface, and she complained to her sister-in-law Rose. "Everyone around us seemed wealthy," Rose said. "Everyone seemed wealthy, but us."

Before long, Nathan and Sarah moved to a two-bedroom apartment with a sun parlor. Their shelves filled with books; the Victrola played Mozart and Schubert. Sarah and cousin Jenny sang arias at family affairs. Friends gathered in their parlor to discuss art, literature, and politics. They read poems by the young Chicago poet Carl Sandburg and debated the social implications of Sinclair Lewis's books. Sarah and Nathan were building a life together—the kind of life of which Nathan had only dreamed of, the kind of life Sarah expected. Proud to be U.S. citizens, they tried to erase all traces of their accents; they registered to vote—Democrat. As much as Sarah strove to change her speech, dress, and thought, she still bore emotional scars from the pogroms. To survive, one had to be strong, self-reliant, and superior, both intellectually and physically. Although attracted by the allure of the American dream, Sarah was driven by fear.

❧

On April 24, 1918, their first son, Henry Seymour Kaplan, was born. Sarah had assumed her child would be perfect. She called him Zinu, "adorable son" in Yiddish. And he *was* adorable, with curly blond hair, dark eyes, and a sweet disposition. But he wasn't perfect. He had two giant fingers on his right hand and several enlarged toes on his left foot, making it a full size bigger than the right one. Sarah blamed herself. She talked about his fingers incessantly. What had she done wrong? Anuta had five normal children, and she hadn't even wanted all of them. Sarah had only wished for one special child. How had she inflicted these defects on her son? Every time she looked at his fingers, she winced. "She ached so for Henry," a friend said. "She just ached for him every living minute."

Usually rational and self-possessed, Sarah lost all sense of proportion; she became preoccupied with her son's fingers. A congenital deformity, the pediatrician told her. Congenital—present at birth—the term challenged her conviction that she could control her child's destiny. Worse yet was the word "deformity." She associated imperfection with inferiority and weakness. In Russia, her son would have been ridiculed and likely victimized. How could Zinu, with his large, malformed fingers, become a physician, a dentist, a pianist? Some thought her reaction a manifestation of the Brilliant "mental strain." "She was a self-centered, slightly paranoid, very superior lady who had a child with a defect," a family friend observed. "Can you imagine what that must have meant to her?" Her son's hand became an obsession, which dominated his early childhood.

At first, guilt drove her to hide his disfigurement. A studio portrait of young Hank, as relatives called him, shows a husky child with a Buster Brown haircut, holding a sailboat, smiling. On closer inspection, one notices his right hand is awkwardly positioned behind the boat. This photograph of a happy child is also a picture of Sarah Kaplan trying to conceal her son's deformity. But before long Hank would start school, and she couldn't hide his hand forever. Now instead of contriving ways to conceal his fingers, she became preoccupied with correcting them. She consulted a number of specialists, most of whom told her nothing could be done. Finally, she found an orthopedist who applied a brace to straighten the fingers and retard their growth. After six months, however, they had grown larger. In desperation, Sarah tried to persuade a surgeon to amputate her child's fingers. "She would be excising her guilt, her horror," a family member suggested. The surgeon refused. Sarah eventually returned to the family pediatrician. He took one look at the little boy, a metal brace immobilizing his right hand, and said, "Take that off this child and leave him alone. Just make him strong."

Henceforth, Sarah had a new goal—making her son strong. Henry would accomplish such feats in science or law that his hand would become insignificant. She told him God had made a mistake with his fingers but had given him a bigger brain to make up for it. "She always felt that Henry was going to be one of the great men of the world," Cousin Claire said. "Henry was going to be a genius, because Sarah said so." Listening to records or taking a walk became an educational exercise. What symphony is this? How is the age of a tree determined? At age five, he was reading *The Book of Knowledge*.

Sarah instilled the Brilliant attitude of superiority into her son. She rarely allowed Hank to play with neighborhood children; she considered their games silly, a waste of time. When she took him for walks in Humboldt Park, two-year-old Hank, his sailor suit spotless and his golden curls combed, pointed to children playing in the sandbox and said, "Dirty boys," or to children shouting at a game of tag and said, "Loud boys." Whenever Max Crocker visited, he always found Henry on the floor, surrounded by books. "He didn't have any friends," Max recalled. "He didn't seek any. He was primarily interested in books. He was a loner."

While Sarah was nurturing Hank's curiosity, his father taught him to laugh. Nathan regularly kissed and tickled him, pinched his cheek. Their long walks together weren't educational, simply playful. They went fishing, and Hank caddied for Nathan at the public golf course. In the evenings, Hank sat on his father's lap while Nathan read *The Pilgrim's Progress*. His father was soft and smelled of tobacco; his voice was happy. As a child, Hank watched his father tease a young patient, gently reassure an elderly woman, refuse payment when he knew a man couldn't afford groceries. Hank adored his father, and years later, he would treat patients with the same consideration and compassion.

Family members described Henry Kaplan's early childhood as idyllic. To escape the summer heat, the Kaplans rented a cottage at Union Pier. Within walking distance from Lake Michigan, the cottage had a great room with a fireplace and was surrounded by a screened porch, perfect for sleeping. Cows grazed in a nearby meadow; at night, a cool breeze blew off the lake. While his cousins played in the sand dunes and went berry picking, Hank read. In the evenings, he and his mother walked to town to watch the train come in and get the daily mail. At night, Sarah and her friends gathered to discuss literature and politics. Hank's vocabulary broadened as he heard talk of things like the Teapot Dome Scandal and the Communist Party. He likely preferred the nights when the children sat around the fireplace telling ghost stories. On the weekends, his father came to the beach, and the cottage filled with his laughter. Hank loved to hear his father call his mother "sweetheart" and "honey."

Sarah was almost satisfied with her life. Nathan's practice was growing; she had a group of cultured friends; she spent summers at the lake. Hank was the sweet and gifted child she had known he would be. And then Sarah became pregnant again. She did not want another baby, but Nathan had insisted. As the pregnancy progressed, Sarah became increasingly anxious. What if her second child had deformities? In 1924, when Hank was six years old, Richard Kaplan was born. As Sarah awoke from anesthesia, the first thing Nathan said was, "He's perfect; all his fingers are perfect."

Richard Merle Kaplan was a handsome child with olive skin, thick blond hair, and dimples. As much as Hank physically resembled their grandfather Henry Brilliant, Richard resembled their grandfather Motell Kaplan. When Sarah took Richard out in his carriage, strangers raved about her beautiful child. But as he grew up, Richard came to see his attractiveness as a curse. Whenever he asked his mother to help him solve a problem, she replied, "Why should you have problems? Look at your hands." Although bright, he was considered the good-looking kid, the athlete; his brother, the scholar. Hank thought his younger brother a nuisance; he disrupted their household. Sarah used to tell of the time when after baby Richard had been crying for hours, Hank looked up from a book and said, "Throw that kid into the ocean." For a long time, Richard thought his name was "Brat."

As Richard grew older, his relationship with his brother vacillated between pedagogical and contentious. Modeling himself on his mother, Hank tried to improve his younger brother's mind. Once six-year-old Richard needed help with his math, and Hank decided to teach him algebra. When Richard could not comprehend a quadratic equation, his brother said, "You're an idiot, a damn fool." Sarah had instilled intolerance of ignorance into Hank. "You could be mean," Richard said years later, "but not dumb. That was unforgivable." Sarah didn't intervene when Hank criticized Richard; she never corrected the impression that he was intellectually inferior to Hank. But as soon as she left the room, Richard retaliated. "Big fingers, big fingers," he yelled, and ran.

With a second child, the family atmosphere changed. Hank had been easy and agreeable, "such a sweet child," his Aunt Rose said. Richard challenged Sarah's authority, and they often locked horns. Dinnertime was particularly stormy. Hank always ate what his mother placed before him. If she tried to force her second child to clean his plate, he refused. This contest of wills resulted in screams, threats, and bent silverware. Nathan opened his arms to his younger son, but this sensitive child longed for his mother's love, a love she had invested totally in her firstborn.

Those who saw the Kaplan boys together never guessed that they were brothers. Richard was slender and graceful. He smiled easily, like his father, and turned girls' heads. Hank was stocky with a large left foot and two deformed fingers. He had a slight overbite and rarely smiled. He was not charming and had no interest in being so. But when they spoke, it was clear they came from the same household. Both were opinionated and masters at using words. That, too, was a Brilliant trait. And both seemed to have a layer of arrogance just below the surface.

The biggest difference between the two brothers was that Richard craved his mother's love, and Henry had it. From the day her first son was born until she died, Sarah's energy and love centered on him, almost to the exclusion of anyone else. "You can't understand Hank," Richard said, "unless you understand my mother's pushing him and encouraging him to be normal, even more than normal—super . . . and unless you understand that my mother encouraged him to think that he was the smartest boy in the world. And you can't understand Hank without understanding my mother's drive to see that he didn't suffer from those deformed fingers about which she felt so guilty." Henry bent to his mother's will yet did not feel dominated; no one recalls a harsh word between them. He never shrank from his mother's incessant drive for him to be the best, because he wanted to be the best. "She pushed him in the direction he wanted to go," Cousin Claire said. Richard rebelled regularly, mostly in attempts to get his mother's attention. He never learned, as his brother and father had, that you never won a fight with Sarah. These two talented boys could have bonded together to face the troubles ahead, but Hank rarely asked about his younger brother's activities or feelings. Perhaps his biggest sin in Richard's eyes was that he ignored him. The result for Richard was an insecurity that took years to resolve and a smoldering anger waiting to flare.

⌒

Sarah was never content on the West Side. She watched her friends' husbands build up their businesses from little markets to fashionable shops to chains of stores. Most had relocated to better neighborhoods. They could, too; Nathan would just have to raise his fees. So the Kaplans moved to Hawthorne Place on the North Side, one block from Lake Shore Drive, with elegant mansions at the end of their street. A few families had chauffeurs; one had an electric car. In winter, some flooded their backyards to make ice-skating rinks. Their neighbors included the Hettlers, who owned a lumber business; the Barretts, a family of prominent lawyers; and the Meyercourts, whose clothing patches brought them a fortune. The Kaplans lived in a modest red brick, two-family dwelling, the second home in from the streetcar line. But they lived on the North Side.

Hank and Richard attended Nettlehorst Grammar School on Broadway. Most students came from the high-rent district—the kind of children with whom Sarah thought her sons should associate. Having skipped several grades, Hank was younger than other classmates, but it didn't take them long to find out how smart he was. "Mrs. Hayes, our fourth-grade teacher, asked the class a question," his friend Herb Trace recalled, "and typically, Hank's hand went up even before the question was finished." Influenced by his mother's training, Hank was confident he could excel at anything, and he did—at stoopball, tennis, swimming. Herb marveled at the intricate arts and crafts Hank did in Boy Scouts and how he spent hours patiently sorting stamps and gluing them into his album. But mostly, Hank and Herb talked about how they planned to be doctors—not just ordinary doctors, but great scientists.

When Sarah chose Hawthorne Place, she may have pushed Nathan beyond the family's means, but she chose well. Sarah had carefully selected an environment in which her sons would flourish. Everything was finally under her control—until the cousins came. And the Depression.

Sarah had always been jealous of her older sister's good fortune. Anuta had a prosperous husband, an elegant apartment, and five normal children. Repeatedly Sarah compared their home with that of their "rich cousins." But Anuta also suffered from the Brilliant "mental strain." High-strung and intelligent, she was never happy with the husband her father had chosen for her. Benjamin Kalom might be a successful pharmacist—an excellent match—but she didn't love him, and she couldn't learn to. After years of despondency, Anuta became deranged. She tried to jump out a window; she set fire to their apartment. Ben Kalom had to commit his wife to North Shore Sanitarium. Possible paranoid schizophrenia, he was told. Her mind wandered back to Russia; she thought the sanitarium was her estate, the nurses, her servants. Shock treatments didn't work, and Anuta never returned home, leaving behind her a bewildered husband and five teenagers. Benjamin Kalom could not manage the household, and Sarah offered to look after the children. In 1929, when Hank was eleven and Richard five, four of the cousins came to live on Hawthorne Place. And they stayed.

Anuta's eldest, Arnold, was a licensed pharmacist and already married. The second son, Henry, was sixteen, an athlete who wore a sweater displaying his varsity letters. Richard idolized him. Henry taught his young cousin to throw a baseball and shoot basketballs. Sarah called him a *tivel*, devil. Once he coated the kitchen floor with butter and slid across it. Sarah was relieved when he left to become a pharmacist too. Fifteen-year-old Lawrence was the Kaplan family favorite. A talented pianist, he entertained them with Chopin and Mozart. He picked up Richard from school, made him a snack, amusing him with popular songs like "Play Gypsy Play" and "The Donkey Serenade." And he treated his Aunt Sarah like a queen. Years later, a physician, he drove from the suburbs into Chicago every Wednesday and took her to dinner and the theater. Seymour, a fourteen-year-old with reddish-blond hair and freckles, was a baseball fanatic who always seemed to be swinging a bat or listening to a Chicago Cubs game. He was barely out of his teens when he was killed by a hit-and-run driver.

The fifth cousin, twelve-year-old Lucille, was a sweet girl on the verge of becoming a young lady when her mother was committed to an insane asylum.

Sarah never had a daughter, and they could have developed a special relationship, but they didn't. No matter what Lucille did, it was never enough. If she practiced the piano for half an hour, it wasn't long enough. If she practiced for two hours, it was long enough, but not good enough. No matter whom she brought home, he didn't meet Aunt Sarah's standards. She built a fence that Lucille couldn't climb. In the end, Sarah's drive for perfection squeezed the joy out of her.

When it became clear Anuta would never recover, the Kaplans moved to a larger apartment a few blocks away. Rose noticed that it was decorated with some of Anuta's loveliest pieces of furniture. Ben Kalom paid Sarah thirty-five dollars each week to cover expenses. That was a lot, considering that streetcar fare was seven cents. The Kaplan household changed overnight. The noise of doors slamming, a radio blaring, the phone ringing filled the apartment. Sarah worried that the chaotic atmosphere would interfere with Hank's studies. But she didn't need to worry. Hank had already developed a voracious appetite for knowledge and seemed oblivious to the confusion around him. He read several books a day, with Sibelius playing in the background, the louder, the better.

Mindful of Hank's intellect, his older cousins treated him with respect. But the boys in the Rogers Park neighborhood didn't—at first. This husky boy with tortoise-shell glasses who walked down the street reading a book was too good a target to pass up. "Hymie Einstein! Hymie Einstein!" they yelled from the top of a tree, from behind a fence, from a stoop. Hank didn't hesitate to express his low opinion of them, using words they didn't know, but the meaning of which they could guess from the tone of his voice. One winter day, a gang ambushed him, threw him down on the ice, and beat him. Hank got a good look at each of the five boys before he heard the crunch of his glasses under someone's foot. They laughed when he said he'd get even. They didn't know Henry Kaplan never forgave a wrongdoing and never made a threat he didn't intend to keep. He washed the blood from his broken nose and made up a story about slipping on the ice so as not to upset his mother. Hank could have enlisted the help of his cousins; they loved a good fight. But he never asked someone else to fight his battles. Over the next several weeks, Hank waited, he observed; he learned when each boy was likely to be alone. Then he rolled those large fingers into a fist and pummeled the boys one by one. After that, the neighborhood boys stepped aside when Henry Kaplan walked down the street, his broken nose buried in a book.

Hank had no time for dating or competitive sports. Science fascinated him, and he knew he had much to learn. He and friend Joseph Izenstark performed biological experiments in Joseph's basement. Once they dissected a chameleon, trying to discover how it changed color. At one point, Hank became intrigued with taxidermy. His room was littered with dead squirrels and birds and bottles of arsenic used to prepare the skins. Hank valued people with strong commitments, and at Lakeview High School, he found friends with similar academic interests. On the five-mile walk to school, they talked about their ambitions. And most of their dreams came true: Benjamin Narodick became a successful physician, Joseph Izenstark chief of staff at a California hospital, Glen Rose a motion picture producer, and Marvin Kahn, despite cerebral palsy, a major California developer.

During his senior year, Hank attended the University of Chicago High School, a private school for superior students, located on the university campus. He loved the academic repartee. He considered himself a pure analyst, repudiating new ideas until proven. His political views, like Sarah's, were left of center. And, like his mother, he rarely moderated his opinions. Hank preferred discussing the theory of relativity or the principles of Marxism to high-school dances or neighborhood gossip. "His favorite word was 'bourgeois,'" Richard recalled. "He said it with relish and with scorn."

There was only one person who teased Hank and made him laugh—his father. "I think the gentleness and kindness in Hank came from his father," a friend said. Nathan enlivened the apartment with his stories. Hank and his cousins looked forward to Sunday dinner, the one time they all ate together. If Nathan wasn't there, however, there was little conversation. He spent less and less time with his family; he preferred to play cards with his Brother Freemasons, or fish or ride horses in the country. The minute he came into the apartment, Sarah began her tirades. He wasn't an adequate provider; he drank too much; he joked with other women. She never stopped nagging.

The year the cousins came to live with the Kaplans, the stock market crashed. At dinner, they talked about the increasing number of unemployed and the daily suicides. At first, a historian wrote, "You could feel the Depression deepen, but you could not look out of the window and see it. Men who lost their jobs dropped out of sight." But one only needed to look under the Michigan Avenue Bridge to know that the Depression had hit Chicago. There, men and women wrapped themselves in newspapers to keep warm. After a while, it came closer—veterans sold apples on street corners; bread lines extended down the block. Finally, the Depression reached the upper-class neighborhoods of the Gold Coast, Lakeview, and Rogers Park. "Everyone knew of someone engaged in a desperate struggle, although most of the agony went on behind closed doors," an account of the times read. "The stories were whispered. There was something indecent about them."

When men began coming to the Kaplan's back door, asking for a sandwich, Sarah fed them. Their presence, however, frightened her. What would she do if Nathan couldn't work? Almost a third of the total workforce was jobless. They could barely cover expenses, and Nathan's income was dwindling. As the number of outstanding dental bills increased, so did dinner table fights. Always the same: Nathan explained that a patient had recently lost his job but was certain to pay when his situation improved. "He's such a nice guy," Nathan said. Sarah interrupted, calling Nathan a sucker, a patsy.

When the Depression worsened, there were more and more nice guys. The Kaplans lived in an almost non-cash economy. "Even five or ten cents was a big thing," Richard said. Sarah felt she couldn't rely on Nathan. She hadn't escaped from Russia, she hadn't moved up from the West Side to falter now. She had created a suitable environment in which to raise her sons, and she wasn't about to lose it because her husband didn't collect his bills. Sarah Kaplan returned to work. She spent her days helping in her brother-in-law's pharmacy and her evenings in school studying for a pharmacy license. What would she do if Nathan couldn't work? She soon found out.

Nathan started to have pains in his back. "Lumbago," his doctor said, a form of rheumatism. But the pain increased and spread to his legs. His feet turned bright red, and he began to drag one foot when he walked. A specialist diagnosed Buerger's disease, an illness that afflicted smokers. "I virtually can't remember my father without a cigarette in his hand," Richard recalled. "He used to get those Lucky Strike flat fifties . . . and it was nothing for him to go through one pack a day." Patients with Buerger's disease suffered intense pain, caused by obliteration of small blood vessels in the hands and feet. Skin ulcers and even gangrene followed. The possibility of an amputation gave Sarah nightmares. Without his legs, Nathan couldn't practice dentistry; and if he couldn't work, they would starve. A specialist prescribed diathermy, the delivery of heat deep into the tissues using high-frequency electromagnetic waves. At the end of the day, when Nathan's legs were throbbing and burning, young Richard wrapped heavy foil sheets around them and turned on the diathermy unit. This big machine, with its various switches and dials, made Richard feel important. When the heat increased the circulation in Nathan's legs, the pain lessened, and he smiled at his worried son. When the pain subsided, he began to kid him. But his jokes became less and less frequent.

Sarah's nightmare was coming true. Now she had to become the breadwinner. She needed her own pharmacy. People might not buy a new dress or matching shoes and purse, she reasoned, but they still bought grandma's gall bladder pills and junior's cough syrup. Sarah had seen a small store on Broadway, and she intended to get it. She began to borrow money from friends and relatives—ten dollars from one, fifty from another.

During the summer of 1934, Nathan's health deteriorated. The cousins, now grown, had moved out, and Sarah sent Richard to a sleep-away camp. Although a financial drain, "it was the thing people with money did," Richard said. Nathan wrote his son regularly. At first, his letters only mentioned minor pains, as an aside to family news. But soon head pains, burning in his chest, and doctors' visits dominated his letters. No one in Chicago could identify the cause of his illness. Sarah insisted Nathan go to the Mayo Clinic for an evaluation. People with means went there for treatment.

On Thursday, August 21, 1934, Nathan wrote from the Hotel Zumbro in Rochester, Minnesota:

> I was down in the Clinic and registered. My number is 101. . . . From what I have observed so far, this is a highly developed factory, with a system equal to none. Go to desk no. 22 and to the ninth floor South, back to desk no. 11, and so on down the line. See how foolish I am. Here I come to my room to lie down and sleep, and instead I am writing to you. But it makes me feel closer to you. . . . Cheer up, kid. I just wanted to see the Mayo Clinic. . . . It sure is a beautiful place to stay away from, and if I never see it again, it will be too soon. Lots of love and kisses for you and my sweet son.

Five days later, a second letter arrived:

> I woke at four A.M. . . . I tossed and twisted and could not sleep, so figured I could make my day seem shorter and not so lonely, and I found that writing to you would solve both things in one. For how can I be lonely when I talk to my most precious thing in the world, my wife, whom I love better than my own life. . . . I am sure my health will be restored to me, and I will again begin to live and enjoy life with you and my two little treasures. Right now there is a little fire burning in my chest. I can feel the heat from it radiating to the surface, and my bed is splitting in two as I sit up and open the windows and write. . . .

Nathan concluded the source of his trouble was his teeth. He thought dental extractions would solve his problem and wrote:

> When I think of how I will again be well and able to walk down the street in my own natural gait without lowering my shoulder or dragging my leg, nothing else matters. . . . I would give ten dollars just to look at you all. Hearing your voice last night was delightful. I clung to the phone long after you said good-bye to me. It somehow made me feel closer to you. . . . Right now I feel I could have a big breakfast, but for twenty cents, you get two slices of dry toast and coffee, and who wants to spend more than that. . . .

A few days later, a final letter came from Hotel Zumbro:

> Just came down to my room from a three-hour examination, and in a way they told me the news. It is not the best, but I will try to make the best of it. I may be home in a few days. . . . Be brave, dear, and don't worry. I am coming home. I am so hungry for you all, to hold you, squeeze you, and love you.

At the age of forty-five, Nathan Kaplan was diagnosed with advanced lung cancer. He returned home to die. Sarah took Richard to meet him at the train station, and when he first spotted his father, he was stunned. His father's skin was sallow, his temples sunken, his smile gone. In the taxi on the way home, his mother and father were crying. Sarah spoke about his illness only to Hank and her closest friends, and she spoke in whispers. "In those days, you didn't talk about cancer," Richard said. "It was as if someone had something immoral, like syphilis." Whenever Richard missed school because of his father's illness, Sarah sent a note saying her son had been sick. She didn't want the neighbors to know Nathan was dying of cancer. "I actually felt guilty," Richard said, "tainted." Richard didn't know how his mother felt; she never told him. But Rose knew. Her sister-in-law's reaction was a mixture of sadness and bitterness. The more debilitated Nathan became, the greater the bitterness.

Nathan never returned to work, and Hank became his mother's confidant and his father's nurse. He read and played records for him, and when Nathan got weaker, he fed him and carried him to the bathroom to bathe him. Nathan smoked incessantly, and one day his mattress caught fire. Before long, his skeletal arms and legs stuck out from his bloated stomach. Although Hank tried to make his father comfortable, he stood by helplessly as his father writhed about with uncontrollable pain.

Soon Nathan's breathing deteriorated, and he had to be hospitalized. As Hank carried his father out to the waiting taxi, Richard said good-bye to the dearest person in his life. He never saw him again. Only Hank was allowed to visit their father; he had already become the male head of the house. When Nathan's breathing changed to gurgling and gasping, and the hospital called Sarah to come, she even forbade Hank to go with her. He pleaded. Trying to spare her Zinu more grief, Sarah refused. That evening when she returned home, she said nothing. Her mouth was set, her eyes dry. The next morning Sarah took Richard into the bathroom and leaning against the radiator told him his father was dead. The sun, shining through the window, gave the illusion that a flash of light emanated from his mother, a flash that felt to Richard like anger.

At sixteen, Henry Kaplan had lost his father, and it would be some time before anyone made him laugh again.

~

Brother Freemasons gave Nathan Morris Kaplan the finest of funerals. His casket lay in a funeral parlor on Lawrence Avenue. Such a large crowd of people came to pay their last respects that they spilled out into the street, and streetcars had to be stopped. Solomon Goldman, a celebrated rabbi, conducted the ceremony. The long line of chauffeur-driven black cars made Richard feel important. But when he heard the first shovel of dirt hit the coffin, he understood that his father was never coming home.

Following the funeral, friends and relatives packed into the Kaplans' apartment. They brought deli meats, casseroles, and homemade desserts. People laughed and enjoyed themselves, just as Nathan would have wanted. "It was one of the most festive times I can remember in that apartment," Richard said. Hank was polite, but unusually quiet. After the relatives and friends had gone, Sarah and Richard sat alone, staring at the plates of food and baskets of flowers. The room was silent. Hank entered, and the first thing Richard noticed was how tightly his teeth were clenched. He stood before his mother and brother and announced, "Someday I'm going to cure cancer."

5   Roentgen's Rays

Researchers had been trying to cure Hodgkin's disease for three decades—ever since 1902 when Dorothy Reed had written: "No therapeutic measure has been discovered which influences . . . the course of the disease." Progress in its treatment had been hampered primarily by two obstacles—confusion regarding the basic nature of the disease and limited therapeutic tools. A few physicians believed it to be a malignant neoplasm; most still considered it an inflammatory disorder. Some thought that local treatment of affected lymph nodes was sufficient. Others considered Hodgkin's disease a systemic illness and concluded that therapy should encompass the entire body.

Surgeons had been among the first to attempt a curative approach. The premise underlying surgical therapy was based on the belief that infectious agents or irritants entered the body from a specific source—inflamed tonsils or decayed teeth—and spread toxins throughout the system. Enlarged lymph nodes were thought to represent an inflammatory reaction to these poisonous substances. In 1917, J. L. Yates and C. H. Bunting, two prominent Wisconsin surgeons, recommended radical resection of nodes in the neck, axilla, or groin to "extirpate so thoroughly all eradicable involved tissue" as well as the tonsils or teeth to "eliminate the portal or portals of entry of the infection." They reported that 20 percent of their patients had significant improvement. Consequently, surgeons recommended radical resections for Hodgkin's disease.

But the fundamental hypothesis was erroneous. There was no portal of entry for Hodgkin's disease; patients underwent needless dental extractions and tonsillectomies. And although surgery may have controlled disease in a few patients with localized nodal involvement, most patients had more widespread disease than could be determined by physical examination. Within months after resection, disease recurred in adjacent lymph nodes or liver or lung. Eventually, it became apparent that even the most extensive surgical procedure could not eradicate disease in the majority of patients. By the 1930s, the role of surgery had been reduced to a diagnostic biopsy.

More commonly physicians recommended drug therapy for patients with Hodgkin's disease. Those who still believed its origin to be the tubercle bacilli that caused tuberculosis treated patients with quinine, iron, and cod-liver oil. Some advocated arsenic, based on the observation that arsenic poisoning was associated with shrinkage of normal lymphoid tissue. One popular arsenical was called Salvarsan, which meant "saved by arsenic." But patients weren't saved by arsenicals, and long-term use caused numbness and weakness of patients' feet and legs from nerve damage. Others injected lymph nodes with caustic chemicals, such as potassium iodide, silver nitrate, or carbolic acid, often resulting in abscess formation. Frustrated by the ignorance concerning the biology of this disorder and discouraged by lack of effective therapies, most practitioners considered Hodgkin's disease fatal and provided supportive care only.

A small group of scientists refused to concede. They viewed Hodgkin's disease as a battle between the otherwise healthy patient and some unknown toxic substance. Instead of attempting to excise the undetermined source of the toxin, they maintained that one needed to increase the body's natural ability to repel the poisonous material. Thus began the era of vaccine therapy for Hodgkin's disease.

In 1928, University of Pittsburgh researchers Andrew Wallhauser and J. M. Whitehead hypothesized that since affected lymph nodes contained toxins, injections of extracts from these nodes might stimulate the body to produce antibodies against the substance. To test their theory, they excised an involved node, macerated it, pressed it through a filter, and injected small amounts of nodal extract into the same patient. Having no way to determine the concentration of the supposed toxin in the preparation, they selected the dose by trial and error. Too much of the solution produced fever and shaking chills; too little had no effect. But, if by chance, they injected the proper dose, nodes softened and shrank.

Within months, researchers in England, France, America, and Australia rushed to produce vaccines for patients with Hodgkin's disease. Each had his own hypothesis, each his own technique. Scientists minced nodes and pressed them through various filters in order to extract toxins, or elementary bodies, or some infectious agent they thought caused the disease. They injected patients with extracts from their own lymph nodes, or solutions from other patients' glands, or mixtures from several patients. Papers on sensitized lymphadenomatous gland filtrates and autogenous glandular extracts appeared in the most reputable journals. At scientific meetings, researchers touted the activity of their vaccines, predicting that Hodgkin's disease would soon be controlled. But responses were short-lived, and others couldn't confirm the results. Reports became less impressive, fewer in number, and were published in obscure journals.

Some postulated that injection of nodal extracts had failed because humans couldn't form antibodies against Hodgkin's disease. They thought this problem might be circumvented by inducing animals to make antibodies. Among the best-known trials of serum therapy were those conducted by Leslie Utz and Leila Keatinge at St. Vincent's Hospital in Sydney, Australia. Based on the assertion that Hodgkin's disease originated from a strain of tubercle bacillus also found in fowl, Utz and Keatinge chose chickens for producing antisera against Hodgkin's disease. They injected lymphoid tissue from a patient into the thigh of a hen, and after twelve days—during which time the animal supposedly was making antibodies against Hodgkin's tissue—they bled the hen and separated clear serum from the blood. They proceeded to treat patients with up to forty-nine injections of serum and reported that they had observed almost complete regression of enlarged nodes within weeks. Patients reacted to the chicken serum with fever, itching, redness at the injection site, and prostration. The more severe the toxicity, the better the response. When Utz and Keatinge published their results in the *Medical Journal of Australia*, physicians raised concerns over the ethics of treating patients with chicken serum. An investigation ensued, but they were exonerated. Unfortunately, other investigators could not repeat their results, and by the early 1930s, only a few champions of vaccine therapy remained.

It is not surprising that these early treatment approaches failed. Misconceptions regarding the nature of the disease had resulted in a series of false leads. The first major mistake was believing Hodgkin's disease to be an infection. Bacteria found in patients with Hodgkin's disease were actually secondary infections or contaminants. So treatment for tuberculosis and other infections inevitably failed. The second misconception was assuming the disease to be limited to sites that could be palpated. Surgical excision or injection with caustic chemicals only briefly controlled growth, because undetected disease was already present in other tissues. Identification of all sites of disease, later called staging, would prove crucial in planning therapy. But these early physicians had no accurate way to assess disease status—no means to detect enlarged nodes in the chest or abdomen. So they didn't know where to direct therapy.

⌣

The first major breakthrough in the treatment of this disease came about through the work of Wilhelm Roentgen (1845–1923), a leading German physicist, who had never thought about Hodgkin's disease. Having conducted brilliant work on gases, heat, and crystals, Roentgen was fifty when he began research on the physics of cathode rays.

Late one November day in 1895, his laboratory darkened by afternoon shadows, Roentgen covered a vacuum tube with black paper. When he turned on the current, a faint light on a nearby table caught his attention. This puzzled Roentgen, because light from the cathode tube could not have penetrated the thick black paper. Upon further investigation, he discovered the unexpected light emanated from a piece of cardboard lying on the table. That cardboard, used for another experiment, had been covered with a chemical that phosphoresced when struck by some form of energy. He suddenly realized he was observing a new kind of ray—invisible to the eye, unique in its power of penetration—that had emanated from the cathode tube, passed through the black paper, and caused the cardboard to glow. He named these mysterious rays "x-rays."

Six weeks after his initial observation, Roentgen submitted an article titled "Über eine neue Art von Strahlen" (On a New Kind of Ray) for publication. Within days after it appeared, his work made headlines around the world. "Sensational Discovery," the *Frankfurter Zeitung* announced. London's *Daily Chronicle* acclaimed "the marvelous triumph of science reported from Vienna." Roentgen had taken an x-ray of his wife Berta's hand, and photographs of the image caught the public's attention. The press speculated as to the medical implications of x-rays—diagnosis of fractures, locating the exact position of a bullet without the usual surgical probe. "In all probability," the *Nation* concluded, "the process can be perfected and modified so as to photograph the heart, lungs, liver, and other internal organs, and thus determine their precise condition." Despite Roentgen's protestations, a senior scientist insisted that x-rays be renamed "Roentgen rays."

A celebrity, Roentgen received thousands of congratulatory letters, scientific inquiries, and requests for public demonstrations. Reporters violated his privacy; strangers stole photographs and equipment from his laboratory. Entrepreneurs encouraged him to obtain a patent and exploit his discovery commercially, but he refused. "According to the good tradition of the German University professors," he said, "I am of the opinion that their discoveries and inventions belong to humanity." Roentgen received numerous prizes and medals. Thirty-four scientific societies made him an honorary member; towns conferred honorary citizenship; several streets bore his name. In 1901, he was awarded the first Nobel Prize in physics. By the time Roentgen died at age seventy-six, he had seen his discovery dramatically change the field of medicine.

⌒

If the value of Roentgen rays for medical diagnosis was immediately obvious, their therapeutic potential was not. Before long, however, physicians noticed that following prolonged exposure to diagnostic x-rays, patients developed skin burns or hair loss in the area beneath the x-ray tube. This led surgeons to utilize x-rays like a cautery to burn off cancers. The therapeutic x-ray tube resembled that for diagnostic radiology: a high voltage of electrical current was applied to accelerate electrons between the cathode and anode, hitting a target and causing electrons to give off energy in the form of x-rays. When tissues were exposed to x-rays for several minutes, changes occurred inside cells, releasing chemical products. These interacted with DNA, resulting in cell death. Although scientists of the early nineteen hundreds didn't know about electrons and DNA, they did observe the end result—death of cancer cells.

Soon after Roentgen's discovery, Swedish researchers announced regressions of skin cancers using Roentgen therapy. A prominent New York surgeon treated twenty cases of recurrent breast cancer with radiation. Many responded, and the disease disappeared entirely in one. Reports of successful treatment of stomach cancer were released from France, nasopharynx cancer from Germany, throat cancer from America. One case that caught the attention of the medical community was a thirty-nine-year-old New Haven schoolteacher with a uterine sarcoma. The tumor was so large that she appeared to be seven months pregnant. With x-ray treatments, it regressed completely.

William Allen Pusey, professor of dermatology at the University of Illinois in Chicago, had been treating patients with skin cancers for months when a four-year-old boy with Hodgkin's disease was referred to him. The child had had enlarged neck nodes for at least a year, and a surgeon had already removed those in the right neck. When Pusey examined the boy, he noted "a mass of glands on the left side as large as a fist." He exposed the tumor to x-rays for ten minutes daily, and in this first report of radiation therapy for Hodgkin's disease, published in 1902, he wrote, "In two months the glands were reduced to the size of an almond." Pusey included a photograph of the child, his neck distorted by massive nodes, and a follow-up photo of a normal-looking child.

A year later, Nicholas Senn, professor of surgery at Rush Medical College in Chicago, treated a forty-three-year-old saloonkeeper with Roentgen rays. The glands in his neck had grown so large that they obliterated his jawline, fusing his face with his neck. Enormous axillary nodes pushed his arms out from his chest, and his immense spleen distended his abdomen over his belt. Labored respiration indicated extension of the disease to bronchial nodes. He was dying of Hodgkin's disease.

"I prescribed, as usual, arsenic and iron," Senn wrote, "and, in view of the heretofore hopelessness in such cases, advised in addition the use of the Roentgen ray." Warned that he might sustain severe burns, the patient consented to the treatment. X-rays were applied daily to his neck, axillae, groin, and spleen, and by day ten of the therapy, the nodes had shrunk appreciably. The skin of his chest blistered, and his armpits turned dark brown; pus drained from his nipples. After thirteen more treatments, radiotherapy was suspended. The patient returned two weeks later with improved appetite and breathing. Senn could no longer feel any enlarged glands. His subsequent report included this patient and a similar case. In conclusion, Senn wrote, "The eminent success attained in these two cases . . . can leave no further doubt of the curative effect of the Roentgen therapy in the treatment of pseudoleucaemia [Hodgkin's disease]."

The melting away of massive nodes was impressive but transient. Irradiated nodes eventually enlarged again, and patients went on to die from the disease. This lack of long-term efficacy resulted from the technical inadequacies of Roentgen therapy. Those who administered it had no understanding of the physical nature or biological effects of these mysterious rays. They had no method to measure dose and no agreed-upon unit of dose. Equipment was unreliable. X-rays produced were of such low energy they had limited penetration. Doses concentrated in the skin, causing superficial burns with minimal effect on underlying tissue. "The prescription of dosage was so uncertain," one cancer specialist wrote, "and the results apparently so capricious that all one could really do was to place the patient under the machine and hope for the best. Patients were burned from unexpected leaks, and on one or more occasions, it is said, they were actually electrocuted on the treatment table."

Health hazards to those working with x-rays also gradually became apparent. At first, physicians viewed passage of x-rays through the body as that of light through glass. Since they couldn't see or feel the rays, they assumed them to be harmless. They used no protection and tested their equipment by taking repeated radiographs of their own hands. In time, they began to notice that the skin on their hands reddened and cracked, but they attributed these changes to electric current from the induction coil. Blisters erupted that wouldn't heal. A number of physicians developed aggressive, relentless skin cancers on their fingers and underwent a succession of amputations—first the fingertips, then whole fingers, then arms. Eventually they died of metastatic cancer. Radiation affected them internally as well. The cumulative effect on bone marrow resulted in marrow failure in some, leukemia in others. When the number of treatment failures increased, and disastrous side effects were reported, initial optimism about the wonders of Roentgen therapy was succeeded by a wave of pessimism. Radiation therapy might have been abandoned had it not been for two important advances.

The first was the development of the Coolidge tube in 1920. A major technical limitation had been the low electrical energy that x-ray tubes could withstand—fifty to seventy-five kilovolts. As a result, they emitted rays that penetrated only the superficial layers of tissues. In order to treat a tumor deep within the abdomen, x-ray exposure had to be prolonged, resulting in severe skin burns. The Coolidge tube could bear energy as high as two hundred kilovolts and thus emit more penetrating rays, which lessened this complication. Physicists designed more reliable machines and agreed upon a standard measurement of radiation, the roentgen. Most therapeutic plans for treating cancers, however, still consisted of a single high dose. Internal damage was marked. Vomiting, low blood counts, and intense swelling of organs necessitated prolonged bed rest. Enthusiasm for radiation therapy again began to wane.

The second important advance came from studies in radiation biology conducted by Claude Regaud at the Fondation Curie in Paris. He set out to investigate alternate strategies to the commonly employed single large dose. Regaud selected the ram testicle as his model, hypothesizing that with its high rate of cell turnover, sperm production mimicked malignant growth. He irradiated ram testicles with different doses at varying intervals and demonstrated that sperm production could not be totally eradicated with a single high dose of radiation. A smaller dose delivered over longer periods of time did produce sterilization. So he began to treat patients with small daily doses of radiation, given over several weeks, and found improved therapeutic effect with less toxicity. This concept of fractionated irradiation heralded the birth of clinical radiation therapy. Using two-hundred-kilovolt machines and fractionated irradiation, therapists of the early 1930s began to report excellent results with cancers of the throat, tongue, and breast. But success in Hodgkin's disease would remain limited until researchers could unravel the perplexing progression of this disease and plan therapy accordingly.

6   A Spartan Existence

The Chicago winter of 1934 was so cold that water froze in the fire hydrants. The temperature was below freezing for eight consecutive days, and the chilling wind from Lake Michigan, known as "the Hawk," blew down Lake Shore Drive at fifty-seven miles an hour. Hundreds of homeless lived under double-decked Wacker Drive with little protection from the record snowfall. The unemployed numbered more than 800,000 in Cook County; payrolls fell by 75 percent, foreclosures quadrupled, and there was no relief in sight. Chicago was in the midst of the "dismal decade." According to one account, there were "1000 men eating in bread lines food that costs 4½ cents a day, and these men are from the so-called gold coast." Despair prevailed; suicide was commonplace.

On December 24, 1934, seven weeks after Nathan's death, Sarah Kaplan received a letter from the New York Life Insurance Company. Expecting a check, she was surprised to learn that her husband had cashed in his life insurance policies in April 1930. Unable to afford the cottage at the lake, the duplex on Hawthorne Place, sleep-away summer camps, Nathan had invested their savings in the stock market in hope of turning a profit. His friend Joe Katz had told him that he couldn't lose. But he did. Their savings gone, he had taken out a loan on his life insurance policy—just until better times, when he planned to pay it back. But better times never came. His estate consisted of outdated dental equipment and a small amount of cash—barely enough to cover funeral expenses. When Nathan Kaplan died, he left Richard a pair of hairbrushes and a Masonic belt buckle; he left Henry his prayer shawl; he left Sarah penniless.

A widow at thirty-nine with two sons to support, Sarah faced a mortgage payment and a stack of medical bills. Her life changed quickly, radically. She packed away the samovar and tried to forget life as a Brilliant. They moved into a studio apartment, and her bitterness grew when she had to sell her elegant dining set and her own bedroom furniture. Looking out the window at boarded-up storefronts, she missed the stately trees lining Hawthorne Place. She felt herself sinking. Penniless, destitute—the words were terrifying, humiliating. She talked of suicide. Richard lived in fear—fear he'd become one of those children under Wacker Bridge, fear his mother would kill herself, and he'd be left an orphan. For the two boys, a relative said, "childhood vanished overnight."

Sarah could have become paralyzed, but when she looked at her Zinu, bent over his books, her determination returned. After all, she was a Brilliant, and she would survive. She went to work, keeping the drugstore open seven days a week, including evenings. At 5 A.M., she unloaded stock and prepared for the breakfast crowd. At midnight, she washed dishes and swept the floor. "She was a woman who had a job to do," a relative said. "Her job was to run the drugstore and keep the boys in school. It was just that simple." But she didn't do it alone. Henry, then a freshman on scholarship at the University of Chicago, worked at the store evenings and weekends. He didn't ask for a winter coat or money for the movies. He saved ten cents a day in carfare by walking the last mile of his commute to the university. Eliminating milk from his lunch, he saved another dime. But Henry never complained. "He's my rock," Sarah used to say.

Family and friends helped, as well. Joe Katz and Sarah's sister-in-law, Rose, formed a committee to save Kaplan Pharmacy. They collected contributions from relatives and neighbors to help pay the mortgage and stock the drugstore. "I gave her the few pennies I had," Rose recalled. But when they presented the gift to Sarah, they got no thanks. It was an affront to her dignity. She took the money but insisted upon a list of contributors. Each received a promissory note, and in time, Sarah paid back every cent.

The main reason Kaplan Pharmacy prospered was because of Sarah's industry. "She was a sharp businesswoman," Max Crocker said. One winter morning, cardboard lining her shoes to cover the holes, she visited the Hydox Ice Cream Company. When she came out, she had a deal: Hydrox would finance a soda fountain in her pharmacy, and she would sell its ice cream exclusively. Eventually, it funded a counter, ten stools, and two booths as well. Next, Sarah approached the Post Office to authorize a substation in her pharmacy as a service to the neighborhood. Once established, she charged the postal service rent. When customers walked to the back of the store to buy stamps, they often picked up a magazine or cigarettes as well. Furthermore, Sarah made arrangements with a traveling rental librarian to locate a lending library in her store. In the magazine rack, next to *Li'l Abner* and *Look Magazine*, lay *Lost Horizon*, *Lust for Life*, and *Good-bye, Mr. Chips*. With good books came educated people and their business.

Kaplan's remained open long after others had closed. It was the only place to get Vicks VapoRub late Saturday night or Bromo Quinine on Sunday morning, and it offered home delivery. At seven o'clock, Sarah fried eggs and grilled pancakes for men who worked downtown; at eleven o'clock, she served hot coffee and sandwiches to men coming off the evening shift from the dairy across the street. Before long, Kaplan Pharmacy had become an integral part of the neighborhood.

Sarah insisted on quality. Even if she wasn't sure she could pay the next month's rent, she provided first-rate products, and her customers came to expect them. She served the thickest hot fudge, fresh-baked bread, grade A eggs. "She spoke of Walgreens with contempt," Richard recalled. "She said they had their bread sliced especially for them—thinner, so they could get more slices per loaf." Catering to neighborhood women, Kaplan's offered a variety of cosmetics and toiletries displayed on glass shelves. When Sarah made a small profit, she ordered the better perfumes, like Shalimar and Chanel, and she began to attract customers with money to spend.

The first year in business, the boys were Sarah's only helpers. Richard dusted the counters, stacked magazines, made ice cream floats, and delivered prescriptions. Hank worked in the postal substation. "I remember people waiting in line at the post office for stamps," his Aunt Rose recalled, "and Henry's got his face in a book." He also filled in as pharmacist. Measuring out liver pills and cough syrup in his white coat and tortoise-shell glasses, he looked like a doctor. And customers began to treat him like one.

Sarah and her sons became increasingly resilient. She never missed a day at the store, even when she broke her leg. She survived several robberies. One night a nervous young man pulled out a gun and held it to Sarah's head. "Hey, that's a real gun," Richard blurted out at which point the man swung around and aimed the gun at Richard. "Now, he's only a boy," Sarah said calmly. "He doesn't know what he's talking about. If you just ignore him, I'll give you all the money." But if she gave him all the money, she couldn't pay for incoming orders. So at the risk of getting shot, she reached into the cash register and took out a stack of one-dollar bills, leaving the tens and twenties in the register. The robber grabbed the money and ran. Few could outwit Sarah Kaplan.

The pharmacy flourished, but for years the earnings just covered the mortgage payments and new inventory. The boys adjusted to their spartan existence. Hank slept in the kitchen on an army cot, stretched between the sink and stove. He studied at the kitchen table, a bare light bulb overhead. But with his chemistry text in front of him and Chopin on the radio, Henry was happy.

⌐

At the age of sixteen, after only three years of high school, Henry entered the University of Chicago. Its intense student body maintained an atmosphere of academic exhilaration. In describing a model undergraduate, one university president wrote: "He must be bright . . . in some extravagant and unusual way. He must have read and pondered esoteric things far beyond his years. He draws a sharp breath when reference is made to Aristotle, St. Thomas, John Donne, and James Joyce. He wears glasses, does not dance, deplores sports, and has advanced ideas on labor and the theory of relativity."

The freshman class had a grade point average of 95 percent, and for the first time, Henry met classmates who answered questions before he could. In addition, he belonged to the most competitive group—Jewish premedical students. Though unacknowledged, a Jewish quota for medical school admissions was known to exist. His freshman year was difficult—the long commute, trudging several blocks in freezing weather, late hours at the pharmacy, and a bad case of pleurisy, requiring weeks in the infirmary. When he got his first B on an exam, he was upset. More hours of study followed, and by the end of the academic year, Henry Kaplan stood fourth among the "ten brightest freshmen" at the university, according to the *Chicago Daily News.* Even so, he knew he could do even better. For the next two years, he spent countless hours at the kitchen table bent over his books and was rewarded by election to Phi Beta Kappa. At the University of Chicago, Henry learned that he was not always right, and that the world was more exciting with a receptive mind, important lessons that his mother had not taught him. The university fostered in him a budding inclination—the desire to investigate.

At first, Henry had limited time to socialize. He mainly befriended upper-middle-class Jewish intellectuals from the North Side: the Linn brothers, Bob Leibler, Gladys Adelman, Mirielle and Niecy Fein. Commuting together, they carried on a "six-way elitist conversation," a friend said, debating the New Deal's potential to restore prosperity, the political implications of Roosevelt's Good Neighbor Policy. They argued about almost everything, but among all those profound polemics was one ongoing dispute—was it cloudier on the North Side or the South Side?

On weekends, they gathered to play anagrams, listen to classical music, and talk. There was always an air of playful competition. "We'd listen to symphonic music," a former girlfriend recalled, "and Hank would ask, 'Who wrote it? In the first few phrases, you ought to know.' I had to know the difference between a Brahms and a Schubert or I was in trouble." Although reserved, Hank was thoughtful. He warned fair-haired Irwin Linn of the dangers of excessive exposure to the sun. "Of course if you get skin cancer," he told Irwin, "I'll take care of you." When Mirielle Fein Linn, as a young bride, confided in Hank that she "didn't know a lamb chop from a steak," he took her to a butcher shop and instructed her on the various cuts and grades of meat. "If you needed a friend and knew Hank, you were lucky," Robert Linn said. But if Hank found a conversation dull or a newcomer to their group pedestrian, he didn't hesitate to sit in the corner and read.

Eventually, he began to date—Vera Rooney, Florence Yard, and Mirielle Fein. Hank had reached his full height of just over six feet. Slimmed down, with dark, curly hair, he was almost handsome. He dated sparingly, because it cost too much. Besides, he was a bit awkward with girls. After an evening with Hank, Florence Yard told a friend, "He didn't allow himself to be social." Another girl complained to Irwin Linn that Hank was a bore. In truth, girls were a distraction. He spent most of his time in class, at the pharmacy, or studying. "Hank wasn't very light in those days," his brother said. He didn't have much fun—until Max Crocker moved his family to Chicago.

Max had a son, Norman, who was Hank's age. Shorter and slighter than his cousin, Norm had wavy brown hair, an easy smile, and a relaxed manner. Good-looking and sociable, "he was going out on dates when Hank didn't know what girls looked like," Richard said. Although Norm wasn't a genius, he attended the University of Chicago and was smart enough to gain his cousin's respect. What particularly attracted Hank to Norm was his enjoyment of life. His cousin awoke a sensation deep inside him that had withered when his father became ill. It was something akin to levity. Under his cousin's tutelage, Hank flowered. The two became inseparable. "I brought him the key to having fun," Norman said. "And I brought him wheels."

Norman had a 1927 Pierce-Arrow, a large gray car with black fenders, leather seats, bright red spoke wheels, and a rumble seat—the so-called "Mercedes of the twenties." Hank had never imagined he could love a car, but he loved that car. On Saturday nights, they jumped into the Pierce-Arrow, drove to Chinatown, and had what they considered a feast—for a dollar. Or they rode to the movies for a free triple feature, compliments of a classmate's father. Or they just cruised around. "I liked Hank more when he was with Norman," Richard said. He actually became playful.

Sarah encouraged the friendship. By then, she could afford help in the pharmacy, and she wanted her son to enjoy himself. She even gave him a couple of extra dollars when she could. In summer, Hank and Norman played tennis or met the gang at the beach. In the fall, they ushered at University of Chicago football games, and even though Chicago always ranked at the bottom of the Big Ten, their enthusiasm never waned. And Norm introduced Hank to music written after the eighteen hundreds. One rainy night, he took Hank to a small hotel for a drink. The room was practically empty. A young musician named Benny Goodman took center stage and played for an hour. "Hank went out of his mind," Norman said.

Hank and Norman always stopped by the drugstore for a milkshake before Sarah closed at midnight. She delighted in hearing about the evening's adventures. She didn't resent the growing affection between the two. She still remained central to Hank's life—his confidante. And Sarah couldn't resist Norman with his gentle teasing, his ready laughter. He was one of the few who could put his arm around her shoulders.

Despite their tomfoolery, Hank's grades didn't suffer. Norman, too, was a serious student, and they shared a love of intellectual repartee. Hank admired his cousin's sophistication, his ease with people. As their relationship deepened, they shared confidences. Hank asked advice about girls. Once he confessed that he couldn't dance, but he had always wanted to learn. Norman was talented at tap as well as ballroom dancing. He offered to teach his cousin. Pulling down the living room shades, he turned on the radio and showed Hank a few steps, but he just couldn't get the beat. Norm took the woman's position, and arm in arm, the two waltzed around the room, bumping into furniture, tripping over each other's feet, laughing. For several years, Hank and Norman were together daily. They shared nonstop banter, from the esoteric to the ridiculous. "Hi, Stinky," they greeted each other. With his cousin, Hank could be silly; he could be young. And with his cousin began a lifelong pattern of male intimacy.

⤳

In 1937, after three years of undergraduate education, Henry Kaplan was admitted to Rush Medical College, at the time affiliated with the University of Chicago. The faculty, which included a number of distinguished scientists, might have been brilliant, but the physical plant was not. Rush Medical College consisted of two square brick buildings, distinguished only by an ornate wooden entrance. The Rawson building contained the laboratories and the central free dispensary; the Senn building, two amphitheaters and the clinics. One side of the school abutted the hospital; the other faced the Pinks—a bright pink apartment complex that housed a large Italian population. The air smelled of nearby stockyards.

With high expectations, the class of 1940 began their preclinical years. Among them was nineteen-year-old Henry Seymour Kaplan. The excitement soon dissipated; they faced full days of lectures and nights of rote memorization. The stimulation to think creatively, to question, so prevalent during the undergraduate years, was now dulled by the droning litany of anatomy: *peroneus longus, flexor retinaculum, vastus medialis.* Students spent hours in the anatomy laboratory with their cadavers. The sweet, pungent smell of formaldehyde permeated their books, clothes, and hair. Physiologic chemistry was no better, with pages upon pages of biochemical formulae that seemed to have no relevance to patients.

At first, Henry Kaplan did not stand out in his class like gregarious Frederic de Peyster, the class president, or Dick Korney, who kept two rattlesnakes in his room, or lovely Julie Olentine, for whom achieving an A seemed easy. Classmates noticed his abnormal hand, but no one remembered its hindering his intricate dissections in anatomy or his ability to suture. In the lecture hall, Henry rarely asked questions. He didn't have to; "he knew the answers," de Peyster said.

As sophomores, the class encountered more of the same—hours sitting through pathology, pharmacology, and neurology lectures. They memorized extensive charts that mapped the course of each nerve from its origin in the brain to its site of innervation. They reviewed hundreds of microscopic slides until they could distinguish hepatitis from cirrhosis, glomerulonephritis from pyelonephritis. They made their first trip to the morgue to observe an autopsy. Their professors showed them brain slices, gallstones, kidney stones—but never a patient. Although most found the preclinical years tedious, Henry became intoxicated with basic science. He wasn't content just memorizing the names of cells he saw under the microscope, he wanted to know how they functioned, what made cells of one organ behave differently from cells of another. And he was particularly interested in cancer cells—what stimulated their growth; how could it be stopped? He planned to have his own laboratory one day; he planned to find out.

Finally, the class put on their white coats and entered the wards. "It was as if the pearly gates of heaven opened," de Peyster said. They learned clinical medicine from George Dick, a brilliant researcher, who had found the cause of scarlet fever. On his "Professor's service," he stressed excellence in general medicine. In the operating room, they observed Vernon David, who had devised the classic operation for rectal cancer. For two years, the class rotated through internal medicine, pediatrics, psychiatry, obstetrics and gynecology, and surgery. On the wards, they obtained laboratory specimens before eight o'clock rounds and then spent the day examining patients, performing minor procedures, attending operations. The most thrilling rotation was the home delivery program, dubbed "going into the district," in which pairs of medical students delivered the babies of dispensary patients at home.

On the wards, in the clinics, in the district, Henry Kaplan learned to be a doctor. In his meticulous way, he sharpened his clinical skills until he could perform a physical examination as well as he could solve a biochemical problem. But he enjoyed more than just making the correct diagnosis; he loved hearing patients' stories. He understood why his father was happy going to the office each day. And he made another discovery: when he cared for others, he got something intangible back in return.

Henry's best friend in medical school was Abraham Braude. Hank could see through the three-piece suit, Phi Beta Kappa key, and rimless glasses. Abe's innate brilliance, coupled with his exuberance and humor, attracted him. To dampen the boredom of anatomy laboratory, they played trivia while they dissected. Braude was an inveterate tease, who occasionally took unsuspecting young ladies to the anatomy lab late at night and watched their reactions when shown the glass cases filled with hearts and kidneys. Hank and Abe entertained classmates with their medical spoofs; they were proud co-owners of an old Studebaker. Like Henry, Abe was a fervent man—about politics, music, science, and their friendship. During the war, after Abe had been on leave, Henry wrote to him:

> Those two or three days we had together were wonderful—the kind of days I had been dreaming about for two years. And although I begrudged every moment you spent meeting relatives and other people, it was still one of the best times I've ever had. Only we didn't seem to realize, at the moment, just how short the time really was. Now that you're not here anymore, I can think of dozens of things I wanted to say. . . . I didn't have time to really say goodbye. I rushed for a train and got on and waved and then you were gone.

Medical school entailed hours of study, insufficient sleep, and a constant shortage of cash. Pleasures were few. During their third year, however, a classmate's girlfriend arranged a blind date for Henry with a senior at University High School. That evening, a doorman ushered him into a fashionable apartment building at 4300 Lake Shore Drive. He entered a living room decorated in high rococo, with pastel pink walls and delicate French furniture. The love seats were arranged to accentuate the magnificent view of Lake Michigan. Henry stood motionless as a willowy young woman with dark eyes and full red lips walked into the room. Her thick, brunette hair fell to her shoulders. She wore a pink cashmere sweater. "Hello, I'm Leah Lebeson," she said extending her slender hand to Henry. She was the most beautiful woman he had ever seen.

Everything in Leah's appearance spoke of wealth—silk stockings that accentuated her long legs, a scarf from Marshall Field's designer boutique casually tied around her neck. When she put on her fur coat with its high collar and padded shoulders, she looked as if she had stepped off the society page of the *Chicago Tribune*. At parties, young men surrounded her. "Effervescent" was a word used to describe her. Had that been all, Henry would have found her tiresome. On their first date, however, he discovered that she could discuss current events and art. And she had the most wonderful, spirited laugh. It seemed to burst forth, travel across the room, settle in your ear, and make you smile.

Despite the trappings of wealth, Leah was without airs. She liked people far more than material things. When she entered a room, she became the center of attention, but she didn't seem to notice; she focused on others. Henry couldn't help observing the way she leaned over when she spoke with someone, looking directly into the person's eyes. Whether discussing the stock market with a sober schoolmate or a hopeless romance with a distressed girlfriend, she had a knack for making people feel good. She had much in her life that Henry had never known—money, class, social grace, popularity—yet she maintained her modesty and humor. Leah Lebeson was a spectacular young woman, and Henry was in love.

7   The Courtship of Leah Lebeson

Henry Kaplan was in love. "I don't love her [just] for her beauty," he wrote Abe Braude, "but for her unselfishness, her sensitive consideration . . . of others, her intellectual curiosity." So great was Leah's joie de vivre, Henry never would have suspected her tragic family secret. He had her father, Harry Lebeson, to thank for that.

At eleven, Lebeson had emigrated from Russia to escape the pogroms. A stocky, energetic young man, he supported himself through veterinary school. Initially, he worked as a government livestock inspector, but he dreamed of having his own business. During the Depression, he was able to buy the Allied Screw Machine Company, a bankrupt Chicago manufacturing firm. He speculated that since jobs were scarce and the future for many white-collar careers uncertain, men would be seeking to retrain for manual jobs. Using his factory as a classroom to teach the tool and die trade, Lebeson established the Allied School of Mechanical Trade, one of the first private vocational training schools in America. When the prewar buildup of tanks and planes began, Lebeson increased the production end of his operation, turning it into a lucrative sheet-metal plant. Now financially secure, he married Sarah Greenberg, a cheerful, pretty woman. On April 23, 1921, their first daughter, Leah Hope, was born, followed by Shirley two years later.

A delicate child, Leah always seemed to have a cold or tonsillitis. When she was seven, a chest x-ray was interpreted as showing a congenital heart defect. Specialists told her parents nothing could be done; her heart would gradually fail. To help prolong her life, they should reduce the strain on her heart. So while Shirley ran off to the beach, Leah lay in bed. Her father sent her to a fresh-air school that had cots in the classroom for children to rest between lessons. After school, her mother took her for sun treatments at Edgewater Beach Hotel. When they went shopping, she insisted Leah ride in a wheelchair. But Leah didn't get sicker; she grew stronger and taller than her classmates and eventually refused a wheelchair. She skipped rope and played hopscotch without becoming short-winded, without her fingertips turning blue. Years later, Henry Kaplan obtained her early x-rays and discovered that they had been taken at an angle, producing the false impression of an abnormal cardiac shadow. Leah had never had a heart defect.

As her daughter's health improved, Sarah's deteriorated. Doctors couldn't find the cause of the facial pain that plagued her for years. One suggested dental problems, another sinusitis. They recommended root canals, dental extractions, heated poultices, cold packs. Nothing relieved her. A hand brushing across her face or her husband's kiss triggered paroxysms of pain in her lips, gums, and cheek. Finally, a specialist made the diagnosis—tic douloureux, a neuralgia of unknown cause that affects the facial nerve. Patients suffer intermittent lancinating pain, causing them to wince, as if with a tic. In constant torture, Sarah could barely think about her family. She became despondent. In desperation, she agreed to an operation. A surgeon cut through the base of her skull and severed the nerve. Sarah came home from the hospital with her head bandaged, her scalp partly shaved. Her facial muscles were paralyzed; the right side of her face sagged. She couldn't close one eyelid, so that when she slept, the white of that eye was exposed, creating an eerie stare. She had a crooked smile; she drooled. And she still had unbearable pain.

A few days after her mother's return home, Leah's uncle unexpectedly picked up the girls from school. He said he was taking them to visit their grandmother in Michigan. As he drove away, the questions began. Why were they going to grandmother's? Where were mother and father? Why was uncle crying? Several miles out of Chicago, he pulled off the roadway. He told Leah and Shirley that their mother had fainted and hit her head against a radiator. Blood had gone to her brain, and she was dead.

During the funeral and the weeks that followed, Leah sensed something was amiss—the way relatives lowered their voices when she and Shirley entered the room. Years later, she confronted her father. He sobbed as he told her the truth: When their mother had returned from the hospital, she was severely depressed. Surgery had failed to relieve her pain and had left her with a grotesque scar and facial paralysis. One morning, after the girls had gone to school and Harry to work, she had sent the housekeeper to the store and hanged herself from the rafters.

At the time, Harry Lebeson was working twelve hours a day, building his business. He didn't know how to starch pinafores or braid hair. Most men of that time would not have considered rearing children by themselves and would have remarried or sent their children to live with relatives. Not Harry Lebeson. He had been raised by a stepmother who never cared for him, and sending his daughters away was unthinkable. He resolved to give them a loving home. After a series of incompetent housekeepers, he hired Mary Williams, a black woman with a warm sense of humor and enough energy to handle his two high-spirited daughters.

Nine-year-old Leah was tall and gangly, often tripping as she dashed off to some new adventure. Close at her heels ran seven-year-old Shirley. After school, they rode their bikes over to the Edgewater for chocolate sodas; on Saturdays, they took a bus downtown for chicken salad sandwiches at DeMets. They always seemed to be giggling about something, and their laugh—a full-bodied, joyous staccato—was unique. Once, a total stranger, hearing Shirley laugh, asked if she had a sister named Leah.

Harry tried to raise his daughters the way he thought his wife would have done. He sent them to a fashionable summer camp to learn horseback riding, golf, and tennis, and to a finishing school to learn proper social behavior. And he secured their admission to the elite University of Chicago High School. Their Aunt Gertie was charged with selecting their wardrobes. No shoes fitted Leah's oversized feet; dresses wouldn't button around Shirley's plump figure, and each shopping ordeal ended in uncontrollable giggles in a Marshall Field's dressing room. Once, when Leah was approaching puberty, a close family friend asked her to lunch. Leah idolized the woman, a successful psychoanalyst. Their conversation drifted to the facts of life, and the woman explained them in a gentle and natural way. Years later, Leah discovered that her father had planned the luncheon. Above all, Harry Lebeson gave his daughters affection. Although he usually finished work after the girls had gone to bed, he frequently stopped at a grocery and picked up ice cream. Shirley remembered him standing in their bedroom doorway with two Dixie cups and wooden spoons, hoping they would awaken.

Before long, Harry's two little girls had matured into lovely young women. Shirley's baby fat disappeared, and a dark-haired beauty emerged. Leah's spindly legs became slender; her bob grew out to shoulder-length, wavy hair; her mischievous look became enchanting. And boys began to call.

When Hank Kaplan met Leah, she had just been voted "most popular senior" at University High School, and she could barely fit him into her social schedule. Young men from the Gold Coast and Hyde Park picked her up in their own cars; Hank came by streetcar. Boyfriends made reservations at fine restaurants; Hank took her to public museums. Suitors came to her door in evening coats and cravats; Henry wore the same long, black overcoat he had worn for the past six winters. And he sold his own blood to a transfusion service—"blood money" he called it—so that he could afford to take Leah to the movies. Although the Lebesons lived only a few blocks from the Kaplans, walking to their apartment, Richard said, "was like crossing the world."

Every date was an educational exercise. They never merely listened to a symphony; they analyzed the violin solo or noted the discordant rhythm of the tympani. On the way to a movie, they talked about capitalism; on the way home, they talked about socialism. Leah found Hank far too serious. "When I first met him," she recalled, "he wasn't the sort of guy you'd want to spend a lot of time with." Henry, on the other hand, found Leah captivating. She delighted in a new sonata, a snowfall, a funny old man selling hot dogs, a stray cat; she enjoyed life more than anyone he had ever met. And she loved to laugh. She and her sister teased him mercilessly, calling him "the bear that walks like a man." He, in turn, called them "the Sisters Karamazov." Leah Lebeson crept into Henry's mind as he studied. His step became lighter; he hummed to himself more often.

Hank could hardly wait for Norm Crocker to come home at Thanksgiving. He invited Leah and Shirley to go out with them. "They were two of the most delightful, sexy, beautiful, funny girls [I'd] ever seen," Norm said. By Christmas, however, Henry was distraught and sought Norm's advice. He was crazy about Leah, but she had a number of wealthy guys chasing her, willing to spend a fortune, and she had grown up with fine things. "Mr. Lebeson's got money he hasn't even counted or folded yet," Hank told him. To make matters worse, Leah had begun to affect his work. He couldn't concentrate; his career was threatened. "I told him there was only one thing to do," Norm said, "stop seeing her." So without an explanation, Hank quit calling.

Leah, then a freshman at the University of Chicago, was busy with classes and college activities. For a while, she didn't miss him. After several months, however, her boyfriends began to seem immature, their conversations boring, their concerns trivial. Her thoughts turned toward Hank. Here was a man who stepped on her toes when they danced, whose tie was crooked, who brought her old records instead of flowers and candy. He would never join the family business or vacation at Miami Beach, but he was a man who became so excited hearing violinist Jascha Heifetz that he didn't notice what he was eating, who walked ten blocks in the snow, his feet wet, to see a new exhibit at the Chicago Institute of Fine Art. And, in contrast to most of the men Leah knew, he had passion, a defined purpose to his life. She found herself thinking more and more about Henry Kaplan.

Leah hadn't seen Hank for months. She dragged her sister to the hospital and sat in the luncheonette, sipping coffee, waiting to bump into him "accidentally." Hours later, he walked in with a nurse, and Leah, acting surprised to see him, made a few casual remarks. Obviously uncomfortable, he failed to grasp her intent.

When Norm Crocker attended Hank's medical school graduation, he spotted a group of pretty coeds among the parents and guests. Looking more closely, he saw Leah and Shirley Lebeson. After the final procession, Leah boldly walked up to Hank, shook his hand and expressed her sincere congratulations. Perhaps it was her touch or the way she looked at him that made him realize their meeting was more than just chance. Although Hank had long since stopped talking about Leah, he had never stopped thinking about her. When Norm saw them together, he knew he had given his cousin the wrong advice. Leah told Norm she would be at a strawberry festival, hosted by one of the fraternities, that night. Later, he asked Hank to go to the festival with him to celebrate. As they stood dipping fresh strawberries into bowls of powdered sugar, in walked Leah Lebeson. And she headed straight for Henry. "Hank and Leah ended up in a car necking," Norm said.

↫

Henry had found the girl he planned to marry. But just when the two wanted to be together all the time, his internship began. For an entire year, he immersed himself in medicine. Along with Abe Braude and Ed Laden, he interned at Michael Reese Hospital, located on the South Side in a run-down neighborhood adjacent to the Illinois Central railroad tracks. Why did these three top students choose this internship, instead of a more prestigious one at a university hospital? "If you planned to practice in Chicago," Laden said, "and if you were Jewish, you wanted to be on the staff at Michael Reese," where most of the Jewish physicians admitted their patients. Besides, a Jewish quota existed. "We probably couldn't have gotten internships in many places," he said.

Like most new graduates in the 1940s, Henry took a rotating internship, divided among five services: medicine, surgery, obstetrics and gynecology, pediatrics, and psychiatry. On the surgical service, he drew blood and prepared patients for surgery before dawn; he assisted all day in the operating room, holding retractors. In the evening, he changed dressings on the surgical patients and sewed up lacerations in the emergency room. On the medical wards, he cared for fifteen to twenty-five patients with heart failure, syphilis, diabetes, or tuberculosis. If lucky, he slept a couple of hours each night. These were the days before penicillin, when pneumonia was a deadly disease. The ravings of schizophrenics mystified physicians. Confined on the lockup ward, they were wrapped in cold, wet sheets. Cancer was considered a hopeless disease.

Henry lived in the hospital, assigned a sparse, single room. Most interns thought this a deprivation. Not Henry; for years he had slept in the kitchen. The compensation for working every day and every other night was free room and board. But the food was so tasteless that Henry covered everything with ketchup, calling it "local anesthesia."

During internship, Henry had little time for the symphony, museums, tennis, or Leah. They shared a hurried meal in a neighborhood Greek restaurant, a quick kiss in a vacant corridor. Leah could count on his falling asleep at a slow-paced movie. Once, Hank arranged for Leah's admission to an observation room so that she could watch him assist at an appendectomy. All she saw of her beloved that evening was a masked figure holding retractors. The stolen moments together seemed to intensify their relationship. One balmy spring evening after a movie and a snack, they parked at a favorite spot. Hank suddenly said, "Leah, let's get married." Full of hamburgers and root beer, Leah unintentionally burped. "I assume that means 'yes,'" he said.

Now they had to obtain their families' blessings. The first time Hank brought Leah to the pharmacy, Sarah ignored her, busying herself with customers. Undaunted, Leah walked back to the postal substation and introduced herself to sixteen-year-old Richard. "So, how are you?" she asked. He thought Hank's girl was gorgeous, but he ignored her. When she again asked, "So how are you?" he snapped back: "You already asked me that." He later admitted to being jealous: Hank got everything—brains, medical school honors, their mother's affection, and now a stunning girl who lived on the Gold Coast and had her own car. But Leah soon won Richard over when she asked about him—his friends, his track meets—and when she teased his high-and-mighty brother. Besides, he liked Henry better when he was with Leah. "It's hard to imagine somebody as young as Hank picking a wife who complemented him as much as she did," Richard said.

Sarah, ever the good businesswoman, weighed Leah's assets and liabilities. Although she appeared healthy, Leah had had a heart condition that kept her bedridden as a child. Sarah worried that someday Hank might be nursing an invalid, conjuring up images from *Ethan Frome*. On the other hand, Leah's life exemplified what Sarah's would have been had her family prospered, had she married the right man. Leah came from an affluent Jewish family; she wore clothes advertised in magazines; and she talked about the economy and opera—Henry had given Leah a crash course in the latter subject. And her son appeared happier than he had ever been. He could do worse. So Sarah didn't object.

At first, Harry Lebeson hadn't paid much attention to Henry Kaplan. He was just one of many young men who called upon his daughter, perhaps a bit more serious than most. But Lebeson's impression changed after the evening they first played cards. Leah was taking a long time to dress, and the two men sat in the pink rococo living room making idle conversation, something neither did comfortably. Lebeson, who considered himself a master at gin rummy, nonchalantly asked Henry to play. He replied that he had never played before, but would like to learn. When Henry won the first hand, Lebeson didn't mind;

he felt benevolent toward the well-mannered fellow who called him "sir." Hank, however, proceeded to beat him at every game. Lebeson appreciated not only the keen mind of this young man who surpassed him at gin rummy but also his willingness to trounce his date's father. In fact, Lebeson enjoyed the competition so much that he began to monopolize Hank whenever he came to visit. Shirley knew how much Hank disliked cards, yet he spent hours playing with her father while courting Leah. "I often thought 'a greater love hath no man,'" Shirley said.

Leah anticipated her father's objection to their marriage. "Dad," she said to him one evening at dinner, "Hank and I would like to get married." Before he could say a word, she continued, "and he's going to be a resident, making thirteen dollars a week. If you give me a job at twenty to twenty-five, we can get along." That was the first Lebeson had heard of their engagement. He had always hoped his daughter would marry someone who would join him in the family business. He worried she was marrying a man who would be secluded in a basement laboratory with rats and test tubes. "But I liked the idea because I liked him," Lebeson said. "And so I told her I'd think about it."

Lebeson did think about it. He didn't want Leah to quit school to work, but he knew Henry would never take a handout. So he devised an ingenious plan. His company and school employed over a hundred workers and had a thousand students. On-the-job injuries occurred frequently, and loss of labor cut productivity. Lebeson called Henry to his office. "Look," he said, "we've quite a few people working here, and I'd like to set up a first aid station where any of my employees could get an examination. If you could spare one or two afternoons to supervise it, I could offer you something." Henry agreed. He organized a health service, hired a nurse, and provided medical care for the workers. Lebeson's employees appreciated it; the school's prestige increased; Lebeson paid Henry three hundred dollars a month, and he gave Leah and Henry his blessing.

Two years after they first met, Leah and Henry married. She was twenty; he was twenty-three. The wedding took place on June 21, 1941, with seventy-five guests crowding into the Lebeson apartment. Flowers covered the entire wall facing the lake, a canopy in the center. Posing for wedding pictures with Harry Lebeson were three other short, stout men—Leah's pediatrician, the rabbi, and the family lawyer. Without a wife's guidance, Harry had looked to them for help. The pediatrician gave Leah her premarital checkup, the rabbi a premarital lecture, and the lawyer advice on budgeting—something she had never done. Leah referred to them as "the three wise men."

The wedding proceeded smoothly, although Sarah insisted that Hank walk her down the aisle, indicating that she was giving away her son. Leah didn't laugh once during the ceremony, and when Henry crushed the glass, he sealed a marriage that lasted the rest of his life. As Harry Lebeson hugged his new son-in-law, Hank said over his shoulder to a friend, "He just loves me because I'm going to support his daughter."

Sarah had always hoped that Hank would open a medical practice in Chicago. She disparaged a career in academic medicine where he would be working for someone else. "My mother understands so little of what I'm all about," he told Leah. But Lebeson understood; he knew about determination. His son-in-law said he planned to cure cancer, whatever it took. So Lebeson wasn't surprised when after two years of radiology training at Michael Reese, Hank announced their move to Minneapolis. There he would study with an eminent radiologist, Leo Rigler, and begin his research on the cause of cancer.

8   Headway with Hodgkin's Disease

In 1940, Charles Craft, a radiotherapist at University of Minnesota's Department of Radiology and Physical Therapy, reported that roentgen therapy could prolong the lives of patients with Hodgkin's disease. He compared survival of 179 patients treated with x-rays between 1929 and 1936 with a group who had received supportive care alone. At five years, 23 percent of those treated were still alive, while 94 percent of the untreated patients were dead. "These significant differences should convince even the most dubious of the effectiveness of roentgen ray therapy in Hodgkin's disease," Craft wrote.

Craft's improved survival rate resulted from forty years of progress. As the quality of radiographs improved, physicians discovered sites of disease involvement beyond those they could palpate. Chest x-rays revealed enlarged nodes in the chest—mediastinal nodes—in half the patients. This finding explained the difficulty breathing and swallowing some patients experienced. Skeletal radiographs showed that affected bones reacted with intense new bone formation, causing "ivory vertebrae," as radiologists called the characteristic bright white bones. But x-rays could not visualize abdominal contents well, and intra-abdominal lymph node enlargement went undetected until a mass obstructed the kidneys or bile duct, causing renal failure or jaundice. By then, it was too late for treatment to be effective.

Better radiologic evaluation triggered the concept of stage—the initial extent of a patient's disease—and how it influenced survival. Those whose disease was confined to lymph nodes in the neck lived longer than those who had generalized disease. But occasionally clinicians noted that disease in patients of the same age, sex, and initial stage behaved differently. Of two young men with Hodgkin's disease confined to the right neck, one was alive and healthy twenty years after treatment, while the other lost weight, became markedly short of breath, and died within months. Researchers began to suspect that all cases of Hodgkin's disease were not alike. Two Harvard professors showed this to be the case.

In 1944, Henry Jackson and Frederic Parker reviewed the pathologic material and case histories of 259 patients diagnosed with Hodgkin's disease at Boston City, Collis P. Huntington Memorial, and Pondville Hospitals. After correlating the appearance of lymphoid tissue under the microscope and the clinical course, they identified three distinct subtypes of Hodgkin's disease, which they termed granuloma, paragranuloma, and sarcoma.

The subtype that displayed the more commonly seen pathologic characteristics described by Dorothy Reed—bands of fibrous tissue and Reed-Sternberg cells—they called granuloma. These patients usually had disease localized to a single node or nodal group, which spread insidiously to involve spleen, liver, bone, or lung. Survival averaged three years. As an example, Jackson and Parker described a twenty-two-year-old housepainter whose disease had begun as a painless, walnut-sized lump in his left neck. Six months later, he began to have attacks of fever every six weeks, the so-called Pel-Ebstein fever. During attacks he became bedridden. A chest x-ray showed a small mediastinal mass, which regressed following radiation treatments. Four months later, however, he developed an enlarged liver and spleen. Jaundice and inanition followed, and the patient died a year after diagnosis.

They identified a second subtype—paragranuloma—which appeared far less aggressive. Microscopically, lymphoid tissue from patients with this subtype contained abundant lymphocytes, the cells normally found in lymph nodes. They were not, however, organized in an orderly pattern; instead, the lymph node was totally effaced. Jackson and Parker found only rare diagnostic Reed-Sternberg cells. Clinically, these patients also had disease confined to a single site, but they survived an average of eleven years. The authors wrote of a thirty-six-year-old woman who had had enlarged lymph glands removed from her right neck at age ten. Twice during her youth, nodes in her right neck had become enlarged and again were resected. She was still alive and free of disease twenty-six years after its onset.

The third and most malignant variant of Hodgkin's disease—the sarcoma subtype—contained abundant Reed-Sternberg cells and other large cells of varied size and shape. Patients with this type survived an average of six months. Jackson and Parker described a thirty-seven-year-old man who had gone to his doctor complaining of stomach pains. The physician felt an orange-sized mass in his abdomen and massive nodes in the neck and axillae. The patient was treated with low doses of irradiation to all these sites, resulting in dramatic regression. Six months later, the pain recurred, and the lymph nodes measured up to ten centimeters in size. Three weeks before his death, the patient suffered constant fevers. A mass protruded from his skull. At autopsy, Hodgkin's disease was found in his lymph nodes, liver, pancreas, kidney, bowel, and bones.

Jackson and Parker published their remarkable findings in the *New England Journal of Medicine*, and the Jackson-Parker system was widely adopted as the first major pathologic classification system. It would remain unmodified for the next two decades. But the underlying cause of Hodgkin's disease remained a puzzle. By mid 1930, researchers had divided into two camps—those who considered Hodgkin's disease a cancer and those who considered it an inflammatory reaction.

In the meantime, the field of radiation therapy had entered a new era—that of treatment planning and dosimetry, the measurement of tissue dose. Prior to the 1920s, therapists had treated patients empirically; now they had guidance from radiation physicists. Using ionization chambers, physicists computed accurate radiation dose by measuring the quantity of ions produced by a particular x-ray beam. They developed isodose curves—diagrams that displayed distribution of radiation in the body and its variation with dose, distance between the x-ray tube and patient, machine energy, and thickness of filters. They found that normal cells recuperated from the effects of radiation faster than cancer cells. Thus, dividing the total dose into smaller fractions given over several days allowed normal tissues to recover between doses, while cancers continued to regress.

Physicists of the 1920s had determined that the higher the energy of x-rays, the better the penetration into underlying tissues. Major cancer hospitals rushed to acquire the most modern equipment—the 250-kilovolt machine. Even with its high energy, the skin received a substantial radiation dose. Burns limited the total amount of roentgens that could be delivered. To avoid this disproportionate radiation dose to skin, physicists devised new techniques, such as crossfiring, whereby therapists directed the beam from two or three different angles. This evolved into rotational therapy—crossfiring from multiple angles. Touting its advantage, I. Seth Hirsch of New York City's Bellevue Hospital calculated that if one irradiated a roast beef with the beam and roast stationary, the surface intensity would be about twenty times that in the center. If, on the other hand, the x-ray tube revolved around the roast, the surface dose was significantly reduced, while that in the center doubled.

By the 1930s, many of the basic principles of radiation therapy were understood, but radiologists differed substantially in their approach. While most still considered irradiation merely a palliative tool, others designed aggressive treatments. The concept of rigor as applied to clinical research was in its infancy. Most published small studies with limited description of their patients and techniques and almost no standardization of therapy. Definitions of tumor response, duration of response, and survival varied from report to report. Few described toxicity in detail. Data were rarely reproducible from one center to the next. It is not surprising that these reports engendered minimal enthusiasm.

In 1924, Bernard Schreiner and Walter Mattick from the New York State Institute for the Study of Malignant Disease reported on forty-six patients treated with low doses of roentgen rays to small circular ports that encompassed involved nodes. While irradiated nodes were regressing, disease was progressing to other sites. They concluded palliation was the best one could hope for. At the other end of the spectrum, a handful of radiologists were applying total body irradiation, introduced in Europe in the 1920s by Werner Teschendorf. He maintained that his method, called the "x-ray bath," eradicated "all wandering malignant cells or early metastatic foci without destruction to the host." But most European clinics soon abandoned the technique because of serious and often fatal reactions—prolonged vomiting and severe bone marrow suppression leading to overwhelming infections and bleeding.

Even as the x-ray bath was being rejected in Europe, Arthur Heublein was introducing total body irradiation, called "Heublein therapy," in America. In 1931, Lloyd Craver and Fred Medinger at Memorial Hospital in New York City began using his techniques. Patients were housed in a small lead-insulated hospital room, equipped with only a bed and an x-ray tube mounted on the wall three meters away. For a week, they sprayed the patient with continuous low-dose radiation twenty hours a day, allowing four hours for meals, baths, and visitors. At first, patients felt no effects. But by the sixth day, they began to retch uncontrollably; weakness, fever, often hemorrhage followed. Craver and Medinger reported treating ninety-four Hodgkin's patients; over half had reduction or stabilization of disease. But total body irradiation merited only a brief chapter in the history of Hodgkin's disease. Craver and Medinger's responses proved short-lived. By the time their report was published, most of their patients had died.

The strategy that established the grounds for modern-day radiotherapy was developed by René Gilbert of Geneva. In 1937, he read his landmark paper at the Fifth International Congress of Radiology in Chicago. He condemned the two most popular radiotherapy techniques for Hodgkin's disease: small doses given weekly over months and massive doses given at one sitting. Based on scientific principles determined by radiation biologists, he recommended roentgen therapy with high-energy rays, using a 250-kilovolt machine, at 180 roentgens per day for fifteen days. Gilbert observed that in patients treated just to the sites of involved lymph nodes, disease often recurred in adjacent nodes. So he advocated treating a field that included not only the involved lymph node chain, but also contiguous nodes. And if the patient had persistent symptoms, such as fever, sweats, or weight loss, he presumed that the abdomen contained occult disease and irradiated the abdominal nodes and spleen as well. This con-cept of prophylactic irradiation to contiguous nodes was revolutionary.

Gilbert carefully reported all toxicities—low blood counts, scarring of the lungs, heart damage, and early menopause. He stressed the patient's quality of life and advocated adapting the treatment program to individual patients. "This is a question of clinical flair and restraint," he said. "On the one hand, it is essential to irradiate widely enough to be reasonably certain to subject to the action of the rays the entire invaded region; on the other hand, one must con-stantly strive to save the general condition of the patient." Gilbert reported that 34 percent of his Hodgkin's patients treated this way were alive at five years. De-spite these superb results, American cancer specialists did not readily accept his therapeutic approach. "It is impossible to predict future sites of involvement," two prominent radiotherapists wrote. "For this reason, we believe that prophy-lactic irradiation is contraindicated." Another suggested that Gilbert's survival rates were high because he had eliminated some patients from analysis.

Three years later, Craft at the University of Minnesota demonstrated pro-longed survival for Hodgkin's disease patients treated with radiation therapy. Published in an obscure journal, his remarkable data went unnoticed. So, for the most part, both Craft's and Gilbert's reports were disregarded—except in Toronto, Canada, where a young radiotherapist at Princess Margaret Hospital, Vera Peters, applied Gilbert's principles in an even more methodical way. But it would be eleven more years until she presented her results and the medi-cal world finally acknowledged the curative potential of radiation therapy for Hodgkin's disease.

9   The Fledgling Investigator

Leah Kaplan was freezing. She could hear her feet crunch the ice but could no longer feel them. Minneapolis was much colder than she had expected, and unprepared for the below zero temperature, she had gone apartment hunting in shoes and stockings. Far from the hotel, her legs were becoming heavy and numb. She panicked. She rang the bell of the nearest house and asked, "May I come in? I'm freezing."

In the winter of 1943, Leah and Henry Kaplan moved to Minneapolis, where Henry began advanced radiology training and Leah continued her under-graduate studies at the University of Minnesota. Their first time living away from home, without advice from Harry Lebeson or Sarah Kaplan, they found themselves somewhat bewildered. They rented a room at the Radisson Hotel downtown. Leah felt comfortable among the brocaded sofas and velvet-covered chairs. But their savings soon ran out, and with only Henry's small stipend, Leah began to search for an inexpensive apartment. She had gone from being the daughter of a wealthy businessman to the student-wife of a poor trainee. No longer could she drop by the tearoom for lunch or buy the fur-collared coat she saw in the store window. Household budgeting was a foreign concept to her. But she was determined to be a good wife, and she viewed their life to-gether as an adventure.

Leah finally found a few rooms near campus. They occupied the first floor and basement of a two-story house with a shared bathroom on the second floor. At night, she heard mice scratching behind the walls, and in the morning, Henry swept the droppings off the basement steps before she spotted them. The sparsely furnished rooms looked shabby compared with 4300 Lake Shore Drive, but after they put their books and records on the shelves and set out the lamps Leah's father had sent, they began to consider it their home. "Our screen porch was repaired last week," Henry wrote his mother in the spring. "Saturday I carried all the old junk away . . . and we put some chairs and a small table out there. There's a plug for a radio and lamp, and it really looks nice and feels swell on hot evenings." He installed a shower in the basement, and Leah bought a used card table with a checkerboard top and a chess set. Leah's father frequently found a reason to visit Minneapolis and took them to dinner at Harry's, one of the best restaurants in town. "Eat hearty," he always said. "I won't be back for a couple of months."

Hank wrote his mother religiously—during a lull in reading radiographs, while waiting for Sunday morning breakfast. He described details of his day—the macaroni and cheese Leah had fixed for lunch, what he thought about "The Devil and Daniel Webster," how they had listened to Beethoven's *Emperor Concerto* with the McCloskys. He asked for decorating suggestions and drew her a picture of the living room with "ain't it pretty" written underneath. He asked about her health and gave advice about running the pharmacy. "We're dusting off the couch," he wrote, urging her to visit, "all ready for you to lie down on . . . to just read or nap with a heating pad on your feet and a comforter to keep you warm . . . and all your loved ones around to keep you company." He finished letters with "your super-loving son" or "a dutiful son of a beautiful ma" or "my mice send all their love." No matter what he was writing about, however, he always came back to his favorite topic—Leah.

Leah the "gracious hostess," Leah an "eager student"—Henry never stopped talking about her. He liked to watch her study. Leah was completing her requirements for a degree in political science, taking courses entitled "European Dictatorships" and "Corporation Economic Systems." While Hank wrote of her "intellectual curiosity" and "desire for knowledge," Leah described herself as struggling to pass. To Sarah, Henry wrote:

> Leah finished her exam today, thank God, and once again I can walk around happy and unburdened without such horrible worries as "Oh, Hank, when will I ever get time to study?" or "Do you think the exam will be subjective or objective?" . . . I really think I ought to get a B.S. in political science at the same time she does, if only for the worrying I shared with her. After exams, she got a hair cut . . . and she looks cute as the devil, and she's my little honey once more.

At the same time, he teased her and delighted in her accomplishments. He bragged about how she officiated at the section on war information at the Workers' Institute exhibition in Minneapolis and about her work for the Bureau of War Information. Henry deeply loved his wife. "It's amazing," he said, "but the longer we're married, the more I fall in love with her." Early in their marriage, Henry laid a strong foundation, which sustained Leah during the challenging times ahead.

Sarah could easily have tired of Hank's exultations, felt displaced by Leah. But she wanted the best for her beloved son, including the best wife. Besides,

Leah poured out affection for her mother-in-law, calling her "Taddy Queenie" and signing her letters "Love Love Love Love Love." When Sarah visited, she taught Leah to cook pot roast and bake a cherry pie. They washed and set each other's hair. Leah bought her a sweater to keep her warm; Sarah sent cologne. Their close relationship pleased Hank. "I'm glad she loves you so much," he wrote his mother, "and that you feel the same way about her. Because you're my two best girls." But this honeymoon period didn't last forever, and before long, Leah was added to Sarah's long list of those who didn't do anything right.

The first few months after they moved to Minneapolis, Leah longed for her Chicago friends. She especially missed her sister; they had never been apart. Leah suggested that Shirley enroll at the University of Minnesota, and she moved into a room upstairs. Soon there were three places at the Kaplan table. Their father sent bicycles, and the two sisters explored the town. "Leah and Shirley are running around together like two busy little bees," Henry wrote. "It'll do Leah good to have some companionship."

Before long, Richard, too, moved to Minneapolis, where he rented a room across the street from Leah and Henry. Now there were four places at the dinner table. With distance and time, Hank and Richard had drawn closer. It began through letters, with Hank asking his mother about Dick's schoolwork and activities, always sending him regards. At first, Dick just added a note to his mother's. "I got your letter today," Hank wrote, "and laughed uproariously at Dick's letter inside." Soon they were corresponding directly once or twice a week. Hank began to appreciate his brother's quick wit and gift for writing. They began to talk on the phone, and Hank urged his mother to send Dick to Minneapolis: "I'm dying to see the kid again," he wrote. "I want to talk to him, play tennis with him, and show him the school and the mouse laboratory." Nineteen-year-old Richard was eager to leave Chicago and his nagging mother. He had graduated from high school at seventeen and followed his brother into premedical studies at the University of Chicago. But he had performed poorly. When Richard developed severe headaches, Hank insisted that he move to Minnesota where he could watch out for him.

Richard's life changed overnight. He enjoyed the laughter at meals, the outings, the way his sister-in-law listened to him. "It gave me a sense of home for the first time," he said. Gone was the obnoxious youth who had called him "idiot" and "brat"; in his place was a patient and attentive brother. "Dick just came in and had breakfast with us," Henry wrote to his mother one Sunday. "Now we're all reading or writing letters in our cozy little house with the old-fashioned curtains and listening to the Philharmonic symphony on the radio." Hank took care of Dick's migraines, counseled him regarding career plans. Clearly, Dick didn't excel at science, and despite their mother's expectations,

Hank thought medicine a poor choice for him. He encouraged Dick to use his writing skills, perhaps to work as an editor. When Dick took a job as a record salesman instead, Hank expressed enthusiasm for that as well. And he built his brother's confidence further by dispelling the myth that he himself excelled at everything. Dick regularly trounced him on the tennis court; he translated a 1912 German report that Hank needed for a seminar; and when Leah took pictures to send their mother, Hank said, "Why do I always look like a monkey, and Dick invariably looks handsome?"

Now that Hank had gotten his brother out of Chicago and improved his self-esteem, he set about trying to mend Dick's relationship with their mother. He knew Sarah would consider Dick's rejection of medical studies a failure, so he took on the responsibility for the decision himself. "I'd like to get him into some sort of literary work and get the idea of medicine out of his head," he wrote Sarah. "I don't see the point in his beating his head against a wall when he neglects fields in which he has definite ability and talent." But when Richard announced his decision to study journalism, Sarah belittled him. Hank had long ago learned how to respond to his mother: "I nearly died laughing at your letter," he wrote on one occasion. "It was typical of you—first you call me the most perfect human being and then you fill in four or five pages full of criticisms of me. A guy as inferior as all that can't really be called perfect." But Richard couldn't make light of his mother's caustic remarks, and she refused to answer his letters. "I know you are exasperated with him," Henry wrote after Dick had taken a job filling orders for a drug company, "but nothing can ever stop you from loving your sons, *both* of them." In the end, no matter how hard Henry tried to be a brother to Richard, their mother's one-sided love always came between them. The time the two brothers spent together in Minneapolis was the best they would ever share.

Besides family, Henry and Leah cherished their friends. They told Sarah about picnics at Cedar Lake, football games where they froze, tennis until closing time, and dinner with the first cellist of the Minneapolis symphony. On Saturday nights, friends often gathered at the Kaplans' for dinner. While a Prokofiev violin concerto played in the background, they analyzed whether Roosevelt would run for a fourth term, argued about the basic concepts of democracy, and played "three-fourths of a ghost." Most evenings ended with talk of the war. Increasingly, the words "Dachau" and "Buchenwald" entered the conversation, as reports from the underground told of firing squads and mass graves.

Henry became restless. While he was studying radiology and listening to Bach, Jewish scientists and musicians were being gassed. "Sometimes I feel ashamed of myself for being so happy," Henry said. No longer could he just talk about the war; he decided to enlist. He appeared to be an excellent candidate—a twenty-five-year-old physician in good health with only one dependent and eager to serve. But the chief officer at the induction board told Henry they would only take him on one condition—he must have his deformed fingers amputated. Henry was dumbfounded; he had already sewn lacerations, started intravenous lines, set broken bones. "It doesn't make sense," Henry told the examining physician. "My hand doesn't interfere with what I can contribute as a doctor."

"*You* don't understand," the officer replied. "You have to be able to give a snappy salute." Henry Kaplan was classified 4F. All the army allowed him to do was to volunteer at Fort Schilling's military hospital. He came home humiliated and angry. In the meantime, the best he could do was push ahead with his research and improve the health of those who survived.

⌒

Henry Kaplan had come to the University of Minnesota to study with Leo G. Rigler, chairman of the Department of Radiology and Physical Therapy. Rigler was said to have trained more residents destined to be chairmen of academic departments than any other radiologist. After reading hundreds of x-rays with Rigler, Henry developed the facility to see what other radiologists couldn't. But diagnostic radiology failed to challenge him. At twenty-five, he had an ambitious goal—to discover how healthy cells transformed into malignant ones. Somehow biology went awry. Neatly organized cells were replaced by larger, irregular ones that only faintly resembled their parents. They no longer grew in an orderly manner but multiplied uncontrollably, resulting in tumor masses. They spread to other parts of the body, where they grew and crowded out healthy cells. What switched them on? How did these cells escape the body's normal controls? Only by answering these questions could scientists hope to prevent cancer or cure it once established. And these puzzles could only be solved in the laboratory. Thus, while working all day as a diagnostic radiologist, Henry began to spend nights and weekends learning basic skills in cancer biology.

He knew exactly with whom he wanted to work. Anatomy professor Arthur Kirschbaum, a researcher with immense drive, was studying the genesis of leukemia in mice. He accepted Kaplan into his laboratory, making it clear that he expected the highest level of precision. But Henry didn't know how to anesthetize or irradiate mice, how to inject chemicals into the abdominal cavity. He had to learn the painstaking task of performing autopsies on mice, dissecting out the spleen and tiny lymph nodes. He came home exhausted, but euphoric. "My research is starting," he wrote Sarah, "and I'm really very happy about it. If you pray for me and stay well and my luck continues to be wonderful, maybe

I'll get some worthwhile results and start to carve out a name for myself (that is, some name other than 'Stinky')."

The aim of his first project was to determine whether exposing mice to total body irradiation could induce tumors of lymphoid tissue—lymphomas and leukemias—and if this was a good system with which to investigate the basic mechanisms of carcinogenesis. Under Kirschbaum's direction, Henry maintained a colony of 946 mice. In his first experiment, he irradiated 114 for eleven days each, performing autopsies on those that died. He and Kirschbaum demonstrated that total body irradiation did generate lymphomas and leukemias. In addition, they found that some mouse strains were more likely to develop these malignancies and concluded that in mice, genetic constitution determined susceptibility to cancer. Years later, he said of his work with Kirschbaum: "We published some early papers together, largely the result of his scientific input and my perspiration." The mouse leukemia-lymphoma model proved to be a good one in which to study carcinogenesis, so good that Kaplan used it throughout his career. "I'm still working my fanny off," he wrote his mother. "This Saturday is the big day. I have to talk for an hour to the Department of Anatomy on 'The influence of radiation upon experimental leukemia in animals.' Hope it goes across well."

A few days later, he wrote:

Dear Mom,
    Yesterday I delivered my lecture at the anatomy seminar, and I'm glad it's over. It was pretty good—Art Kirschbaum said it was the best one of the year. . . . So my first venture in public speaking was fairly successful. I'm enclosing the announcement in the school paper (but please promise you won't post it on the store window).

At home, Leah listened patiently as Henry described his experiments. Although she rarely understood, his enthusiasm was contagious. Now while the family listened to the Philharmonic on Sunday afternoons, he went to the laboratory. He played fewer games of tennis with Richard. His love affair with research had begun, and henceforth, Leah would have to share him. But she never protested. "I knew it was going to be part of his life," she said. "It was something I accepted from the beginning." What made it easier was his continued adoration. "I love her so much," he wrote, "I go around singing inside all day."

Henry relished his years in Minneapolis. At one point, he told his mother:

I'm the happiest guy who ever lived—I've got a swell job, a nice home, freedom, recreation and fun, but far more important, I've got a family that loves me, a mom that I adore and am deeply proud of and am lonesome for, a brother I've grown to like and to respect and whose company I really enjoy and a wife who is . . . the best companion I've ever known.

His job may have been "swell," but Henry still worked in Kirschbaum's laboratory under Kirschbaum's direction. He wanted his own laboratory where he could plan and execute his own experiments. He finally got the opportunity in 1945, when he assumed his first academic appointment at Yale University.

↬

The chairman of Radiology at Yale, Hugh Wilson, had a reputation as a brilliant diagnostic radiologist and dynamic teacher. "His manner in the classroom was probing," Kaplan said, "dissatisfied with glib and superficial answers." Wilson himself referred to his teaching method as "education by scarification." It was not enough to identify a barely perceptible mediastinal mass on a chest x-ray; the student had to know the entire list of possible diagnoses based on where in the mediastinum the mass was located. "I'm not sure" was unacceptable. And just when a student had finally struggled through a difficult case and started to sit down, Wilson put up another film. Intimidated, most failed to notice the amusement behind his scowl.

But Henry Kaplan wasn't intimidated; he found Wilson stimulating. He liked being quizzed about an unusual x-ray or provoked to pursue a new technique. Unbeknown to Wilson, his new instructor—whom he described as "Jewish, but a nice young person"—was very much cast in his own mold. Kaplan began to challenge Wilson's judgment, and increasingly they were heard arguing about cases, usually tempering the altercation with a dime bet. "Henry won more than I think Hugh would have liked," a former resident recalled. They enjoyed sparring. In time, Kaplan's teaching techniques and diagnostic acumen became remarkably similar to Wilson's.

Although engaged in clinical work and teaching, Henry was anxious to set up a laboratory. Lionel Strong, an anatomist and geneticist, gave him a few shelves in his large mouse facility, affectionately known as "L. C. Strong's mouse house." At the time, research grants to cover staff salaries and supplies weren't readily available. "When I arrived at New Haven," Kaplan said years later, "I was given a budget of three hundred dollars a year to take care of my animals, which meant taking care of them personally. I cleaned the cages, replacing the dirty with clean sawdust and put in fresh food and water." His mice numbered in the hundreds. Undaunted, Kaplan proceeded to plan his experiments. "He was so excited about his research," Leah said, "but I was turned off by it." When Henry came home with the smell of mice permeating his clothes, hair, and skin, Leah held her nose until he showered and scrubbed. Lebeson's fear that his son-in-law would be secluded in a laboratory with mice and test tubes had become a reality.

At Yale, Henry continued his work on radiation-induced leukemias and lymphomas in mice. He used a special strain of inbred mice, C57 blacks, which had a low chance of developing malignancies spontaneously. In his initial experiments, he investigated the relationship between age at time of exposure to radiation and susceptibility to lymphoid malignancies. He irradiated C57 black mice for twelve consecutive days, sacrificed the animals at intervals, and performed autopsies. He dissected out each organ and lymph node group and examined them under the microscope. Although he was investigating the effect of age, he made an important observation that had relevance to human disease.

At that time, there was controversy over whether tumors of lymphoid tissue spread from a single focus or arose simultaneously from multiple foci. The latter was widely believed to be true, leading to the conclusion that lymphomas were systemic at onset and thus incurable. Kaplan noted in his mice that lymphomas first appeared in the thymus gland, a small gland in the anterior chest, or mediastinum, where lymphocytes were thought to originate. From there the lymphoma spread to adjacent lymph nodes, then to other tissues, and finally into the bloodstream where it appeared as a lymphocytic leukemia. In mouse after mouse, he found the exact same route of spread. "These findings are incompatible," he concluded, "with the theory that lymphoid tumors ... are, from their inception, systemic diseases of the lymphoid tissues." The observation that lymphomas originated in and remained confined to the thymus for some time before disseminating to other tissues suggested that they might be curable with local therapy. If true in humans as well, this finding had major implications for treatment.

Despite the long hours of work and meager income, the years at Yale were happy ones. Leah finished graduate studies in International Relations at Yale and obtained a master's degree in Psychiatric Social Work at Smith College. They played tennis, attended concerts in the Berkshires, and tried to learn Russian. As always, Henry did everything with gusto. He played tennis as if each game were Wimbledon. He debated dialectical materialism at his Russian study group with such zeal that a frustrated fellow debater once yelled, "If there's a revolution, you'll be first on the list." He and Leah had lively friends, like Don Seldin, who years later became one of the premier medical chiefs in the country. Henry and Don enjoyed friendly competition: who could shoot pool more skillfully, who had the best recording of Bach's *Goldberg Variations*, who could hold his liquor better. The Kaplans and Seldins frequently went to New York City for a weekend of theater, chamber music, tea dancing, and dining, which they called their "cultural binge."

Surrounded by dynamic people, Henry and Leah found it hard to leave Yale.

But when an opportunity arose to work with Egon Lorenz, a leading scientist in carcinogenesis at the National Cancer Institute (NCI), Kaplan accepted his offer. Lorenz's laboratory was so stimulating that a few months later, when Kaplan received an offer to become chairman of Radiology at Stanford University, he said he wouldn't even consider it.

10   The Unlikely Aftermath
                                    of Mustard Gas

In early December 1943, a fleet of Allied cargo ships lay berthed in Bari harbor on the eastern coast of Italy, one hundred and fifty miles from the front. One quiet evening, with the Adriatic lapping against the vessels, the faint sound of aircraft could be heard in the distance. Before an alarm could warn the sleeping sailors, the Luftwaffe attacked. Hundreds jumped or were blasted into the chilly waters. Fuel tanks ignited, and ships exploded, scattering debris into the sea. As flames lit up the sky, men grabbed onto floating wreckage, the blare of sirens echoing in the background. Although the Luftwaffe destroyed sixteen supply ships, 600 men were rescued. How fortunate they must have felt, settled at the hospital with warm blankets and coffee. Four hours later, pandemonium broke out.

At first, some seamen complained of intense itching. Nurses noted their skin looked diffusely red, as if it had been scorched from the explosion. Their axillae and genitalia were the areas most severely affected. In a short time, the skin blistered and with scratching or movement against bed clothing, rubbed off. Nurses rushed from one screaming patient to another, applying cold compresses. When they removed the dressings, they discovered blisters the size of eggs and large open ulcers.

On other wards, patients complained of a gritty sensation in their eyes. The doctors assumed they had been irritated by salt water or bits of debris. Washing with boric acid didn't help, and no fragments could be found. Despite eye patches, the burning intensified, and when nurses changed the bandages, they observed the eyelids to be red and swollen. As they lifted the lids to apply ointment, patients became terrified. They couldn't see. On closer inspection, doctors found their corneas cloudy and ulcerated.

Many sailors had entered the hospital coughing; some had rapid pulse and temperature. The staff expected a few cases of pneumonia, given the lengthy exposure in the water. But soon, a number of men developed loud, croupy coughs and complained of choking. Some had purulent mucous covering the throat and larynx "so thickened that only a knitting needle [could] pass [through]," one observer wrote. Others began to wheeze and gasp for breath, bubbling foam from their mouths. On examination, doctors found pulmonary edema—fluid building up in the lungs.

Meanwhile, the Allied ship *Bisteria* had picked up thirty sailors and continued out to sea, destined for Taranto in southern Italy. Safe aboard ship, survivors slept or exchanged war stories. Five hours out at sea, the sailors from Bari began to rub their irritated eyes and complained of blurred vision. Soon the crew of the *Bisteria* began to experience similar symptoms. As their sight dimmed, panic ensued; men had to grope their way up to the deck. When they reached Taranto, they had great difficulty docking. Almost the entire crew was blind.

Fourteen hours after the attack at Bari, the hospital to which most of the injured had been admitted received a call from port authorities. While inspecting the wreckage, they discovered broken mustard gas shells. The SS *John Harvey* had surreptitiously been carrying one hundred tons of mustard bombs. When the ship exploded, hundreds of gallons of mustard gas solution had spread across the harbor, bathing the sailors waiting to be rescued. Some recalled smelling garlic—the characteristic odor of mustard gas—while they bobbed in the water. By the time the hospital had been notified, it was too late—decontamination with bleaching agents was beneficial only within the first few minutes after exposure. The first sailor had already died. In the case of the *Bisteria*, clothing of the rescued men had been saturated with mustard solution. When the liquid evaporated, it filled the air with mustard vapor, secondarily exposing the crew. This amount of gas, concentrated in close quarters, had been sufficient to blind everyone below deck. Casualties from the attack at Bari totaled 83 deaths, 534 serious injuries.

> Never take some chances if
> Garlic you should strongly sniff
> Don't think Mussolini's passed
> Man, you're being mustard gassed!

During World War I, German chemists had reported that sulfur mustard had toxic characteristics that made it ideal for gas warfare. Called "mustard" because of its irritant and vesicant properties, the chemical could burn, blind, and asphyxiate the enemy. Mustard gas soaked through rubber, canvas, and leather, thus penetrating gas masks and protective clothing. It was so potent, one historian wrote, that "a drop the size of a pin head" could "produce a blister the size of a quarter." And gassed areas remained contaminated for weeks.

On July 12, 1917, the Germans first used mustard gas against the unsuspecting Allied forces at Ypres in Belgium. British doctors found a red blush over the skin of the injured and feared an outbreak of scarlet fever. But when large blisters erupted, they realized that something far worse had occurred. The Germans had launched a new form of chemical warfare. They used mustard gas at Verdun, and such quantities were used to capture Armentières that it was said to "run in the gutters like water." The most potent chemical agent used in the war, mustard gas caused an estimated 400,000 casualties. The effects of mustard poisoning—disfiguration, suffocation, blindness—generated revulsion around the world. In 1925, thirty-two nations signed a treaty outlawing use of poisonous and asphyxiating gases.

As a result, mustard gas was rarely used during World War II, although U.S. intelligence was cognizant of Japanese and German research programs in chemical and biological warfare. The SS *John Harvey* was carrying one hundred tons of mustard bombs to Allied command centers in Europe to be held for retaliation in case the Germans reinitiated gas warfare. The six hundred casualties resulting from the explosion of the SS *John Harvey* were not disclosed to the American public because of the secrecy surrounding the chemical warfare program.

But the incident wasn't kept from Major Alfred Gilman and First Lieutenant Frederick Philips at Edgewood Arsenal in Maryland, where they were conducting research on mustard gas. The military authorized them to determine the basic cellular actions of the agent in order to develop antidotes. When Gilman and Philips reviewed medical information from the attack at Bari, they found the expected injuries—blistering of skin, blindness, and pulmonary edema. These arose from vesicant properties of mustard gas. When they read the detailed autopsy reports, however, they discovered toxic effects not previously described. Lymph tissue, including bone marrow, had been obliterated. Hoping this clue might help them elucidate how mustard gas kills cells, Gilman and Philips pursued this unusual finding in animals. "These studies revealed a type of action on cells which can be likened to that of no other chemical agent," Gilman wrote. They found mustard gas and one of its chemical derivatives, nitrogen mustard, had a propensity to kill rapidly dividing normal cells, such as bone marrow. This led them to look beyond chemical warfare to the most rapidly growing cells—cancer. But with the war ongoing, work with chemical warfare agents was considered classified. Gilman was impatient. So under strict secrecy, he and colleagues at Yale University treated six terminally ill patients with infusions of nitrogen mustard. Two with lymphomas responded.

Theirs, however, was not the earliest use of mustard gas compounds against cancer. James Ewing of New York's Memorial Hospital had conceived of its therapeutic potential while serving at the Army Medical Museum during

World War I. He noted that the reaction from one drop on the skin lasted five to ten days; he had never seen anything like it. Ewing suggested to two young researchers, Frank Adair and Henry Bagg, that this chemical might eradicate neoplastic growths. They obtained concentrated mustard gas solution from the U.S. Army's Chemical Warfare Service and began animal experiments. Subsequently, they treated thirteen patients, using it to burn off superficial cancers.

Among them was a thirty-one-year-old government clerk who had noted a lump the size of a pea on his anus. It was excised and found to be malignant. Three months later, numerous crusted nodules erupted over his trunk, arms, and legs. Biopsy revealed cancer that had metastasized from the anus. They applied a drop of mustard gas solution to two large lesions, and they vanished. Next, the investigators treated two patients with penile cancer who had relapsed following radiotherapy. One week prior to scheduled amputations, they applied mustard solution to the cancers. After penectomy, the pathologist examined the specimens and found no malignant cells. Given these amazing results, they treated two more patients who had irradiation-resistant penile cancers with mustard solution, this time without amputation. The tumors regressed completely.

"We believe that mustard-gas solution offers another agent for fighting cancer, provided the lesion is localized," Adair and Bagg wrote in 1931. Superficial application of mustard gas solution, however, didn't cure cancers; it couldn't eradicate deeper foci of disease. In time, most recurred. Mustard gas solution never did replace surgical excision or radiotherapy for cancers of the anus and penis as they had hoped. Besides, this chemical agent could extirpate surface cancers only. In order to treat most cancers, they needed to give a chemical agent systemically, by vein. But mustard gas solution was highly volatile and caustic, making it too dangerous to inject intravenously. Use of chemicals to treat cancer seemed to have reached a dead end until the more stable derivative, nitrogen mustard, was synthesized, permitting its intravenous delivery. After Gilman's experience at Yale, the National Research Council, in cooperation with the Chemical Warfare Service, authorized further clinical research on nitrogen mustard. Investigators noted some brief responses in leukemias and other cancers. But the most dramatic results occurred in patients with Hodgkin's disease.

L.W., a thirty-three-year-old housewife, had been diagnosed with Hodgkin's disease in 1941 when her doctor found enlarged lymph nodes in her axilla, neck, and mediastinum. Radiotherapy relieved her symptoms, but within a year, she returned with shortness of breath. The chest mass was growing. Despite more treatment, she developed coughing spasms and such labored respiration that she became bedridden. Several months later, she was admitted to the hospital cyanotic and gasping for breath. "The face and neck were greatly swollen and distorted, and the left side of the neck bulged with a hard irregular mass," her physician wrote. "Both axillae were occupied by hard, irregular masses. . . . The breasts were large and edematous. The right arm was greatly swollen and completely paralyzed." Louis Goodman, a colleague of Gilman's, treated her with intravenous nitrogen mustard on four consecutive days. After a second dose, her breathing improved, the cyanosis resolved, and the nodal masses shrunk by 75 percent. "The disfiguring edema of the face and neck entirely receded," Goodman reported, "and the hugely swollen right arm returned almost to normal size."

Classification of nitrogen mustard research as "confidential" kept results such as these from being published until after the war. In August 1945, three months following Germany's surrender, investigators working with this, the first chemotherapeutic agent, came together at Gibson Island, Maryland, to share their findings. Putting the field in perspective, the keynote speaker reviewed chemical approaches tried thus far: organotherapy with Aristotrop, an extract of animal pancreas and stomach, and Splendothelan, a preparation of animal spleen; Carcinolysin, a plant enzyme; heavy metals; vitamins and snake venoms. Of most therapies, he said, "After a few . . . apparent miracles, the treatment was abandoned."

Following his address, investigators presented laboratory studies showing that degree of cell kill from nitrogen mustard was related to the growth rate of cells. Thus, because cancer cells grew rapidly, they were particularly susceptible. This observation also explained why the bone marrow and gastrointestinal tract, tissues with high growth rates, were the organs most often injured by nitrogen mustard. A group from the University of Chicago reported on twenty-six Hodgkin's disease patients whom they had treated with the agent. Ninety-four percent had shrinkage of lymph nodes, decrease in mass on chest x-ray, or resolution of bone pain. As impressive as these responses were, they proved short-lived. David Karnofsky from Memorial Hospital reported similar results. And Louis Goodman reviewed collaborative efforts from Utah, Tufts, the University of Oregon, and Yale. Almost every patient with Hodgkin's disease had responded, some dramatically, but remissions lasted last seven months at most. Even L.W. died four weeks following her remarkable response.

Next they turned to toxicity. "The efficacy of a chemotherapeutic agent in controlling a disease cannot be judged only by the period of remission it will produce," an investigator said. "The toxic reactions must not endanger life or delay recovery of general health." Participants at the meeting reported observing similar toxicities: Patients suffered severe nausea and vomiting, which lasted for hours. The drug irritated veins, causing phlebitis, and if it leaked into surrounding tissue, burns and ulcers resulted. The most serious toxicities emerged two to three weeks following treatment. Injury to bone marrow caused the white blood cell count to fall, often to a level below that needed to fight infection. Damage to marrow also resulted in decreased platelet counts, sometimes so low patients reported nosebleeds and blood oozing from their gums when they brushed their teeth. Toxicity appeared to be dose-related—the higher the dose, the more depressed the blood counts—and the margin of safety was narrow. Permanent destruction of bone marrow would be lethal; patients would die of infection or bleeding. But miraculously, on the third week after treatment, a few cells reappeared in the marrow, and by the fourth week, the bone marrow was repopulated with normal cells. Investigators found they could treat patients a second or third time, and the bone marrow again recovered. They could infuse nitrogen mustard intermittently for months, and patients dying of Hodgkin's disease gained six or eight more months of life.

Where did nitrogen mustard fit into the management of Hodgkin's disease? David Karnofsky, a leader in the cancer field, said he still considered irradiation the best therapy for localized disease, since it induced remissions that lasted years. Participants agreed that radiotherapy should remain the primary treatment for Hodgkin's disease, reserving nitrogen mustard for patients with widespread disease or those in whom irradiation had failed. True, it caused marked reduction in tumor masses and provided relief of symptoms, but only temporarily. "The use of these agents seems to represent a definite but limited advance," Goodman concluded at the end of the conference.

The field of chemotherapy had had an inauspicious beginning. In the 1940s and 1950s, only a handful of cancer specialists showed interest in nitrogen mustard. Its role had been relegated to palliation.

11   The Stanford Wooing

When the dean of Stanford University School of Medicine asked Henry Kaplan to consider becoming head of radiology, he initially declined without much thought. His laboratory work at the National Cancer Institute was progressing well. He planned to take a faculty position at some point, but few medical investigators thought that academic medicine existed west of Chicago. "Henry had barely heard of Stanford Medical School," Leah said. Relatively young, it had no ivy-covered buildings, endowed chairs, list of famous alumni, or tradition. But Dean Chandler insisted that Kaplan at least visit. He finally agreed; he had never been west. On his first trip, Henry found two surprises: He fell in love with San Francisco. And he perceived a dormant potential in the school, although it was considered second-rate by both researchers and clinicians.

Originally established in 1859 as the Medical Department of the University of the Pacific in San Francisco, this was the first medical school on the West Coast. Its founder, Elias Samuel Cooper (1820–62), disdained the current state of medical education, which consisted of several months of lectures followed by an apprenticeship. This bold and inquisitive Ohio surgeon dreamed of establishing a medical school of distinction—not just another "diploma mill," churning out large numbers of barely qualified physicians. He planned a progressive curriculum that included dissection of cadavers to learn anatomy and vivisection—practicing surgical skills on live, anesthetized dogs. Having moved west for his health, Cooper approached the Board of Trustees of the University of the Pacific, and they agreed to establish a medical department. The San Francisco medical community, possessive of its patients and threatened by his novel approaches to medicine, reacted with hostility. Despite their attempts to incite a public outcry against the school by exposing his practice of exhuming bodies for dissection, Cooper persisted.

Following Cooper's death four years later, his nephew, Levi Cooper Lane, a brilliant surgeon and scholar, took his place. Over the next thirty years, the school, which Lane named Cooper Medical College after his uncle, changed substantially. It instituted a four-year curriculum, hired academic faculty, offered free public lectures, and had a five-story modern medical building and hospital built in the fashionable Pacific Heights section of San Francisco. The school improved to the point where faculty dared compare it to eastern schools. "We are glad to learn," the *American Journal of Medical Sciences* editorialized, "that the noble example of Harvard has borne good fruit on the distant shores of the Pacific." By the early 1900s, Cooper Medical College owned properties valued at almost nine million dollars. But academic faculty required laboratories, equipment, and staff. The task of maintaining facilities and supporting faculty salaries became increasingly difficult. So when David Starr Jordan, president of Stanford University, approached Lane about a potential union, he appreciated the security it might bring. In 1908, Cooper Medical School became the School of Medicine of Leland Stanford Junior University.

The school's first dean, Ray Lyman Wilbur, believed medicine should be taught, not as a trade, but as an academic subject by university professors. He had inherited a faculty totaling twenty-seven; five years later, they numbered a hundred, mostly trained at Johns Hopkins. His successor, William Ophuls, took further steps to mold Stanford into a research-oriented medical school. He stressed scholarship and medical education designed to train successful investigators, attracting a distinguished group of faculty, who made significant contributions to medical science. Ophuls also strengthened clinical training. A new 180-bed hospital opened adjacent to Lane Hospital, and patients soon filled the clinics. When Ophuls died in 1933, Loren Chandler, a Stanford-trained surgeon, became the third dean. Scientific investigation continued to thrive, and Chandler boasted that 83 percent of graduating students went on to further professional training.

During the 1920s and 1930s, Stanford gained a reputation as a research-based medical school with excellent clinical training, and eastern schools began to consider it a serious competitor. But with the start of World War II, progress stopped. Stanford responded to the national mandate to train practicing physicians. As a result, its special luster faded. Funds for nonmilitary investigation all but disappeared; research programs disintegrated. The Stanford School of Medicine lost its momentum.

❦

When Henry Kaplan visited Stanford in 1948, the school emphasized training for clinical practice—"a bit of a trade school" one faculty member called it. With its poorly lit hallways and chipped paint, Lane Hospital, once described as "elegant and modern," no longer seemed a desirable place for private physicians to admit patients. High ceilings caused voices to echo, and patients were housed on large open wards.

Kaplan found Radiology located at the back of Lane Hospital. The small, dilapidated unit contained three primitive diagnostic x-ray machines. Unprotected wires dangled from the ceiling. Considered a technical service, Radiology had been established as a division in the Department of Medicine. What a contrast to Minnesota or Yale, where Radiology was a distinct, well-staffed department with modern equipment, where Leo Rigler and Hugh Wilson were respected as superb teachers and clinical investigators. At Stanford, Radiology had no full-time faculty; it was in essence an embellished private practice. A Marin County radiologist came into the city a few times a week to treat cancer patients. Leo Henry Garland, a radiologist with the largest practice in town, supervised an affiliated service at San Francisco City Hospital. Most staff assumed that Dean Chandler would choose this quick-witted socialite, popular among private radiologists, to be chief. But Chandler resolved to rebuild his school and raise it out of mediocrity. He wanted to recruit an academic radiologist who would combine clinical service and research. He wanted Henry Kaplan.

Leah remembered what she called the "wooing" as a social whirlwind. For a week, they stayed at the elegant Fairmont Hotel atop Nob Hill. Every night, Leah, then just twenty-six, and Henry, twenty-nine, attended a different catered affair in the home of a senior faculty member, all of whom seemed older than their parents. Before one dinner party, the hostess called Leah to inquire whether she had brought a formal gown. Leah didn't tell her that she didn't own a formal, only that she hadn't brought one. When she and Henry arrived at the three-story Victorian home in Pacific Heights, Leah noticed all the women were wearing long gowns, except her and the hostess.

Because of her background in psychiatric social work, Leah was always seated next to the chairman of Psychiatry, George Johnson. Leah thought him boring and obsessive; he took forever to choose something from a platter. A staunch advocate of shock therapy, Johnson had little to say to Leah, who adhered to the school of psychoanalysis. They ran out of conversation the first night and sat in uncomfortable silence. On their third evening together, Johnson asked Leah what she thought about the upcoming presidential election. Lukewarm about both candidates, Leah laughed and said, "It could be worse; we could have Hoover."

"Not only was Herbert Hoover one of our greatest presidents," Johnson replied, "but he's a personal friend of mine." The room suddenly became silent. Leah looked down the long dinner table, covered with china and silver, to Hank, sitting next to Dean Chandler's wife. "If you want this job," Leah's expression conveyed, "you'll have to get it on your own." After a week of faux pas, she concluded, "They certainly didn't offer Hank the job because I was a charmer."

There was one person, however, who did not woo Kaplan—Henry Garland. Although associated with the department for twenty years, he had not been asked to consider the position. After Kaplan's visit, he wrote a letter full of feigned concern:

> It seems to us out here that whoever takes the department must expect to put in two to three years practically full time in administrative work in order to get it straightened out. After that, if past experience is any guide, he will have to spend about half time in administrative work and half time in clinical radiology. He will have very little time for organized teaching and none for research. These are the sad facts.

And Garland freely divulged his disdain for Dean Chandler in a letter marked "personal and confidential":

> I have suggested to the dean that the department could support and deserves at least three senior full time men, who could share the load of teaching, clinical radiology and research, but my suggestions have fallen on barren soil. . . . the profit from the department does seem to be more essential than good radiology! It is a very sad and extraordinary state of affairs. I deeply sympathize with whoever takes the heavy load upon himself.

But Kaplan liked Chandler. He had shepherded Stanford through the Depression and World War II. He clearly loved the school and was determined to resurrect it.

On March 26, 1948, Dean Chandler formally offered Henry Kaplan a position. "We are confident that we have a splendid opportunity both for you and the School," he wrote. But the dean had to be prepared to provide a lot more than just the position. Henry Kaplan bargained like a Brilliant: Radiology had to be established as a separate department with the same powers as the departments of Medicine and Surgery. Given the dilapidated condition of the unit, he would need approximately $100,000 to refurbish the current space. Transforming a second-rate unit into a major academic department required constructing a new hospital wing to house diagnostic and therapeutic radiology units, research laboratories, and teaching space. Since he planned to treat an increasing number of cancer patients, who had special nursing needs, he pressed for a dedicated cancer ward. He also requested a discretionary fund to develop new programs and required space for his laboratory. Finally, he wouldn't consider the position unless appointed on a full-time, salaried basis, making him one of the first radiologists in the country to be paid in this manner. He wanted to avoid the conflict inherent when faculty profited from private practice, even if it meant a salary of only $15,000. "It has been most difficult for me to arrive at a decision about moving West," Kaplan wrote to Chandler, "since . . . I have been subjected to increasing pressure to stay on here, including a personal appeal from the new Surgeon General and the future chief of the National Institutes of Health." Nevertheless, he said he was "inclined to accept the appointment" if Chandler agreed to his requests, which he considered the minimal requirements for building a first-rate radiology department. Chandler agreed to them all.

Why, when he was gaining recognition for his investigative work on carcinogenesis, did Henry Kaplan leave the National Cancer Institute? There he had modern laboratory facilities, funding, superb scientific colleagues, and no administrative duties. As a department chairman, paperwork and patient responsibilities would curtail his research time. He could return to his laboratory only after the budget had been submitted, the broken orthovoltage machine repaired, the patient with an obstructing lung mass treated. But he missed the academic atmosphere of a university, the youthful enthusiasm of medical students, and above all, patients. Besides, he couldn't do research in a vacuum; clinical problems generated new questions, and patients drove him to answer them. He wrote to Hugh Wilson, his former chief at Yale, for advice. "I am definitely prejudiced in respect to believing that you do not belong at a cancer institute," Wilson replied. "I feel strongly that your talents in both teaching and clinical service to patients should have an outlet."

But why Stanford? As one of a handful of academic radiologists, Kaplan could have taken a position at the University of Chicago, Yale, or Harvard. Why would he agree to chair a department that was considered a service unit, housed in a far corner of an outdated hospital? And why would he come to what one faculty member called "a parochial, rather undistinguished regional medical school"? Because Henry Kaplan had a vision, born of dissatisfaction with the existing state of medicine. He had learned from Leo Rigler and Hugh Wilson what an excellent radiology department was, but he imagined what an academic radiology department could be, and no department in the country met his expectations. Of course it should provide service to patients—not just diagnostic x-rays, but inventive treatments, as well. He considered the current state of cancer care deplorable. A modern radiology department should think of its patients as a research base for clinical investigation. It should support laboratory research in carcinogenesis, isotope development, and biophysics, and relate to other basic science departments, like biochemistry and engineering. And it should train the next generation of academic radiologists and radiation therapists, not private practitioners. Henry Kaplan could see beyond the hanging wires and chipped paint. At Stanford, he saw a place where he could create his ideal of an academic radiology department. And looking down the

Peninsula to the immense resources of land, academic space, basic science faculty, laboratories, and libraries on the main campus, he felt confident he could play a major role in creating a first-rate academic medical center. "I [am] excited and enthusiastic," he wrote to Hugh Wilson, "about the prospect of working with a team of young men over a period of years in a re-birth of a medical school."

So on September 1, 1948, Henry Kaplan came to Stanford. Some faculty were pleased; most were indifferent. Not Henry Garland. Livid that Dean Chandler had passed him over, Garland pledged to drive Kaplan from San Francisco.

12   The Outsider

Stanford University School of Medicine was located in Pacific Heights amid brightly colored Victorian houses, overlooking San Francisco Bay. Henry Kaplan appreciated the cloudless azure skies, the bay stippled with sailboats, the crisp breeze with a scent of seawater, the impatiens in bloom. But once he stepped inside, everything was a dark, faded green. Stanford Hospital didn't meet modern-day fire and safety standards, and the adjacent Lane Building was condemned a few years later as unfit for patient care. The stark lobby contained an information desk with an arrow pointing to restrooms. Beyond the information desk, a sign read "To X-Ray and Zander." Zander, Kaplan learned, was director of physical therapy. Tucked in a back corner of the hospital, beyond Zander, behind swinging wooden doors, was the Radiology Department.

Henry Kaplan had set out to build one of the finest radiology units in the country. He soon realized just how overwhelming the task would be. His space consisted of three rooms for diagnostic work and one for therapy; patients waited in the corridor. At the end of the hall was Kaplan's office, barely large enough for a desk and chair. To reach it, he had to pass patients in wheelchairs or on stretchers, crowding the hallway, waiting for x-rays to be taken, treatments to be delivered.

His unit was highly inefficient. Without an automated processor, technicians developed radiographs by hand, dipping the heavy films one at a time into various solutions and then hanging them on racks to dry. This process took up to two hours. The diagnostic x-ray machines dated from the 1920s, and at least one always seemed to have broken down. When Kaplan first arrived, he found "bare wires, carrying up to 200,000 volts, dangling above the patient." Dean Chandler had agreed to replace the machines, but that took months. In the meantime, Kaplan worried that a patient would get shocked or electrocuted. "I had more nightmares than in all the rest of my life put together," he said. "Every single one . . . ended in a brilliant blue-white flash."

If diagnostic radiology at Stanford was a nightmare, therapeutic radiation therapy was even worse—"a disgrace" Kaplan called it. He had only a 250-kilovolt machine with which to treat patients. Because of its low energy, long exposure times of up to thirty minutes were required to deliver adequate doses. The poor penetration of these low-energy x-rays caused accumulation in the skin of high doses, almost twice that delivered internally. Patients suffered burns from the large surface dose and damage to internal organs from radiation scatter. Few were cured.

While struggling to bring his unit to a level of passable safety and efficiency, Kaplan had to deal with a large clinical service—patients at Stanford Hospital in addition to those at the Veterans Administration and county hospitals. Before Kaplan's arrival, the radiology service had been a glorified private practice, where a small group of staff radiologists supervised the residents and took home the revenue. Three residents read the majority of x-rays and performed most procedures with minimal supervision. Kaplan instituted an unpopular change: no x-ray henceforth left the department without being read by a staff member and resident. And a portion of the income from clinical service went to the department, not to the private radiologists.

In the midst of organizing his department, Kaplan began to assemble his laboratory. When he became chairman, most radiologists did no basic scientific investigation. "The only thing being called research by diagnostic radiologists," Kaplan said, "was to sit on their butts in front of a viewing box and look at films and perhaps collect one or two cases of some rare malformation." Kaplan believed the combination of a clinical base and research programs was essential if radiology were ever to be viewed as an academic discipline, not just a technical service. He had to serve as a model. Besides, he was eager to continue his studies on radiation-induced lymphomas.

As promised, Dean Chandler gave Kaplan a laboratory in the Lucie Stern Research Building, a renovated Victorian house. Henry had acquired enough grant funding to hire his first laboratory assistant, and he recruited Mary Brown, an outspoken young woman he had known at Yale. She was no-nonsense from her haircut to her shoes to her dealings with people. When his lab was small, she did small tasks, like preparing slides and cleaning mouse cages. When his lab became big, she did the big tasks, like training new technicians and managing budgets. Called Kaplan's "major-domo" by staff and trainees, Brown controlled his laboratory and protected him from interruptions. "You could only get to Dr. Kaplan through Mary," a former student said.

The first time Brown entered Kaplan's laboratory, she was shocked to see an empty, dirty room with no cabinets, animal cages, or glassware. The windows faced the wall of an apartment building. The room was stifling. The ventilation system had been shut off ever since a microbiologist had accidentally contaminated it with *Coccidioides*, a fungus that causes pneumonia.

Essential to Kaplan's research were his mice—the C57 blacks that he had inherited from L. C. Strong and had continued to breed at the National Cancer Institute. By 1948, the colony had grown quite large. As soon as Mary had prepared stacks of cages to house them, she had the mice shipped from Washington, D.C. One morning at 2 A.M., Henry and Mary went to San Francisco International Airport to receive them. When the sun came up, they were still in the lab—unpacking mice, labeling each one, and placing them in their specific cages.

In his early years at Stanford, Henry did most of the technical research work himself. Brown marveled at how deftly he performed delicate procedures; his enlarged fingers posed no problem. Time and again after Brown had locked up the lab late Friday, Kaplan returned and spent the evening planning experiments, all day Saturday operating and reading slides. On Monday morning, when Brown opened the lab, she found an entire week's work completed. "Work was his hobby," she said. "It was his golf course."

Kaplan's vision for a comprehensive cancer program included not only an updated radiology unit and research laboratories, but also a dedicated cancer ward. He had explicitly requested such an arrangement in negotiations with Chandler. But when he arrived, he found his patients were admitted to the medical wards under the supervision of Professor Arthur Bloomfield, chairman of Medicine.

The son of a Johns Hopkins professor, raised in an upper-class eastern family, Bloomfield was rarely heard to raise his voice; yet "the Professor," as he was called, ruled the wards. He examined every patient admitted to the medical service and reviewed the treatment plan for each. Trained in the European school, where students revered their professors, Bloomfield observed rigid protocol. Use of Christian names was forbidden; interns communicated with him through the chief resident. "He was coldly intellectual and stylized," a faculty member recalled.

No one who trained at Stanford Hospital during his reign ever forgot Bloomfield's rounds. Every Friday morning, all faculty and residents from the Department of Medicine, professors from other departments, and private physicians gathered for medical grand rounds. Bloomfield entered the wards, escorted by the chief resident, and stood at the head of the bed on the patient's right. The chief resident faced him; the assistant resident stood two feet behind; the interns assembled at the foot of the bed. Rounds started so promptly that a practitioner at that time recalled, "You could set your watch by Bloomfield's arrival and departure." No visitors were allowed on the wards; Bloomfield insisted on absolute quiet. Unfortunately, the garbage collectors had the same timetable, and the clatter of trash cans regularly interrupted the silence.

After a trainee presented the case, the Professor examined the patient, usually finding a soft heart murmur or tiny skin nodule everyone else had missed. Then he proceeded to discuss the case. "In freshly donned, newly cleaned white coat, hands clasped behind him, teetering on his heels, he went to work," a former student wrote, "and within the hour made complex topics simple." Bloomfield embellished his medical discourse with classical references. When he lectured about typhoid fever, he read the original description from an eighteenth-century French text, translating as he read. When someone rushed to accept a new therapy, he cited Hamlet: "Let us rather bear the ills we have, than fly to others we know not of." No one else spoke except select senior faculty, like Chief of Surgery Emile Holman, a Johns Hopkins graduate and Rhodes Scholar.

Into this established routine, this formal atmosphere, came Henry Kaplan. Bill Creger, then an intern, recalled the first day Henry attended Bloomfield's rounds wearing a slightly wrinkled lab coat and a bow tie. How this Chicago Jew contrasted with the well-born, well-bred faculty. And at that first grand rounds, Creger noticed something else—Henry didn't hesitate to contradict Bloomfield. Looks of astonishment passed from face to face. Everyone was deferential to the Professor, but "deference was not a quality Henry could ever be accused of possessing," a prior resident said. And he wasn't even a professor of medicine; he was a radiologist. Some found his interruptions annoying, calling him "an outsider." Others thought his presence delightful. "Bless him," Creger said. "He was always interesting." Closing ranks around Bloomfield, the senior professors tested Kaplan, baited him. They soon learned he had an encyclopedic knowledge of medicine.

Kaplan knew the faculty expected him to behave like a radiologist and just show the radiographs. But he wouldn't accept this role; he was a doctor, too. If he integrated the findings to arrive at a diagnosis others had overlooked, he didn't intend to keep quiet. After all, the patient's health was his major concern, not protocol. And he brought something new to those rounds—he incorporated basic scientific principles. But most faculty didn't appreciate his challenging long-established medical tenets; they just wanted him to read x-rays. Once on ward rounds, a medicine professor made light of his interpreting the pathophysiology of some disease process found on the radiograph. "Gentlemen," Kaplan said, "radiology is not photography; it's a branch of medicine."

Of those who baited Henry Kaplan, none was as malignant and persistent as Leo Henry Garland. President of the local medical society, he dominated the radiology community in San Francisco. Garland owed his success to "his brain and his tongue," one radiologist said. "He had a significant amount of blarney and some brilliance." He enlivened cocktail parties and medical meetings with stories told in Irish brogue. Women found him irresistible; men did too. He had married the daughter of one of the wealthiest retailers in San Francisco, and aided by her connections, he built the city's largest downtown radiology practice.

But Garland wasn't content with his lucrative practice and his gracious homes in the city and Marin County. He wasn't content with being the director of the radiology service at San Francisco City Hospital. He wanted to be head of radiology at Stanford University. When he traveled to international meetings, he presented himself as a clinical professor from Stanford. Often he was mistakenly called the chairman of Radiology, and he didn't correct the error. When the chairmanship became available, Garland's friends and colleagues began congratulating him. Chandler's appointment of Henry Kaplan surprised and humiliated him.

Garland was used to being in charge. "There was no one in his immediate environment," one radiologist said, "whom he didn't wish to control." A faculty member recalled a party at Garland's home: guests were lingering about the pool when Garland turned to an associate, dressed in a fine suit, and told him to dive into the swimming pool. At first the man laughed, thinking it a joke, but something in Garland's look checked his laughter, and he jumped in. A resident told a story of dining at Garland's home. After brunch, he said to his wife, "Go upstairs and get my cigarettes." She turned to call one of the children to fetch them. "No," Garland snapped. "I told *you* to get my cigarettes."

Henry Garland set out to win over Henry Kaplan, but Kaplan didn't succumb to charm. He treated Garland like any other staff member, writing him that the role of a radiologist at a teaching hospital was different from that of a private practitioner. His prime job was to teach and do research. He suggested that Garland present his results from treating cervical cancer, which he had been quoting. But Garland hadn't done anything that resembled clinical research. When Kaplan suggested that he teach general practitioners the basics of x-ray interpretation, Garland responded that in his experience, courses for nonradiologists "tend to result more in the production of half-baked amateur radiologists than in the production of physicians with a better insight. ... Granted these fellows were no geniuses." And then Kaplan announced that staff could no longer keep all revenue from radiologic procedures.

Garland soon realized that he couldn't manipulate his chairman. Kaplan didn't accept his advice and clearly didn't revere him. Since Garland couldn't control Kaplan, he set out to destroy him. He began to spread rumors about Kaplan's incompetence. He took films and reports to other radiologists and said, "Look what the shining light of Israel read." When he couldn't find errors, he fabricated them. "He was capable of making misstatements with a level of assurance that was beyond belief," a prior trainee said. Garland depicted Kaplan as a near-sighted scientist, calling him a "mouse radiologist." But community physicians found Kaplan's radiology seminars stimulating. They began to appreciate his superb diagnostic skills and his willingness to share new information. Since Garland's verbal attacks weren't effective, he began to sabotage Kaplan's unit. Stories circulated among trainees that Garland entered the Radiology Department late at night and mixed up films.

With friends, Kaplan called Garland a "malignant son-of-a-bitch," but in public, he ignored him. This infuriated Garland even more; no one had ever disregarded him. Garland stopped whispering about Kaplan behind closed doors and became publicly vocal. "He was snide, nasty, and backbiting," Leah said. He began to taunt Kaplan, trying to lure him into battle. But Kaplan wouldn't fight; he didn't need to. At a large dinner party for a distinguished English radiologist, Garland gave the opening address, referring to Kaplan as "the professor from Palestine." Kaplan said nothing and continued eating. On another occasion, when Garland made an offensive comment, Kaplan looked straight at him and without an inflection in his voice said, "It is well known that all carcinogens are irritants. How fortunate that not all irritants are carcinogens."

No matter how frustrating his day had been, Henry knew that when he climbed the hill to his apartment, he'd find Leah willing to listen—ready to laugh at Garland's latest escapade or to sympathize about an experiment that had failed. Leah didn't complain when Hank failed to notice her new blouse, when he forgot to kiss her. That was the price for marrying a man with a destiny. "There aren't enough superlatives," she wrote Sarah, "to use in describing your son."

Leah and Henry had always assumed they'd have a family, but after ten years of marriage, they remained childless. Early on, they had enjoyed the freedom this gave them. On Leah's twenty-fifth birthday, however, she and Hank had decided to have a baby. When several years passed without success, they began to worry. Leah hoped that the difficulty lay with her, but a fertility workup determined her husband to be the infertile one.

Henry had been somewhat cavalier with regard to radiation exposure. In the 1940s, radiation safety was just a vague concept. Film badges were available to gauge exposure, but Kaplan seldom wore his, although he irradiated large numbers of mice and patients daily. In addition, he likely had absorbed a great deal of radiation while a resident at Michael Reese Hospital. Residents had to keep account of the radium needles—radium sources encased in platinum tubes, each engraved with a code. "The damn things were about the size of a paper clip," a former resident said, "corroded and dirty, so you would have trouble seeing the engravings. You got a lot of exposure by the time you had gone through twenty." To make matters worse, when Kaplan's desk at Yale was checked with a Geiger counter, it clicked loudly. Tucked in the back of a drawer were hot, unshielded radioactive needles. No one knew how long they had been there. Any of these exposures could have caused sterility. Henry had chosen the field of radiation therapy because he wanted to cure cancer. As of 1950, he had made little progress, but he was already paying a price for his choice.

↜

After six months, Kaplan's department began to resemble a modern radiology unit. "Had it not been remodeled soon," a colleague speculated, "we would have been condemned as obsolete." Staff remember Kaplan's delight when shock-proof diagnostic machines arrived, followed by an automated film developer. Each new piece of equipment required changes in the wiring, protracted calibration, and thorough inspection for radiation leaks. Walls had to be reconstructed to meet radiation safety standards. Every time Henry signed another work order, he saw his development fund dwindle. "The next time I remodel an x-ray department," he wrote to Leo Rigler, "it will be done while I'm on a six-month vacation."

Kaplan wanted to create an academic department in which faculty taught, did research, and provided clinical care. This was impossible with his current staff. So he set out to replace the private physicians with full-time academicians. Initially, he had funds to hire only one, and he chose Henry Jones, whom he had known at Yale. At first glance, most people underestimated this thin, pale young man with wire-rimmed glasses, close-cropped hair, and a crooked tie clasp. His expressionless face matched his dry wit. On an instructor's salary of $5,000 a year, Jones supervised the entire clinical service. Staff were welcome to interrupt him with difficult x-rays at any time. And he was loyal to his chief. Once while on vacation, he received a note from Kaplan saying, "shortly after you left, all hell broke loose. . . . Would appreciate it tremendously if you could make every effort to revise your travel plans." He returned immediately.

In time, Kaplan hired more full-time faculty. Among them was Herb Abrams, a hard-working and exceptionally bright resident who was advancing the new technique of cardiac angiography—the radiographic examination of blood vessels after injection of radio-opaque dye. He exemplified the kind of academic radiologist Kaplan sought. After he had strengthened the clinical program, Kaplan added research scientists to broaden the investigative activities. He planned to build a radiobiology section to probe the fundamental mechanisms of radiation effects. Few departments in the country could boast a slate that included prominent men such as Robert Kallman, who developed transplantable tumor models to study radiobiologic principles; J. Eugene Robinson, who studied the influence of nutritional alterations on the radiosensitivity of cells; and Kendric Smith, known for his studies comparing DNA from normal and irradiated tissues.

Despite his enthusiasm for research, Kaplan never lost sight of the underlying reason for such an effort—the patients. He told his faculty that the quality of patient care in the department had to be first-class, and he spent as much time as they did reading films, and even more treating cancer. And woe to anyone who ever harmed a patient. Mary Brown recalled the day an unattended patient in the Radiology Department fell off a stretcher. When Henry received the telephone call, he stormed out of his lab, rushed across the street and down the hospital corridor. His anger was so great, Brown said, "that a nurse rushed behind him passing out tranquilizers."

Once the department had been renovated and new faculty had been hired, Kaplan could spend more time in his laboratory. His ideas emerged so quickly that he and Brown could not perform all the experiments he had conceived. So he hired two more assistants—Barbara Hirsh and Susie Nigarada. From the beginning, he treated them like a research team. While other investigators credited their technicians in footnotes, Henry made them his co-authors. He sent them to scientific meetings, stimulated them to try new techniques, to plan their own experiments. But often he pressed too hard. "He was a very strict taskmaster," a student said. "That lab was a beehive." He expected everyone to work at top speed at all times, and he wouldn't tolerate sloppiness or stupidity. "He just couldn't suffer fools," Abrams said. He was patient the first time he explained a technique, but staff and trainees learned never to ask the same question twice. The ever-present tension dissipated when Henry traveled, and the research team began to look forward to his trips. When he returned, however, he passed out stacks of three-by-five cards on which he had jotted down experiments he had planned on airplanes, in taxis. Gradually the distance between Kaplan and his staff widened. He became increasingly intense. "He was like an old man at age twenty-nine," a student said. His staff no longer called him Henry; they addressed him as Dr. Kaplan. In his absence, they referred to him as HSK.

When Kaplan wanted to add a postdoctoral fellow to the group, Mary pointed out that the crowded laboratory, smelling of mice and sawdust, was already unbearable. He appealed to Chandler for an additional room in the Lucie Stern Building. The dean said the space had been committed to other activities to which Kaplan responded: "there [are] 28,000 mice, two physicians, and three technicians, adding up to 28,005 breathing, living organisms in 700 square feet." Chandler gave him another room. Then just as the technicians were beginning to reorganize the laboratory, Kaplan brought in more people. "There wouldn't even be a chair for them," Brown said. "We called it the ghetto complex."

Out of that tiny, two-room laboratory, however, came some impressive work. Kaplan's major emphasis continued to be the study of carcinogenesis using C57 black mice. Now that he had discovered that radiation-induced leukemia and lymphoma began in the thymus gland, he concentrated his efforts specifically on those thymic cells. He wasn't interested in lymphoma or leukemia per se; he was using them as a model to study the earliest stages of malignant transformation. In his next set of experiments, rather than administering total lymphoid irradiation, he directed the radiation beam to the thymus gland only. To his surprise, these irradiated mice did not develop lymphomas; they remained healthy. The results didn't make sense; scientists thought radiation caused cancers by direct damage to the irradiated tissue. Instead, he had found a paradox: radiation delivered to the whole body induced a cancer in the thymus gland; whereas radiation to the thymus gland itself didn't. Why not? He tried changing the dose, the fractionation, but still no cancers developed. Kaplan concluded that the prevailing theory was wrong. These tumors were not caused by direct radiation damage, as always thought, but by some indirect mechanism.

Intrigued by this finding, he changed the focus of his work. To prove that indirect stimulation generated these lymphomas, he and his research group performed an elegant series of experiments. First, they removed the thymus glands from a group of C57 mice and treated them with total body irradiation. Then they transplanted thymus glands from healthy mice that had never been exposed to radiation into the irradiated mice. Lymphomas developed in the transplanted thymus glands even though the glands themselves had not been exposed to radiation. Kaplan concluded that radiation-induced cancers of mouse thymus originated not from cells damaged by direct x-ray exposure, but from some systemic, activated factor that transformed normal lymphocytes into malignant ones. What was this activated factor? This mystery intrigued him, and he could barely stand to leave his laboratory.

During his first seven years at Stanford, Kaplan published thirty-nine papers. "I used to think he was an authentic genius," biophysicist Robert Kallman said. "Then I discovered he wasn't really a genius, just a very smart man who worked awfully hard—twenty-four hours a day." He had the capacity to perform several tasks simultaneously. His early years working in the drugstore while commuting to school had trained him well. "He had that rare ability to make use of little snippets of time," Brown said. Between patient cases, he ran across the street to the lab, read a stack of slides, then dashed back across the

street. "The lab was his haven," she recalled. If one of the x-ray machines broke down, if a patient suffered a complication, he took care of it, then trudged across Clay Street, and without a word, began operating on his mice.

And Henry found refuge in Leah. She remained cheerful despite his long hours and their infertility problem. Henry halfheartedly suggested adoption. Leah had begun reading articles on how to tell a child he was adopted when she became pregnant. On Christmas Eve 1951, she went into labor, and considering how she and Henry felt about finally having a child, they thought it appropriate that the "Hallelujah" chorus played continuously in the background. When Henry held his daughter Ann—a tiny, dark-eyed beauty—for the first time, he sighed, "She's perfect." "I realized he meant the fingers," Leah said.

Leah felt awkward with the new baby. Not Henry; he approached fathering with his typical self-confidence. He read baby books and showed Leah how to change diapers, prepare formula, and feed their daughter. An adoring father was one of Ann's earliest memories. Since their first conception had taken five years, Henry and Leah immediately planned for a second child. To their delight, a son, Paul, was born sixteen months later.

～

Kaplan could have concentrated his efforts on his own department, and the other senior faculty would have been content. But he devoted himself to raising Stanford from a mediocre school to the stature envisioned by its founder. At first, the process seemed hopeless. Arthur Bloomfield and Emile Holman were outstanding clinicians and teachers but lacked his vision of an academic medical school. The other faculty were a small, close-knit group who had long ago stopped challenging one another. He found himself up against "good-old-boy cronyism," one colleague said. Most ate lunch together in the faculty dining room, located in an old Victorian house. "A chummy family," one young faculty member called them. "And when you hear 'chummy family' in a scientific institution, watch out."

But change did eventually occur. In 1953, Loren Chandler retired, and Windsor Cutting, chairman of Pharmacology, became dean. In the next two years, five department chairmen, including Bloomfield and Holman, retired, and Kaplan became one of the senior faculty. Every time the dean needed to fill a position, Kaplan was there to advise him. He wanted to be certain Cutting hired research-oriented faculty. He knew faculty were more important to Stanford's viability than its buildings and landscape.

Kaplan's tenure at Stanford might have been short-lived. The more he published and presented at national meetings, the more his reputation grew. Before long, other institutions began to offer him positions, good positions with more

space, bigger budgets, and better laboratories than Stanford could provide. But despite his frustrations, budding inside him was a loyalty to the school that would grow into a love affair. Now Leah had two loves with which to contend—his research and Stanford.

Faculty split in their opinions of Kaplan. Some felt he was too dogmatic. He had "an eastern aggressiveness, an assertiveness that was rather foreign," one recalled. They found his self-confidence irritating, thought him too eager to wield power. Other colleagues called him "a good citizen of the school." "He was a giver, not a taker," one said. They appreciated that he exhibited only "modulated excitement" about his own successes. They acknowledged that he wanted power—not to control others, but so that no one could control him. Whatever the opinion of Henry Kaplan—a man of commitment or an egoist—all agreed that he was "a man to be reckoned with."

13   Vera Peters: Daring to Cure Hodgkin's Disease

By his early thirties, Henry Kaplan had accomplished more than many scientists do in a lifetime. Already nationally recognized for his work on radiation-induced murine cancers, he might have been satisfied, but he wasn't. He felt as if he had just started. On July 27, 1956, he attended the Eighth International Congress of Radiology in Mexico City, where he heard Vera Peters from the Ontario Institute of Radiotherapy present a paper entitled "A Study of Hodgkin's Disease Treated by Irradiation." Her data suggested a cure rate of 60 percent in patients with early-stage disease using new radiation techniques. Peters was advancing the field of cancer treatment; he was not.

When Vera Peters addressed the International Congress of Radiology, she was scared. At this, her first major presentation, she faced an audience that included many of her strongest critics. Cancer specialists from around the world had come to hear this Canadian woman who had challenged the status quo, boldly stating that she had cured patients with Hodgkin's disease, which most still considered fatal. Many thought her doses and fields too aggressive. But data she had published in 1950 had been intriguing, and they had come to learn if, six years later, any of the patients were still alive.

The audience likely expected an outspoken, self-righteous woman of prominent carriage. But nothing about her suggested her importance. Her dress and demeanor were inconspicuous. Slight in build, she had a cap of brown curls surrounding a face one might describe as cute. She spoke with simple clarity and humility. Those who got to know Peters were drawn in by her affability. Lacking pretenses, she seemed as comfortable as an old friend. Despite her slightly crossed front teeth, she smiled freely. She liked a cold beer, country-western music, and a good joke. Deep in conversation, she barely stamped out one cigarette before she lit the next. The sole evidence of any self-awareness was an occasional glance at her hands. She was pleased they didn't look blemished and desiccated, a common consequence of prolonged exposure among radiation therapists. Those who got to know Peters were drawn out by her conversa-

tion, the way she spoke of everyday things. Only later, after she left, did they remember she was one of the foremost radiation therapists in the world.

~

Mildred Vera Peters, the fourth child of an indigent farmer, was born on April 28, 1911, in Thistle Town, Ontario. Her father struggled to make a living from a small herd of dairy cattle and a few acres of hay. The closer they edged toward poverty, the more her mother, a prior teacher, stressed education. They had no electricity or telephone and wore homemade clothes; yet Vera's mother always corrected her English. Considered a tomboy, Vera had an impish smile and preferred playing pranks to lessons. Yet even as a child, she had an immense capacity for hard work. She didn't mind milking cows at 4 A.M. while the icy wind rushed across the prairie or picking corn under the hot August sun. She imagined she could be happy farming for the rest of her life. But when she was eleven, that notion changed. Her father suddenly died.

Memories of that night haunted her for years. Her father had always been strong and stoic. Then one evening, he complained of stomach pains and started vomiting. He suspected tainted food, but in a few hours, the pain became excruciating, the retching constant. The nearest house was miles away. By the time her brother reached it to phone a doctor, their father was dead from intestinal obstruction. Vera knew that her father would have survived if they had had a telephone to call for help or a car to drive him to a hospital. That summer, as Vera and her mother, brother, and sisters labored to keep the farm afloat, she vowed never to be helpless again.

In the fall, Vera returned to the one-room school no longer a mischief-maker, but a serious student. She mastered all eight grades in six years and attended a collegiate high school in Toronto, where she excelled in mathematics and the sciences. Her brother suggested she consider a career in medicine, although the cost was almost prohibitive. The family pooled its resources, and in 1928, Vera entered the University of Toronto, completing her undergraduate and medical education in six years.

Then during her second year of medical school, her mother developed breast cancer and underwent a mastectomy. Vera saw the way physicians whispered about cancer in the hallway, how they treated the disease, not the patient. "Quite apart from the medical disadvantages of mastectomy," she wrote years later, "is the associated emotional trauma, frequently raw and bleeding long after the physical wound becomes a scar." She decided to devote her life to cancer patients, and following graduation, she took a residency in surgery, the main avenue to a career in the cancer field.

During Vera's residency, her mother's cancer recurred, causing painful ulcers

across her chest wall. At Toronto General Hospital, she underwent treatments with a radium jacket—a corset interlaced with radium needles that delivered high doses of superficial radiation to the skin. Vera appreciated how her mother's doctor, Gordon Richards, the chief of Radiology, blended competence and compassion. And she became fascinated by the new tool he used to treat cancer. Since there was no formal training program in radiotherapy at the time, Peters asked for an apprenticeship with Richards. At the age of twenty-five, she had found her life's work—radiation therapy—and a mentor, Gordon Richards, who would change her life.

When Peters met Richards in 1936, he was already well known in his field and could have chosen any one of a number of bright young men as his trainee. Instead, he chose her. Richards appreciated her combination of innate intelligence and a seemingly limitless capacity for work. And she shared his fervor for curing cancer. As an apprentice, Peters received a monthly salary of $100, not enough to cover her expenses. So she took a job at a private hospital managing night emergencies in exchange for room and board. Following her apprenticeship, Richards asked Peters to join him as a colleague.

In her last year of training, Peters married Kenneth Lobe, a high-school principal. The couple led a quiet life, centered on family and work. Vera brought stacks of papers home every evening. Their two daughters became accustomed to the piles of patient charts on the dining room table. Vera calculated survival rates and wrote manuscripts while children played around her. She made some of her most astute observations with the record player blaring in the background. "Mom will never hear that," her daughters used to tell friends. "She doesn't hear anything."

During the early years of marriage and motherhood, she was treating up to forty patients daily. The cancer Peters found most challenging was Hodgkin's disease. In treating it, Richards was influenced by the Swiss radiotherapist René Gilbert. Gilbert recommended irradiation to affected lymph nodes with 180 roentgens daily for two weeks, followed by low-dose prophylactic irradiation to adjacent, uninvolved nodes. Richards taught Peters to go further. He treated involved lymph node regions to a total dose of 3,000 to 4,000 roentgens. And having observed that in patients with lymph nodes in the mediastinum (central chest), the disease progressed in the upper abdomen, he began to treat abdominal nodes prophylactically. "You can never extinguish a fire by pouring water into the center of the flames," he used to tell Peters. If a patient had diseased nodes in the chest and abdomen, he treated all lymphoid regions.

One day, Richards told Peters that he had just seen a patient he had treated ten years earlier for Hodgkin's disease. The thirty-five-year-old woman had presented with a large mediastinal mass, and he had designed a treatment that delivered high doses to her mediastinum with minimal scatter to her lungs. Now, ten years later, she had no evident cancer. Richards told Peters he thought that they might have cured a number of patients, but they needed an in-depth analysis to prove it.

Peters set out to review the records of 257 patients treated in their department over an eighteen-year period. Although the work was tedious, she said, "I enjoyed every chart I read, because each was a patient." Halfway through the project, she noted that systemic symptoms, such as fever, night sweats, itching, and weight loss, seemed to affect outcome. She had not kept track of these, so she had to start over, reading the charts again. After two years, she was ready to analyze the data.

What she found astonished her: half of the patients were alive at five years. When she plotted a survival curve for the entire group, she noted that after eight years, it ran parallel to the survival curve for healthy, age-matched adults. This meant that if cancer hadn't recurred by eight years, the chances of doing so were exceedingly small. At ten years, 35 percent of their patients had not had a recurrence. These results looked superior to those from Memorial Hospital and the University of Minnesota, where ten-year survival rates ranged from 3 to 8 percent. When she showed the data to Richards, he confirmed what she barely dared to believe. Others had hinted at it, but she and Richards had proved the curability of Hodgkin's disease. He sent her back to probe further: Did certain subgroups of patients fare better? How did stage at presentation and symptoms affect outcome? Had any new long-term effects of irradiation surfaced?

Peters divided the cases into subgroups by survival and looked for common characteristics within each. "I was fascinated with the different patterns of disease," she said. Although age, sex, and pathologic subtype influenced prognosis, extent of disease involvement at the time of diagnosis had the most striking effect on outcome. Peters proposed assigning patients a stage based on initial sites of disease. To do so, she devised a staging system: stage I—involvement of a single lymph node region; stage II—involvement of two or more lymph node regions, both located in either the upper or lower half of the body; stage III—involvement of two or more lymph node groups in both the upper and lower trunk. Richards reviewed the data and agreed. Grouping patients by this system, Peters found that a high percentage of patients with stage I disease survived ten years; a fifth of those with stage II were still alive; everyone with stage III had died. No one had ever proven statistically that the anatomic extent of involvement at presentation influenced survival. It was time for Peters and Richards to reveal their findings.

Peters's excitement, however, was dampened by Richards's failing health. At sixty-four, he was dying from aplastic anemia, failure of the bone marrow to produce blood cells. Not much attention had been paid to radiation exposure in the early nineteen hundreds. Few long-term side effects had been described in therapists, except skin damage. Richards's hands were shriveled and discolored. The more serious injury—that to his bone marrow—had been insidious. Obliterated by radiation, it no longer produced blood cells. He suffered from progressive weakness, repeated hemorrhages, and recurrent infections.

From his hospital bed, Richards encouraged Peters to publicize their findings. In 1949, she presented their data at a Toronto General Hospital staff meeting. Richards was wheeled down to hear her seminar. "He sat in the front row," Peters recalled. "His face was very white, but he looked proud as punch." She described the patient population studied, radiation techniques, and statistical methods. Then she showed the survival curves, comparing their results to those at other institutions. "In light of present knowledge," she concluded, "the diagnosis of Hodgkin's disease should not be regarded with despair and the patient treated as incurable." When she finished, the audience applauded politely. She knew they didn't believe her. After a few civil questions, the attack began. Cure of Hodgkin's disease—impossible; the pathology must be incorrect, follow-up data wrong. Fortunately, Richards had already returned to his hospital room.

Gordon Richards died soon thereafter, and Peters had to defend their stand on the curability of Hodgkin's disease alone. She submitted a paper—later considered a classic—to the *Canadian Medical Association Journal*, but it was rejected with the comment that it contained too many tables. Following its publication in an American radiology journal, she received numerous letters calling her conclusions and recommendations outrageous. Some felt threatened by this complicated therapy, which could only be administered by specially trained radiotherapists. Others called it cruel to give false hope to patients who would, in time, die of their disease. Even academic radiotherapists sounded skeptical. A professor from the University of California wrote in a prestigious journal: "The reasons for the exceptionally high survival in the Toronto series are not evident from the published report. . . . The figures are so much at variance with other experiences that questions of selection and sources of bias must be raised." Peters knew her data were accurate—she had read every chart herself. Without Richards, she felt alone, discouraged. Then she received a letter of congratulations from René Gilbert, which bolstered her flagging determination.

Despite barbed remarks from academic radiotherapists, Peters continued to treat patients aggressively. She concentrated her efforts on modifying her techniques, using multiple fields and different angles to increase tumor dose and diminish normal tissue damage. And for the next six years, she kept collecting data. The stacks of charts on her dining room table grew, and the database, kept by her own hand, increased to 291 patients. Gradually, cancer specialists became more interested in her results, and in 1956, Peters was invited to present her updated analysis at the International Congress of Radiology in Mexico City.

"It has been the custom to regard the prognosis of this disease as a tale of unrelieved gloom," she began. "One of the objects of this paper is to dispel something of that gloom and to demonstrate the value of early diagnosis [and] energetic initial therapy." With an increased number of cases, her data still demonstrated excellent survival rates—almost a third of the patients were alive at ten years. She pointed out that patients who survived that long without recurrence had almost no chance of relapse. Likely they had been cured.

Peters presented her staging system and demonstrated the influence of stage on survival. In addition, she said, she had become impressed with the dramatic differences in survival based on presence or absence of constitutional symptoms—fever, night sweats, itching, or weight loss. She added the notations A (absence of symptoms) and B (presence of symptoms) to her staging system. Because of Richards's foresight in requiring detailed records and Peters's keen insight in reviewing them, she had made several other important observations. Three patients had developed thyroid dysfunction as a result of neck irradiation. Subsequently, yearly evaluation of thyroid function became routine. She described herpes zoster, or shingles, a reactivation of the chicken pox virus, as the most frequent infection in her patients and noted that the painful blisters often heralded a recurrence of Hodgkin's disease. She reported that two patients had developed acute leukemia years later. And she described treatment of thirteen pregnant patients, using a plan that assured the safety of the fetus without risking the mother's welfare.

The major focus of Peters's talk at the Congress was her therapeutic approach to Hodgkin's disease. She recommended that 3,000 roentgens be delivered over a two-week period to all involved lymph nodes. This dose usually eradicated the known disease. Then she went a step further. As Gilbert had reported years earlier, she and Richards had found the first site of relapse, with few exceptions, to be in adjacent nodal groups. So she prescribed 1,000 roentgens to contiguous, clinically uninvolved nodes. "If indicated," she said, "segmental irradiation of all the chief lymphatic chains is advised to supplement the radical treatment of the involved areas." She was advocating irradiation of lymph nodes seemingly unaffected by disease. To substantiate her revolutionary approach, Peters compared the survival of patients treated to areas of involved nodes only with those who had received prophylactic irradiation to contiguous uninvolved sites as well. Prophylactic irradiation increased survival rate by at least 20 percent.

This time the audience believed her. Those who had read her initial report had waited to see if her survival data still held up years later. It had. "The former prevailing attitude of skepticism gradually evolved into optimism," Peters said. "They all rushed home and analyzed their own experience and found we were right." Her three-stage staging system received prompt acceptance. Within a few years, excellent survival data were being reported by other investigators using Peters's intensive radiotherapy techniques.

⸕

In the audience at Mexico City sat Henry Kaplan. He asked perceptive, probing questions. "He was very clever," Peters said, "and I had tremendous respect for him—until I got involved at meetings with him." Kaplan returned to Stanford and collected the charts of 109 patients treated since 1928. He wanted to validate Peters's findings. Although Stanford patients had been treated over a thirty-year period by several radiologists with different machines, fields, and doses, Kaplan found that 16 percent had survived ten years, 43 percent if disease involved only one or two nodal groups. Peters had been right. "Clinically localized Hodgkin's disease should be considered a potentially curable tumor," he wrote in the *Stanford Medical Bulletin*.

Was Peters correct about the importance of dose too? Kaplan found that in most patients treated with less than 1,000 roentgens, cancer recurred at the treated site within a year. Finally, he questioned the utility of Peters's staging system. But after he divided his patients into the three stages and calculated survival, he had to agree. "Although the staging definitions and the survival figures have both undergone modification in the course of time," he wrote years later, "the basic observation of Peters, that the anatomic extent of disease is the single most important factor influencing survival of patients with Hodgkin's disease, still holds true today."

No one remembers when Henry Kaplan first became intrigued with Hodgkin's disease. His father's death had challenged him to cure cancer, and in his initial laboratory work, he sought to elucidate the basic mechanisms underlying carcinogenesis. His first study of Hodgkin's disease, however, appeared soon after Peters presented her compelling statistics. "Peters was the first to arouse widespread interest in the curative potential of radiation for Hodgkin's disease," he said.

Peters's data and his own experience convinced him of the importance of radiation dose. Peters had used doses as high as 4,000 roentgens without undue toxicity. Why not higher, Kaplan thought, particularly in patients with large masses? Yet he couldn't forget the young woman sent to him with the sudden onset of shortness of breath and chest pain. A chest x-ray had revealed massive involvement of her mediastinal lymph nodes, extending into her lung and invading the pericardial sac around her heart. A biopsy confirmed Hodgkin's disease; her prognosis was grim. Kaplan had treated her with 4,000 roentgens. The mass decreased in size but did not regress entirely. He pushed the dose higher—up to 5,500 roentgens—the highest dose yet reported for this disease.

The patient's breathing had improved, her chest pain resolved, and her mass disappeared. Kaplan delighted in watching her return to a normal life. But a few years later, her breathing became labored again. An x-ray demonstrated damage to her lungs resulting from radiation scatter. In time, she became confined to bed with shortness of breath—a respiratory cripple. Five years following treatment, she died, and an autopsy revealed severe pulmonary fibrosis, her lungs replaced by scar tissue. The pathologist found no evidence of Hodgkin's disease. Radiotherapy had cured her cancer, but the woman had died from complications of the treatment.

Henry Kaplan was upset. The fact that the patient had lived five years free of disease brought him no solace. He knew dose to be crucial, especially for large masses, and yet with the kilovoltage machine, delivery of 5,000 roentgens to the tumor resulted in too much injury to adjacent tissues—skin, bone, lung, heart. He needed a way to deliver high-energy radiation so that he could direct the beam to the tumor target with minimal damage to normal tissues. He believed that he could cure more patients with Hodgkin's disease if he had a more powerful machine.

One evening at a cocktail party, Kaplan overheard several people talking about a new atom smasher being developed by physicists on Stanford's main campus. The device for which he had been searching might be right there at his own university.

14   The Cancer-Killing Cannon

In his later years, Henry Kaplan said three events led to his success in treating Hodgkin's disease. The first was development of the linear accelerator.

In order to design what he considered an ideal radiotherapy machine, Kaplan had to solve two major problems: how to produce and harness high-energy x-rays and how to direct them to the target with precision. At the time, radiotherapy units were primitive, producing radiation of such low energy that it barely penetrated the skin. "The early x-ray therapy equipment," Kaplan wrote, "not unlike the automobiles of that era, was highly unpredictable in performance." And most treatments were administered by surgeons and dermatologists who had no understanding of the physical aspects of radiation. They measured dose by skin redness. Popular units included the Chaoul Apparatus, a shockproof 60-kilovolt machine, and the Newton Victor G X 10, which produced a maximum energy of 140 kilovolts. In 1926, W. D. Coolidge designed a vacuum x-ray tube that operated at an unprecedented 200 kilovolts. After it was adapted for radiotherapy units, radiologists began to report better results with throat and skin cancers, but they still could not treat deep-seated tumors effectively. By the 1930s, it became apparent that in order to make significant advances in cancer therapy, machines that operated at greater energies were needed. But production of high-energy x-rays was beyond the capability of radiation physicists at that time.

Radiotherapists might have been stuck in the kilovoltage era had not a new scientific field blossomed—nuclear physics. Scientists had long sought ways to accelerate electrons in order to split atoms and investigate the properties of nuclear energy. Charles Lauritsen of the California Institute of Technology built a 750,000-volt transformer for his physics research. Recognizing that the high-energy x-rays produced by this apparatus might have useful biological effects, he contacted Albert Soiland, a radiologist at the Los Angeles Tumor Clinic. Soiland asked permission to treat a man with advanced rectal cancer. Standard kilovoltage radiotherapy had a low chance of controlling his disease and would produce burns and ulcerations around his anus and scrotum. Following treatment with Lauritsen's machine, the patient's cancer regressed with minimal skin reaction. Two years later, Soiland reported that the patient had only "a vestige of the old lesion present." The era of megavoltage radiation had begun.

Kilovoltage and megavoltage machines produced radiation in basically the same way—by accelerating electrons to high speed in a vacuum tube and crashing them into a metal target. Electrons collided with atoms in the target, releasing energy in the form of x-rays. Lead shielding reduced dispersion of radiation in all directions except that of the exit beam. When x-rays were absorbed by living cells, they transferred energy to the cells, making them electrically charged or ionized. Ionization produced biological changes that resulted in cell death. X-ray dose was measured in roentgens, the unit of ionizing radiation transmitted in air.

Megavoltage or supervoltage radiation referred to x-rays or gamma rays generated at energies greater than a million electron volts. Its advantages over kilovoltage radiation were considerable. The higher the voltage used to accelerate electrons, the higher the energy of the radiation produced. And the higher the energy of x-rays, the deeper they penetrated into tissues. As machine energies increased from 250,000 volts to several million, the point of maximum radiation concentration centered deep below the skin surface. This made delivery of high doses to tumors located in the chest, brain, and abdomen possible, while sparing the skin excessive exposure. No longer did patients suffer severe radiation burns. Measurement of x-ray dose was changed to rads (radiation absorbed dose)—the amount of ionizing radiation absorbed by, not transmitted to, the tissue. These high-energy beams had sharply defined edges with less radiation scatter, making them more precise. Since megavoltage radiotherapy produced fewer toxic effects than kilovoltage, higher total doses could be delivered. Cancer patients, once treated for pain relief only, could now be treated with curative intent.

Within a few years, several megavoltage devices were designed: the betatron, the Lauritsen tube, and the Van de Graaff generator. But transition from the physicist's laboratory to the clinic was not easy. These machines were immense and inflexible. The betatron, which used enormous magnets to accelerate particles, weighed several tons. The Lauritsen unit at Caltech occupied an 8,000-square-foot room. One of its four transformers was so large that it had to be sunk into a pit to clear the fifty-foot ceiling. The early Van de Graaff generator, called a "magnificent monster," was housed in an airship hangar and mounted on railroad cars for transport.

In the meantime, radiotherapists were exploring a different source of radiation—gamma rays emitted from radioactive material. Radium had been used for decades, but its scarcity made it inordinately expensive—one-thirteenth of an ounce cost $120,000. Work at nuclear reactors led to a substitute, cobalt 60, which was quickly adopted for medical use. Radiologists considered cobalt 60 perfect: it emitted gamma rays in the 1.2 million volt range and could be housed in a relatively compact machine. The usual price of a cobalt unit, $40,000, made it attainable, and units were soon set up in cities throughout Canada and the United States. Most radiologists were satisfied; they considered this the ultimate machine for radiation therapy. But a handful of radiotherapists dreamed of a better device to deliver megavoltage radiation, one with even higher energy and more precision. Among that small, dissatisfied group was Henry Kaplan. He referred to the cobalt unit as a "shotgun." He wanted a rifle.

~

The foundation for the linear accelerator—the machine Henry Kaplan dreamed of—was laid prior to World War II. After Hitler began to rearm in blatant violation of the Treaty of Versailles, the British rushed to design an early warning system to detect approaching enemy aircraft, later named radar ("radio detection and ranging"). Four scientists were housed at Orford Ness, a spit of land located ninety miles northeast of London and accessible only by boat. Sir Henry Tizard, Chairman of the Aeronautical Research Committee, charged them to design an early warning system as quickly as possible. Configuration of a radar set was straightforward: A transmitter produced electromagnetic waves which were emitted from an antenna. When they struck an object, the signals were reflected back to the antenna where a receiver amplified the weak echoes and displayed them on a screen. The time required for echoes to return was converted into a measurement of distance. Since the strength of returning pulses was only a few millionths that of the transmitted pulses, the group's first task was to build a more powerful transmitter. They pieced together parts from ship radios and old x-ray units. Working around the clock, they devised the first crude set within a month, and in less than a year, they had constructed a workable ground radar system.

Soon thereafter, Tizard set up a string of radar stations, the Chain Home System, along the eastern and southern coasts of Great Britain. At night, however, atmospheric conditions limited the range of ground radar, and Tizard knew once the British used their system to detect and destroy enemy planes by day, the Germans would switch to night raids. But the range of ground radar was limited at night. They needed a radar unit small enough to install in planes so the Royal Air Force could patrol the coastline. The transmitters in their ground radar system weighed several tons; antennae stood at least seventy-five feet high, and associated equipment filled a room.

Wavelength of the signals posed yet another challenge. To be functional, an airborne radar system required a narrow beam. Otherwise it picked up stray echoes from the ground, which obliterated signals from approaching aircraft. To produce such a beam, the group at Orford Ness needed signals with wavelengths as short as ten centimeters, so-called microwaves. Their radar set produced signals fifty meters long. And even if they could produce a signal of short wavelength, it wouldn't travel far enough unless it had immense power behind it. In order to proceed, the group needed a compact device that could generate microwave signals at enormous peak power. This obstacle seemed beyond the scope of their expertise. But not far away, at Birmingham University, Mark Oliphant was working on a device to produce microwaves based on an instrument invented by Russell and Sigurd Varian in Palo Alto, California. Their apparatus—which they called a klystron—could produce extremely short radio waves of significant power. Oliphant developed an even more compact microwave radar transmitter—the magnetron—which used magnets to bend electron beams, increasing their intensity. These two powerful sources of microwave signals, the klystron and magnetron, made airborne radar finally feasible. And with this sophisticated system, the British battered the Luftwaffe, winning one of the most decisive battles of the war.

After the war, physicists in Great Britain and the United States began designing microwave linear accelerators for fundamental research, using powerful new microwave sources, the klystron and magnetron. Among them was Stanford professor Edward Ginzton, who had worked with the Varian brothers while a graduate student. He collaborated with physicist Bill Hansen to build a klystron a thousand times more powerful than the original. This device became the heart of a linear accelerator they constructed for physics research.

The basic element in the linear accelerator was a waveguide, a large, corrugated copper pipe into which electrons were injected from a cathode. Radarlike waves were pulsed into the waveguide from a klystron, and electrons rode the waves down the pipe. Ginzton drew the analogy to a boy on a surfboard who, drifting in still water, reached shore without much speed. If, however, the boy rode the surfboard on a wave, he obtained substantial speed. Electrons gained velocity in a similar way and exited from the waveguide with enormous energy. The accelerator could push particles up to speeds of 185,000 miles/second—close to the speed of light. The result was an atom-smashing beam of particles equivalent to six million electron volts.

In the early 1950s, Henry Kaplan began to hear about this atom smasher. There, at his own university, was the potential source of high-energy x-rays he had been seeking. He set up a meeting with Ginzton and the chairman of the physics department and described the current status of radiotherapy to them.

Conventional kilovoltage therapy controlled some superficial cancers, often at great expense to normal tissues. In order to direct radiation to deep-seated tumors, large fields had to be used, resulting in injury to nearby organs. If they reduced the dose, they decreased the therapeutic effect of x-rays. Megavoltage radiation allowed higher doses to be delivered, enhancing their ability to eradicate cancers. The available megavoltage units, however, were large, expensive to build, and costly to maintain. In addition, they lacked mobility and flexibility, which made treatment from different angles almost impossible. The properties of Ginzton's accelerator made it ideal to adapt for medical purposes. "You could accelerate electrons with these high energies," Kaplan said, "and you could hit a heavy metal target and make them into x-rays." By constructing the proper x-ray head, beam width could easily be controlled. No longer would generators, pumps, or massive magnets be necessary. The beauty of the linac lay in the relative simplicity with which one could produce and use high-energy x-rays. "I became convinced that this was to become the radiotherapy machine of the future," Kaplan said, "[and] by the end of that luncheon, I had convinced all of them."

Ginzton and Kaplan began traveling the thirty miles between San Francisco and Palo Alto almost daily, and with each trip, their excitement grew. Within a few months, they had drawn up blueprints for a medical linear accelerator. Now they needed funds to build it; Kaplan estimated $100,000. They sent a grant request to the NIH outlining the need for such a machine. In the budget justification, they projected relatively low construction costs, proposing to use some components from old radar sets. Nevertheless, the NIH disapproved the grant. Kaplan replied to the criticisms and resubmitted it; again he was turned down. For two years, he wrote grants, called government agencies, traveled to Washington, and waited. With each rejection his anger increased. They were proposing a plan that would revolutionize the field of radiotherapy, and they were being blocked by shortsighted reviewers and red tape. (He later learned that one grant reviewer held stock in the company that made Van de Graaff generators.) Kaplan and Ginzton had reached an impasse.

Around this time, Kaplan learned from Carl Von Essen, a former student of his who was training at Michael Reese Hospital, that Eric Uhlmann was building a medical linear accelerator there using gift funds from a wealthy patient. He was taken aback by Kaplan's response; he had never seen him so mad. "It took us more than two years in the richest country on earth to raise $150,000," Kaplan said years later.

At the same time, Great Britain's minister of health recognized the possibility of using the magnetron to power a linear accelerator for medical use. He understood that in order to develop the accelerator expeditiously, it needed to be built by scientists in industry who had the talent and motivation to produce a marketable device. He coordinated three groups: The British Atomic Energy Research Establishment provided the design, the Metropolitan Vickers Electrical Company built the machine, and the Medical Research Council directed the clinical projects. The British government financed the entire endeavor. Now they were preparing to install the linear accelerator at Hammersmith Hospital in London.

Henry Kaplan had only an idea, one collaborator, and no money. Finally, after two and a half years, he and Ginzton received grants from the NIH and the American Cancer Society totaling $63,000 for the first year. The funding covered only two-thirds of their projected needs, but it was a start.

In 1952, a team consisting of three faculty members and seven graduate students began building a medical linear accelerator in the Microwave Physics Laboratory on the Stanford campus. Ginzton supervised construction; Kaplan took responsibility for clinical design. He emphasized simplicity and accuracy. Although he had no background in physics or electrical engineering, he learned quickly. Each day, after he had finished treating patients, attending to departmental business, and planning experiments with Mary Brown, he drove from San Francisco to Palo Alto to work with Ginzton. Kaplan wanted to be involved in every aspect of the project. "I was interested in having a machine that was functional therapeutically, not just a gadget," he said. He appreciated Ginzton's willingness to innovate. Other physicists and engineers tried to discourage Kaplan, explaining why his ideas wouldn't work. Ginzton always asked, "Why not?" Ginzton's colleagues wondered why he was constructing this "junior-sized" linear accelerator for clinical use instead of spending more productive hours in basic research. They told him he shouldn't be wasting time on practical applications; his academic career would be jeopardized. Friends in industry teased him about the immense effort he was expending on this unmarketable machine, calling it "Ed's passport to heaven."

Ginzton and Kaplan planned a six-million-volt accelerator with four main sections: a source to emit electrons, a klystron to generate microwaves, a six-foot length of waveguide, and a metal target. They used old parts from radar sets, kilovoltage units, and Ginzton's previous linac. "I wish I could give you some really enlightened information about how to design a linear accelerator," Kaplan wrote to Hugh Wilson at Yale, "but we are flying blind on our own design." What a contrast to the sophistication of the Medical Research Council in Great Britain, which had teams of physicists and machinists devoted solely to dosimetry, x-ray heads, patient setup, and safety features.

A major limitation of most megavoltage machines was their inflexibility. Kaplan impressed upon the group the importance of creating a maneuverable machine so that they could rotate the beam in various directions, allowing them to treat deep-seated tumors from different angles, while minimizing damage to vital organs. A linac on a movable base would be unique, but seemingly impossible to achieve. The waveguide had to be kept in a vacuum to allow electrons to attain their maximum velocity, and maintaining a constant vacuum required large mechanical pumps, liquid nitrogen, and other bulky equipment. If the Stanford team planned to make a movable waveguide, they had to find a way to seal the waveguide permanently and eliminate the vacuum pumps. "This has never been done," Ginzton remembered thinking, "but—maybe it could be." In a few months, he created a sealed tube by electroplating the waveguide, securing all joints with gold, and baking it under compression. This vacuum-sealed tube eliminated the need for cumbersome, costly accessories, required less space, reduced operations costs, and provided the flexibility that Kaplan insisted upon.

They suspended the two-ton linac from the ceiling of a radiation-shielded chamber, where it rested on an electrically operated cradle that allowed it to be moved to different heights and angles. A lead diaphragm at the front of the accelerator could be opened for large fields or narrowed to pinpoint size. They designed supporting devices to hold the patient motionless. At the control panel outside the chamber, an operator could view the patient through a three-inch lead glass window.

Within two years, the medical linac was ready, and Kaplan and Ginzton issued a press release. Headlines on January 10, 1954, proclaimed:

ATOM CANNON WILL BECOME CANCER PISTOL
—Los Angeles Examiner

OFFICE-SIZE A-SMASHER BEING MADE
—Los Angeles Times

Kaplan and Ginzton emphasized the linac's spectacular capabilities, while trying to placate practicing radiotherapists by touting its affordability at less than $18,000 per unit. But press coverage generated minimal public excitement.

Kaplan and Ginzton now encountered their next major problem—where to house their accelerator. They needed a special facility with eighteen-inch concrete walls and a three-foot-deep concrete trench for radiation protection. The estimated construction costs were $75,000. Meanwhile, a decision had been made to relocate the medical school from San Francisco to the main Stanford campus in Palo Alto. Although the scheduled move was still four years away, no one wanted to pay for temporary installation of the accelerator in the city. Kaplan was told to wait until they had built the new hospital in Palo Alto. But he couldn't be set back four years in his attempts to cure cancer. He had reached the peak of frustration when the Irvine Foundation agreed to finance construction of a radiation vault behind the Stanford Hospital in San Francisco.

In 1955, Kaplan and Ginzton dismantled the linac and moved it from the Stanford campus to San Francisco. "Our linear accelerator is finally being installed," Kaplan wrote a friend. "It was moved up here last week, and now the millions of parts are being put together in noisy fashion by a gang of physicists." Most of the medical staff didn't know what was going on in the concrete block behind the hospital. "Something was being built there," internist Joe Kriss, recalled, "and nobody knew exactly what it was."

They had barely reassembled the linear accelerator when Kaplan got a call from an ophthalmologist named Earle McBain. He had just diagnosed retinoblastoma in a seven-month-old boy. He remembered reading about the linear accelerator in the newspaper. Could Kaplan treat the child on his new machine?

⌒

Helen Issacs felt certain something was wrong with her infant son, Gordon. She thought she saw a white object in his right eye, and when she fed him, his eyes appeared luminous. The family physician said he was fine. A few weeks later, Mrs. Issacs returned. She said Gordon rubbed his right eye frequently, and she didn't think he could see. The doctor assured her the baby was normal. In desperation, she looked for an ophthalmologist in the Yellow Pages and called Dr. Earle McBain in San Rafael. He told her to come to his office that afternoon. McBain examined the baby and identified cat's-eye reflex and cottage-cheese calcifications—findings diagnostic for retinoblastoma, a malignant eye tumor. The cancer had obliterated the vision in his right eye. McBain found at least two tumors in the left eye, but Gordon's sight appeared intact. He advised that the right eye be surgically removed. Regarding the left eye, he told Mrs. Issacs that they had three choices: It, too, could be removed, and Gordon most likely would be cured, but blind. It could be irradiated using cobalt, but in his experience that usually did more harm than good. Growth of the bony orbit was retarded, distorting facial structures; teeth failed to erupt; cataracts eventually developed. Or he had heard that a Stanford radiotherapist had a new radiotherapy machine, which possibly could cure Gordon while preserving his sight.

When Helen Issacs met Henry Kaplan, she was immediately impressed with his gentleness and honesty. He told her the linac would be ready in about thirty days, and her son would be the first to undergo therapy. Treatment would require six weeks of hospitalization with daily anesthesia to immobilize Gordon. He offered to pay for treatment and hospitalization out of his research budget. Helen Issacs gave her consent, and Kaplan told her to bring her son back after Christmas.

Physics professor Mitchell Weissbluth, who had responsibility for calibrating the machine and determining isodose curves, estimated they needed a year to finish the task. Kaplan said they had a month. That December was hectic, Weissbluth remembered. They had designed a lead block to shield vital areas, but it weighed too much to lift. "I don't think I will ever forget the puzzled look on the face of the garage owner down on Fillmore Street," Kaplan recalled, "when I asked him to borrow a heavy-duty automobile jack, and then explained that it was to carry a huge block of lead with a pinhole in it to enable us to position the pinhole day after day for six weeks directly opposite the tumor in the baby's eye."

In January, Helen Issacs brought her son back to Stanford University Hospital. The momentous time had arrived—the first treatment with the linear accelerator. "When the doctors gathered around the machine just before the treatment was to begin," Ginzton recalled, "they realized they did not know how to pinpoint the x-ray beam onto the tumor without destroying the rest of the retina." Ginzton suggested they tape a photograph of the child's eye to his temple. With that roadmap, they felt they could aim the beam with sufficient accuracy to proceed. For thirty-eight days, Gordon lay under the accelerator with six million volts pointed at his tiny eye. Kaplan treated the tumors with 5,800 rads. On June 19, 1956, he wrote in the chart: "The lesion at 12 o'clock appears to be entirely calcified, and there is no evidence of spread at this time." And three months later, he wrote: "the mother states that he can see very tiny objects."

No one remembers any festivities after the first patient finished treatment on the linear accelerator—no speeches, no ceremony. "We were deeply satisfied," Ginzton said. "What needed to be done was done." Mrs. Issacs knew that Dr. Kaplan was pleased with the results when she saw his "quiet little smile." Five years later, when Kaplan considered Gordon cured, he called Helen Issacs to say he had just opened a bottle of champagne.

On April 27, 1956, headlines read:

NEW CANCER-KILLING CANNON UNVEILED
AT STANFORD HOSPITAL
—*San Francisco Examiner*

STANFORD RESEARCHERS HAVE NEW CANCER GUN
High Success Rate Already Indicated
—*San Francisco Chronicle*

The benefits of the linear accelerator seemed substantial: sharply defined beams with less scatter, ability to pinpoint deep-seated tumors, less absorption by normal tissues, and increased potential to plan complex fields. But not everyone reacted enthusiastically to this remarkable achievement. "It is not my purpose to belittle the effort now being made by the several research institutes ... but to warn against too hasty conclusions drawn from insufficient experimental and clinical evidence," a radiotherapist said at a meeting of the Illinois State Medical Society. "There is a common belief, held by both the medical profession and the laity," a noted radiologist complained to the Minnesota State Medical Society, "that higher and higher voltages are synonymous with better and better treatments, and more and more cures of cancer. This popular feeling is stampeding radiologists into procuring apparatus capable of producing higher and higher voltages." Besides, community radiotherapists felt comfortable with cobalt. Cobalt units required no additional equipment, less radiation protection, and minimal technical understanding of dosimetry or physics. The prevailing attitude was, as physicist Jacob Haimson expressed it: "Here's a black box—you just open the jaws, and you've got irradiation. We don't want to fool with microwaves and vacuums." And cobalt was easy to obtain, whereas linear accelerators were still beyond the reach of private practitioners.

San Francisco radiologists were quick to criticize Kaplan, and the loudest voice was Henry Garland's. He accused Kaplan of using publicity hype to steal patients from practicing physicians. Warning about the dangers of the linac, he spread rumors that Kaplan was engaging in gross malpractice. He went so far as to hint of dangerous rays contaminating the local community. At a California Medical Association seminar, Garland reviewed radiation therapy results for cancer of the larynx. His first slide showed two of Kaplan's residents dressed in green scrub suits. One was holding a surgical scalpel, the other a butcher knife. "This is the comparison between the 250 kilovoltage machine," he said, pointing to the scalpel, "and the linear accelerator," he said, pointing to the butcher knife. "If you were to have your larynx cut out, which would you choose?"

Radiologist Henry Jones couldn't help laughing at the irony. Kaplan carried out radiation therapy meticulously, spending hours on each treatment plan, using intricate fields and precise shielding. Garland was a proponent of larger, simple fields, or as Jones called it, "the slop-through-it school." Kaplan resented the time he had to spend answering press questions instigated by Garland, but this was the last time Henry Garland would harass him. He died a few years later of metastatic colon cancer.

~

"I'd like to be remembered as the co-developer of the medical linear accelerator," Henry Kaplan said in his later years, "... and for developing not just the machine, but the standards for its use." Kaplan's place in the history of megavoltage radiotherapy has been a source of controversy for decades. Many have ascribed him with inventing the first medical linear accelerator, an assertion that annoyed British radiotherapists. "That piece you sent me about linear accelerators was wildly inaccurate," Sir David Smithers wrote an American radiotherapist. The Medical Research Council had installed its linear accelerator in Hammersmith Hospital a year and a half before the press announced Kaplan's "cancer pistol" and had treated its first patient almost three years before the "new cancer-killing cannon" at Stanford. C. W. Miller and P. Howard-Flanders had described its basic design in the *Metropolitan Vickers Gazette* in 1953. And W. J. Meredith of Manchester had presented his paper on medical linear accelerators at the Eighth International Congress of Radiology in 1956. The two machines did differ, however. The British used a magnetron as the microwave power source; Kaplan used a klystron.

Although many credited Kaplan with development of the linear accelerator, he qualified his achievement as the first medical linear accelerator in the Western Hemisphere. Even that caused controversy. Eric Uhlmann contended that he had built the first linac at Michael Reese Hospital. Both Kaplan and Uhlmann installed their machines in 1955, but Uhlmann's machine produced electrons, useful in treating superficial cancers, not x-rays.

Most agree that Kaplan was responsible for moving the linear accelerator from the laboratory to the clinic. He and Ginzton wanted the rest of the world to have access to this powerful tool, but they could not interest any corporation in manufacturing these machines. Ginzton went on to co-found Varian Associates and helped build the fledgling electronics business from six employees into a billion-dollar company that became the world leader in producing linear accelerators. Kaplan didn't have a patent; he didn't receive stock in the company or consultant fees. "His only compensation for his advice and counsel," Ginzton said, "was in the form of knowledge that his ideas were now about to be used on a broad scale." But Kaplan knew that the mere availability of megavoltage machines wouldn't further the field unless standards were set for their use and therapists trained appropriately. He persuaded the NIH to fund such training programs.

So Henry Kaplan didn't invent the first linear accelerator. He and Ginzton may have built the first self-contained medical linear accelerator or the first klystron-driven medical accelerator in the world, or at least the first x-ray-producing medical linear accelerator in North America. But it didn't matter to Gordon Issacs whether Kaplan had been first or not. He could see, and for Kaplan, that alone was credit enough.

15   Moving to the Farm

Henry Kaplan said the second event that contributed to his success in treating Hodgkin's disease was the Medical School's relocation to the main Stanford campus. Although he believed in the move and supported it avidly, he nonetheless left his home overlooking San Francisco Bay with regret.

When he and Leah first came west, they had planned to buy a home in San Francisco, where they would be close to work and could take advantage of the symphony and theater. They had both grown up in city apartments. "We were used to going to the park to see grass," Leah said. They began looking at houses, but all seemed ordinary. Henry wanted their first home to be special and concluded that they should build their own. When he stood on an empty lot in Sausalito, just north of the city, and looked across the fields to the Bay, he knew he had found the perfect site.

They interviewed five architects, all of whom showed them conventional floor plans. Then they met Mario Corbett who told the Kaplans that building a house was like molding a sculpture. He designed a spectacular home for them—three-story, cube-shaped, with cathedral ceilings and a central spiral staircase—an award-winning design later featured in architectural magazines. It was perched on the crest of a steep hill, the side facing the Bay constructed entirely of glass. "The view became part of your life," Leah said. It was magnificent—a panorama of deep blue water with Angel Island in the foreground and the Berkeley Hills in the distance. Henry loved to sit in his living room and watch the fog creep over the Bay. To him, his home was a work of art.

There, Leah and Henry began to raise their children. Leah described herself as a caring, but self-conscious, new mother. "I would never say I was a natural," she remarked. Despite her training in child psychiatry, Leah was overprotective and fretful. "When I was looking for help," she said, "if Anna Freud herself had applied, she wouldn't have qualified." Henry, on the other hand, felt perfectly at ease with children. He played their games and roughhoused, yet talked to them as if they were young adults, asking their opinions about a recent sporting event or a piece of music.

Annie was a miniature Leah, with curly brown hair and dark eyes. She brought out the gentle side of her father as they took walks through the Marin hills or translated French stories together. Paul, a stout little boy with a deep, booming voice, made his father laugh. He learned early on that curiosity pleased his father. At the age of five, he could tell Bach from Vivaldi. He could rattle off the names of dinosaurs his father hadn't even heard of. A favorite pastime on family car trips was "animal, mineral, vegetable," a game in which one person thought of a word, and the others asked questions trying to guess the answer. The family groaned when Paul's turn came, since he invariably chose a dinosaur with a barely pronounceable name, like pachycephalosaurus. His face lit up when no one guessed it. If they protested the use of extinct animals, he picked obscure living ones like the emu or the Malaysian flying snake.

Most family outings had a strong educational component. Paul and Annie never ambled through a gallery; their father covered the name of the artist and quizzed them. And he approached most activities with dogged determination, such as the time he decided the family should learn to ski. On their first day at Lake Tahoe, the blowing snow stinging their faces, Henry led them to the top of a steep hill. He had read a book on skiing and proceeded to instruct the family on the snowplow turn. Leah was fussing over the children, afraid they might fall and get wet or break a leg. The ski lesson was progressing far too slowly for Henry. At lunch, he said, "Dear, why don't you go get your hair done this afternoon?"

Leah readily agreed. After the children had put their skis back on, Henry asked, "Do you see your mother anywhere?"

"No, Daddy," Anne and Paul replied.

"All right, goddamn it—fall down," he commanded. So the children fell to the ground.

"All right, goddamn it—get back up." Soon they were skiing.

Paul and Annie had to share their parents more than they liked. Company was a part of their family's fabric. "Henry and Leah gathered friends in extraordinary numbers by some remarkable power of attraction," a colleague said. They frequently attended cocktail parties and buffet dinners. Paul hated putting on his scratchy red wool suit to go visiting. He preferred it when his parents entertained at home, except that all their friends seemed to be intellectuals—architects, political scientists, psychoanalysts. Paul sat through innumerable dinner parties racked with boredom. He recalled pushing his peas from one side of his plate to the other when what he really wanted to do was load them onto his spoon and pelt a stuffy dinner guest. Paul began to resent living in this adult world, with its constant pressure to appear clever. "I would have welcomed someone who was not intelligent," he said.

The Kaplan children also had to share their father with his work. All too often he was absent. Annie, like her mother, accepted early on that that was just the way it was. Paul couldn't. He thought that if he tried harder, if he asked better questions, his father would spend more time with him and love him. Attempting to gain his father's attention, six-year-old Paul went to work in his laboratory on Saturdays. The days were long; Henry usually worked for eight hours straight. He gave Paul small tasks such as carrying trays of specimens or counting cell cultures, but Paul's frequent interruptions and questions became annoying, and Henry relegated him to cleaning mouse cages. The experience did not beget a stronger father-son relationship. Instead, Paul struck up a friendship with Tony, the Filipino animal caretaker, with whom he spent afternoons chatting. The Kaplan children didn't understand that their father was a man of destiny. They simply missed him.

⤿

Kaplan was working hard to build his department. The number of patients treated in his unit steadily increased. Physicians referred cases from cities throughout Northern California and Nevada. Enlarging his faculty roster, he recruited Malcolm Bagshaw, a graduate of Yale Medical School. Bagshaw arrived with his pediatrician wife in a car loaded with children, the family rock collection, and a guitar he had made to play flamenco. Kaplan described him as having "a deceptively quiet, easygoing manner that covers a tremendous amount of drive and determination." Together they devised new techniques to treat cancers of the prostate, pituitary gland, and nasopharynx. Kaplan and Ginzton designed a 70-MeV linear accelerator that produced high-energy radiation called electrons, and Kaplan hired Carl Von Essen, a former Stanford student, to investigate the clinical uses of electron therapy. He expanded his radiobiology group to the extent that his department's laboratories occupied almost the entire Lucie Stern Building. And his own research on leukemogenesis continued to be productive.

Then, in 1952, President Wallace Sterling told Kaplan he was considering relocation of the Medical School to the main Stanford campus and asked him to serve on an advisory committee. Kaplan favored the move. He knew that Stanford Medical School was mediocre, with antiquated facilities, a provincial curriculum, and few faculty one could call scientists. Medicine was at the threshold of a new era, ready to apply the basic sciences to medical care. This could only take place if collaboration between laboratory researchers and clinicians were facilitated. But integration was impossible with the chemistry and physics laboratories thirty miles from the Medical School. "I saw no alternative," Kaplan said. "The school must move down to campus if it were to try to become anything but a third-rate clinical medical school." And having reached that conclusion, he supported it wholeheartedly. "This school is going to make some big leaps," he told radiobiologist Robert Kallman. "It's going to become an outstanding medical school."

When the president announced his decision to move the Medical School, there was an immediate outcry. Most of the clinical faculty had private practices and taught part-time. They didn't want to abandon their patients or their Victorian homes. They didn't want to uproot their families and move from one of the most vibrant cities in the country to this small California town where some people rode horses instead of driving cars, and where neighbors talked about the rattlesnake problem. In short, they didn't want to relocate to "the farm," as the campus had long been called. Bloomfield, Holman, and other senior faculty exerted great pressure on Sterling to change his mind, calling this the "worst decision imaginable" and predicting that "it would be the death of the medical school." Dean Chandler couldn't agree to the plan and resigned. But Sterling held fast. He appointed a new dean, Windsor Cutting, chairman of Pharmacology, to lead the move.

Colleagues described Cutting as gentle and kindly. "He had a folksy, a homey quality that evoked memories of big front porches and rocking chairs," one recalled. Many felt that he made an excellent start in planning the relocation of the Medical School. But, "being a modest man, he had a modest vision," hematologist Bill Creger said. His dream wasn't as grand as Kaplan's, and from the beginning they clashed. Cutting reached decisions by consensus. Kaplan found this galling. He agreed that the dean's role was to implement the will of the faculty, but he should have the wisdom to implement the will of the *right* faculty. "Cutting wanted to build mediocrity," Kaplan said, "in the absence of argument and debate." Kaplan considered this a death knell for an academic medical school.

One of Kaplan's first conflicts with Cutting came over a decision he had made to appease the Palo Alto City Council. At the same time that Stanford was building a new medical center, the City Council wanted to expand the private Palo Alto Hospital. The dean and City Council agreed that constructing one large hospital to house both services would be more cost-effective, but both wanted to maintain control over their part of the hospital. Kaplan was out of town when he heard of this. He wrote a forceful letter to Cutting outlining why he thought it inadvisable to have two owners of one hospital. Cutting responded, "Perhaps it's not possible for you to be happy at Stanford, and you should think about going somewhere else." In recalling the letter years later, Kaplan said, "I was hurt, but then I considered the source."

Once the resolution had been made to build one wing for Stanford faculty and one for Palo Alto private physicians, a decision had to be reached concerning supporting services such as Pathology and Radiology. Kaplan attended a joint meeting of the Palo Alto City Council and the University Board of Trustees to discuss the issue. "Do you believe that there should be two departments [of radiology] under one roof in this hospital, or do you feel they should be amalgamated into a larger, stronger department?" Kaplan was asked. Stressing the words "larger" and "stronger," they expected him to choose the latter. But Kaplan had just rid his department of private radiologists, and he didn't intend to re-create that situation. "I don't believe in two departments of diagnostic radiology under one roof in one hospital," he replied. "But this isn't one hospital. This is two hospitals owned by two owners. If you can put up with anything as silly as that, then you ought to be able to put up with . . . two departments of diagnostic radiology."

A month later, while Kaplan was examining a patient, he was interrupted by a call from Cutting. "Henry," he said, "it's been decided to unify diagnostic radiology into one department after all."

"That's interesting," Kaplan replied. "Did you decide that?" Cutting said the decision had been made at the level of the trustees by David Packard.

"Would you mind giving me his phone number?" Kaplan asked. "I'd like to call him up."

"That's not necessary," Cutting replied. "David Packard is right here in my office."

Minutes later, Kaplan stormed into the dean's office in his white coat. "Hello, David," he said. "I understand you decided to unify the departments of radiology after all." Packard tried to defend his decision, but Kaplan cut him off. "You don't have to explain all that to me," he said. "You are the president of the Board of Trustees of Stanford University. It's entirely within your power to make that decision." Packard and Cutting must have relaxed, thinking he was going to be reasonable. Kaplan took off his white coat. "But there are other decisions that need making." He handed his coat to Packard. "For instance, there are a lot of patients down in the radiology clinic in need of care, and you've just become the chairman of the Department of Radiology by default. So you'd better get down there and start taking care of them."

At first, Packard didn't seem to understand; he looked at Kaplan incredulously. "What's all this?" he asked.

"It's very simple," Kaplan said. "In any of these situations there can be only one president of the Board of Trustees, and there can be only one chairman of Radiology. Who is it, you or me?"

Packard stared at Kaplan, trying to assess if he was bluffing. But Henry Kaplan never made a threat he didn't intend to keep. Packard handed back the white coat. "You are the chairman, and we'll do it your way."

Henry Kaplan had established his rightful power over his own department. But he wanted more. He wanted to help shape the school's faculty. He respected the teaching and clinical skills of the San Francisco faculty, but those were only two legs of the three-legged stool of academia. Faculty needed to do research as well. For Stanford to become an outstanding medical school, they had to recruit the best faculty. This wouldn't be just a relocation of the Medical School; it would be a reincarnation.

The current faculty roster contained a handful of researchers, among them the Harvard-trained Avram Goldstein, who had succeeded Cutting as chairman of Pharmacology. A superb scientist, Goldstein had discovered opiate receptors in the brain, shedding light on pain control and narcotic addiction. He had come to Stanford encouraged in part by Kaplan's enthusiasm. Together, he and Kaplan pushed to recruit more basic scientists, but Dean Cutting didn't feel the same urgency. They had an ongoing argument over biochemistry. Cutting thought the Department of Chemistry faculty could teach medical students. Kaplan and Goldstein insisted that a separate department of biochemistry—the heart of a medical school—was essential. Cutting remained intractable.

At about that time, Dean Berry of Harvard University Medical School asked Kaplan to become the chairman of Radiology and direct radiology services at all Harvard-affiliated hospitals. The offer was attractive; Berry agreed to all his requests. Cutting made no attempt to retain him, but when Stanford's provost, Frederick Terman, heard about the offer, he called to meet with Kaplan. When he started talking about more space and money, Kaplan made it clear that he didn't want anything for himself. "I told him what I wanted were intellectual playmates," Kaplan said. He used the biochemistry department as a case in point. Every modern medical school had a biochemistry department, and they had identified the ideal chairman—Arthur Kornberg, well-known for his work on DNA replication and repair. He said Kornberg was content at Washington University in Saint Louis and he doubted Stanford could recruit him. "I hope you'll pardon my being cynical," Kaplan told Terman, "but I've watched how Stanford does some of its recruiting. . . . You wait until you hear that the guy has been invited out to give a seminar at Berkeley so that you won't have to pay his plane fare, and then you invite him across the bay to the farm, and you talk to him about the sunshine, the climate, and the bay, and you won't offer him any budget or any space, and then you don't understand why he won't come."

"What would you like us to do?" Terman asked.

"I'd like you to invite Mrs. Kornberg with Arthur on the first visit," Kaplan said. "I'd like them to come first class. I'd like to have a car waiting for them at the airport, preferably a convertible. I'd like them to have a suite at Rickey's. . . . I want you to promise him every square inch of space and every dollar of budget that he asks for, because I know Arthur well enough to know that he won't ask for more than he can use." Terman said nothing. "I'll make it very simple for you," Kaplan said as he got up to leave, "if you recruit Kornberg successfully, I'll stay. If you fail, I'm going to Harvard." Shortly thereafter, the Kornbergs visited Stanford, and Terman did everything Kaplan had asked. Before he returned home, Kornberg accepted Stanford's offer. And Henry Kaplan turned down Harvard's. "This is the first note of encouragement I've had concerning the future of Stanford," wrote the director of Harvard's Cancer Research Foundation.

The hiring of Kornberg foreshadowed the fall of Cutting. Kaplan had gone over the dean's head. Deans, he thought, were "a necessary evil—somebody to run the office and be a kind of postman," and he was especially contemptuous of Cutting. Plans for the Medical School move were progressing too slowly for Kaplan, and he felt Cutting's desire to appease everyone would ensure mediocrity. His negotiations with the Palo Alto medical community gave practicing physicians too much control over the hospital. And he committed space and funding to current faculty that could have been used to develop programs in the new fields of immunology and genetics. Those who sided with Kaplan agreed that Cutting's goal seemed to be "to move the same jolly bunch of old folks down to the campus."

One day President Sterling asked Kaplan to meet with him. Unexpectedly, Sterling asked him what he thought of Cutting as a dean. "I said he was an embarrassment and a catastrophe," Kaplan recalled. Sterling told him he planned to request Cutting's resignation, and, knowing that Kaplan himself would never accept the position, asked which of the current faculty he recommended for the deanship. Kaplan suggested the chairman of Pediatrics, Robert Alway.

Many faculty detected Kaplan's hand in Cutter's termination, and he began to acquire a reputation for being a dean killer. They regarded Cutting as a nice man with good intentions pitted against two fiercely ambitious men—Kaplan and Goldstein. Others thought Cutting wasn't capable of leading the Stanford Medical School to eminence and appreciated Kaplan's efforts. "He played an important part in bringing about the change in deanship," one faculty member said. "That was an absolute prerequisite to establishing a new school here on campus, not merely the old one in a prettier location."

So Robert Alway became the next dean. He was a small, energetic man who did not engage in idle conversation. In meetings, he had "the unsettling effects of an explosion," the *Palo Alto Times* wrote. With a zest for life, he swam every morning before work and went horseback riding with one of his five children at the end of the day. Alway hadn't aspired to be dean, but Sterling was insistent. Sharing Kaplan's opinion that the faculty was the Medical School, Alway set out to attract the best. During his seven years as dean, he appointed 126 full-time faculty and seven new department chairmen, all accomplished scientists. In his commitment to building a superior institution, he sought the advice of only a few faculty, and among the most influential were Goldstein and Kaplan. "Kaplan said he wasn't cut out to be a dean," one of his colleagues said, "but he sure was cut out to be the power behind the throne." He constantly badgered Alway about faculty recruitment, distribution of funds, and space. "Henry and Avram were the two people who would use their spurs on me," Alway said. "They were never satisfied."

The hiring of Arthur Kornberg started the snowball effect that Kaplan had hoped it would. Kornberg brought five research scientists with him, including a young biochemist, Paul Berg, who won a Nobel Prize in Chemistry a few years later. Joshua Lederberg, a brilliant geneticist from the University of Wisconsin, soon followed him. Lederberg had already declined an offer from Stanford when he learned of Kornberg's acceptance. Kaplan and Kornberg were attending a farewell party at Paul Berg's home in Saint Louis when a call came from Lederberg. He asked Kornberg about Stanford: "It seemed like the same old sleepy place," Lederberg said, speaking of a prior visit. "Now I hear that Henry is staying and you are going [there]. I want to find out what's happening to inject this degree of excitement." Lederberg joined the Stanford faculty, and in 1958, he won the Nobel Prize in Medicine. A year later, Arthur Kornberg traveled to Stockholm to receive the Nobel Prize for the synthesis of DNA. "We perceived the new era of medicine as one in which science would change almost everything," Goldstein said.

Goldstein and others thought the school needed a new curriculum to match its new character. If Stanford's mission was to generate knowledge, then it should train students accordingly. Under his leadership, the curriculum committee designed an innovative five-year program in which students would be taught a basic core of knowledge, leaving them free to pursue subjects of interest in depth. This allowed faculty to train research scientists. Kaplan invited promising students into his home every Tuesday evening for research seminars. Students took turns analyzing recent publications, and Kaplan debated with them as if they were colleagues. Afterwards they ate cookies and listened to music in his study. These students called it one of their most memorable experiences in medical school, and many went on to become distinguished scientists. More and more students spent their extra year in the laboratories of Kornberg, Lederberg, Goldstein, and Kaplan. "We went mad for science," Bill Creger said.

Kaplan not only wanted to shape his own department, the faculty composition, and medical students' careers, but he also wanted a say in the design of the new medical center. He dreamed of creating a place that was functional, yet aesthetically distinguished. He was thus delighted when asked to chair a committee to select the architect. Ignoring political pressure to hire a Palo Alto firm, he traveled around the country searching for the right person. And he found Edward Stone. A well-known New York architect, Stone had designed the United States Pavilion at the Brussels World Fair and the American Embassy in New Delhi. Kaplan thought his work strikingly attractive and asked him to plan Stanford's new medical center.

Stone's design blended with the landscape. The center was located on fifty-six acres of farmland, and he preserved most of the eucalyptus trees and California oaks. He set the hospital a quarter mile back from the main road, allowing for a gracious, gently winding drive through a park-like setting. In front of the main entrance, he placed a thirteen-thousand square-foot reflecting pool, with floating gardens and fountains. The 434-bed hospital was H-shaped, with a wing extending forward on each end. He overlaid the entire face of the hospital with a grill of forty-four-inch concrete blocks, creating a patterned screen. Large colonnades and hanging gardens added height to the three-story structure. He connected the seven separate buildings, covering sixteen acres of floor space, with expansive breezeways that had the same lacy grillwork, imparting a cloister-like effect. Between the buildings, he laid out seven individual courtyards, each with a different arrangement of fountains, flowering trees, and gardens, designed by Thomas Church, a well-known San Francisco landscape architect. When finished, the medical center was more magnificent than Kaplan had ever envisioned.

On September 18, 1959, the faculty moved in with great fanfare. With the change in orientation from strictly clinical work to first-rate research, some faculty felt the atmosphere became cold and unfriendly. No longer did they gather in the doctors' dining room for lunch; most ate bag lunches at noon conferences or in their laboratories. For many, the move wasn't a happy one. They had to sell their homes in Pacific Heights and move to modern stucco houses on what they called "the farm." Kaplan loved San Francisco, too, but he believed in the move. He had a vision of what the medical school should be, and that required relocation on the main campus. Only there could it become a true academic center. Kaplan held the conviction that the medical school, as part of a great university, had a special mission—to innovate, to discover. He agreed with Goldstein who said, "This research mission . . . is the heart and soul of our enterprise." To that end, HSK fought hard, whether against faculty, the Dean, the City Council, or the Board of Trustees.

By the early 1960s, Stanford was in the spotlight. Numerous scientific achievements made headlines: an infectious viral DNA synthesized in the test tube, heart transplantation in dogs. The proportion of graduates entering academic medicine increased yearly; several Nobel laureates could be counted among the faculty. Soon Stanford University School of Medicine was being mentioned in the same breath with Harvard. Stanford had entered the big time, and Henry Kaplan had played a major role. "He was the symbol of our aspirations," Goldstein said.

Portrait of Sir Thomas Hodgkin in
the Gordon Museum, King's College,
London. Courtesy the Curator, Gordon
Museum.

Dorothy Reed as a medical
student at Johns Hopkins.
Courtesy Alan Mason Chesney
Medical Archives, Johns Hopkins Medical Institution.

Sarah Brilliant Kaplan. Courtesy the Kaplan family.

Sarah Brilliant, ca. 1916. Courtesy the Kaplan family.

Nathan Kaplan. Courtesy the Kaplan family.

Henry Kaplan and playmate, 1921.
Courtesy the Kaplan family.

Leah and Shirley Lebeson, ca. 1925.
Courtesy the Kaplan family.

Hank, Dick, and their Uncle Will, 1927. Courtesy Sherman Keats.

Canadian radiotherapist Vera Peters.
Courtesy American College of
Radiology.

Hank and Leah, ca. 1940. Courtesy the
Kaplan family.

Henry, Leah, Paul, and Ann Kaplan, 1953. Courtesy the Kaplan family.

Henry Kaplan working on the Stanford linear accelerator, ca. 1953. Courtesy Lane Medical Archives, Stanford University Medical Center.

Gordon Issacs, the first patient treated with Stanford's linear accelerator, 1956. Courtesy Lane Medical Archives.

Paul Kaplan. Courtesy the Kaplan family.

Stanford Medical School and Hospital in 1959. Courtesy Lane Medical Archives.

16 Saul Rosenberg: A Promising Young Oncologist

Henry Kaplan had built a powerful tool to treat cancer, and the Medical School had moved to the main campus. The third factor to which Kaplan attributed his success in treating Hodgkin's disease was the arrival of oncologist Saul Rosenberg.

‿

Born to eastern European immigrant parents in 1927, Saul Allen Rosenberg grew up in a three-room apartment in East Cleveland, Ohio. His father, a buyer in men's wear, could barely support his wife and three children. Rosenberg's childhood memories were as colorless as East Cleveland. No one read to him from *The Book of Knowledge*. No one called him "adorable son" or "the smartest boy," and no one told him he was perfect. When the neighborhood gang called him "kike" and "Jew-boy," he didn't dare yell back. He just wanted to fit in, but short for his age and athletically inept, he didn't. Rosenberg saw one person in his community command respect—the family doctor. So he began to talk about becoming a physician, an improbable career choice as no one in his family had attended college, and they had no savings. But he was determined; being a doctor would give him prestige—and a ticket out of the east side.

At age sixteen, Rosenberg entered Adelbert College of Western Reserve University in Cleveland. He found college work easy and received an "A" in almost every course. A superb ballroom dancer with a look of innocence that attracted young women, he soon garnered the popularity he sought. He pledged the top Jewish fraternity, Zeta Beta Tau, whose brothers came from Shaker Heights and other posh neighborhoods. Soft-spoken, articulate, and meticulously dressed, Rosenberg appeared wellborn, and he didn't dispel that notion. But at initiation, one of his fraternity brothers learned he came from East Cleveland, and several members tried to expel him.

In 1945, during his second year at college, Rosenberg applied to medical school. To mitigate the wartime shortage of doctors, schools had reduced the entrance requirement to two years of premedical courses. He wrote to thirty schools, confident that his almost perfect academic record would assure him of admission. But Rosenberg did not receive a single application, not even from his own university. The Jewish quota was barring him. He watched gentile classmates with inferior academic records enter medical school. Discouraged and embittered, he abruptly left college and enlisted in the Merchant Marine Naval Academy. In his haste, he did not formally withdraw from Western Reserve, and as a result, his transcript registered four failing grades.

World War II ended before he saw active duty. Without a degree, Rosenberg returned to East Cleveland to work for his father as a bookkeeper in his children's clothing business. But his father's health and the business soon failed, and he took a job at a smelting plant. Analyzing lead samples day after day, he once again contemplated a medical career.

Since medical schools now required a college degree, Rosenberg attended night classes in chemistry and physics at Cleveland College, while working in a smelting plant during the day. When he graduated in 1948, again no medical school accepted him. This time, he called on the dean of Admissions at Western Reserve University, John Coy, and challenged his refusal. Coy agreed to give him a chance to prove himself by working for a year in one of Western Reserve's research laboratories. If he did so successfully, he could reapply.

Rosenberg began working in an Atomic Energy Commission laboratory headed by radiobiologist Hymer Friedell. As his lab technician, Rosenberg prepared radioactive compounds and cared for animals treated with radioactive isotopes. Faculty were beginning to explore the use of these compounds for basic research and clinical care. They could only obtain them from Friedell's laboratory, specifically from Rosenberg. He showed internists how to use radioactivity to measure blood volumes; he prepared tiny radioactive applicators for ophthalmologists; he taught radiotherapy trainees about radioisotopes. While working with Friedell, Rosenberg became interested in Kaplan's elegant work on radiation-induced lymphomas in mice, and his career goals crystallized—he wanted to do radiobiology research with Kaplan. That year he proved himself to Coy and gained admission to Western Reserve's medical school.

Rosenberg excelled in medical school and continued to work in Friedell's laboratory, publishing four scientific articles. He graduated as one of the top five students, received three research prizes, and was elected to AOA, the honorary medical society. Faculty assured him he was a candidate for the most competitive medical internships. On intern selection day, however, he didn't match for a single spot.

Humiliated, Rosenberg stayed on at Western Reserve in an extra position created for him. He proved to be an excellent intern and was offered a medical residency for the next year at Peter Bent Brigham, a Harvard hospital. Feeling vindicated, he had just moved to Boston when the Korean War started, and he was drafted. He pleaded his case at the Naval Personnel Office, pointing out that with his expertise in radiobiology, he should be stationed at a research laboratory. He was assured of such. A few weeks later, his orders arrived. He was to report to boot camp in North Carolina. From there he was shipped to North Camp Fuji, Korea. Rosenberg's company never did engage in active combat. As the infantry battalion surgeon, he mainly treated venereal disease and injuries inflicted in drunken brawls. A year later, he was assigned to a naval hospital in Southern California where he met and married Shirley Strahl.

After the war, Rosenberg returned to Boston to complete his medical training. He then took a fellowship at Memorial Center for Cancer and Allied Diseases in New York City, where he hoped to work with lymphoma specialist Lloyd Craver. But Craver retired the year Rosenberg arrived. Memorial had one of the largest populations of lymphoma patients in the world, and during his fellowship, Rosenberg abstracted data on this group and published "Lymphosarcoma: A Review of 1269 cases," the most comprehensive series to date. Following his fellowship, he served as chief medical resident at Peter Bent Brigham Hospital, his final stepping-stone to an academic career. Now with an impressive curriculum vitae, Rosenberg hoped to return, triumphant, to Western Reserve University as a professor. But the chairman of Medicine there told him that they already had a faculty member with his expertise. Rebuffed again, Rosenberg wrote Henry Kaplan, inquiring about a position. Kaplan welcomed this promising young oncologist, and at the age of thirty-four, Saul Rosenberg came to Stanford as an assistant professor of medicine.

༄

Rosenberg found Kaplan to be a courteous and thoughtful man. He and Leah included Saul and Shirley in their social gatherings. Charming hosts, they tried to make the somewhat shy couple feel welcome. Although Rosenberg held an appointment in the Department of Medicine, it was Kaplan who provided initial financial support for his research, as well as his first office. He even offered him a joint appointment in Radiology. Saul Rosenberg had promise, and Kaplan set out to foster him.

Kaplan seemed pleased with his new colleague. Rosenberg was smart, one of the few academicians trained in the new field of medical oncology; he understood the intricacies of the lymphomas, having published two extensive reviews on the subject. And Kaplan soon discovered that Rosenberg was an astute diagnostician with superb clinical skills. At the bedside, his quiet words and soothing touch calmed the most agitated patient. "Saul was the complete physician," a colleague said. Increasingly, Kaplan sought Rosenberg's opinion, and he never asked anyone's opinion unless he wanted it.

Those who worked with Kaplan and Rosenberg observed the contrast in their personalities and style. Kaplan's demeanor was forceful. "His presence demanded that you pay attention to him," a resident said. Rosenberg was shorter and slighter with a gentle countenance. His sad eyes and shy smile imparted a vulnerable look. Kaplan's gait was lively and firm; Rosenberg's subdued, humble. When talking to a colleague, Kaplan looked directly into his eyes; Rosenberg had the habit of averting his glance. Kaplan openly expressed a range of emotions—he laughed out loud or bellowed a string of curses. Rosenberg's face rarely revealed his feelings; he spoke softly, his voice almost monotone. Residents couldn't determine if he was pleased or disappointed. It was apparent to trainees and colleagues, however, as dissimilar as the two men were in temperament, Kaplan had a special fondness for his new colleague.

In 1961, they began their collaborative work on Hodgkin's disease. At that time, cancer specialists approached treatment of Hodgkin's disease with minimal enthusiasm. A widely used pathology textbook described it as "a progressive condition leading inevitably to death." This pessimism led to the prevalent notion that it didn't matter who managed Hodgkin's disease. Patients were treated by radiotherapists, hematologists, or surgeons, with almost no communication among specialists. The major determinant of a patient's therapy was the attitude of the initial consulting physician. If a surgeon performed a biopsy and found Hodgkin's disease, he might order radiotherapy or send the patient home, "thus avoiding the upset of the patient by x-rays," as one prominent British physician wrote. If sent to a hematologist, the patient might receive chemotherapy. Radiotherapists looked upon this treatment with disdain, citing its limited benefit. Since any physician could prescribe chemotherapy, it was often used improperly, resulting in death from toxicity. At Memorial Center for Cancer in New York, surgeons and oncologists often filled out prescriptions for radiation doses, drew fields on their patients with marking pens, and sent them for prescribed treatments without even asking the radiotherapist's opinion, treating them like technicians. Controversy and suspicion among specialists were the norm. The absence of a collaborative effort was a major stumbling block in treating Hodgkin's disease. Fragmentation of care and its delivery by physicians with limited experience resulted in death for most patients, which, in turn, reinforced the concept of this disease as "inexorably fatal."

Henry Kaplan knew he couldn't cure Hodgkin's disease alone; he needed a team of experts: a surgeon, pathologist, radiologist, and oncologist. He sought a radiologist who would do more than just interpret films, someone who would improve the radiologic assessment of Hodgkin's disease. Chest x-rays demonstrated involvement in the lung or mediastinal lymph nodes, but evaluation of the abdomen posed a bigger challenge. Kaplan had read of a technique reported by J. B. Kinmoth at St. Bartholomew's Hospital in London whereby he introduced dye into the abdominal lymphatics to illuminate them. Lymphangiography, as it was termed, allowed one to visualize intra-abdominal nodes, significantly improving clinical assessment. But few embraced the procedure, because it required technical skill to inject dye into tiny lymphatic vessels in the foot and diagnostic skill to interpret the results. Initially, Herb Abrams took on this task, then Ronald Castellino, a young radiologist who developed proficiency in performing and interpreting lymphangiograms and devoted his career to assessment of lymphomas. Kaplan wanted a surgeon bold enough to test his ideas and strong enough to withstand criticism from surgical colleagues. He found Thomas Nelsen to be perfect—superb technically and loyal. And in 1968, Ronald Dorfman, an academic pathologist renowned for his expertise in lymphomas, completed the team.

Shortly after Rosenberg's arrival, he and Kaplan established a weekly conference at which they reviewed all new cases of Hodgkin's disease and other lymphomas with this group. Although the dynamics and participants changed with time, the format of that meeting remained unaltered for decades. Unique for its comprehensive approach and research orientation, Stanford's lymphoma staging conference became a model for the multidisciplinary approach to cancer.

Staging conference took place every Monday morning at eight o'clock in the Radiology Department. Visitors who came to observe this legendary conference years later were surprised at the setting—a fifteen-by-thirty-foot basement room with bare walls, linoleum on the floor, a folding table, and metal chairs. Rosenberg arrived early to arrange the chairs and discard leftover coffee cups. Throughout the years, the seating never changed, although not assigned. Kaplan and Rosenberg sat opposite each other at the front end of the table. Beside Kaplan sat an associate radiotherapist, then pathologist Ron Dorfman, his resident, then other radiotherapy faculty. Next to Rosenberg sat a junior oncologist, then his oncology nurse. Behind Kaplan were seated the radiologists. Trainees occupied chairs in an outer circle. Surgeon Tom Nelsen stood at the back of the room. "Even if Kaplan or I were absent," Rosenberg said, "no one sat in the empty chair. And if a visitor or new student took the wrong seat, he was suddenly hoisted out of it." By eight o'clock, everyone had taken their places. A few minutes after eight, Kaplan arrived. Everyone stopped talking. "A lot of people felt they should stand when he entered," a trainee observed.

After a brief nod to colleagues, Kaplan asked for the first case, and a resident rose to the podium to present the history and physical findings. Rosenberg made notations on a staging sheet, filling in pertinent information and recording the exact location and size of lymph nodes on a body diagram. No one interrupted the presentation. At its completion, Kaplan and Rosenberg asked for details: What percentage of total body weight had the patient lost? Was the lymph node located in the inguinal or femoral region? Residents agonized as they stood before Kaplan; he didn't tolerate imprecision. Next, a pathology resident, with Dorfman's able guidance, presented slides of all biopsy material. He had to demonstrate the pathognomonic Reed-Sternberg cells; there could be no doubt about the diagnosis. Then they reviewed the radiographs. Kaplan enjoyed pointing out subtle abnormalities the resident had missed.

The case presented, pathology and radiographs reviewed, Kaplan and Rosenberg determined the stage, based on sites of involvement. They devised their own staging system, modified from Vera Peters's. Because stage had such important implications for therapy and prognosis, Kaplan and Rosenberg deliberated, sometimes disagreed, over what stage to assign. Staging completed, they decided on therapy. This was where they differed the most. Rosenberg agreed that patients with early-stage disease might live longer if treated with radiotherapy; otherwise, palliative chemotherapy was the best they could offer. Kaplan believed that they had the tools to cure almost any patient.

Before Rosenberg came to Stanford, Kaplan had treated a number of patients with what he called radical radiotherapy—irradiation to involved lymph nodes and uninvolved adjacent nodes as prophylactic treatment, based on Gilbert's and Peters's scheme. But he used much larger ports and doses. Peters treated involved nodes with 3,000 rads, uninvolved with 1,000 rads. With the linear accelerator, Kaplan could deliver up to 5,000 rads safely. And Peters treated each nodal group with a separate radiation port in patchwork fashion. This took months; irradiating all lymph node groups required nine separate fields. Radiotherapists had minimal enthusiasm for undertaking stage III patients—those with disease both above and below the diaphragm—because by the time they had finished treating lymph nodes in the neck and chest, abdominal nodes had enlarged.

"It is highly desirable," Kaplan wrote, "to treat multiple lymph node chains in continuity with as few fields as possible." He designed two ports whose shape allowed several lymph node groups to be irradiated simultaneously, while avoiding normal tissue. He included five lymph node sites (right and left neck, right and left axillae, and mediastinum) in one port—the mantle—so named because its shape resembled a sleeveless cloak. The mantle encompassed all major lymphatics of the upper torso, while sparing the lung, heart, and spinal cord. His second port—the inverted Y—was shaped to cover major lymphatics in the abdomen (para-aortic nodes) and those in both groins. Therapy to all lymphoid groups, which took others six to twelve months, could be completed by Kaplan in two. When he compared outcome in Stanford patients treated with radical radiotherapy to those who had received low-dose therapy prior to his arrival, he found an 80 percent improvement in survival. "The onus of responsibility," Kaplan said, "now rests with those who persist in treating localized Hodgkin's disease palliatively." He planned to treat all new Hodgkin's patients with radical radiotherapy.

When the two began making treatment decisions together, Rosenberg initially deferred to Kaplan. He appreciated his innovative approach. "HSK had the courage to do things differently," Rosenberg said. Before long, however, he began to question Kaplan. The issues they debated most often were dose and ports. Practicing therapists gave several hundred rads, at most a thousand. Kaplan was suggesting doses five times greater. "The selection of dose levels," Kaplan wrote, "is an empirical process, in which a balance is struck between two conflicting goals: the use of a dose high enough to be maximally effective against a tumor and a dose low enough to cause little or no lasting damage in normal tissues." Although Rosenberg found Kaplan's stance compelling, he was cautious, concerned about potential long-term toxicity. They also debated the appropriate treatment field. Kaplan advocated prophylactic irradiation to adjacent, uninvolved nodes, using his mantle and inverted Y ports—radiation ports never before employed. Rosenberg was leery of this; he thought Kaplan was moving too fast. "Saul was a treatment gentleman," an oncology fellow observed. "Kaplan was willing to treat in excess in attempts to cure."

Every Monday morning at staging conference, these discussions took place. No one remembers when the intellectual disagreements gave way to arguments. But they did. These weren't directed at each other; they always addressed patient care or science. Rosenberg called them "friendly debates." Initially, Kaplan had determined the therapeutic plan, and Rosenberg served as a medical consultant. He finally told Kaplan that if they were going to care for patients together, he couldn't do so with a clear conscience unless he had a say in their initial treatment plan. Their interactions, which had begun as polite deference, in time resembled a joust. "They enjoyed one another's combativeness," a resident said, "intellectual combativeness, that is." Kaplan emphasized how much better his patients had done with radical therapy—an 80 percent improvement in survival compared with the group treated palliatively. Rosenberg agreed that the results were good, but regarded them as statistically flawed. Kaplan had drawn his conclusions from only twenty-three patients, treated by different physicians over different time periods. This made Rosenberg question an improvement of 80 percent.

Kaplan became impatient. He wanted to leap to new ideas. Rosenberg thought his ideas intriguing, but insisted on evaluating each new approach methodically in a series of patients. "Saul began to put some structure on a very enthusiastic Dr. Kaplan," a trainee said. Although Peters's data had been provocative, her credibility had been challenged. Radiotherapists accused her of selection bias, choosing the most favorable cases, who would have done well even with a more conservative approach. Rosenberg argued that they might face the same criticism. To prove superiority of a particular therapeutic plan, they needed to carry out randomized trials, whereby they assigned patients of comparable age, sex, and stage to one of two different treatments, pitting the new therapy against standard treatment. Only then would others believe their results. To date, no such trials had been done in Hodgkin's disease. Rosenberg convinced Kaplan that randomized trials had to be performed in order for treatment of Hodgkin's disease to advance. Although Kaplan considered his approach superior, he agreed to test several postulates concerning radiation dose and fields. "It was to Kaplan's credit," Rosenberg said, "that he was willing to test the alternative option to what he thought best."

From then on, every new Hodgkin's disease patient was asked to participate in a trial. Kaplan and Rosenberg outlined the specifics of each—eligibility criteria, required staging procedures, treatment plans, and statistical analysis—in a document called a protocol. On Monday morning, after they had determined the patient's stage, Rosenberg's oncology nurse opened a sealed envelope containing the assigned treatment. This blind selection process, termed randomization, eliminated potential for bias. And Kaplan and Rosenberg no longer argued over every treatment decision.

In 1962, the randomized clinical trials at Stanford commenced, opening a new chapter in the history of Hodgkin's disease.

17

The L-1 Protocol: Christine Pendleton and Douglas Eads

When Christine Pendleton bent over to make her bed, she felt a sharp pain in her chest. She thought she had pulled a muscle. That evening at a PTA meeting, she experienced a rattling sensation when she took a deep breath and worried that she had "walking pneumonia." The next morning she saw her internist, Bill Fredell. Although the symptoms had disappeared, and her lungs sounded clear, he sent her for a chest x-ray on her way home. The following day, he called Christine back to his office. She suspected something serious when Dr. Fredell apologized for not having reached her husband, Red. He proceeded to show her the chest x-ray, pointing out a large mass, which he called a tumor. He said it should be removed, and he had tentatively scheduled surgery at Stanford Hospital later that week.

Pendleton was stunned. "I felt as if I were watching a grade B movie," she said. She considered hers a storybook life, and this was the wrong script. Only that morning, she had been a busy Palo Alto housewife, concerned with getting her children to school on time and finishing a community project for the Junior League. By evening, she had become a patient with a deadly disease.

Christine felt terrified. Hospitals reminded her of her sister, Suzanne, who had died of staphylococcal septicemia on Christine's twelfth birthday. She had been afraid of hospitals ever since. "That's where you go to die," Christine thought. Now she had to overcome that fear. "Not surviving was out of the question," she said. "I had four children to take care of." Her determination faltered when the thoracic surgeon told her after surgery that she had inoperable lung cancer and that he had asked a radiation therapist to consider palliative treatment. He gave Red Pendleton more details: his wife had a virulent type of lung cancer. At best, she might live two years; more likely she would be dead in two months.

Christine was lying in her hospital bed trying to comprehend what was happening to her. Cancer, palliation, death: these words were foreign, frightening. Dinner, homework, birthdays: that was her world. Only forty-three-years old, she had rarely smoked. How could she be dying of lung cancer? Her thoughts were interrupted by a young physician who seemed to bounce into her hospital room, introducing himself as Scotte Doggett, a radiotherapy resident. His broad smile seemed inappropriate. He spoke so rapidly Christine caught only a few words: "Dr. Kaplan," "Hodgkin's disease," "80 percent." Piecing together his utterances, she began to understand that a Dr. Kaplan had been asked to treat her with radiation. He had reviewed her slides himself and disagreed with the pathologist's diagnosis of lung cancer. He felt certain she had Hodgkin's disease, a malignancy of lymph tissue, which he might be able to cure. Doggett proposed that Pendleton participate in a clinical trial. All Christine heard was "80 percent chance of survival." She accepted.

Christine Pendleton had consented to participate in the L-1 protocol, the first randomized study initiated by the Stanford group. Rather than debate dose and field on every new patient, Kaplan and Rosenberg had agreed to resolve these issues through clinical trials. They had designed L-1 to test whether prophylactic irradiation delivered to uninvolved nodes adjacent to affected regions—which they called extended field irradiation—could improve duration of remission and survival. L-1 included patients with stages I and II disease; that is, disease in one or two sites in either the upper or lower torso, with the diaphragm as the dividing line. Patients were randomized to either arm A—4,000 rads to involved fields or arm B—4,000 rads to extended fields. Kaplan regarded arm A as standard therapy, even though it did entail high doses. "What was considered a conservative treatment arm by our group," Rosenberg said, "was considered radical at other centers."

Shortly after Pendleton entered the trial, Doggett presented her case at staging conference. A pathologist reviewed her biopsy slides and confirmed Kaplan's diagnosis. The remainder of her evaluation, including blood counts, blood tests for liver function, a bone marrow biopsy, and a lymphangiogram was negative. She was designated as having stage IA Hodgkin's disease. Rosenberg's nurse opened the sealed envelope containing her assigned treatment: the B option—extended field irradiation. She would receive 4,000 rads over four weeks to a mantle field, followed by 4,000 rads to her para-aortic nodes and spleen.

Kaplan designed Pendleton's treatment plan with rigorous attention to detail. His success didn't result solely from his use of high doses and unique fields—the mantle and inverted Y; his methodology contributed too. He shaped Christine's port to shield as much lung as possible, interposing five-centimeter lead blocks between her and the radiation beam. He irradiated her from front and back on alternate days to minimize skin dose. As a result, she experienced mild sunburn, not the blistering predicted at those doses. Each week Kaplan reviewed her progress, readjusted machine settings, and sent the technicians back to recut her lead blocks. He required absolute precision; he would not tolerate even a half-centimeter deviation. "If other therapists would . . . use my methods," he told a colleague, "they could cure many more patients." Kaplan gave Pendleton more than just his technical expertise, however; he gave of himself, as well. "Dr. Kaplan had a bedside manner like no other doctor," she said. He expressed interest in her children, her husband, their vacations. And he never hurried. At clinic visits, even if three other doctors were in the exam room and an overhead page was repeating Kaplan's name, he focused entirely on her. "When he was talking to me," Christine said, "I was the only person in the world."

At first, Pendleton found the radiation treatments scary. She lay on the table while technicians arranged lead pieces around her. Then they left, shutting the heavy door and leaving her in the silent, sterile vault. "I was alone with that big machine," Christine recalled. "Those three minutes of having to lie absolutely still getting radiation were the longest minutes in the world." But the treatments turned out to be easier than she had thought. She drove herself to Stanford; afterward she went shopping and made dinner. The side effects—hair loss at the nape of her neck and superficial skin redness—were a nuisance at most. She didn't even worry about the electric shocks up and down her spine once Dr. Kaplan explained she had Lhermitte's syndrome, named after a French neurologist who first had described these symptoms. Presumably, they arose from radiation effects on the spinal cord. Kaplan assured Pendleton that the symptoms would not progress to nerve damage and would eventually disappear. If she didn't flex her neck quickly, she could continue to hike and ride her bike.

After a few weeks, however, her condition changed. Her stomach became so irritated that she consumed bottles of antacids. Insufficient saliva from damaged salivary glands made the inside of her mouth feel like cotton. She had to wash food down with sips of water. Her tongue stuck to the roof of her mouth when she talked for more than a few minutes. Before long, esophageal swelling reduced her intake to a liquid diet. Most intolerable was the overwhelming fatigue. "I felt like I had been run over by a truck," she said. For two months, Christine rarely left the living room sofa. "Doing a crossword puzzle was the extent of my activity," she said.

Kaplan expressed concern about her symptoms, but he didn't let up. His goal was cure. So was Christine's. At completion of mantle irradiation, the mass in her chest had shrunk substantially, but it had not disappeared. Doggett worried that Pendleton had not achieved a complete remission, but Kaplan said that he had seen a number of patients with a residual mass, which turned out to be scar tissue. He was right. Eleven years after her diagnosis, Christine sent

Dr. Kaplan two snapshots—one of a toddler in the kitchen, surrounded by pots and pans; the other of an infant, snug in his blanket. "These pictures of our two grandchildren," she wrote, "are to show you two more reasons why we are so thankful for the work on Hodgkin's disease you've done so successfully."

⌐⌐

Douglas Eads spent the summer of 1965 working in a fruit-packing plant. So when Dr. McCarroll, the family physician, told him that the lump in his groin was a hernia, he wasn't concerned. He was scheduled for a routine hernia repair before returning to his senior year at San Jose State College.

Eads lay in his hospital bed after surgery, waiting for his doctor. He knew something was wrong. "Dr. McCarroll walked to the door of my room, paused, and then walked away," he said. "He did this twice. The third time, he came in and broke the news." McCarroll was carrying a medical textbook and appeared troubled. "You've got something called Hodgkin's disease," he said. He confessed that he didn't know much about it and read a description from the book, ending with "runs a course of about three years and is invariably fatal."

How could this robust young man with bright eyes and a peaches-and-cream complexion have a life-threatening illness? He should be playing baseball, going out on dates. Instead, Doug began replanning his life. "I imagined that the clock was running," he said, "and in three years, I'd be dead." This wasn't the first time he had faced a serious situation. During infancy he had undergone emergency surgery for pyloric stenosis—a blockage of his stomach, which had almost killed him. When he was five, his parents had divorced. In his teens, he had been blinded in his right eye by BB shot. And his half-sister had recently died in an automobile accident. "I was resigned," Douglas said. "Death is a little bit easier to face when there is no alternative."

Three weeks later, McCarroll called to say that he had heard about a research program at Stanford and had arranged for a Dr. Kaplan to see Douglas. At the initial visit, a resident described a protocol study and the potential of high-dose radiotherapy in optimistic terms. He went on to say that they weren't certain about the acute and long-term effects. Douglas didn't pay much attention to the explanation; he agreed to participate. "I've got nothing to lose," he reasoned. His composure was shaken, however, when he was admitted to the hospital for further tests. His roommate had advanced Hodgkin's disease. "He didn't have long to live," Eads said, "and he knew it. He was crying regularly. I don't think he felt any pain; he just didn't want to die. I thought, 'this might be me in a few years.'"

Then Douglas met Henry Kaplan. When talking to him, Kaplan placed his hand firmly on Doug's shoulder and looked into his eyes. He told Doug that he planned to cure him. "He inspired confidence with his manner," Eads said. Tests indicated disease confined to lymph nodes in the groin and pelvis—stage IIA. Like Christine Pendleton, he was randomized to the B arm of the L-1 protocol, extended field irradiation. Kaplan treated his enlarged pelvic nodes and adjacent, uninvolved areas—para-aortic lymph nodes and spleen—with 4,000 rads. In contrast to Pendleton, he experienced few side effects, just mild nausea and fatigue. His most unpleasant memory was the strong smell of ozone in the linear accelerator vault.

Once in remission, Eads still anticipated recurrence of his disease. A year passed, and Mrs. Eads sent Kaplan a college graduation announcement. After that Doug attended graduate school in public administration and became an administrative aide in Saratoga, California. Shortly before his five-year mark—the time Kaplan considered him cured—he finally believed he was going to live. He married his college sweetheart, had two sons, and went on to become assistant city manager of Fremont.

Years after his treatment, when they passed in the hall, Dr. Kaplan addressed Doug by name. "He must have seen thousands of patients," Eads said. "How could he remember me?" A rumor circulated among patients that Dr. Kaplan had a photographic memory and tracked their blood counts in his head. Douglas also noticed how he kept trainees on their toes. When he entered the exam room, Dr. Kaplan often had two or three residents in tow, and he usually asked the same question. He pointed to Ead's tiny abdominal scar and asked for what condition had he undergone surgery. Eads detected the hint of a smile when no one correctly answered, "pyloric stenosis." "Once a resident did guess," Douglas said, "and he almost seemed disappointed." He noticed that Kaplan insisted technicians be attentive to every detail. "I'll bet he wasn't the easiest person in the world to work for," Eads said. "I can well imagine him being difficult, but it's the kind of difficulty I have to be thankful for."

⌒

Ninety-six patients entered the L-1 protocol. Not everyone did as well as Eads and Pendleton. Several recurred and underwent repeated courses of radiotherapy and/or chemotherapy. Of the patients who received extended field irradiation, 60 percent remained free of disease, compared with 46 percent of those who had received involved field irradiation only. Because some who relapsed were controlled for years with further treatment, survival was similar in both groups—approximately 55 percent. There was one exception. Patients with systemic symptoms—fever, night sweats, or weight loss—did much worse with involved field irradiation; in over 80 percent, the disease recurred. This group fared substantially better if they had received extended field irradiation.

Hearing results of this trial, many radiotherapists concluded that since there was no difference in survival, they should treat stage I and II patients with involved field irradiation only. Kaplan interpreted the data differently. The almost 20 percent reduction in recurrence would eventually translate into a 20 percent improvement in cure. In his view, these results confirmed the benefit of extended field irradiation, and he set out to discover why any patients in this arm had recurred. He carefully tabulated patterns of relapse. "Kaplan was good at doing failure analysis," a colleague said, "going back and trying to learn lessons from his past mistakes—not really mistakes, but lack of complete understanding." He quickly found the problem: An unexpectedly high number of patients with disease in the low neck, called the supraclavicular area, recurred in para-aortic nodes. He hypothesized that a lymphatic connection existed between low-neck nodes and abdominal nodes. This explained why extended field, as he had designed it, had been inadequate in some patients. Thus, while others said results of L-1 indicated that the Stanford group had given excessive radiation, Kaplan concluded that they hadn't given enough.

18 The L-2 Protocol: Petra Ekstrand and Joey Radicchi

For eight months, Petra Ekstrand had an itch. At first she wasn't concerned, since she didn't have a rash, but in time, the itching intensified, keeping her awake at night. The twenty-four-year-old didn't have the energy to manage the children at her day-care center or even her three-year-old daughter. Then a small lump appeared on her chest, to the left of her breastbone. When it grew to the size of an orange, she became scared and saw a doctor. A biopsy revealed Hodgkin's disease. By the time Petra was referred to Stanford, she had multiple enlarged lymph nodes in her neck, axillae, and groin, as well as a five-centimeter chest wall mass. To complicate the situation, she was four months pregnant. If she proceeded with radiotherapy, the fetus would likely die or be born with multiple congenital abnormalities. If they delayed therapy for five months while awaiting delivery, she might die, and both mother and child would be lost. Petra's cancer was growing so rapidly, she reluctantly agreed to have the fetus aborted. She had to consider her young daughter. Three days after the abortion, she began undergoing tests: a bone marrow biopsy and liver tests were negative; a lymphangiogram showed enlarged para-aortic and pelvic nodes—stage IIIB. Most such patients died within a year or two. Trusting Kaplan, Petra agreed to participate in an experimental trial.

The L-2 protocol, which began at the same time as L-1, caused even more controversy. Its goal was to determine whether high-dose irradiation was more effective than palliative doses for patients with stage III disease, defined by Stanford's staging system as disease both above and below the diaphragm. Most radiotherapists believed these patients to be incurable; they had too much disease to irradiate. They considered patients' comfort the primary goal, hence the standard approach of low-dose irradiation to relieve symptoms. The L-2 protocol was the first effort to try to cure such patients. Kaplan planned to employ high doses to both mantle and inverted Y fields—total lymphoid irradiation. Rosenberg expressed concern about potential toxicity; he could imagine the outcry from the radiotherapy community. So Kaplan agreed to test total lymphoid irradiation in a randomized trial. Patients on arm A would receive standard therapy—1,500 rads in two weeks to involved nodes only; those on arm B would receive 4,000 rads in twelve weeks to all major lymph node groups and the spleen.

Total lymphoid irradiation was untried, its toxicity unknown. "When we first initiated the total lymphoid technique of radiotherapy for stage III Hodgkin's disease," Kaplan wrote, "it was with a great deal of trepidation." He knew the potential morbidity from the mantle and inverted Y fields alone, but not combined. Mantle field irradiation resulted in dry mouth, sore throat, and lassitude. Inflammation of the lungs, resulting in fever, cough, and shortness of breath, occasionally severe enough to require oxygen, was among the more serious side effects. Radiation injury to the sac around the heart could cause pericarditis, manifested by chest pain and fluid collection, often large enough to threaten the heart's normal function. Damage to blood vessels might precipitate premature narrowing of the arteries. Although some toxicities occurred during or shortly after therapy, others might not become evident until years later. A patient could be cured of Hodgkin's disease and later become a respiratory or cardiac cripple.

The inverted Y technique caused nausea, vomiting, and fatigue. Kaplan had seen two patients develop stomach ulcers; several had bloody diarrhea. Following pelvic irradiation, men experienced a reduction in sperm count. Ovarian function ceased after only 800 rads, and young women became prematurely menopausal. Disturbed by this, the Stanford group routinely recommended an oophoropexy, a surgical procedure to move the ovaries away from lymph nodes into the midline of the abdomen where they were protected with lead blocks. With this procedure, 70 percent of women resumed menstruation.

Another concern was blood count depression from radiation effects on the bone marrow. Kaplan calculated that with total lymphoid irradiation, 60 percent of the marrow would be irradiated, lowering blood counts to less than half their normal value. If the white blood count fell too low—leukopenia—patients had a high probability of developing a serious infection. Something as innocuous as a splinter or a dental procedure could cause an overwhelming infection in the bloodstream. If the platelets fell too low—thrombocytopenia—the blood was unable to clot properly, and patients could suffer bleeding gums, nosebleeds, or brain hemorrhage, resulting in paralysis or coma. Kaplan also worried about the delayed effects of radiation on the bone marrow, especially leukemia. In the early years of roentgen therapy, cases of leukemia were noted in radiologists who had repeated radiation exposure. And studies had just been published citing a significant number of leukemia cases among atomic bomb survivors. Kaplan thought this threat varied with type of radiation, its intensity, and duration of exposure. An atom bomb explosion liberated large quantities of gamma rays and neutrons, showering the entire body. But they needed a longer period of observation before determining the leukemia risk after treatment with his techniques.

The potential hazards of total lymphoid irradiation were staggering. No one had attempted such a radical approach before. "A priori," Kaplan wrote, "the delivery of tumoricidal doses of about 4,000 rads to virtually every lymphoid structure in the body seemed prohibitively dangerous." After lengthy deliberations, he convinced Rosenberg that although total lymphoid irradiation was risky, these patients would probably die without it, and on balance, the risk seemed justifiable. Stanford hematologist Bill Creger publicly criticized Kaplan for overtreating patients with advanced disease and exposing them to dreadful toxicities. Kaplan's own technicians felt uneasy. One resident overheard faculty saying things like "They'll never survive" and "You'll kill people." Reports circulated to other academic centers, and outsiders began to wonder what was going on at Stanford. "Kaplan was considered a bizarre maverick by some," a radiotherapy colleague said. "Others thought him a nut."

Everyone in Radiation Therapy loved Petra Ekstrand, the young Scandinavian with long, honey-colored hair, a dainty nose, and an engaging smile. So when she entered the L-2 protocol and was randomized to total lymphoid irradiation (TLI), staff felt apprehensive. Even more concerning, because of the large mass in her chest wall, Kaplan planned a boost to that area, bringing the total dose to 5,000 rads. During therapy, Petra lost hair at the nape of her neck and suffered persistent vomiting. Still, she smiled in a way that made physicians and staff caring for her happy. And she continued to be flirtatious, even with Henry Kaplan. Her compliments made him blush.

Ekstrand didn't develop any of the severe acute toxicities Kaplan had worried about—bone marrow suppression, inflammation of the lung or heart. Early in the course of therapy, her itching resolved, and by the end of treatment, the lymph nodes had returned to normal, the large chest mass disappeared. This young woman, whom others would have treated palliatively with no expectation of cure, had achieved remission.

Kaplan's joy in seeing Petra remain disease-free was dampened by the chronic toxicities she subsequently experienced. To begin with, irradiation left her sterile. "Kaplan was exceedingly proud of the women who went on to have children," recalled a trainee. "He just reveled in those who came back with babies." Then Petra began to have increasing difficulty breathing from recurrent fluid collections, which impaired the ability of her lungs to expand. Drainage tubes were inserted into her chest several times. A heart biopsy revealed degeneration of her heart muscle—a chronic effect from the 5,000 rads. Kaplan was disturbed; he wanted to cure patients, but at what price? He could have given up on total lymphoid irradiation, retreated to a more conservative stance. Instead, he developed maneuvers to minimize them. He devised special lead shields—"thin-lung blocks" and "subcarinal blocks"—to protect the lungs and heart from excess dose. Petra Ekstrand was one of the last to experience such profound cardiopulmonary toxicity. Five years following her therapy, although she still got winded climbing stairs, she continued to be free of disease—a cure.

↜

Half the patients on the L-2 protocol were randomized to total lymphoid irradiation as Ekstrand had been; the others were assigned to standard low-dose therapy. Among this group was Joey Radicchi.

This thirteen-year-old from Santa Cruz was the only son of Italian immigrants, Nello and Annunziata Radicchi. Joey was a handsome child with rosy cheeks, his father's hazel eyes, and long, thick lashes. His mother parted his straight, dark hair on the side and slicked it down. Although his sisters pampered him, Joey was loving and easy-going. When he was eleven, the family moved into a middle-class neighborhood. Joey and his friends played ball in the street until dark. On Sunday afternoons, the family picnicked with aunts, uncles, and cousins in the Santa Cruz Mountains and hiked among the redwoods. On hot days, his sister took him to the beach. Joey was an avid baseball fan; he even preferred hamburgers and hot dogs to pasta.

When Joey lost his appetite and grew listless, Mrs. Radicchi became concerned. He refused her apple pie, and after school, instead of grabbing his bat and ball, he lay on the sofa. She took him to Dr. Morris, the family doctor. He found Joey slightly anemic and reassured her by saying that he was going through a growth spurt and just needed iron. She proceeded to feed Joey steak and spaghetti, but he became increasingly fatigued and lost more weight. She took him back. Morris said Joey needed more iron. Joey's father didn't trust doctors and decided to examine his son himself. When he pushed on his belly, Joey winced. The next morning, Mrs. Radicchi returned to the doctor. "My husband find a spot that hurts," she said. "Can you x-ray it?" Morris reexamined Joey, and this time he palpated an enlarged spleen. An x-ray confirmed the presence of splenomegaly. Morris told Mrs. Radicchi that possible causes included leukemia, lymphoma, and Hodgkin's disease. Mrs. Radicchi didn't know what lymphoma and Hodgkin's disease were, but when he mentioned them in the same breath as leukemia, she knew they must be bad. She was devastated. "I know the disease is cancer," she said, "even though he don't say so." Dr. Morris told her there was hope; he was sending Joey to a specialist at Stanford University, Dr. Saul Rosenberg.

When Rosenberg first examined Joey, he found a cachectic child with a fever, an enlarged left cervical lymph node, and a palpable spleen. A biopsy revealed Hodgkin's disease, and on March 15, 1965, Joey was admitted to Stanford Hospital for blood tests, a chest x-ray, lymphangiogram, liver scan, and biopsies of his liver and bone marrow. Rosenberg determined that he had stage IIIB disease. He discussed the L-2 protocol with the Radicchis as a treatment option. They had almost agreed to the trial when a new intern was assigned to Joey, and Mrs. Radicchi asked his opinion. "He's going to die sooner or later," the young physician said. "Hodgkin's disease is terminal, and treatment won't do much good." She rushed downstairs to Rosenberg's office. He took her hand and reassured her. (He said nothing about the intern, but the Radicchis never saw him again.) Yes, Joey had a serious illness from which many patients did die. "But we have to try," Rosenberg said, "because if we don't, he will die. You have to give him a chance." So Mrs. Radicchi signed the consent form, and Joey was randomized to arm A—low-dose irradiation.

Mrs. Radicchi told her son he had Hodgkin's disease and that the doctors could control it with radiotherapy. She didn't say how serious his illness was; after all, he was just a boy. Shortly after therapy began, Joey's fever abated, his appetite improved, and he began to gain weight. He received 1,500 rads to a mantle and inverted Y over forty-three days with nausea as the only toxicity. Joey Radicchi had the same stage of disease as Petra Ekstrand; yet he received one-third the total radiation dose that she did.

Mrs. Radicchi felt fortunate to have been sent to Saul Rosenberg. "He didn't say much on rounds," she recalled, "but I knew where his office was. Every time I saw big words I don't understand, I go and ask him." He answered all her questions and in terms she could comprehend. But Mrs. Radicchi noticed he kept using the word "arrest," not the word she longed to hear—"cure." For Joey, Rosenberg always had a kind glance and gentle words. He sat on the edge of Joey's bed and explained how they used blue dye for the lymphangiogram and why he needed to do a bone marrow biopsy. "Joey's my special person," he told Mrs. Radicchi. Twenty years later, Rosenberg still had the rose quartz Joey had given him from his mineral collection.

When Mrs. Radicchi talked about Dr. Rosenberg, she expressed fondness; when she recalled Henry Kaplan, she laughed. She loved to watch Dr. Kaplan tease her son. "I've got a daughter born on the same day as you, December 26," he said one day on rounds. "Of course, she's much prettier than you." And they had a standing joke on his follow-up visits: "How are you doing, Joey?" Kaplan used to ask.

"Fine," Joey replied.

"You must be coming here for the ride," Kaplan said, "since you're always fine."

When Kaplan examined Joey, Mrs. Radicchi always noticed his two giant fingers. "What happened to your fingers?" she asked one day. The other doctors in the room seemed to stop breathing, but without embarrassment Kaplan replied, "I was born with them. They make me a little different."

After Joey completed therapy, the lymphoma team reevaluated him at monthly intervals. He returned to school and played baseball. Then nine months later, his fever reappeared, and an x-ray indicated enlargement of lymph nodes in his chest. The Hodgkin's disease had recurred, and he would need further treatment. Rosenberg was sad, but he had expected it. Kaplan felt sad, too. More than just sad, he felt terrible. And every time he saw Joey, this feeling compounded. He had treated the boy with a therapy he thought inadequate.

Joey Radicchi was the fifteenth patient with stage III disease randomized to low-dose, palliative radiotherapy. Hodgkin's disease recurred in eleven; Joey was the youngest. Only half the patients in the other arm, total lymphoid irradiation, relapsed—results far superior to any reported to date. And the toxicity had been much less than Rosenberg and Kaplan had anticipated. Henry told Rosenberg that he thought they should modify the L-2 protocol and treat all stage III patients on the B arm. He had been reluctant in the first place to conduct a trial where half the patients received low-dose treatment. The word "palliative" stuck in his throat when he talked about a curable disease. He couldn't treat another patient with what he knew to be inferior therapy just for the sake of continuing the trial. He grimaced whenever a patient was randomized to arm A.

Saul acknowledged that total lymphoid irradiation had turned out to be less toxic than he had feared, and he was delighted it seemed to be more effective. But he still had two major reservations. First, the period of observation had been too short to thoroughly evaluate long-term toxicity. Although 4,000 rads to the chest hadn't produced acute respiratory problems, years later fibrosis might render patients as compromised as those with severe emphysema. The electric shocks patients felt down their spine might portend crippling nerve damage. Kaplan countered that at least the patients would be alive. Secondly, Rosenberg cautioned against drawing early conclusions from small numbers of patients. Only thirty had entered the study. The statistician had calculated they needed approximately a hundred to prove a significant difference between the two arms. He thought they should continue the trial to completion. If they stopped now, the study would never be scientifically valid, and if they didn't prove superiority of high-dose total lymphoid irradiation in a randomized trial, the radiotherapy community would never believe them. After all, many considered Kaplan a radiotherapeutic zealot.

Leah remembered lengthy evening telephone conversations between Saul and Henry, debating early closure of the trial. She thought it ironic that Saul, the patient advocate, was arguing for science, while Hank, who prided himself on being a scientist, was pressing for patient welfare. "When I can't feel good about what I'm offering a patient," he said, "then I can't treat him." But Rosenberg's intense concern for patients drew him to his position. Because he cared deeply for these young people, he did not want to subject them to potentially profound toxicity until he was sure the gain was worth the risk. Of course he wanted to cure patients, but he could accept that Hodgkin's disease eventually killed patients with advanced stage; Kaplan could not. Rosenberg felt they had to verify the superiority of an experimental approach. "I'm the voice of 'you have to prove it before you do it,'" he said. Kaplan couldn't be bound by the rigidity of clinical trials; there had to be flexibility. And he abhorred a study that accepted failure in one arm.

Reasoning led to pleading. Kaplan said he had already seen too many young men and women die from this disease. Leah heard Henry use every possible argument, his voice rising in frustration. "What if it were your wife?" Kaplan asked. He hung up the phone exasperated. Finally, one morning he said to Leah, "That settles it. When this interferes with my sleep, and I'm up nights stewing, it's time to stop." In the spring of 1965, Kaplan closed arm A of the L-2 protocol and treated all subsequent stage III patients with high-dose total lymphoid irradiation.

The closure of the L-2 protocol was a turning point in Kaplan and Rosenberg's relationship. Initially, Kaplan had seemed genuinely pleased to have Rosenberg as a colleague. He was a fine clinician and a conscientious clinical investigator. But he lacked verve, daring. In their battle against cancer, Rosenberg wanted to pick off his foe slowly, one at a time; Kaplan wanted to attack with all barrels blasting. Perhaps Rosenberg's greatest sin in Kaplan's eyes was his scientific conservatism. "Saul was an evolutionary scientist," a former trainee observed; "Henry was revolutionary." The L-2 protocol underscored this difference.

Rosenberg thought that Kaplan had wanted a colleague, but collegial meant "with power shared equally," and it had become clear Kaplan didn't want to share the power. He wanted smart people around him who would do his bidding. At first, Rosenberg thought their relationship had great promise. He found Kaplan's ideas exciting, if a bit radical. And Kaplan listened patiently to his opinions, appearing to weigh them heavily. If they disagreed, he was courteous. But his behavior had changed. Rosenberg felt rebuffed. If Kaplan didn't respect his viewpoint, then Kaplan didn't respect him. Although co-investigators, they were not equals.

The termination of L-2 was more than the closing of a trial; it was the closing of a door. Whatever friendship Saul had hoped for would never come to be. Maybe they never would have been friends anyway. When Henry invited the Rosenbergs to dinners, Saul couldn't help noticing that the Kaplans' friends were worldly people with enormous vitality. They never drank a glass of wine without debating its virtues and deficiencies. They didn't just show pictures of their trip to Europe; they boasted of finding a superb, but relatively unknown museum on a back street. Henry liked to dine in a room charged with energy. Saul liked to tend his garden, fish a quiet stream, dine alone with his wife. Although Kaplan formed intense, lifelong friendships with several men, he was never intimate with Rosenberg. Kaplan's friends called him "Hank," but Rosenberg would always address him as "Dr. Kaplan."

At first, Rosenberg tried to stand his ground. Kaplan respected strength. Their contest of wills played out at staging conference as well as at departmental parties. On one occasion, Kaplan organized a water polo match. Staff watched as he and Rosenberg grabbed the ball and disappeared under water. A few bubbles rose to the surface; minutes passed. Finally, they emerged, slightly blue, both still holding the ball. "I'm sure he tried to drown me," Rosenberg recalled. With his friends, Kaplan was competitive in a flamboyant way; he loved a good joust. Rosenberg took the competition personally. "I never felt angry," he said, "only guilty."

Faculty and trainees began to notice more arguments at staging conference. Most stemmed from Rosenberg's conservative stance clashing with Kaplan's eagerness to forge ahead. Kaplan became increasingly frustrated and openly criticized Rosenberg, offending him. But seemingly Kaplan was not conscious of the effect he had. For him, personal issues were never at stake—only scientific and moral principles. "Even when we had serious clinical or scientific arguments," Rosenberg said, "he was always pleasant to me on a social basis." Both men rejoiced over the Christine Pendletons and were deeply saddened by the Joey Radicchis. Both men wanted to cure Hodgkin's disease, and it was this desire that would keep them together for years to come.

19   International Cooperation

Henry Kaplan wanted to cure Hodgkin's disease, but he knew he couldn't do it alone, not even with his lymphoma team. He needed international cooperation. The Stanford group had an organized approach to the disease, with specific protocols for each stage. But practices accepted at Stanford as the norm—rigorous clinical evaluation, prophylactic irradiation, optimal dose, randomized trials—seemed foreign to most cancer doctors. They remained stuck in the palliative mode. Even those who considered the disease curable treated each patient differently, with almost no standardization, making their techniques difficult for others to follow.

In the mid 1960s, four distinct groups of specialists—hematologists, surgeons, radiation therapists, and medical oncologists—managed patients with Hodgkin's disease. In many places, radiotherapists were still regarded as technicians. When several began touting long survivals of Hodgkin's disease patients, hematologists and surgeons responded with allegations of misdiagnoses, flawed analyses. If progress were ever to be made in treating this disease, cancer specialists had to work together, develop a common language, a coordinated approach. So when Maurice Tubiana, chief of the Radiation Department at the Institut Gustave Roussy outside Paris, invited Henry Kaplan to participate in the first international conference on Hodgkin's disease, he readily agreed.

Tubiana was organizing this meeting in response to a challenge from Jean Bernard, secretary-general of the French Hematologic Society: Can you really cure Hodgkin's disease? Since skepticism ran high, Bernard had suggested a symposium at which this question would be put to the test. He proposed that all investigators submit their pathology slides and data for review. Let their work withstand the critiques of pathologists and statisticians. Tubiana knew he could convert doubters to believers and move the field forward only if he could attract the most prominent cancer specialists. Unfortunately, he had no funds to offer for travel, lodging, or honoraria. But once Henry Kaplan agreed to participate, the others felt they had to come, likely to defend their positions.

So Tubiana got the headliners he wanted—Vera Peters, David Smithers, Robert Lukes, Eric Easson, and Henry Kaplan.

Most regarded Peters as the reigning queen of Hodgkin's disease. She had the greatest experience treating this disorder; her name was attached to the most commonly used staging system. David Smithers, an eminent radiotherapist from London's Royal Marsden Hospital, had played a central role in developing supravoltage radiation. Robert Lukes from the University of Southern California was one of the world's foremost lympho-pathologists. British radiotherapist Eric Easson had caught the attention of cancer specialists two years earlier with a paper boldly entitled "The Cure of Hodgkin's Disease." And Tubiana was a draw himself.

On February 15, 1965, the Paris meeting on Hodgkin's disease took place at the Hôpital Saint-Louis. Built in the seventeenth century, it was a historical monument—impressive, but not particularly comfortable. A hundred and fifty guests sat on benches in an amphitheater where anatomical dissections had been performed for decades. Twenty-two speakers from nine countries presented data in a marathon session from seven in the morning until 2 P.M. the next day, with short breaks for meals and sleep.

Many of the attendees considered Hodgkin's disease incurable, alleging that reported successes resulted from errors in interpretation of the pathologic material. Thus, the first issue addressed was whether patients with long survivals actually had Hodgkin's disease. An international panel of pathologists, headed by Robert Lukes, had reviewed these patients' biopsy slides sent from the investigators prior to the meeting. His panel concluded that only a small percentage of cases had been misdiagnosed. Tubiana had been shrewd in putting Lukes first. Once the concern over inaccurate diagnosis had been dispensed with, the mood changed from skepticism to guarded enthusiasm.

The group then turned to the second question: Were long-term survivors actually cured? Most cancer specialists agreed that if Hodgkin's disease remained in remission for five years, it rarely recurred. Tubiana asked three leading radiotherapists who contended that they had cured a subset of patients to present their data. Eric Easson went first. Between 1934 and 1956, over eight hundred patients had received radiotherapy at Christie Hospital in Manchester. Of those with disease localized in one lymph node region, 40 percent were still in remission at ten years. Patients with early-stage Hodgkin's disease, he said, "require immediate radical x-ray therapy while they are still localized if the opportunity for cure is not to be lost."

Peters followed in her understated manner. She had already published her results with prophylactic irradiation—extending treatment to uninvolved nodes. In Paris, she presented an update, which included patients who had far more advanced disease than Easson's group. Her results—35 percent disease-free at ten years—had stood the test of time. Following Peters, Henry Kaplan addressed the group. Although his demeanor did not invite critique, his attempts to speak French endeared him to the audience. Reviewing patients treated at Stanford, he, too, had found a substantial number who had lived at least five years beyond treatment without relapsing.

Results from these three contrasted sharply with the large number of earlier papers reporting high death rates. Explaining how Hodgkin's disease had come to be regarded as hopeless, Easson said, "Many of the earlier published studies . . . were made by morbid anatomists working backwards in time from the autopsy table! To draw conclusions about survival from a population of dead patients is a singularly fallacious approach." To address the skepticism regarding these three reports, Tubiana had asked a group of statisticians to scrutinize the data. They reported finding no errors; the conclusions held. And the second consensus of the conference was reached: selected patients with early-stage Hodgkin's disease could be cured with radiotherapy.

With the two major challenges of the conference behind them, the group turned to pathologic classification. For the past twenty years, pathologists had used the Jackson-Parker system. Although it divided Hodgkin's disease into three categories—the indolent paragranuloma, the virulent sarcoma, and the intermediate granuloma—90 percent of cases were classified as granuloma. Thus, the system made minimal distinction among patients based on pathologic grounds. Robert Lukes proposed a new classification that divided patients into six distinct groups. To many, including Kaplan, a more decisive classification had great appeal. But Luke's classification, with terms such as "lymphocytic and/or histiocytic (L&H) type, diffuse with lymphocytes predominating," seemed too complex for most.

Next they addressed clinical evaluation. An exciting new technique was introduced at the Paris meeting—the lymphangiogram. Participants sat enthralled as many saw abdominal lymph nodes for the first time. Few investigators had tried the procedure; fewer yet had mastered the intricate technique. The Stanford group led in experience with this procedure. Excitement generated by lymphangiograms served as the perfect prelude for Saul Rosenberg's talk. A relative newcomer, he reviewed the Stanford experience with clinical assessment of newly diagnosed patients, so-called staging. In his paper, "La classification clinique des maladies de Hodgkin," he outlined the laboratory tests and radiographs he considered requisite. He showed how the lymphangiogram had almost doubled the detection rate of positive abdominal nodes compared to standard radiographs, quadrupled that found by physical examination. Logical and rigorous in his approach, articulate in his presentation, Rosenberg converted the audience to his position. He had made his first major contribution to the management of Hodgkin's disease—setting high standards for the thorough and accurate evaluation of patients. This was Rosenberg's debut in international cancer research. Henry Kaplan appeared to have a smart, adept associate, and their collaboration—a medical oncologist working with a radiotherapist—showed the advantages of a team approach to cancer. No longer did investigators speak of the Kaplan trials; they referred to the Stanford trials.

Having reached consensus on recommended staging procedures, the group turned to a more controversial topic—optimal, or at least acceptable, therapy. Kaplan recommended 4,000 rads and made the case for the superiority of the linear accelerator. He pointed out that Easson had delivered 2,500 rads and used a 250-kilovolt machine. No wonder he had achieved good outcomes with stage I disease only. As for Peters, he questioned how much better her results might have been had she used a linear accelerator and given higher doses. Peters felt her cheeks flush. Hadn't Kaplan been listening? Even at 3,000 rads, four of her patients had died of cardiopulmonary toxicity.

Kaplan proceeded to present an early analysis of the L-1 and L-2 protocols. This was the first time most had heard of the mantle and inverted Y. Many radiotherapists would consider these innovative fields among Kaplan's greatest contributions to the management of Hodgkin's disease. And just as participants were digesting the idea of including so many sites in one field, he introduced the concept of total lymphoid irradiation. Hematologists and surgeons sat bewildered as interest among radiotherapists grew. Delighted as she was to see this about-face in the treatment of Hodgkin's disease, Peters couldn't help noticing that gradually she was receiving less and less credit for her work. In time, most radiotherapists attributed prophylactic irradiation to Kaplan.

The Paris conference was a milestone in the history of Hodgkin's disease. The critical question of potential curability had been answered, and other important issues—pathologic classification, staging, and appropriate therapy—had been addressed. The conference sparked an interest in the disease and ushered in what Vera Peters called the "age of resolution." The encouraging treatment results stimulated investigators around the world to undertake a more systematic study of Hodgkin's disease. Perhaps not appreciated at the time was the major influence Kaplan and Rosenberg had on the future of clinical trials in stressing the imperative for randomized studies. The rigor with which their L-1 and L-2 protocols were conceived and carried out set a new standard. And the Paris meeting introduced the notion of specialists collaborating.

Henry Kaplan was emerging as the foremost investigator in the field. Smithers thought he was assuming this position not because he was the most experienced or innovative, but because of his effectiveness as a speaker, problem-solver, and coordinator. Kaplan could absorb twenty-two talks, sift through the data, and identify the core issues. He persisted in questioning every speaker in detail. Tubiana liked the way Kaplan attacked Hodgkin's disease. "He decided that he was going to beat this disease," Tubiana said, "and he was a stubborn fighter." Rosenberg felt that Kaplan became the leader because he led so well. He didn't necessarily intend to dominate the field, but he didn't want someone less competent to assume that role. Vera Peters disagreed. She saw how Kaplan delighted in new insights and creative approaches; how he reveled in debating intricacies of treatment; how he synthesized vast quantities of information, distilling out what he considered the fundamental management principles; and how, in the end, he mandated them. Whichever perception was right, Kaplan's force was beginning to be felt at the Paris meeting. Henry Kaplan wanted to cure Hodgkin's disease, and now there was a cadre of cancer specialists worldwide devoted to that effort.

⌐∽

After the Paris meeting, investigators returned home enthusiastic about the prospects for an international effort. In order to capitalize on the spirit of cooperation, Kaplan obtained funds from the American Cancer Society and the National Cancer Institute and scheduled another conference to be held seven months later. Organization of that meeting bore Kaplan's mark. To begin with, this was to be a working meeting—no audience, just forty-two selected participants. And he invited only the most innovative or influential researchers in the field. He didn't want to waste time listening to or arguing with undistinguished cancer specialists. Conspicuously few in number were surgeons and hematologists. Radiotherapists, pathologists, and medical oncologists filled the list of attendees. From then on, they would take the lead in managing Hodgkin's disease.

Kaplan selected Westchester Country Club in Rye, New York, as the meeting site. Its isolation ensured that attention would not be divided between their work and other business. Attendees ate together, which fostered an informal exchange of ideas. And Kaplan added another detail that encouraged consensus—participants sat around one large table. Twenty-seven papers, grouped by topic, were scheduled over three days. Kaplan limited lecture time, allowing ample opportunity for open-ended discussion in order to critique the data. Small committees were selected to reconcile specific problems and report back to the entire group. Sidney Farber of the Children's Cancer Research Foundation in Boston moderated. Known as "silver-throated Sidney" because of his resounding voice, Farber could be counted on to keep the meeting on course. Kaplan titled the Rye Conference "Obstacles to the Control of Hodgkin's Disease."

First on the agenda was agreement on the pathologic and staging classification systems that would be used for future trials and published reports. Investigators needed to speak the same language. Lukes was asked to chair the committee on pathologic classification. He had a reputation as an open-minded pathologist, a good listener who invited the opinions of others. A number of different classifications had been used over the previous four decades, including the popular Jackson-Parker system, but each had major flaws—either it could not be reproduced by other pathologists or it didn't separate patient subgroups with different clinical courses. Farber allotted the committee just two hours to reach consensus on a classification scheme. He knew Lukes favored six pathologic subtypes. As the committee was retiring to another room, Farber took Lukes aside and said, "Most clinicians have trouble remembering six names. Could you pare it down to four?"

As soon as the committee convened, Henry Rappaport, an esteemed pathologist from the University of Chicago, suggested they just accept the Jackson-Parker system with which everyone was familiar and add a fourth subgroup. Lukes squirmed. In Paris, he had outlined the deficiencies of the Jackson-Parker system, and he thought he had convinced most pathologists that it didn't meet clinicians' needs. Fortunately, others rejected Rappaport's suggestion. Following Farber's advice, Lukes began to think how he could consolidate and simplify his six groups. "Those with lots of lymphocytes have the best prognosis," he said. "How about calling them 'lymphocytic predominance?' And those with few lymphocytes do the worst. We could name them 'lymphocytic depletion.' Those that are in between and contain an admixture of cells we could call 'mixed cellularity.'" That left one subgroup—those with wide bands of fibrous tissue that formed nodular masses. He suggested calling them "nodular sclerosis." "That sounds great," one pathologist said. "I vote we accept it." And in twenty minutes, they had a new pathologic classification system—the Rye Classification—which would remain unaltered into the next century.

Concurrence on a clinical staging system was not as easy to achieve. When Lukes finished his work, he joined the committee on staging and found it deep in deliberation. Each had come with his or her own proposal and was unwilling to compromise in order to formulate a single international system. Many used Peters's three-stage system: stage I—involvement of a single lymph node region; stage II—involvement of two or more lymph node regions, both located in either the upper or lower half of the body; stage III—involvement of lymph node groups in the both the upper and lower half of the body, or an organ, such as the lungs or liver. The designation A indicated absence of systemic symptoms, and B the presence of symptoms—fever, night sweats, and/or weight loss. This seemed a good starting point. Rosenberg proposed the Stanford classification in which patients with organ involvement were called stage IV. Peters found it difficult watching her long-standing system be altered in an instant. She considered this area her province. "Henry came out with his own classification," Peters recalled, "which was similar to mine, but which, as you can imagine, had to be different." Yet, she understood the value of the Stanford modification. Besides, she liked Saul Rosenberg. He was a gentleman; he listened to her, respected her point of view. She trusted him and felt they could work together. After lengthy debate, the committee finally voted to try the Stanford four-stage system. "It is therefore hoped," Rosenberg wrote in the summary, "it will be . . . found acceptable for international adoption."

But it wasn't found acceptable. After the meeting had adjourned, Canadian radiotherapists proposed that stage II be divided into two subgroups, and the British insisted that anemia be considered a B symptom. The French wouldn't approve either modification. Months after the Rye meeting, Rosenberg was still sending suggested compromises to Europe and Canada. With confusion mounting, Kaplan stepped in. Although he had not been a member of the committee on clinical staging, he could no longer tolerate the obstinate positions different groups had taken. He flew to New York City, Toronto, and London, achieving American, Canadian, and British agreement. Then he wrote to Maurice Tubiana: "I have sufficient admiration for your prowess as a diplomat to hope that . . . you will be able to persuade the others." Tubiana did convince the European groups, and Stanford's four-stage classification was finally adopted.

Another important issue addressed at the Rye Conference was how Hodgkin's disease spread. Swiss radiotherapist René Gilbert had postulated that it spread from an involved lymph node to adjacent lymph node groups in an orderly fashion. Gordon Richards and Vera Peters had based prophylactic irradiation on this belief. Others, led by David Smithers of the Royal Marsden Hospital, believed it could arise in several different sites simultaneously, termed "multifocal origin." Saul Rosenberg sought to resolve this controversy with facts. He had plotted the initial site of disease involvement in a hundred patients and the subsequent sites of disease in those who relapsed. In most, spread of disease was predictable, just as Gilbert had suggested. Hodgkin's disease appeared to start in a single site and spread along lymphatic channels in an orderly fashion. He called this "contiguous spread." Kaplan asserted that they could construct a "road map for successive sites of involvement."

Smithers challenged him. How did they explain a patient who had disease in the neck that spread to the abdomen, skipping the chest? Kaplan hypothesized that disease spread through the thoracic duct, which connected lymphatics in the left neck and abdomen. "HSK promulgated the theory of contiguous spread—the relentless marching from one node to another," one young investigator recalled. "When he ran into cases that didn't fit his hypothesis, he came up with a new explanation." Determining how Hodgkin's disease spread was more than just an intellectual debate. It would dictate the principles for treatment planning.

Although the pattern of spread remained unresolved, the group turned to treatment. The major objective of the Paris meeting had been to establish that Hodgkin's disease could be cured. At the Rye conference, investigators were trying to reach concurrence on general principles of treatment so that therapy could be standardized. Kaplan felt they had to address all three therapeutic modalities—surgery, radiation therapy, and chemotherapy—but he planned to dispense with surgery as quickly as possible. George Pack, a leading New York cancer surgeon, had been invited to present his results.

Pack contended that early-stage Hodgkin's disease could be eradicated successfully by surgical excision, demonstrating superior outcome compared to irradiation. Kaplan pointed out the flaws in his data. In response, Pack became defensive, but Kaplan kept needling him, pointing out the lack of scientific method in his approach. Participants began to feel uncomfortable. "When Kaplan was through with Pack," one oncologist said, "surgery was clearly out." It was probably at this meeting that Henry Kaplan began to acquire a reputation as a shark. Researchers became reluctant to argue with him. "If you are going to debate Henry Kaplan," David Smithers said, "you should know your business very well."

Participants proceeded to debate two major radiotherapy issues: optimal dose and appropriate field. Kaplan stated emphatically that 3,500 to 4,000 rads over three and a half to four weeks should be the minimally acceptable dose, although he preferred 5,000 rads. Concerns were raised over giving such high doses. Then he proposed treating stage III patients with 4,000 rads to all lymph node groups—total lymphoid irradiation. "Where does aggressiveness cease?" Easson asked. "Five years ago," Kaplan responded, "I would have regarded our present treatment of virtually every lymph node in the body with 4,000 rads . . . as insane. But this is now being done without apparent serious injury to the patients." His results for stage III disease looked far superior to any reported to date.

Participants also debated whether prophylactic irradiation should be given to uninvolved adjacent areas for patients with stages I and II disease. Rosenberg's contiguity theory supported this approach. If a patient initially had disease in a single lymph node chain, he reasoned, and one could predict the next area of spread, why not irradiate the area as a preventive measure? Some argued that this was excessive. "The hazard of not irradiating an area which may already be minimally involved has been exaggerated by Dr. Kaplan," said a hematologist from Roswell Park Memorial Institute in Buffalo. "These areas can usually receive tumoricidal doses just as effectively at a later date." He reminded the group that although Kaplan had found a lower relapse rate with prophylactic extended field therapy, he had not yet demonstrated improved survival. "During this phase of ignorance," Kaplan replied, "therapeutic philosophy must give the patient the benefit of the doubt. This means to me that areas adjacent to the original focus should be treated aggressively." But, he went on to say, "These differing views constitute the best argument for a prospective randomized comparative trial."

Finally, attendees heard preliminary reports from chemotherapy trials. Kaplan had allocated a smaller amount of time for this topic, reflecting what he thought of its importance. For years, nitrogen mustard had been the only available drug to treat Hodgkin's disease, and although it caused tumor shrinkage, the effect was short-lived. Besides, shrinkage was no longer the goal; cure was. Those discussing this relatively new modality were tentative in presenting their data. "It should be mentioned at the onset," Daniel Miller of Sloan-Kettering said, as he began his talk on chemotherapy, "that there is no question as to the primacy of radiation therapy in the treatment of Hodgkin's disease." By 1965, several new chemotherapeutic agents had been introduced, and laboratory studies suggested better responses if several drugs were combined. Emil Frei III reviewed preliminary results from the National Cancer Institute on a promising four-drug regimen. Would chemotherapy have a significant role in treatment of Hodgkin's disease? Kaplan was skeptical, but allowed that the data were premature.

Henry Kaplan felt pleased with the Rye conference. Much had been accomplished. Pathologic and staging classification systems had been agreed upon. The contiguity theory had been well received, and Rosenberg had stimulated others to examine patterns of spread in their own patients. Kaplan had come closer to convincing radiotherapists that high doses and extended fields should be employed. And he and Rosenberg had challenged investigators to follow their lead and prove the efficacy of treatment through randomized trials.

Kaplan had planned this meeting well. He had established the goals and selected the perfect environment in which to accomplish them. They had come closer to overcoming the obstacles to the control of Hodgkin's disease, with few controversies and a great sense of camaraderie. Robert Lukes described the symposium as the most outstanding of hundreds he had attended during his career. Vera Peters remembered it as one of the most pleasant meetings in which she had participated. The Rye conference represented the best cooperative effort of investigators to work together unselfishly to overcome Hodgkin's disease. There would never be another like it.

20   A Famous Father

Henry Kaplan was becoming famous. Not yet fifty, he had been elected president of the American Association for Cancer Research, the Association of University Radiologists, and the Radiation Research Society. The list of international awards was growing. Among them, Kaplan especially cherished the Chevalier de la Legion d'Honneur. Since the Paris Conference, Kaplan had maintained a strong relationship with the French scientific community, inviting so many French scientists to Stanford that colleagues used to joke about Stanford's metastases to France. "His name is associated with scientific rigor, exceptional talent, and great personal distinction," the French consul general wrote. "His nomination to the Order of the Legion of Honor reflects the gratitude, admiration, and friendship ... of the most distinguished political and scientific personalities in France."

With increasing eminence came an expanded travel schedule. Societies asked Kaplan to organize their meetings; foreign governments sought his advice on their cancer programs. He was an active member of seven national organizations, whose charges varied from radiation safety to training requirements for radiation therapists. He served on several advisory boards, including the Oakridge National Laboratory in Tennessee and the National Academy of Sciences in Washington. Never a passive participant, he tried to attend each meeting and proved influential in shaping each group. He lectured throughout the world on the management of Hodgkin's disease. From Kansas City to Oslo, he rarely declined the opportunity to teach techniques for the mantle and inverted Y, to spread the word that Hodgkin's disease could be cured. Leah called it his "missionary work."

Traveling companions marveled at Kaplan's stamina. After eighteen hours in an airplane, he insisted on a trip to a museum or monument, and returning home, he stopped at his office to catch up on paperwork. When called to advise the NCI director, Kaplan took the red-eye (before the era of commercial jets), worked all day in Washington, D.C., and returned home the same night. Prior to a trip, Kaplan read about the history, culture, and architecture of his destination. When in France, he tried to speak French; he even addressed scientists in their native language. He supplemented his high school French by reading murder mysteries. He joked that his French was adequate as long as he only needed to say, "Drop that gun" or "Up against the wall." At one symposium, he began his presentation by remarking, "The words you hear are not mine; they are the words of Inspector Maigret."

Years later, Leah still laughed about a dinner in Japan where, as the guests of honor, they were served fish heads cut so that they stood on the plate eyes staring upward—the pièce de résistance. She was picking at her fish when a geisha girl offered to help her. With a chopstick, the girl popped out the fish eyes, and they rolled onto Leah's plate. Knowing she would offend her host if she left them untouched, Leah waited until no one was looking, made a hole in her rice, rolled the eyes into a little cave, and covered them up. She peeked over at Henry to find him eating his fish eyes with apparent relish.

Although Kaplan tried to intersperse the rigors of work with sightseeing, this became more difficult with time. Almost everywhere he went, physicians sought his advice. They considered him "the Messiah of Hodgkin's disease." Kaplan couldn't walk between conference rooms at a meeting without being stopped a dozen times. Once while visiting Israel's Weizmann Institute, he and Leah stayed in a guesthouse on the premises. Someone was always knocking on the door, seeking consultation. "He couldn't go to the bathroom without being interrupted," Leah said.

Even when Kaplan was vacationing, local physicians and scientists found out where he was and called upon him. He reviewed a difficult case or gave an impromptu lecture or dropped by a laboratory to look at data. Seemingly, his life had spun out of control. Not so. Kaplan rarely lost control of anything. He had just mixed his pleasure with his work for such a long time that they eventually became inseparable. He began to spend more time in airplanes and conference rooms than at home. Letters to friends often started, "I'm on my way to . . ." or "I just came back from. . . ." Colleagues at Stanford introduced him as a visiting professor. Henry Kaplan had attained preeminence. Some of his family reveled in that fact; others struggled with it.

⬳

His mother continued to live alone in Chicago, still running the pharmacy. Henry called less often and sent fewer letters, but when he did, he included newspaper clippings about his awards. No longer did he ask, "Are you proud of me?"

His brother Richard had forged a new relationship with Henry and Leah after moving to Minneapolis. They had embraced him when he was floundering, made him part of a family. They had encouraged him to enroll at the University of Minnesota, where he studied political science and journalism and wrote for the college paper. Dick began to idolize Hank. "He was the framework of my life," he said, "the be-all and end-all." But in the process, he lost his own identity. Years later, he described himself as a satellite orbiting a bright star. At his graduation, Richard planned to show his family the campus and introduce them to faculty and friends. He wanted his mother to know that her second son had done well too, had made a name for himself among the University of Minnesota's 23,000 students. But Sarah insisted on shopping for a girdle at the Dayton Hudson store in Minneapolis. They arrived late to graduation and never saw the rest of campus or met his friends.

After graduation, Dick took a job as a foreign correspondent for United Press in Mexico City. When Hank and Leah moved to Washington, D.C., he did, too, living two blocks away from them. They encouraged him to study law. Three years later, the family attended his graduation from the University of Michigan Law School. Again Sarah insisted on shopping, this time for antiques. Richard had to run ahead of them with his cap and gown to catch up with his classmates at the ceremony. In the company of her beloved first son, Sarah practically ignored Richard.

Following law school, Richard moved to the Bay Area, eventually becoming a successful trial lawyer in San Francisco. Busy at Stanford, Hank had less time for him and didn't realize how troubled his brother's relationship with his mother had become. Although Richard and Hank had drawn closer in Minneapolis, Sarah continued to wedge herself between them. When Richard tried to emulate his brother, she pointed out the futility of his trying to do so. In time, Richard, who had once thought Hank godlike, began to harbor a grudge against him. This went on for years. Focused on his work, Henry never perceived his brother's rancor until it culminated at a dinner party in the Kaplans' campus home.

Among the guests that evening were Berkeley political science professor Herb McClosky, his wife, and Richard. Annie and Paul were downstairs playing pool with Danny McClosky when they heard loud voices upstairs, which escalated into yelling, a slamming door, squealing tires. Later Annie learned Richard had had too much alcohol and had begun insulting the McCloskys. When Hank asked him to curb his language, Richard turned on his brother, suggesting they step outside to settle the argument with their fists. Henry asked him to leave, and after a vicious verbal barrage, Richard stormed out. Hank never understood what caused his brother to lash out at that dinner party. The bitterness and jealousy pent up for years had spewed forth.

His children, too, suffered from Kaplan's success. When they moved from Sausalito, Paul, or Paulie as his parents called him, started first grade and Annie third at Stanford Elementary School. With his mop of curls, sweet smile, and remnant of baby fat, Paulie looked like a cute, happy child. Annie easily made new friends and excelled in her schoolwork. They didn't have as much company as in Sausalito, and their father seemed to have more leisure—for a while. Annie liked to hear him practice the cello; Paulie looked forward to the evenings when his father sneaked up and tickled him until he cried for mercy. He taught the children to swim and after each lesson, flipped Annie and dunked Paulie, starting a free-for-all. The children looked forward to the Sunday morning pancake ritual. It started when their father would announce with great flourish that he was making pancakes. He sheepishly discarded the first batch—uncooked because the skillet was too hot. The second batch stuck to the pan because it was too cold. Paulie, barely reaching up to the stove top, would take over the spatula and produce perfect pancakes.

But after Henry got busier, they no longer roughhoused in the swimming pool; he forgot to tickle Paulie. He even skipped the Sunday morning pancakes if he had a plane to catch. Even when their father came home, the children felt the intrusion of his work. Annie's friend Tracy recalled a typical scene in a letter she wrote to Kaplan years later:

> I remember sitting at your kitchen table . . . when you came in after work. You looked very tired and were about to retreat to your study with a drink, but I remember you kissing us all, then standing between Annie and Paul with one hand on Paul's shoulder and the other cupping Annie's cheek and asking us all about our day, listening gravely and encouragingly to our little frustrations and triumphs.

Tracy had sensed that he wanted to sit and talk, but his work pulled him away.

More and more, Leah had to raise the children alone. Although she commuted two hours to work as a psychiatric social worker in San Francisco, the children always knew she would be there, loving and forgiving. Leah was a good mother, but perhaps a better wife. Although she knew Hank didn't pay enough attention to the children, she had more concern for him as he gave up tennis, then his art discussion group, then the cello. "I don't care whether you spend more time with me," she said. "I just want you to relax and do something you enjoy." "You don't understand," he replied. "I enjoy my work." Leah didn't complain when Henry fell asleep at the symphony or came home just long enough to put clean socks and underwear in his bag. She had married him, instead of some light-hearted young man, because he had a passion, and she never lost sight of that.

Paulie and Annie felt they never had enough time alone with their father. "Our home was often shared with patients and scientists," Paul said. The student research seminar group was an example. Henry found the weekly meeting exhilarating; for the Kaplan children, it meant one less evening with their father. Leah rushed home from San Francisco, and with her eye on the clock, hurried Paulie and Annie through their dinner, then banished them downstairs. She set out refreshments and slipped into her bedroom just as the students arrived. As Paul and Annie fell asleep, they heard their father in lively debate with the students upstairs. "Trying to learn why he gave so much of himself to other people, to the university, and to the world was no easy task for us," Paul said.

Several times Henry invited patients undergoing therapy to live with them. Some came from as far away as Israel and Greece and couldn't afford housing. Others needed extra care, such as the medical student, recovering from an operation, whom Kaplan found living alone in a one-room walk-up. Annie and Paul couldn't help noticing the tenderness their father showed his patients. Once a family moved in with their seventeen-year-old daughter, and a few days later, Henry came home looking ashen. The girl's cancer had spread, and he had to tell her parents that he couldn't cure her. "I saw a piece of him die that day," Annie said.

Although she wanted more of her father, Annie seemed to understand his commitment and developed a protective feeling for him at an early age. She watched him come home exhausted, only to face a dinner party. Sometimes he could barely keep his eyes open, yet the guests stayed. She wanted to tell them to leave and let him go to bed.

When Paul was nine and Annie ten, Henry took the family to Europe for three months on his sabbatical. They rented a Citroën and drove about the countryside, stopping for picnic lunches. "The cheese you ate yesterday came from this town," he told Annie. "This is where Joan of Arc was burned at the stake," he instructed Paul. Henry never just sat at a sidewalk cafe enjoying the ambience of a new place. He made every outing a learning experience. "When it came to exploring archeological ruins," Paul said, "the 499th Greek temple . . . was just as fascinating as the 401st . . . an opinion not always shared by the rest of us!"

When they visited the larger cities, however, physicians and scientists wanted to meet with Kaplan, and he began to spend time touring a new radiation facility or evaluating a difficult patient while Leah, Paul, and Annie waited in the lobby. Country picnics were replaced by luncheons with researchers. Family suppers in a quiet café were supplanted by formal dinners in the home of a French radiologist or a Swedish biologist. Paul and Annie began to resent these scientists. This was supposed to be a family vacation, not a series of visiting professorships.

The children might have more easily adjusted to an absent father if they had been surrounded by loving, supportive relatives. But they weren't. They looked forward to visits from Aunt Shirley; she and their mother always seemed to be laughing over some shared memory. And they considered trips to grandfather Lebeson's summer home a treat. Visits from Sarah proved more problematic. Ann had fond childhood memories of her grandmother: museums, galleries, cooking dinner together using her old recipes. She loved hearing her grandmother's stories about growing up in Russia and her many suitors, conjuring up images of a Russian Jewish Scarlett O'Hara. But Ann hated the way her grandmother criticized their mother. Her work, her home, her cooking—nothing Leah did was good enough for Sarah's son.

Paul had mixed feelings about his grandmother. She fascinated him with her knowledge of the world and her ability to remember minute details of things she had read. "She had an intensity," Paul said, "a drive and enthusiasm for living that was unmatched by anybody I've met." But she had strong opinions about everything. "My grandmother was carved out of granite," he said. "No one could ever win an argument with her." Worse yet, she ignored him, making him feel part of the background, "like the wallpaper," he said.

Richard, on the other hand, paid special attention to Paul. Leah continued inviting him to family events for the children's sake. She had tried unsuccessfully to mediate a reconciliation between her husband and her brother-in-law for years. But Henry couldn't excuse Richard's juvenile behavior. And Richard couldn't forgive Henry for capturing all their mother's love. Leah persisted until Paul's eleventh birthday. Richard had invited him to go skiing. His bags packed, Paul waited on the front steps with great anticipation for his Uncle Richard's car. Hours passed. Richard never came. Later he called to say he couldn't go, no excuse. Paul felt crushed. Ann wrote to her uncle, calling him immature and saying that he should not take out his anger at her father on them. If he couldn't separate the two, she wanted nothing further to do with him. Henry and Leah didn't know about the letter until Richard called Leah and chastised her for putting Annie up to it. After that, Leah's attempts at reconciliation ceased. The fragile link between the two brothers broke. Henry didn't speak to his brother again until Sarah suffered a stroke nineteen years later. The family circle was shrinking.

The limited time Henry spent with his children posed one impediment to his parenting. The way they spent their time together presented another. Paul learned early on that to be with his father meant entering his sphere of interest. That included the laboratory and the symphony, not Scouts and the Three Stooges. At dinner, when Henry asked about their day, Paul sensed a genuine interest if he described an art class, but only passing enthusiasm for a newly built fort. Paul spent hours listening to his father's scratchy, old 78 rpm classical records because it meant being with him. After dinner, Henry usually retired to his study. Paul tiptoed to the door, peeked in at the stern figure bent over his desk, and tried to decide from his expression whether or not to disturb him.

Henry couldn't easily shift from a driven adult environment to a child's world. Paul recalled his father's reaction when halfway through a dinner party, he described a horror movie in which a scientist delivered large doses of radiation to an octopus. It grew to giant size and ate the Golden Gate Bridge. He asked his father if radiation could make animals grow that large. "No," Henry answered bluntly. "That's nonsense. If you irradiated an octopus, it would die."

Paul remembered another instance when the family was vacationing at his grandfather's summer home in Eagle River, Wisconsin. He had started to build a balsa wood airplane, which had hundreds of pieces and pages of instructions. His father was pacing in the background. Paul spread out all the pieces and was beginning to glue tab A to tab B when he realized his father was looking over his shoulder. Within a short time, he was giving Paul a great deal of unsolicited advice. Half an hour later, Paul moved out of his seat, and over the next three days, his father built the airplane by himself.

Perhaps Kaplan had difficulty playing with his children because he had never had a childhood. His mother had raised him in an adult world where reading books and visiting art galleries were appropriate; climbing trees and wrestling were not. So he spent hours teaching Paul art history, not realizing that his son really wanted to play cards and tell jokes. The Kaplan children felt their father's high expectations, and they didn't want to disappoint him. For Annie, that seemed to come easily, but not for Paul, and his father's failure to recognize why proved tragic.

Knowing Paul as a child, one might have predicted that he would become a duplicate of Henry. Learning seemed to be effortless as evidenced by his encyclopedic knowledge of dinosaurs, reptiles, and fossils. And he had an aptitude for figuring out how things work. The family boasted that if something broke, whether the swimming pool filter or toilet, Paulie could fix it. Nobel Prize winner Arthur Kornberg found himself explaining DNA to a little boy. When political scientist Herb McClosky came to dinner, Paulie asked him to explain how polling was done. "I had a great deal of genuine curiosity," Paul said, recalling his interactions with his parents' friends, "plus an ordinary desire to show off." When he started kindergarten, the teacher reported that Paul worked effectively with minimal assistance. So the following year, Leah and Henry were shocked when the principal called to say their son was flunking first grade.

Paul's teacher reported that he was the only child in her class who couldn't read, and that he had begun to misbehave. His writing was illegible. When asked to add numbers in a column, he wrote answers anywhere on the page.

She assumed Paul was mentally slow, but the principal pointed to his superior scores on achievement tests. The teacher concluded that he was lazy and careless. When she asked him to read a phrase such as "See Tim go," he read "Tim go see," and classmates laughed. Paul might have been funny and the center of attention, but beneath his smile, he felt humiliated. The teacher began to yell at him, belittling this sensitive child who was used to praise. Paul began to fear that he was stupid.

Henry found it inconceivable that his son couldn't read. He felt sure that Paul could surpass his peers if only he applied himself. He decided to tutor his son, to motivate him. After dinner, Henry selected an enjoyable book, such as *The Story of Babar* or *Ferdinand the Bull*, and they retired to his study, Henry calm and full of good intentions. As Paul struggled through a page, Henry reviewed each word several times. He made Paul spell a difficult word and sound it out again and again until he seemed to have learned it. A few minutes later, Paul would stare blankly at a word they had just studied. Sometimes he couldn't remember a word as simple as "cat." Henry's jaw tensed. He didn't notice the droplets of sweat collecting on his son's forehead. When Paul stumbled over "which" a second time, Henry corrected him, speaking in a slow, steady voice. "Just concentrate; buckle down," he said. The third time Paul confused "which" and "when," Henry pounded the book. Paul became terrified; he loathed these sessions with his father. They confirmed his fears: he was retarded, defective. "When patients would talk about my father," Paul said years later, "saying what a wonderful doctor he was with a great bedside manner, a man who made them feel at ease, I would wonder if we were talking about the same human being."

The after-dinner reading ordeals became more problematic, and a hush fell over the table as they finished dessert. Annie cleared the dishes and slipped away. She couldn't understand what was happening; she had always thought Paul was smarter than her. Henry's anger and Paul's silence caused Leah great anxiety. She comforted Paul, but he craved his father's warmth and approval. Finally, Leah intervened and hired a tutor, regretting that she had waited so long. Even then, Paul could not learn to read.

The principal at Stanford Elementary School did not accept the teacher's appraisal and had Paul tested by a series of psychologists, but none could diagnose his reading problem. One psychiatrist told Leah that Paul suffered from "fear of success." Henry couldn't understand the concept. Traveling home from a vacation on an ocean liner, the Kaplans met Freda Owen, a child psychologist who had just accepted a job in the Palo Alto school system. Leah told her about Paul's problem, and on board, she had ample opportunity to observe the engaging little boy. When she began working at Stanford Elementary School, she was assigned his case and almost immediately diagnosed dyslexia.

In the early 1960s, dyslexia was poorly understood, even among psychologists, and the disorder was practically unrecognized in the public school system. Freda Owen reviewed the situation with the Kaplans. She assured them that it wasn't hopeless and described experimental techniques that had been successful in some cases. Henry and Leah felt a mixture of relief and guilt. All the time, Paul had been trying far harder than most children. Paul sensed a sudden change in his parents' attitude. Dinnertime became more relaxed. His mother laughed more often. His father became gentle and supportive. He likened Paul's dyslexia to his deformed fingers and drew closer to Paul, as if they had a special bond.

After a series of unsuccessful tutors, Leah found Dr. Marion. She taught Paul the technique of auditory memory and helped him develop muscle memory of letter shapes by duplicating the motion of writing a letter with his hand— "much like a dancer memorizes choreography," she told him. She spoke calmly and made Paul feel like an important person even if he didn't remember what w-h-o spelled. Paul thought her wrinkled face and arthritic fingers beautiful. Before long, he could read. In two years, he caught up to his classmates. But the damage had been done. His self-image had been marred, explicitly by his teacher and implicitly by his father. His sense of identity was based on being retarded, someone born to fail. He could never lift his chin and say, "I'm going to cure cancer." At the age of nine, Paul Kaplan didn't think he could succeed at anything.

A prominent scientist, outstanding clinician, superb teacher, and academic leader, Henry Kaplan approached everything with vigor and enthusiasm. There was seemingly no problem he couldn't solve. This brilliant man, who could comprehend the impediments to health care in Iran, who could comfort a newly diagnosed cancer patient, failed to recognize his own son's needs. He couldn't appreciate that Paul just wanted to be loved for himself.

Kaplan made an earnest attempt to draw closer to his son during a trip to Israel. When Paul turned twelve, Henry and Leah began discussing whether he should have a bar mitzvah. They decided that developing an appreciation for Jewish history and culture would be far more meaningful than an elaborate affair with sculptured chopped liver and an aging rock band. When they proposed a trip to Israel instead, Paul felt relieved. He had seen the wide-eyed, forlorn look of friends as they struggled to read Hebrew in front of the congregation. As far as he could tell, the most he would gain from a bar mitzvah was a lot of new fountain pens. So instead of trudging to Hebrew school every day, chanting prayers, and watching boys throw spitballs behind the cantor's back, Paul studied Jewish history with his father. They retired to his study after dinner and read about the Ottoman Empire under Suleiman the Magnificent and the establishment of a homeland for Jews as a result of the Balfour Declaration. Henry made each narrative vivid and fascinating to his son. He told Paul the entire country was a museum, where construction workers uncovered ancient tombs in Jerusalem suburbs; where a shepherd, exploring a cave, had made one of the great archaeological discoveries of all time, the Dead Sea Scrolls. He said details of entire periods of history had been reconstructed from fragments of clothing, pottery, and documents found inadvertently by local residents. Paul cherished these evenings alone with his father—no visiting scientists, no patients, no shouting.

In April 1966, Paul and Henry spent two weeks touring Israel with Henry's close friend, Michael Feldman, a biologist at the Weitzmann Institute of Science. At every stop, he regaled them with stories not found in their history books. The mystery and vitality of Israel thrilled them. In Jerusalem, Paul heard five different languages on one city block. His father pointed out two women walking down the street—one hidden by a black veil, the other in a uniform with a gun slung over her shoulder. In Mea She'arim, the quarter of Jerusalem where ultraorthodox Jews lived the way they had done in the shtetls of eastern Europe, Paul saw Hassidic Jews dressed in long, black coats, with earlocks hanging beneath their flat, round fur hats. At Hazor, the ruins of twenty-one strata of settlements going back to the Bronze Age brought to life the history he and his father had studied. As they climbed up to Masada at dawn, Paul recalled the story his father had read to him of the Jewish rebels who in 71 A.D. had sought refuge there from the Romans and, after a two-year siege, died in a final embrace. Even more touching was Yad Vashem, a memorial to the six million Jews murdered by the Nazis. Henry and Paul agreed that the highlight of their trip was attending a Passover Seder at Ein Ha-Horesh kibbutz, most of whose five hundred members were Holocaust survivors. When the entire kibbutz community stood to sing "Hatikvah," Israel's national anthem, meaning "The Hope," Paul watched his father's reaction. He realized how proud his father was to be a Jew, and how Israel symbolized being Jewish for him.

During their two weeks in Israel, Paul and Henry traveled to dozens of towns, excavation sites, and museums. Paul demonstrated how much he had learned by reciting the history of a dig or the significance of a monument. He asked a thousand questions, displaying inexhaustible curiosity. To Henry, the trip surpassed his expectations. He had succeeded in imparting to his son an appreciation for his heritage. Paul, on the other hand, felt ambivalent—externally ebullient, but unsettled inside, as if a piece were missing. Together he and his father had forged a connection with their cultural origins. In this regard, the trip was a success, but Paul had wanted more. He had hoped somehow his father would become the close companion he longed for. Paul noticed that when he interacted at his father's level—asking questions about an historical event or an archeological find—he had his father's full attention. And if they visited a particularly moving site, like Yad Vashem, Paul felt his father's arm around his shoulder. Paul wanted to keep this closeness alive forever. But his father was constantly drawn back into the world of work—preparing lectures on the airplane, consulting at The Weizmann Institute, writing papers at night. At those times, Paul felt excluded. If he fidgeted or interrupted his father, Henry raised his voice, reducing Paul from traveling companion to naughty child. "My father was able to focus dazzling energy, enthusiasm, and affection for a moment," Paul said, "and then be stern or hostile the next. There was not much of a gradient between the two. It was pretty abrupt." This confused Paul; he never knew where he stood.

Over the years, Paul began to comprehend the significance of their trip on another level. It had helped him understand his father—his greatness as a scientist, as a scholar, but his shortcomings as a parent. Paul finally came to grips with the realization that he would never get more from his father. Henry had taken weeks away from work to devote to his son. He had given all he was capable of giving. At the end of the trip, a new bond had been created between them—the bond of a shared experience. With time, however, the memory faded, and the closeness and sharing gradually slipped away.

21   The Single-Minded Focus
of Vince DeVita

In April 1967, Henry Kaplan attended the yearly meeting of the American Association for Cancer Research, held in Chicago. He had reviewed all the abstracts and was particularly intrigued by one entitled "Combination Chemotherapy in the Treatment of Hodgkin's Disease." Vince DeVita from the National Cancer Institute (NCI) presented the paper. The audience was astonished to hear this young investigator report a complete remission rate of 90 percent in patients with advanced disease. His weapon was a four-drug regimen: mechlorethamine (nitrogen mustard), Oncovin (vincristine), procarbazine, and prednisone. He called it MOPP. If his results were reproducible, chemotherapy had emerged as a major therapeutic tool in the quest to cure Hodgkin's disease.

❧

The story of cancer chemotherapy had begun in the late 1940s, when a few agents, starting with nitrogen mustard, were found to inhibit cell growth. Despite their potential, the drugs generated minimal interest among cancer specialists. The gulf between the chemistry laboratory and the cancer ward was wide, and collaboration between basic scientists and clinicians almost unheard-of. In the decade that followed, brief periods of enthusiasm were followed by stretches of pessimism brought on by the inadequacies of this new modality—poor response rates, short remissions, and significant toxicities. But happenstance led to discovery of several new agents, and lessons learned from mice taught oncologists how to use these caustic drugs, which were of such potency that they were called "poisons." One of the earliest successes was the MOPP regimen. Its composition resulted from the masterful integration of a series of keen observations. None of the four agents constituting MOPP had been developed through organized programs of drug synthesis and screening. Each had been discovered by serendipity.

Nitrogen mustard had been formulated during World War II by Major Alfred Gilman while performing classified research on gas warfare. Studying the effects of mustard exposure in Bari Harbor, he suggested the cancer-killing potential of mustard compounds. He tested one of its chemical derivatives, nitrogen mustard, in six terminally ill patients; two with lymphoma improved. By the 1960s, it was established that nitrogen mustard could produce responses in Hodgkin's disease patients. But they were short-lived; cancer progressed six to ten weeks later. And the drug caused significant toxicities—nausea and vomiting, reduction in blood counts, and skin burns if it leaked out of the vein and infiltrated surrounding tissue.

In 1958, a second chance observation led to discovery of another drug for Hodgkin's disease. Oncovin, better known by its generic name, vincristine, came from a most unexpected source—the periwinkle plant. R. L. Noble at the University of Western Ontario had been studying extracts from plants alleged by Indian folklore to have medicinal properties. He had heard about a West Indian tea made from leaves of *Vinca rosea*, a white-flowered periwinkle, that could lower blood glucose levels in diabetics. He obtained a supply from Black River, Jamaica, prepared a solution from the leaves and injected it into diabetic rats. To his disappointment, it did not reduce glucose levels, and within a week, all the animals died. He performed autopsies on the rats and found widespread infections with liver and lung abscesses. Noble discovered that *Vinca rosea* had suppressed bone marrow function, causing a rapid fall in white blood count, thus the enhanced susceptibility to infection. He postulated that since this chemical suppressed white blood cell proliferation, it might have potential for leukemia therapy. Vinca alkaloids, the class of substances isolated from the periwinkle plant, never played a role in the treatment of diabetes, but they became important antineoplastic agents. Reporting his findings, Noble wrote: "The cancer worker in the smaller institution . . . must view with awe the vast chemotherapeutic screening projects in progress in the United States. . . . Although somewhat irregular in comparison with the systematic prediction, synthesis, and screening of an entirely new series of compounds, chance observations may well be worthy of greater consideration than they have received."

In 1962, NCI oncologist Paul Carbone treated a small group of Hodgkin's disease patients with one of the vinca alkaloids—vincristine—and reported brief responses. He observed, however, something else of significance: vincristine had a different toxicity profile from nitrogen mustard. It primarily affected the nervous system, causing numbness of the fingers and toes and constipation, but did not induce vomiting or lower blood counts in man. "This order of responsiveness in the absence of bone marrow toxicity," Carbone wrote, "is unique." One could consider using more than one drug at a time if they had different side effects. Nonoverlapping toxicities, as the concept was called, would become a major consideration in the design of MOPP.

The third active chemotherapeutic agent in MOPP—procarbazine—originated from a group of compounds synthesized and tested as antidepressants. In the early 1950s, doctors had noted that patients treated for tuberculosis with the drug iproniazid had a striking improvement in mood. Intrigued by this beneficial side effect, scientists investigated its actions and found that iproniazid stimulated the central nervous system by inhibiting a particular enzyme—monoamine oxidase. Psychiatrists began using this antituberculous drug to treat depression. The drug worked, and two chemists at Hoffman-LaRoche Laboratories began synthesizing several hundred different monoamine oxidase inhibitors, searching for even more effective antidepressants. They found that one compound, procarbazine, had an unexpected side effect; it inhibited cellular growth. They tested its antineoplastic effect in animals and in 1963, reported effectiveness against a wide spectrum of transplanted tumors.

Later that year, Gerald Mathé treated twenty-two Hodgkin's disease patients with procarbazine at Institut Gustave-Roussy. Sixty-eight percent had a response, although short-lived. Of more interest, Mathé observed that patients whose cancer had become resistant to nitrogen mustard and vincristine responded to procarbazine, some completely, because it inhibited cellular growth in a dissimilar way. He was describing non-cross-resistance. Combining drugs that kill cancer cells by different mechanisms would become another important consideration in planning MOPP.

Prednisone, the fourth drug in MOPP, came to the attention of cancer specialists as a result of Yale Professor Thomas Dougherty's investigation into the effects of adrenal gland hormones, such as cortisone, in mice. He reported diminished size of all lymph nodes. If cortisone or prednisone could shrink normal lymphoid tissue, investigators postulated that these steroids might prove effective in treating pathologic lymph nodes too. In 1965, Thomas Hall of the Children's Cancer Research Foundation in Boston treated fourteen Hodgkin's disease patients with high doses of prednisone. Over half had tumor responses lasting four months on average.

For almost two decades, cancer specialists had been tentative in their use of chemotherapy. These drugs did not damage cancer cells solely but indiscriminately impaired any rapidly dividing cell. The margin of safety was small. The dose and scheduling of chemotherapeutic drugs were, for the most part, empirical. Ignorance surrounding chemotherapy administration resembled that of radiation therapy in its early years. Cancer specialists knew that they had a powerful tool in chemotherapy but did not understand how to use it properly. Deterred by its overwhelming side effects, they approached it cautiously, giving drugs one at a time in low doses.

Chemotherapy might have remained in its own kilovoltage age had not it been for Howard Skipper. Work coming from his laboratory in Birmingham, Alabama, provided a scientific basis for chemotherapy administration. Skipper used leukemia in mice to study the kinetics of cell kill. With this tumor model, he determined that a single dose of chemotherapy killed a constant percentage of neoplastic cells. Thus, if a tumor consisted of a billion cells, and if one dose killed 90 percent, one hundred million cells still remained; after the second dose, ten million were left. Repeated drug doses were required to rid his mice of leukemia. Skipper also observed a clear dose-response relationship between individual drug dose and survival, concluding that the highest tolerable dose should be used. By changing drug scheduling from daily to intermittent dosing, normal cells recovered between treatments, reducing toxicity. Finally, Skipper addressed the problem of drug resistance, which limited the duration of response. If agents that killed cells in different ways were combined, he reasoned, tumor cell growth could be inhibited at several points and the emergence of drug resistance delayed. Thus, Skipper's model predicted enhanced therapeutic effect from a high-dose, intermittent, repetitive dose schedule employing multiple agents. These new concepts challenged the traditional use of single drugs in low doses. His brilliant observations established the principles that would become the framework for modern combination chemotherapy. Few cancer specialists embraced his ideas at the time, but those who understood his work realized that he had given them a new, more logical way to attack cancer. Emil (Tom) Frei III and Emil J. Freireich at the NCI applied Skipper's concepts to the treatment of childhood leukemia, raising the complete response rate to an unprecedented 84 percent. For the first time, children with leukemia survived more than a year.

By the mid-1960s, the stage was set for a major breakthrough in the chemotherapeutic approach to Hodgkin's disease. Four agents with different mechanisms of action and nonoverlapping toxicities had been found effective. The basic principles for combination chemotherapy had been determined in mice. All that was needed was a lead player who would link these observations, who was willing to take risks and withstand criticism because he knew he could do better, because like Henry Kaplan, he didn't accept tumor shrinkage; he wanted cure. That man was Vince DeVita.

↩

Vincent T. DeVita, Jr. was born on March 7, 1935, in the Bronx, eldest son in a family of second-generation Italians. Hard-working and ambitious, the DeVitas exemplified the promise of the American dream. Vince's grandfather, Ernest LoNano, had immigrated to the United States at age sixteen and obtained a job restoring antiques. Eventually he owned an interior design company which

Rockefeller commissioned to help renovate historic Williamsburg, Virginia. Vince's father was equally determined. Having dropped out of high school to help support his immigrant family, he attended night school, entered banking, and eventually was promoted to manager at First National City Bank. Young Vince admired his father who was also a superb athlete, onetime New York City handball champion. The DeVitas lived in a rented duplex in the Bronx. Vince's childhood memories included Giants games at the Polo Grounds, swimming at Orchard Beach, crabbing with his father at City Island. When he was seven, his family moved to Westchester County. On Sundays, aunts, uncles, and cousins sat at tables in the backyard, eating and playing cards. The family picnicked at Peach Lake; in the evenings, his mother played Italian arias on the piano.

In grade school, Vince began to show an interest in science. His mother often found him in the basement, tinkering with his chemistry set, or on the front steps, dissecting a frog. She informed relatives, friends, and neighbors that Vince was going to be a great physician. "I always knew I was going to be a doctor," DeVita said. "My mother told me."

When Vince entered Roosevelt High School, he found students divided into warring gangs. He slicked his black hair back in a ducktail and lifted weights so he had something to show when he flexed his muscles. On weekends, he and friends went looking for trouble, which usually involved a girl. They partied often, and not infrequently Vince slipped up the back stairs with liquor on his breath. At the same time, he excelled at his studies and felt increasingly drawn to the sciences. If known, this would ruin his popularity. "I spent a lot of time pretending that I wasn't doing much," he said.

Vince would be the first in his family to go to college. He was looking at New York City schools when he received an acceptance from the College of William and Mary to which he had not thought of applying. He learned that his uncle was restoring antiques in Williamsburg and knew influential people. As Vince left for college, his uncle's parting words were "don't embarrass me."

Vince found the formal atmosphere at William and Mary foreign. Men had crew cuts and said "please" and "thank you." Women wore white gloves and pearls and waited for the door to be held for them. "Yes" was a two-syllable word. Into this civilized world came Vince DeVita with his ducktail and New York accent. "When I arrived at William and Mary," he said, "I went ninety miles an hour. They slowed me down to seventy." And he got a crew cut.

Fearful he would flunk out and disappoint his mother, Vince studied hard, ranking fourth in his freshman class. But the lure of a social life soon seduced him. He pledged Phi Kappa Tau, played varsity baseball, and joined the yearbook staff. A chemistry major, he now rushed through his laboratory exercises and crammed for tests; his grades began to suffer.

The gatekeeper for entrance into medical school was Alfred Armstrong, professor of chemistry, a demanding teacher revered and feared by students. One day, when Vince was walking behind him, Armstrong abruptly stopped, turned around, and said, "Mr. DeVita, I understand you have joined a fraternity." Vince was stunned that Armstrong even knew him. "Your grades are slipping," he said, "and I understand you want to enter medicine." He walked on, leaving Vince to wonder why he had singled him out. He concluded that his professor must have been watching him, must believe he could succeed. That brief interaction gave Vince pause. Did he want to be a doctor—yes. Was his mother working hard to save for medical school—yes. Would he get into medical school—probably not. He started declining social invitations, logged more hours in the library. He returned to his studies with such vigor that he graduated near the top of his class—and was accepted into medical school.

No one, however, had as much influence on taming DeVita as Mary Kay Bush, a poised, petite coed from Louisiana. Smitten, Vince dressed more carefully and refined his language. After graduation and two months of Marine boot camp, he married Mary Kay and entered George Washington University School of Medicine.

There he excelled. The chairman of Physiology, C. Adrian Hogben, recognized DeVita's talent and asked him to join his research group for the summer in Bar Harbor, Maine, where he studied the secretion of hydrogen ions in the swim bladder of the goosefish. Homer Smith, a famed renal physiologist, had a laboratory there called the "kidney shed." On Monday evenings when Smith finished work, he hung out a white flag, and everyone went over to his lab to eat mussels, drink martinis, and talk science. Inspired by these brilliant men, DeVita vowed to devote his life to research. "My life might have taken a completely different turn," he said, "if I had not gone to Bar Harbor that summer."

At Bar Harbor, DeVita met Dave Rall, a pharmacologist from the National Institutes of Health (NIH), a major center for training research scientists located in Bethesda, Maryland. Rall encouraged him to apply for a research position following his medical residency. Fellowships at one of the NIH's eleven specialized institutes were highly competitive and were usually given to young physicians from a handful of elite schools—Harvard, Johns Hopkins, Yale. DeVita loved cardiology and applied to the Heart, Blood and Lung Institute. At the interview, he was so anxious he couldn't recall any details of his goosefish research. He was accepted by the Cancer Institute, mainly through Rall's recommendation.

In 1963, when DeVita began his training in oncology, the NIH was a national effort in biomedical research unequaled in the world. Its atmosphere felt charged with adventure. The Medicine Branch, which tested clinical application of new drugs, was headed by Emil (Tom) Frei III, a zealot in his fight against cancer. Born into a family of artists, Frei had been influenced as a teen by Hans Zinsser's study of typhus fever, *Rats, Lice, and History*, and turned his back on his father's stained-glass company to pursue a medical career. He was recruited to the NCI in 1955 and had already made a major impact on childhood leukemia with his aggressive regimens. An excellent clinician who cared deeply for his patients, Frei pushed on when most doctors had given up. One prior postdoctoral fellow called him an "idea generator," a "seed-sower." If a scheme sounded logical and had cancer cure as a goal, he accepted it. Researchers had free reign to pursue almost any hypothesis. "He took all the rules," DeVita said, "and threw them out the window."

DeVita was one of four clinical fellows who began training in 1963. Jack Moxley, from Boston's Peter Bent Brigham Hospital, would go on to be the youngest dean of a medical school. George Canellos, from Massachusetts General Hospital, would one day direct the cancer program at Harvard. Dean Siebert had come from Dartmouth, where he would return as a dean.

DeVita had entered the NIH planning to become a scientist, but he found he had to be a laboratory technician, pharmacist, chemotherapy nurse, and intern as well. The four clinical fellows provided daily care for all patients admitted to the cancer wards at the clinical center. Soon DeVita was working harder than he had as a resident at a large university hospital. He started intravenous lines, mixed experimental agents, and injected them. Since many had never been given before, he hovered over the patient, uncertain as to what reaction might occur. If a patient developed pneumonia, DeVita treated him; if a child suddenly went into shock, he was called; if a woman started vomiting blood, DeVita inserted a nasogastric tube and lavaged her stomach.

In the laboratory, DeVita began studying drug metabolism. In order to ascertain how the body disposed of a chemotherapeutic agent, he had to collect and analyze all the urine and stool from a patient over a 24-hour period. When he arrived on the wards each morning with his plastic buckets to collect the specimens, the other fellows called out, "Good morning, honey buckets." At first DeVita felt somewhat dispassionate about the field he had entered, but two early experiences changed his view.

The first agent he studied was BCNU, a drug shown to have activity against tumors in animals. DeVita treated patients with advanced cancer to determine the optimal dose. Among them were several patients with melanoma, a deadly cancer resistant to chemotherapy. To his amazement, two achieved complete tumor regression with BCNU. "For the first time in my life, I saw patients go into remission," DeVita said. "I thought I'd been put on this earth to cure melanoma."

Early in his first year, DeVita rotated onto the pediatric leukemia service, where he worked with Tom Frei and Emil J. Freireich. They treated children with drug combinations at high doses, pushing to the limits of tolerance, then supporting them through major infections, bleeding, and relentless vomiting. The two investigators had just started testing a new four-drug regimen, and DeVita saw a high percentage of children achieve remission. It appeared survival rates would increase substantially.

Having seen what combination chemotherapy could accomplish in leukemia, DeVita wanted to design a multi-drug trial for Hodgkin's disease. He discussed his ideas with Jack Moxley. Soon thereafter, Frei called a meeting of the clinical fellows, and when Moxley and DeVita entered the room, they found "Hodgkin's disease" written on the board, along with a list of drugs. Frei said that he thought the disease should be treated with a combination of them. That was the green light DeVita and Moxley needed.

At that time, four classes of drugs had proven effective in Hodgkin's disease, and they selected one from each: cyclophosphamide (a mustard-like drug), vincristine, methotrexate (a new agent with some activity), and prednisone. They called the regimen MOMP. They applied Skipper's basic principles of high doses, drugs with different mechanisms of action, and an intermittent schedule. Influenced by the work of Henry Kaplan, they decided to add radiotherapy, as well. After the first cycle, patients would be irradiated to all known sites of disease and then undergo two more cycles of chemotherapy. Their goal was cure. "Frei was the only senior person in the Medicine Branch at the NCI," Moxley said, "who did not believe that we were inherently insane to talk about curing Hodgkin's disease."

The proposed protocol generated immediate opposition. Paul Carbone, chief of the solid tumor service, proposed starting with a single agent and adding one drug at a time. Ralph Johnson, chief of radiation therapy, argued that no one had shown lasting benefit from chemotherapy in this disease. The group seemed to have reached an impasse with the chief of the solid tumor service on one side and the chief of radiation therapy on the other, neither agreeing with them. DeVita and Moxley held their ground, but Frei had the final decision. A pragmatist, he knew if these two young fellows felt strongly about the trial, they would execute it expeditiously. "What the hell," he said. "Let's get this protocol going."

Before long, patients from around the country were volunteering to be experimental subjects. Although DeVita and Moxley talked with each patient about potential lethality, none withdrew. "I well remember how radical we thought this treatment was," DeVita said. "All patients were hospitalized for the entire course of treatment." While the first patient was receiving chemotherapy, DeVita paced outside the room, worried the patient might not survive. But he did, and in the following months, they saw large neck masses shrink, fevers disappear, and bedridden patients gain weight and return to work. DeVita was thrilled. "Once you see people go into remission," he said, "it gets into your blood and never leaves."

In a year, they enrolled fourteen patients. Half had stage I or II disease; half stage III. Complete regression occurred in almost all. Although no patient died from the treatment, it wasn't easy. Most experienced severe vomiting, low blood counts, hair loss, mouth ulcers, and numbness in their hands and feet. DeVita and Moxley were eager to publicize their results. Because the trial was an equally shared effort, they flipped a coin to see who would make the first presentation and who would be first author on their paper. "My recollection is that I won the toss," Moxley wrote to DeVita years later, "and chose to senior-author the first publication thereby allowing you to be thrown to the wolves in Philadelphia."

In April 1965, the American Association for Cancer Research held its fifty-sixth annual meeting in Philadelphia. DeVita presented their paper, entitled "Intensive Combination Chemotherapy and X-Irradiation in the Treatment of Hodgkin's Disease." David Karnofsky, chief of Memorial Sloan-Kettering Cancer Center and among the most respected oncologists of the day, chaired the session. DeVita was so nervous that he had to hold the microphone tight to keep it from shaking. He reported that thirteen of fourteen patients had achieved a complete remission and concluded that the MOMP combination looked promising.

Karnofsky spoke first: "You can't use 'complete remission' for solid tumors. That's a term borrowed from acute leukemia." "But the tumors disappeared," DeVita replied, surprised by his reaction. Karnofsky proceeded to chastise De-Vita for reporting his data prematurely. Others in the audience pointed out that nine of his patients had received radiotherapy in addition, and that regression could have been achieved by that alone. Few were convinced. But DeVita was. He had seen fevers abate and lymph nodes disappear long before radiotherapy started. He knew he could cure Hodgkin's disease, and he set out to prove it.

MOMP had been more powerful in treating this disease than any chemo-therapy to date, but DeVita wasn't satisfied. The regimen didn't include what he now considered to be two of the most potent drugs—nitrogen mustard and procarbazine, a promising new agent. In consultation with Frei and Carbone, he designed a new four-drug regimen called MOPP. On the first and eighth day of each monthly cycle, patients received nitrogen mustard and vincristine intravenously, and for fourteen days, took procarbazine and prednisone pills. A two-week rest period followed, during which bone marrow could recover. He planned six cycles. MOPP embodied the same basic principles as MOMP: use of four drugs, each of which killed cells in a different way; optimal doses; nonoverlapping toxicities; intermittent administration to allow normal cell re-covery; and enough cycles to ensure complete cell kill.

To forestall the criticism this trial was sure to generate, they enrolled only patients with advanced disease, and each underwent a thorough clinical evaluation. Tests were repeated at completion of therapy, and a patient was designated as having achieved complete remission only when all abnormal physical findings, radiographs, and laboratory tests returned to normal. They specified definitions for complete and partial response, remission duration, and survival. This trial established high standards for the conduct of chemotherapy trials.

DeVita opened the protocol while still a clinical fellow. The first patient to enter was a twenty-year-old man who had disease in lymph nodes, liver, lung, and bone with associated fever, sweats, and weight loss. One week after the first treatment, he abruptly went into shock and died. At autopsy, the bowel was found to be extensively involved with Hodgkin's disease; a perforation had caused his death. Shortly thereafter, a thirty-eight-year-old man with Hodgkin's disease of the lung entered the trial. After the first cycle of MOPP, he developed a lung abscess and died. These two deaths put enormous pressure on DeVita from other NCI investigators. He might have stopped the trial, but then a twelve-year-old girl with extensive lung and liver disease entered complete remission. And he saw more and more of these. "Vince was a treater," Moxley said. "He always believed that cancer can be cured, and you've got to move forward with that as your goal. He used MOMP with that in mind; he used MOPP with that in mind."

DeVita had arranged to finish his training in internal medicine at Yale following his NCI fellowship. Having treated only fourteen patients with MOPP, he was reluctant to leave. Moxley had been appointed assistant dean at Harvard, and Frei had taken a position at the MD Anderson Cancer Center in Houston. Paul Carbone agreed to assume responsibility for the study. A year later, DeVita returned to the NCI as a senior investigator. Carbone had added twelve more patients to the MOPP trial and modified the regimen slightly by changing the schedule of prednisone. The results were impressive. Most who had achieved a complete response were still in remission. MOPP proved effective in teenagers as well as sixty-year-olds; it eradicated disease in the liver, bone, and even unusual sites, such as the bowel and pancreas. Although the study merited report, DeVita hesitated. Stung by Karnofsky's criticism of MOMP, he decided to wait until the trial had matured before publicly reporting the data. By 1967, they had treated thirty patients, many of whom they had followed for over three years. He submitted an abstract to the American Association of Cancer Research (AACR), and it was accepted.

The fifty-eighth annual meeting of the AACR was held at the elegant Edgewater Beach Hotel in Chicago. Twelve hundred attended the conference, including the leading cancer specialists from around the world. Henry Kaplan delivered the presidential address, entitled "On the Natural History of the

Murine Leukemias." Three hundred abstracts of recent scientific advances had been selected for ten-minute presentations.

DeVita felt apprehensive as he approached the podium. He knew Henry Kaplan and other prominent figures sat in the audience. The goal of MOPP chemotherapy, he began, was to increase the complete response rate and prolong the duration of remission for patients with advanced Hodgkin's disease, a heretofore incurable group. The majority of patients on his trial had the worst prognosis—stage IV disease and systemic symptoms. After outlining the regimen, he detailed the toxicity: all patients experienced nausea and vomiting; a third had hair loss; most suffered numbness in the fingers and toes. Depression of white blood counts was occasionally severe, putting patients at risk for infection. Yet some continued to work throughout the treatment period. Twenty-seven patients—90 percent—had achieved a complete response. Only three had relapsed; some had been in remission for over two years. In closing, DeVita drew conclusions more tentative than those he had expressed at the 1965 conference. "It appears," he said, "that combinations of active agents can increase the number of complete remissions obtained in previously untreated advanced Hodgkin's disease." Oncologist John Ultmann recalled the audience's reaction as one of incredulity. Many asked questions regarding the accuracy of staging and management of toxicity. No one was ready to accept MOPP; most still believed that patients with advanced Hodgkin's disease couldn't be cured.

DeVita had been able to test such a novel and aggressive approach only because he worked at the NCI. The staff at most hospitals never would have allowed it. Even some of his NCI colleagues thought him crazy. At a meeting of the NCI-sponsored Lymphoma Task Force, one prominent oncologist asked, "Have any of your patients ever spoken to you again?" A senior hematologist on the National Cancer Advisory Board was outraged and questioned whether MOPP was ethical. DeVita didn't retreat. He knew MOPP could cure patients, and at every chance, he presented his data. Eventually, the furor began to subside, and investigators began to try MOPP. When they saw their own patients enter remission, they began to accept it. In 1970, DeVita published the completed trial in *Annals of Internal Medicine*. "In the wake of that publication," Frei said, "there immediately appeared a 50 to 60 percent reduction in the mortality from Hodgkin's disease." In time, MOPP became the standard therapy for advanced stages of the disease. And following its acceptance, DeVita's career soared.

↜

Over the years, some investigators have contended that DeVita received more acclaim for MOPP than was his due. Does credit for developing MOPP belong to Vince DeVita or was he simply the team member most in the spotlight?

Jack Moxley considered the MOMP trial a joint endeavor but felt that MOPP was clearly Vince's achievement. He and DeVita appreciated Frei's enthusiasm, remembering him as "paving the way." Paul Carbone recalled the story differently: Tom Frei, then chief of the Medicine Branch, wanted to explore the concept of combination chemotherapy for Hodgkin's disease and organized the work for the junior people. Frei, too, saw MOMP and MOPP as a collaborative effort between DeVita, himself, and Carbone, although in 1977, he wrote, "Vince deserves . . . a lion's share of the credit for the MOPP program." All agree that Frei and Freireich created an atmosphere at the NCI that fostered innovation. "Great outspoken characters," Canellos called them. "Unfettered by the medical diplomacies of the times, they were fearless." Frei constantly threw out ideas and provoked young investigators to pursue them. With regard to MOPP, Canellos said, "Tom Frei was the spark, but Vince DeVita was the fuel." Besides, Frei left the NCI to go to MD Anderson Hospital in March 1965, at which point only one patient had been treated with MOPP.

And what about Carbone? How much credit did he deserve? Carbone felt he had made some substantive changes in the protocol, but others remember him as initially obstructive, later merely nurturing the trial along in Vince's absence. DeVita felt miffed that once MOPP proved successful, everyone wanted credit. "While I was away, the protocol had to be retyped," he said. "The guy that retyped it used to say that he wrote the protocol for MOPP."

In reality, no one person was totally responsible for MOPP. Researchers had discovered the four chemotherapeutic agents by chance. Howard Skipper had established the basic principles for chemotherapy delivery from his mouse leukemia model. The concept of combination chemotherapy had been tested in childhood leukemias by Freireich and Frei. The significance of DeVita's work was that he took Skipper's principles, modified them, and applied them to a disease considered incurable with chemotherapy. Someone had to believe that the disease could be cured and persevere despite censure. That person was Vince DeVita. "Who actually designed MOPP is less important," an NCI investigator said, "because it was clear that Vince really believed in it and had a single-minded focus in pursuing it." He disputed the prevailing palliative approach avowed by most oncologists and hematologists, and he challenged the supremacy of radiotherapy as the only curative modality for Hodgkin's disease.

Vince DeVita was to medical oncology what Henry Kaplan was to radiation therapy. They were, however, yet to meet.

22   A Walking Textbook of Radiation Morbidity

"In my opinion," Henry Kaplan wrote in the *New England Journal of Medicine*, "patients with . . . Stage III-A or III-B disease have a significant chance for cure by the techniques available." Kaplan felt that he had failed Joey Radicchi; his initial treatment should have been more aggressive.

In May 1965, thirteen-year-old Joey had completed low-dose total lymphoid irradiation on the L-2 protocol. Kaplan objected to having a low-dose, palliative arm. He preferred to treat everyone with his high-dose approach, but Rosenberg had convinced him they needed a randomized trial to prove its superiority. Nine months after completion of treatment, Joey developed a fever, and a chest x-ray showed enlarged lymph nodes in his mediastinum—recurrent Hodgkin's disease. Since Joey's disease was confined to the lymph nodes, Kaplan still considered him curable. He treated Joey again, this time with the doses and ports of the high-dose arm. Between March and June of 1966, Joey received 4,000 rads to a mantle and inverted Y, bringing his total dose to an unprecedented 5,700 rads to all lymphoid groups.

This was much harder than low-dose irradiation. Treatment to the mantle field gave Joey a continually sore throat and damaged his salivary glands, causing thick, scanty saliva. Even his mother's spicy spaghetti sauce seemed tasteless. During irradiation to the abdominal field, chronic nausea further diminished his enjoyment of food. The most problematic symptom, however, was the overwhelming lassitude that came on an hour after each treatment. Every afternoon, Joey had to nap. Evaluations and treatments became so time-consuming that Joey and his mother moved into a motel close to Stanford Hospital. Kaplan paid the bill, as well as the expenses for gasoline, from his grant, but he couldn't ease the disruption to Joey's family. Nello Radicchi had to care for their four daughters alone; five-year-old Kathleen only saw her mother on weekends. So they felt relieved when at completion of therapy, Kaplan told Mrs. Radicchi that her son was in remission.

Joey just wanted to be a normal teenager and attend school, go to the beach with friends, hunt quail with his father, and date. But repeated complications confined him to the hospital, and a series of debilities limited his activities. Radiotherapy to his bones arrested his development, and Joey stopped growing at five feet. Radiation affected the growth centers unequally, resulting in asymmetrical maturation of his bones. His arms and legs lengthened normally, but his trunk was stunted. Impaired development of his breastbone and collarbones made his chest concave. His neck looked emaciated, his spine twisted. Despite these "skeletal stigmata" of therapy, as they were called, Joey never complained.

Then, just as he was regaining his strength, Joey broke out in blisters on his chest wall. They were so painful that he couldn't stand to wear clothing. The local doctor called it poison oak, but Mrs. Radicchi knew poison oak didn't hurt. She drove Joey back to Stanford Hospital, where a radiotherapy resident diagnosed herpes zoster, or shingles. He explained that after a child had chicken pox, the virus remained dormant in the body. Suppression of the immune system could reactivate it. They had seen this complication in 15 percent of irradiated patients with Hodgkin's disease. Fortunately, the infection did not spread to Joey's lungs or liver, but he suffered weeks of burning pain and was left with scars from his breastbone to spine.

Months after completing radiotherapy, Joey experienced further side effects: a shrunken left kidney, damaged by scatter from irradiation to the spleen; weakness of his left arm, attributed to nerve injury from mantle irradiation. Then he developed a hacking cough and shortness of breath. A chest x-ray showed a collection of fluid between the two layers of tissues lining the lung. These pleural effusions were thought to result from radiation pneumonitis, a pulmonary reaction to radiotherapy. A resident performed a thoracentesis, inserting a needle between Joey's ribs and threading a catheter into the pleural space to drain off fluid.

Shortly thereafter, Joey became so winded that he could only walk a few steps before resting. His cardiac exam revealed a scratchy sound with each heartbeat. Termed a friction rub, this finding indicated inflammation of the pericardium, the sac surrounding his heart. A series of x-rays revealed an enlarged heart shadow, and he underwent cardiac catheterization, which showed fluid filling the pericardium. A cardiac surgeon inserted a needle next to Joey's heart and removed a pint of fluid. The final diagnosis was radiation pericarditis. High-dose irradiation had damaged the pericardium, resulting in scar tissue that acted like a steel sock around the heart, limiting its ability to contract properly and causing heart failure. In the spring of 1967, while his friends were dancing to the Beatles, Joey was wheeled into the operating room for a pericardiectomy, stripping a thick, fibrotic peel from around his heart. He came home from the hospital having lost forty pounds, his skin taut over his bony prominences. Although the staff saw Kaplan smile when Joey came for follow-up visits, it was painful for him to see the boy suffer almost every known complication. "Joey was a walking textbook of radiation morbidity," radiotherapist Eli Glatstein said.

Just when Joey seemed to be recovering, he began to have intermittent fevers up to 104°, requiring more hospitalizations. No infection was found, and Kaplan and Rosenberg began to suspect recurrent Hodgkin's disease, but tests revealed nothing. In the spring of 1968, two years after his radiotherapy, they recommended exploratory surgery in attempts to determine the cause. When Rosenberg entered the surgical waiting room, Mrs. Radicchi looked at his face and knew that they had discovered Hodgkin's disease. He gently explained that the surgeons had found two spots in the liver, each the size of a quarter, and the abdominal nodes and spleen were involved, as well. They had given Joey a radical course of irradiation, and still his disease had recurred.

"What do we do next?" Mrs. Radicchi asked. Rosenberg could not be optimistic. He had not observed long-term remissions from chemotherapy. "Drug therapy should be reserved for palliation," he had written in 1966, "and has no established value as a curative approach." Initially, Kaplan had not been impressed with chemotherapy either. At the time when DeVita was beginning to analyze his results with MOPP, Kaplan had stated: "At present, radiotherapy is the only modality known to offer a significant chance for cure. Thus, a decision to attempt cure is tantamount to a decision to use radiotherapy." His opinion, however, had begun to change after he heard DeVita present the MOPP data in Chicago. Initially skeptical, he analyzed DeVita's data from every angle. Besides judging the data, Kaplan took notice of the man. He liked smart people, and he appreciated how DeVita persisted despite intense criticism.

Kaplan concluded that if they were going to give Joey Radicchi chemotherapy, they should try MOPP. Rosenberg was reluctant. He usually treated with one drug at a time; MOPP combined the four most active agents simultaneously. And MOPP required high drug doses, whereas Rosenberg used the smallest dose possible to control symptoms. If he knew a patient wasn't curable, quality-of-life issues were the primary consideration. Why strip a patient of his dignity by making him bald during the last months of life? How could a patient enjoy his family if he was continuously nauseated? These toxicities were only tolerable if the outcome was cure, and he wasn't yet convinced that MOPP would achieve this. He was waiting to see what happened when DeVita treated a larger number of patients. But once Kaplan had made up his mind, he was impatient. He criticized Rosenberg for his conservative approach and badgered him until he agreed to try MOPP.

The first patient to receive the regimen had had multiple recurrences and reached the limits of radiotherapy. Joan Bull, a senior oncology fellow, helped Rosenberg treat patients. "I remember giving those first syringes of MOPP," Bull said. "I felt like I was setting off an atom bomb." They anxiously awaited the potential reaction. That first patient had a dramatic response, superior to anything they had seen with single drugs. The most difficult toxicity was vomiting, which lasted for hours. The team had only treated a handful of patients with MOPP when Joey Radicchi relapsed.

Rosenberg told Mrs. Radicchi that they could give Joey a chemotherapy regimen called MOPP, but it was experimental, and the side effects could be substantial. She understood that if it worked, at least her son had a chance; if they did nothing, the disease would progress, and in a few months, he would be dead. Nello Radicchi said he didn't want his son to be a guinea pig any more, but they left the decision up to Joey. "I'll take it," he said. "What have I got to lose?"

The next six months were more difficult than anything Joey had endured. Two days each month, he received intravenous injections of nitrogen mustard and vincristine, and for two weeks he took procarbazine and prednisone pills. With each injection, he suffered hours of retching followed by weeks of chronic nausea. The first time he took antinausea medicine, he had an allergic reaction, and his tongue swelled until it almost choked him. His hair thinned; his blood counts fell dangerously low. But Joey never complained. His positive outlook and sense of humor touched the oncology nurses. No matter how sick he was, he insisted on the five-bed ward, instead of a private room. He comforted other young men who were just beginning treatment. The hospital became the social center of his teenage years.

By that time, Joey understood the seriousness of his situation. Interested in learning more about Hodgkin's disease, he asked for reading material. "Mom," he said one day when she came to visit, "you didn't tell me I have cancer."

"I told you you have Hodgkin's disease," she replied, "and you done good so far."

Joey had his mother's indomitable spirit. And he enjoyed practical jokes. One April first, he enlisted the help of nurse Maureen O'Hara and radiotherapy resident Norman Coleman in order to play a trick on the senior resident, Eli Glatstein. They taped a urinary catheter in the palm of Joey's hand and strung the tubing down his shirt, attaching it to a large syringe. He lodged the syringe, filled with saline, between his knees. Then they bandaged his hand with gauze and waited. Following the lymphoma staging conference, Dr. Glatstein made hospital rounds on the patients with the younger residents, students, and nurses. As he approached Joey's bed, Maureen said, "I feel terrible. We dropped an IV bottle and cut Joey's hand." When Glatstein bent over to examine his hand, Joey squeezed the plunger between his knees, squirting him in the face.

"April Fool!" he cried. All the patients on the ward laughed. Joey's roommate had to hold a pillow over his recent incision to keep from pulling his stitches. Eli shook his head as he chuckled affectionately. "You got me," he said.

In February 1969, Joey completed chemotherapy. All he wanted to do was return to Santa Cruz and be like other eighteen-year-olds. He attended Cabrillo College and pursued an interest in gems and minerals. Lynette, a distant cousin, wrote to him frequently. He invited her to family parties, and when the family went to Lake Tahoe, he took her to see Diana Ross. But these good times were cut short when the vincristine began to affect his nerves. At first he had numbness and tingling in his legs, then weakness, requiring a cane to walk. The neuropathy progressed until he couldn't pick up his feet and had to use leg braces. When they went fishing, his father had to carry him.

Joey had battled Hodgkin's disease for four years, much of which time he had spent in a drenching sweat or in a hospital bed vomiting. He had been robbed of a foot of height and the use of his legs, and he had a scar down the center of his chest and another crossing his abdomen. He often labored to breathe. Yet he was thankful to be alive. Following six months of MOPP chemotherapy, he went into remission, and his Hodgkin's disease never recurred.

23   Living Autopsies

Cancer specialists around the world were beginning to regard the Stanford team as the avant garde of lymphoma research. But when a 1969 publication from the group recommended that a major operation—staging laparotomy—be performed on newly diagnosed Hodgkin's disease patients, many considered it crazy. And the first author was a relatively unknown radiotherapist—Eli Glatstein. While still a trainee, he opened a new chapter in the history of Hodgkin's disease.

Born in Muscatine, Iowa, in 1938, Glatstein met Kaplan when he attended medical school at Stanford. He began his residency in the Department of Radiology there in July of 1967. His nickname—"Mr. Wonderful"—captured his essence. Glatstein was bright as well as facile with the literature. "He knew absolutely everything," a fellow resident said. And he worked thirteen-hour days, arriving at six-thirty in the morning and staying until seven-thirty or eight, even on Saturdays. It was his buoyancy, however, that made him so appealing. Glatstein took immense pleasure in whatever he did. He could be heard whistling while checking port films. And only Glatstein could get away with putting his arm around the chief technician, who stood a head taller, calling her "toots." When he entered a room, he infused it with his joie de vivre.

During Glatstein's first year of residency, Kaplan took a sabbatical leave to write a book on Hodgkin's disease. He and Herb Abrams read most lymphangiograms, but Abrams had left to become chief of Radiology at a Harvard hospital. The remaining radiologists felt less confident about interpreting lymphangiograms, and reports came back labeled "suspicious" or "worrisome," instead of definitively positive or negative. The lymphoma team relied on these radiographs to determine the presence of Hodgkin's disease in intra-abdominal nodes. If they were interpreted inaccurately, the therapeutic plan might be inappropriate: a stage III patient erroneously thought to be stage I could have disease below the diaphragm left untreated. A stage I patient mistakenly called stage III might receive more aggressive irradiation than necessary.

Glatstein was working in the lymphoma clinic with Saul Rosenberg at the time, and he became frustrated with equivocal lymphangiogram interpretations. Rosenberg told him that over the years, to help determine stage, they had sent selected patients for an operation called exploratory laparotomy. With this procedure, the surgeon removed suspicious nodes, and the pathologist determined whether or not they were involved with Hodgkin's disease. Rosenberg and Glatstein began to request this procedure on more patients—twenty-five in a six-month period. And they suggested that as long as the surgeon was exploring the abdomen, he might as well remove the spleen. As far as was known at that time, it had no important function. Its presence made radiotherapy technically more difficult, since including the spleen in the radiation port subjected the nearby kidney to radiation injury. And they asked the surgeon to biopsy the liver, which occasionally harbored disease.

Glatstein and Rosenberg hadn't anticipated the findings. A number of newly diagnosed patients with normal-sized spleens were found to have unsuspected disease in the spleen at laparotomy. Had these patients not had exploratory surgery, they would have received insufficient treatment. Intrigued by these observations, Eli decided to review the records of all Hodgkin's disease patients who had undergone laparotomy at Stanford and to determine how accurate their clinical assessment had been. He tabulated initial physical findings, laboratory and x-ray results, and reviewed the detailed operative and pathology reports, correlating findings, site by site.

When Kaplan returned, Glatstein presented his data at a seminar. He described thirty-seven patients with Hodgkin's disease who had been subjected to laparotomy because of an ambiguous lymphangiogram interpretation, suspected liver involvement, or a slightly enlarged spleen. All had undergone complete clinical evaluation and been assigned a clinical stage. At surgery, splenectomy had been performed, as well as biopsies of the abdominal nodes and liver. Glatstein reported the following: prior to surgery, twenty-three patients had had enlarged spleens, assumed to be involved with Hodgkin's disease. Upon splenectomy, nine of them had no malignant cells. Of the fourteen patients with spleens of normal size—thus assumed to be negative—nine were found to contain Hodgkin's disease. Thus, clinical examination had been highly inaccurate in predicting splenic involvement. He had discovered clinical assessment of the liver to be equally erroneous. Twelve patients were considered to have hepatic Hodgkin's disease based on an enlarged liver or abnormal blood tests, but at surgery only five proved positive. The others had benign liver conditions. "It is disheartening to see how unreliable routine liver function studies have been in the detection of liver involvement," Glatstein remarked.

Lymphangiograms had been more accurate, but not infallible. If the radiologist had called a test positive, he was right 70 percent of the time, and if he read it as negative, he was correct 82 percent of the time. Where the radiologist had been uncertain and interpreted a lymphangiogram as "equivocal," abdominal nodes were positive in a third of patients. Glatstein calculated that approximately 20 percent of patients in his study had more extensive disease than anticipated by clinical assessment and would have been undertreated. Twice this number were found to have less disease at laparotomy. He concluded: "Laparotomy, splenectomy, liver biopsy, and para-aortic lymph node biopsy may be valuable supplements to the diagnostic evaluation of selected patients with Hodgkin's disease." For short, they called this operation staging laparotomy.

The implications of Glatstein's data were profound. The Stanford trials had been based on the premise that most patients could be cured if evaluated precisely and treated aggressively. Glatstein had detected inaccurate clinical assessment in a high percentage of cases. After the presentation, Kaplan sought him out and said, "That was a very good seminar. I think you ought to write it up for publication." He paused and smiled. "Then we'll let you burst forth on an unsuspecting world."

Glatstein worked hard on his paper and felt satisfied his sixth draft was good enough to give to Dr. Kaplan. Two days later, Kaplan handed it back, riddled with red. He had such tiny handwriting that Glatstein almost needed a magnifying glass to read it. "Kaplan could probably write *War and Peace* on one page," he said. Kaplan had crossed out words, inserted conjunctions, moved paragraphs, and scribbled in new phrases. No sentence was left untouched. Glatstein was sitting in the resident's room, staring at the paper when Gerry Hanks, a young faculty member, walked in. "What's the matter?" he asked. "You look depressed." Glatstein held up the paper. "Oh," Hanks said. "You've given a manuscript to the great man. Lots of red, huh?"

"Every page," Glatstein replied.

"Don't feel bad," Hanks said. "The first time I gave him a manuscript, he stopped on page three and gave it back to me with a note that read, 'Put this in English.'"

Kaplan might have criticized Glatstein's grammar, but he took no issue with the content. This young resident had shaken up the field of Hodgkin's disease. Not only had he shown how inexact their clinical evaluation had been, but he had demonstrated the value of staging laparotomies. Kaplan concluded that they should perform this procedure on all newly diagnosed patients. Rosenberg hesitated. What if a potentially curable patient died from operative complications? But Kaplan had great confidence in his surgical team, led by Tom Nelsen. "Kaplan was off and running," Glatstein said, and beginning in 1968, staging laparotomy was performed routinely on all new patients, unless they had had a positive bone marrow or liver biopsy prior to surgery.

As word that the Stanford team was subjecting patients to this operation spread, cancer specialists expressed mixed reactions. "There were a lot of raised eyebrows," Rosenberg recalled. Some considered this a major step. Most, however, thought the procedure unnecessary. At every major cancer conference, Kaplan had to defend it. Ralph Johnson, chief of the Radiation Branch at the National Cancer Institute, accused the Stanford team of performing "living autopsies."

But they persisted, and in time, they reported results on almost three hundred patients, confirming that laparotomy altered the stage in almost 20 percent of patients and ultimately influenced treatment in a third. Moreover, the data obtained allowed Rosenberg and Kaplan to make important observations about the spread of the disease. They plotted initial sites of disease and sites of recurrence, adding to Rosenberg's previous database. With this information, they substantiated their premise that Hodgkin's disease progressed in an orderly fashion. And these data lent more credence to their belief that contiguous nodes should be included in the radiation field along with diseased nodes.

⌒

Even though staging laparotomy was becoming routine at Stanford, Rosenberg still felt uneasy sending a debilitated patient like Mary Murray for a major operation.

Mary considered the fall of her senior year at California State Hayward idyllic. She spent four months in France, traveling with French Professor Elie Vidal. Shy and somewhat introverted, Mary had grown up in a middle-class Catholic family in San Leandro, California. Living abroad boosted her self-confidence. She thought about applying to law school or joining the diplomatic corps. "The world was opening up for me," Mary said. At twenty-one, she had become a beautiful woman—willowy with fine blond hair hanging almost to her waist.

But after she had been in Paris a while, her stamina began to wane. She couldn't understand why she slept twelve hours a day. At times her lassitude became embarrassing. Once Elie and friends planned an outing to show her Normandy; Mary slept in the car for the entire trip. Strange phenomena began to occur. She awakened at night in a drenching sweat; her left shoulder and armpit ached when she drank wine.

In January 1969, after she had returned to college, Mary found a painful lump under her left arm and went to the student health service. The doctor said she likely had mononucleosis, but the blood test came back negative. He then attributed the lump to an infected pore and gave her penicillin. But the mass grew. Mary couldn't concentrate on her studies; when she sat down to read, she fell asleep. When she woke up, her armpit ached. She went to see her old family physician. By now, she had a painful lump in the other armpit, and her left breast was swollen. He told her he suspected Hodgkin's disease. A biopsy confirmed his suspicion.

Hodgkin's disease—Mary didn't understand what he meant when he called it a disease of the lymphatic system. All she knew was that she felt terrible and didn't have the means to pay for further tests or therapy. Someone suggested she go to Stanford Hospital where she might be treated free of charge on a research grant. Mary hesitated to cross the Bay and seek care at this large medical center where she knew no one, but Elie urged her to go. In March 1969, nine months after her symptoms had begun, Mary enrolled as a patient at Stanford Hospital.

When the radiotherapy resident examined Mary, he found multiple nodes in both sides of the neck. He felt a three-centimeter mass in the right axilla and a five-centimeter mass in the left with resultant swelling of her breast. Those nodes had caused the pain she felt in her armpits when she drank alcohol—a rare, but characteristic symptom of Hodgkin's disease. An x-ray revealed a large mediastinal mass in her chest. The resident felt no enlarged abdominal or groin nodes and determined her to have stage IIB disease. A staging laparotomy was recommended.

Tom Nelsen made an incision from Mary's breastbone to her navel and explored her abdomen. He found a massive cluster of rock-hard nodes adhering to the aorta. Tumor nodules covered the spleen and stuck it to the diaphragm. After removing the spleen and taking biopsies, Nelsen moved the ovaries behind the uterus to protect them from future irradiation.

Mary Murray had stage IIIB Hodgkin's disease, and the doctors began to talk to her about possible therapies. "I wasn't really aware of what was going on at the beginning," Mary said. "It was just a slow accumulation of consciousness of how serious it was." When one resident alluded to Hodgkin's disease as a "first cousin to cancer," she realized the graveness of her situation. Frightened and confused, Mary cried for an entire day despite the resident's reassurance and the nurse's attempts to comfort her. Then she met Henry Kaplan. He sat down, took her hand and asked about her: her family, her life, her fears. He told Mary about Stanford's new treatments and their successes, giving her hope. He told her he would direct her therapy, and she could always count on him.

Stage IIIB Hodgkin's disease—Mary had nodal involvement above and below the diaphragm. The staging laparotomy had revealed more disease than had been apparent. Had she not undergone the procedure, she might have been undertreated. Systemic symptoms made her prognosis worse. Even with total lymphoid irradiation, fewer than 10 percent of patients were cured. Staging laparotomy had shown Kaplan just how extensive the disease was in this young woman. Now he had to devise a scheme to eradicate it.

It was at about this time that Kaplan seriously considered adding chemotherapy to radiotherapy in attempts to improve curability. In the early 1950s, David Karnofsky at Memorial Hospital in New York City had treated a small number of early stage patients with nitrogen mustard and irradiation. But the disease still recurred. Concluding that chemotherapy added nothing to radiotherapy, Kaplan lost interest. "Mustard is for hotdogs," he used to say. Then DeVita's work on MOPP caught his attention. If MOPP proved effective in patients with stage IV disease, Kaplan postulated that its potential for stage III disease might be even greater. Total lymphoid irradiation (TLI) cured an unacceptably low percentage of patients with disease in the spleen, particularly if they had systemic symptoms. He began to talk of treating these patients with TLI, followed by six cycles of MOPP. And when Kaplan had an idea that excited him, it wasn't long before he wanted to test it.

Once again, Kaplan was moving too fast for the rest of the cancer community. Radiotherapists were leery about delivering 4,000 rads to all lymphoid groups. Most chemotherapists, hesitant about trying MOPP even in advanced disease, continued to use single agents. The controversy over staging laparotomy was still raging when Kaplan announced his new protocol. Most thought it inconceivable that patients could tolerate a year of such treatment. But Kaplan ignored public opinion. "The rest of the world didn't count," one resident said; the important discussions took place across the table at lymphoma staging conference, where Kaplan and Rosenberg continued to argue about protocols. Kaplan proposed the H-5 study for stage III patients—randomly assigning them to receive either total lymphoid irradiation, plus 3,000 rads to the liver, or the same radiation therapy followed by six cycles of MOPP. Rosenberg demurred. This trial underscored their different approaches to cancer: Kaplan anticipated unprecedented success; Rosenberg worried about potential morbidity. But Kaplan prevailed, and in August 1968, the H-5 study began.

The likelihood of Mary Murray being cured was slight, and she would normally have been given palliative treatment. Kaplan offered her the H-5 protocol. Although the potential side effects sounded formidable, Mary accepted them as necessary for survival. Besides, most were transient; she just had to endure them for the months on therapy, except one—possible infertility. That she couldn't accept. Mary loved her nieces and nephews and imagined herself surrounded by children of her own. For the first time since coming to Stanford, she wavered. Mary and Elie spent hours talking about this, the most unacceptable side effect. Even the fear of death didn't grieve her as much as the prospect of life without children.

Nonetheless, Mary agreed to participate in the H-5 study; she was the sixth patient. At staging conference, she was randomized to receive total lymphoid irradiation and MOPP. On April 14, 1969, she began daily treatments to a mantle field, which encompassed the nodes in her neck, axillae, and mediastinum. Within two weeks, her fevers, sweats, and fatigue had markedly improved. Then, just when she was feeling stronger, she developed severe abdominal pain. Radiographs showed that while disease in the radiation field was shrinking, the abdominal nodes were increasing.

Kaplan faced a dilemma: The chest and abdomen could not be irradiated simultaneously. Should he interrupt the mantle therapy and treat the abdomen? This would leave a large axillary mass untreated for weeks. Or should he finish the mantle irradiation and treat her abdominal pain with narcotics? If the nodes grew larger, they might obstruct blood vessels or the kidney. Most radiotherapists would have called this a treatment failure and sent her for palliative chemotherapy. Not Kaplan. He devised a new strategy, hoping to get Mary out of this precarious situation. He treated the upper abdomen with just enough radiation to control the enlarging nodes, finished the mantle, and then proceeded to the inverted Y, completing total nodal irradiation in less than four months. Now Mary faced six months of MOPP.

When the nurse started an intravenous line and injected two syringes of harmless-appearing clear liquid, Mary could not imagine how overwhelming the reaction would be. She suffered repeated bouts of vomiting, intense jaw pain, severe constipation, and numbness of her fingers and toes. "It was beyond my capacity to think that anything could make me feel that bad," she said. Rosenberg reduced the dose of chemotherapy, but still she had severe nausea, resulting in weight loss and fatigue.

Elie, her family, and friends brought food, helped her dress, and encouraged her to continue. But no one knew how it felt to be stuck with needles day after day for blood tests and chemotherapy, leaving the arms bruised and aching. They couldn't imagine months of constant nausea and uncontrollable vomiting that left her limp. Her feet became so weak that she found the simple act of walking awkward, and her fingers were so numb that it took several minutes for her to button her blouse. She felt as if she crawled from one day to the next. "It was a very lonely experience," Mary said. But every time she saw Dr. Kaplan, he took her hands in his and patiently listened to her concerns. He told her he understood how sick she was and how discouraged she felt. Then he said he knew she could go on.

One year after beginning therapy, Mary had completed total lymphoid irradiation and six cycles of MOPP. Kaplan examined her, reviewed her x-rays, and pronounced her in remission. She started attending classes again. Although she seemed fully recovered to friends, she still felt the psychological burden of her disease. "When you're going through treatments," she said, "you live day by day. When the treatments are over, you have this big, empty time, and now you're thinking, 'This is great, but what's going to happen a year from now.' And everyone around you is wondering too." Mary never felt really free of her disease until Henry Kaplan pronounced her cured at her five-year checkup. She and Elie married, and she pursued her studies, earning a PhD from Berkeley, followed by a professorship at Princeton. She was left, however, with two permanent scars, one from the laparotomy and the one she feared most—infertility.

She and Elie decided to adopt, but they found it wasn't so easy. Agencies focused on Mary's cancer and closed their doors. During the entire ordeal, Henry Kaplan was sympathetic and supportive, making calls and sending letters on their behalf, emphatically stating that Mary Vidal was cured. When she and Elie finally adopted twin three-year-old French girls, Mary felt her life was complete.

↬

The H-5 study had been a good outcome. Of patients with stage IIIA disease, 70 percent randomized to receive total lymphoid irradiation remained disease-free, compared with 86 percent who had received TLI and MOPP. Of patients with systemic symptoms—stage IIIB—only 8 percent randomized to TLI remained disease-free, compared with 51 percent of those treated with combined irradiation and chemotherapy. Incorporation of chemotherapy into the primary treatment program had been a success. And it had another subtle effect at Stanford. With the radiotherapy trials, Rosenberg had been involved in the design and analysis, but now he played an essential role in the patient's primary treatment. Drug delivery, dose calculations, and management of side effects required the finesse of a well-trained oncologist. Rosenberg was one of the best, and now Henry Kaplan drew upon that talent. "As chemotherapy became part of the treatment program," Rosenberg said, "and the total medical care of patients was important, Kaplan depended on me and my colleagues, knowing that the studies could not be carried out without medical oncologists." And Kaplan appreciated Rosenberg's mettle. After all, Rosenberg had been the one who had started sending patients for staging laparotomies in his absence. And he had agreed to the H-5 study, standing firm despite barbs from oncologists around the world. Residents began to notice a change in their relationship.

The Stanford lymphoma group had made major strides in the management of Hodgkin's disease. Cancer specialists were coming to recognize the value of staging laparotomy. Acceptance of the contiguity theory of the spread of Hodgkin's disease followed. And researchers worldwide began experimenting with combinations of radiation therapy and chemotherapy. These rapid changes in the field led to the 1971 Ann Arbor Conference, the next great international meeting on Hodgkin's disease.

24   Protégés

Henry Kaplan was a world-renowned cancer specialist, an international star. What did not appear on his curriculum vitae or in *Who's Who in America* was his role as a mentor. Yet he considered his students and residents among his greatest accomplishments—and his greatest joys. Kaplan was a model physician and teacher, exciting students to answer questions through research, fostering their careers. "Kaplan boys," as some referred to his successful trainees, became leaders in the cancer field.

When residents began working with Kaplan in the lymphoma clinic, they expected him to explain the mantle and inverted Y techniques, but the first thing he talked about was the most basic medical skill—the physical exam. He repeatedly pointed out findings they had missed, and which he trusted they would never miss again. Kaplan expected his trainees to exhibit the same thoroughness in everything they did. "He made you reach for the best inside you," said John Glick, who went on to become a prominent oncologist.

Chart rounds epitomized Kaplan's insistence on exactitude. Every Wednesday afternoon, the faculty, residents, and technicians divided into groups and reviewed all patients under therapy, including treatment plan, radiation ports, and side effects. Kaplan conducted his rounds with great rigor. "As residents, we always tried to please him," Harvard-trained Sarah Donaldson recalled, "so when he checked the port films, they were just right. We thought we had drawn a mantle perfectly. Then in chart rounds, he would move the field a millimeter to the left." Rounds often continued into the evening. "Time was not the critical thing," she said. "Precision was."

Residents found Kaplan's voluminous knowledge of medicine from infectious diseases to cardiology astounding. What impressed them most, however, was the way he related to patients. An imposing figure, Kaplan seemed to fill the examination room when he entered. He directed his total attention to the patient, and with a remarkable kindness and efficiency of words, he found out how the person was doing and conveyed his concerns. "The way he talked to patients and his relationships with them became one of the models in my life," Glick said. But Kaplan did more than just express his concerns; he acted upon them. When he and Donaldson were evaluating a child from Lebanon with Hodgkin's disease, Kaplan learned that the family was practically destitute, without enough money for lodging or food. He recalled that Danny Thomas, with whom he had worked on St. Jude's Children's Hospital advisory board, was a Lebanese American. He called Thomas, and a check for the family arrived a few days later.

Zvi Fuks, a dashing young Israeli radiotherapist, had come to Stanford in 1968 to learn cancer biology and new radiotherapy techniques, but he discovered something more important. The first time Fuks saw Kaplan talk to a young patient, it touched him deeply. In telling her about the treatment, Kaplan recognized how the disease had interfered with her life plans and helped her piece her shattered dreams back together. "He didn't approach her as a medical problem, but as a human being," Fuks said. "Doctors are busy and save time by moving straight to the point. Henry moved straight to the heart."

Some colleagues might have considered Henry Kaplan intimidating and occasionally brutal, but he was beloved by his trainees. "When I was a young postdoctoral fellow, I called on him . . . to borrow some white rats," G. J. Nossal, director of the Institute of Medical Research in Victoria, Australia, recalled. "It was absolutely typical of Henry that he warmed to a young upstart, full of new ideas, because he never changed in his devotion to fundamental science and his sponsorship of young workers." A former student told of her devastation when she gave birth to a severely handicapped child. "Henry came to town," she said, "and I picked him up at the airport and filled his ears with my grief and fear and lack of courage." He listened and responded openly with no sign of embarrassment. "In a few words, he conveyed to me his grasp of what caring for [my child] had meant to me . . . the wordless blend of lost opportunities for myself [and] commitment to my child. . . . I don't know anyone who has understood that as deeply as he did."

Occasionally, however, Kaplan's counsel backfired. He had advised Sarah Donaldson that in preparation for a career in pediatric radiotherapy, she should spend a year studying with Odile Schweisguth, the grand dame of pediatric oncology, at the Institut Gustave Roussy. As Donaldson was planning her trip, Kaplan recommended that she learn some French; her new colleagues would have more respect for her. He gave her several mysteries by Georges Simenon, featuring Inspector Maigret, and told her that he had learned French by reading them. Sarah tried his method and arrived in Paris feeling that she had mastered enough French to carry on a simple conversation. When she was introduced to Maurice Tubiana, chief of the radiation department, he said, "Bonjour, Mademoiselle," taking her hand and bowing slightly. "Bonjour, Monsieur," Sarah replied. She proceeded, she thought, to ask, "How are you, sir?" Instead, having learned her French from a detective story, she asked, "How you doin', kid?"

A few weeks later, as a protégé of the great Henry Kaplan, Donaldson was invited to a formal dinner with French dignitaries. When the hostess pressed her to take a second serving, Sarah replied, "No thank you. I'm too full" using her best French. Unknowingly, she had said, "No thank you. I'm pregnant." The hostess smiled and patted her arm. Sarah went on to say it was just a little problem, which would be over in a few hours. At that, the hostess became alarmed and whisked her into the powder room. Donaldson found herself surrounded by a group of women talking simultaneously and giving all kinds of advice about how to handle her problem. Weeks later, she learned they had thought she was talking about an abortion. When Donaldson returned Dr. Kaplan's mysteries, she thanked him but said next time she planned to study French the conventional way.

Kaplan watched proudly as newly trained radiotherapists left Stanford every year and began treating patients around the country. Especially rewarding were those who went on to make advances in the cancer field. While still a resident, Norm Coleman published several important observations on radiation injury to the spleen and bone marrow. "Kaplan had a great way of conceiving of an idea," he said, "making you think it was yours, leading you to the next experiments, and then letting you do them and get credit for them." Beginning his career, Eli Glatstein asked Kaplan what advice he had for someone entering academic medicine. He replied, "I have three principles I follow in my work: only fight one battle at a time, never trust anyone completely, and don't ever make a threat you don't intend to keep." As close as many trainees felt to Henry Kaplan, none of them called him "Henry" or "Hank." They addressed him as "Dr. Kaplan." But they referred to him among themselves as HSK.

⌐⌐

Sarah Donaldson's professional career flourished with Kaplan's prompting. She had not considered pediatric radiotherapy until, as a resident, she treated twenty-month-old Roberto. A Brazilian woman in a cotton housedress arrived unannounced at the radiotherapy clinic carrying a baby. She spoke only Portuguese. Kaplan and Donaldson learned that the woman had already lost a four-year-old, and when the doctors said her baby had a terminal illness called Hodgkin's disease, she had sold everything to buy a ticket to Stanford.

The four leading pediatric textbooks of the day recommended irradiation to the primary lesion and adjacent nodes for children with early-stage Hodgkin's disease. For stages III and IV, they suggested low-dose irradiation to bulky sites or single-agent chemotherapy for palliation. They described the prognosis as grave.

Kaplan didn't see why he couldn't achieve the same excellent results with children that he was having with adults. He set out to manage twenty-month-old Roberto like a twenty-year-old, recommending a lymphangiogram and laparotomy. Pediatric faculty reacted with outrage. No one had ever performed a staging laparotomy on a baby. Besides, the child would likely die from the malignancy in months. But Kaplan proceeded and confirmed that Roberto had stage IIIB disease. He planned to use total lymphoid irradiation with 4,400 rads, similar to his adult program. "It was clear," Donaldson said, "that one couldn't give extended field, high-dose irradiation to this baby who still had a teething ring in his mouth." She questioned Kaplan's proposal. His own data showed inhibition of bone growth. If Roberto reached puberty, he would have a midget trunk with relatively long arms and legs. He would look like a freak.

Kaplan considered Donaldson's concerns. "Maybe we could lower the radiation dose," he suggested, "and make up the difference with experimental chemotherapy." Donaldson agreed, and they treated Roberto with 1,500 rads of total lymphoid irradiation, followed by six cycles of MOPP chemotherapy—the first child in the world treated in this fashion. Eleven years later, when Kaplan was attending a conference in Brazil, he examined Roberto and, to his delight, found him still disease-free. "Some decreased growth of clavicles with slightly narrow shoulders," he scribbled in the chart, "but looks about normal."

A month after Roberto arrived at Stanford, Mark R., a four-year-old Mexican American boy from San Jose, was referred to Kaplan. His mother had noticed large bruises on his legs and arms, and he was vomiting blood. The pediatrician found his platelet count to be dangerously low. Assuming that the boy had idiopathic hemolytic anemia, a disease in which the spleen destroys platelets, he recommended emergency splenectomy. It revealed Hodgkin's disease. After further staging, Kaplan and Donaldson confirmed stage IIIB disease and treated the child with 2,000 rads of total lymphoid irradiation, followed by six cycles of MOPP. Eight years later, he remained disease-free and could not be distinguished in physique from his playmates.

After Mark and Roberto achieved remission without life-threatening toxicity, Kaplan encouraged Donaldson to write a protocol combining low-dose, involved-field radiotherapy and MOPP chemotherapy for children under fifteen. Pediatricians openly criticized Donaldson for this. They called subjecting children to staging laparotomy unnecessary, dangerous, and practically immoral. Donaldson countered with data showing that laparotomy changed the stage in a third of adult patients. When they said MOPP had never been given to children and was excessively harsh for palliative treatment, she responded that her intent was not palliation but cure. Most remained skeptical. Kaplan had prepared Donaldson for opposition and prompted her to defy prevailing doctrine for the sake of all children with Hodgkin's disease. "Don't let anyone talk you out of what you believe," Kaplan advised her. Donaldson withstood the bullying, and when pediatricians saw her results, they gradually began referring patients.

The radiotherapy community considered the pediatric Hodgkin's disease trial revolutionary. No one had ever proposed using chemotherapy to reduce radiation dose. After they had treated twenty-eight children, Donaldson reported preliminary results: all but one was alive, and the children had almost no growth abnormalities. Cancer specialists considered these results phenomenal; due in large part to her work, most children with Hodgkin's disease could be cured. Her achievements hadn't ended with Hodgkin's disease, however. She became a leader in the treatment of other childhood cancers as well. "When I first see a child with cancer," Donaldson said, "I'm thinking about him graduating from high school, going to college, having a career, and getting married." Considered one of the foremost pediatric radiation oncologists worldwide, Donaldson served as president of several scientific societies, and could have directed her own department, but she chose to stay at Stanford.

⌒

Zvi Fuks, a young Israeli radiotherapist, made a similar impact on mycosis fungoides (MF), a lymphoma of skin. In the late 1960s, not much was known about MF; a leading hematology textbook devoted one paragraph to the disease. Eczema-like lesions progressed to produce diffusely red, scaly skin, which disfigured the patient. Eventually, MF spread relentlessly to other organs, and cancer specialists regarded it as incurable. At Stanford, radiotherapist Malcolm Bagshaw, using a novel six-field technique, treated 107 patients with 3,000 rads to the entire skin. Working with Bagshaw while a visiting fellow, Fuks reviewed the results and discovered that 70 percent of patients with limited disease and 45 percent of those with widespread disease had achieved complete remissions. He submitted a paper to the Radiological Society of North America, and it was accepted for presentation at the December 1970 meeting in Chicago.

On the morning of his presentation, Fuks found the convention hall full. When he stepped to the podium, anxiety overcame him, and he forgot every word. Then he spotted Kaplan sitting in the second row. He looked straight at Fuks and coaxed him on with his hand. Fuks felt like a struggling musician with Kaplan as his conductor. When he began to speak, he remembered his entire talk. He described the techniques and initial responses and reported that some patients had remained free of disease as long as eleven years. "It appears highly probable," he concluded, "that they have been cured."

His data, the first to suggest that mycosis fungoides could be treated effectively, maybe cured, astonished the audience. The resounding applause surprised Fuks. As he stepped down from the stage, a crowd gathered around him. People introduced themselves, famous people; they were congratulating him and shaking his hand. Fuks felt overwhelmed; he had not expected this response. He had put a tremendous amount of energy into his talk, and in fifteen minutes, it was over. "I had a sense of emptiness," he recalled, "as if all the air had gone out of my balloon."

Fuks rushed out of the hotel and started walking. He soon found himself at the Chicago Art Institute. "On that afternoon," he said, "a very strange thing happened. I couldn't see any pictures inside the frames; they were empty." He felt a hand on his shoulder and turned to see Henry Kaplan. He told Zvi he was proud of his presentation. "Afterwards," he said, "I understood what happened to you." He had followed Fuks out of the hotel, down the street and into the museum. "I saw you wandering among the pictures," Kaplan said. "Let me show you something." He took Fuks by the hand and walked with him through the museum. "You know, I was born in Chicago," he said, "and this is my museum." He stopped in front of a Monet. "This is my favorite," he said. Fuks looked at it. A stunning picture now filled the frame.

Fuks joined a long list of Stanford trainees who became leaders in radiation therapy. "HSK loved his young people," Norm Coleman said. "He nurtured them without smothering them." When Fuks returned to Jerusalem to build a radiotherapy unit at Hadassah Hospital, Kaplan called it his gift to Israel. In time, Norman Coleman would become chief of Radiation Therapy at Harvard; John Glick, director of the Cancer Center at the University of Pennsylvania; and Eli Glatstein, head of Radiotherapy at the National Cancer Institute. Henry Kaplan populated the cancer community with superb clinicians who reflected his style of patient care and teaching. And as his legacy, he sent forth a cadre of physician-scientists who, like him, were dedicated to curing cancer.

25   Intellectual Playmates

Henry Kaplan was a paradox: although beloved by patients, revered by scientists around the world, praised by students and young researchers, he was called egotistical and belligerent by some of his closest colleagues. Friends thought him selflessly devoted; those with whom he did battle found him relentless. "Viewed from one side," he told a reporter late in his career, "I think I was a kindly physician, a role model. Viewed from another side, I was a malignant son-of-a-bitch that drove deans to despair."

∽

In 1959, when Stanford University School of Medicine moved from San Francisco to Palo Alto, its character changed. In San Francisco, faculty had prided themselves on patient care and bedside teaching. On the Stanford University campus, the school acquired a third dimension—an investigative focus. Henry Kaplan and Avram Goldstein, chairman of Pharmacology, led the transition. Both appreciated the uniqueness of a university. "In truth," Goldstein said, "the faculty is the university, who carry forward the search for knowledge . . . who train the next generation of researchers and practitioners." He and Kaplan had set out to populate the school with first-rate clinicians, teachers, and scientists—so-called "triple threats." To begin, they needed to recruit outstanding department chairmen who, in turn, would attract other luminaries and promising young trainees.

They had started at the top, recruiting Arthur Kornberg as chairman of Biochemistry and Joshua Lederberg as chairman of Genetics, both later Nobel laureates. As chairman of Medicine, Kaplan favored Halsted Holman of the Rockefeller Institute, a bench immunologist who was assumed to be an outstanding clinician like his father, Emile Holman. And as chairman of Psychiatry, Kaplan helped recruit David Hamburg from the National Institutes of Health. Hamburg had a reputation as a superb mediator, and his strong science background allowed him to converse easily with the biochemists. These chairmen, as one science writer said, "shared the vision of Stanford as a new avatar of scientific medicine."

A wonderful camaraderie suffused the Medical School. Dean Robert Alway created this climate; his primary ambition was to promote the faculty. He had almost no interest in the power of his position and decentralized control to the departments. "When we were a little group," Kaplan said years later, "the seven departments were calling the shots on everything." Kornberg found Stanford more tolerant of innovation and less concerned with protocol than eastern schools—an ideal place to build his department, free from bureaucratic interference. "There was tremendous idealism and a willingness among us to give up things for the greater good," Kaplan said. "The school improved dramatically because of that." Researchers shared equipment and pooled funds to help promising young scientists. Increasingly, lead articles in the foremost journals bore the names of Stanford faculty. Professors acquired more research grants than ever before. Patients from all over the United States traveled to Stanford for heart surgery or cancer treatment. And with its innovative curriculum, Stanford was beginning to compete for the best medical school applicants. "The Alway years," Goldstein recalled, "were characterized by great collegiality."

Socially, faculty enjoyed each other, too. Hal Holman and Henry attended ballgames with their children. When the Lederbergs came to the Kaplans' for dinner, they occasionally stayed overnight. And no party was complete without Norman Kretchmer, chairman of Pediatrics. This talkative man loved to clown around. Arthur Kornberg enjoyed dinner parties at the Kaplans', where he and his wife met artists, writers, and political scientists. The Kaplans looked forward to picnics with the Kornbergs, and they regularly shared Thanksgiving dinner. Henry spent weekends house hunting until he found the perfect home for the Kornbergs. Arthur and Henry were more than just colleagues; they became devoted friends. They argued about art and baseball, and at scientific meetings, they stayed up half the night talking. Life at Stanford had turned out just as Henry had hoped—he was surrounded by "intellectual playmates" at work, blessed with a group of invigorating, loyal friends.

But in time, the wonderful esprit de corps eroded. Faculty performance did not match expectations; personalities that had formerly been stimulating became grating. To begin with, Kaplan became disenchanted with David Hamburg. When they had first met at the NIH, Hamburg had charmed Kaplan with his personality. It became clear to Kaplan, however, that Hamburg's reputation as a great consensus builder resulted from his rarely taking a stand on an issue. And although impressive in planning, he never seemed to complete projects. Years later, Kaplan said, "One of our most terrible mistakes that started us on the road to losing our momentum was the selection of David Hamburg as Professor and Chairman of Psychiatry." Nor did Kaplan hide his disappointment with Halsted Holman. Enamored with basic science, the chairman of Medicine had been heard to say clinical experience was inconsequential. On the other hand, Kaplan had decreed that patient care had to be absolutely first-rate. "I had some memorable fights with Halsted Holman," Kaplan said, "on issues relating to that."

And the fastidiousness and authoritarian stance of his friend Arthur Kornberg was beginning to irritate Kaplan too. He felt his friend believed that winning the Nobel Prize gave credence to his opinions on any subject. Kornberg was quoted in newspapers and interviewed on television about topics as diverse as the country's economic destiny, anti-intellectualism, and the buffoonery of creationists. Leah recalled one evening when Henry and Arthur were arguing about politics. "Arthur," Henry said in frustration, "when it comes to biochemistry, I'll get down on my hands and knees before you, but when it comes to politics, you're as ignorant as anybody else."

Kaplan had set out to make Stanford an unparalleled research university, and he would not tolerate mediocrity. To that end, he continued to badger Dean Alway. When the dean resigned in 1964, many thought that Kaplan and Goldstein had pushed him to the point of exhaustion. Faculty resentment festered for years. But Alway didn't feel that way. "The medical school is truly most indebted to Henry and Avram," he later wrote, "who kept the spurs and whip at ready use."

The Dean's Selection Committee, composed of Hamburg, Holman, Kornberg, Lederberg, and Kretchmer, initiated a nationwide search for Alway's replacement. After a year of intense work, they announced their choice to be Robert Joy Glaser. A graduate of Harvard College and Medical School, Glaser had become dean of the University of Colorado School of Medicine at thirty-nine, one of the youngest deans in the country. Six years later, he assumed responsibility for all the Harvard hospitals. He came to Stanford at forty-seven with a reputation as an administrative genius. Glaser was a brash, energetic man whose limp, resulting from a childhood amputation of his lower leg, did not slow him down as he moved through a crowd. He capped his political savvy with an earnest manner. The Dean's Selection Committee saw Robert Glaser as one of a new breed, a modern dean to lead Stanford into the next decade.

Henry Kaplan wasn't opposed to Glaser's appointment. They shared similar views on the requisites for a first-rate academic medical center. Each thought he was acquiring an ally in his cause. What Kaplan didn't appreciate was the extent to which Glaser planned to centralize control. Leah noticed sooner than her husband how deftly Glaser assessed the sources of power. At a party, she watched him nodding while someone was talking to him, his eyes focused over the person's head, checking out the room. And what Glaser didn't realize was how difficult it was for Kaplan to compromise when he felt strongly about something. Glaser was set to accept Stanford's offer when Kaplan left for a European conference. Neither suspected that they were about to collide.

The issue at stake was the Medical Service Plan, which determined disbursement of professional fees. When the medical school had first moved to Palo Alto, there was no plan to manage the financial aspects of the medical practice. Faculty didn't care until they collected almost $2 million in one year. Before long, they began to argue about distribution of profits, and Alway appointed a committee, chaired by radiologist Herbert Abrams, to devise a medical service plan.

Alway had asked Abrams to write the medical practice plan because of his proficiency with the financial aspects of medicine and his impeccable integrity—he never modified his opinions for the sake of politeness or political gain. Abrams's committee hired legal counsel and spent a year devising a scheme they thought equitable. They proposed a faculty-run group in which only physicians could be members, thus excluding the basic scientists from sharing the profits. This forced the latter to fund their research from grants, not from payments for patient care. A substantial portion of net income would be allocated to the clinical departments that had earned the income. The dean would determine how the remainder was used. Kaplan was willing to share funds with other chairmen, but he wanted full authority over how his hard-earned income would be spent.

The Medical Service Plan had been in effect for almost two years when Glaser was offered the deanship. During his interviews, Abrams explained Stanford's practice plan and its faculty endorsement. Glaser assured him that he would not change this arrangement until he had worked with it for at least a year. Abrams considered his assurance binding. But after Glaser returned home, he realized that Stanford's practice plan would impose significant constraints on his ability to implement new programs. On January 22, 1965, he wrote to President Wallace Sterling, proposing a plan whereby all professional fees would be transferred to the dean, who would use this income to benefit the whole school, not selected high-earning departments. Glaser's acceptance seemed contingent on adopting his plan. On January 28, the Executive Committee, composed of all department chairmen, accepted his proposal by majority vote. Those from the basic science departments favored his scheme, since under it, they would share income they had not helped generate. Those clinical departments with unprofitable clinical activities also readily agreed. Kaplan was out of town at the time.

When Herb Abrams learned of these negotiations, he became livid and wrote to Glaser. "I have read . . . your eloquent letter to the President with great interest," he began. "I have serious reservations about [your plan's] feasibility in this state. I believe it is almost certainly illegal." In California, he explained, payments for patient care by any physician belonged to that physician. "A system in which the medical school employed physicians to render patient care for money irrevocably channeled into the medical school coffers," he said, "could be construed as the corporate practice of medicine." He implied that faculty had legal grounds on which to contest Glaser's plan. In closing, Abrams wrote, "Obviously, this is a personal letter of concern about a matter which I had thought already intelligently resolved in a spirit of amity and cooperation. Once again let me emphasize that the enthusiasm for your appointment runs very high, which surely portends very well indeed for the solution of the problems which you will confront at Stanford."

Radiobiologist Robert Kallman would never forget the day the storm broke. He was sitting in his office on a Friday afternoon when he heard a loud commotion next door. Several members of the search committee charged into Kaplan's office yelling, "Where's Kaplan? Where's Abrams?" Both were away—Henry lecturing in England, Herb skiing in Squaw Valley. Glaser had already accepted Sterling's offer when he received Abrams's letter. He called the president and threatened to withdraw his candidacy. He didn't want to confront a lawsuit the minute he arrived at Stanford.

Sterling contacted Abrams at Squaw Valley to find out why he had written such a letter. "The man has made a commitment," Abrams said bluntly, "and if he doesn't keep it, he's not the kind of man you want to be dean." Sterling immediately called members of the search committee, who were outraged. They didn't believe Abrams had acted alone and suspected Henry's hand in the affair. After all, he had a reputation as a dean killer, and who but Kaplan would display such blatant disregard for the private negotiations of a search committee. As further evidence of his involvement, they noted that the letter had been written on Radiology Department stationery. Abrams received an urgent call from his colleague Joe Kriss, saying that he should return to Stanford immediately. Kaplan was under attack and about to be condemned.

Abrams met with the Dean's Selection Committee early the next day. The Saturday morning quiet of the Medical School was accentuated by the silence he encountered when he entered the conference room. Kornberg, Lederberg, Hamburg, Kretchmer, and Holman were seated around a large table. Arthur Kornberg looked stern, with a crease between his eyebrows, his lips pressed tightly together. He opened the interrogation by asking Abrams to explain why he had written to Glaser. Abrams said he felt it imperative to advise Glaser of possible ramifications of his actions. The committee probed further, trying to ascertain his real motivation. Abrams suddenly realized that they hadn't brought him there to clarify the situation but to extract a confession. Had they known him better, they would have realized that he was not a man with a hidden agenda. "The letter spoke for itself," he said. "It was absolutely precise." They shouldn't want a dean who didn't keep his word. Kornberg accused Abrams of purposely interfering with their work. Incensed, Abrams replied, "I have never come across a more self-righteous prick than you." No one spoke. Some committee members stared down at the table; others shifted in their seats. They had expected an apology from Abrams, but none was forthcoming. He had no regrets.

Next they turned to Kaplan's role. Despite Abram's protestations, they sensed Kaplan's Machiavellian touch and denounced him as an accomplice. Abrams looked from one committee member to the next in disbelief. How could Kornberg and Lederberg, supposed friends of Kaplan's, impugn him? Hamburg should have been sensitive to the effect this accusation would have on Kaplan, but he posed no objections. It didn't matter what Abrams said; the committee had already drawn its conclusions and called for a vote of censure. "I simply will not hear any more of this nonsense," Abrams said, and he walked out.

Unaware of what had transpired, Kaplan returned from England to find himself a pariah. David Hamburg was selected to speak to him; as a psychiatrist, he had expertise in dealing with difficult people. Leah Kaplan recalled the morning Hamburg came by their house. Henry was exhausted after almost twenty-four hours of travel. They went into Kaplan's study and closed the door. Leah didn't know when Hamburg left, but half an hour later, Henry came out of the study. His teeth were clenched; his face looked pale. He told Leah what had happened: Hamburg had begun the conversation by saying, "You were so good to me when I first came to Stanford." He proceeded to inform Kaplan that they knew of his devious maneuverings and had resolved to give Glaser full allegiance. Leah was shocked at Hamburg's brusqueness, at his disregard for the pain he was inflicting.

Henry was crushed. Colleagues had seemingly overnight become adversaries, attempting to expel him from the Executive Committee. He couldn't understand how he could have worked so hard for the school and generated such animosity. These weren't just associates; many were his friends, men with whom he had shared holidays, attended Stanford football games, argued baseball. He couldn't fathom what had happened. "He expected them to understand that his interests were those of the school," Abrams said, "as they always were. And if he had had a role, which he didn't, it would have been in the best interests of the school. He expected them to understand that and found it beyond the pale that they did not."

Several weeks later, the subject of dispute seemed to have been resolved. Glaser, assured by the Executive Committee of their full support, agreed to come to Stanford. Abrams left to become chief of Radiology at Harvard. Kaplan became uncharacteristically quiet. He wasn't brooding over the financial plan or the hiring of Robert Glaser. The crux for Kaplan was broken loyalty. He was terribly hurt. He and Leah stopped socializing with faculty; Henry constantly ruminated about the affair. What upset him most was the manner in which he had been attacked—behind his back, behind closed doors, without a chance to defend himself. He would never have treated anyone that way. He didn't begrudge his colleagues a good fight, but he expected them to look him square in the eye, not hide behind an Executive Committee resolution. He lived by what he considered a strict moral code; apparently, they played by a different set of rules. "He was utterly simple," Goldstein said, "in a way you don't see much anymore—absolute honesty and integrity." Henry Kaplan had been betrayed by his colleagues, and he would never forgive them.

⌒

On July 1, 1965, Robert Glaser became dean and vice president for Medical Affairs at Stanford University School of Medicine. He had visions of building a school to surpass all others. At the first meeting with the Executive Committee, he outlined his long-range plans, and the chairmen assured him of their full support. He thought the controversy over Abrams's letter would soon be forgotten as they delved into their work. Glaser had come to Stanford with an agenda, an organizational plan, and a timetable.

Before long, however, he ran up against Kaplan. Glaser had enormous regard for him as a clinician, teacher, and scientist, and the two held similar views on what constituted an academic medical center and what kind of faculty should populate it. But they had different views on how to achieve these goals. Kaplan thought the drive should come from strong chairmen who had the freedom to maneuver. Glaser believed in centralized authority. "The Executive Committee changed," Avram Goldstein said, "from a collective group who were trying to hammer things out to Bob Glaser's executive committee. He was a professional dean."

For a while, Kaplan and Glaser related to each other in a cordial manner. "Your memorandum . . . just arrived," Glaser wrote to Kaplan in Israel, "and while I sit here in splendid solitude in my office . . . I thought I would respond to it." After updating Kaplan on Medical School affairs, he mentioned that he was traveling to Australia for a conference. "If memory serves me," he wrote, "you may also be planning to be there, and if that is the case, perhaps we can see one another." He closed with "all warm regards." Kaplan replied promptly.

He was arranging for Glaser to visit several Israeli medical schools, hosted by Michael Feldman. Regarding Glaser's takeover of the hospital from the city of Palo Alto, he wrote: "My sincere congratulations on a job well done!" He also responded to Glaser's plans to develop a "meaningful incentive program" for clinical income. "I would infer from this," he wrote, "not all of the other clinical departments are doing as much as the Department of Radiology to pull hard on the oar. . . . I think you will agree that it is a tribute to the Department of Radiology that we have not ever let our efforts flag, despite our fundamental difference of opinion about the change in professional service income policy."

But Kaplan resented Glaser's authority over his budget, and he asked the dean for more and more resources for his program: a novel form of high-energy radiation used an enormous magnet to capture and bend electron beams. A new field of therapy was emerging—implantation of radioactive seeds deep into cancers. Both required physicists and sophisticated computerized equipment to calculate doses. In the laboratory, radiobiologists were developing powerful new chemicals, called radiosensitizers, to enhance cell kill. They needed more space.

Glaser felt that Kaplan exaggerated his needs. "The way Kaplan talked," he said, "you'd think he was using the original Roentgen tube." Glaser tried to grant his requests, but radiation therapy machines were expensive. Besides, Stanford's Radiology Department already surpassed most nationwide with regard to space and equipment. Glaser was trying to build a balanced medical school. He had recently bought Palo Alto's share of the hospital for $1 million and signed an agreement to construct a pediatric research center. Kaplan cared deeply about the school, but he wanted to cure cancer, and he couldn't have his hands tied. If Glaser acquiesced to his demands, Kaplan cooperated for a while, but six months later, Glaser could expect another call, and if he didn't grant Kaplan's request, Henry became belligerent, once calling him a son of a bitch. Kaplan felt patronized. He wasn't the only unhappy chairman. After constant run-ins with the dean, Avram Goldstein resigned as chairman.

But Kaplan was determined the new dean wouldn't control him and the future of his department. "Look," he said to Glaser once during an argument, "my father died of cancer, and nobody's ever told me what to do since." He chose Executive Committee meetings as his battlefield. The issues at stake were always valid and of importance to the school, but whatever small shred of tact Kaplan had once had vanished. Like a wounded lion, he became ferocious. Instead of working together, the chairmen were breaking into small fighting factions, and several felt that the principal cause was Henry Kaplan. "He'd come sailing into Executive Committee meetings with all guns blazing," Holman said. They didn't accomplish much, because Glaser had trouble maintaining control.

He had always had amiable relationships with faculty; he didn't like conflict. "Henry seemed to enjoy controversy," Glaser said.

Others viewed Kaplan differently. Robert Chase, the new chairman of Surgery, admired Kaplan's tough stance; it was the only way to accomplish anything in that climate. And John Wilson, associate dean for faculty affairs, recalled how important Kaplan was to the school in those days. "He always came down on the right side," Wilson said, "perhaps a little too vigorously." Faculty split on almost every subject, but most inflammatory was the budget. Glaser asked David Hamburg to chair a budget review committee to counsel him with regard to faculty salaries, professional service income, and long-range financial planning. When Hamburg presented the final budget proposal to the Executive Committee, Kaplan objected to every point. He called the practice plan a "dean-run practice carried out by the faculty as hired hands." He complained that Hamburg's own Department of Psychiatry did not earn sufficient income and virtually accused committee members of advancing their own concerns. "It's time to blow the whistle," he told a reporter.

Kaplan began attacking departmental chairmen, saying their departments were not doing their share of clinical work. In addition to teaching and conducting research, Radiology faculty spent thirty hours a week reading radiographs and performing radiologic procedures, while many professors in the Department of Medicine saw only ten patients a week in clinic. Yet the dean split their profits equally. "Is that fair?" Kaplan asked. He felt that Glaser rationalized this practice as a means to strengthen the weaker departments, and that it was impeding the growth of the more productive ones. If Glaser kept this up, Kaplan predicted, the school would slide back into mediocrity. "He made it an absolute issue that he take over the [faculty practice] program," Kaplan later said. "That very nearly destroyed the school, and it almost led to my departure. . . . The faculty was given no incentive to give a damn. They were helpless."

Faculty and deans of other medical schools watched this drama unfold with great interest. "Robert S. Glaser and some other members of the faculty," wrote a reporter in *Science*, "dominate the *haute politique* of academic medicine." Stanford was described as "setting the pace in American medical education." A subsequent article noted: "The main complaint in these clinical departments is not that they are underpaid . . . but that what they regard as a fair share of funds earned by their departments is not returned to finance research and needed expansion or renovations of facilities. And what they seem to find most galling is their belief that their colleagues in other departments are not putting sufficient time and effort into medical care to pay their department's way."

Yet another confrontation occurred when Kaplan proposed dividing Radiology into two departments—Diagnostic Radiology and Radiation Therapy—in line with the national trend. Glaser appointed a committee, which included Kornberg, Lederberg, and Hamburg, to evaluate criteria for creating new departments. They concluded that the dean should form no additional departments; resources should support existing ones. Kaplan objected, stating that the committee had been appointed to sanctify a decision already made by Glaser without representation from departments most affected. The executives passed the resolution, with Kaplan's as one of only two dissenting votes. At times, it seemed as if others voted against Kaplan simply to oppose him.

No subject was spared, no decision arrived at easily. The hospital needed a new wing, and Glaser appointed a hospital committee to choose an architect. The Executive Committee approved the architect's plan for a six-story building, but Kaplan objected, not only to the blueprints, but to the architect as well. He thought the new building pedestrian, a blight on Stone's beautiful work. To the executives, this represented one more example of Kaplan's egotism. Kaplan saw it differently. He felt if he gave in, he would be compromising the quality of Stanford Medical School. "I want to be remembered," Kaplan said years later, "as somebody who was tough enough to be willing to fight the battles ... that were needed to create and maintain high standards, not just for our department, but for the school."

Perhaps he didn't realize just how much his friends' betrayal had affected him. His style of fighting had changed. Increasingly caustic, he didn't seem to care what anyone thought. "Henry had a sharp tongue," Kornberg said, "and with a rapier-like ability, could dissect people in a rather bloody way." He ridiculed Kornberg publicly, contending that through its clinical income, the Radiology Department made it possible for the school to indulge in the Biochemistry Department. He called Hamburg "the original three dollar bill."

When Kaplan got wound up, he became merciless. At Executive Committee meetings he stood up, paced around, yelled, and waved his fist. "There were shouting matches," Kornberg said, "that were inappropriate and unbecoming for people of intelligence and stature." Glaser didn't know what to do. In all his years of administrative work, he had never faced such a difficult situation. Kaplan essentially crippled the Executive Committee as an operating unit. Finally, he just wore everyone down. Colleagues found it too tiring to fight with him. "I consider Kaplan," Holman said, "the single most destructive force I've encountered since I've been at Stanford." Glaser couldn't grasp his behavior; it seemed he almost relished altercations. But recalling those days, Kaplan said, "I never enjoyed fighting with deans; I never enjoyed it for one minute. It took an awful lot out of me."

Neither Glaser nor any of the executives understood the effect the breach of loyalty had had upon Kaplan. They could never comprehend the depth of feeling this strong, independent man had for his friends. He would have given freely from his own funds if one of them had needed financial assistance. He would have flown halfway around the world if one of them had called for help. But he could never forgive a betrayal. He had felt devastated when he learned that they thought him conniving and meddlesome. Lederberg and Kretchmer tried to apologize, but it was too late. Henry couldn't trust them.

Years later, when Kornberg tried to reestablish his friendship, he was also rebuffed. "I don't understand why Hank took offense," he complained to Leah. "It was a small amount of money."

"Arthur," Leah replied, "you're talking about money. You've missed the whole point."

Kaplan became embittered, and he inadvertently ended up stymieing the growth of the school he loved so dearly. "As much as Henry did for this place," Glaser said, "nobody stops to think how much more he could have done."

Robert Glaser had come to Stanford full of enthusiasm, with plans to build an outstanding medical center. He was prepared to bring all his creative talents and energies to bear. Five years later, he gave up.

26   Peace Now!

On April 30, 1970, only six months after he had asked the country's "silent majority" to support his plans to end the war, President Richard Nixon disclosed
that American forces had begun bombing communist sanctuaries in Cambodia. Anti-war protests had been escalating for five years, and that day the barely
contained rage erupted on college campuses. "University strikes against President Nixon's Cambodian policy took on national proportions last night," the
Stanford Daily reported, "as many of the country's most prestigious universities
prepared to end 'business as usual.' "

Nationwide, student leaders advocated boycotts, and ten university newspapers, including the *Stanford Daily*, printed a joint editorial urging immediate
action, saying: "We do not call for a strike against the University but a strike *by*
the entire university." Students and faculty at Harvard, Ohio State, Berkeley,
Amherst, Smith, and Columbia were mobilizing. Campuses were seething; over
four hundred colleges and universities were shut down.

The press described Stanford's strike rally as the largest on the West Coast.
This was no surprise; the apparently bucolic university had repeatedly made
headlines for its anti-war radicalism going back to the mid 1960s. With the
bombing of Cambodia, previously restrained emotions seemed to explode
overnight, and student violence followed. A crowd of protesters blocked the entrance to the main administration building. Angry employees stepped on them
to gain entry, and one student, brutally kicked in the back, was taken away by
ambulance. Shotgun blasts tore into the house of the ROTC commander. Demonstrators randomly shot marbles at cars, and a motorcyclist, sprayed with
mace, crashed into a ditch. Stanford police scanned the campus in helicopters.
When forty deputies in full riot gear proved insufficient to control the scuffles
breaking out all over campus, the Milpitas police were called in.

Stanford's President Kenneth Pitzer, only recently appointed, feared the intended strike might provoke further havoc. "The wave of protest set in motion
by President Nixon's decision to invade Cambodia," he said in a public state-

ment, "has broken most strongly in the universities of the nation. Stanford is among those most directly in the path of the storm." He warned that although some considered a strike a nonviolent act, it could provoke retaliation. But Pitzer's plea to respect the university as a "center for reasoned discourse" went unheeded, and he began preparing for the worst.

Medical students joined the campus demonstrations. Protesters blocked classroom doors in attempts to shut down the Medical School. Associate Dean John Wilson, a gentle, soft-spoken man, had been left in charge. He met with the Executive Committee in an emergency session to determine how the Medical School should respond. Faculty were bewildered; most had never been confronted with political unrest and potential anarchy. They looked to the Executive Committee for direction, but it seemed rudderless until Henry Kaplan stepped forward.

Still aggrieved from the Executive Committee's rebuke during Glaser's recruitment, Kaplan could have retreated into his laboratory. But he still cared deeply about Stanford and refused to stand by and watch its destruction. Although incensed by the Cambodian bombings, he opposed transforming the Medical School into a political machine. Damage to university property was inexcusable; discontinuation of learning unreasonable; disruption of patient care and research unacceptable. Kaplan suggested that they confront student hostilities immediately rather than let them snowball. "He had a very positive effect on the faculty," said Professor of Surgery Larry Crowley. "Even though he was an administrative maverick and a thorn in the side of every dean and almost every chairman, when the going got tough, he stuck with the administration." Kaplan helped organize a convocation for the entire Medical School community, to be held on the evening of May 4. Its purpose was to provide information regarding the events occurring in Cambodia and discuss the planned student strike. Some thought it foolhardy to call together a large group of angry students, poised for action. As Kaplan was preparing his remarks, a news release reported that four students had been shot at Kent State.

By 5 P.M., a thousand students, faculty, and staff had gathered in the courtyard outside the dean's suite. A podium had been placed at the far end of the courtyard looking out toward the hanging gardens and the university beyond. The balmy evening and sweet fragrance of laurel, however, didn't mask the air of volatility. Some students sat cross-legged on the grass, but most stood, arms folded across their chests. To begin, a professor of anthropology reviewed the history of the war. The crowd cheered when he condemned the policy of expansion into Cambodia. But his suggestion that they work through their congressmen did not satisfy them. They wanted action.

When Henry Kaplan stood at the podium in his white coat, he faced a hostile audience. He cleared his throat and with a commanding voice began to speak of the medical community's relationship to current world problems. Although doctors traditionally thought of themselves as "above politics," he reminded them that they had chosen a medical career because of the "humanitarian purpose of alleviating sickness, suffering and saving human lives," and that was at odds with taking an apolitical position. He used his own work as an example. He had set out to cure cancer, and he and his colleagues had made significant strides. "And yet today I am confronted with the irony that more people are being killed in Vietnam in a week than I can save in a lifetime." Describing his frustrations, he said: "I feel a sense of irrelevance." Yet his work had to go on. He spoke of the university's role and decried taking out international problems on the school. "You don't destroy your institution to make a point," he said. "It makes no sense. The university isn't your enemy." Nevertheless, he shared their sentiments. They should be angry. "We feel increasingly that our entire lives are being made meaningless by all that is transpiring around us, and it is for this reason that physicians . . . must take a serious, continuing and meaningful interest in political and social questions in the world that surrounds us. Because without political involvement on our part, our entire lives today are increasingly in danger of becoming a mere mockery." When he stepped back from the podium, the courtyard was silent.

Later in the evening, Kaplan joined a group of students and helped direct their energy into positive endeavors, instead of destructive acts. That night, what became known as "the movement" emerged from the School of Medicine, coordinated through the newly formed Stanford Medical Community for Peace (SMCP). Anarchy had been averted; students and faculty started working as a united front. "Genesis of a Movement" announced headlines in *The Goose,* a medical student newspaper. "Since the President announced the US involvement in Cambodia," it read, "there has grown within the Stanford Medical Center an impressive piece of machinery whose purpose is to organize and verbalize the will of . . . the Medical community to change current policies in SE Asia." Beside the article was a picture of Henry Kaplan.

⌒

Expression of a social conscience was not new for Kaplan. Its development had begun in childhood when his mother fostered an awareness of a world beyond his, reading to him from *The Book of Knowledge.* Sarah had helped immigrants settle in Chicago through the Jewish People's Institute. During the Depression, Henry had watched his mother hand out food to those who came to the door hungry. And she occasionally slipped medication to a regular customer who, when laid off, couldn't afford it.

If Henry's mother had planted the seed of social conscience in him, his wife and friends had nurtured it. Part of his attraction to Leah had been her intense concern for others, leading to a career in psychiatric social work. In Minneapolis, when friends gathered at the Kaplans' apartment, conversation had often turned to the violent negation of human rights by the Nazi Party in Germany. During escalation of the Cold War, Henry joined a Russian study group at Yale. And at their Sausalito dinner parties, political scientist Herb McClosky could always be counted on to start a debate over public policy. But Henry had learned from Sarah that talk was meaningless without action. True to his convictions, Kaplan disregarded potential personal consequences. Such had been the case in 1956, when he testified as a character witness for Stanford radiology professor Joseph Kriss.

Caught in the frenzy of McCarthyism, Kriss was charged with disloyalty and political chicanery, based on three pieces of "evidence": He had signed a petition protesting methods used by the House Un-American Activities Committee to interrogate citizens. He took a woodworking class at the California Labor School, located across the street from the Soviet embassy. And his parents were Russian. Kriss thought the charges preposterous, but his lawyer suggested he get the most impressive character witnesses possible. He asked Henry Kaplan to testify.

The investigation was conducted at the U.S. Naval Station on Treasure Island in San Francisco Bay. Most witnesses attested to Kriss's fine qualities as a physician and loyalty as an American citizen. Kaplan was incensed by the proceedings, however, and when put on the stand, he answered defiantly, directing attention away from Kriss and toward himself. The examiner asked his position with respect to loyalty oaths. Instead of simply responding that he had taken the oath, which he had, Kaplan said that he considered it an indignity. "It is basically an un-American idea because there is the implication in the loyalty oath that one is guilty until he has sworn he is innocent." He went on to say there was a bill pending before the state senate that required every physician to take the loyalty oath in order to get a license. He was deeply opposed.

"You objected to the requirement of a doctor's loyalty oath?" the examiner asked.

"I did, and I still do," he replied. "I signed a petition." The examiner probed further, asking if Kaplan had ever held a commission in the armed services. When he learned Kaplan had been rejected, it piqued his interest.

"Will you state what the basis of that rejection was in your application for the Army?" the officer asked.

"I was told by the examining physician that I could not turn out a snappy salute." With that, Kaplan raised two giant fingers to his forehead. The courtroom became silent. The examiner looked down and said, "That's all I have, Doctor." In the end, the examiners exonerated Joseph Kriss.

In 1962, Kaplan had been invited to speak at the plenary session of the Eighth International Cancer Congress in Moscow. The Soviet Union had just violated the U.S.–USSR treaty on nuclear test suspension by exploding a 58-megaton hydrogen bomb. Kaplan thought it ironic that he should be asked to present his work on enhancing cancer cures in a country that by its recent action might generate thousands of new cases. He boycotted the Congress and urged other scientists to do the same. Furthermore, he published his letter canceling his talk in *Science*, a widely read journal.

Most Stanford colleagues didn't appreciate the intensity of Kaplan's convictions until they heard his passionate speech to the medical community following the Cambodian bombings. His contact with students who were working diligently for peace may have propelled him into his next action.

On May 24, 1970, the Tenth International Cancer Congress opened in Houston, Texas. Scientists and physicians from all over the world attended this meeting, sponsored by the International Union Against Cancer / Union internationale contre le cancer (UICC). There leading cancer specialists presented their latest scientific discoveries. The National Organizing Committee, chaired by former Texas governor John B. Connally and R. Lee Clark, president of the University of Texas's MD Anderson Hospital & Tumor Institute, had planned the largest congress to date. Speakers from seventy-two countries would present 1,740 papers. As researchers began to gather and exchange ideas, enthusiasm for conquering cancer swelled.

Lee Clark had planned an impressive event for the thousands visiting Texas. On opening day, the United Nations Postal Administration issued two "Fight Cancer" stamps. A sculpture by Alexander Calder entitled "The Crab" was featured at the entrance to the Albert Thomas Convention Center, where 254 scientific exhibits were displayed. Vice President Spiro T. Agnew was to give the welcoming address. Extensive press coverage had been arranged.

On May 24, six thousand gathered for the opening ceremonies at Sam Houston Coliseum. Because of the vice president's visit, security was heightened, and attendees had to pass through an electronic device that screened for concealed weapons. Men in gray slacks and blue blazers stood on the balcony holding rifles at their sides. The coliseum was full from the floor to the bleachers on three sides. An enormous stage had been set up at the far end of the hall. Heavy curtains that reached to the ceiling made an impressive backdrop, on which was suspended a large banner with the letters UICC. Eighteen dignitaries sat across the front of the stage.

After a laudatory introduction, Agnew stepped to the podium. "On behalf of the President," he said, "I bid our eminent visitors welcome." James Holland, president of the American Association for Cancer Research, who was sitting on the stage with other international leaders, had his attention suddenly drawn from Agnew when a man in a suit and bow tie rose from his seat on the far right and began striding down the aisle. He had both hands raised high, making two V signs, and in a booming voice shouted, "Peace now! Peace now!" Holland was shocked when he recognized Henry Kaplan. Agnew abruptly stopped speaking as Kaplan marched toward the front, continuing his call for peace. Holland saw Secret Service agents in the balcony raise their rifles. Kaplan had almost reached the podium when he was surrounded by plainclothesmen and escorted out of the coliseum, still shouting, "Peace now!" Several hundred participants followed him.

The incident wasn't reported in newspapers or played up by local television stations. The preliminary session continued without further disruption. But during the entire conference week, Kaplan's action was a topic of conversation. Many were astonished by this outburst from such a dignified scientist. He was not known to be an activist. Several Europeans attending the conference praised Kaplan's courage. They told him that in their respective countries, such actions would have serious repercussions. American colleagues who agreed with his views said they planned to do something in their own way. Most never did. Some thought the walkout had no impact on Agnew, but he later blocked Kaplan's nomination as director of the National Cancer Institute.

Many puzzled as to why Kaplan had chosen this mode of expression. He could have written Agnew or circulated flyers denouncing the war or published an editorial. Why did he risk being condemned by the world's leading scientists? Why did he take the chance of being shot by Secret Service agents? Anyone who had heard his speech two and a half weeks earlier knew why. He had told Stanford students and faculty that the war made him feel irrelevant. Then he found himself in Houston sitting with thousands who had devoted themselves to saving lives, listening to a man who, as Nixon's vice president, bore responsibility for more deaths than all the scientists in the coliseum could ever hope to avert. The irony must have been unbearable. As Kaplan had said, without political involvement, his life could become a mockery.

27   Mary Lasker's Moon Shot
                              for Cancer

Two days before Christmas 1971, President Richard Nixon spoke to the American public from the White House State Dining Room. "We are here today," he said, referring to the group of congressmen and special guests, "for the purpose of signing the National Cancer Act. I hope that in the years ahead we look back on this day, and this action is shown as being the most significant action taken during this administration." The National Cancer Program did become one of Nixon's finest achievements. Television cameras and national attention focused on Nixon as he signed the bill. In the front row, out of the cameraman's view, sat the real architect of the Cancer Act—Mary Lasker. Who would have suspected that this seventy-year-old woman, wearing a strand of exquisite pearls, her dark hair coiffured in a bouffant flip, wielded such power. Advisor to presidents and benefactor to Nobel laureates, Lasker was a woman of strong convictions, with the money and influence to pursue them. Through her efforts over forty years, billions of federal dollars were allocated to medical research. In 1969, she had decided it was time to cure cancer.

⏤

Though not particularly tall, Mary Lasker was a woman of stature. "Her presence," one scientist said, "caused us all to perk up as if the sun had just come out." Born into an advantaged family, successful in business, and married to a wealthy advertising executive, Albert Lasker, she could have divided her time between travel, luncheons, and garden parties. But her mother had instilled into her an obligation to serve the community. Although Mary contributed substantial efforts to the arts, it was her endeavors on behalf of medical science that had the greatest impact on the American public.

Mary never forgot the day she accompanied her mother to visit their cleaning woman who was dying of breast cancer, a disease whose name people only whispered. Years later, her own cook developed cancer, and doctors told her that the woman's disease was terminal. Tired of hearing "Nothing can be done," she decided it was time to act. Lasker was later described as having "a rare passion for beauty and a rare rage against disease."

Mary had witnessed numerous technological advances, which had come about through substantial research and development. A bridge had been built that spanned San Francisco Bay; a jet engine had been designed; the atom had been split. She believed similar progress could be made in medicine by expanding scientific investigation. Yet in the early 1940s, the United States was spending less on cancer research than her husband's clients were spending to advertise toothpaste. "Medical research is a gift," she wrote, "a legacy that we leave to the next generation." Mary began her crusade, and a few years later, her husband retired to join her. They established the Albert and Mary Lasker Foundation, through which they provided resources to promising investigators. "When I think of Mary Lasker," Jonas Salk said, "I think of a matchmaker between science and society." But their foundation could not provide enough funds to make significant progress against heart disease, cancer, and stroke, the three most common causes of death in the United States.

The Laskers gathered together friends who shared their goal of promoting medical science. Known as the "benevolent plotters," the group included wealthy businessmen, prominent physicians, and several with strong political connections. They encouraged press coverage of medical advances by sponsoring an annual seminar to bring journalists and scientists together. They urged legislation that established the National Heart Institute. And they determined to break what they called the cycle of cancer incurability: since not much could be done for the cancer patient, enthusiasm for cancer research had stagnated. This required a considerable amount of money, and Mary and her friends set out to secure it.

They started with the American Cancer Society, at that time an elite organization supported by a few wealthy New Yorkers. The society concentrated on educating the public about the warning signs of cancer. Lasker thought this tactic pointless unless treatment was available. She approached the directors and asked how much of their $350,000 yearly income they spent on research. When they answered "none," she made a deal with them. She would direct the next fund-raising campaign if they would allocate one-quarter of the receipts to research. They reluctantly agreed. Lasker proceeded to hire a professional advertising firm and encouraged *Reader's Digest* to print a series of articles on cancer, followed by an appeal for donations. The Laskers persuaded the Radio Corporation of America to use the word "cancer" on the air to help demystify the disease. As a result, over $4 million was donated to the American Cancer Society. But first-class cancer research required billions of dollars, and there was only one place to obtain that much—the U.S. government.

Mary Lasker was already well known to presidents. When President Harry Truman signed the bill creating the National Heart Institute, he had appointed Lasker as the first lay member of the advisory board. She had served on several presidential boards for President John F. Kennedy. When his brother Edward was elected to the Senate, JFK gave him the following advice: "Have lunch with medical school professors, have dinner with Nobel Prize winners, but if you really want to know about . . . medical research . . . talk with Mary Lasker." And at Lasker's insistence, President Lyndon Johnson had created the Commission on Heart Disease, Cancer, and Stroke as a national network for research, education, and patient care. "I am opposed to heart attacks and strokes," she said, "the way I am opposed to sin." President Johnson later awarded her the Medal of Freedom.

While the Laskers were pushing for more research funds to overcome cancer, a malignancy was silently growing in Albert's colon. After he died, Mary's zeal to eradicate cancer intensified. The National Cancer Institute was mired in layers of bureaucracy; there were only four cancer centers nationwide; research dollars were diminishing. Influenced by Solomon Garb's 1968 book *Cure for Cancer: A National Goal*, Mary insisted that they had to find a better approach. The United States had just put a man on the moon, and Garb drew three conclusions from the space program: finding a cure of cancer required a specific plan; substantial funds to direct scientific talent toward this goal; and management by an independent agency, free from bureaucracy, reporting directly to the president. In short, they needed a "moon shot" for cancer. Lasker sent copies of Garb's book to her friends, and in 1969, she organized them into the Citizens' Committee for the Conquest of Cancer. They hired a Washington lobbyist, and shortly thereafter, a full-page notice appeared in the *New York Times*:

MR. NIXON: YOU CAN CURE CANCER

If prayers are heard in Heaven, this prayer is heard the most: "Dear God, please. Not cancer." Still more than 318,000 Americans died of cancer last year. This year, Mr. President, you have it in your power to begin to end this curse.

They arranged for Garb to testify before Senate and House appropriations committees to urge an NIH budget increase. And they persuaded Senator Ralph Yarborough, chairman of the Committee on Labor and Public Welfare, to appoint a National Panel of Consultants on the Conquest of Cancer. Its express purpose was to recommend a national program to achieve cure of the most common cancers by 1976, the bicentennial year.

Mary knew makeup of the panel was crucial in achieving credibility and assuring incorporation of their recommendations into law. She advised Yarborough in his appointments—scientists, philanthropists, representatives from organized labor, individuals with advertising expertise, members of the press, and enough Republicans to assure presidential support. To make certain they would reach rapid consensus, Mary weighted the list with veterans of her prior initiatives. Yarborough asked Benno Schmidt to chair the panel. Schmidt, a venture capitalist tailored on Park Avenue, retained his Texas down-home charm. Having engineered many successful civic activities, and serving as chairman of the Board of Trustees of New York City's Memorial Hospital, he moved easily in the arena where high finance and politics overlapped.

Joe Burchenal, vice-president of the Memorial Sloan-Kettering Cancer Center, recommended that Henry Kaplan be added to the panel. Kaplan's accomplishments impressed Lasker, and she approved his appointment. She would soon learn that Kaplan's zeal to cure cancer equaled hers. She didn't yet realize, however, that no one told Henry Kaplan how to think or what to say.

Senator Yarborough convened the Panel of Consultants on June 29, 1970. "There was hardly an individual among the laymen," Kaplan later wrote, "who was not in a position of substantial political influence in one or the other of the two major national parties. And it was apparent immediately that this committee was not about to generate a report that would not be read carefully in Washington." Yarborough formally charged the panel with assessing the adequacy of cancer research funds and determining the steps needed to cure the disease. He requested a complete report in three months. Benno Schmidt divided the group into subcommittees to address scientific proposal, budget, and administrative structure. Although not an official panel member, Lasker made it clear that she expected a goal-oriented research plan, a request for substantially increased funding, and centralized authority.

Schmidt assigned Kaplan to the subcommittee responsible for preparing the scientific plan. Kaplan knew the idea of developing a program in three months that would lead to the eradication of cancer within six years was unrealistic. The notion Lasker and her group had popularized—"Why, if we could land a man on the moon, can't we cure cancer?"—was driven by emotionalism, not objectivity. The success of the space program had resulted from an intense exploitation of existing technology. Scientists already had the requisite tools. Stamping out cancer required unraveling the mystery of the malignant process first. "An effort to cure cancer at this time," a Columbia University scientist said, "might be like trying to land a man on the moon without knowing Newton's laws of motion." Kaplan knew cancer couldn't be cured by the bicentennial, as did the other scientists on the panel, but that didn't dampen their enthusiasm. They welcomed a national focus on cancer research, especially if funding followed.

Theirs was an intensive endeavor, carried out with the fervor of a crusade.

During the summer of 1970, Kaplan logged thousands of miles to the East Coast. "I virtually lived on the 'red-eye special,'" he said. And in just over two months, his subcommittee submitted a cancer plan to Schmidt. In it, they recommended continuing the investigative programs already funded by the NCI; providing increased support for prevention, early detection, treatment, and research; and building cancer centers across the country in which to carry out the work.

This wasn't the detailed plan Mary Lasker had hoped for. It didn't specify the exact research that should be conducted and by whom. It didn't outline a roadmap to reach the endpoint of cancer cure. The plan left too much to the discretion of individual investigators and placed too much emphasis on basic research. Lasker stood firm that funded research should be directly applicable to patients. When she supported scientists, she expected results that could ultimately be measured in terms of human lives saved. Lasker favored a central agency that distributed contracts to scientists for specific projects, that is, directed research. She advocated an administrative model similar to NASA's. Substantial funds had helped NASA attract top scientists. Goal-oriented directors used the task-force approach to science, instead of relying on what Lasker considered the vagaries of independent investigators. And the chief of NASA reported to the president. Using this model, Lasker proposed a National Cancer Authority, separate from the NIH.

Kaplan argued for scientific freedom, not directed investigation. He thought gifted scientists should be given autonomy and railed against what he called the "managed approach to big science." He preferred the academic peer-review model, where scientific excellence and ingenuity were rewarded with grant funding, as opposed to the product-driven model of industry. Great science didn't emanate from the creativity of bureaucrats. "The really good ideas, the sudden intuitive perceptions of connections between seemingly unrelated bits of information," one cancer center director said, "occur in individual minds, and they cannot be programmed or planned." Furthermore, Kaplan thought directed research undervalued the role of serendipity—the unanticipated observation, the surprising twists and turns a contract didn't allow a scientist to follow. "What emerges unexpectedly in experiments is often the most critical," echoed a scientist. No one had directed Roentgen to discover x-rays, and who would have predicted that wartime mustard gas casualties would give rise to the field of chemotherapy? In each case, a scientist had pursued an unusual finding while working on something entirely different. "Funding patterns of science," Kaplan said, "influence the way in which scientists feel free to behave as citizens."

But Mary Lasker considered the current NIH structure cumbersome and inadequate. She calculated that less than 2 percent of federal funds allocated for research were spent on cancer. And, she contended, the research talent that could be applied to the cancer problem had barely been tapped. Mary recommended that the president centralize the cancer effort, appointing someone who reported to him and had the authority and money to carry through the plan to its conclusion rapidly. At the September 18 meeting in New York, Schmidt attempted to persuade panel members to support this proposal. Henry Kaplan and the other basic scientists opposed the idea. Kaplan argued that it wasn't because of poor coordination that cancer hadn't been cured, but from lack of fundamental knowledge. In the long run, he said, it would be detrimental to sever the relationship between cancer researchers and basic scientists in other branches of the NIH, since collaboration with virologists and molecular biologists was critical to deciphering carcinogenesis. And he opposed creation of a cancer authority appointed by the president. Scientists, not political appointees, should determine scientific priorities.

Given these objections, only five panel members concurred with Schmidt, so he and Lasker set to work. Over the next two weeks, Mary lobbied members of the panel, many of whom were her friends. Schmidt told the scientists that the bill wouldn't pass without unanimity among panel members, and cancer funding would remain unacceptably low. One by one, they agreed. Henry Kaplan was the last to capitulate. "I found out personally how difficult it was to oppose the majority view of this powerful panel," he said years later. "It was said to be my duty to go along with the committee on an issue with which I had a great deal of misgiving from the beginning."

At their next meeting, the entire panel voted to recommend an independent authority. Before long, Kaplan began to regret his acquiescence. He thought the panel had been railroaded into concurrence. He wanted to see cancer research emphasized, but he thought the panel's position would decimate the NIH in the end. He insisted on a special meeting to debate the point. "My powers of persuasion were so effective," he lamented, "that the committee finally voted 25–1 against me to continue with its recommendation for an independent agency." In the end, Henry Kaplan could not agree to a proposal that threatened scientific freedom and the vitality of the NIH. Despite her charm, political savvy, and power, Mary Lasker could not alter his conviction. Kaplan insisted that a minority report be written.

On December 4, 1970, the panel presented its final report to the Senate Committee on Labor and Public Welfare. It contained three recommendations: initiation of a comprehensive cancer plan; appropriations of substantial funds, reaching over $1 billion by 1976; and creation of an independent National Cancer Authority, reporting directly to the president. The cancer program was touted as "a whole new ball game." Kaplan thought otherwise.

The work of the panel might have been over, but for Lasker and Schmidt the harder job had begun—guiding the act through Congress and securing support from the president. Yarborough was not reelected, and the cancer act would have to be introduced by the next chairman of the Subcommittee on Health, Ted Kennedy. A longtime supporter of the Kennedys, Mary knew that the senator had an interest in health care and would champion the cancer bill. He was prepared to introduce S.34—the Conquest of Cancer Act—to the 92nd Congress. Cancer had now entered the political arena. Everyone wanted legislation that would hasten its cure, and it became a race among politicians to see whose name would be associated with that accomplishment. Lasker understood that fact, and she used the insight well.

She and Schmidt turned their attention to the president. For six months, Nixon's health advisor had been urging him to engage in the cancer problem. So Nixon pledged his support in his State of the Union message. Echoing Lasker, he said, "The time has come in America when the same kind of concentrated effort that split the atom and took a man to the moon should be turned toward conquering this dread disease." He announced his request for an additional $100 million to find a cure for cancer. Nixon hadn't previously mentioned cancer in his political career. When the press inquired about his sudden interest, he replied he had been affected by his Aunt Elizabeth's death from cancer. Making this announcement three days before Kennedy introduced the cancer bill to the Senate, Nixon had grabbed the limelight. If the Panel of Consultants reveled in the certainty of presidential support, that joy was short-lived. Yes, Nixon had given cancer the national priority they sought, and he had committed considerable resources. But influenced by his science adviser, who told him that the medical community strongly supported the NIH, he concluded that the cancer program should remain within that agency.

On March 10, 1971, Kennedy opened subcommittee hearings on S.34. At the onset, he stated that the proposal came with a unanimous recommendation from the Panel of Consultants and the support of fifty-two senators. The surgeon general testified first. He said that the administration concurred with the panel on all but one point—organization. He reaffirmed the president's belief that formation of a separate authority would be a mistake. Panel members testified on the second day. Schmidt began with an emotional call to arms and concluded by saying, "The scientists and professional men who have spent their lives working in this field feel that the time is especially right today for an intensified and accelerated effort." Following him, five distinguished scientists from the Panel of Consultants made prepared comments. Schmidt had asked Henry Kaplan to present the scientific plan. Although Kaplan found appearing amenable to creation of an independent authority difficult, Kennedy did not ask his opinion.

Sides had been drawn—those who agreed with the panel and Kennedy in support of a separate agency and those who concurred with the administration in keeping the cancer program within the NIH. The NIH director encouraged scientists to petition their senators. When the outpouring of mail and calls began to threaten S.34, Lasker and her colleagues planned a counterattack, using the press. The *Wall Street Journal* published a heart-wrenching letter from a man whose son had leukemia, pleading for more support for cancer research. And Ann Landers wrote an entire column on the disease, stating, "Cancer claims the lives of more children . . . than any other illness." She urged her readers to write their senators in support of S.34. Almost a million letters swamped the Senate.

On May 11, Nixon announced he was sending Congress alternate legislation, Senate bill S.1828, to establish a Cancer Cure Program within the NIH. By mid-May, the two groups seemed at an impasse. Then, in a stroke of political genius, Kennedy broke the blockade. He combined the two approaches and suggested that a Conquest of Cancer Agency be formed within the NIH, but with independent budgetary status, reporting to the president. On July 7, S.1828 passed the Senate, each side declaring victory. The bill's quick passage left the expectation that the House would rapidly follow.

Representative Paul Rogers, a Florida Democrat, served as chairman of the House Subcommittee on Public Health. He knew national sentiment compelled the House to pass cancer legislation, but he did not plan for it to be Senate bill S.1828. Impressed with the achievements of the NCI, he feared that an independent agency would erode its integrity. And he resented the way Lasker and her group thought they could steamroll this bill right past him.

The House hearings opened on September 15. Most of the same arguments were recapitulated, again focused on organization. Thirty-one House members gave testimony supporting the bill, many telling tragic stories of friends and family who had died of cancer. It appeared that the bill would ride through the House on a wave of emotion. On the third day, the Panel of Consultants added its strong support. Henry Kaplan had not been included. But Rogers had read Kaplan's minority report and called him to testify. Rogers reviewed Kaplan's impressive credentials and asked him to comment on the pending legislation. At last, Kaplan could state his opinion publicly.

Kaplan began by underscoring the necessity for expanding cancer research and agreed with the panel's emphasis on increased financial support, a comprehensive plan, and efficient administration. To accomplish this, the panel had recommended an independent agency—"a conclusion," he said, "with which I concurred very reluctantly." They had had only three months to prepare a report. "It is perhaps not surprising," he said, "that today, with the clarity born of hindsight, one can appreciate that there were certain gaps in the thoroughness with which various options were explored." He would have preferred a proposal to strengthen the current NIH structure. The panel could have determined the specific procedures that caused inefficiency in the NIH, but they hadn't. They could have asked the NIH director to propose methods to streamline his operations, but they hadn't. Kaplan went on to point out that creating an independent agency within the NIH, as proposed by the compromise bill, presented a contradiction. "The agency," he said, "if it is truly independent, is not in any functional sense within the National Institutes of Health; conversely, if it operates within the guidelines of the National Institutes of Health, it is not independent." He predicted that this ambiguity would lead to administrative conflicts, resulting in a more encumbered system and diverting them from the goal of curing cancer. By the time he had finished, Kaplan had discredited part of the panel's work and contributed to the death of S.1828.

A new compromise bill had to be drafted, requiring a joint Senate-House conference. Meanwhile, President Nixon made it clear to Rogers that he expected a cancer act on his desk before Christmas. Rogers proceeded to write new legislation. A rapid series of maneuverings between him and Kennedy ensued—what one historian called the "politics of compromise." Nixon received his cancer legislation just before Christmas.

The final bill substantially increased federal funds for cancer research. It made the NCI director a presidential appointee and specified that the NCI budget would be passed directly to the president for review. It created the National Cancer Advisory Board, empowered to advise the NCI director on all aspects of its programs, and the President's Cancer Council, a small group that would link the NCI and the Advisory Board to the president. It did not, however, create a separate, independent agency.

On December 23, 1971, 137 guests gathered in the State Dining Room of the White House for the signing of the National Cancer Act. With millions of Americans watching on television, the president said:

> Hope and comfort, the relief of suffering and the affirmation of life itself—these are the qualities which have traditionally been associated with the Christmas season. There could be no more appropriate time than this to sign into law the National Cancer Act of 1971. For this legislation . . . can mean new hope and comfort in the years ahead for millions of people in this country and around the world.

Seated in the audience were Kennedy, Rogers, and other congressmen involved in passing the legislation. Mary Lasker was among the honored guests as well as many from the Panel of Consultants. Henry Kaplan had not been invited.

⌐╕

Mary Lasker should have been pleased. Over the next two decades, the government spent billions of dollars on cancer research, and cancer became a household word. But she was not. Lasker never achieved her "moon shot," and cancer was not eradicated by the bicentennial. Most researchers knew that the goal had been unrealistic, but Lasker still believed that had they committed to a NASA-type effort, cancer could have been cured. The final Cancer Act did not have all the components she had envisioned, and Henry Kaplan had been a major stumbling block. Kaplan's mission was to cure cancer, and he pursued it relentlessly. He considered scientific autonomy crucial, and it was that freedom for which he fought so hard. Mary Lasker also wanted cancer eradicated. What the two could never reconcile was how to reach that goal, and both felt vehemently about their position. Mary Lasker usually prevailed. So did Henry Kaplan.

Kaplan didn't have political power, but he had confronted those who did. He didn't respond to emotionalism or political maneuvering. He simply stood his ground and spoke out, and in the end, his persistence and intellect had triumphed. The "Great Persuader" had not been able to control Kaplan, and she seemingly never forgave him. He suspected that Lasker had deleted his name from the White House guest list for the signing of the Cancer Act. And although nominated many times, Kaplan never received a Lasker Award—"a serious sin of omission," one of Lasker's closest friends wrote years later. He was never asked to serve on the National Cancer Advisory Board or the President's Cancer Council. His nomination was blocked at higher levels. To Kaplan, these were petty actions, but he couldn't help feeling disappointed. Yet no amount of pressure would have induced him to act against his conscience. He believed in freedom of inquiry and willingly risked his reputation to preserve it for all scientists, whether at Stanford, in Washington, D.C., or around the world.

28   A Cancer-Causing Virus

Nixon's war on cancer couldn't have come fast enough for parents nationwide. In 1971, headlines reported an outbreak of a cancer called Hodgkin's disease among teenagers in Albany, New York. A colleague had called Nicholas Vianna of the Center for Disease Control and Prevention—the national watchdog for infectious diseases— and told him about the cases. Intrigued by the possibility that Hodgkin's disease might be transmitted like an infection, Vianna set out to determine whether there had been any contact between students who had come down with the disease. What he discovered was disturbing: of the 317 students in the 1954 graduating class of one high school, two had died from Hodgkin's disease—a surprising number for this relatively rare cancer. Furthermore, two close friends of one of the students had also died from this illness. And another two classmates had relatives living with them who contracted the disease. One of these relatives attended a different high school, and one of his classmates had developed Hodgkin's disease, as had the sister of yet another of his classmates. The more Vianna probed, the more cases he found. Vianna postulated that one student from the class of 1954 had passed some infectious agent to five other students. Three showed signs of overt malignancy; two others became carriers who passed the illness to relatives. "This outbreak," Vianna concluded, "has all the features of an infective-disease condition with a carrier state and a long incubation period." His report soon had the medical world buzzing.

Vianna wasn't the first to report possible transmission of a lymphoid malignancy between individuals. A decade earlier, two Pennsylvania physicians, Hugh Gilmore and Gabriel Zelesnick, had investigated an extraordinary occurrence in a small south-central Pennsylvania town. It involved two adjoining houses—one brick and one frame—both built in the 1860s. The two houses were similar to others in the neighborhood—two floors, an attic, a basement, and a small garden. But the grief suffered in those homes over a decade was remarkable, and the story Gilmore and Zelesnick told of the families living there provided a new clue to the cause of Hodgkin's disease.

The S—— family resided in the frame house, the mother having been raised there. Their firstborn had died of Hodgkin's disease in 1948 at the age of eighteen. A year after her death, their second child married and moved out of the house. Nine years later, he, too, died of Hodgkin's disease. At age seventeen, their fifth child developed many of the same symptoms his older brother had had. He was found to have infectious mononucleosis.

The A—— family had lived next door in the brick house since 1907. Three of their children had died in infancy—one from poliomyelitis, one from pneumonia, and one from an unknown cause. After their oldest daughter moved away, the parents divided the house and continued to live on one side. A granddaughter who moved in with them developed mononucleosis at age eleven. Then in 1950, Mrs. A—— died of Hodgkin's disease. Following her death, her husband rented the other half of the house to a family with two daughters. Shortly thereafter, both girls died of leukemia; one was seven, one five. After the parents moved away, Mr. A—— rented to a family of six. The youngest daughter died of leukemia a year later.

When Gilmore and Zelesnick first learned of these deaths, they became intrigued and set out to investigate the origin. They began by analyzing all cancers that had occurred in this town of 2,500, and, to their astonishment, they found that over a thirteen-year period, every case of a lymphoid malignancy had been confined to these two houses with the exception of an elderly neighbor who had died of chronic leukemia. Searching for an underlying cause, they first explored potential environmental toxins. The town had four companies— a shoe factory, a machine and tool business, a cigar factory, and a furniture company—none located in the neighborhood. They checked for radioactivity inside the two houses and in the surrounding soil but detected no trace. Both homes had city sewers and water, and on chemical analysis, the tap water was no different from that in houses miles away. Second, they considered a genetic predisposition. But the S—— and A—— families were not related, and each had large numbers of relatives, none of whom had contracted a lymphoid cancer. Gilmore and Zelesnick never could explain this phenomenon. In 1962, they reported their findings in the *Pennsylvania Medical Journal*. Some scientists thought the finding of these cancers afflicting six children and adults in two adjacent homes suggested an infectious cause, and Gilmore and Zelesnick's observations gave rise to the hypothesis of possible person-to-person transmission of lymphoid malignancies.

Other sporadic cases among people living together or in close contact emerged. An attendant who cared for a patient with Hodgkin's disease contracted the illness and died within a month. Two medical school classmates developed the disease; both died. Two University of Texas students who had occupied the same room successively were afflicted. A French cheese maker was diagnosed with Hodgkin's disease at age thirty. His sister developed the disease ten years later. And five instances of this malignancy involving both partners in married couples were reported.

One such story involved a forty-two-year-old man who had noticed a swelling in his neck and experienced recurrent temperatures that reached 104°. He attributed these symptoms to bad teeth. In just a few months, however, he lost twenty-five pounds and could barely walk. He was admitted to the Bronx Veterans Administration Hospital, where a diagnosis of Hodgkin's disease was made. Radiation therapy provided no relief, and he soon died. Three years later, his wife was admitted to Binghamton City Hospital with lymph node swelling, high fevers, a cough, and breathing so labored that she couldn't lie down. Two liters of fluid were drained from her chest, and a biopsy revealed Hodgkin's disease. Despite radiation treatments, the disease spread. Six months later, she died.

Vianna knew of these reports when he set out to investigate the Albany high school cases. After his 1971 publication, he conducted a study that was even more compelling. He reviewed all cases of Hodgkin's disease recorded in Albany County during the prior two decades, 1950–70, which totaled 208. To determine if any relationship had existed among the patients, he interviewed their friends, relatives, and teachers, and examined school files and yearbooks. Vianna found that during that twenty-year period, thirty-one patients, or 15 percent of all new cases of Hodgkin's disease in Albany County, were linked through direct contact or a mutual friend. These cases became known as the "Albany cluster."

Epidemiologists rushed to find other concentrations of Hodgkin's disease, and clusters were soon reported in Los Angeles, New Orleans, and Darby Township, Ohio. Critics called Vianna's work anecdotal. "Other studies have been conducted along related lines," wrote two prominent epidemiologists, "but they have . . . tended to generate heat rather than light and the epidemiological picture still remains murky." Some pointed out that a disease could appear in high incidence in certain places just by random distribution. "Hodgkin's disease: a clue or a fluke?" the *British Medical Journal* asked. In order to prove that transmission occurred between individuals, a larger region needed to be studied.

And that was what Vianna did. He evaluated the 777 public schools in the two major counties of Long Island—Nassau and Suffolk. Reviewing all hospital admissions between 1960 and 1970, he found 465 cases of Hodgkin's disease, forty-nine of whom were teachers and students. When he looked at the distribution of these forty-nine by school, he discovered that if one student or teacher developed Hodgkin's disease, the number of subsequent cases in the school involved was two to three times that anticipated. "The results," he concluded, "support the concept that some form of transmission may be important in the occurrence of Hodgkin's disease." Not everyone agreed. "The apparent impressiveness of the linkages described in studies such as those of Vianna may be illusory," a Harvard epidemiologist suggested.

But Henry Kaplan found Vianna's work intriguing. He thought Hodgkin's disease might be caused by a virus, and if so, Epstein-Barr virus (EBV) seemed a likely candidate. EBV was known to cause infectious mononucleosis, a disease manifested by fatigue, fever, and enlarged lymph nodes and spleen. Kaplan had heard of a young woman with concurrent mononucleosis and Hodgkin's disease, and David Smithers of the Royal Marsden Hospital had spoken of four similar cases. Gilmore and Zelesnick had reported cases of mononucleosis in the two Pennsylvania houses. The possible connection between EBV and Hodgkin's disease fascinated Kaplan, and he began to ask every new patient if they had had mononucleosis. In 1964, he found his first case in which the two diseases coexisted.

Ronald F——, a twenty-five-year-old machine operator from Mountain View, California, noticed a lump on the left side of his neck above the collarbone. He ignored it until he was involved in an automobile accident, and the examining physician noted neck adenopathy. A few weeks later, Ronald returned to the hospital with fever and fatigue, and a physician found enlarged nodes in his right axilla as well as in the left side of his neck. He performed blood tests and diagnosed mononucleosis. The fever and fatigue eventually resolved, and Ronald returned to work. Over the next three months, the nodes increased in size and became painful. A biopsy revealed Hodgkin's disease, and he was referred to Stanford.

Then came nineteen-year-old Gary T—— of San Jose. He and his wife were expecting their first child when he developed painful neck nodes and a sore throat, which persisted for weeks. His physician told him that his mononucleosis test was positive. After the pharyngitis resolved, Gary felt better, although the enlarged nodes persisted. A biopsy was consistent with mononucleosis. Four months later, the lymph nodes increased in size, and a second biopsy demonstrated Hodgkin's disease.

Kaplan kept a list of his Hodgkin's disease patients who had had mononucleosis, and over an eight-year period, he found twenty-nine cases. Nineteen were men; the average age was twenty-four. Several had been diagnosed with Hodgkin's disease within months of recovering from mononucleosis, whereas in others, the interval between the two was years. In several, he observed Hodgkin's disease in a lymph node that had remained enlarged following the infection. Kaplan reported his series—the largest to date—in 1972. Was there an association between the two diseases or were these cases coincidental—"a clue or a fluke?"

To find out, epidemiologists Roger Connelly and Barbara Christine undertook an extensive investigation in Connecticut, where doctors were required to report all cancers and all communicable diseases. The two scientists found 4,529 cases of infectious mononucleosis diagnosed there between 1948 and 1964. When they cross-checked the names with the state tumor registry, they discovered that patients who had had mononucleosis developed lymphoma (predominantly Hodgkin's disease) at a rate almost four times that of the general population. At the same time, Danish investigator Nils Rosdahl carried out an even more extensive analysis. As in Connecticut, Danish physicians were required to report all new cancer cases. But in addition, a single laboratory performed all mononucleosis blood tests for the entire country. Rosdahl matched the names of 17,073 people who had had a positive mononucleosis test with names in the cancer registry. He, too, found the incidence of Hodgkin's disease quadrupled in people who had had mononucleosis. "Our findings," Rosdahl concluded, "support the suggestion that infectious mononucleosis and Hodgkin's disease may be associated."

The common factor appeared to be the Epstein-Barr virus. Supporting that hypothesis, a Brazilian researcher found elevated levels of antibody to the virus in 98 percent of patients with Hodgkin's disease. Several scientists argued that many healthy people have measurable EBV antibodies, probably from a low-grade infection earlier in their lives. Another group, however, reported antibody levels in patients with Hodgkin's disease to be higher than in the general population. And those with the highest levels had the most advanced disease. But the presence of antibody to EBV in cancer patients didn't prove that the virus actually caused the cancer. Scientists needed to go one step further: They had to demonstrate DNA from the Epstein-Barr virus in lymph nodes from Hodgkin's disease patients. This ultimate test failed. And the mysteries of case clustering and the association between Hodgkin's disease and mononucleosis remained unsolved.

⁓

Although epidemiologic studies provided clues to the etiology of Hodgkin's disease and other lymphomas, Henry Kaplan knew that this puzzle could only be solved in the laboratory. Early in his career, he had begun probing the basic biology of cancer cells by inducing mouse lymphomas and leukemias with radiation. At that point, he hadn't been interested in lymphomas per se; he was just using that malignancy as a model to investigate the mechanism by which radiation induced cancer. Radiation biologists believed radiation acted directly on targeted cells and transformed them into cancerous ones. Kaplan had set out to ascertain how that happened when he began his work with C57 black mice. None of his early publications even mentioned the word "virus."

Kaplan had found that mouse lymphomas originated in the thymus gland and subsequently spread to other organs. When he directed radiation to the primary site in the thymus, however, he discovered that these tumors were caused not by direct radiation damage, as thought, but by some indirect mechanism. To prove this theory, he had removed the thymus glands from a group of mice and treated them with total body irradiation. Then he reimplanted the healthy glands, which had never been exposed to radiation, back into the irradiated mice. Lymphomas developed in the transplanted thymus glands even though the glands themselves had not been irradiated. Thus, the accepted theory for radiation-induced carcinogenesis was wrong. Normal thymus glands had been transformed into malignancies, not by radiation directly, but by something in the irradiated host environment. Kaplan focused his work on discovering what in the host had converted normal cells into malignant ones. Three thousand miles away, Ludwik Gross, working in the basement of the Bronx Veterans Administration Hospital, asserted that a virus caused leukemia in mice. No one believed him, not even Henry Kaplan.

Among the most ubiquitous of organisms, viruses are parasites that live in the cells of other organisms. Composed only of a core of DNA or RNA and a protein coat, a virus can't reproduce by itself. Yet once inside a living cell, it can multiply hundreds of times. A virus infects a healthy cell by attaching to the cell surface and propelling its own viral RNA or DNA inside. The virus then takes over the cell's protein-making process and orders the production of hundreds of copies of itself. Eventually, the cell is damaged irreparably, and viruses released from the dying cell go on to infect hundreds of other cells. This simplest of organisms killed twenty million people in the 1918 influenza epidemic and left a hundred thousand children crippled from polio in the 1940s and 1950s.

The first connection between a virus and cancer had been discovered by serendipity. In 1908, Danish veterinarians Vilhelm Ellerman and Oluf Bang were studying the spread of leukemia in hens. At that time, leukemia was thought to be an infection, and they were searching for the responsible microbe. They made suspensions of diseased tissues and passed them through filters that trapped leukemia cells and bacteria. When they injected healthy hens with these filtrates, the hens developed leukemia. Because they thought the infecting agent was so small that it slipped through filters, they categorized it with the group of mysterious microbes called viruses. Neither they nor their colleagues understood the implications of their findings: they had demonstrated transmission of cancer by a virus.

Three years later, Francis Peyton Rous, a microbiologist at the Rockefeller Institute, began investigating the cause of fowl sarcoma, a disease known to be malignant. He made solutions of minced tumors collected from Plymouth

Rock chickens he found at a market near his laboratory. After passing the mixture through filters impermeable to cancer cells, he inoculated this cell-free filtrate into the breast muscle of healthy young hens. Nothing happened. Then he did something ingenious: he serially transplanted the sarcoma in several generations of chickens, producing a more virulent cancer in each subsequent generation. After each transplantation, he made a cell-free filtrate and inoculated another group of healthy hens. Fourteen months later, in the eighth generation of Plymouth Rock hens, he detected tumor nodules. Under the microscope, the growths resembled the original sarcoma. In 1911, Peyton Rous reported that he had isolated a tumor-producing particle responsible for transmission of sarcoma in fowl.

If viruses caused cancer in fowl, why not in humans? Despite substantial efforts, Peyton Rous and other scientists could not detect viruses in human tumors, and interest waned. "For many years," a biographical account read, "scientists scoffed at Rous's discovery. They believed cancer couldn't be caused by a virus because it wasn't contagious." Peyton Rous had inaugurated the field of cancer virology, but no one believed him, and he himself eventually turned to other areas of research. His finding was considered an avian oddity, and its significance was not recognized for decades. (This discovery, later termed the Rous sarcoma virus, earned Peyton Rous the Nobel Prize in 1966 at the age of eighty-seven.)

Tumor virology lay dormant until the 1950s, when the next major finding was made by Ludwik Gross, a Polish surgeon. During his surgical training, Gross had resected a large number of lip cancers and noticed that they always seemed to spread to lymph nodes in the neck like infections. He began to search for an infectious agent in these cancers, and when he could not see one under the microscope, he concluded that a virus had generated the cancers. Certain his hypothesis was right, Gross spent most of his life trying to prove it. His research took him to the famed Pasteur Institute in Paris, where after eight years of investigation, he came up empty-handed. He tried to secure a research position in the United States but was repeatedly rejected. No one believed his viral theory of carcinogenesis, and no one wanted to invest in him. After Germany invaded Poland in 1939, he emigrated to the United States and joined the army.

Assigned to the Bronx Veterans Administration Hospital, Gross set up a laboratory in a basement storeroom to which he retreated after finishing his medical duties. He was determined to prove that a virus caused cancer. His experiments involved taking the AK strain of mice that spontaneously developed leukemia, and using Peyton Rous's techniques, mincing their tumors, making a cell-free filtrate, and injecting it into the C3H strain of mice, known to have a low incidence of leukemia. If the second group contracted leukemia from the filtrate, he could deem a virus the likely agent. Scientists had been trying to transmit cancer between strains of mice for twenty-five years, and most had abandoned the work.

In 1944, Gross started to breed AK and C3H mice. It took him four years to build a large enough colony to begin his experiments. He injected cell-free filtrates from AK mice into C3H mice, but he could not induce leukemia. So he tried again. By then he had so many mice, he kept them in coffee cans in his room and car. Colleagues began to ridicule him for his tenacity. "There were even rumors that I would be shipped out," he recalled, "because I had crazy ideas."

Then one day a breakthrough came from an unanticipated source. Gross was attending a lecture on neurologic complications of a particular viral infection in mice. The visiting scientist said he could produce paralysis only if he inoculated newborn mice whose immune system had not matured. "I did not wait until he finished his lecture," Gross said. "I ran to the laboratory." The immune system had been the stumbling block. "It was going to work," he said. "I knew it." Now he planned to inject newborn C3H mice with filtrates from AK mice. "In the crucial experiments that followed," he recalled, "I frequently came to the laboratory late at night because pregnant female mice gave birth to newborn litters very often in the middle of the night." Still no tumors appeared. He made eighty different filtrates from the diseased organs of almost a hundred AK mice. After eighteen months of experimentation, he came to the lab one day to find a mouse stricken with leukemia; more followed. In 1951, two decades after beginning his search, Gross announced he had isolated what he called the murine leukemia virus (MuLV).

Other investigators had difficulty replicating his results, in part because of the long latency period between injection of filtrates and development of leukemia. "Gross's early work was greeted with reactions ranging from skepticism to outright disbelief," Henry Kaplan said, "and I must admit that I shared in this skepticism." One of Kaplan's research assistants hung a cartoon mocking Gross and his virus in their laboratory. Some scientists went so far as to attack Gross's integrity. He was declined membership in the major cancer research society. Years later, however, the murine leukemia virus could be detected by electron microscopy. "The discovery of MuLV by Gross in 1951," one historian wrote, "was the pay-off par excellence of intuition, faith, perseverance, and hard work."

Henry Kaplan had found that something had induced lymphomas and leukemias in his mice after they had been exposed to radiation. Although he initially didn't believe Gross's assertion that a virus caused murine leukemia, he began to follow the virologist's work closely, and with time, found the theory more compelling. Seemingly overnight, Kaplan's staff saw a transformation from cynicism to enthusiasm. The Gross cartoon disappeared from the laboratory. Now Kaplan embraced the viral theory of carcinogenesis: "Confronted by the paradox that radiation acts by an indirect mechanism," he said years later, "and stimulated by Gross's discoveries, we were led to consider the possibility that an agent similar to the Gross virus might play a role in the indirect development of thymic lymphomas." Radiation might produce leukemia by activating that latent virus.

Kaplan knew investigation of this hypothesis would be laborious and thrust him into an entirely new area of experimentation. He was a radiation biologist, not a virologist. If he entered the tumor virology arena, he needed a research associate who had both experience with viruses and the diligence required for this work. And he needed an assistant who believed, as he did, in the viral theory of carcinogenesis, an unpopular and risky research endeavor for someone just starting his or her career. When Henry Kaplan hired microbiologist Miriam Lieberman in 1959, he selected the perfect person with whom to begin this journey. Neither would have predicted they would work together on radiation-induced leukemia for the rest of their academic lives.

Lieberman came to Kaplan's lab with a PhD from Berkeley. They made a perfect team—he on the theoretical side, she on the practical. Kaplan designed the experiments; Lieberman executed them meticulously. Together they published over thirty articles. Some research staff found Kaplan too directive. That didn't bother Lieberman. She had been raised and educated in the traditional academic milieu of eastern Europe where senior scientists were referred to as "Herr Professor."

Although many on his research team felt intimidated by Kaplan, Lieberman understood her boss. When Kaplan suggested experiments that Lieberman thought theoretically sound but unworkable, she simply maneuvered around him, making changes in the design, sometimes so subtle as to be imperceptible. While Kaplan was regularly bursting with new ideas, Lieberman plodded along from one trial to the next. "He was the brains; she was the hands," Kaplan's research associate Alain Declève observed. Together Kaplan and Lieberman performed what would be a landmark experiment in viral oncology.

Setting out to prove that a virus generated the radiation-induced lymphoid malignancies found in mice, they began by applying whole body irradiation to C57BL mice. As expected, 80 to 90 percent developed lymphoma. Following Gross, they then sacrificed the mice and prepared solutions of minced lymphomatous tissue—filtered to eliminate cancer cells. Then they inoculated unirradiated newborn mice with the filtrate. If Kaplan's suspicion was correct, the filtrate should contain a virus that would eventually cause the newborns to develop leukemia.

At first nothing happened. But they didn't expect immediate results. Viruses require months to induce tumors. Six months passed, and still they detected no cancer. At a year, they began to doubt whether such a virus existed. Was the filtrate they had injected actually sterile? Had they had been watching the mice for over a year for naught? By now they had a colony of almost a hundred mice. At eighteen months—the point at which Gross had finally detected his cancers—they still saw no evidence of lymphoma, and Kaplan became so discouraged that he contemplated giving up. Then, at two years, the first thymic lymphoma appeared in a C57BL recipient, and before long, 17 percent had tumors that looked identical to the original lymphoma.

Kaplan was elated. The waiting had paid off. He postulated that C57 mice carried a latent virus, which they passed to their offspring. Although the virus was capable of causing leukemia, the host-viral relationship somehow prevented spontaneous tumor growth. Total body irradiation altered that relationship so that the virus converted normal thymus cells into neoplastic ones. "The essence of what we discovered," Kaplan said, "is that mouse leukemias, which were ostensibly caused by x-rays and certain chemicals, were in fact due to latent viruses ... triggered into activity by exposure to x-rays.... The animals can live a completely normal life span without ever evincing the fact that they harbor these viruses, if they are not exposed." In a broader sense, he had confirmed the viral theory of carcinogenesis in mice. That was in 1959. Henry Kaplan had been studying murine leukemia for sixteen years.

Next Kaplan set out to identify the type of virus with electron microscopy. Nine years later, in 1968, he and colleagues identified an RNA virus in the thymus gland and then in the filtrates themselves. Furthermore, these viruses could be detected months before the appearance of leukemic cells, lending more evidence to his theory of a latent virus. He called this new agent radiation leukemia virus or RadLV. Joining the ranks of pioneering tumor virologists, Henry Kaplan had not only discovered a new cancer virus, but also had established a link between an external cancer-causing agent—radiation—and a virus.

Henry Kaplan had started out trying to discern how radiation induced cancer as a means to solve the mystery of carcinogenesis. Along the way, he had stumbled across an unexpected finding. Instead of discounting it, he pursued it. As a result, he found a cancer-causing virus in mice. Like Gross before him, Kaplan then became obsessed with finding a virus that causes cancer in man. And his fervent quest for the human tumor virus began.

29   The Ann Arbor Conference

In April 1971, the third pivotal meeting for key investigators engaged in Hodgkin's disease research took place in Ann Arbor, Michigan. It had been almost six years since the highly successful Rye conference. Throughout that earlier meeting, a great esprit de corps had prevailed, and when it was over, participants left determined to continue working together to overcome this disease. Experts in radiation therapy, medical oncology, and pathology communicated regularly in attempts to standardize therapy. No cancer had been attacked with such a multidisciplinary, collaborative effort. "There was no holding back," said Sir David Smithers of the Royal Marsden Hospital, "everything out in the open, everybody helping. I think the advances in the treatment of Hodgkin's disease came more from these group meetings than from anything else."

The hallmark of their endeavor was scientific rigor. "The fragmentary, anecdotal, inadequately characterized clinical studies which had filled the older medical literature," Kaplan said, "gave way to studies of large numbers of . . . meticulously staged patients. Collectively, these rigorously designed studies have yielded unambiguous evidence concerning virtually every clinical aspect of the disease." This academic approach and the subsequent high-quality trials generated optimism regarding a possible cure for Hodgkin's disease.

Beyond that, camaraderie had developed among leaders in the field. Paul Carbone of the NCI recalled a colloquium at Brown University at which he and Kaplan were to debate therapy for Hodgkin's disease. Carbone dreaded facing this formidable opponent. When he arrived, he found, to his dismay, that he had forgotten some of his slides. Kaplan suggested they pool their slides and present and defend each other's data. The audience enjoyed the interchange, but no more so than Kaplan and Carbone. Kaplan invited David Smithers and Maurice Tubiana to stay at his home whenever one of them visited California. And if Henry found Vera Peters alone at a meeting, he asked her to join the Stanford group for dinner. Peters, Kaplan, and DeVita often spoke at the same conferences, where they enjoyed each other's company. Vince recalled the time they had attended the dedication of a new radiation therapy center in Chapel Hill, North Carolina. After the opening ceremonies, they went out for drinks. "There was only one bar in all of Chapel Hill," DeVita said, "and it was a dump. There we were—HSK in a suit and tie and Vera in a large fur coat—drinking beers, listening to country music. And I think Vera was the most comfortable."

But in the years since the Rye conference, some of the smooth working relationships had become worn, and the cooperative effort began to dissipate. Working together wasn't as easy as they had anticipated; tempers began to flare. Kaplan frequently spoke at the same conferences as Ralph Johnson, chief of the Radiation Branch at the NCI. He had no respect for this self-important man and became annoyed every time Johnson presented data on total nodal irradiation, acting as if he had conceived of the technique. Once when DeVita and Kaplan were sharing a taxicab to the airport, Henry blurted out, "Ralph Johnson is a pig. He gives 4,000 rads through an anterior port and has a high rate of pericarditis, as anybody in their right mind would know he would. Then he presents a paper on the management of pericarditis. Only Ralph Johnson would capitalize on an error." Johnson regularly maligned the Stanford group, accusing them of "burning bodies" when they introduced total lymphoid irradiation, calling staging laparotomies "living autopsies."

Now leaders in the field were about to meet again in Ann Arbor. The conference had been planned as a three-day working meeting by Saul Rosenberg, Paul Carbone, pathologist Henry Rappaport from the University of Chicago, and Jack Milder of the American Cancer Society. They had invited twenty-nine current leaders in the field. The main purpose was to conclude a piece of unfinished business from the Rye conference—international adoption of a uniform staging system. Rosenberg and Carbone had asked Vera Peters to set the stage for the conference with a keynote speech on the topic. A series of talks and informal discussions would follow. Participants would then break into three committees—initial clinical evaluation, a universal staging system, and pathologic criteria for diagnosis—and propose recommendations to the full group. In addition, the conference would serve as an intimate gathering to discuss the latest, as yet unpublished, research on Hodgkin's disease. Above all, the meeting would provide an opportunity to recapture the collegial spirit engendered by the Rye conference.

Saul Rosenberg looked forward to the Ann Arbor conference. This would be an opportunity to establish himself internationally as a colleague equal in stature to Henry Kaplan. At forty-four, Rosenberg had been working with Kaplan for ten years. Their collaboration had shown researchers the effectiveness of bridging the disciplines of radiation therapy and medical oncology. During that time, Rosenberg had made several significant contributions to the field, starting with the 1965 Paris meeting. There his elegant presentation on the need for precise clinical assessment of Hodgkin's disease had convinced cancer specialists. At the Rye conference, he had substantiated the concept of contiguous spread by showing his analysis of diseased sites in newly diagnosed patients. Additionally, he had proposed adopting Stanford's staging system, calling it the Rye classification system. Since that conference, two procedures—the lymphangiogram and staging laparotomy—had greatly enhanced the accuracy of patient assessment, and he had taken a lead in publicizing them. Despite these accomplishments, he was still viewed as Kaplan's junior associate. Of eleven papers they had published together, Rosenberg was first author on only four.

As the Ann Arbor conference drew closer, Kaplan, preoccupied with the Cancer Act, said he didn't know whether he'd attend. This was Rosenberg's chance to shine. He planned to present two reports, including an update of the Stanford data obtained from staging laparotomies. He hoped to secure consensus about and then publish guidelines for assessing new patients. And because he had designed much of the Rye classification, he anticipated a major role in finalizing an international staging system.

Vera Peters went to the Ann Arbor conference with high expectations too. For years she had been talking and writing about the need for a uniform staging system. Now she would be the keynote speaker. She had planned her address carefully. First, she would review the evolution of staging systems and the deficiencies of those currently used. Then, she would unveil her proposal for a completely different classification—the TNM system—which she thought rectified these flaws. This would culminate years of deliberation on her part. So Saul Rosenberg and Vera Peters anticipated leaving Ann Arbor feeling gratified. They envisioned a meeting that rivaled the success of the Rye conference. Neither happened.

On April 26, 1971, investigators from as far away as Rotterdam and Paris gathered in Ann Arbor at the University of Michigan's Center for Continuing Education. They couldn't help contrasting the setting with that at Rye: a sparse classroom instead of a country club; low-hanging clouds and crusted snow instead of blue skies and fall colors. That didn't dampen their enthusiasm, however; they came ready to adopt a new staging system. The need for consensus was obvious. Without common definitions, comparing clinical trial data among investigators was problematic. And if researchers couldn't build upon each other's results, progress in the field would be stifled. But participants came to Ann Arbor with differing positions. Several European groups already were arguing among themselves. Vera Peters' new proposal would be a radical departure. And Kaplan had specific views on which he did not intend to compromise. If consensus were to be reached in three days, either some extraordinary mediation or tricky maneuvering would be required.

Peters's keynote address opened the conference. She examined prior staging systems, including that developed at the Rye conference. Many centers had begun using this four-stage scheme, but she pointed out its limitations: It didn't distinguish stage determined by physical examination and laboratory studies from stage based on findings at laparotomy. It didn't take into account factors that affected prognosis, such as size. And it didn't distinguish extent of disease. A patient with a single lung lesion and one with multiple lung nodules were both called stage IV. The former could be cured with local irradiation; the latter required chemotherapy. Peters proposed adopting the TNM system, which had been used in staging other cancers for years. In this, T described size and extent of the primary tumor, N the extent of nodal involvement, and M the presence or absence of metastatic disease. She suggested that each Hodgkin's disease patient be assigned two stages—a clinical stage, based on physical exam and laboratory tests, and a pathologic stage if the patient had undergone a laparotomy.

Just as Peters was starting to make her most important points, Maurice Tubiana, chairman of the session, interrupted and said she had exceeded her allotted time. Peters was baffled; her invitation had suggested a forty-five minute address, and she was just halfway through. She had not yet pointed out the major advantages of the TNM system, nor had she shown the detailed tables she had drawn for charting the stages of individual patients. Flustered, she sat down, unable to sense the audience reaction to her proposal. She consoled herself that she would make her points in the small working committee.

Although most participants weren't enthusiastic about the TNM system, they were courteous. Kaplan said nothing, but he thought Peters's proposal unworkable. Its adoption would require reassigning stage for all past patients. This meant reviewing hundreds of records at Stanford alone, thousands around the world. Results of published studies would need to be reanalyzed using the new system and the design of ongoing studies reassessed. The resulting chaos would set efforts back years. They were moving toward overcoming this disease, and Kaplan didn't intend to take a detour. But he did not confront Peters in public. To the surprise of many, he sat quietly while she introduced her radical proposal. Later that morning, however, as Peters passed Kaplan in the hall, he said, "Vera, you'll never get me to use the TNM classification for Hodgkin's disease—never." She suspected then that it was Kaplan who had managed to have her talk stopped prematurely. (Months later she found out that Tubiana had been instructed to limit presentations to twenty minutes. He hadn't been told that the keynote address was an exception.)

Following Peters's address, the group turned to the first major topic—initial clinical evaluation, so-called staging. Rosenberg presented Stanford's most recent data on over two hundred patients who had undergone staging laparotomy and splenectomy. He emphasized that this procedure had resulted in a change of stage for a substantial number of patients. Without precise staging, he concluded, published results of new treatment programs would be uninterpretable, hindering progress.

Peters spoke up first. She didn't agree that most patients needed to undergo a laparotomy, and based on her own experience, she could not recommend the procedure routinely. She could predict intra-abdominal disease from the histologic subtype and findings on physical examination and chest x-ray. After the initial Stanford report, she had subjected all newly diagnosed patients to a laparotomy. After analyzing the first seventy cases, she found that she had predicted who had intra-abdominal disease with almost complete accuracy. They hadn't needed surgery. Only one group benefited from the procedure—patients with the nodular sclerosing type and disease confined to the mediastinum. In these cases, she could not determine who had intra-abdominal disease. These patients, she concluded, were the only ones who should undergo a staging laparotomy. Rosenberg countered that Stanford had by far the largest group who had undergone laparotomies, and no one factor stood out as an absolute predictor for results.

Sir David Smithers, the best-known radiotherapist in England and a friend of Kaplan's, echoed Peters's concerns about performing laparotomies in patients at low risk for having abdominal disease. He worried about the procedure's safety. Surgeons had reported anesthetic complications in patients with large mediastinal masses, postoperative infections that delayed treatment, and even death. He agreed that the staging laparotomy might improve interpretation of data; however, this did not benefit every patient. "It seem[s] more useful for knowledge's sake," he said, "than for the sake of the patient."

These criticisms, coming from esteemed colleagues, were painful for Rosenberg. Fewer than 10 percent of Stanford patients had suffered complications. He tried to emphasize that without accurate staging, up to a third would be either overtreated, subjecting them to unnecessary toxicities, or undertreated, reducing their chance of being cured. In that case, Tubiana countered, laparotomy should influence subsequent therapy. He asked Rosenberg whether they refrained from irradiating the abdomen in patients with negative laparotomies, and if so, what had been the outcome. Rosenberg responded that at Stanford, such patients still were enrolled in trials that assessed the value of prophylactic abdominal irradiation. Ralph Johnson pounced upon this point. "Unless information is contributed which regularly alters eventual treatment," he said, "staging laparotomy is scarcely so innocuous as to be routinely justified."

Rosenberg's frustration grew. Why couldn't they understand how crucial accurate staging was if they expected clinical trials to be meaningful? Kaplan did not engage in this debate; he let Rosenberg defend their stance. Nothing would be gained by yet another heated exchange. DeVita saw Kaplan frequently sitting alone, preoccupied. He left the room several times to take calls about the Cancer Act. He even flew to Washington, D.C., and back in the middle of the conference. Rosenberg was on his own. Kaplan would assume leadership of the Ann Arbor conference, but not over this issue.

At lunchtime the first day, Paul Carbone, chairman of the Program Committee, announced the members of the three working groups. The committee on staging procedures included Vince DeVita, Ralph Johnson, Saul Rosenberg, and several others. Rosenberg did not want to argue with Johnson anymore, but Kaplan had asked him to lead this group, saying he would take care of the committee on staging classification. Rosenberg was disappointed. He had planned to have a major role in determining the Ann Arbor classification. Kaplan had expressed no enthusiasm for the conference. "But as so often happened," Rosenberg said, "once he arrived, Kaplan took over." Rosenberg's leadership had been usurped.

Next Carbone announced the members of the committee on staging classification. Peters had assumed that she would be appointed to that group, probably chair it. After all, she had been asked to deliver the keynote address on the subject. She sat stunned when Carbone announced the names: David Smithers, Maurice Tubiana, Karl Musshoff, and Henry Kaplan. Carbone would chair the committee himself. Not only had Peters been omitted from the staging committee, but she was one of the few participants not assigned to any group. A Dutch radiation oncologist sitting next to her whispered, "That's rotten." Peters was humiliated. "It was a slap in the face," she said. She suspected that Kaplan had persuaded Carbone to exclude her from the group. All the members of the committee on staging classification were either his friends or admirers.

On the last day of the conference, Rosenberg reported back for his committee on clinical evaluation and staging procedures. They had quickly reached consensus regarding most recommendations: each biopsy should be reviewed by a pathologist with expertise in Hodgkin's disease, each new patient examined by an experienced cancer specialist. Initial tests should include a blood count, tests of liver function, a chest x-ray, a lymphangiogram, and a bone marrow biopsy. They had not agreed on the role of staging laparotomy. Their consensus statement read: "In view of the known and possible complications of exploratory laparotomy and splenectomy, the procedure would be considered required for diagnostic purposes if the therapeutic philosophy is to limit radiotherapy to only the known sites of disease." Although Rosenberg couldn't help feeling discouraged, he predicted that once physicians became more comfortable with the procedure and observed its usefulness, they would recommend it more often. He was right. Within a few years, staging laparotomy did become routine at most cancer centers—even, despite Ralph Johnson, at the NCI.

Next, Paul Carbone reported his committee's recommendation for a new staging classification system built upon the Rye four-stage system. It specified: stage I—involvement of a single lymph node region; stage II—involvement of two or more nodal regions on the same side of the diaphragm; stage III—involved nodes on both sides of the diaphragm; stage IV—disseminated disease. B would still be used to designate systemic symptoms—fever, night sweats, or weight loss—and A the absence of these symptoms. They proposed two modifications that addressed the limitations pointed out by Peters. First, the new system differentiated between organ involvement that resulted from generalized spread of disease and localized involvement of an organ by extension from a nearby lymph node, which they termed an extranodal, or "E," lesion. Thus, a patient with multiple lung nodules would still be designated as having stage IV disease, requiring chemotherapy. On the other hand, a patient with local extension into the lung from mediastinal nodes would be designated I_E and treated with irradiation. Second, the new system distinguished between clinical stage, determined by physical exam, blood tests and radiographs, and pathologic stage, determined by laparotomy.

The rapidity with which the committee members had agreed and the precision of the report were due in large part to Kaplan. "Henry was instrumental," Carbone said, "in trying to make the scheme logical." Participants congratulated the committee on their design of a comprehensive classification, which seemed to address all the inadequacies of the Rye system. The Ann Arbor staging system was accepted. Their report never even mentioned consideration of the TNM system.

⌒

The Ann Arbor conference would assume its place in the history of Hodgkin's disease as the time when researchers from around the world joined forces to develop a new staging classification. The Ann Arbor staging system had universal acceptance and would stand the test of time unaltered. At the meeting's conclusion, David Smithers wrote, "The main business of our conference has been satisfactorily resolved. . . . It was a valuable and most cheerful meeting." Although the group left Ann Arbor having accomplished their main goal, it was nevertheless with a sense of resignation on the part of some.

The conference had been a personal disappointment for Saul Rosenberg. He had anticipated a more pronounced role. Much of the Rye classification had been of his design, and the Ann Arbor system simply represented a modification. Yet he had received no recognition. "Ann Arbor" was stamped indelibly on the staging system. And because Paul Carbone had appointed himself chairman of the committee, he was the first author on the publication. More discouraging, Kaplan had once again emerged as the leader in Hodgkin's disease. "I was one of the initiators of that meeting," Rosenberg said, "but I got overshadowed by Henry Kaplan. He took over as spokesman for Stanford."

Vera Peters considered those three days among the worst in her life. She felt brushed aside. "I think Kaplan respected me," she said, "but he understood my shortcomings and took advantage of my personality. He knew I wouldn't fight back." Maurice Tubiana perceived their cooling relationship. He attributed it to the contrast in styles—Kaplan loved to debate; Peters, who was somewhat shy, didn't like to spar in public. Even if unhappy, she remained charming. At Ann Arbor, Peters was more than unhappy, she was mortified. She left the conference with a simmering resentment of Henry Kaplan. "He wanted to be the king of Hodgkin's disease," she said, "and he didn't want to share the crown."

Several years later in Paris, Kaplan invited Peters to join him and four other researchers for dinner. They were having a lovely time when Henry leaned across the table and said, "Vera, I think you should stop writing about Hodgkin's disease and concentrate on breast cancer." Peters was shocked. She had treated more Hodgkin's disease patients than anyone in the world. She had been first to demonstrate that the disease could be cured. She had devised the earliest staging classification, which became the foundation for the Ann Arbor staging system. She had emphasized the importance of dose and prompted use of prophylactic radiation, the predecessor to total lymphoid irradiation. Vera Peters had been writing about Hodgkin's disease for over twenty years, and now Henry Kaplan was suggesting she just stop. She graciously muttered something about breast cancer being a full-time endeavor. That was the last conversation she ever had with Kaplan. And after that, she published only one other article on Hodgkin's disease.

Vera Peters went on to have a major impact on the field of breast cancer. She led the movement for breast-conserving therapy—local excision and radiation instead of mastectomy. Considered the foremost radiotherapist in Canada, Peters received numerous honors. The one blight on her otherwise stellar career was the Ann Arbor conference. "It was the lowest point of my career," she said.

And what of Henry Kaplan? Did he sense Saul's disappointment or Vera's bitterness? Probably not. Many remembered his repeated tributes to Peters as a pioneer in Hodgkin's disease. "Kaplan credited a Toronto doctor, Vera Peters, with bringing about some of the important advances in treatment," the *Toronto Star* noted. But in his single-minded zeal to cure Hodgkin's disease, he was oblivious to the needs and feelings of Rosenberg and Peters. As it had been when he set out to transform Stanford into a first-rate medical school or to preserve the NIH intact during the battle over the Cancer Act, he just didn't have the time or inclination to be diplomatic. "HSK achieved his goals," one radiation oncologist said, "not by stepping on people, but by stepping over them."

Once Kaplan had decided to go to Ann Arbor, he focused on one objective, and he had achieved it. The Ann Arbor staging system allowed clinical research to progress more rapidly, no longer hampered by use of several different classifications. But a price had been paid. The field lost Vera Peters's insight and creativity. And never again would this group of prominent investigators work together toward a common goal.

30   Bookends

Henry Kaplan was approaching his prime. In the early 1970s, his list of awards extended over pages. The Shabanou Award, bestowed by the empress of Iran for his major advances toward the cure of cancer; Italy's Ordine al Merito della Repubblica (Order of Merit of the Republic); the Atoms for Peace Award, which he received along with President Eisenhower. And he was the first radiotherapist inducted into the National Academy of Sciences. His name was a drawing card for any conference. His radiation therapy program attracted the most talented trainees, and scientists from around the world lined up to spend sabbatical time with him. Nearly 70 percent of patients with Hodgkin's disease achieved long survival; whereas fifty years earlier, 90 percent had died. Elegant work on the radiation-induced leukemia virus continued to emerge from his laboratory—a prelude to his hunt for a human tumor virus. And his ultimate goal—the cure of cancer—seemed near.

Kaplan's family was also flourishing. Leah was gaining recognition for her efforts to help students at Stanford's Counseling and Psychological Services. She still entertained regularly, and friends considered an evening at the Kaplans' a treat. Henry adored Leah. "The longer we're married, the more I fall in love with her," he wrote. And he enjoyed teasing her so that he could hear her burst of joyful laughter. He once told her that he had considered dedicating his book *Hodgkin's Disease* to her, with the inscription: "To my wife, Leah, without whom this book would have been completed two years earlier."

Annie was excelling in her studies at Stanford University and trying to decide between law and psychology. Paul had found his niche in art. Henry had accepted that his son was not destined to be a scientist and had begun to appreciate Paul's potential as a photographer. After graduation, he entered Antioch College West, a small, liberal arts school in San Francisco affiliated with the unconventional parent college in Ohio. Henry envisioned his son as being well on his way to becoming a renowned photographer and began to treat him as such.

Especially dear to Kaplan were his friends. Estranged from his brother and often distant with his own son, Kaplan developed intense friendships with a number of men. Most colleagues were unaware of these relationships, likely assuming that a man with such self-confidence had no need for companionship and perhaps doubting that a man with his strong ego had the capacity. But his firm sense of self may have been precisely what allowed Kaplan to open himself to such closeness. He had several close male friends, including Abe Braude, Ed Ginzton, David Karnofsky, and later Vince DeVita. Above all, however, he cherished his friendship with Michael Feldman.

Kaplan and Feldman had met in 1959 at a research symposium at the Weizmann Institute. Neither had yet achieved fame. A son of Russian immigrants, Feldman was a developmental biologist. He was eight years younger and a head shorter than Kaplan, with dark, unruly hair, which curled about his ears. He bristled with vitality. "The year Monet died," he once told Kaplan, "I was born. This planet couldn't take both of us." His eyes and hands seemed in constant motion, and he walked with such buoyancy that gravity didn't seem to hold him. His speech exuded imagination, colorful language, and warm humor. Michael was immediately attracted to Henry. "I was introduced to him," he said, "and we started to talk, and within ten minutes, I felt he was one of those rare people with whom I could find a common language." Following the seminar, they toured Israel together, and a friendship began that would last a lifetime.

The two corresponded regularly, writing about science, families, politics, human rights, and Israel. At forty, Feldman had become dean of the Graduate School at the Weizmann Institute. A professor of cell biology, he was renowned for his work on lymphocytes and antigen production. Although the relatedness between his and Henry's work was tangential, they continued to seek ways to collaborate. "I am interested in your thoughts," Henry wrote Michael, "about [a] model system for the development of Hodgkin's disease and other malignant lymphomas. . . . What would be really ideal would be an opportunity for us to work together on them."

When apart for too long, their letters expressed their eagerness to reunite. "Looking back at the last few months," Michael wrote after sabbatical time spent at Stanford, "seems to me like having been a dream." Henry replied, "Your office is still vacant and waiting for you, and so is everyone else here in the lab!" They compared travel schedules in attempts to spend time together. Henry wrote:

> I am due to participate in the symposium on carcinogenesis . . . in Amsterdam about the middle of May and would welcome the opportunity of seeing you if your travels take you in that direction. . . . I will be going to Brazil . . . immediately after attending what looks like a very interesting symposium on virus oncogenesis to

be held at Saratoga Springs. . . . Is there any chance that your travel to Washington . . . could be modified to include a visit to upstate New York? . . . Finally, I must go to Florence in late September. . . . It is at least conceivable that I could squeeze in a brief visit to Israel.

In another letter, Kaplan wrote, "I look forward to seeing you again in Corfu. . . . I hope we will find time for some good walks and talks."

Together they toured Europe and the Far East, adding a few days to each conference for sight-seeing. They tried to provide each other with new, exhilarating adventures. Their conversations sparkled as they rapidly moved between science, art, and politics. If their wives left the room, they didn't notice. They always seemed to be chuckling over some episode, like the three days they had spent in Tahiti on their way home from a symposium in Australia. They had visited a botanical garden, where Henry spent hours taking pictures of exotic flora. He insisted that they return later in the afternoon to catch certain plants in a different light. While Michael paced, he took almost twenty minutes to compose each picture. Back home, Henry found that the camera had no film. For years afterward, Michael called Henry "the Gauguin of photography."

Few knew of Kaplan's and Feldman's friendship. Though thousands of miles apart, Henry shared his thoughts with Michael from his frustrations in the laboratory to his distaste for deans to family affairs. "There have been so many times in the past few weeks when I wanted very much to talk with you," Henry wrote, "and I find it absolutely impossible to communicate much in the frustrating form of a letter." These two brilliant men, continued to invigorate each other throughout their lives. They talked softly, laughed out loud, argued over a work of art or an experiment, continually inspiring each other. "You could have dropped the two of them anywhere on earth at any time in history," Paul Kaplan said, "and they would have found something that interested them at a high level of intensity. They were a pair of bookends."

Dear friends, a loving wife, success in his work—Henry Kaplan had reached the pinnacle of his life. He had achieved greatness by anyone's measure. But greatness had its costs. He logged hours on airplanes before jet travel, and often Leah saw him only long enough to put a clean change of socks in his bag before he rushed to the airport again. On Annie and Paul's birthdays, he called from Brussels or Hong Kong. His classical music collection gathered dust; he never again took an extended family vacation. "Whatever he was working on," a friend said, "was *the* most important thing." He had a battle to win, and he didn't stop to tend those, like Saul Rosenberg or Vera Peters, wounded along the way. As a result, professionally Kaplan received respect from colleagues, but not necessarily their affection, and ultimately not their loyalty.

Henry Kaplan had made great strides in combating cancer. But he couldn't fight alone. To be most effective, he had to be a good leader, but in this regard Kaplan was hampered by a tragic flaw: his single-mindedness blunted his insight into the hearts and minds of many colleagues, alienating them and isolating him. This single-mindedness, which had fostered his success, proved to be a liability, especially when it came to fulfilling his dream of building a cancer center at Stanford.

31   The Cancer Center Debacle

On December 23, 1971, President Richard Nixon signed the National Cancer Act, launching his war on cancer. The cornerstone of that campaign was the comprehensive cancer center. Fifteen such centers, established at medical schools across the nation, would bring together a critical mass of scientists and clinicians dedicated to the eradication of cancer. The government's investment would be substantial: funding to construct new facilities, plus long-term support for research, patient care, and training of cancer specialists. At the time, there were only three cancer centers nationwide—Roswell Park Cancer Institute in Buffalo, MD Anderson Cancer Center in Houston, and Memorial Sloan-Kettering Cancer Center in New York City. All were free-standing, not embedded in a medical school and substantial in size.

Roswell Park employed several hundred clinicians and scientists and spanned eight city blocks. In one three-year period alone, a basic science building and a clinical research center were dedicated at a cost of $5 million, and construction began on a seven-story building for viral research. MD Anderson Cancer Center treated over 4,000 new patients yearly. It boasted one of the first hyperbaric oxygen chambers, where oxygen levels in tumors were increased, making them more susceptible to irradiation, and a "life island," a sterile environment which proved life-saving for patients with dangerously low blood counts. Memorial Sloan-Kettering, supported heavily by philanthropy, had a long-term building plan, the "Center of Tomorrow," which included thirteen buildings in the center of New York City. A nineteen-story hospital was under construction.

How did Stanford University compare? The Medical School had no cancer hospital. Investigators housed their research patients in a fifteen-bed unit; other cancer patients were admitted to wards throughout the hospital. There was no radiation therapy center; oncology was allotted six examining rooms in the medical clinic, afternoons only. Cancer investigators had no facility for viral research; in fact, there was no cancer research building at all. The number of faculty in the medical school—375—was less than the number of cancer physicians at MD Anderson.

But Stanford professors were conducting a substantial amount of first-rate research—all the more impressive considering that it was one of the smallest medical schools. Faculty promulgated innovative cancer treatments through journal articles and symposia. Their training programs were producing world-class scientists. Recognized as a major referral center for cancer therapy, Stanford attracted patients from as far away as Italy and Japan. The lymphoma staging conference exemplified the multidisciplinary team approach. "Stanford was already a cancer center," Rosenberg said, "with research, patient care programs, and recognition equal to or greater than almost any center in the world. It was a cancer center without walls." With Henry Kaplan's reputation and leadership, it was certain to be designated an NCI cancer center.

The rewards would be considerable—as much as $15 million over a three-year period, renewable three times. With these resources, Stanford could construct modern laboratories and recruit cancer biologists, epidemiologists, statisticians. Kaplan envisioned a comprehensive program, which included researchers who could fully investigate the cause of cancer at the molecular level and clinicians who could apply the latest advancements to patient care. He imagined multidisciplinary teams for all cancer types. And patients could receive beyond state-of-the-art care in one center—a comfortable, modern facility, adorned with gardens and artwork, yet technologically advanced. Henry Kaplan wanted to cure cancer, and this center would be the vehicle to accomplish that goal. With millions of federal dollars within his grasp, this was the opportune time to make his dream come true.

As a member of the Panel of Consultants, Kaplan had actually known almost a year earlier, in 1970, that with enactment of the National Cancer Act, substantial funds would soon become available to construct cancer centers. The time was right for Stanford to begin preparing a cancer center proposal. Robert Glaser had resigned to become a Commonwealth Fund executive, and the acting dean, John Wilson, a mild-mannered surgeon, believed in decentralized administration. At Kaplan's prompting, he convened the Cancer Research Center (CRC) Planning Committee. Members included Saul Rosenberg, Malcolm Bagshaw, Joshua Lederberg, biochemist Paul Berg, pharmacologist Robert Schimke, surgeon Larry Crowley, and pathologist David Korn, with Kaplan as chairman. Since all were dedicated to curing cancer and professed to be intent on building a cancer center at Stanford, Kaplan assumed that the task of writing a proposal for a cancer center grant would be relatively easy. In his excitement, he didn't take time to size up his committee. Each had reasons to feel indebted to Kaplan; several, however, had reasons to resent him.

Saul Rosenberg, chief of the Medical Service and director of the internal medicine residency program, had been working with Kaplan for ten years, and their names were linked in a substantial record of accomplishment. Despite his international reputation as a superb clinical investigator, however, Rosenberg had never felt himself to be a colleague of equal standing. Kaplan didn't perceive this festering resentment and assumed he would have Saul's full support.

He also thought he could count on Malcolm Bagshaw; he always had. Bagshaw had organized the solid tumor programs while Kaplan managed the lymphoma protocols and patients. In their fifteen years' working together, they had never argued. Bagshaw appeared to be among the happiest of faculty members, yet he still stood second to Kaplan. Although Bagshaw had recently been appointed director of the Division of Radiation Therapy, few seemed to recognize him as their leader, mainly because of Kaplan's strong presence as department chairman. Bagshaw was grateful for the opportunities given him, even though Kaplan seemed to take him for granted.

Kaplan had helped recruit Joshua Lederberg, but their friendship had ended abruptly when Lederberg accused him of trying to scuttle Robert Glaser's recruitment. Paul Berg had come to Stanford as Arthur Kornberg's postdoctoral fellow. He went on to win the Nobel Prize in 1980. Kaplan appreciated Berg's genius, although he thought the biochemist frequently put his department's interests before those of the school. Robert Schimke had been recognized by Kaplan years before as a promising medical student. He had helped Schimke obtain a position at the NIH, which had launched his career. Now chairman of Pharmacology, Schimke took a dim view of those who concentrated on patient care while dabbling in research, and he didn't mince words, calling them "pseudoscientists."

The youngest of the group, thirty-seven-year-old David Korn, had been at Stanford only two years, yet was quickly building one of the foremost pathology departments in the country. Kaplan had been instrumental in the recruitment of this summa cum laude Harvard graduate, who had recently been honored with the Distinguished Young Scientist Award at the NIH. He had helped Korn hire several valued colleagues. But at one point, Kaplan promised a scientist a position in Korn's department without even asking him. Korn felt that he had overstepped his authority, and they never resolved the misunderstanding.

Thus, these committee members had several common attributes: They were bright and accomplished, leaders in their respective fields. Each was intensely devoted to Stanford University and would go on to spend much, if not all, of his career there. And all were ambitious. This group would determine the fate of Stanford's cancer center.

The CRC Committee began deliberations, and on February 17, 1971, after a few hasty meetings, Kaplan presented a proposal to the Executive Committee. He began by informing them that Yarborough's Panel of Consultants had submitted a report recommending expanded budgetary support of cancer research and construction of cancer centers. Why should Stanford apply for a center's grant? He moved right to the compelling argument—academic competition. Although Stanford had one of the strongest programs for clinical investigation in radiation therapy, and, he said, "to a lesser extent" in medical oncology, "there is spotty and relatively sparse basic science support in cancer research." If the NIH designated Stanford as a cancer center, it would invest millions of dollars in new laboratories and recruitment of basic scientists, raising the school to elite status. He went on to address the administrative structure. The CRC Committee recommended that the cancer effort be housed in a single facility. And because the Cancer Act stipulated centralized administration under one individual, the committee proposed a dean-appointed director who would be a voting member of the Executive Committee and have authority to recruit faculty and assign space.

The Executive Committee gave the CRC Committee the go-ahead to develop a more detailed plan, and Kaplan immediately obtained a $75,000 planning grant from the NIH. Now all he seemed to talk about was the cancer center. He met with almost every faculty member involved in cancer care and research, and a blueprint for a comprehensive center began to evolve. "The plan was full of excitement," a colleague said. Kaplan described a specialized research center with animal-care facilities, centralized computing services, and the most modern equipment. He proposed fourteen interdisciplinary research teams, modeled after the lymphoma group. Inpatient beds would quadruple in number, and outpatient care would take place in a new ambulatory center, with facilities for diagnostic tests, drug infusions, and radiotherapy. A hoptel, consisting of forty single rooms and ten mini-care suites, would house patients and their families. To staff such a comprehensive center, he calculated, thirty-nine new faculty would be required.

As the specifics of his proposal began to unfold, the CRC Committee members became alarmed. They suddenly realized how big his plans had become. After only a few meetings, Kaplan was moving ahead at breakneck speed. Although they all wanted an NIH-sponsored cancer center, Kaplan appeared to be planning a cancer empire, and they set out to stop him before he started laying the foundations.

Their concerns centered on two major problems: the establishment of an academic structure foreign to Stanford and a potential imbalance between cancer and non-cancer-related programs in the school. Historically, the School of Medicine was opposed to the concept of centers. It ran counter to the traditional academic structure in which all faculty belonged to either a basic science or a clinical department. Chairmen, appointed by the dean, recruited faculty and determined the departmental agenda; the major business of the school was carried out at the departmental level. In fact, Henry Kaplan, as one of the architects of the Medical School, had long been a strong proponent of departmental control. To be successful, a chairman needed financial resources, space, and faculty positions or billets, all of which were divided among departments by the dean. "The enterprise of academic medicine," said David Korn, "is carried out in billets, space and dollars." And therein lay the first problem. Chairmen found it difficult enough vying with one another; they didn't want another competitor, namely the cancer center director.

Kaplan contended that the center would bring millions of dollars into the system, and that the NIH would build research laboratories and clinics; they wouldn't be competing for space. They countered that the autonomy specified in Kaplan's proposed structure gave the director almost as much control over space and faculty as the dean had. How could they be certain that resources would be distributed fairly if the director had ultimate control? Kaplan responded that to create the type of program envisioned, the director had to be free from departmental bargaining and bickering. Besides, if Stanford wanted to have a cancer center, it had to have an autonomous director; the NIH mandated it.

Faculty billets were an even greater sticking point. Korn didn't want the cancer center director to hire pathologists; that was his province. Chairmen recruited faculty for their research accomplishments, not because of programmatic need. "A star system emerged at Stanford," one journalist wrote, "which . . . made the medical school organizationally more like a galaxy than a universe." Kaplan had helped create this culture with the recruitment of Kornberg and Lederberg; he had fostered the attitude that luminaries should be given carte blanche and left alone to excel. Now he was touting teamwork. But Lederberg wanted to be able to recruit the most promising geneticists, not necessarily the most promising cancer geneticists, and Berg the best biochemists, not just biochemists focused on cancer. Kaplan reminded them that the NIH required interdisciplinary research teams. He reiterated the vision of a center where scientists and clinicians interacted regularly, clinicians bringing perspective to basic scientists, and they, in turn, developing new therapies for clinicians to test at the bedside. But the committee didn't rush to embrace his view. Whether one called it defense of departmental identity or intellectual elitism, the traditional departmentally based structure was ingrained at Stanford. "There was an anti-center sentiment at Stanford," said a later dean, "and that feeling was hard to overcome."

The second major objection voiced by the CRC Committee was the sheer size of the proposal. Kaplan had interviewed almost everyone involved in cancer research and patient care to determine their current needs and future plans, and by the time he had finished, the list had grown quite long. He taped index cards on his office wall showing programmatic requirements and relationships. Cards soon covered the entire wall. He wanted a comprehensive center, and the field was expanding exponentially. "Basically," Malcolm Bagshaw said, "it got too damn big."

Balance became a recurring theme. Committee members worried that if Stanford Medical School became known as a tumor institute, it would be harder to recruit faculty in other fields. Rosenberg reiterated that medical students and residents needed to gain expertise in general medicine. If the number of beds devoted to cancer patients quadrupled, exposure to other kinds of patients would decrease. "Rosenberg was extremely conscientious about maintaining the vitality and wholeness of the medical school," Schimke observed. "In opposing Kaplan, he put the welfare of the medical school above personal interests." At the same time, Schimke and Berg pointed out that a proliferation of clinical faculty would dilute the academic environment. "The basic scientists were kingpins around here," said Larry Crowley, the surgeon on the CRC Committee. "They wanted things kept small and concentrated on research."

Kaplan argued that his plan would enhance the basic science effort. A center would provide seed money for new investigators, and interactions with clinicians could stimulate new areas of inquiry. But no amount of counterargument would have swayed the CRC Committee, because it had another agenda. Its members just didn't want Kaplan to have that much control. Although they discussed billets and hospital beds, in the final analysis, the debate was really about Henry Kaplan. "My impression," Robert Glaser said, "is that a lot of people opposed the center because they were afraid it was going to be the 'Kaplan Center.'" Some on the CRC committee had vivid memories of bitter altercations between Kaplan and other chairmen throughout Glaser's deanship. Some still blamed him for Glaser's resignation. Several expressed concern about Kaplan's apparent singleness of purpose. "When Henry came up with what looked like his own institute," Schimke said, "we all backed off."

Individual committee members may have had more personal reasons for not wanting Kaplan to direct a large center. David Korn had already seen Henry cross the line between assistance and control when he began selecting his faculty. Saul Rosenberg said he disagreed with Kaplan on allocation of cancer gift funds, but radiobiologist Robert Kallman speculated that Rosenberg's objections had deeper roots. "Henry respected Saul's clinical prowess," he said, "but he insulted him right and left. Saul envisioned Henry's rising up to be czar of everything. He would be deeper in his shadow." Rosenberg suddenly had the power to restrain Kaplan with his vote. Malcolm Bagshaw thought a compromise could be reached. He proposed that a small group—Kaplan, Rosenberg, and himself—direct the center. Kaplan responded with an unequivocal "no." The legislation specified that the cancer director alone should control all resources, and diluting this authority would jeopardize their ability to compete for a center grant. At that point, Bagshaw could no longer fully support him.

So CRC Committee members already knew that they would never grant Henry Kaplan the power he insisted upon for the director. But they didn't confront him with this fact. They didn't talk of his leadership style or his aggressiveness; instead, they talked of billets and balance. It was easier to address academic structure than to acknowledge the deeper, interpersonal issues. "I know exactly what happened," said Halsted Holman. "Henry wanted desperately to have a cancer center, and the reason we didn't had nothing to do with anything other than the fact that *he* wanted to have a cancer center."

Kaplan's dream of curing cancer made him oblivious to the sentiments of his colleagues. He was busy designing a pediatric sarcoma team with the orthopedic surgeons, determining the optimal square footage for a modern radiobiology laboratory with Robert Kallman. While he was moving cards around on his walls, the CRC Committee was planning mutiny.

For months, Kaplan pressed them to reach consensus on the cancer center proposal. When President Richard Lyman announced that Clayton Rich, an endocrinologist from the University of Washington, would be the new dean of the Medical School, committee meetings took on a more urgent character. Kaplan had been granted immense freedom by Acting Dean John Wilson; he didn't know what Rich's stance would be. Would the new dean want a firm hand in directing the school's activities like Glaser or did he believe in decentralization like Wilson? Kaplan didn't want to take any chances; he planned to have the cancer center plan approved by the executives before Rich arrived. But that didn't happen. The committee seemed to get bogged down in minutiae, and on September 1, 1971, Clayton Rich took office.

It didn't take Kaplan long to size up this pleasant man in a blazer and bow tie with his prep-school diction. In contrast to Glaser, whom he considered a power broker, Rich espoused consensus and cooperation. Rich had met Kaplan during his recruitment and was immediately impressed. "Stanford was packed with hyper-achievers," he said, "but Henry was extraordinary." He had barely moved into his office when Kaplan started pushing him to accept his cancer center proposal. The new dean, however, was facing more urgent issues. Stanford had recently made national headlines when a violent protest threatened to destroy the hospital.

The incident had begun when Sam Bridges, a black maintenance worker, was fired for unexcused absences, sleeping on the job, and verbally abusing a co-worker. Two groups of hospital employees, Alianza Latina and the Black Advisory Committee, called the dismissal racial discrimination. Protestors took over the administrative offices of the hospital director, Thomas Gonda. They placed guards in the corridors and harassed staff who tried to pass. They blocked access to vital hospital services; patients on ward West 2 had to be evacuated.

After a day of failed negotiations, Gonda invoked the trespass law and called in police. "More than fifty demonstrators," *Campus Report* recounted, "some swinging clubs, caused an estimated $100,000 property damage to an administrative office area at the Stanford University Hospital late Friday . . . when Palo Alto police broke through barricades to end a thirty-hour sit-in." Protestors had smashed all the furniture and used chair legs as clubs. Riot police had to resort to mace; twenty-three demonstrators were arrested; twenty people suffered injuries. "It looked like a war zone," Dean Rich said. "Every window that could be reached by a stone was broken." Hostility swelled. President Lyman's office in Building 10 was bombed.

These were frightening times for the faculty. The Black Panthers barged into an Executive Committee meeting and ringed the room, arms folded, waiting to hear the response to their demands regarding workers' rights and affirmative action. "I wondered if I would make it home that night," one chairman said. Most felt intimidated, but not Kaplan. He agreed to represent the executives in negotiations with the Black Advisory Committee and Alianza Latina. Though sympathetic to their claims of racial inequities, he stood firm that the university would not be dismantled or patient welfare hindered for a political agenda. Leah began to worry about Henry's safety. Window washers cleaning their home discovered bullet holes in the window of his study.

Shortly after his arrival, Dean Rich faced other difficulties. The School of Medicine had just begun building a new hospital wing when OPEC raised the price of oil, doubling the cost of construction. Then, in the middle of the project, the architectural firm collapsed financially. So the cancer center proposal was hardly the most pressing matter on his agenda. Kaplan argued that the school could not be derailed by these events. But Rich was beginning to sense faculty dissension; the last thing he needed was to lose support of his executives over the appointment of a cancer center director. He took the position that he would agree to Kaplan's plan if he found unanimity between the executives and CRC Committee. When several expressed concern about Kaplan, the dean remained neutral.

In the meantime, the CRC Committee proposed diminishing the director's role—restricting his authority over faculty recruitment and space. Several suggested that the dean be principal investigator on the cancer grant. Kaplan found this laughable; the NIH would never approve a cancer center grant with an endocrinologist at the helm. In the midst of this debate, Kaplan surprised everyone when he announced his intent to resign as chairman of Radiology. Some thought this expressed his indignation at the dean. Others thought he wanted to spend more time designing the cancer center, that he was stepping down in order to step up. But Kaplan told Eli Glatstein the department was so strong that this was the best time to make the change. At a subsequent Executive Committee meeting, after the social work budget and audiovisual instructional aids had been discussed, a resolution was passed: "The Executive Committee extend[s] its gratitude to Dr. Kaplan for his long and devoted service." This was the extent of the executives' acknowledgment for the man who had served the school for twenty-four years as chairman of Radiology and who, through his relentless insistence on excellence, had thrust Stanford into the elite circle of research-oriented medical schools.

Meanwhile, the CRC Committee's deliberations began to drag on. Kaplan became frustrated. Nixon was to sign the Cancer Act in a few months, and medical schools would rush to compete for cancer center grants. Stanford had only to submit a proposal, and millions of dollars would be theirs. He began goading the committee. Most meetings had a similar pattern: Kaplan presented his view in a calm, straightforward manner with supporting facts. When he couldn't persuade the committee to accept his position on a particular issue, he spoke faster and with great precision, but with less tact. And when committee members openly opposed what he considered a good idea, his face reddened, and he became more dogmatic, raising his voice. The gulf between him and the rest of the committee widened. When committee members seemed to check Kaplan's every move, his language became abusive. "We wrangled with increasing passion and ill temper," Korn said. This dissension leaked to the press. "Internal pressures building at Stanford," the journal *Science* reported, "could dismember the medical school."

Late in the fall of 1971, Kaplan had had enough of debate. He saw his dream slipping away, and in a desperate attempt to hold on to it, he called an emergency meeting of the CRC Committee. Bagshaw was out of town. When the others had gathered, with no introductory remarks, Kaplan demanded a vote. Would the cancer center director be principal investigator for the center grant—yes or no? Would the director have control over space, faculty appointments, and gift funds—yes or no? He still assumed the committee wanted a cancer center, and while idling, was drifting off course. He thought if given an ultimatum, they would acquiesce. But the committee voted unanimously against him. He said nothing. He didn't need to. "None of us failed to recognize that war had been declared by that vote," Korn said.

In January 1972, right after Nixon signed the Cancer Act, the Cancer Research Center Planning Committee presented a formal cancer center proposal to the Executive Committee: The dean would serve as principal investigator and annually appoint a director who would be a nonvoting member of the Executive Committee. The director could not hire faculty, and a policy committee would have approval authority over the director's budget and programs. The Executive Committee unanimously approved the proposal. Henry Kaplan had lost on every point.

For a while, Kaplan didn't comprehend what had happened. He thought the CRC Committee were being obstinate, and that he could eventually persuade them to adopt the administrative structure stipulated by the NIH once the printed guidelines became available. He didn't yet realize that they would never approve a cancer center of the magnitude he envisioned; they would never endow a director with the authority he deemed requisite; and they would never give such power to him. But Kaplan persevered. Throughout the winter, he continued working with an architect to determine the square footage needed by each program. Although disillusioned, he couldn't walk away. Stanford deserved a cancer center. And as far as the NIH was concerned, it was his for the asking.

Over the spring and summer, Kaplan's exasperation grew. Committee members said they were too busy to make meetings; calls weren't returned. Dean Rich had already turned his attention to other issues. By the fall of 1972, Kaplan realized the vote wasn't just an obstacle to maneuver around; it was an expression of no confidence. There would be no cancer center at Stanford. His demand for a vote had forced the CRC Committee to admit that fact, and in time, Kaplan concluded that the unanimous "no" vote represented one thing—a breach of loyalty. What irony. He had been instrumental in building the basic science departments, helping to recruit David Korn and Joshua Lederberg, obtaining a position at the NIH for Schimke early in his career. He and Bagshaw had worked side by side for fifteen years, during which time they had never failed to agree. Yet when it came to a public show of support, Bagshaw hadn't spoken up for him. Kaplan, however, was disappointed most by Saul Rosenberg. With this cancer center grant, they had planned to recruit clinical researchers, expand the cancer programs, create a special environment for patients. What happened to the vision they had shared? Trust and loyalty seemed to mean nothing. Rosenberg had turned on him.

But Kaplan didn't confront the committee members. Only his closest friends knew of his profound sadness. He told DeVita that the CRC Committee had stripped him of his ability to do anything; the cancer center director would be a mere figurehead. When Michael Feldman came to visit, they walked for hours around the campus. Although Kaplan spoke calmly, almost analytically, Feldman knew his friend well enough to appreciate how hurt he felt. And late at night, Henry turned to Leah and asked, "Why? What were they afraid of?"

Kaplan became unusually quiet around colleagues, which some interpreted as acquiescence. Then, in November 1972, eleven months after the Cancer Act had been signed, when medical schools across the country would soon begin breaking ground on new cancer centers, Kaplan resigned from the CRC Committee. Committee members were surprised; there didn't seem to be a specific precipitating event. "One day," Bagshaw recalled, "when things seemed to be going well and there were billions of cards all over the walls, Kaplan just walked in and said, 'I resign.'"

Kaplan stopped talking about a cancer center. "The subject was taboo," Bagshaw said. And he no longer expressed interest in medical school affairs. Just six months earlier, he had readily engaged in battle over faculty promotions, distribution of clinical income, space allocation. Now his concern over departmental business waned, and he relinquished decisions seemingly overnight. Except for the weekly lymphoma clinic, Kaplan spent almost no time in the department. Constrained from building a center that would bring colleagues together, Kaplan withdrew to the position of individuality that characterized Stanford faculty. He moved into a research laboratory located across the street from the Medical Center. "Henry essentially seceded from the Medical School," heart surgeon Norman Shumway said.

The curtain had dropped on his magnum opus before the final act. There would be no cancer center, and when full comprehension of that fact sunk in, Kaplan's dismay turned to anger. "He was very bitter," Crowley said; he felt he had been deceived and became resentful. "Kaplan was on nonspeaking terms with a number of people after that," Bagshaw said. Their relationship cooled perceptively. Kaplan couldn't fathom why the man to whom he had entrusted his department had stood by and passively watched the cancer center effort fail.

Much of Kaplan's overt resentment focused on one person—David Korn. Korn was baffled; he hadn't been particularly outspoken or taken the lead in efforts to block Kaplan. But if the two attended the same meeting, even if seated beside each other, Kaplan acted as if Korn didn't exist. He told DeVita he blamed Korn for the cancer center's collapse; he told Bob Kallman he would hate Korn even after he himself had died. Maybe Kaplan found it easier to express enmity toward Korn because he wasn't a close associate. Some speculated that Korn had led Kaplan to believe he fully agreed with the proposal, and that when he voted against him, Kaplan construed it as an act of duplicity, which was anathema to him. Whatever the reason, Korn perceived himself as the scapegoat for the committee. "I became the personification of his rage," Korn said.

With regard to Rosenberg, Kaplan thought he had not dealt openly on the whole issue of the cancer center. That was especially painful, but he never revealed his sentiments to Saul; he never had. He began speaking to him only when necessary, rarely looking directly at him. He never asked why he had essentially voted against an NCI cancer center. Kaplan had already accepted that Rosenberg wasn't a visionary like DeVita, but he had never thought that he would obstruct the advancement of cancer research.

Kaplan's unspoken resentment surfaced under a different guise. Disagreements at the lymphoma staging conference increased in number and had a sharper edge. It seemed as if Rosenberg barely finished a sentence before Kaplan challenged him. He quizzed Rosenberg about a subtle radiographic abnormality in the same way he did a resident. He contradicted his opinion on management, citing unpublished data he had just heard from DeVita or Smithers. He asked his "esteemed colleague" why the staging sheet hadn't been completed on a patient. Bagshaw became uncomfortable watching Kaplan berate Rosenberg and stopped attending the conference. Rosenberg fought back, and their duels so embarrassed trainees, many said they felt like crawling under the conference table. The relationship between the two men had changed irrevocably.

Kaplan's vexation climaxed two years later at his home, where faculty and trainees from Radiation Therapy and Medical Oncology had gathered to discuss cancer research and plan joint trials. At this quarterly meeting, the postdoctoral fellows learned the craft of protocol design as well as the value of interdisciplinary interaction. They considered themselves privileged to watch their mentors at work. Some of the best trainees, including Norman Coleman, Ed Gilbert, and Carol Portlock, contributed by asking questions or tentatively suggesting alternative approaches. Portlock always enjoyed these evenings until one particular meeting—the one that would be the last.

Twenty faculty, residents, and fellows had gathered in Kaplan's living room with beer and chips. Chairs were arranged in rows along two sides of the L-shaped room with Kaplan and Rosenberg seated at the front. After discussing a protocol for colon cancer, Kaplan suddenly turned to Rosenberg and asked, "Why won't you let Ed do that project?" Most people in the room didn't know what he was talking about. He was referring to the radiotherapy resident Ed Gilbert, who had designed a protocol to spare bone marrow from the effects of chemotherapy. Gilbert had placed a tourniquet on the thigh of a patient just prior to administration of nitrogen mustard and performed a bone marrow scan to determine the distribution of marrow following chemotherapy. He found normal marrow in the femur of the leg with the tourniquet and no residual marrow in the other femur. Excited by this result, he proposed blocking the blood supply to the femur during chemotherapy to reduce damage to the bone marrow. Rosenberg had already said he thought it illogical. To Gilbert, it seemed that the more enthusiastic Kaplan became, the more Rosenberg disparaged the project. He would not consent to having his patients participate in it.

Kaplan's anger erupted, and he began berating Rosenberg's conservatism. Rosenberg struck back, practically calling the approach foolhardy. Both voices rose to high volume. Portlock was shocked; she had never heard Rosenberg speak with such agitation, and over a subject that hardly seemed important. Gilbert, too, felt confused. Why were these two giants having a major altercation over his protocol? But within seconds, the argument moved beyond Gilbert's project, and Kaplan let loose a barrage of criticisms ranging from Rosenberg's lack of creativity to the disappointment he'd been throughout the years. Don Goffinet, a new faculty member, was dumbfounded. "You could see everyone backing away," he said. Gilbert felt himself turning green. "We loved both of these were men," he said, "and to watch this—I thought I was going to throw up." At the peak of the altercation, Kaplan blurted out, "You've never made any significant contribution to the cure of cancer." Rosenberg gathered his papers and walked out. Kaplan's pent-up bitterness over the cancer center had finally been unleashed.

In November of 1972, when Henry Kaplan resigned from the CRC Committee, he essentially walked away from the medical school in whose history he had played a major part. He had encouraged the move to Palo Alto and selected the architect who designed a strikingly beautiful medical center; he had helped recruit a cadre of brilliant scientists and built the foremost radiation therapy department in the country. Poised to put the crowning touch on his medical school, he was felled. He felt wounded, betrayed. So he turned away from the school he loved. Stanford University School of Medicine didn't have a cancer center, and Henry Kaplan never fulfilled his dream.

32 Deadly Complications

The cancer center debacle was a major blow for Kaplan. The razing of this center, already built in his mind, left him dispirited. Furthermore, the vote of no confidence by the Cancer Center Committee devalued his efforts, and him. He took down all the cards on the wall and threw them away. A lesser man might have said, "To hell with it" and left Stanford. But Henry Kaplan only needed to walk into a patient's room to regain his determination. Patients restored his vitality. He continued to ask them about their college and career plans. He kept wedding announcements, Christmas cards, snapshots of children born after therapy. Now, more than ever, he needed to see those he had cured—young people who would live long, productive lives.

In his files, he kept an article entitled "Winning a Battle with Cancer," in which Mrs. C. J. Collins of Redwood City, California, related the story of her teenage son David, who had been diagnosed four years earlier with Hodgkin's disease. She recalled the shock when the surgeon told her and her husband that their son had cancer. Worse yet, he had stage III disease—"generally regarded as incurable," she said. The Collinses already knew of Kaplan's work; David's father had helped build the Stanford linear accelerator. "If the accelerator hadn't been built," Mrs. Collins said, "David . . . probably wouldn't be alive today."

David Collins entered the H-5 protocol and underwent a year of total lymphoid irradiation and MOPP chemotherapy. "The first time David received radiation therapy at Stanford was scary," Mrs. Collins recalled. "Entering the x-ray treatment center through a door in a four-foot thick cement wall and lying on the treatment table was a devastating experience." But her son trusted Dr. Kaplan. "David was one of the first twenty-eight people who was cured while Dr. Kaplan was working under a research grant," Mrs. Collins reported. When asked about her son's career plans, she replied: "I don't think it matters what his plans are. What really matters is that he has been given the opportunity to have a future so that he can make plans."

Around the same time, Mary Harvey, a twenty-six-year-old TWA stewardess, told Dr. Kaplan that she had started flying again. The previous year, a routine chest x-ray, performed at her company checkup, had shown a shadow. On Thanksgiving Day, she had been admitted to the hospital for a biopsy. She was told she had a cancer called Hodgkin's disease. Harvey underwent a staging laparotomy, and after two and a half months of intensive radiation treatments, she was in remission. Four years later, an article in the *Nevada State Journal* showed a picture of a petite blond, standing on a beach. "Cancer Victim," the caption read. "Mary Harvey, a stewardess from California, donned a bikini to appear on an American Cancer Society television spot in which she tells about how her life was saved from Hodgkin's disease." Harvey credited Dr. Kaplan. "The worst thing cancer did for me," she said, "was give me a twelve-inch scar that hardly anyone notices—not even in a bikini. It could have killed me."

For years, Kaplan kept these newspaper articles and those on many other patients in his office. He might not have established a cancer center at Stanford, but these patients were living reminders of his most important accomplishments. Then, in 1972, Vince DeVita told him that several of his patients, cured of Hodgkin's disease, had developed second malignant tumors. He worried that they might have resulted from the treatment.

⌒

The first patient who attracted DeVita's attention was a fifty-three-year-old commercial artist who had come to the NIH in 1968 with an abdominal mass, diagnosed as IIB Hodgkin's disease. Following abdominal irradiation, he relapsed and received more radiotherapy and MOPP chemotherapy. Nine months later, the patient developed a neck mass and a skin ulcer in front of his ear. A biopsy revealed squamous cell cancer of the skin, and he underwent what was thought to be a curative resection. A few months later, the cancer recurred, and within the year, it had invaded a major blood vessel in his neck, and he bled to death. That the man had developed skin cancer was not remarkable. What stood out was its unusual invasiveness.

Before long, DeVita saw another of his patients develop a second malignancy. The twenty-three-year-old man had come to the NCI in 1966 with stage IIB Hodgkin's disease. Five months after total lymphoid irradiation, he relapsed in the liver. DeVita's team treated him with MOPP, and he achieved a remission. Almost five years later, he developed pain in his left shoulder. A radiograph demonstrated a dense lesion in his clavicle, which looked like Hodgkin's disease. While it was being evaluated, nodules appeared throughout his lungs, and his legs became paralyzed from a mass compressing his spinal cord. The lung nodules grew rapidly, and he died of respiratory failure. An autopsy revealed widespread cancer but no evidence of Hodgkin's disease.

Then, just two months later, DeVita learned of yet another case. This fifteen-year-old student had been diagnosed with stage IIIA disease in 1968. Following total lymphoid irradiation and MOPP, he was judged to be in remission. Two years later, he noticed a small lump over his sternum. He ignored it, and within a month, an eight-centimeter necrotic mass had eroded his sternum, extending into his lungs. A biopsy revealed fibrosarcoma, a cancer of fibrous tissue. Despite chemotherapy, the cancer progressed, and the young man died. An autopsy revealed no Hodgkin's disease.

DeVita and his colleague George Canellos were alarmed. These patients had likely been cured of one malignancy when another appeared. And these were far more aggressive than anticipated. "It was clear to us," Canellos said, "that something was happening in this patient population; these were vividly morbid cancers. Their gruesome nature and inexorable course were very disturbing." James Arseneau, an NCI trainee, had seen people die of cancer, but he described these three as particularly "nasty and fast-growing." Something had gone awry, and he wanted to determine what had happened.

On rounds, DeVita postulated that these cancers might, in part, have been caused by radiation therapy. Radiation was known to be carcinogenic dating back to the early days of roentgen therapy, when radiologists had developed skin and bone cancers. Several investigators had addressed the question of increased susceptibility to second cancers among Hodgkin's disease patients. They found that approximately 2 percent developed another malignancy and concluded that this risk was no greater than the chance of developing a cancer among the general population. Henry Kaplan had cautioned in his book *Hodgkin's Disease* that "the risk of late radiation-induced leukemia after extensive high-dose irradiation of the bone marrow is one that must be taken seriously in the light of the evidence from survivors of the atomic bombings." But, he went on to point out, unlike Hodgkin's disease patients, who received a smaller dose of radiation to a specific port over a month, "atomic bomb survivors obviously received single, relatively massive, total-body exposure."

One physician had tried to sound an alarm. In 1969, William Crosby of Tufts–New England Medical Center reported a tenfold increased incidence of acute leukemia in Hodgkin's disease patients treated with radiation. He had sent letters to twenty-five medical centers asking if any of their Hodgkin's patients had developed leukemia. Among 10,000 patients treated over a twenty-year period, he found seventeen cases—substantially higher than the number in healthy adults. Crosby published his results in an abstract without details. Thus, his warning went largely unnoticed.

Now three NCI patients had been diagnosed with second tumors in rapid succession. DeVita encouraged Arseneau to review their experience in order to determine if their Hodgkin's disease patients did have an increased chance of developing subsequent cancers. Arseneau examined case records of 425 patients going back to 1953 and compared the number of secondary malignancies in this group with the number of new cancers expected in a comparable normal population of similar age and sex. What he discovered was that Hodgkin's disease patients were three and a half times more likely to develop another cancer. DeVita proposed two hypothetical causes: First, as a consequence of chemotherapy and radiotherapy, these patients were immunosuppressed for prolonged periods of time. Recipients of renal transplants, another group undergoing chronic immunosuppressive therapy, were known to have an increased incidence of cancers. Second, radiotherapists had long known of the carcinogenic potential of radiation. And chemotherapy had been shown to cause cancer in animals.

When Arseneau showed DeVita the data, he suggested that Arseneau go back and determine if any particular subgroups had greater susceptibility. His data were startling: he found the risk in patients treated with more modern therapy—intensive irradiation and chemotherapy—to be twenty-nine times greater than that expected in the general population. To make matters worse, the chance of developing a second cancer increased with each year of follow-up. "My main concern," DeVita said, "was I didn't know when it would stop." If the incidence of second cancers continued to rise, it might negate the advantages of modern therapy. For all he knew, the majority of his Hodgkin's disease patients could succumb to another cancer.

They consoled themselves, Canellos said, with the thought that "at least the patients had lived long enough because of MOPP chemotherapy to get these complications." DeVita agreed. "We had people who were surviving," he said. "We had never had that before." They had to keep reminding themselves of all the patients they had cured, lest this new finding demoralize them and stymie further progress. DeVita and his team took stock. To retreat to a palliative approach seemed unthinkable. They could not let themselves become discouraged, reluctant to try new therapies. The NCI group concluded that use of intensive radiation and chemotherapy "must be balanced against the risk of development of a second primary tumor." For patients with advanced disease, this risk might be considered acceptable because of the poor prognosis. Putting patients with localized disease at risk was another matter.

In 1972, when the NCI group reported in the *New England Journal of Medicine* that curative treatment for Hodgkin's disease could cause cancer, the Stanford team was dismayed. What they had considered a possibility, the NCI group called an inevitability. Straightaway an outcry arose from Stanford, but not from Henry Kaplan. This time, Saul Rosenberg confronted the NCI team.

"Saul called us up and told us we were discrediting the field," Canellos said. Arseneau felt intimidated when Rosenberg approached him at a national meeting and made a caustic remark about overzealous young investigators.

No wonder the NCI report upset Rosenberg. He and Kaplan had treated a large number of patients with combined therapy, and their current protocols included MOPP and subtotal or total lymphoid irradiation for almost all groups of patients—even those with stage I disease. "There is now little doubt," Kaplan had stated at an international meeting prior to the NCI report, "that modern techniques of intensive megavoltage radiotherapy and combination chemotherapy have sharply improved the prognosis of patients with Hodgkin's disease and that . . . actual permanent cure is being obtained in a high proportion of patients thus treated." If the NCI contention proved true, Stanford's aggressive programs might prove disastrous in the long run.

Rosenberg didn't believe the problem to be of the magnitude DeVita alleged; they had not seen a single second malignancy at Stanford. Moreover, he knew that the consequences of a premature conclusion could be substantial. Community physicians might be scared off, stop referring patients, and treat them conservatively at home. This news might instigate an exodus from academic centers and drastically reduce the number of patients entering clinical trials. In the rush to publish their findings, the NCI group might not have considered these potentially damaging repercussions. "In my opinion," Rosenberg said, "they exaggerated the risk in a very small series of patients."

Three months after the Arseneau report, Rosenberg published a letter in the *New England Journal of Medicine.* "We have been concerned," he wrote, "since we first heard from Dr. Vincent T. DeVita that other malignant tumors were being observed in patients with Hodgkin's disease treated with both intensive chemotherapy and radiotherapy." These data had now been widely publicized. "It is important for investigators in this field to know," Rosenberg went on to say, "that the experience at Stanford University does not yet confirm that there is such an association." He emphasized that the NCI conclusions had been drawn from a small "selected subgroup" of only thirty-five patients. Stanford had already treated fifty-two patients with intensive combined therapy. "If the true risk of second malignant tumors were as high as three in eight, as suggested by Arseneau and his co-workers," Rosenberg wrote, "we probably would have seen such an occurrence."

Arseneau didn't know how to respond. After all, he was just a trainee; Rosenberg was an internationally known figure. "Let me handle this," DeVita told him. "Quite frankly, you're too much of a pipsqueak to take on these guys." Vince wrote a rebuttal to the *New England Journal of Medicine*: "We share Dr. Rosenberg's uncertainty," he wrote, "about the importance of the . . . cases of cancer in a population of patients selected by virtue of the type of therapy received. We also think we have the obligation to monitor closely and report any late effects of therapy, real or suspected."

While Rosenberg continued to criticize the NCI report publicly, Kaplan was more guarded in his opinion. But he began to worry about David Collins and Mary Harvey and the all the other patients he had treated aggressively. In the meantime, their protocols continued as planned.

33   High-Dose DeVita

Vince DeVita was a man on the rise. By 1972, at the age of thirty-seven, he had already published elegant pharmacokinetic studies on several new chemotherapeutic agents, developed the first effective regimen for non-Hodgkin's lymphomas, and demonstrated the chemotherapeutic cure of Hodgkin's disease. As chief of the Medicine Branch at the National Cancer Institute—just steps away from the directorship—he was in a position to have a major impact on cancer therapy nationwide. And he did.

DeVita resolved to cure cancer; not reaching that goal was unthinkable. He couldn't bear to see people die, particularly in the prime of life. Called a "magnificent clinician" by one trainee, he was devoted to his patients and frequently found on the wards tending to them. As he rose through the ranks of the NCI, however, DeVita also acquired a reputation for toughness, which began to isolate him from subordinates. Some dubbed him the "Italian boss."

Present at the dawn of chemotherapy, DeVita became ardent about using this new modality to treat cancer. If they could achieve dramatic responses in leukemia and Hodgkin's disease with chemotherapy, he reasoned, why not in other malignancies? They just needed to develop more new agents and give them in the greatest tolerable doses. Pushing far beyond what others considered standard, he became known as "high-dose DeVita." He maintained that any cancer could be cured; one only had to try hard enough. "He was a believer," a prior trainee said, "in an era where few people believed." His excitement about treating cancer with chemotherapy became contagious, and he spawned a generation of academic medical oncologists enthralled with clinical research.

Like Henry Kaplan, Vince DeVita was becoming a forceful figure in the cancer field. Many anticipated a collision between this man who considered chemotherapy the key to eradicating cancer, and Kaplan, the man who had harnessed radiation to treat it. No one would have predicted the intimacy that developed between these two strong individuals. Despite the seventeen-year difference in age between them, Kaplan and DeVita had many similarities. Both cared deeply for their patients and took great pride in their clinical skills. Both understood how basic science could be applied to clinical problems. Each was intolerant of sloppiness, stupidity, or even carelessness of thought, and neither hesitated to express his opinion vehemently. Their mothers had engrained in them the belief that they could accomplish anything they set out to do. And both were fighters.

In the summer of 1972, DeVita spent two months at Stanford as a visiting professor while Rosenberg took a sabbatical. He attended ward rounds, oncology clinics, and the lymphoma staging conference, which he found a challenging experience. "Henry really kept me on my toes," he said. At first, he didn't comprehend the fun Kaplan was having; Henry had found an "intellectual playmate." Then the two began to take leisurely lunches together. Sitting around Kaplan's swimming pool, they discussed his attempts at establishing human cell lines to study lymphoma, argued over the optimal sequence of chemotherapy and irradiation for Hodgkin's disease. At Kaplan's favorite Chinese restaurant, they debated national policy on cancer. With time, their conversations turned to art and travel. Vince began to appreciate the many facets of Henry Kaplan—those seen by his patients, trainees, and friends. "He was a different sort of person," DeVita said, "from the one you heard about—the Henry Kaplan who would chop your head off. I saw the warm side of him." And he didn't need permission to call him "Henry."

Although DeVita hadn't even been born when Kaplan vowed at his father's funeral to cure cancer, the age difference between them seemed inconsequential. DeVita felt comfortable teasing him. "I enjoyed seeing you in Chicago," he wrote after one symposium. "Arguing with you is something akin to teasing a grizzly bear. I always feel like I want to count my fingers and toes after I leave the podium."

That summer at Stanford, Vince crossed over onto what he considered hallowed ground—friendship with Henry Kaplan. Bruised by breaches of loyalty from those he had considered friends, Kaplan had become wary of intimacies. But something about DeVita invited his confidences. Appearing invulnerable to the outside world, he unburdened himself. He told DeVita how exhausting it had become juggling his laboratory, clinical, and administrative work, and he revealed the depth of his disillusionment over the cancer center. DeVita began to appreciate the triumphs and failures that constituted Kaplan's career.

On the verge of ascending to the most powerful political position in the cancer field, DeVita needed a friend. He could never be certain what motive underlay advice he received from others. Always forthright, Kaplan helped him make the best decisions for science and patients nationwide, not for himself. That summer marked the beginning of a friendship, one DeVita had never experienced and one to which Kaplan was drawn despite his caution. Mutual admiration, trust, and a passion to cure cancer—these bonded the two most powerful men in the cancer field.

~

One evening soon after the DeVitas had returned to Bethesda, Vince noticed a bruise on his young son's arm. When he looked more closely, what he saw shocked him: Teddy was covered with bruises. "Leukemia" was his first thought. Distraught, he called the NIH Clinical Center, and Teddy was admitted. Blood tests revealed severe anemia, a diminished white blood count that rendered the boy highly susceptible to infection, and a platelet count so low that he was bleeding under his skin. A bone marrow biopsy was performed, and Vince and Mary Kay anxiously awaited the results. To their relief, the biopsy indicated no evidence of leukemia. Teddy had an uncommon disease called aplastic anemia, a disorder in which bone marrow cells have been destroyed and replaced by fat. Since bone marrow contains stem cells for platelets and red and white blood cells, all three elements drop to low levels. Some patients experience a return of blood counts within weeks; others die from infection or hemorrhage within months.

At the time Teddy was diagnosed with aplastic anemia, not much was known about its cause. Several agents could damage bone marrow, including radiation, chemical toxins, a few drugs, and tuberculosis, but in over half of the cases, no history of exposure could be determined. Although the NCI doctors found no explanation for Teddy's disease, Vince felt responsible. Just before they had left Stanford, the family dog developed severe diarrhea and got better with clindamycin, a new antibiotic. When Teddy became sick a few days later, Vince gave him the same antibiotic. One case of aplastic anemia had been reported after clindamycin use. Was his son the second? Vince would never know, but he would live with that uncertainty and guilt the rest of his life.

DeVita familiarized himself with every known therapy for aplastic anemia. Steroids and testosterone had been used to stimulate growth of bone marrow cells with some success, but responses were short-lived. In reality, there was no known effective therapy. Patients merely received supportive care—red blood cells for anemia, antibiotics to treat infections, and platelet transfusions to prevent a fatal hemorrhage—until the bone marrow spontaneously repopulated with normal cells. While awaiting recovery, patients needed complete protection from the outside world. There was only one way to accomplish this—isolation in a sterile room.

An environment free of micro-organisms could best be obtained in a laminar airflow room, a so-called life island. A polyvinyl chloride shell, supported by posts, was placed in a hospital room and inflated with air, creating a large bubble. Fans constantly blew filtered air through the space, preventing stagnation and buildup of bacteria or fungi. But life islands required enormous resources. Staff had to go through an elaborate procedure of scrubbing and gowning before entering the unit. Sterilization of food drove up food service costs fivefold. "The logistics and expense of maintaining patients in life islands," one hematologist wrote, "are almost forbidding." The NCI had recently completed a trial demonstrating a reduced incidence of infection among leukemia patients hospitalized in laminar airflow rooms. Based on this observation, the Pediatric Oncology Branch began to test the rooms' use for patients with aplastic anemia.

Vince and Mary Kay DeVita could not image confining their son in an isolation room. He was only nine years old. Conflicted, they hesitated to enter Teddy into the NCI study. It meant separating him from family and friends, preventing him from touching another human being at a time he most needed comforting. Teddy began transfusions as an outpatient, but within a week, he developed a severe infection in his bloodstream and had to be hospitalized. After long, painful discussions with expert hematologists, the DeVitas consented. On September 15, 1972, Teddy DeVita entered the laminar airflow room. "I'll never forget the night Teddy went into the bubble." DeVita said. "My life has never been the same since."

Vince began to call physicians all over the world, looking for effective treatment. "I was driving people crazy," he said. But not Henry Kaplan. He understood the depth of Vince's agony. "It was very touching," DeVita said. "His support was one of the reasons Henry was so special to me." While others told Vince they were sorry that nothing could be done, Kaplan joined him in the hunt for successful therapy. He talked to experts in the field, hypothesized new approaches. Neither Vince nor Henry would ever give up hope. They assumed they would find a way to cure Teddy and release him from the life island.

34   The S-5 Protocol: Chris Jenkins

In 1974, Stanford's second series of Hodgkin's disease trials reached completion. The remarkable results advanced the field another giant step. Designated the H studies, these trials had been designed by Kaplan and Rosenberg in 1968 to determine whether relapse rate could be reduced and survival improved with the addition of chemotherapy to irradiation—so-called combined modality therapy. Two hundred and fifty-four patients, evaluated by staging laparotomy and found to have stage I, II, or III disease, had been randomized either to irradiation alone or to irradiation followed by six cycles of MOPP. When they analyzed their data, Kaplan and Rosenberg found their assumption to be true: the outcome improved significantly when chemotherapy was added to irradiation. The results were most striking for the subgroup of patients with stage IIIB disease—those with widespread nodal disease and systemic symptoms. Following irradiation alone, disease progressed in 90 percent of patients, as opposed to just half of those treated with the combination.

Every patient on protocol received chemotherapy under Saul Rosenberg's supervision, and he came to realize just how intolerable MOPP could be. This intensive combination chemotherapy left no one unscathed. A grandmother reported that her fingertips had become so numb she no longer could knit sweaters for her grandchildren. A young woman suffered a third-degree burn on her forearm when nitrogen mustard leaked outside the vein. An accountant, whose wife was pregnant with their first child, developed such severe constipation that he required a nasogastric tube threaded through his nose into his stomach to relieve the gas and secretions he couldn't pass. Debilitated from vomiting and consumed with gas pains, he subsequently lost both his job and his wife. A nun turned to drugs and alcohol to get through MOPP. Yes, Saul Rosenberg wanted to cure patients, but MOPP had its costs, and at times they seemed too great. He set out to design an alternate regimen, based on the same principles as MOPP, but which afforded a better quality of life. In planning it, he chose less toxic drugs—procarbazine, Alkeran, and Velban—hoping to reduce acute side effects. He called his new regimen PAVe.

PAVe did live up to Rosenberg's expectations. He treated a small group of patients and observed no disabling numbness or constipation. The vomiting diminished substantially, and burns from chemotherapy infiltration into skin all but disappeared. PAVe appeared to be a good alternative to MOPP, and Rosenberg was preparing to test it in a larger group of patients. Once he established its response rate and toxic effects, he could consider PAVe for their combined modality trials. Impressed with the results, however, Kaplan wanted to incorporate it into their trials right away. "Kaplan thought PAVe was much better than MOPP," Rosenberg said, "and he pushed me to use it long before I was ready." Although Rosenberg thought PAVe might be equivalent to MOPP, he didn't know for sure. But Kaplan was impatient; he wouldn't relent. Rosenberg finally acquiesced, and they tested PAVe in their next generation of combined modality trials—the S studies.

The main objective of the S trials was to maintain the excellent results with combined chemotherapy-radiotherapy, while reducing the acute toxicity. The S studies pitted PAVe against MOPP. Patients with stages I, II A and B, and IIIA would be randomized to radiation therapy followed by either MOPP or PAVe. With regard to IIIB disease, the lymphoma group was dissatisfied with results to date. Even with total lymphoid irradiation (TLI) and MOPP—the most aggressive therapy imaginable—only half of the patients in the H study had survived. Because of the extent of disease, while they were irradiating a mass in a patient's chest, tumors often grew in the abdomen. To avert this they decided to treat IIIB patients with two cycles of chemotherapy followed by TLI and then four more cycles. Again, half would receive MOPP, half PAVe.

As soon as he learned of the studies, Vince DeVita wrote to Rosenberg:

> I have no problems with the overall design of your current trials, but the selection of PAVe, to me, doesn't make a great deal of sense. [Alkeran] is the most . . . carcinogenic alkylating agent I know of . . . and procarbazine, of course, we know is a potent carcinogen. To remove alkylating agents that cause nausea and vomiting in favor of those that will probably produce greater long-term carcinogenicity . . . does not make sense to me.

Rosenberg disagreed. He suspected that Vince felt defensive because PAVe threatened to displace MOPP. They locked horns. DeVita criticized him at a national meeting, publicly saying that PAVe might be more carcinogenic than any combination to date. Rosenberg defended his regimen. The Stanford group had yet to document a single treatment-related second cancer from MOPP, and he had no reason to suspect that his new regimen would be any different. Only one of them could be right. Meanwhile, Stanford's S trials were already under way.

One of the first patients randomized to TLI and PAVe was Chris Jenkins, a thirty-one-year-old who had come to Stanford in September of 1974 with a nine-month history of fatigue, drenching night sweats, and weight loss. A wan, spindly young man with unkempt blond hair, a beard, and wire-rimmed glasses, he seemed exceedingly frail. When he spoke, he selected his words carefully, the gentle quality of his voice almost dreamy. But behind this passive demeanor was a man of courage. A lifelong idealist, Chris had acted upon his beliefs and gone to Vietnam to work with Vietnamese students. There he had survived one of the bloodiest battles of the war. Now his fortitude was about to be tested again.

⁓

Chris Jenkins was born in 1943 in Bryn Mawr, Pennsylvania, where his father, a graduate of Yale and Harvard Business School, ran an insulation business. Family life at the Jenkins's was as tidy and orderly as the manicured lawns in their neighborhood. Dinner was served at precisely the same time every evening; Chris and his brother were required to wear coats and ties. While they ate, their father recounted the events of the day. As teens, Chris and his brother were sent to Taft School, a Connecticut prep school their father and grandfather had attended. "My father," Chris said, "was very rigid in his values and feelings about how the world should be ordered." Isolated behind picket fences and stone walls, Chris never thought to challenge him.

When he was eighteen, Chris traveled to England as an exchange student and found the world vastly different from what he had been taught. When he returned home, he announced that he would not attend Yale, as his father expected; he was going to Stanford University. Three thousand miles from home, Chris felt liberated. He became involved in the civil rights movement, culminating in his participation in Martin Luther King Jr.'s Washington march. He returned home with shoulder-length hair, wearing jeans and sandals. His father's greatest fears about California had materialized—his son had become a hippie. Chris talked about spending the summer in Mississippi, registering blacks to vote. His father refused to let him go. In a soft, but earnest voice, Chris tried to explain to his father that the only way for black people to improve their lives was through political power. It was their right. His father retorted that Negroes had no rights.

From then on, Chris rarely went home. During his junior year, he studied in Tours, France. There he heard students talk about Vietnam, a country he vaguely recalled from his stamp collection. He had arrived in France shortly after the Gulf of Tonkin incident; bombing of North Vietnam soon followed. President de Gaulle called for withdrawal of U.S. forces, and the mood in France became increasingly anti-American. French newspapers wrote of rice fields destroyed with herbicides to starve the North Vietnamese—not just the Vietcong, but women and children as well. In the south, Agent Orange defoliated large regions of rain forest in order to expose Vietcong hideouts. Farmers and their families fled from their hamlets into the cities, where they lived in filth and often survived by begging or prostitution. Chris had thought America was fighting communism in Vietnam; he had never realized how this war affected innocent people. Even more distressing were accounts of modern weaponry. On impact, a cluster bomb discharged hundreds of high-velocity pellets that ripped apart the body of anyone in range. Napalm roasted victims alive. Chris was appalled. "I got caught up in the ethical questions surrounding Vietnam," he said. What were we really doing there? He had to find out for himself.

Back at Stanford, Chris attended teach-ins at White Plaza; he picketed the napalm factory in Redwood City. And he joined ten thousand demonstrators, each carrying a single candle, silently marching through Palo Alto to protest the senseless deaths in Vietnam. Chris Jenkins was a quiet warrior. While other students screamed anti-war slogans and then went to the movies, he protested quietly, and in June 1966, he boarded Pan American flight #1 for Saigon.

For two years, Chris taught English and participated in community projects, first through Stanford's Volunteers in Asia, then with the International Volunteer Services. Assigned to Dalat, he began to doubt the veracity of the stories he had heard. Built by the French as a resort, Dalat was as yet untouched by the war. This mile-high city in the central Vietnam highlands was surrounded by pine forests and waterfalls. Swiss-style villas dotted the hillsides surrounding a lake. But when Chris joined a Vietnamese student work group, which took food and medical supplies to peasants in the surrounding countryside, he saw firsthand what war had done to the country. Working side by side with the students, he developed an immense respect for the Vietnamese. Though their country was ravaged by war, they still had a quiet pride. Chris began to speak their language, eat their food, and wear their clothes.

Chris especially admired Tran Khanh Tuyet, one of the student leaders, who worked in a jungle hospital and organized student groups to aid peasants in remote hamlets. Chris watched her bargain with Vietnamese officials for supplies and orchestrate meals for a hundred. They became friends, although they had to keep their distance in public. Any Vietnamese woman who befriended an American was suspected of prostitution, and an American involved with a Vietnamese youth group leader would come under CIA surveillance. In the evenings, Chris sneaked into Tuyet's apartment, where they fried squid over a kerosene lamp, shared a bottle of beer, and read Vietnamese poetry. Chris passed information to Tuyet regarding supplies given by USAID to local Vietnamese officials. These facts gave her bargaining power in trying to obtain goods for local citizens. Working together, Chris and Tuyet became soul mates.

In January 1968, a medical student invited Chris to spend Tet, the Vietnamese New Year, with her and her family. The Nguyens lived in Hué, a city of 140,000 located south of the demilitarized zone. The imperial capital during the 1800s, Hué contained palaces and tombs of past emperors. In the center of town stood an ancient fortress, the Citadel. On the eve of Tet, the city was ablaze with fireworks, set off to drive away evil spirits for the New Year. Noise from the celebration obscured the sound of automatic weapons as the Vietcong attacked. When Chris looked out the window the next morning, the streets were empty except for soldiers dressed in black pajamas. The yellow-starred Vietcong flag fluttered above the Citadel. "I suddenly found myself in enemy territory," he said. From a hidden radio, he learned of the Tet offensive. In the predawn hours of January 31, in violation of a truce to observe the New Year, seventy thousand Vietcong had taken part in surprise attacks on more than a hundred cities throughout South Vietnam. Two thousand Americans, four thousand Vietnamese soldiers, and uncounted civilians had died. Three weeks later, the Vietcong still occupied Hué.

For the first few days, the city was deathly still, the silence punctuated by isolated gunshots and muffled cries, indicating another execution. Vietcong began house-to-house searches, rounding up civilians suspected of aiding Americans and marching them to the jungles or riverbeds for execution. The family dressed Chris in black pajamas and sandals and instructed him to speak Vietnamese. Then they waited. Some of Chris's colleagues staying in a nearby home were marched up the Ho Chi Minh trail into North Vietnam, where they were imprisoned for five years. And they were the fortunate ones. In all, three thousand people were shot, decapitated, or buried alive.

The Vietcong already knew of Chris's whereabouts. They had infiltrated Hué months before the offensive began and compiled an execution list. So when a Vietcong soldier appeared at the Nguyens' door, he was looking for the American who worked for the International Volunteer Services (IVS). He sat down and began talking casually with the old man and his daughter about politics. Gradually he got around to IVS—who were they; what were they doing in Hué? Chris was hiding in the next room. Would he be shot, his body dumped into the river, or forced to march hundreds of miles to the Hanoi Hilton, the infamous camp for American prisoners, there to die of malaria, cholera, or starvation? But his friend was shrewd. Members of IVS had signed a letter protesting the war. "You ask about the IVS," she said, handing a copy to the Vietcong.

"They sent this letter to President Johnson." It was good to have subversive Americans inside South Vietnam. The solder said nothing and left. Chris had been spared.

Over the next fifteen days, bombing and artillery fire hammered Hué as American marines tried to take back the city. "People were being killed all around us," Chris said. A cousin staying with the Nguyens died, hit by flying shrapnel as he prayed at the family altar. "Houses were collapsing, and families were fleeing," he said. "Children were trapped under the rubble, and parents could hear them screaming. They were still alive, but they couldn't get to them." And napalm was being dropped indiscriminately on Vietcong and Hué citizens alike. The siege of Hué was a massacre.

Twenty-five days after the communists had captured Hué, a marine suddenly appeared in the Ngyuens' backyard. He started hustling Chris out, yelling that the neighborhood was about to be bombed. Chris insisted that the marine take the Nguyen family with them. "You can't leave these people," he screamed. "They saved my life." But the marine refused, not even giving him time to say good-bye. As they drove to a villa outside Hué, Chris was horrified to see much of the ancient city reduced to rubble. To save Hué, American forces had destroyed it.

At U.S. headquarters, authorities interrogated Chris. He was still wearing black pajamas and thongs. "I looked like an American Vietcong," he recalled. Determined not to cooperate with the military, he remained silent, sitting cross-legged. They thought he was shell-shocked and evacuated him to the U.S. air base at Phu Bai. There Chris agreed to talk to an ABC newsman, and in New York his sister-in-law spotted him on the nightly news. That was the first the Jenkins family had heard of their son since he had disappeared into a town called Hué during the Tet offensive. Two months later, he left Vietnam.

Chris's experience intensified his commitment to the Vietnamese people. To prepare himself for a more effective role, he entered a graduate program in Asian Studies at Berkeley. In addition, he volunteered for an organization that brought Vietnamese children to America for plastic surgery. The children needed a translator, and Chris suggested hiring Tran Khanh Tuyet, who had immigrated to the United States. No longer restrained by Vietnamese taboos, she and Chris began a courtship and three years later married in a traditional Vietnamese ceremony. They subsequently moved to Washington, D.C., to work for the Indochina Resource Center, interpreting events in Vietnam to the press and briefing journalists being sent to Indochina. In the summer of 1973, they returned to Berkeley to set up a western branch and start a family.

In the spring of 1974, Tuyet entered her last trimester of pregnancy, but it was Chris who felt fatigued. He got winded just riding his bike to work. He attributed his exhaustion to middle age. When he started coughing, he became concerned and went to the hospital. A physician diagnosed a viral infection and prescribed aspirin, but the cough worsened, and he began losing weight. Again he was told he had a virus. He began waking up at night soaking wet. He told a psychiatrist friend, John Champlin, that he thought he was having anxiety attacks over the upcoming birth of their child. When John came to visit, he was shocked by Chris's sickly appearance and told him to insist on having a chest x-ray.

A few days later, a nurse called Chris at work to report a shadow on his lung. She rattled off a list of potential diagnoses—all of which sounded serious. The subsequent evaluation stretched over months. In the meantime, Chris could barely speak without coughing, and his clothes hung loose from all the weight he had lost. As the baby was growing inside Tuyet, he began to feel a tumor was growing inside his chest. On July 19, Melinh was born; six weeks later Chris's doctor ordered a biopsy.

Chris was frightened the day he went to see the surgeon. So far his physicians had been dispassionate; he hoped this woman doctor would be different. She asked a few questions and while examining him, muttered, "nice narrow chest," as if sizing him up for surgery. Then, without a glimmer of emotion, she said, "We've narrowed it down to lung cancer or Hodgkin's disease." Chris left her office stunned. Sitting in his parked car, unable to drive, he realized he didn't even know what Hodgkin's disease was. When he finally got home, he and Tuyet clung to each other and cried. They knew the dismal prognosis from lung cancer; Tuyet's father had died of the disease in just four months. Would Chris live to see Melinh ride a bike or just smile at him for the first time?

To make a diagnosis, the surgeon scheduled a bronchoscopy, a procedure by which she would look into his bronchial tree. When Chris arrived at the hospital, the first question she asked was, "Did you eat breakfast?" When he replied that he had, she said, "Didn't anybody tell you you weren't supposed to eat?" Irritated, she cancelled the procedure. Days later, she performed a mediastinoscopy, making an incision in Chris's throat and inserting a scope behind his breastbone to biopsy his mediastinal nodes. But the procedure did not reveal the cause of his illness. Finally, the surgeon performed a thoracotomy, opening Chris's chest to obtain a larger piece of tissue. Six months after his symptoms had begun, a diagnosis was made: Chris Jenkins had Hodgkin's disease.

A few days later, a medical oncologist came into his hospital room. "We're going to start your chemotherapy tomorrow," he said. Before Chris could digest the news and ask questions, the doctor left. Melinh was only two months old, and he was going to begin chemotherapy and perhaps die.

Chris was to undergo treatment about which he knew almost nothing, for a disease he didn't understand, under the care of doctors he didn't trust. Bewildered and paralyzed, he again turned to his friend John Champlin. "You don't always have to do what the doctor tells you," he said. "Take control." He encouraged Chris to go to Stanford, but when Chris asked his oncologist for a referral, he advised against it. He told Chris that the Stanford doctors would recommend a laparotomy and likely he would contract pneumonia and die. Tuyet had called a contact at the NCI and found that this wasn't true. But the oncologist spoke only to Chris, never even acknowledging her presence. If the oncologist thought he was dealing with a meek, uneducated immigrant, he had underestimated Tuyet. She insisted that her husband be referred to Stanford. She had read in the *Stanford Daily* that Dr. Henry Kaplan had just received over $1 million to study Hodgkin's disease. Kaplan appeared to be the best, he worked at Stanford, and that was where they planned to go.

Chris was anxious the day of his Stanford appointment. Up to that point, physicians had been brusque and insensitive. Annoyed by his questions, they either ignored them or answered in highly technical terms. He found his new role as a patient humiliating. Now he was going to be evaluated by one of the world's greatest cancer doctors. He anticipated that Dr. Kaplan would have even less time and patience. To his surprise, Kaplan seemed unhurried. He put his hand on Chris's shoulder and asked what he did and how the disease was affecting him. After examining Chris, he went into the waiting room and invited Tuyet to join them. He showed them the chest x-ray, pointing out the large mass that represented what he called mediastinal lymph nodes. He recommended irradiation to the chest mass to reduce its size, followed by a staging laparotomy to determine the extent of his disease. He described their protocol studies and gave them optimistic figures about success rates. And he said Chris's medical expenses would be covered by his grant. When Tuyet posed questions, Kaplan answered in terms they understood. Then he asked, "Mrs. Jenkins, have you had your lunch?" When she said no, he suggested she and Chris discuss his recommendations over lunch, taking whatever time they needed; he would be available all afternoon.

Chris started irradiation to a mantle field, and within ten days, his fever and sweats disappeared, his energy improved. Dr. Kaplan showed him his chest x-ray, pointing out that the tumor was shrinking. As happy as Chris felt, his elation deflated when he entered the waiting area. There he sat with a group of strangers, all wearing hospital gowns. "You felt like you were looking at people in different stages of their own deaths," he said. Especially difficult to watch were the children—helpless, often bald. He became tearful whenever he saw a child taken from his parent's lap to be put in the radiation suite alone. His anger at his own situation faded.

After 2,600 rads, the mass in Chris's chest had shrunk sufficiently to make surgery safe, and Kaplan scheduled him for a laparotomy. The evening before his operation, he was lying in bed, staring at the ceiling, scared, when Maureen O'Hara pulled a chair to his bedside and asked if he would like to talk. This round-faced young woman with freckles and green eyes spoke soothingly. She said something he never forgot: "If you had to get cancer, this is the best one to have."

Following his operation, Chris had so much pain, he walked bent over like an old man. Maureen tried to make his recovery more tolerable by breaking hospital rules. She looked the other way when Tuyet crawled into bed with Chris and pulled the curtains around them. Maureen gave Tuyet access to the small kitchen on the floor so that she could make Chris's favorite Vietnamese dishes. And she let Tuyet smuggle Melinh into his room. Tiny Melinh brought her father strength when he felt helpless.

Kaplan told Chris that the results from his laparotomy indicated stage IIIB disease. On the S-5 protocol, he had been randomized to alternating PAVe chemotherapy and irradiation. He would be among the first so treated. By July 1975, Chris had completed mantle irradiation and two cycles of PAVe, after which Kaplan deemed him to be in remission. He went on to receive inverted Y irradiation and three more cycles of chemotherapy. Just as Kaplan had predicted, he had few side effects. One more cycle, and he would be free. He eagerly anticipated having more energy for Tuyet and Melinh, who was just starting to walk. During the last cycle of PAVe, however, Chris suddenly developed abdominal pain and fever. The resident on call at Stanford felt an enlarged liver and thought the most likely cause to be recurrent Hodgkin's disease. He admitted Chris to the hospital. A day later, blisters broke out on his abdominal wall; he had herpes zoster, or shingles.

Chris required constant medication to control the pain. Because the virus attacks nerve roots, the skin is exquisitely sensitive, and as in Chris's case, pain could precede the blisters by days. At that time, there was no antiviral drug to halt the progression of shingles. The resident observed Chris closely for complications, especially bacterial pneumonia, which could be fatal. Because shingles is highly contagious, Chris was put in isolation. For three weeks, he could not touch Tuyet or Melinh; they could only wave through the window in his door. Lying flat on his back day after day, in too much pain to move, Chris felt like a prisoner. The situation reminded him of Hué—confinement over which he had no control, with the threat of death looming. He had survived that ordeal and emerged more determined. But this was different; he was alone. His hospital gown felt like a prison uniform; he had lost his identity. He was the patient at the end of the hall.

Then one night, a new nurse came on duty. While taking Chris's temperature and blood pressure, she told him that she had just completed chemotherapy for Hodgkin's disease herself. Surprised, he asked, "How do you have the energy to work?" "Sometimes I don't," she replied. That brief encounter was just what he needed. After weeks of solitary confinement, his only contact being healthy nurses and doctors, here was someone like him, someone with a malignant disease to whom terrible things had happened. Yet she was part of the real world again. Perhaps he could be too.

35   Inconsolable

Eleven years had elapsed since Joey Radicchi had first come to Stanford at the age of twelve. After two recurrences of Hodgkin's disease, necessitating total lymphoid irradiation and intensive chemotherapy, he had been in remission for more than five years—likely cured, his family was told. He had suffered almost every known complication of therapy, from pericarditis to crippling nerve damage, but he hadn't been hospitalized for over a year.

Twenty-three years old, Joey stood five-foot-one with a concave chest and wry neck. Scars crossed his torso and abdomen; he needed braces to walk. Yet he attended Cabrillo College, planning to become a jeweler. Joey relished every day. When he sat in a boat with his father looking out over Lake Tahoe at sunrise or smelling pine trees in the Santa Cruz Mountains, he considered himself the luckiest man alive.

Then in July 1975, he began vomiting. He felt hungry, but when he tried to eat, he developed cramping pain in his mid-abdomen. Just when he thought he had found a food his stomach could handle, he threw it up hours later, undigested. Nothing stayed down, not even water. When he began to feel dizzy standing up, his mother called Stanford, and Joey was admitted to the Clinical Research Center (CRC).

The on-call resident encountered a thin, pale young man, in obvious discomfort. He noted several abnormal findings chronicled in the old chart—skeletal deformities, foot weakness, visible pounding of the heart through the chest wall— but nothing suggestive of recurrent Hodgkin's disease. The resident did find signs of severe dehydration, and when he palpated the abdomen, Joey winced. Listening with his stethoscope, he heard no bowel sounds, suggesting intestinal obstruction. An abdominal film indicated something blocking the stomach so that food, water, and even air could not pass into the intestines. The resident threaded a nasogastric tube through Joey's nose into his stomach and attached it to a pump to relieve the gas and secretions. Finally, Joey slept without retching.

Rosenberg and Kaplan were notified. They thought the likely cause of obstruction to be scar tissue from prior surgery. The next day Joey underwent an upper gastrointestinal series. When barium flowed down the esophagus and into the stomach, it stopped. A gastroenterologist was consulted. "I suspect the problem is adhesions," he wrote in his note. He performed a gastroscopy, passing a gastroscope through Joey's mouth, down his esophagus, and into his stomach. He couldn't advance the scope more than midway through the stomach, which he described as "rigid with thickened irregular folds." He took a biopsy, and a few days later, the pathologist called—undifferentiated lymphoma he said. Joey Radicchi had a second cancer.

After Arseneau had published the NCI findings showing an increased number of second cancers among Hodgkin's disease patients, Kaplan had stepped up his surveillance. At the time of the NCI report, Rosenberg said he hadn't seen a single case at Stanford. Then a twenty-year-old woman treated for Hodgkin's disease developed a lymphoma. She had been diagnosed at age thirteen with IIB disease and received subtotal nodal irradiation. When she relapsed, Rosenberg treated her with MOPP. Seven years later, she developed a lymphoma which had spread from her lymph nodes to her spleen, kidneys, bowel, lungs, and bone marrow. She died shortly thereafter. Now Joey Radicchi had a second cancer.

Kaplan was worried. What if Arseneau was right? He was so concerned, he kept the names of afflicted patients on 3 × 5 index cards which he carried in his breast pocket. Anytime they found a new case, Kaplan added a card. He wanted absolute accuracy in determining the case rate at Stanford. Meanwhile, one of DeVita's oncology fellows, Norman Coleman, came to Stanford to train as a radiotherapist with Kaplan. He had been taking care of Joey Radicchi when he developed a lymphoma. Before long, he saw two other patients with second cancers; one had leukemia, the other, a sarcoma. Coleman suggested to Kaplan that he do an in-depth analysis. He and oncology trainee, John Krikorian, reviewed the records of every Hodgkin's disease patient treated at Stanford since the early 1960s. They tracked down each one, calling the local doctor if the person had returned to the community, writing to South America and Europe, and doggedly obtaining autopsy reports on all patients who had died. The number analyzed totaled 680 patients—half treated with irradiation alone and half with irradiation and chemotherapy.

What they found was disturbing. For all patients, the chance of developing acute leukemia at ten years was 2 percent; lymphoma risk was 4 percent—over a hundred times the national average. Among those 344 patients who had received irradiation and chemotherapy, the risk was even higher—3.9 percent for leukemia, 15.2 percent for lymphoma. Those afflicted ranged in age from fifteen to sixty-seven. In each case, the chemotherapy used was MOPP. All but two were in remission from Hodgkin's disease when their second cancer was diagnosed. Response to subsequent chemotherapy was poor; the average survival for those with leukemia was only four months. DeVita had been right. Hodgkin's disease patients did have an increased chance of developing another cancer. The Stanford group had to conclude this might be another late risk of their therapy. They published their findings in the *New England Journal of Medicine*—five years after Arseneau's original publication.

Rosenberg and Kaplan were discouraged. These data challenged everything they had achieved. "You can't help but feel responsible about a life-threatening toxicity which has been induced by your treatment," Rosenberg said. "Some were patients we had followed for many years and were very fond of, so it was a very emotional experience." Like DeVita and Canellos, they had to look to their accomplishments for solace. "We had to handle it like other complications," Rosenberg said. "These were problems of success." After all, of the over six hundred patients they had treated with Hodgkin's disease—once called "invariably fatal"—the majority were alive at five years. "Of course," Rosenberg said, "that only slightly reduced the tragedy of the event."

Rosenberg was somewhat philosophical, but Kaplan became despondent. They had encountered side effects before, and he had analyzed them, corrected them, and pushed on. Now the cost had become too great. Kaplan loved seeing his patients return to normal lives. That's why he kept every graduation announcement and wedding invitation. He expressed particular pride in the young women who had faced possible death, were cured, and went on to have children. It was as if propagation of the next generation represented an affirmation of his work. Returning from a brief sabbatical, Kaplan learned that a couple of patients had developed second cancers and were dying. "He was overcome," trainee Carol Portlock remembered. After that, she noticed a change in him. Before, he had seemed light-hearted when he went into an exam room to see a patient he assumed to be cured. Now, he entered the room cautiously, as if he weren't sure what he might find.

The appearance of these treatment-induced cancers curbed the lymphoma team's enthusiasm over their recent results. They had been moving toward near total cure at meteoric speed. What had gone wrong? How many would be stricken? Once the champions of the combined modality approach, they now concluded: "There is currently a trend toward the use of combined modality therapy for all stages of Hodgkin's disease, and . . . it remains to be seen whether or not [it] . . . can be justified as initial treatment . . . or whether single modality, with the second reserved for salvage treatment of relapses, would be a better approach, thereby exposing a smaller proportion to the high risk of leukemia."

Kaplan set out to determine what had happened. "It wasn't the 95 percent of patients who won," Coleman said, "but the other 5 percent that got him. It wasn't the victories, but the losses that drove him." Kaplan began to investigate the problem in detail, looking at effects of radiation dose, different drugs, and sequencing of the two modalities. He wouldn't accept a lower survival rate, but they clearly had to take a different tack and develop regimens with less carcinogenicity. They had to reduce this risk. With each new case of a treatment-related cancer, he was devastated. One day when Norm Coleman stopped by his office, he was surprised to find Kaplan in tears. He had just learned of another patient with a secondary leukemia. "Norman," he said, "we have to do better."

Joey Radicchi, beloved by Kaplan, Rosenberg, Glatstein, Coleman, O'Hara, and every other physician and nurse who had cared for him, now had a second cancer—undifferentiated lymphoma. Another malignancy of lymph tissue, this type was far more aggressive than the one he had survived. It spread through the body in an unpredictable manner, invading vital organs. The most effective treatment at the time was irradiation, but the disease often progressed. And the success from chemotherapy in Hodgkin's disease had not been duplicated in lymphoma.

Joey's mother could always predict whether news would be good or bad from the look on Rosenberg's face. So she expected bad news when he told her the results of the biopsy. "We found a tumor in the wall of Joey's stomach," he said. "It may be caused by the radiation or chemotherapy. I'm not sure."

"I knew what was coming," Mrs. Radicchi said. "For the first time, I realized Joey might not make it." They never talked about the implications of the diagnosis, but she thought her son knew. That afternoon he took communion in the hospital chapel.

Rosenberg recommended a new chemotherapy regimen he had been testing in advanced lymphomas. It was composed of three drugs: cytosine arabinoside, adriamycin, and 6-thioguanine; he called it CAT. Although he had seen responses in over half the patients, second cancers were less responsive to therapy. He told Joey that the side effects would be similar to MOPP, except for one other potential toxicity, which worried him: Adriamycin could damage the heart muscle, and Joey had already sustained substantial radiation injury to his heart. Joey replied just as he had when Rosenberg asked him about MOPP years earlier—what did he have to lose? With an obstructed stomach, he was starving to death.

On August 2, 1975, Joey began CAT chemotherapy, and within five days, he could keep down liquids. A few days later, he was eating a soft diet and was discharged home after three weeks of intravenous feedings. He subsequently received six more cycles of chemotherapy and underwent a repeat upper gastrointestinal series, which showed complete relief of the obstruction and no tumor. Before long, Joey returned to cutting gems and fishing with his father.

Then, just a few months later, Mrs. Radicchi called. Joey had become winded just talking. Rosenberg's greatest fear had materialized—Joey developed congestive heart failure. His heart muscle could not contract normally, leading to fluid collection in his lungs. A heart biopsy confirmed severe muscle injury. Rosenberg knew the damage was permanent. All he could do was stimulate the remaining muscle fibers with digitalis and control the backup of fluid with diuretics.

Over the next few weeks, Joey's health deteriorated. An electrocardiogram showed first-degree heart block; the electrical impulses had gone awry. Then his heart began to skip beats. Another EKG showed second-degree block. His heart was getting weaker. Despite diuretics, fluid continued to collect in his lungs. But Joey never complained. He was admitted to the hospital several times in the spring of 1976, and although the CRC nurses offered him a private room, he insisted on the five-bed ward. "More often than not," Maureen O'Hara said, "he was the sickest one there, and yet he was the biggest morale booster for everyone else on the ward." Meanwhile, Rosenberg increased his diuretics, and once his heart stabilized, let Joey go home.

Upon return to the lymphoma clinic on June 14, Joey told Eli Glatstein that he had lost his appetite. X-rays showed a mass in the upper abdomen and several spots on the liver. Joey's lymphoma had recurred. Rosenberg recommended no further therapy. There was none left to give. "He is stable," Glatstein wrote in the clinic chart, "and we will see him again in approximately one month." He was never to see Joey again.

Two weeks later, Joey was admitted to the CRC extremely short of breath with a dangerously slow heart rate. An electrocardiogram showed no electrical current between the chambers of his heart—complete heart block—and a pacemaker was placed emergently. "He couldn't breathe no more," his mother said. "I was expecting his death, but you hope until the last." Joey's oxygen level dropped, and he became confused. Hope had run out. A decision was made not to intubate him. His heart had been irreparably damaged by radiation and chemotherapy; he had a treatment-induced cancer, resistant to all therapy. Oxygen was discontinued, and on a sunny July afternoon in 1976, Joey Radicchi died.

Not long afterward, Carol Portlock spotted Henry Kaplan in the lymphoma clinic. He was sitting bent over with his head in his hands. "I don't know if I can take this anymore," he said.

36   Without a Spleen

Sadness hung over the CRC the day Joey Radicchi died. But Chris Jenkins didn't notice; in a nearby room, he lay close to death himself.

Chris had never fully recovered after his hospitalization in July 1975. The pain from his shingles hadn't abated; he felt as if someone intermittently applied electric shocks to his nerves. Anything that merely touched his skin, no matter how lightly, incited the pain. That summer, he and Tuyet were starting to look for a house in Berkeley, and the realtor was a bit surprised that her client wore no shirt. Chris's sister came from the East Coast to visit, and whether they drove to the wine country or ate in a cafe, Chris went bare-chested. At night, when the fog rolled in, the cool air made him shiver, but he preferred that to the sharp twinge provoked by contact with bedclothes.

To make matters worse, Chris developed diarrhea from radiation damage to his intestines. He had to rush to the bathroom ten to twelve times a day. As a result, he didn't absorb nutrients properly. A thin man to begin with, he now looked gaunt. He couldn't return to work; he declined social invitations. His whole life centered on his bowels. Since he could not digest solid foods, his diet consisted mostly of Vivonex—an orange-flavored liquid high in calories and nutrients. Chris felt miserable. When he thought he could no longer bear these problems, however, he reminded himself how desperately ill he had been from Hodgkin's disease. At least now he was in remission.

On a special dietary regimen, Chris's diarrhea eventually decreased, and he stopped losing weight. It took a year for his intestines to heal and the pain from his shingles to diminish. In the summer of 1976, he felt well enough to return to work at the Southeast Asian Resource Center. With the end of the Vietnam War, it focused on educating the public about normalization of relations with Vietnam and human rights violations in Laos and Cambodia. Chris and Tuyet moved into their first home in Berkeley where he could enjoy a bike ride and dinner with friends.

A week after he had returned to work, Chris awoke in the middle of the night with a dull headache. He tried to ignore it, but toward morning, if he tried to sit up, pain reverberated through his head. When dawn came, light increased the intensity. He kept the shades drawn, his eyes shut. By afternoon, his temperature reached 103°, and muscle aches kept him awake most of that night. Chris thought he had the flu, and despite Tuyet's urging, he would not go to the hospital. The next day, his fever persisted. He started shaking. Tuyet became alarmed and telephoned the resident on call. "Come to the emergency room immediately," she was told. Chris lay in the fetal position in the back of their station wagon as Tuyet drove the too familiar route back to Stanford. Any bump or jarring of the car detonated what felt like an explosion inside his head.

On July 8, 1976, Chris was again admitted to the CRC. The on-call resident described an "emaciated, febrile, shaking male with closed eyes." Concerned about a possible bacterial infection, he ordered cultures of blood, sputum, urine, and stool, and performed a lumbar puncture. When the resident inserted the needle into Chris's spine, clear fluid flowed into the collection tube. Meningitis seemed unlikely, but the next morning on rounds, the team found Chris writhing in pain. He didn't know where he was or who he was. The nurse reported that he had just vomited. His temperature was 104°, his pulse so rapid she could barely feel it. On examination, his neck was stiff; the resident could not bend it even a few degrees—a sure sign of meningitis. He repeated the lumbar puncture. This time a white, milky fluid dripped out. He ordered penicillin and moved Chris into isolation. The laboratory soon confirmed the diagnosis. In fifteen hours, the white blood cell count in the spinal fluid had shot up from one to 429, and it was heavily infiltrated with bacteria. The same bacteria were growing in his blood, a condition termed sepsis. The nurse reported falling blood pressure. Chris had meningitis, and he was going into shock.

Why had Chris Jenkins contracted such a fulminant infection—likely because his spleen had been removed at his staging laparotomy.

~

The spleen, a crescent-shaped organ of lymph tissue in the left upper abdominal cavity, had long been considered nonessential. This was the prevailing attitude until 1952, when surgeons at Indiana University reported that five infants on whom they had performed splenectomies had developed meningitis or sepsis. Two had died. The surgeons concluded that there must be a cause-and-effect relationship between splenectomy in infancy and sepsis. For the next ten years, academicians argued over whether or not splenectomy increased susceptibility to infection. In 1962, pediatric hematologists in Melbourne reported the largest series to date. Of 141 children who had undergone splenectomies, 12 percent had subsequently developed a serious infection. Four years later, British physicians identified two specific organisms that caused most postsplenectomy infections—*pneumococcus* and *Haemophilus influenzae*. Worse yet was the rapidity with which these infections spread. "[It] slays so quickly," one physician wrote, "many patients are found dead in bed or on arrival at the hospital." These reports made pediatricians reluctant to subject children with Hodgkin's disease to staging laparotomies. But no one had found this to be a problem in adults.

Then, in December 1970, Sarah Donaldson, a radiation therapy resident at the time, was on call for the CRC and admitted twenty-two-year-old Judith Hurt for evaluation of a fever. Just a month earlier, Kaplan had told the young woman that she was in remission. With that good news, Judith had returned to college with the goal of teaching nursery school. Shortly thereafter, she began vomiting. She attributed it to the chili she had eaten for dinner. A severe headache, muscle pains, and diarrhea followed. When she started shaking with chills, she became alarmed and called the CRC.

Donaldson found a drowsy, slightly confused young woman with a high fever who screamed in pain with the slightest movement. The constellation of fever, muscle aches, and diarrhea suggested a severe case of the flu. But Donaldson suspected something more serious. She set to work quickly, culturing blood, urine, and sputum. And because Hurt was a bit disoriented, she performed a lumbar puncture. The spinal fluid was clear, but Donaldson knew that if meningitis was even a consideration, she needed to repeat the spinal tap a few hours later. This time when she inserted the needle, the spinal fluid dripped out slowly; it looked like curdled milk. Within minutes, she gave the first dose of penicillin. The laboratory confirmed the diagnosis—clumps of bacteria and ten thousand white blood cells—bacterial meningitis.

Despite antibiotics, Hurt's temperature rose to 105°, and she became delirious. Nurses wrapped her in a cooling blanket, trying to avoid a seizure. Then she began to bleed from her gums; bruises spontaneously appeared all over her skin. Her platelet count had fallen to a dangerously low level. Donaldson infused blood and platelets, but Hurt's blood pressure was falling. She knew that if Hurt went into shock, she'd lose her. There was nothing Donaldson could do but continue to support her with blood products and antibiotics—and wait. In the early morning, Hurt opened her eyes. For the first time since admission, she responded to her name. When Kaplan arrived for rounds at 9 A.M., Hurt's temperature was down, her blood pressure stable.

Donaldson and Kaplan discussed the puzzling aggressiveness of Hurt's infection. She had a normal white blood count, and she was not on chemotherapy, yet she had no ability to combat the bacteria. Donaldson recalled how her Harvard pediatrics professor had warned her about pneumococcal infections in splenectomized infants. Judith Hurt had no spleen. Did that put her at increased risk, even though she was an adult? If that were the case, they should be able to confirm it, since Stanford had a large number of adult patients who had undergone a splenectomy. Donaldson told Kaplan that she would analyze their records and tabulate the number of infectious episodes. Kaplan agreed; it was crucial to determine whether they had uncovered yet another long-term complication of their treatment.

Donaldson began her investigation by searching for prior publications on the subject. She found a 1969 report in an Australian medical journal about seven adults who had developed pneumococcal infections up to fourteen years following splenectomy. Five had died within hours of becoming ill.

By then, the spleen was known to have a special role in eliminating a particular bacterial species, which included *pneumococcus, Haemophilus influenzae,* and *meningococcus.* Donaldson examined records of the Stanford patients looking specifically for infections with these organisms. Within a few months, she had reviewed the hospital charts of almost five hundred patients who had undergone splenectomy during a three-year period, beginning in 1968. Half had had Hodgkin's disease or non-Hodgkin's lymphoma. Twelve patients with Hodgkin's disease or lymphoma and twenty-one with other diseases had developed infections in the bloodstream. Thirteen had died. Donaldson calculated the risk of sepsis following splenectomy to be about 7 percent. Because the time between removal of the spleen and a subsequent infection could be years, and the number of affected patients was relatively small, this fatal complication in adults had gone largely unnoticed. Kaplan considered a 7 percent chance of sepsis unacceptable and determined to find a way to mitigate it. Donaldson hoped her results would alert cancer specialists to the potential seriousness of fever in splenectomized patients. She didn't anticipate the furor that ensued.

When Donaldson published her findings in the *New England Journal of Medicine* in 1972, it added fuel to the controversy over staging laparotomy. Researchers at the University of Chicago wrote in the *Annals of Internal Medicine*: "In many treatment centers . . . evaluation in Hodgkin's disease or lymphoma has come to include diagnostic laparotomy and splenectomy. Introduction of this method has generated a lively controversy. Further controversy is certain to be raised by the reports . . . [that] suggest that splenectomy . . . may pose a special long-term risk for severe infections."

The routine use of staging laparotomy became a subject of more debate at national and international meetings. Community physicians used this complication as a reason not to send patients to Stanford. "To the rest of the world," Donaldson said, "the conclusion from my work was: 'You shouldn't do staging laparotomies because they are bad.'"

Chris Jenkins had undergone a splenectomy, and now he lay in the CRC critically ill. An infectious disease consultant diagnosed meningitis and sepsis from pneumococcal bacteria. "Among acute bacterial meningitides," he wrote in Chris's chart, "pneumococcal disease has the worst prognosis with mortality in up to twenty percent of cases." He told the team to be prepared for convulsions. The resident explained the gravity of the situation to Tuyet. Chris might not survive. All they could do was wait, hope the penicillin worked fast enough. Tuyet sat outside Chris's room, unable to touch or even see her husband. She tried to interpret the expressions on the faces of the doctors and nurses who rushed in and out of the room.

Jenkins lay on a precipice. He couldn't make sense of what people were saying. Drenched in sweat, he felt as if someone were hitting his head with a sledgehammer. At one point, he awoke to find Dr. Kaplan standing at his bedside. "This is a very serious infection," he said, "but we can treat it." Kaplan's words calmed him.

Chris drifted in and out of consciousness. Whenever he opened his eyes, someone took him away for a test. He couldn't understand what was happening to him, and he couldn't put words together coherently enough to ask. He felt scared. His hospital room, which once he had considered a prison cell, now became his refuge. "The room seemed much nicer—all soft colors," Chris recalled. "Everything turned white, and filtered light came in through gauzy curtains. It didn't feel like a hospital."

On the third hospital day, Chris became more somnolent, and a nurse reported that he had lost most of his hearing. The nurses tried to comfort Tuyet, but she could see the sadness in their eyes. Two days later, Chris passed bloody urine and went into renal failure. Radiographs demonstrated markedly enlarged kidneys without an obvious cause. The nephrologist and ward team discussed a kidney biopsy but deemed it too dangerous. The nephrologist concluded that the most likely diagnosis was an unusual reaction to penicillin. The drug had to be stopped and another, less effective antibiotic substituted.

Chris's mental state continued to wax and wane. He began hallucinating. The team performed a mental status exam several times a day. Chris loathed it. "Who are you? Where are you? What day is it?" The resident asked him to count backward from one hundred, to list the last five presidents in order, to subtract seven from a series of numbers. Sometimes he could do it; sometimes he could not. And they had to shout, since he was almost deaf.

Just as Chris began to think and speak more clearly, he suffered yet another series of medical problems. On the sixth hospital day, his platelet count plummeted. A hematology consultant was called. Tests indicated that his body was destroying platelets as fast as he made them. The platelet count reached such a low level that Chris could spontaneously bleed to death. He had already begun having nosebleeds. Then Chris said he couldn't take a deep breath. A chest x-ray showed a fluid collection in the lining of one lung. The resident performed a thoracentesis, inserting a needle into the space between Chris's lung and chest wall to remove the fluid. Afterward, he could breathe more freely, but the procedure induced a pain that felt as if someone were rubbing sandpaper inside his chest whenever he took a breath. Tests on the fluid did not reveal either an infection or Hodgkin's disease. Two days later, the resident detected a scratchy sound over his heart. He told Chris he had pericarditis—an inflammation of the sac around his heart. An x-ray demonstrated fluid there, and the doctors considered inserting a needle to withdraw a sample. Chris didn't know how much more he could take.

On the ninth hospital day, the resident told Tuyet that Chris would survive the meningitis, but he continued to spike fevers. Cultures revealed nothing. He developed diffuse joint pains and couldn't move his right wrist and left shoulder. Rheumatologists and orthopedic surgeons were consulted. Evaluation for every known arthritic condition proved negative. Then tests indicated damage to his liver; his white and red blood cell counts began to drop. Something was injuring multiple organs. Although Chris protested, the resident persuaded him to undergo bone marrow and liver biopsies. They, too, revealed nothing. Jenkins's case was discussed at oncology conferences and radiation therapy rounds. Pathologists showed his slides to other colleagues in the department. Specialists made calls to other specialists. Despite the best Stanford could bring to bear on his case, Chris Jenkins remained an enigma.

By now Chris's mental state had improved enough for him to become upset over the barrage of tests and annoyed by the number of teams rounding on him daily. He had been in the hospital twenty-two days, evaluated by nephrologists, gastroenterologists, pulmonologists, cardiologists, rheumatologists, orthopedists, hematologists, and infectious disease specialists. Each team included at least one medical student, a resident, and an attending physician—all of whom examined Chris. "Why don't the doctors talk to each other," he asked, "instead of bothering me?" Once a new intern came in and questioned him for forty-five minutes, going all the way back to his initial diagnosis. Chris found his awkwardness and insecurity amusing. Following the interview, the intern scurried down the hall and tripped over a cart; instruments and bottles crashed onto the floor. At that, Chris did something he thought he might never do again—he laughed.

Chris Jenkins had been hospitalized for almost four weeks when his medical problems—anemia, low platelets, kidney failure, abnormal liver tests, joint pains, fever, and hearing loss—all began to improve. The specialists never could diagnose the specific cause of these symptoms; they attributed them to the overwhelming infection and to toxicities from the antibiotics. Chris Jenkins had survived against all odds. On August 4, 1976, he returned home. In his absence, Melinh had learned several new words.

The suffering this gentle man had endured disheartened the lymphoma team, no one more than Kaplan. "HSK felt responsible for this problem," Eli Glatstein said of postsplenectomy sepsis. But he didn't concede on the necessity for staging laparotomies. Postsplenectomy sepsis was a rare event, which could be managed with antibiotics if diagnosed early. Although Kaplan's critics rushed to condemn laparotomy, the Stanford team kept their perspective: a 25 percent chance of undetected disease in the spleen, a 7 percent risk of sepsis with the procedure. "We weren't going to stop doing laparotomies," Donaldson said. But Kaplan couldn't tolerate inadvertently causing even one death. "He felt terribly guilty," Glatstein said. "He went after the problem with a vengeance."

At first, Kaplan contemplated prophylactic antibiotics to prevent infection, but cases had already been reported of splenectomized children dying despite long-term use of penicillin. Besides, hundreds of patients would have to be treated, and several were sure to develop an allergic reaction, which could be fatal. In 1977, a vaccine against *pneumococcus* became available, and within a year, researchers had tested it in patients with Hodgkin's disease. To their disappointment, they found that the ability to produce an antibody to *pneumococcus* was severely impaired following splenectomy and treatment. Kaplan postulated that the vaccine could protect against sepsis if patients were immunized before therapy commenced, and he started vaccinating all patients prior to splenectomy.

At the same time, Kaplan began investigating what colleagues considered an outrageous idea—reimplantation of splenic tissue, termed "splenosis." It had been observed that in patients who had undergone a splenectomy for traumatic injury, small pieces of tissue left behind could implant themselves and become functional—a "born-again spleen," it was called. Kaplan proposed inducing splenosis in Hodgkin's disease patients. During staging laparotomy, a pathologist would examine the spleen in the operating room. If he detected no disease, a piece of spleen would be inserted into the abdominal cavity, where it would grow and restore the immune response. But the Stanford team considered this too radical to test in patients and insisted that he prove his hypothesis in animals first. Even more intriguing to Kaplan was a splenic peptide called Tuftsin—named after Tufts University where two scientists had isolated the substance. When they removed Tuftsin from the spleen of a normal animal and infused it into a splenectomized animal, it restored antibody production. Unfortunately, Tuftsin's activity was too short-lived to be of benefit.

While working to find a solution for postsplenectomy sepsis, Kaplan warned physicians and patients about the dangers of any fever in splenectomized individuals. "Until such time as the efficacy of these modalities can be adequately tested," Donaldson wrote in 1978, "prompt recognition and early antimicrobial treatment . . . remain the most reliable means of managing infections." Despite their warning, and despite the pace at which scientists worked to prevent postsplenectomy sepsis, it was not fast enough for Petra Ekstrand.

⌒

By 1978, Petra Ekstrand made only yearly follow-up visits to Stanford. At thirty-five, this lovely Scandinavian woman had been in remission for years. Cure had seemed improbable when in her early twenties she had come to Stanford with stage IIIB disease, a large mediastinal mass eroding her chest wall on the verge of blocking her bronchial tubes and major blood vessels. To complicate matters, she was pregnant. In 1966, when she had been diagnosed, most patients with IIIB disease received palliative care. Kaplan had treated Ekstrand with high-dose total lymphoid irradiation—including radiation to the spleen.

Ekstrand's Hodgkin's disease never recurred. But high-dose radiotherapy had left its mark—low thyroid function, chronic radiation pericarditis, pneumonitis, and a shrunken, nonfunctional spleen. The CRC nurses marveled at Ekstrand's buoyancy and amicability despite these complications. And she always looked elegant, even when a resident was draining fluid from her lung. When Kaplan saw her in lymphoma clinic in July 1977 for her yearly follow-up visit, he wrote, "She has no complaints today other than mild dyspnea [shortness of breath] on exertion although she is still able to ride horseback four times per week."

One June evening in 1978, Ekstrand called the CRC. She told the nurse she had developed a cough, sore throat, headache, and shaking chills. Her husband had taken her temperature—104°. And something else—the light hurt her eyes. The nurse told her to come to the Emergency Room. Then she called the ER and asked that the CRC resident be notified as soon as Ekstrand arrived.

Petra's husband brought her to Stanford an hour later. Her temperature had almost returned to normal, and the ER resident found nothing abnormal on examination. Petra's appearance may have misled the resident into underestimating the severity of her situation. She didn't know that even when ill, Petra dressed smartly and wore lipstick. The resident diagnosed a viral syndrome, prescribed Tylenol, and sent her home. She did not notify the CRC resident. The next morning, Petra felt so dizzy she couldn't stand. Her husband laid her in the backseat and drove to the Stanford ER. When the orderly brought a stretcher out to the car, he found the young woman inside dead.

An autopsy revealed massive numbers of *pneumococci* in the bloodstream, invading many organs, as well as widespread hemorrhages into the nose, eyes, bronchial tree, kidneys, and adrenal glands. The spleen was small and scarred. The pathologist found no Hodgkin's disease.

Henry Kaplan was beside himself. The next morning, as the ward team sat down to review charts, he stormed into the conference room. "What happened to Petra Ekstrand?" he demanded. The team stared blankly at him. No one had called them about a patient named Ekstrand. Kaplan looked pale and agitated. He proceeded to blurt out the story of a young woman, cured of Hodgkin's disease, who had died that morning because of the stupidity of the resident in the emergency room. He knew the whole story. His question—"What happened?"—was more a question to himself.

Colleagues had never seen Kaplan so distraught. He kept talking about Petra. He could not console himself that he had cured hundreds of patients with Hodgkin's disease. He could not put her death in perspective as a rare event. She was a vibrant, loving woman whom he had cured and then somehow failed. He had spent his entire adult life fighting cancer. He had made great strides and was honored and applauded everywhere he went. But all that meant nothing to Henry Kaplan if he couldn't save Petra Ekstrand.

37   Kaplan's Moby Dick

Leah never knew about Joey Radicchi. Ann and Paul never heard of Petra Ekstrand. Henry Kaplan rarely shared his sadness with his family—a pattern he had established early on. By the time he came home in the evening, Ann and Paul were eating dinner. He briskly kissed Leah's cheek, patted the children's heads and retreated to his study. There were times, however, when Leah sensed that something sad had happened to a patient. Instead of retreating to his study, he stopped in the kitchen. After hugging Ann and putting his arm around Paul, he sat down and asked about their school activities and friends. At these times, he found solace in his family.

As years went on, the children saw less of their father. "In his heart he put his family first," Ann said, "but in reality he put his work first." Now at a time when Henry needed his family's support, it was too late. The children had grown up, and Leah had her own career. Their lives no longer centered on his. Leah had evening meetings to attend; the children only came home on holidays and occasional weekends. Henry had encouraged his family's independence, and he delighted in their achievements. He kept newspaper clippings about Leah in his office files; he invariably closed letters to friends with a paragraph about his children.

Leah had been the perfect wife for Henry—talented and independent, yet supportive of everything he did. Although she called his laboratory his mistress, she never felt jealous. She had allowed, even encouraged, her husband to be single-minded in his quest to cure cancer. But now she was busy with her own work. In 1974, after counseling Stanford students for ten years, Leah had become assistant dean of student affairs. People were her passion. Henry proudly showed friends a *Campus Report* article in which President Donald Kennedy said of Leah's work as a dean: "She is known far and wide in this community for her ability as a counselor and for her extraordinary sensitivity." Given his own reputation for being a "dean killer," Henry used to tease Leah that he was now sleeping with the enemy.

She served as director of the Help Center and received the Dinkelspiel Award, the highest recognition for service to undergraduate education at Stanford. Henry felt especially proud of Leah's work on sexual harassment. Her guidelines had been adopted as university policy long before most schools even recognized the term.

Ann had grown up to be an accomplished woman. Following her undergraduate education at Stanford, she had attended law school. She married a businessman, Robert Spears, and became a successful trial lawyer with a large San Francisco firm. And Paul, who had matured into a six-foot, four-inch man, was busily pursuing a career in film making. Henry was loath to burden them with his problems.

In the Kaplan family, problems were not discussed, only solutions. Sarah had instilled that ethos into her son at a young age. This was clear from her reaction to his deformed fingers and from Henry's response to Paul's dyslexia. In this family, achievement was presumed; no one spoke of failure. "The pressure I felt," Paul said, "wasn't to follow in my father's footsteps. The pressure I felt was to be excellent." What had been a clarion call for their father became a burden for them. From the time Ann and Paul were youngsters, their father had said over and over again, "We don't care what you do as long as you do it to the best of your ability." Implied in his statement was that they should succeed. Both were doing well in their careers, but the road had not been smooth.

Although Ann had excelled at Stanford, when she was ready to graduate, she had no plans for her future. She had no passion, no proverbial mountain she wanted to climb. Henry suggested law, pointing out that in her sociology and psychology classes, she had been attracted to the criminal aspects. Ann found the prospect of a law career interesting, but intimidating. She thought only the brightest people studied law, and she didn't consider herself particularly intelligent. She had chosen an unreasonable basis for comparison—her father. Besides, she had heard that many law students didn't pass the first year. "My father had high expectations," she said. "I didn't like to do anything that had the potential for failure." Ann was a Kaplan; she wasn't supposed to flounder. "My mother was open to other people's frailties," she said. "I knew if I screwed up, she would still love and accept me. That was harder to work out with my father." Eventually, however, Ann entered law school, where she flourished.

Paul, on the other hand, did have a passion—photography. He wanted to explore it in his own way, at his own pace, but his father constantly tried to focus his goals and quicken his stride. "I didn't start out planning to become a hotshot photographer," Paul said; "I just enjoyed it." The summer after his first year at Antioch College West, Paul was accepted into the Ansel Adams Workshop in

Yosemite—his first contact with serious photographers. The group was electrifying, "a smorgasbord of 'Who's Who in Photography,'" Paul recalled. They often stayed up all night talking, arguing, never satisfied. Paul worked harder then he ever had. Wanting to devote all his energy to photography, he dropped out of college. Although disappointed, Henry tried to remain supportive. "Paul is deeply immersed in landscape photography," he wrote Michael Feldman.

Paul began to study Adams's zone system with the renowned San Francisco photographer Oliver Gagliani. With this approach, a subject was seen as a series of zones or contrasts from light to dark. This radical approach elevated photography from a craft to a science. And that was the appeal to Paul. "I started learning about technique as something integral to vision," he said. With the zone system, he could apply the same scientific rigor to his photography that his father applied to radiotherapy. Every photograph was an experiment; the darkroom was his laboratory. Paul felt accomplished. He belonged to a profession that required creativity and intelligence, one in which he was not impeded by dyslexia. Like his father, Paul had found a language, culture, and world of his own. Before long, he had produced a large body of black-and-white landscapes and abstracts. The youngest in Gagliani's class by ten years, he was regarded as precocious. Paul had found his niche; he felt on the verge of an important personal discovery.

Excited when he saw what Paul had done, Henry thought it was time for a public appearance. In the spring of 1972, he urged Paul to show his work at Stanford. Reluctantly, Paul agreed. He received praise for his exhibit—"A Fourteen Month Retrospective"—and the photographs sold very well. To Henry the show was a great success; to Paul it was a disaster.

Paul had been enjoying photography, finding new artistic pleasures daily. Suddenly his work was shared with others. Strangers bought his favorite photographs and took them away. Trying hard to enter and share in Paul's new domain, Henry was talking about the zone system and previsualization. "It was something that I could look at that was truly mine," Paul said, "and it ended up being sort of owned by him." Paul was only nineteen. "I would have preferred to photograph in anonymity for fifteen years," he said, "attaining a sense of my own self worth, rather than receiving so much attention." But anonymity wasn't Henry's way. If you had the chance to reach your goal, you grabbed it. In his genuine desire for Paul to succeed, he unwittingly robbed his son of the chance to experience the vicissitudes of youth, to find himself, to excel on his own. He had entered the private place Paul had carved out for himself.

After the show, photography was never the same for Paul. Those who knew his work were disappointed; Paul had talent. Had he persevered, he might have made his mark in the field. But when his father's enthusiasm peaked, Paul's

interest waned. Over the next few years, he rambled, exploring several different fields. Where most fathers would have lost patience, Henry, to his credit,
expressed genuine interest and encouragement over each change in direction.
When Paul entered Evergreen College in Olympia, Washington, and majored
in anthropology, Henry may have imagined Paul as a future professor. When
Paul attended graduate school at the University of Massachusetts three years
later to study archeology, Henry wrote to a friend in the Netherlands: "Paul
seems seriously interested in his archeology. You can readily imagine the pleasure which his development gives us." But Paul never completed his studies. A
year later, Henry wrote to a colleague in England: "Paul is currently working in
an intensive course in movie-making at the University of California Berkeley."
His eagerness for his son to succeed was suffocating.

To be the child of Henry Kaplan was at times wonderful, at times quite hard.
While he enriched their lives with art, music, and political debate, Paul and
Ann found their father a tough role model. By not exposing them to his failures, he inadvertently perpetuated the image of unmitigated success. Difficulties—whether giant fingers or dyslexia—were to be overcome. He had set this
tone in his home, and now he had to live with it. Thus his children never knew
of his agony when he first learned his treatment had caused a patient to develop another cancer. And they never appreciated the depth of his disappointment when his dream of a cancer center died. Henry Kaplan bore a great deal
of pain in silence.

↬

The cancer center fiasco was the first major failure Kaplan had encountered in
his professional life—"a particularly shameful defeat for him," Michael Feldman said, "because he was at the peak of his fame." How dismayed he must
have felt when he learned that the University of Wisconsin, the University of
Pittsburgh, and a number of other medical schools, many far inferior to Stanford in research accomplishments, had been granted NCI center grants. Every
time he saw "deceased" stamped on yet another chart, he was reminded of his
unfulfilled promise to himself to cure cancer.

Kaplan's senior research scientist, Alain Declève, recalled a conversation he
had with his boss shortly after he had withdrawn from the cancer center effort. Declève had gone to his office to review some experiments. Kaplan barely
greeted him; he avoided eye contact. This thirty-year-old Belgian scientist, indebted to his mentor for his career development, was struck by his loneliness.
"He was like a monument," Declève said, "so proper, trying to hide his emotions." And he hid them well. While most thought of Kaplan as impenetrable,
Declève saw a man—one who was hurting.

Declève insisted they go for a walk. He steered Kaplan down a path to the old Stanford barn. The sun warmed their backs, and they could smell fresh-cut hay. The Medical School in the distance, Kaplan finally began to talk. As he expressed his disappointment, Declève was surprised to realize that Kaplan was apologizing for failing *him*. Declève was to have assisted him in directing all cancer research programs. Now his vision of an entire building of research laboratories had faded. Declève, always forthright with Kaplan, said, "There is nothing you can do about it now. You just have to accept the loss."

Two days later, Declève saw a changed man. "The dream is not over," Kaplan told him. "I'll get my own institute." And he did. Kaplan's Cancer Biology Research Laboratory (CBRL) opened at Stanford in 1975, with Declève as associate director. "Institute" may have been too grand a word for the 11,000-square-foot building, but it was a separate space, located across the street from the Medical School, with the entrance facing the foothills. There he could do what he wanted. The CBRL symbolized the beginning of a new phase of his life.

Henry Kaplan had always wanted to unravel the secrets of carcinogenesis. He had begun making strides in his mouse lymphoma work when, in 1959, he got caught up in the shaping of Stanford's Medical School. For the next fifteen years, he had taken on more and more administrative duties. Now freed from these burdens, he could devote most of his time to science, and the years that followed were his most productive.

Henry Kaplan had spent twenty years treating cancer. By the mid seventies, he and Rosenberg were making excellent progress with Hodgkin's disease, but they had less success with the non-Hodgkin's lymphomas. Despite high-dose irradiation, more than half the patients relapsed. Chemotherapy could induce remissions in those with slow-growing lymphomas, but all eventually recurred. For the more rapidly growing lymphomas, they had tried a number of regimens, but none had significant curative potential. Kaplan wasn't confident that either irradiation or chemotherapy or both combined would ever be able to eradicate the non-Hodgkin's lymphomas. They needed a new approach. So he took this clinical problem into the laboratory seeking solutions.

Kaplan hoped to elucidate what transformed normal lymphoid tissue into neoplastic lymphoma cells, and what controlled their growth. Then he could design rational therapies or perhaps prevent the disease. Kaplan always contended that only through a partnership between laboratory research and clinical investigation would lasting contributions be made to cancer therapy. Neither would succeed in isolation. He had seen too many clinical investigators repeatedly try therapies that had no scientific grounds, and that, not surprisingly, were ineffectual. He had reviewed too many grants from scientists who spent their careers performing experiments that had no clinical relevance.

Decades later, "bench to bedside" research was still regarded by some as a new concept. Kaplan was ahead of his time in suggesting this partnership, and he was unique in being his own partner. Fundamental laboratory research, however, was a full-time endeavor. Most scientists could only hope to succeed in one arena; most worked on just one problem. Kaplan was trying to solve several, juggling clinical and laboratory research. "I guess you have to be a bit schizophrenic to try that," he once said.

Kaplan believed that a virus caused lymphoma. "This is my personal conviction," he told reporters at the dedication of the Cancer Biology Research Laboratory. He spoke of his certainty that a human cancer virus would be found within the decade. Furthermore, if scientists could identify the causative virus, perhaps they could develop a vaccine, as had been done for polio. Cancer prevention might then become possible on a mass scale. As yet, no one had isolated a virus in human lymphomas—a task Kaplan described as "formidably difficult." Nonetheless, he was determined to find it, and this search would span the rest of his career.

In 1976, at the age of fifty-eight, Henry Kaplan looked tired. His hairline had receded, revealing permanent forehead creases. As the skin on his cheeks began to sag, his overbite had become more prominent. Brown age spots dotted his hands. Physically he was aging, but his mind was more robust and creative than ever. Every newly diagnosed patient, every death drove him to find the cause of cancer. "He told me he felt like Captain Ahab," Leah said. "Cancer was his Moby Dick."

38   The Elusive Human Tumor Virus

Henry Kaplan had been investigating lymphomas in mice since 1943 when he had set out to discover how healthy cells changed into malignant ones. He had not started as a virus hunter, but his unexpected finding—that some agent, when activated by x-rays, transformed normal thymic cells into malignant ones—propelled him into the nascent field of viral oncology. After twenty-five years of arduous work, he and research associate Miriam Lieberman had discovered a virus responsible for radiation-induced lymphomas in mice. He believed that a similar virus underlay lymphomas in patients. So late in his career, Henry Kaplan embarked upon a new journey—to find the human lymphoma virus and eliminate it.

Establishing that a virus caused lymphoma was no easy feat. German microbiologist and Nobel laureate Robert Koch (1843–1910), who had identified the bacterium responsible for tuberculosis, had laid down the requirements necessary to prove an organism causes a disease. A hundred years later, scientists still adhered to his criteria, called Koch's postulates: the organism must be detectable in every case of the disease; it must be possible to isolate and grow it in a pure culture; and it must reproduce the disease. Modified for cancer-causing viruses, Koch's postulates dictated that the virus had to be isolated from cancerous tissue, grown in culture, shown to transform normal human cells into malignant ones, and, finally, be identified in these new cancer cells.

The simplest of organisms, a virus was known to consist of only a protein coat and a core of nucleic acid—either DNA or RNA. Scientists presumed that if a virus caused cancer, it did so by attaching to the surface of a cell and injecting its nucleic acid into it. Once incorporated into the cell's genetic machinery, it transformed the healthy cell into a malignant one. So, at the onset, a virus needed to be identified inside cancer cells. Kaplan knew that this would be exceedingly difficult. The body's defense mechanism, the immune system, produces antibodies in response to invasion by a microbe. Antibodies induced by a virus in turn bind to them, masking their detection. Kaplan needed to grow lymphoma cells outside the body in an environment free of antibodies; he had to grow lymphoma cells in culture. But he couldn't obtain these cell cultures from another researcher or simply order them from a scientific supply house. He would have to cultivate his own.

Growing lymphoma cells in culture was tricky. They required a delicate balance of nutrients, growth factors, and culture conditions to be sustained outside the human body. And cases of mistaken identity occurred frequently. If cultures were contaminated by other viruses, normal lymphoid cells could be stimulated to grow in a manner that superficially resembled lymphoma. Kaplan was entering a new area of science in which he had no experience or expertise. Then, in 1971, a bright, energetic MD-PhD student, Alan Epstein, asked to work with him on tissue culture techniques. While doing his required course work, Epstein spent nights and weekends in Kaplan's laboratory, teaching himself about cell cultures. His early attempts failed. Then he came across a report of an old method, the feeder layer technique, used to grow animal cells. He didn't know why it hadn't been used by scientists trying to culture human tumor cells, but it made good sense to use a "feeder layer" of normal cells as a carpet on which to grow lymphoma cells. The method worked, and within a year, Epstein had developed a successful culture technique for human lymphomas.

The first cell line established by Epstein and Kaplan came from the malignant pleural fluid of a ten-year-old boy with non-Hodgkin's lymphoma. They called it SU-DHL-1 for Stanford University and the type of lymphoma from which the cells had been derived. Two more lines followed. Under the microscope, these cells resembled the tumors from the patients, and when Epstein injected the cells into mice, lymphomas developed. Henry wrote to Michael Feldman: "The lymphoma cell lines are growing magnificently." Now he had a tool with which to set about fulfilling Koch's postulates. "An important laboratory advance . . . was reported Tuesday," Stanford's News Bureau announced in January 1975. "Researchers have grown tumor cells from lymphoma patients in the laboratory. They will pave the way for studies of drugs . . . radiation treatment, and improved methods of diagnosis. In addition, the cells can be used in a search for cancer-inducing viruses."

Kaplan expressed concern about his research team's safety. "If we really do succeed in isolating a human cancer virus," he told the press, "it would be potentially a very dangerous agent." What if a laboratory accident occurred? If they freed a virus from the body's controls by growing it in culture, what would keep it from infecting others—research staff, a deliveryman, the rest of the Medical Center? This was risky work. Kaplan made the case that tumor virology research must be conducted in a facility designed to contain biohazardous materials. That was how he got his own building.

On October 4, 1975, Kaplan celebrated the dedication of the Louis B. Mayer Cancer Biology Research Laboratory (CBRL), funded in large part by the Louis B. Mayer Foundation in memory of the movie mogul, who had died of leukemia. The laboratory sat on eight acres of land at the edge of the Stanford Medical Center, surrounded by mature California oaks. From his window, Kaplan had a panoramic view of the foothills. He loved his new laboratory. In its design, special consideration was given to the containment of hazardous materials; sophisticated ventilation systems and laminar airflow biohazard safety cabinets were installed. The CBRL housed laboratories for seven scientists, including his dear friend, Michael Feldman, who was developing techniques to transform normal lymphocytes into tumor-killing cells. "The most exciting news," Henry wrote Michael, "is that my new Cancer Biology Research Laboratory was completed this week. Your office, Room 109, already contains a desk, a credenza, some bookshelves, and three chairs; I believe you will be very pleased with it." With the CBRL and three lymphoma cell lines, Kaplan was primed to isolate a human lymphoma virus.

⤻

In the 1970s, the number of scientists searching for a human tumor virus was small; few believed that a virus caused cancer. Scattered around the world, these cancer virus hunters became a brotherhood, corresponding regularly regarding techniques and interpretation of their findings. Among them were Robert Gallo of the NCI, Michael Anthony Epstein of the University of Bristol in England, and Henry Kaplan. Relative newcomers to the field, Kaplan and Gallo worked on RNA viruses. Epstein had already made his mark years earlier when he had described an association between a DNA virus and a rare African lymphoma. The path to that discovery had begun by mere chance when in 1961, Epstein, a pathologist at London's Middlesex Hospital, read the following announcement: "Mr. D. P. Burkitt from . . . Uganda will talk on 'The Commonest Children's Cancer in Tropical Africa. A Hitherto Unrecognized Syndrome.'"

Denis Burkitt was a surgeon with a missionary's heart. In 1911, he was born in a small town in Northern Ireland, the son of a country surveyor. Having devoted his life to healing the sick, he dreamed of practicing in Africa. When World War II broke out, he was sent to Kenya to care for African troops after which he joined the Colonial Service. Assigned to a town in the East African bush, Burkitt assumed responsibility for a quarter million Africans. In 1948, he was transferred to the Mulago Hospital in Kampala, Uganda, to head a surgical unit.

Burkitt had been working there for almost ten years when a colleague asked him to see a five-year-old boy with a difficult, undiagnosed case. Four large masses protruded from his jaws, distorting his face, impairing his ability to eat. Burkitt thought the boy had some form of cancer, far too advanced to operate. To his surprise, a few weeks later, when he was visiting a hospital fifty miles away, he saw another child with large tumors erupting from his jaws. Despite his enormous workload, Burkitt began investigating this unusual disease that was disfiguring and killing African children.

Colleagues sent every new case to him for examination. What he saw was shocking. A five-year-old Mdigo boy's face was so distorted by tumor that it looked as if a balloon had been blown up inside his cheek. A four-year-old girl had a tumor filling her mouth, with her teeth embedded in a fungating mass. A six-year-old Luhga boy had cheeks four times normal size. A tumor extended upward into his right eye, creating a gelatinous mass. Among the worst was a four-year-old Mkamba boy whose upper lip, nose, and left eye had been replaced with a smooth, glistening tumor. It seemed a blessing that these children died quickly.

Burkitt sent biopsy and autopsy specimens to several pathologists, who reported a remarkable similarity among all the tumors. Although under the microscope they resembled lymphomas, they had a distinct appearance: large clear cells interspersed among the lymphocytes, imparting a "starry sky" pattern. When a distinguished physician from South Africa visited Kampala, Burkitt showed him photographs of the children and the pathology slides. The physician said he had never seen such a malignancy in South Africa. This intrigued Burkitt. Somewhere between Uganda and South Africa a line had been drawn. Above it, children seemed susceptible to this disfiguring lymphoma; below the line, they appeared to be protected.

To refine his observation, Burkitt printed 1,200 pamphlets with photographs of stricken children and sent them to doctors throughout Africa with an attached questionnaire asking: "How long have you worked in your hospital, and have you seen this condition?" He hung a large map in his office, and as cases came in, he plotted them with pins. When he stood back and looked at the pattern, he observed a belt across equatorial Africa where the tumor commonly afflicted children. He thought if he could define the exact edge to this belt, he might find some environmental factor to be the cause. In 1961, he and two colleagues embarked on a ten-thousand-mile safari over ten weeks, visiting twelve countries and fifty-seven hospitals, performing one of the greatest feats of epidemiologic detective work. "It was a milestone in geographic pathology," a historian wrote.

What Burkitt found astonished him. Depending on the area, no cases occurred above a certain altitude—an altitude barrier, something unheard of. Plotting the same data against temperature, Burkitt noted that in regions where the temperature fell below 60°, children rarely developed the tumor. Moving into West Africa, he noted another strange finding: few cases occurred in the driest areas; rainfall seemed to be another confounding variable. Burkitt covered a map of Africa with chalk. He cleared off the areas where the temperature fell below 60° and yearly rainfall was below thirty inches. The portion of the map that remained covered with chalk looked almost identical to the tumor map.

Then an unexpected clue came from a seemingly unrelated event. An epidemic of O'nyong-nyong fever—a painful, but rarely fatal, illness, in which patients feel as if all their bones are breaking—spread across Africa. No one living above five thousand feet, however, contracted the disease. O'nyong-nyong fever was known to be a viral infection, carried by mosquitoes. When Burkitt looked at a mosquito map, he could superimpose areas of heavy infestation on the tumor map. He began to speculate that a virus, borne by mosquitoes, produced this strange lymphoma in African children.

Shortly after finishing the safari, Burkitt returned to England for a brief period, and during that trip, he gave a lecture on what he called the "Commonest Children's Cancer in Tropical Africa." His detective-style story of the search for the disease's origin caught Michael Epstein's attention. "After he had been talking for ten minutes," Epstein recalled, "it was absolutely clear that he had something tremendously important." For over a decade, Epstein had been searching for a tumor virus in his laboratory. The key to finding it might lie in the hands of this African missionary doctor. He invited Burkitt to tea. Delighted to have stimulated the interest of this reputable virologist, Burkitt agreed to send fresh tumor samples to Epstein.

Up to that point, the British medical establishment had virtually ignored reports of this rare tumor affecting African children. But when Burkitt published his findings in the widely read journal *Cancer* in 1961, the medical world took notice. This might be the first malignancy found linked to a virus. Burkitt described the reaction that followed as a "bombshell." The *New York Times* picked up the story; television reporters and magazine writers rushed to Africa. What had been cast as a bizarre finding by a missionary doctor soon piqued the interest of cancer specialists across the world; they called this newly described malignancy Burkitt's lymphoma.

As the initial step in fulfilling Koch's postulates, Epstein needed to find a virus in these lymphomatous tissues. To do that, he had to grow lymphoma cells outside the body in tissue culture. As yet no scientist had performed this task; it would be years before Henry Kaplan announced that he had grown lymphoma cells in culture. Undaunted, Epstein began. For two years he tried to grow the tumor samples in cultures, using different combinations of nutrients and conditions. But this malignancy, which quickly laid waste a human being, could not survive on its own. Then one day in 1963, he entered the laboratory to find tumor cells growing in one of the cultures. By replicating the exact conditions he had used in that culture, he was able to sustain growth of Burkitt's lymphoma cells thousands of miles from the child who had borne the tumor. He and his associate, Dr. Yvonne Barr, prepared samples for electron microscopy, and when they scanned the cells, they found them teeming with viruses.

Once found, the virus was not difficult to classify—it belonged to the herpes family, a DNA virus known to produce chicken pox and shingles. They called this new member of the herpes group Epstein-Barr virus (EBV). Did EBV cause Burkitt's lymphoma? Epstein needed to confirm his findings. He sent cultures to two of the most respected virologists—Gertrude and Werner Henle at the Children's Hospital of Philadelphia. They, too, found DNA virus in the lymphoma cells. The Henles further postulated that if EBV induced Burkitt's lymphoma, they should be able to detect elevated antibodies to the virus in serum from infected children.

Burkitt sent the Henles serum samples from his patients, and the excitement must have reverberated between Philadelphia, London, and Kampala as the Henles reported elevated antibody levels in every single case. Then came the blow. Burkitt also sent serum from healthy African children as controls, and they, too, had antibodies to EBV. Furthermore, the Henles detected levels in healthy adults in Philadelphia. They found the EB virus to be ubiquitous. Whether they tested Tirio Indians from the forests of Brazil, Icelandic farmers, or Yale College students, the Henles found antibodies in almost 85 percent of them. "After this remarkable series of discoveries, perhaps unparalleled in the history of virology and human disease," a scientist wrote, "the flow of new findings diminished, and innovative research essentially stopped." In trying to prove that the Epstein-Barr virus caused Burkitt's lymphoma, Anthony Epstein had hit a roadblock.

While Epstein was trying to unravel the mystery of EBV, another virologist was attracting attention. An emerging star from the NCI, described by colleagues as charismatic and aggressive, Robert Gallo was the youngest of the tumor virus hunters.

✑

Born in 1937, Gallo grew up in Waterbury, Connecticut. He was a handsome and athletic young man—a success on the basketball court and popular with girls. His carefree teen years, however, were suddenly disrupted when his younger sister developed leukemia. Robert felt helpless watching his beloved sister suffer from vomiting, baldness, nosebleeds, eventually to die. The experience changed him forever. He vowed to find the cause of leukemia.

Gallo's research endeavors began in a homemade laboratory above the family garage and extended to a local Catholic hospital, where he shadowed a pathologist. Assisting at autopsies, he learned what it meant to think critically. This young man who had cared nothing for academics attended Providence College, graduating *summa cum laude*. Excelling at medical school in Philadelphia and a medicine residency at the University of Chicago, he took a position as a clinical associate at the NCI.

Robert was initially assigned to the children's leukemia ward, where he provided daily care to patients and evaluated new therapies. He had to relive his sister's experience over and over. He couldn't bear watching children undergo intense chemotherapy with all its complications. And he couldn't bear another death. Gallo didn't want to treat leukemia; he wanted to get into the laboratory and find what caused this deadly disease. Before long, he got his chance.

Convinced that leukemia had a viral origin, Gallo joined the ranks of tumor virologists. One would have thought his dynamic temperament not well suited for this field, where a single experiment could take years to complete, but he began the ponderous process of scanning diseased tissue searching for viral particles. Gallo had barely begun this work when in 1970, Howard Temin of the University of Wisconsin and David Baltimore of MIT blew open the field of cancer virology by discovering reverse transcriptase, an enzyme that allows cells to make DNA from a strand of RNA. When inserted into a normal cell, that DNA takes over. This explained how RNA tumor viruses could invade normal cells and change their genetic makeup, transforming them into cancer cells. And reverse transcriptase did something else of vital importance; it left a footprint in cells infected by these viruses. By staining for reverse transcriptase, virologists could screen large numbers of malignant cells, singling out those presumably infected with a virus for further electron microscopic study.

Within a few months of this discovery, Gallo reported reverse transcriptase in the blood of three leukemia patients, suggesting that a virus had generated the leukemia. This finding propelled him into the elite circle of cancer researchers and came at a propitious time—the rising tide of cancer virology. The NCI dedicated such a large proportion of its funding to virology that many felt that this area dominated biomedical research. Even among virologists, a hierarchy developed, with cancer virology at the top. A perceived inequity generated jealousy, some of which focused on Robert Gallo when, in his mid-thirties, he became director of NCI's new Laboratory of Tumor Cell Virology.

Eager to succeed, Gallo seemed in constant motion. He was a temperamental man, often heard shouting at colleagues and staff. He hardly fit the mold of the patient scientist. Some admired his commitment; others found his self-assurance grating. "First came God, then came Gallo," one researcher said. Others felt he spent too much time searching for the spotlight. Yet somehow he focused his enormous energy and talents on one intent—the pursuit of the virus that causes leukemia.

Gallo had demonstrated reverse transcriptase in leukemia cells from three patients. Now he had to find the virus that had left its mark in these leukemic cells. Like virologists before him, he struggled to grow cancer cells in culture, until he finally found a successful mixture of nutrients. Using his new culture medium, Gallo was able to grow the leukemia cells of a sixty-one-year-old woman from Texas. They stained positive for reverse transcriptase, and scanning with electron microscopy, Gallo found an RNA virus. He passed the culture through filters that trapped all the leukemia cells, resulting in a cell-free filtrate, which presumably contained the virus. He exposed healthy cells to this filtrate and could barely contain himself when he detected the same virus in these infected cells. Gallo felt certain he had fulfilled Koch's postulates. He had found the first true human tumor virus. He called it Human Leukemia 23 virus (HL23V).

In 1975, Gallo published his findings in three journals known for their scientific rigor—*Science*, the *Proceedings of the National Academy of Science*, and *Nature*. Scientists around the world applauded his work and began to request samples to study. Now that he had found the human leukemia virus, his fame secure, Gallo supplied others with specimens. He was thirty-eight and had been a serious research scientist for only nine years.

When other researchers began to study Gallo's virus, they reported a disturbing finding: HL23V wasn't a human virus after all; it was a woolly monkey virus—a contaminant, perhaps from a laboratory animal or a pet. Gallo couldn't believe it. He considered himself a careful scientist; his laboratory had the latest in biohazard protection. How had a monkey virus infected his cultures? Humiliated and distraught, Gallo called this "the lowest point of my life" aside from his sister's death. Some researchers were privately pleased, calling him a "grandstander." His perceived arrogance galled many who thought it blinded him to the truth. Former colleagues avoided him at meetings; no one now requested cell cultures or asked his assistance with new techniques. "His career took a nose dive," one historian wrote. "He had become the fading star of the NCI."

⌒

While Gallo was trying to recoup his reputation, Henry Kaplan, having established a number of lymphoma cell lines, was forging ahead. In the summer of 1974, one of his cultures tested positive for reverse transcriptase. When he examined electron micrographs of the cells, he could discern small, round particles near the cell membranes. He concluded that they must be viruses, and by their appearance, of the RNA type. Before Kaplan announced the discovery he had dreamed of for years, he sought the counsel of an old acquaintance, Michael Epstein:

> I am writing at this time to impose on you for a small favor. . . . My main concern is . . . whether these are, in all likelihood, virus particles or not, and if [so] . . . do they sufficiently resemble the . . . leukemia virus ? I did not want to draw any conclusions . . . without the advice of an expert whose opinion I really respect and whose discretion about discussing these very early and incomplete findings I could also rely upon implicitly.

Lastly, he inquired about Epstein's work on EBV: "I have been [a]waiting further development in this exciting field."

Kaplan anticipated Epstein's reply, and eight days later, it came. "There is no doubt," he wrote, "that a virus is present in one of your cell lines." Kaplan must have been delighted until he got to the fifth paragraph where Epstein said, "As to the nature of the virus . . . it would appear that you have a new type of agent in your culture. . . . It was indeed interesting to see this unusual agent in human-derived material." Crestfallen, Kaplan realized Epstein was politely saying that his virus was a contaminant. "Yes," he wrote in closing, "the Herpes oncogenesis field is moving fast."

The race was in full swing. "Any man or woman," a popular writer asserted, "who found and proved that a particular virus causes a particular human cancer could be sure of scientific immortality." Robert Gallo took another step forward when he discovered interleukin-2, a natural substance that stimulates lymph cells to multiply and stay alive in culture. Kaplan was now trailing Gallo, and soon they would have their first encounter.

In 1977, Vince DeVita, then director of the National Cancer Institute, announced that all NCI research programs would be reviewed by outside scientists. Gallo's lab was among the first scheduled for a site visit, and the chairman of his review committee was Henry Kaplan. Gallo concluded that he had been fingered for removal. Having read all of Kaplan's work on the mouse leukemia virus, he thought him brilliant. And he had seen enough of Kaplan at scientific meetings to know how formidable and hypercritical he could be. Besides, Gallo knew how badly Kaplan wanted to find a human tumor virus, and he couldn't help thinking this might color the evaluation of the man who would judge his work, determine his fate.

Gallo became increasingly tense; their approach to tumor virology differed significantly. "His was intellectual," Gallo said, "mine more gambling and daring." At the site visit, Kaplan was thorough and asked probing questions, especially regarding the alleged contamination with woolly monkey virus. He concluded that Gallo probably had isolated an RNA virus from a leukemic patient, but in passing the virus through animal cells, it had likely been altered in such a way that scientists could no longer identify it as the original leukemia virus. In his final report to DeVita, Kaplan recommended only a small budget reduction. "The trimming was hardly noticeable," Gallo said. "It was like cutting my nails." In addition, he found that Kaplan's comments forced him to focus his work. Instead of facilitating Gallo's dismissal, Kaplan had strengthened his position. And with Kaplan's blessing, Gallo was once again invited into the elite scientific ranks.

"Gallo . . . had the courage to continue investigations in this field," Kaplan wrote five years later, "in the face of its numerous pitfalls and difficulties and the thick pall of skepticism." Gallo attributed that courage, in part, to Kaplan. While others scoffed, Kaplan believed that he had isolated a leukemia virus. Kindred spirits in their endeavors, they became friends. Gallo thought of Kaplan as an older brother. "When I got into trouble," he said, "I always knew to whom I could turn." And the field of tumor virology moved forward with Kaplan's intellectual leadership and Gallo's daring.

⌇

By now, Kaplan had expanded his research team. Miriam Lieberman could not possibly learn all the new methodologies required for experimental virology. More and more, Kaplan turned to Alain Declève. This Belgian scientist, who had joined his laboratory, mastered the crucial techniques. Obsessed with finding the human lymphoma virus, Kaplan expected results, and Declève worked such long hours, he often slept in the lab.

Not long after Kaplan had established his lymphoma cell lines, he and his group began to see what looked more convincingly like viral particles in SUDHL-1, the cell line his student Alan Epstein had cultured. Having had his hopes dashed previously when Anthony Epstein had implied that his tumor virus was a contaminant, Kaplan tempered his excitement. He made no public announcement; he published no early results. Instead, he spent the next two years gathering evidence to support his assertion that he had found a human lymphoma virus. Kaplan could demonstrate reverse transcriptase activity in the particles. And when he scanned the particles containing this enzyme with the electron microscope, he found what looked like RNA viruses. At last, Kaplan felt he could announce his breakthrough. "A team of Stanford University scientists has successfully isolated and purified a virus from tumor cells of a patient with . . . lymphoma," a press release read on June 27, 1977.

Henry Kaplan thought he had entered the home stretch in his quest for the human tumor virus. He had isolated the virus and demonstrated its presence in continuously growing cell cultures. "To our knowledge," he wrote in the *Proceedings of the National Academy of Science*, "this is the first reported instance of the spontaneous and sustained release of [an] ... RNA virus by a permanently established human neoplastic cell line." Midway through fulfilling Koch's postulates, all he needed to do was transform normal human cells into lymphomas with cell-free filtrates and demonstrate the virus in these new lymphomas.

Kaplan had become a bit secretive. He had always shared his experimental plans and results with his entire team. Now he no longer held open lab meetings. And he restricted his downstairs lab to a couple of technicians. "He was like a mountain climber," Declève said, "who wants to climb the last hundred yards by himself." He worried that in his haste, Kaplan had become sloppy, occasionally spilling substances. No one knew whether these viruses were contagious and, if so, to what degree. This problem particularly concerned Declève, because he had become Stanford University's first biohazard safety officer. His apprehension increased when he heard that Kaplan had drawn blood from one of the secretaries. Was Kaplan going to infect his secretary's cells with the virus? Declève became alarmed. Henry would be taking risks by transforming cells from someone who worked in the building.

The final experiment Kaplan needed to perform to prove that his virus induced a lymphoma was to take the cell-free filtrate from the lymphoma cell line (presumably containing a tumor virus) and infect normal cells. If they became lymphomatous and could be shown to contain the same virus, he would have fulfilled Koch's postulates. But how could he tell that the lymphoma cells came from the donor and not a few from the lymphoma cell line that had slipped through the filter? Kaplan's strategy was ingenious but simple. Since the lymphoma cell line came from a male, Kaplan would attempt to transform normal female cells. If the new lymphoma cells turned out to be female, they had to have arisen from the donor, not the cell culture. Distinguishing sexual origin of cells was straightforward. Female cells have two X chromosomes, one of which is inactivated, resulting in a small mass in the nucleus of each cell. This spot is called a Barr body, after the scientist who originally described it. Because males have a single X chromosome, Barr bodies are not seen in their cells.

Weeks passed, and Declève heard nothing from Kaplan's laboratory. Then one day he learned that Henry had called a news conference. He had reserved the largest auditorium in the Medical Center, and a rumor was circulating that he planned a major announcement. Declève, the associate director of the CBRL, was in the dark.

Several days before the scheduled press conference, Kaplan caught Declève in his lab. The hour was late, and everyone had gone home. Kaplan told him that he felt certain he had transformed healthy lymphocytes into a lymphoma with their virus. He wanted to know what Alain thought. Declève wondered why Henry was asking him to look at his results at this late date. But it soon became clear that he had gotten cold feet and needed Alain's confirmation. Declève scanned the cells under the microscope and agreed that they were lymphoma cells. Then he looked for Barr bodies—proof that these cells had originated from a female. He could find none. He said nothing. For days, he reviewed Kaplan's slides over and over, but the lymphoma cells all seemed to be of male origin. There could be only one of two conclusions: either Kaplan had not used his secretary's cells, or these cells had come from the original cell line, in which case, he had not transformed cells after all.

Declève had to confront Kaplan before the news conference, and late one evening, he went to Kaplan's lab. "Henry," he asked, "why would you use another male's cells as a target?" Kaplan went white. "I've got to know where the target cells came from," Declève continued. "Were they female cells?" Kaplan confessed he had used his secretary's cells. Declève then went over every slide with Kaplan. They could detect no Barr bodies, no female cells. There could be but one conclusion—these lymphoma cells had arisen from the original cell line. In preparing the cell-free filtrate containing the virus, at least one lymphoma cell must have slipped through the filter. Kaplan walked back and forth in silence. Then he picked up Declève's notes, wadded them into a ball, tossed them across the room into the wastepaper basket, and walked out.

There was no big announcement. When the press gathered in Fairchild Auditorium, they heard an update on Hodgkin's disease. For two weeks Henry didn't speak to Alain. "I thought my career was finished," Declève said. He couldn't discuss his dilemma with anyone; this was between him and Kaplan.

Weeks later, Henry walked into Declève's office and put a rose on his desk without a word. Then he returned to his lab to continue his search for the elusive human tumor virus.

39   The Quiet Conviction

Henry Kaplan loved his laboratory. There he worked undisturbed on tumor-causing viruses. Fully funded, he had total freedom to pursue his science. Like many investigators, he could have been consumed with his own work—presenting data, publishing results, garnishing recognition. But he wasn't. Kaplan viewed science as a means to aid mankind, whether through controlling the elements or eradicating disease. But to advance science, investigators needed training, resources, and autonomy. To properly treat patients, clinicians needed modern facilities and technical support. So Kaplan came out of his laboratory and traveled around the world to help. He was passionate enough to care and bold enough to think he could make a difference.

Kaplan readily assisted bright young researchers who could not obtain adequate training in their own countries. He instructed a steady stream of foreign postdoctoral students, welcoming them into the Stanford scientific community and his home. He assisted senior physician-scientists from overseas, inviting radiotherapists to spend a few months at Stanford to learn treatment planning, helping laboratory investigators learn new techniques. Yet he knew these physician-scientists often returned to outdated radiotherapy units, laboratories lacking the most basic equipment. So for two decades, he served on advisory committees and governing boards worldwide. He traveled repeatedly to Israel, where he helped centralize cancer care in Tel Aviv, develop research programs at Ben Gurion University's new medical school, and organize an oncology department for Hadassah Medical School. In São Paulo, Brazil, he gave technical and operational advice to the Institute of Radiotherapy at the Hospital Osvaldo Cruz. In 1977, he led a delegation of scientists to China in one of the earliest scientific exchanges. Traveling for nearly a month, they held seminars on modern cancer therapy and advised scientists setting up laboratories. Kaplan helped establish an exchange program, which began a lifelong relationship with the Chinese scientific community.

It troubled Kaplan to see scientists with potential hampered by lack of proper instruction and resources. But when he heard of physicians who had lost their freedom, he felt sickened. Sheila Cassidy, a British surgeon working in Chile, was arrested by security police, thrown into solitary confinement, and tormented with electric probes. Her crime—she had treated the bullet wounds of a leftist sympathizer. António Agostinho Neto, an African physician in Angola, had reportedly fallen into disfavor with Portuguese officials when he tried to improve health care services for fellow Africans. Police broke into his home, flogged him while his family stood by helpless, and dragged him away. When Kaplan read of such egregious acts, he couldn't put them out of his mind. Though incensed, he felt impotent. So when he and Leah received a mailing from Amnesty International, they readily joined.

Ginetta Sagan, founder of the western chapter of Amnesty, impressed Henry and Leah with her dedication and fearlessness. At first, they assisted her by letter-writing and raising funds for prisoners' families. In 1973, Amnesty turned its attention to human rights violations in Chile. Following the overthrow of Marxist President Salvador Allende Gossens, hundreds of leftist sympathizers had been sent to secret detention centers. Amnesty learned that the military used torture to interrogate and intimidate prisoners, although the government denied such allegations. Sagan was working hard to publicize this political repression, but Amnesty had no definitive evidence. Kaplan suggested that the group enlist the help of Chilean physicians to examine prisoners after their release and document physical damage. That way, when offenders eventually came to trial, there would be records to prosecute them.

Kaplan was appalled when Amnesty International discovered that some Chilean physicians actually participated in torture. Psychiatrists assisted in interrogations and committed political dissidents to psychiatric hospitals. Worse yet, some physicians certified prisoners as physically fit for torture; others revived victims so that they could be tormented further. Amnesty urged medical associations around the world to set formal guidelines of ethical conduct condemning torture. Astonishingly, most U.S. physicians had never thought about the issue. But Sagan and Kaplan persevered and persuaded the California Medical Association to adopt a declaration that read, "Resolved: That the California Medical Association urges all physicians of all countries, and their respective medical organizations, to refuse to allow their professional or research skills to be used in any way for the purpose of torture or punishment of prisoners." Next, Kaplan prevailed upon the American Medical Association to adopt the resolution, and following that, he confronted international medical associations. Even Chile's medical establishment eventually accepted it.

In 1970, at Stanford's anti-war rally, Kaplan had said, "Physicians must take a serious, continuing and meaningful interest in political and social questions in the world that surrounds us." True to his word, he spent significant time and energy helping scientists and physicians abroad. He became so involved that at times the distinction between his role as an advisor and his work as an activist blurred. Many aspects of Kaplan's life were public. He readily spoke to the press about his cure of Hodgkin's disease, about his impending discovery of the human tumor virus. His fights with deans and his sharp tongue became infamous. But he rarely told reporters or even his colleagues about his international efforts to aid physician-researchers. He didn't seek recognition or expect thanks; he simply wanted talented scientists to thrive and patients to receive the best care possible. Leah referred to this as his "quiet conviction."

Among all the human rights issues with which he became involved, none disturbed Kaplan more than the plight of Argentine physicians and scientists. He had first learned of the country's human rights violations in the mid-1960s, when an Argentine researcher working in his laboratory told him of forcible police entry into the University of Buenos Aires. The totalitarian regime that had usurped power ordered books burned and professors incarcerated. In 1966, Kaplan wrote to California Senator Thomas Kuchel, urging that the United States withdraw recognition of the Argentine government.

For a while, the situation seemed to be improving. Kaplan heard little more until almost ten years later, when he learned that eight scientists at the Argentine National Atomic Energy Commission had been arrested for no apparent reason. As a member of the National Academy of Sciences' Committee on Human Rights, Kaplan wrote to protest their disappearance: No charges had been brought against the scientists; they had no legal representation. After intense international pressure, seven were released, although they were dismissed from their jobs. The scientists told of their imprisonment in Villa Devoto in a ten-by-eight-foot cell. They had been beaten; one had lost his teeth. The eighth scientist, Antonio Misetich, had not yet been released. He had recently accepted a position at the Massachusetts Institute of Technology, and when the laboratory director wrote to the U.S. Embassy in Buenos Aires, he received a note saying that the Argentine government had no record of Misetich's whereabouts.

Kaplan heard more and more such stories. Neighbors reported that scientist Eduardo Pasquin and his wife, a psychoanalyst, were missing. Physicist Federico Alvarez Rojas and his wife Hilda were abducted by a group of armed men, leaving behind their three children. His father, a British Council scholar, made appeals to Argentine authorities, the Red Cross, the Catholic Church, and the American and British embassies. Rojas and his wife had not been charged with any offense; they simply disappeared. Kaplan could no longer just write letters of protest. For Argentine physicians and scientists, he was willing to risk his reputation—and his life.

cord the latest breakthroughs. A boycott of the event was sure to attract media attention.

Before agreeing, Kaplan consulted colleagues who had emigrated from Argentina concerning the consequences this action might have for scientists left in the country. They told him international events, such as the Cancer Congress, aided the military in projecting a favorable image abroad. International pressure from high-level scientists might be an effective way to deter the military from torturing and killing more researchers and physicians. Convinced of a boycott's potential effect, Kaplan agreed to join Rappaport. In turn, he enlisted the help of David Baltimore and Howard Temin, recent Nobel Prize recipients, and Emil Frei III, the physician-in-chief of Harvard's Dana-Farber Cancer Institute.

Rappaport and Kaplan wrote to Abel Canonico, president of the UICC, requesting a change in location for the upcoming congress. Canonico replied that the host country had been selected with no political motive. He stressed the enormous interest in the meeting among South American cancer specialists. "It will be very difficult for young professionals," he wrote, "to understand that there are scientists who would refrain from passing on their knowledge." Thirty-five hundred had already registered. "The participation of a scientist," he went on to say, "does not necessarily imply that he identifies himself with the politics of the host country."

Undaunted, they petitioned the largest American cancer organizations to pressure the UICC to relocate the meeting. Senior scientists of the American Cancer Society voted to boycott the conference, but the 2,500 members of the American Association for Cancer Research voted to proceed. When Kaplan learned that the National Cancer Institute had pledged $1 million to support the Congress, he wrote requesting that it rescind its pledge. The U.S. State Department, however, advised the NCI to continue its support, which it did. When these attempts failed, the five world-renowned researchers appealed directly to physicians and investigators. They submitted letters to the prominent journals *Science* and *Nature* calling for scientists worldwide to join them in boycotting the meeting. Kaplan drafted a petition, which they circulated at research institutes and medical schools. It read:

> The undersigned physicians and scientists engaged in cancer research and patient care are deeply concerned by the flagrant abrogation of human rights in Argentina, the country in which the 12th International Cancer Congress is scheduled to be held. . . . Recent reports . . . leave little doubt that scientists, physicians, professors, journalists, intellectuals, and other citizens have been arrested, imprisoned without benefit of habeas corpus, often tortured, and sometimes executed without trial. We cannot in good conscience . . . participate in an International Cancer Congress, however worthy its cause, if it is held in Argentina.

Within a week, they received hundreds of signatures. *Le Monde* printed a similar petition signed by 291 French doctors. The National Academy of Sciences and the Federation of American Scientists both formed human rights committees. Medical journals worldwide published letters to the editor protesting the situation in Argentina. Still, the site of the conference remained unchanged.

Henry Kaplan was helping to draw international attention to the *desaparecidos*. Likely the junta knew of his role in these activities. Had he been an Argentine scientist, he would have been punished—tortured, mutilated, and dumped in the river. But he was safe—miles away in the United States. Why then did he choose to travel to Argentina right before the conference and put himself in peril?

The junta's strategy of extinguishing people, leaving neither records nor remains, was ingenious. There were no martyrs around whom citizens could rally, no stories for the international press. Names and faces were missing. That made it easier for diplomats and even Argentine citizens to ignore the situation. The junta had effectively created the appearance of normalcy. As a result, no demonstrators called for sanctions; no foreign governments broke off diplomatic relations. The regime successfully kept the Argentine people in line. But they couldn't control foreigners who came snooping.

Leon Schwartzenberg, professor of *cancérologie* at the University of Paris, had a long-standing interest in human rights. He decided to organize a small delegation that would travel to Buenos Aires and attempt to secure the release of imprisoned scientists. He invited four colleagues he knew to be passionate about human rights: Dirk van Bekkum, director of the Comprehensive Cancer Centre in Rotterdam; British psychiatrist Gerald Low-Beer; Colette Auger, a French attorney; and Henry Kaplan. Schwartzenberg, who had joined the Resistance during World War II, regularly addressed human rights issues and had published two books on the topic. Van Bekkum brought social issues to the attention of physicians through his editorials in well-read journals. Low-Beer, a psychiatrist of international repute, spoke out regarding the political use of psychiatry and unethical behavior by psychiatrists. And Auger, a highly respected human rights attorney, had extensive experience in international law.

Schwartzenberg proposed that they travel to Argentina ten days before the Cancer Congress and petition for the release of scientists, physicians, and other health-care workers. They could make the case that such an action would be viewed as a goodwill gesture at the opening of the Congress. He already had a list of 185 people—60 known to be in prison, 125 who had "disappeared." None had been charged formally with committing a crime; none had been brought to trial. The list had been compiled from information provided by four human rights organizations, and Schwartzenberg had been assured that no one on the roster of names had participated in terrorist acts. Henry showed the list of names to Leah. "My God," he said, "each one is part of a family. It's someone's loved one who disappeared without a trace." He didn't hesitate to accept the invitation.

The French ambassador to Argentina planned meetings with the minister of the interior, who managed the prisons, the minister of social welfare, and the chief justice of the Supreme Court. The delegation's goal was to convince authorities that the October 5th opening of the Congress provided a perfect opportunity to show leniency toward the prisoners. "If their release would be timed with the cancer congress," Kaplan told the *Miami Herald*, "it would be an event hailed by physicians and scientists around the world." He anticipated the junta would see the article.

On September 25, 1978, Henry Kaplan flew to Buenos Aires, where he and the four others were met by First Secretary Healy-Martin of the French Embassy. He drove them to the Plaza Hotel in the embassy car. On the way, the group got its first glimpse of Argentine life under the junta. Contrary to their expectations, everything seemed peaceful. "Buenos Aires is a normal looking city," Low-Beer wrote colleagues, "with full shops and . . . little extreme poverty." In the car, Healy-Martin warned them to stay together and to avoid taxis and talking to strangers. Their individual citizenships did not guarantee their safety. Behind the aura of normalcy, the atmosphere felt menacing.

The first day they checked in at their respective embassies. The British secretary received Low-Beer warmly and briefed him about the situation. When Low-Beer asked about the large number of psychiatrists on the list, he was told that many terrorists came from the middle class, where psychoanalysis was common. If a psychiatrist had a patient believed to be subversive on his roster, the psychiatrist was punished. The secretary went on to say that kidnapping of physicians was still prevalent. The day before Low-Beer's arrival, a doctor at a local clinic had been dragged out of his office, beaten up in front of his patients, and taken away. He had no known association with terrorists. These stories made Low-Beer feel vulnerable, and the secretary offered his help. When Henry Kaplan checked in at the U.S. Embassy, he got quite a different reception. First Secretary Tex Harris was an obese young man with a Texas drawl who drove around in an American station wagon. He was not as forthcoming, and his seeming lack of interest reinforced Kaplan's opinion that the United States was ignoring the situation.

As he got a closer look at Buenos Aires, Kaplan was surprised that the military's presence was not more conspicuous. This did not look like a country at war. There were no tanks on the Avenida 9 de Julio, one of the world's widest boulevards. The National Museum of Fine Arts and the Teatro Colón opera house were not bombed out; the beautiful mansions in the northern suburbs had not been reduced to rubble. Finely kept parks and plazas gave the city a sense of tranquility. "We observed," Kaplan wrote, "that there was no crime in the streets, that people appeared to be happy and well-fed, and we certainly concur that many people are happier with the 'law and order' of the present regime than with the terrorism of the [Isabel] Peron regime." He may have begun to doubt the veracity of the reports of concentration camps and houses of torture.

When the delegation visited the Plaza de Mayo in the heart of Buenos Aires, however, Kaplan saw the first signs of persecution—the Madres de la Plaza de Mayo, mothers of the disappeared. This group of grief-stricken women gathered every Thursday in front of Casa Rosada, which housed the presidential offices, awaiting President Videla. They marched two by two, some silently, some crying, some carrying posters with their children's pictures, all with faces of anguish—"a collective funeral," one reporter wrote. None knew if her child was alive or dead, and if dead, where his or her body lay. Kaplan felt heartbroken when he saw the Mothers; the despair on their faces moved him deeply and gave more purpose and urgency to the group's mission.

The delegation was eager to meet with officials. With the list of the disappeared in hand, they prepared to confront them. But Argentine authorities refused to see them, giving what Kaplan called "some convenient political excuses." The day before their arrival, French scientists had announced an alternate cancer congress to be held in Paris for those who planned to boycott the Buenos Aires meeting. The announcement angered the junta. "The Paris conference stuck in their throats," Low-Beer said.

The delegation did meet with two human rights groups—the Association for Human Rights and the League for Human Rights—at great risk to both. Emilio Mignone, director of the Association for Human Rights, told the group that they counted approximately four thousand people imprisoned in camps at that time, and that the *desaparecidos* numbered at least fifteen thousand. The League for Human Rights, a communist-affiliated organization, assisted the persecuted and their families, regardless of religious or political views. Its secretary suggested that the group speak with families of those who had disappeared, and he arranged meetings for the next two evenings.

The delegation met mothers, fathers, sisters, and wives of prisoners and *desaparecidos*. In case after case, they told of sons, husbands, and fiancés who had never engaged in political activities, yet had been abducted. None had been brought to trial, allowed a defense lawyer, or permitted to call witnesses. "They were profoundly grateful," Low-Beer said, "that we took the trouble to see them. Grief-stricken, eager to talk, perplexed, they felt perhaps that we could move mountains." As more Argentineans learned of the delegation, they came to the Plaza Hotel, begging for these esteemed scientists to find out about their loved ones. Some brought pictures. "Let's look at the list," Kaplan said to them. If he found the name, the reaction was incredible. "They would be so relieved," he said. "The world knew; somebody besides themselves knew that the person was missing."

Word got out, and people kept coming. Some showed scars. Some told of masked men coming in the dead of night to abduct their children. "The horror . . . we saw in their faces gave poignant weight to the information we had already gathered," Low-Beer said. Their stories of torture were sickening. Some had been kept hooded, without food, for weeks. Others had been held under polluted water until they lost sphincter control and passed out. Captors used electric shock, working up from their ankles to their eyeballs. "Some of them broke down and cried," Low-Beer said. "Others had cried so much that they were clearly not able to do so any more."

These Argentineans spoke of hearing the incessant hum of airplanes all night over Rio de la Plata. They knew what was happening. Guards needed to erase all evidence. They opened the abdominal cavities of the victims and filled them with stones so that the bodies would sink. Despite these precautions, some resurfaced. "Bodies of decapitated, handless prisoners have washed ashore on the north coast of the La Plata River," Kaplan later told colleagues, "apparently dumped into the estuary of the river at night from planes that regularly take off from the naval base on the south border of the estuary."

The grief and anguish were overwhelming. Years later, Schwartzenberg still remembered the delegation's reaction. "How could one forget these meetings in a hotel lobby," he wrote, "the parents of a young psychologist who had vanished, their voices breaking, and how after warmly thanking them for their confidence in him, Henry Kaplan walked away a few steps and furtively wiped his glasses."

The delegation was stunned to find that while many people were in mourning, their neighbors and co-workers appeared oblivious. The authorities, foreign ambassadors, and even the average citizen acted as if nothing unusual was happening. Low-Beer wrote to the Royal College of Psychiatrists that he considered it a terrible indictment of totalitarianism that it "makes people ignore institutionalized terrorism and support a government responsible for it . . . because they are terrified of the alternative."

Frustrated that they had no access to government officials, members of the delegation went back to their embassies. The French ambassador again requested meetings with the chief justice and ministers of social welfare and the interior, but there was still no answer. The British secretary and Dutch ambassador likewise pleaded their cases unsuccessfully. When Henry Kaplan confronted the American first secretary with his newfound information, Harris's complacency disgusted him. "He was a pig," Henry told Leah, "a pig with no empathy." And the American ambassador, Raul Castro, was no better. When Kaplan recounted the stories he had heard, the ambassador registered no response. Schwartzenberg recalled Kaplan's extreme disappointment in his country: "It is impossible to forget his face-to-face meeting with the U.S. Ambassador, a stuffy government appointee on the one hand, confronted with a scientist proud of his work and his profession . . . a bureaucrat face to face with a human being . . . and the silent sadness of this great American when he left his embassy."

Just when the delegation had almost given up meeting with anyone, the Argentine government contacted Henry Kaplan and suggested he meet alone with a Mr. Arlia, an official responsible for investigating human rights complaints. The French ambassador had warned against being separated from others in the delegation. Kaplan knew he was taking a risk, but this was their first potential breakthrough. So he agreed, selecting a pub opposite and in full view of the hotel. As Kaplan waited alone, isolated from the group, he felt frightened. He knew the fate of those who crossed the junta. When Arlia arrived, however, Kaplan boldly presented the list to him. Arlia said he had no knowledge of the 185 people. Kaplan pressed, and Arlia said that perhaps he could trace twenty on the list. In exchange, he expected Kaplan to encourage specialists to attend the Cancer Congress in Buenos Aires. Kaplan thought twenty was better than none and tentatively agreed. But he never heard from Arlia again. Likely, not even twenty on the list were still alive.

Angered and frustrated, the delegation demanded that the Argentine government account for the several hundred nurses and doctors who had disappeared. They received no response. As their next tactic, they planned to submit a writ of habeas corpus, a document that orders the police to produce a person who has been arrested and formally charge or release him. Recognized in most courts worldwide, the writ obligates the judiciary to investigate a case or be considered accomplices. In short, the judges could never say they didn't know.

Auger prepared a writ for the 185 people with an appended list of several thousand names. It detailed the abrogation of due process, torture, and execution without trial. Before submitting the document, Auger reminded the group that according to Argentine law, a foreigner could be jailed for "causing a nuisance." If the generals found out what the group was planning, they likely would incarcerate them. If they were detained in the country, their respective embassies could do nothing; the junta could cite legitimate laws under which to charge them. Their international stature wouldn't protect them. Already among the disappeared were many top scientists. Some of the country's best lawyers had been slaughtered in public. But the stories the delegation had heard haunted them, and they persevered.

On Friday, September 29, the group registered the writ formally in Tribunal Number 3 fifteen minutes before the courts closed, so that the clerk receiving the affidavits would not have time to notify authorities. Auger warned that they needed to leave the country immediately. Back at the hotel, they found plainclothes policemen in the lobby. They quickly gathered their belongings, and the French consul drove them to the airport in his official car. In the rearview mirror, they spotted police following close behind. At every stoplight, they feared they would be intercepted. For the first time, Henry Kaplan truly felt afraid; later he told Leah that he now understood the term "heart in his throat."

When they tried to board the Air France flight, they were told the plane was full. Only three of them had seats; two would have to stay behind in Argentina. The plane was at the gate, police were in the airport. They had come so close to escaping. Who would stay? His pulse racing, Kaplan felt he had to volunteer. But the French ambassador stepped in and used his authority to bump two passengers.

Only when they landed in Paris did the group feel safe. They would later learn that the military regime, in a special session of the Argentine Supreme Court, had declared the delegation an "enemy of the people." When time came for the group to part, they lamented that they had not been able to talk to anyone in a position of authority; they had not secured the release of any of the 185; they had not even seen one prisoner. Noting their disappointment, Kaplan said, "We didn't come for nothing. Behind their bars, if they're still alive, they know that someone on the outside is trying to help them."

In the end, the UICC refused to change the site, and on October 5, 1978, the Cancer Congress commenced in Buenos Aires. Thousands of U.S. physicians and even more worldwide had signed the petition; many attended the alternate congress in Paris. "More than 8,000 researchers and physicians from 77 countries gathered [in Buenos Aires] to talk about cancer," *Medical World News* wrote, "but the talk of the 12th International Cancer Congress was human rights." The boycott did not stop the Congress, but it did accomplish something even more effective—it focused the international spotlight on the situation in Buenos Aires. Pictures of the Mothers of the Plaza de Mayo appeared in newspapers around the world. Reporters who had come to cover the latest scientific discoveries wrote about the disappearance of scientists instead. "The issue of rights violations in Argentina," one wrote, "hung over the Congress the way allegations of arrests and disappearances of citizens, many of them scientists and doctors, seem to haunt this country."

In 1983, the Dirty War came to a close, and the new government of Argentina arrested several high officials who had been responsible for the *desaparecidos*. Ginetta Sagan wrote Kaplan to say she had recently met with Marcelo Parrilli, a lawyer who had argued the case for the disappeared in recent trials. "Marcelo Parrilli told me that your efforts," she wrote of the delegation, "had been the most important among the ones which had been undertaken, and he asked me to convey to you his warmest thanks." But Kaplan was most touched by the letters from Argentineans, such as that from physician Hipolito Barreiro:

> I understand you went to Buenos Aires . . . and became involved in the defense of human rights there. You went out of your way in trying to secure the release of some Argentinean people and also to know the whereabouts of a hundred others. I also understand you requested interviews with top government officials in Buenos Aires for that purpose, and that in so doing you imperiled . . . your own life. Dr. Kaplan: there is no doubt that for your actions you have shown the noblest qualities. . . . I hereby express to you in the name of the Argentinean people and very specially the physicians and the victims' families our deepest and most sincere appreciation and admiration. One day, we are sure, we will have the great honor to officially thank you back in Argentina.

Henry Kaplan never knew how many lives were saved by their efforts—how many children returned to their mothers, how many husbands returned to their wives. But of one thing he felt certain: if one life had been spared, then it had been worth risking his own.

Oncologist Saul Rosenberg during his medical residency. Courtesy Saul Rosenberg.

Christine Pendleton and her family in 1966. Courtesy Barb Horigan.

Joey Radicchi in 1965. Courtesy
Department of Radiation
Oncology, Stanford University.

Sarah Kaplan flanked by her sons Henry and Richard. Courtesy the Kaplan family.

Vince DeVita and Sarah Donaldson at a medical conference.
Courtesy Saul Rosenberg.

Stanford radiotherapist Eli Glatstein.
Courtesy Saul Rosenberg.

Mary Murray (Vidal), 1969.
Courtesy Department
of Radiation Oncology,
Stanford University.

Saul Rosenberg. Courtesy
Saul Rosenberg.

Chris Jenkins with his wife Tran Tuyet and their daughter Melinh in 1975 after his first treatment for Hodgkin's disease. Courtesy Tran Tuyet.

Robert Gallo and his two sons, 1967. Courtesy Robert Gallo.

Wendy Podwalny.
Courtesy Wendy Podwalny.

Leah and Henry Kaplan in later life. Courtesy the Kaplan family.

Saul Rosenberg and Vince DeVita.
Courtesy Saul Rosenberg.

Radiotherapist Norman Coleman.
Courtesy Saul Rosenberg.

Song of the Vowels by Jacques Lipchitz in front of Stanford Hospital. Photo by Olya Gary. Courtesy Lane Medical Archives, Stanford University Medical Center.

Henry Kaplan in his later years. Courtesy Lane Archives.

40   The Boy in the Bubble

Henry Kaplan sat looking at a letter from Vince DeVita. "We are growing quite desperate," he had written. It was unthinkable—the boy might die. Teddy De-Vita had been ill for six years, and now they had reached an impasse. Every possible treatment had been tried. When he had been diagnosed with aplastic anemia back in 1972, neither Vince nor Henry would accept the high death rate. After all, they had devoted their lives to curing cancer, defying statistics day after day.

When Teddy was first isolated in the laminar airflow room, the so-called life island, Henry had joined Vince in the hunt for an effective therapy, reading everything written on the disease, contacting scientists around the world. Early on, Kaplan talked about Teddy daily, but as his situation stabilized, months passed when he didn't even think about the boy. Now, as he looked at the letter, he likely wondered how he had let that happen. Yes, he was busy. He was designing strategies to push the cure rate of Hodgkin's disease higher. He was trying to develop the first human monoclonal antibody in one laboratory, while continuing to search for the human tumor virus in another. And he traveled regularly to Israel and China to assist in organizing their cancer programs. Henry had vowed to help Vince, but it was already 1978, and what had he actually done?

Teddy DeVita had been placed in the laminar airflow room at the Pediatric Branch of the National Cancer Institute at age nine when his bone marrow suddenly failed. Because he could not produce normal blood cells, he would not have survived more than a few days in an unprotected environment. Microorganisms in the air he breathed and on the people he touched would have quickly killed him. The pediatric team, led by Phil Pizzo, had treated Teddy with androgen, a male hormone known to enhance blood cell production, but the improvement in his blood counts was short-lived.

Then, in 1974, psychiatrists began to report high white blood counts in manic-depressive patients treated with lithium. By some unknown mechanism, the drug stimulated the bone marrow. When Pizzo learned of this, he treated the boy with lithium, and gradually his counts began to rise. When his white count reached a thousand, they began to talk of removing Teddy from isolation. "There was a hopeful expectation that he was recovering," Pizzo recalled, "and that he might leave the room. He felt it, and his parents felt it." They discussed where he would attend school. But just before his release, his white blood count fell to 800, then 500. The effects of lithium could not be maintained. The number of cells kept falling. And then there were none. "It was devastating," Pizzo said, "like relapsing with a malignancy." Only Teddy's indomitable spirit sustained them.

Known as "the boy in the bubble," Teddy DeVita grew up in a cage. A curious, resourceful child, he read avidly, sketched, and taught himself to play the guitar. He had a good sense of humor and enjoyed playing practical jokes on new trainees. It had been years since he had run barefoot in the grass, felt the sunshine on his face, or smelled the salt air at the beach. But he never gave up hope. He was continuing his studies, preparing for the day he would walk free. His father reinforced his optimism. Devoted to his son, Vince spent almost every evening sitting outside his room, waiting.

In the meantime, his career flourished. In 1975, Vince DeVita became director of the Division of Cancer Treatment—one step from director of the National Cancer Institute. NCI Director Frank Rauscher made it known that DeVita would one day head the Institute. A superb scientist and clinician, he had proven himself a capable administrator and charismatic leader as well. Though revered by trainees, staff, and senior colleagues, he also intimidated many of them. DeVita demanded excellence. When he began to reorganize staff and tighten up on review processes, some felt threatened. "Vince was a powerful figure," a colleague said, "who engendered great respect and loyalty on the part of some and great anger on the part of others. He never engendered a neutral response." Yes, Vince DeVita was a powerful man, but he had an Achilles' heel—his son.

In 1976, an anonymous person sent a letter to the *New York Daily News* alleging that DeVita had misappropriated funds for his own child while another had been denied access to a laminar airflow room. The letter appeared just as Vince was beginning to restructure the Pediatric Branch. He suspected the author to be a disgruntled staff physician. Someone wanted DeVita out, and his son's situation was an easy target. To add to the turmoil, someone began spreading rumors that DeVita was planning to curtail several treatment programs, including that for children with acute leukemia.

Distraught over the affair, Vince wrote to Henry. "A somewhat distasteful matter has come up," he said. "Someone has seen fit to write an anonymous letter complaining about the resources committed to my son and made rather serious accusations in regard to the care of another child at the NIH." Kaplan was incensed. He appreciated Vince's integrity better than almost anyone. Vince had taken this job to improve the curability of cancer. He was working as hard as he could with an immense personal problem hanging over him. And Kaplan knew how it felt to be betrayed by those you trusted. He planned to fly to Washington to defend his friend when an investigation exonerated him.

The chief of the Pediatric Oncology Branch, Arthur Levine, prepared a summary of Teddy DeVita's case, justifying his treatment. He pointed out that the decision to put Teddy in the life island had been made at a time when DeVita had no supervisory role in the Pediatric Branch. They had anticipated that Teddy would be isolated for two to three months, not years. When his expected recovery had not occurred, he had been kept alive in the laminar airflow room. Was someone now suggesting that he be expelled from it? He could not fend off even a minor infection. "Removal would now be tantamount to death," Levine wrote. "It seems unthinkable to withdraw him." Moreover, they had accepted Teddy as a research subject, and all patients approved for study by the NIH received care regardless of cost. Their decision had been a medical not a financial one. The inquiry cleared DeVita of all charges. The furor soon died down, but for Vince, the hurt lingered.

Meanwhile, Ted's condition had not improved. The pediatric team concluded that his bone marrow would never recover on its own. Then, in 1976, an international group published a remarkable study of patients with aplastic anemia. They had investigated the efficacy of a relatively new procedure—bone marrow transplant. Two-thirds of those who had undergone a transplant from a matched donor had fully recovered. In comparison, 60 percent of those who had no donor were dead—most within three months. Ted's only hope appeared to be a bone marrow transplant.

A major hurdle to transplant was the possibility that the donor's marrow would be rejected by the patient. The human body has a remarkable system of immunity, in which a whole array of cells are called upon to destroy anything it senses as foreign. Researchers had identified a series of proteins on the surface of cells that must be identical between the donor and the recipient in order for the transplanted marrow to be accepted. If not, the recipient's immune system would consider the marrow foreign and reject it. The ideal donor was an identical twin; a less desirable, but acceptable alternative was a sibling with matching proteins. But only one out of four siblings had a perfect match.

Ted had just one potential donor—his sister Elizabeth. Odds were against them. To the family's immense disappointment, tests indicated that Ted's immune system would reject his sister's marrow. If patients like Ted were ever to accept marrow from a donor who had a close, but imperfect, match, some in-novative way to prevent rejection would have to be devised. Henry Kaplan set out to tackle this problem.

He and the Stanford immunologist Sam Strober had observed that when patients with Hodgkin's disease were treated with total lymphoid irradiation (TLI), their immune systems became partially dysfunctional. They postulated that TLI could blunt the part of the immune response that caused graft rejec-tion, allowing patients to accept unmatched bone marrow. To test the concept, Kaplan adapted TLI for mice. He and Strober found that if they gave doses high enough to inhibit the immune system, they could perform a successful transplant in unmatched animals. Having proved the concept feasible, Kaplan was eager to proceed with patients. When he told Strober about DeVita's son, condemned to life in isolation without a matched donor, Strober understood his impatience.

Before long, a hematologist referred a twenty-five-year-old woman with aplastic anemia to them. Rosa's disease had not responded to any drugs. She had six siblings, but not one of them was a perfect match. Her health was fail-ing rapidly. Kaplan treated her with TLI, delivering 1,800 rads to all her lymph nodes, with almost no toxicity. Then he and Strober infused marrow from a brother with the closest match. Thirty days passed, and Rosa's white count re-mained low. During her prolonged hospitalization, Kaplan and Strober visited her daily. Always cheerful, Rosa never complained. As the days ticked off, their affection for her grew, but their hope that the graft would be successful dimin-ished. Two months following the transplant, Rosa died from a fungal infection. The postmortem examination showed live donor cells in her marrow. Engraft-ment had actually begun. If they had just been able to hold her infection at bay for a few more weeks, she might have recovered. Although saddened by Rosa's death, Kaplan and Strober had demonstrated the validity of their approach: TLI could reduce graft rejection, allowing transplantation with less than per-fect sibling matches.

Now Kaplan faced another hurdle. If patients had previously had blood transfusions, their immune systems were overly stimulated, and they rejected almost any transplant. Most patients with aplastic anemia had had innumer-able transfusions. TLI would not be sufficient. Henry wrote Vince that he was investigating ways to overcome the problem of sensitization caused by prior transfusions. He had just learned of a highly potent immunosuppressive agent, cyclosporin A, being developed in Switzerland. He and Strober planned to combine the drug with TLI, first in dogs and then in patients with aplastic ane-mia. He tried to obtain cyclosporin A through the usual channels, but the drug was in the early phases of testing, and his requests were repeatedly denied. He seemed to have hit a roadblock. In the meantime, Pizzo, learning of his plans, urged Kaplan to redouble his efforts. "While we have been successful in supporting Ted over these past six years," he wrote, "time is beginning to run out."

After almost two years, Kaplan's dogged determination paid off, and he finally obtained cyclosporin A. Despite many competing priorities, he delved into the study of the immune system and transplantation. He was hell-bent on saving Ted DeVita.

In 1980, Vincent DeVita was appointed director of the National Cancer Institute. Having ascended to the most powerful position in the world of cancer, DeVita now set national policy. He determined how millions of research dollars were allocated—what research questions should be asked and who seemed most likely to answer them; he was responsible for the eradication of cancer in hundreds of thousands of patients. DeVita had reached the pinnacle of his career. But his son still remained isolated in the life island.

Ted, as he now preferred to be called, was seventeen years old. A handsome young man with dark hair and eyes, he resembled his father. He had mastered the guitar, read *The Complete Works of Shakespeare* several times, memorizing long passages, and finished high school graduation requirements. Despite his unnatural existence, he behaved like a normal teenager. At 2 A.M. his lights still glowed as he listened to Fleetwood Mac or talked on the phone to one of several disc jockeys, his nighttime companions. His room looked like any other teenager's—an unmade bed, a guitar in the corner, posters of rock stars on the walls. The difference was that he couldn't leave it.

Ted craved independence yet he had to conform to hospital routine. He had to eat on a set schedule; he could only bathe when someone brought him a tub of water. Pizzo tried to let him control his environment whenever possible, such as letting him choose which veins were used for blood draws and who started his intravenous line. After a long battle, Pizzo obtained approval to have a bathroom installed in the laminar airflow room so that Ted could have the privacy of his own toilet instead of a bedside commode. And in his teen years, he took his first shower.

What Ted wanted most, however, was freedom. He yearned to go to movies with friends, to share Thanksgiving dinner with his family. But the air outside the bubble could be deadly. Pizzo ordered a NASA-designed spacesuit for Ted. With it, he thought they could try letting him leave the room for a short time. The day Ted walked out of the life island was a momentous event. His excitement, however, was tempered by public reaction; people openly gawked. He had tried hard to be normal, but outside the bubble, he was constantly reminded that he was an anomaly. "It was a trying experience," Vince recalled. Using a friend's skybox, however, Ted did get to attend his first baseball game. Pizzo kept searching for a less cumbersome protective outfit, and eventually he found a commercially available head unit used by miners to filter air in a high-dust environment. Ted still aroused attention, but he didn't care. Then Pizzo fulfilled one of Ted's dreams—he took him to a rock concert.

Life seemed to settle into a holding pattern. Ted's medical condition remained stable as long as he received weekly transfusions. They were all still waiting for the day when Kaplan's anti-rejection regime of TLI and cyclosporin would permit a marrow transplant. Ted graduated from high school, a Merit Scholar, and he was studying for the college boards. His parents no longer felt they needed to keep a constant vigil. Then one night Vince returned from a Mother's Day dinner to find that Ted had collapsed.

An electrocardiogram revealed the cause to be an arrhythmia—an irregular heartbeat. Ted had developed hemachromatosis, a rare disease caused by excessive amounts of iron deposited in the liver or heart. Blood transfusions contain relatively large quantities of iron. Ted had received so many transfusions that they had lost count. Therapy was limited; the damage had been done. Heart failure could be sudden and swift. Without warning, arrhythmias could cause the heart to stop beating. Vince was beside himself. He had always worried that Ted would contract a life-threatening infection or have a major bleed; he had never anticipated heart failure. Ted looked perfectly healthy, and his mind was as sharp as ever. Vince couldn't accept that his son might die.

Kaplan called Norm Coleman, who had taken care of Teddy while at the NCI, and told him that Ted had heart failure. Coleman thought he had called to commiserate. Instead he asked, "What do you think about a double transplant, bone marrow and heart?" Norm didn't say what he really thought—that the idea was insane. Instead, he said he thought that the likelihood of success was slim. But Coleman knew "Kaplan would go to the ends of the earth to save a patient." Soon thereafter, he phoned a cardiac surgeon and the bone marrow transplant team, trying to mobilize support. "Henry was driving everyone crazy," DeVita recalled. But his optimism and kindness sustained Vince during this difficult time.

Then Ted had a cardiac arrest. Electric shock jolted his heart back into a normal rhythm. It was frightening for the family and terribly painful for Ted. Kaplan picked up his pace. He had almost completed arrangements for heart and marrow transplants. But Ted experienced repeated cardiac arrests. Over the next two weeks, he was subjected to electric shock again and again. His heart was failing; he was too ill to be moved.

Ted was suffering. Vince and Phil Pizzo knew they had lost. There was no miracle, no hope. They knew it was time to quit. Ted was awake and alert. He could see their faces change from panic to hopelessness to sadness. And he told them to stop.

On Memorial Day evening in 1980, Vince, Mary Kay, and Elizabeth gathered at his bedside. The monitor beeped steadily. Ted said his good-byes. And then the next wave of arrhythmias occurred. Pizzo didn't reach for the paddles to shock Ted; he reached for a syringe of morphine. Ted looked up at them and said, "I'm out of here." In a minute, he was dead.

41

The C-1 Protocol: Wendy Podwalny

BEFORE THE DIAGNOSIS

An achromatic autumn
a baby boy born
under the sign of Cancer
Grandparents visiting
breast feeding during the night,
walks, naps in the afternoon.
In the evening, Horowitz and Stroganoff
red wine for a celebration—
three generations of Sergeys.
The dog paced anxiously in the garden,
a frond fell from the palm. The young mother coughed
as she reached to pick a persimmon
burnt orange and plump
on bare, thin branches.
                              —Wendy Podwalny

Cancer, chemotherapy, death—those words never entered the thoughts of Wendy Podwalny when, in July 1981, she cradled her newborn son, Misha. Amply fed by his two grandmothers, he looked like a little Buddha with dimples. Wendy felt thankful that the loose ends of her life had come together.

Born in London to a British mother and an American father stationed in England, Wendy grew up on Air Force bases in Oklahoma and Indiana. As a teenager, she rebelled against her strict upbringing, becoming promiscuous and experimenting with drugs. She married at age seventeen, but the marriage was short-lived; her ex-husband was imprisoned later on drug charges. Wendy enrolled at Indiana University, then Purdue, but she couldn't focus on studies; she preferred to write poetry and paint. She dropped out of school and took a job with an engineering firm, apprenticed to an electrical draftsperson. There she met a thirty-five-year-old electronics designer, Sergey (Gary) Podwalny. After a brief relationship, they married and moved to the Bay Area. Three years later, they had a son. Finally, Wendy felt at peace.

Then, without warning, a nightmare altered her life forever. One day, Wendy was a well person, and the next day, she began to itch. She kept expecting to break out in a rash, but her skin remained clear. She searched the house for fleas or spiders. She threw out her woolen blanket, stopped using detergent and shampoo, changed her diet, all to no avail. A dermatologist diagnosed her problem as a postpartum reaction and prescribed an ointment, but the itch continued. It plagued her day and night. If she and Gary went out to a restaurant, she made several trips to the bathroom to scratch. Before long, scratching with her nails didn't relieve her. She started scraping herself with the edge of a book, with her hairbrush. But she couldn't get at the source. She scratched so hard she abraded her skin and dug deep sores on her arms and legs, which bled. Embarrassed, she hid them with long sleeves and pants. Antihistamines lessened the itching but sedated her to the point where she couldn't care for Misha. In just a few weeks, Wendy had been transformed. Once attractive, with flawless skin, a stylish cut to her blond hair, she now looked slovenly and dull, her body covered with blood-encrusted scabs.

When five months had passed with no relief, a feeling of doom settled over her. She felt it when she woke up, and it held on all day; she couldn't get away from it. This premonition made the itching all the more frightening. Nights were the worst; she felt she was suffocating.

Wendy went to another dermatologist. He was young and didn't even wear a white coat. He began asking the same questions. She thought he would prescribe yet another salve, but instead he pointed out a swelling in her neck and ordered a chest radiograph. A few hours later, he called and asked Wendy to come back to his office with her husband. When she asked why, he mentioned an "abnormal growth." Wendy felt relieved; finally someone had found something to explain the itching. "I thought it was a little cyst, and he was going to pop it," she said. But when the dermatologist showed Wendy and Gary the radiograph, a chill ran through her. He pointed out a mass the size of a Texas grapefruit. She didn't know how something that large could fit inside her chest. He used a term that they had never heard before—Hodgkin's disease—explaining that it was a malignancy that could cause uncontrollable itching. And then he mentioned Henry Kaplan, a name that meant nothing to them. It would grow in importance, however, over the coming months.

"I was so scared," Wendy said. "I remember going to bed that night knowing I had a tumor in my chest." Every breath seemed arduous. "Once I had seen the chest x-ray, it was like there was a beast in there. It was pressing; I could feel it."

Wendy was referred to Stanford, where a biopsy confirmed Hodgkin's disease. After months of being told that she had nothing serious, a flurry of activity ensued. Radiotherapist Richard Hoppe examined her and found enlarged lymph nodes on both sides of her neck. On her chest x-ray, he saw a mass surrounding the trachea and major blood vessels in her chest. Within a week, she underwent blood tests, CT scans, a lymphangiogram, and a bone scan. Following those, Dr. Hoppe recommended a laparotomy to complete the evaluation.

Wendy felt terrified; she didn't know how to sort out the fear, anger, and hopelessness. What would she do about Misha? She was still breast-feeding. One day, while waiting for an x-ray, a social worker invited Wendy to a support group. There Wendy met people who knew what she was going through. They shared their experiences, offered advice on practical issues, demystified procedures. Most important to Wendy, each displayed unflagging optimism.

Two days before Christmas, Wendy underwent a staging laparotomy and splenectomy. The day after, Kaplan came to her room. Sedated with morphine, Wendy still recognized him. She tried to sit up, but pain from the fresh incision pierced her. Dr. Kaplan supported her and laid her back down. The gentleness of such a large man surprised her. A few days later, Wendy developed abdominal pain of such severity that she thought she was dying. She began moaning and screaming; the nurses and residents could not calm her. Dr. Kaplan came to her room and calmed her fears. He said that the pain came from an air pocket where her spleen had been and promised it would go away soon. And it did. A few days later, he gave her some good news: the results from her laparotomy were negative; she had stage IIA disease, giving her a high chance of cure. He went over the treatment choices and asked her to consider taking part in a study.

⌒

In 1980, Stanford's third series of Hodgkin's disease trials—the S studies—had reached completion. Their main objective had been to maintain the excellent results of therapy while reducing toxicity. For patients with the earliest stages of disease, Kaplan and Rosenberg had been able to reduce the extent of irradiation by adding MOPP in a combined radiotherapy-chemotherapy program. For other stages, they showed that PAVe, an alternative chemotherapy designed by Rosenberg, was as effective as MOPP when used in these combined modality treatments. And as hoped, PAVe had fewer acute side effects. With both MOPP and PAVe, however, almost all the men became permanently sterile; over half the women entered menopause. And there was also a more frightening complication—second malignancies.

At about that time, a charismatic young Italian at the Istituto Nazionale dei Tumori in Milan, Gianni Bonadonna, reported on another four-drug combination—ABVD (Adriamycin, bleomycin, Velban, and dacarbazine). ABVD proved to have substantially lower risks of leukemia and sterility, but it had another drawback. Adriamycin, the most effective drug in the regimen, damaged heart muscle, particularly in patients who had had chest irradiation. If a patient developed cardiac failure, it was too late; the heart rarely healed.

The Stanford group stood at a crossroads. In their trials, they had reached what they considered the limits of toxicity. "We're now looking into quality of life," Kaplan told a reporter. "It's a measure of our success that in a disease that once was invariably fatal, we now have the luxury of doing that." So again Kaplan challenged Rosenberg: design a new regimen—one as effective as MOPP or PAVe or ABVD, but without their long-term side effects. And Rosenberg came back with VBM.

The acronym VBM stood for Velban, bleomycin, and methotrexate. Velban could induce mild nausea and muscle cramps; methotrexate might cause fatigue or mouth sores; bleomycin could produce fever and scarring of the lungs. But none of these drugs caused severe vomiting, sterility, or heart damage. And none was known to be carcinogenic. Although each had some activity against Hodgkin's disease, no one had used the three together. Combined, would they be strong enough to do the job? Usually investigators first evaluated a new regimen in patients with advanced disease, where responses could be measured and side effects assessed. Uncharacteristically, Rosenberg skipped the first step and put VBM into trials for early stage disease with no prior testing.

In 1980, the Stanford group announced its fourth series of randomized trials—the C studies. Patients with stages I, II, as well as IIIA disease would be randomized to either total lymphoid irradiation (TLI) or involved field irradiation, just to known sites of disease, followed by six cycles of VBM. Since the Stanford team knew involved field irradiation alone was inferior, they were counting on VBM to eradicate microscopic disease. Normally cautious, Saul Rosenberg was flying blind.

⌒

Wendy Podwalny had IIA disease, and Kaplan offered her two options: She could undergo standard therapy with total lymphoid irradiation, which had a high success rate but carried some risk of infertility. Alternatively, she could participate in a trial in which she would be randomized to either TLI, omitting the pelvic field, or a new treatment consisting of less intensive radiotherapy followed by VBM chemotherapy. They hoped it would preserve fertility, but they had not treated enough young people to know. Wendy chose to enter the trial, hoping for the experimental arm. She wanted to have more children, and she could potentially remain fertile on VBM. But she understood that her assigned treatment would be drawn out of a hat. The consent form warned of a possible risk of other cancers. "At the time," she said, "that didn't mean anything to me." She just wanted to get rid of this cancer, and she trusted Kaplan. Besides, she longed to have more babies. "Even if they had said, 'You will definitely end up with leukemia and breast cancer and thyroid cancer,'" she recalled, "I would have signed the consent." She was the thirteenth patient. At the staging conference, a nurse drew the next card from the protocol box and announced the B arm—involved field and VBM.

Wendy began mantle radiotherapy, and within a few weeks, her itching stopped. The treatment caused a mild sore throat and a small amount of hair loss above the nape of her neck. Toward the end of the course, her saliva dried up, and her mouth felt as though it were stuffed with cotton. But still, the treatment wasn't as hard as she had anticipated. She could even bring baby Misha to the hospital with her.

Spring arrived, and Misha was starting to stand. It was time for Wendy to begin chemotherapy. Oncologist Sandra Horning, Rosenberg's junior colleague, told Wendy that she would receive infusions of VBM twice monthly for six months. The first treatment took just fifteen minutes. It seemed surprisingly easy; Wendy went shopping afterward. That night, however, the side effects struck without warning. Wendy's arms began to burn; she felt as if she had tendonitis in every joint. The smallest movement caused excruciating pain. She couldn't hold Misha; she couldn't even hold a glass of water without screaming in agony. Pain pills gave no relief. "I wanted to bang my head on the wall," she said. Then she started vomiting. She couldn't walk or talk or eat. Her mother called from Indiana and asked if she should come. "Yes," Wendy groaned. "I wanted to see her before I died," she said.

Horning hadn't expected such an intense reaction, and she halved the Velban dose for the next treatment. This made the muscle pain tolerable. Then sores broke out all over the inside of Wendy's mouth. If she tried to drink a cup of tea, she felt as though someone had poured acid down her throat. Horning postponed her treatments. Wendy began to worry about what the lower doses and delays meant for her cancer? But nine months after diagnosis, she completed therapy and was deemed in remission.

CURE

The vinca*
in my garden
grows wild and disorderly
Along the stone steps
Crowds innocent growth
Unfairly

The *Vinca rosea*
Picked, ground and liquefied

Vinca rosea, or periwinkle, is the source of vinblastine, the brand name for which is Velban.

A chemical warfare
against the most dreaded disease
Injected into a vein
Spreads rapidly
through my bloodstream
A raging fire
Wretched violent poison

The vinca
in my garden
a constant reminder
of my dark past
The year of lying
perfectly still
in a dark room
Threads of light
monumental irritants
Agonizing sounds—
a neighbor mowing his lawn
Cheerful coos of my baby
. . .

    —Wendy Podwalny

A year and a half after Wendy was told she had a cancer called Hodgkin's disease, she could go through an entire day without scratching or vomiting or hurting. Misha was walking; her mother had returned to Indiana; friends invited her out to lunch. Life continued, and Wendy was still part of it. But during chemotherapy, her periods had stopped. Her gynecologist told Wendy that she had gone through a drug-induced menopause. She was only twenty-five years old.

⌐

While Kaplan and Rosenberg were pleased with the early success of VBM, others in the field did not accept it so readily. "Stanford's choice of . . . VBM for a proposed study is dreadful," Vince DeVita said at the conclusion of a three-day symposium in San Francisco. He was "personally distressed" at plans to use any but the most potent drugs. This public condemnation of Stanford's latest trial shocked the cancer community. The conference, held in September 1981, had been billed as a showcase for progress in the field. Attendees included prominent investigators from around the world, except for Rosenberg who had planned a vacation at the time. The organizers asked Kaplan to open with a historical perspective and DeVita to end with a critical summary.

Kaplan began the conference on a positive note, tracing the history of Hodgkin's disease therapy from a period of pessimism to what he called "confidence in cure." Over the next three days, researchers spoke on such diverse topics as social class and Hodgkin's disease, chromosomal abnormalities, and a new eight-drug chemotherapy regimen. Optimism seemed high when Kaplan left town for a prior commitment. He didn't hear DeVita's conference summary. DeVita began by thanking the organizers for arranging a meeting "laced with both new information and much controversy." His task was to put this work in perspective so as to point the way for future investigation. "To do this appropriately," he said, "it is more useful to focus on weaknesses in study design than on strengths, with all the inherent danger of injured feelings." A ripple of anticipation ran through the audience. When he said, "My critical comments should not be construed as personal affronts," attendees, as well as the press, whom he had invited, gave their full attention.

After summarizing what he thought had been the highlights of the conference, DeVita turned to the new chemotherapeutic alternatives to MOPP. He said he had known back in 1967 that MOPP was not a treatment they should "keep forever," but he proceeded to point out the shortcomings of other regimens. Finally, he came to the combination of irradiation and chemotherapy, calling Stanford's studies "the most elegant series of clinical experiments" and concluding, "MOPP was the missing tool which allowed Drs. Kaplan and Rosenberg to design the complete therapeutic experiment." Then he lowered the boom—he censured VBM. DeVita contended that three-drug combinations were less effective, besides which VBM contained two weak anti-Hodgkin's drugs. And it had not been tested in advanced disease. His reasons were sound; his rhetoric was not. He used the words "weak," "troubled," and "dreadful." In finishing his criticism of Stanford's new regimen, he said, "radiotherapists do not make such ad hoc alterations to radiotherapy doses and schedules without prior testing. Certainly radiotherapists are not substituting neutrons for photons in a combined program before testing neutrons alone first. These ad hoc choices can serve as a bad example to practitioners whom we frequently admonish for doing the very same things."

Henry first learned of this lambasting when he read it in the newspaper. He was stunned. "I was deeply shocked . . . appalled," he wrote DeVita. He said he understood how Vince might be upset with them for relegating MOPP to "a salvage role." But VBM had arisen from their concern with the toxicities of MOPP and ABVD; they were asking a "legitimate scientific question." How could DeVita denounce VBM with such conviction? "No one is blessed with divine guidance," he continued, "not even you." He reminded Vince how he had criticized their PAVe regimen. "If you were wrong then," Kaplan wrote, "is it not possible that you are wrong again today?" He said DeVita was "denying the right of free inquiry to scientists whose work has been peer-reviewed and approved." Some form of "remedial action" was indicated.

Henry Kaplan was not averse to criticism. He loved a good scientific debate and considered Vince one of his favorite sparring partners. What bothered him was being tried and convicted in the press. Speaking as director of the NCI, DeVita had discredited their work in their own backyard with neither he nor Rosenberg there to rebut him. What would referring physicians think? How would patients who had participated in their trials feel? But what hurt Kaplan most was the breach of friendship. Ever since the cancer center fiasco, he had been wary. So as never again to suffer the pain of betrayal, he kept colleagues at arm's length. But he had considered Vince special. They had shared confidences about work, families, successes, failures. "Saul and I have been good friends," he wrote, "who have come to your assistance on a number of occasions, and this hardly seems a suitable way to recognize our friendship. But even if we were mortal enemies . . . your statements were extremely destructive."

Rosenberg had just returned from Europe when he read the article in the Sunday paper. He, too, was astounded by Vince's behavior. "Our choice of the VBM program," he wrote DeVita, "is a logical step in our studies and is grossly unfairly criticized by you. The purpose should be obvious to you; to reduce or eliminate the risks of acute leukemia or sterility." Rosenberg found the public form of the criticism particularly disturbing. "You and I have had many provocative and productive debates over the years," he wrote. "We will continue to do so, hopefully at medical and scientific meetings . . . and not through poorly informed science writers. . . . You have done me, my colleagues, and patients . . . an undeserved injustice."

A week after DeVita's comments appeared in the *San Francisco Examiner and Chronicle*, the father of a former patient wrote to Rosenberg:

> My son, who presented with Hodgkin's disease at the age of six, was given complete mantle radiotherapy by Dr. Henry Kaplan and when the disease returned was given MOP. . . . He has been in complete remission for five years. . . . I was very disturbed to read the attack made on Stanford methods recently by Dr. DeVita. Is there anything you can tell me which can ease the natural anxieties caused by the newspaper account of Dr. De Vita's accusations?

How many letters would follow? They had treated hundreds of patients. Would those on the VBM study decline further therapy?

DeVita wrote Rosenberg that he was surprised by his letter; Saul had "pulled the trigger a little too soon." After all, DeVita had been asked to provide a critical overview of the conference, and that's what he had done. Because Saul had not attended the meeting, he had missed some of his key points. Vince said he had described the Stanford trials as "the most brilliant series of clinical trials conducted in the annals of the treatment of Hodgkin's disease." And he reminded Saul that over the years he had repeatedly praised the Stanford team.

"Why then," he asked, "should you interpret any critical comment as negating all the previous positive statements? It's like judging a man by the last thing he does as he falls to the ground with his fatal myocardial infarction!" But DeVita did not back down from his criticism of VBM. "[You knew] I disliked it," he wrote. "Two of the three drugs are, in fact, carcinogenic. Your assumption that in the long pull it will be less leukemogenic than other tested combinations, and as effective, is itself untested."

Rosenberg couldn't understand why Vince had behaved this way. Was he trying to assert his power as NCI director? Had the bright lights blinded him? In time, however, Rosenberg was able to put the incident in perspective. After all, he and Vince had a long history of antagonism when it came to the treatment of Hodgkin's disease. "While Vince was talking about dose intensity," he said, "I was talking dose reduction." Although professionally competitors, they were longtime friends. "Vince had a true affection for Henry and me," Rosenberg said, "but it was compartmentalized. On a one to one, he was very warm, but he separated the personal and academic." The two had what DeVita referred to as "our usual soul-searching discussion over a pleasant dinner." Vince acknowledged that the word "dreadful" had been a bit strong. Saul later wrote to him: "Though we did not resolve our scientific differences, I think we better understand each other's motivation." They would remain collegial and continue to argue over the years.

What about Vince and Henry? Kaplan didn't compartmentalize affection. A true friend remained a friend in any situation. DeVita wrote back that he was "shocked" by his letter. "You are known as a person who's quick to criticize," he said. "I always admired this side of you. . . . On occasion, I've felt the brunt of it myself. Nonetheless, I have never felt that your criticism was any more than your honest difference of opinion with a position I had presented. Please don't force me into a box so tight that I am unable to comment on science." Kaplan did not respond.

Rosenberg predicted a permanent rift. "Kaplan never forgot an experience or a negative interaction," he said. "It was always a part of his memory." Throughout his life, whenever he had a major altercation—especially if he felt maligned—he severed the relationship. For him, the individual ceased to exist. The list was long: Henry Garland, David Korn, Robert Glaser, and his own brother, to name a few. But in the end, Kaplan found it difficult to dissociate himself from Vince. They had been through too much together. In their quest to cure cancer, they were fellow spirits, stimulating and challenging each other. Vince had sympathized with Henry's deep disappointment over the cancer center debacle and his frustration when political backbiting excluded him from playing a larger leadership role in the cancer field nationally. It was to Henry that Vince had turned for advice as he rose to the foremost cancer position in the country. Then there was Teddy's illness. As a result, they had feelings for each other far stronger than just collegial. And so Kaplan did something unusual for him—he forgave.

~

Seven years later, the VBM trial would be published. Sixty-seven patients had been randomized to total lymphoid irradiation or radiotherapy limited to involved field followed by six cycles of VBM. As anticipated from previous trials, 30 percent of patients treated with TLI relapsed. What no one expected was how successful involved field radiotherapy and VBM would be. The disease recurred in only 5 percent of patients. Muscle pain had been the major toxicity, but once the dose of Velban was reduced, patients tolerated the regimen relatively well. None lost their hair; no one developed a severe infection. Of nine men who submitted to semen analysis, just one had a low sperm count. Only one woman reported cessation of menses. No second cancers developed. Rosenberg and Kaplan could have flaunted these results to DeVita, but instead the Stanford team cautiously concluded: "Greater patient numbers and longer follow-up are needed to confirm our early experience that VBM is an effective, less toxic regimen. . . . The optimal management of Hodgkin's disease should result in uncomplicated cures for the greatest number of patients."

Wendy Podwalny was one of those patients in remission. She had hoped to retain fertility, but her menstrual periods had not returned, and her gynecologist diagnosed early menopause. She was distraught; she and Gary had hoped to have more children. That had been the main reason for participating in the trial. Then, about a year after she had completed VBM, Wendy became nauseated and fatigued. Her waist began to expand. She thought she was pregnant. "I told my gynecologist," she recalled, "and he laughed." Wendy bought a home pregnancy kit and tested herself. It was positive. Seven months later, she gave birth to her daughter. "When Emily was born," she said, "the first thing I did was to count each of her fingers and toes, and yes—they were all there." Sixteen months later, Alexandra was born. When diagnosed with Hodgkin's disease, Wendy had had two wishes—she wanted to have more children, and she wanted to live to see them grow up. Both came true.

Six years after Rosenberg's VBM regimen had been called "dreadful" in the press, the Stanford group reported that ninety-six children had been born to their Hodgkin's disease patients. At an event celebrating these children, Betty Ann Greenbaum-Miller, a former patient and the mother of two, spoke for all the patients when she said: "Bringing another life into the world after you think yours is going to be taken away is a special miracle."

42   The Quest for the Magic Bullet

Henry Kaplan had received numerous accolades for his discovery of the radiation leukemia virus; his accomplishments in treating Hodgkin's disease would have sustained most scientists for a lifetime. Yet he was not satisfied. Driven by the need to answer questions, to solve puzzles, he had found another: if the human body reacted to an assault from microbes by mounting an immune response that eliminated them, why couldn't it eradicate cancer in the same way? Unlocking the mysteries of the immune system to turn it against cancer, though not a new idea, fascinated and energized Kaplan, now in his sixties.

For decades, scientists had known that when a foreign substance—be it bacteria, a transplanted organ, or malignant cells—invades the human body, the immune system responds. Included in its armamentarium are antibodies—proteins that recognize these substances and target them for destruction. Key to their success is selectivity. These intruders have one or more specific surface markers, called antigens, each of which induces formation of an antibody. This antibody matches with and binds to the antigen, and once attached, sets loose a whole cascade of reactions, which eradicate the invader.

The human immune system, however, didn't seem strong enough to overcome cancer. For centuries physicians had tried to treat malignancies with injections of antibodies from animals or other people. Although antiserum was successful in combating some infections, such as rabies, the difficulty of isolating pure antibody and the small quantity that could be collected from a single donor long hampered its therapeutic use. What scientists needed was a process by which they could manufacture large amounts of a specific antibody.

In 1975, César Milstein and Georges Köhler at Cambridge University astonished the scientific community by developing the first antibody-producing machine in mice. Their technique was brilliant: they injected a foreign protein into a mouse to serve as the antigen, knowing that the mouse immune system would respond by making an antibody. Next they removed the spleen and isolated lymphocytes, the antibody-producing cells. These cells, however, have a short life span and make only small amounts of antibody before dying. How to confer longevity—that was the ingenious part. Milstein and Kohler devised a way to sustain these antibody-producing lymphocytes in perpetuity. They fused the lymphocytes in a test tube with fast-growing cells, and for these they chose myeloma, a bone marrow cancer. What resulted was a hybrid cell—part lymphocyte and part myeloma—which they termed "hybridoma." From the splenic lymphocytes, this hybridoma inherited the ability to produce antibodies; from the malignant cell, the ability to divide rapidly and indefinitely, producing clones, which, in turn, manufactured large amounts of antibody. These were the monoclonal antibodies, so called because each hybridoma makes one kind of antibody.

This proved a major breakthrough for medical science. Monoclonal antibodies seemed as effective as naturally made antibodies, and they could be produced in large amounts. Researchers dreamed of creating antibodies to treat influenza, hepatitis, cancer, and a host of other diseases. There was one hitch, however. The human immune system viewed a monoclonal antibody from a mouse as foreign, triggering the formation of an antibody against it. This rendered the mouse monoclonal antibody ineffective. What was needed was a human monoclonal antibody.

Researchers rushed to see who could make one first. But the task was not easy. To reproduce the Milstein-Köhler experiment in people required a *human* myeloma cell line and *human* spleen cells. Neither of these two cell types was readily available. Human myeloma cells were hard to grow in tissue culture. And removing spleens from human subjects for this purpose was unthinkable. What had been difficult in mice seemed nearly impossible in humans.

Intrigued by the potential of monoclonal antibodies, Henry Kaplan set out to find a solution to this problem which had eluded others. Once again he was delving into a new field—tumor immunology—in which he had limited experience. He teamed up with Scandinavian scientist Lennart Olsson, who had a strong background in immunology and had come to the Kaplan's Cancer Biology Research Laboratory (CBRL) as a postdoctoral fellow. Together they set out to devise a technique for producing human monoclonal antibodies.

They had a head start in this endeavor, because Kaplan possessed both of the essential cell types. He had a myeloma cell line stored in his freezer from an earlier research project. And he had ready access to human spleens from Hodgkin's disease patients who underwent staging laparotomy. Finally, it just so happened that the lymphoma team routinely evaluated the strength of the immune system in patients prior to splenectomy by skin testing with a harmless chemical, DNCB (dinitrochlorobenzene). This meant that the splenic lymphocytes had already made antibodies to DNCB, which identified them and could be traced. This presented a perfect situation for performing the Milstein-Köhler experiment in humans: if antibody to DNCB could be measured following fusion of myeloma cells with human spleen cells in culture, it would prove that they had formed a human hybridoma.

Kaplan and Olsson obtained spleens from the next three patients undergoing laparotomies and isolated the lymphocytes, the antibody-producing cells. Now came the tricky part—fusion—by which they united these lymphocytes and myeloma cells. The process—akin to making two microscopic bubbles come together as one—was "something of an art rather than a precise science," Kaplan said. Olsson mixed the two in culture with a detergent found in antifreeze in order to weaken the cell membranes just enough to make them pliable without rupturing. How thrilled they were to find that some cells fused. What resulted was a culture of hybridomas that produced a variety of antibodies. Their final task was to find the hybridoma that produced the antibody they were seeking—in this case, antibody to DNCB. This would confirm that the system worked.

"The whole process of making monoclonal antibodies was so complex," Kaplan said. "There were so many ways it could fail, that if we failed, we wouldn't know what to change." His entire laboratory felt this pressure, but no one as strongly as Olsson. Anticipation permeated the CBRL; lights could be seen glowing long after midnight. Kaplan stressed the imperative for the experiment to work the first time. And Olsson reported that it did. From the spleens of the first two patients, he isolated hybridomas that produced antibody to DNCB. Kaplan announced their success in July 1980 at the International Congress of Immunology in Paris, making headlines in *Le Monde*: "The first cellular machine to produce human antibodies has been developed in the U.S." The Associated Press reported: "Artificial production of pure human antibodies, announced by Stanford researcher, caps a five-year race involving scientists all over the world." *Time* called monoclonals a step forward in "The Quest for the Magic Bullet."

Researchers hastened to request Kaplan's cell lines. And he was generous. He provided scientists with both the methodology to make human monoclonals and the key ingredient—his human myeloma cells. In their own laboratories, researchers could fuse these myeloma cells with lymphocytes stimulated by any antigen they chose to create hybridomas that could, in turn, produce all kinds of monoclonal antibodies. The biotechnology world took notice; the potential for commercial success was staggering.

Within a few months, Kaplan shipped 250 samples to investigators in the United States and abroad. He anticipated hearing reports of antibodies created for many different purposes, all stemming from his and Olsson's work.

But none were forthcoming. Scientists were unable to fuse lymphocytes from their own laboratories with the myeloma cells Kaplan had sent them. Then Kaplan himself began having difficulty. His research associate of eight years, Marsha Bieber, could measure no antibody to DNCB in their hybridomas. Kaplan couldn't believe it and had her repeat the assay. Again she found no antibody. After further testing, she had disappointing news: the myeloma cell line had become contaminated with mycoplasma, an insidious infection that destroys cell cultures. Kaplan and Olsson faced extinction of their once famous, now infamous, cell line.

"Lab distributed tainted cell line," announced *The Stanford Independent* on February 12, 1982. More than seventy laboratories had already begun working with the myeloma cells, and seven companies had obtained commercial licenses. Kaplan had his work cut out for him. Meanwhile, Olsson had returned to Denmark. "Once they found the contaminant," Bieber said, "Dr. Kaplan had everybody in the CBRL—postdoctoral fellows, technicians, research assistants—working to clean it up." The CBRL had once been a vibrant place. Research staff began to grumble; they hadn't come to the CBRL to work on a contaminant. Tension pervaded the laboratory. After ten months of intense labor, they eradicated the mycoplasma, and the cell line once again grew robustly.

Nelson Teng, a young professor in Obstetrics and Gynecology, had just come to Stanford, hoping to develop monoclonal antibodies to treat ovarian cancer. Kaplan offered him space in the CBRL where he worked side by side with Kaplan—the only Stanford faculty member ever to do so. They spent many nights in the lab after finishing a full day of clinical and administrative work and occasionally ate a late dinner together at the faculty club. A close relationship developed between the two. "We shared many philosophical thoughts," Teng recalled, "about the medical school and science and life."

When Teng began his monoclonal work, he could not get the decontaminated myeloma cells to fuse. In the meantime, Kaplan repeated the original experiment, measuring antibody to DNCB—proof a hybridoma had formed. Bieber could still detect none. Perplexed, Kaplan had Olsson fly back to Stanford to reproduce his results; he couldn't. Scientists had become restless waiting for the cell line. "Many investigators," a British cancer researcher wrote in *Nature*, "have been unable to obtain any hybridomas at all with lines donated by certain laboratories, causing considerable controversy."

What had gone wrong? Some thought there never had been fusion between the myeloma and spleen cells. When Teng studied Olsson's experiments in more detail, he felt certain that Olsson had misinterpreted the data: the DNCB antibody Olsson had measured was probably the small amount produced by the patient's spleen before splenectomy. If Olsson and Kaplan had made clones of hybridomas, they should have been able to measure antibody months thereafter, because the beauty of the hybridoma is its endless production of antibody. "It was logical to conclude they had a hybridoma," Teng said, "but if they had waited three or four months to see if the cell line survived, they would have known it did not." Time was the true test. But they hadn't waited. "Olsson never made a real human monoclonal antibody," Teng believed. "So all those cell lines they gave to other investigators were worthless."

How could this have happened? Kaplan expected the highest level of scientific rigor from his team. "This was completely atypical," Bieber said. "He was always very careful." But Kaplan had a lot on his plate. He had trusted Lennart Olsson and hadn't reviewed the data with his usual scrutiny. The mistake likely would have been detected by a colleague's review of the results, but Kaplan gave no one the opportunity to do so. He had become a solo scientist who relied on the technicians, research assistants, and postdoctoral fellows who worked for him. "He had a lot of 'yes' people around him," one Stanford professor said, "people who would take orders, do what he wanted, and get the results he wanted." Others, including his protégé Ron Levy, were working on monoclonals at Stanford. He could have collaborated or at least communicated with them. Surely they would have questioned his interpretation. But Kaplan didn't want peer review. Nelson Teng was the sole faculty member in his laboratory, and he was judicious in his criticism. "There are only so many times you tell Henry Kaplan he is wrong," Teng said.

Kaplan was close-mouthed about his work. Levy first learned of Kaplan's human monoclonal when he picked up a copy of *Le Monde* at the Paris immunology conference. After failing to create a cancer center at Stanford, Kaplan had isolated himself in the CBRL. Few Stanford faculty knew exactly what was going on there. He seemed detached; some thought him less collegial, even secretive. Perhaps he feared being eclipsed by another investigator. "Kaplan was my greatest collaborator and my greatest competitor," Levy said. Was this a race Kaplan felt he had to win? Some thought the Nobel Prize had eluded him for too many years. Whatever the reason, he made his public statement just two weeks after he thought he had made a hybridoma.

In his scientific endeavors, Kaplan was inventive, but he was impatient. Struck with a new idea, he couldn't rest until he had tested it. No wonder he had been exasperated with Rosenberg, who proceeded cautiously, one step at a time; trials spanned five to ten years. Kaplan wanted to skip steps he considered superfluous. Throughout his career, most of his ideas had proved to be correct. But not all. "He had a couple of windmills he was chasing," Levy said. Kaplan's record of success and overwhelming confidence may have clouded his perspicacity.

Kaplan's haste in this case likely reflected a sense of urgency, which he had expressed to Leah on more than one occasion. He had pledged to find a cure for cancer, and he had not yet done so. Now he had passed the age at which his father had died. So he had rushed to a precipitate conclusion. "It was absolutely essential that the experiment work the first time," he had told a reporter. "I think he realized he was getting older," Bieber said, "and he hadn't figured out what makes people get Hodgkin's disease; he hadn't found the virus that causes lymphoma."

Most scientists, even the best, have their share of failed experiments and ideas that don't pan out. Kaplan, however, had gone public and subsequently sent cell lines to hundreds of researchers. He was cognizant of the precious time and dollars others had wasted on the material he had supplied. This must have caused him significant pain, but no one ever knew how much, because Kaplan said nothing. He didn't talk about the blunder in lab meetings or with research staff who had been with him for decades. Though he showed no emotion, Bieber and Teng could tell that Kaplan was deeply troubled. His jaw was tense, his step less firm. Henry didn't confide in Leah, and if he lay awake at night castigating himself, she never knew. And he didn't call DeVita or write to Michael Feldman as he had often done when faced with scientific problems. He bore his burden in silence.

Another researcher in his place might have blamed Olsson, censuring his work, using him as a scapegoat. Not Kaplan. He had been the senior investigator. Others might have written to the journal that published the work, retracting the manuscript, explaining why the conclusions might have been premature. But Kaplan never went public on the subject of his failure to make human monoclonals. He felt certain that they had made a hybridoma that secreted monoclonal antibodies; they had merely encountered some technical problems. "He believed with some thought and hard work, he could fix it," Teng said.

Retracing his steps, he pinpointed the problem—the human myeloma cell was just too fragile to survive fusion. Kaplan tried several other cell lines, but none had the resilience of the mouse myeloma cell. Not one fused. He needed to develop a more pliable line, but he didn't know how. Then at one of their late night dinners, Teng proposed a way. The mouse myeloma cell line grew fast and had good fusion capability, but its antibodies provoked an allergic reaction in patients. The human myeloma cell could produce human antibodies but didn't thrive. Why not unite a human myeloma cell and a mouse myeloma cell to form what he called a heteromyeloma? In other words, they would produce human monoclonal antibodies using mouse machinery.

The idea was brilliant, but not so simple. They had to combine chromosomes from human and mouse cells and then sift through hundreds of combinations to find the right one. The task was arduous, but at last, they detected one heteromyeloma that yielded a hybridoma that secreted antibodies. Once again it looked as if they had produced human monoclonals. Teng tempered Kaplan's enthusiasm; time alone would prove them right. The entire CBRL was elated when nine months later, the hybridomas were still producing antibody and in substantial amounts. They had constructed a mouse-human hybridoma that secreted human monoclonal antibody. This time there were no press releases, no headlines. With no fanfare, Teng and Kaplan quietly published their results.

"Henry was visionary," Teng said. "He began looking for all types of potential uses for human monoclonals." With a prior classmate, Abe Braude, Kaplan developed an antibody against endotoxin, the chemical that causes shock with bloodstream infections. Kaplan and Teng produced an antibody against Rh factor to prevent the "blue baby" syndrome in infants born to Rh-negative mothers.

This novel technique opened up new vistas; one science writer likened it to the invention of the steam engine. Scientists around the world explored potential uses of human monoclonal antibodies for the detection and treatment of disease: influenza, malaria, diabetes, rejection of transplanted organs. Some predicted that monoclonals would be the great hope for curing cancer. A monoclonal antibody could detect an antigen found on colon cancer cells to screen for this common malignancy. A melanoma vaccine was being investigated, and scientists talked of an anti-lymphoma antibody. Researchers were designing what they called "cruise missiles," antibodies loaded with toxins and targeted against cancer cells. Theoretically, scientists could create antibodies against any antigen. "The sky was the limit," Teng said. "We thought monoclonal antibodies were the wave of the future."

43   The Death of a Difficult Woman

On May 8, 1982, Leah, Paul, and Ann attended "Twenty Years of Research and Progress in the Treatment of Hodgkin's Disease," a tribute to the patients who had taken part in Stanford's clinical trials. Sarah Kaplan would have been proud of her son. She had always said he would accomplish great things. Had she come to that patient reunion, she would have witnessed the embodiment of all that she had aspired to for him. But she could not have appreciated the event. At eighty-seven, Sarah Kaplan was demented.

The change had been gradual, and given her personality, difficult to perceive at first. Sarah insisted upon living alone in Chicago. As she became senile, her energy and determination didn't flag, only her mentation. She ranted about her childhood, and with each recounting, the tales became more distorted. Repeatedly, she told of Hank's beating up the neighborhood bully, twisting it into a story of tyranny. She equated her son's deformity and schoolyard taunting with persecution and pogroms. "It was particularly sad," Paul said, "when aspects of her personality my father most identified with—her interest in life, clarity, sharpness of mind—were replaced by senility of an infantile quality, not infantile funny, but morose, almost gothic." She often forgot what day it was or who people were; she wandered away. But she adamantly refused help.

Sarah's deterioration was painful for Henry. "His feelings were complicated," Ann said. "He had memories of his mother when she was younger, sacrificing everything. He truly loved her and had to reconcile what she had been with the person she became." Whenever Henry talked to his mother, he became increasingly concerned. He could pay her bills, arrange for someone to bring her food and clean her apartment, but from thousands of miles away, he couldn't make sure she took her blood pressure medication; he couldn't protect her from falling on the icy sidewalks or getting lost on the Chicago streets. For years, he had urged her to move to California, but to no avail. So he had to rely on his cousin Claire Edes to watch over her.

One day Claire called and said Sarah wasn't eating; she wore the same dirty dress for days. Henry decided he had to bring her to Palo Alto. He planned to set up a room for her in his study. Paul warned against such a move, trying to paint a realistic picture of life with his grandmother. His parents would become full-time caregivers for a hostile, combative woman; they would have difficulty maintaining their careers, let alone their sanity. Paul predicted that they would murder her within two weeks. His father had to agree, and he arranged for an apartment nearby, with an assistant. On Christmas Day 1982, when Claire went to pick up Sarah to take her to the airport, she found her still in her nightgown. She hadn't packed; she didn't know where she was going.

Sarah had been in Palo Alto a week when she fell and fractured her hip. As the surgeons prepared her for hip surgery, she developed heart failure, followed by a stroke. Henry called Richard—the first time they had spoken in years. The two brothers had avoided each other ever since they had almost come to blows twenty years earlier.

Richard, now a prominent San Francisco lawyer, occasionally ran into Ann at court. He told her about cases he had just won, but he never asked about his brother. He lived with his wife Suzie and two children in upscale Pacific Heights. Richard felt great about himself—as long as he didn't think about his older brother. But now they were thrown together by their mother's illness. They spoke as little as necessary and only about the facts of her situation.

Sarah continued to deteriorate. She had done everything for her eldest son, and now he could do nothing to help her. "The past two weeks have been a kind of nightmare," Kaplan wrote DeVita. Finally, the cardiologist felt that she had improved enough to undergo a hip-pinning procedure, but she suffered a series of strokes afterward. She could no longer swallow; her mental state worsened. One day she thought Henry was her husband Nathan; the next she didn't even recognize him. Then she no longer responded to her name. On February 6, 1983, Sarah Brilliant Kaplan died.

Richard arranged a memorial service at his home. One by one, family and friends reminisced about Sarah. "I didn't like her, but she was a good woman," remarked an old acquaintance. "What I remember about her," Paul said, "was a difficult woman who could be endearing one minute and then turn around an instant later and do something that made you think you just walked in front of a truck. But she had an intensity, a drive, and an enthusiasm for being alive unmatched by anybody I've ever met. Not all of it was good, but all of it was real, and I think that was something everybody respected about her." Then one of Richard's friends spoke. He hadn't known Sarah, but wiping away his tears, he said, "One of the saddest things is that I've not heard anyone mention love." Paul wondered if the man was a professional mourner being paid to make the kind of comments and shed the tears none of them could. Henry remained silent.

Who did mourn the passing of this outspoken, caustic woman? Most found her death a sort of relief. Claire Edes no longer had to watch out for Sarah, who had angrily resisted every attempt to assist her. As a child, Paul had longed for his grandmother's hugs and kisses, only to be rebuffed. For forty years, Leah had put up with her mother-in-law's barbed tongue for Henry's sake. And it had required years of therapy for Richard to reconcile his relationship with his mother.

For Henry the memories were different: reading *The Book of Knowledge* on his mother's lap, walking along the beach at Union Pier, making milkshakes in the pharmacy after closing while he and his cousin Norm recounted their evening's escapades. This was the woman he had called "the swellest mom anyone ever had" and "the mom I adore." When Eve Culberg, a family friend, called from Chicago, Henry could finally share his sorrow with someone who had known Sarah. As he spoke, his voice caught, and then he cried.

◠

At sixty-five, a time when many would be planning retirement, their productive years behind them, Kaplan was more vigorous than ever. His zeal for scientific investigation was at its peak, his creativity barely containable. In one CBRL laboratory, he and Miriam Lieberman continued work on the mouse radiation leukemia virus, while on another floor, he pushed ahead in his search for the elusive human tumor virus. He and Nelson Teng were expanding the potential uses of monoclonal antibodies. He was trying to isolate the malignant cell in Hodgkin's disease tissue so that he could study the basic biology of the malignancy he had nearly cured but barely understood. Along with immunologist Sam Strober, he was investigating a new approach to rheumatoid arthritis—attempting to control the overactive immune system responsible for this disease with total lymphoid irradiation. And he and Saul Rosenberg continued to seek ways to increase survival while diminishing long-term toxicities for Hodgkin's disease patients.

At the same time, Kaplan served on numerous national committees. The chairman of the President's Commission on the Accident at Three Mile Island wrote to him: "Our report has been received with the highest accolades. Its success is a measure of your contributions . . . and the energies you devoted to achieve it." An active member of several international advisory boards, he helped scientists and medical leaders in France, Israel, and China organize their cancer services and strengthen their research programs.

Kaplan still devoted considerable time to human rights efforts, never refusing a request from Amnesty International or the National Academy of Sciences Committee on Human Rights. He wrote to Leonid Brezhnev, urging him to intervene on behalf of biologist Sergey Kovalev, who had been imprisoned in a labor camp for seven years. Co-founder of the Moscow chapter of Amnesty International and editor of an underground human rights publication, Kovalev was confined in conditions Kaplan called "harsh and inhumanitarian." Kaplan also protested the victimization of the physicist and prominent dissident Andrei Sakharov, who had received the Nobel Peace Prize in 1975. He wrote the director of the American Federation of Scientists: "Simply deploring and wringing our hands is not good enough." Kaplan advocated widespread boycott of scientific exchanges with the Soviet Union.

More often than not, Kaplan didn't know the results of his efforts, many of which were aimed at totalitarian regimes. Even so, he persisted. He wrote the president of the Republic of Liberia urging release of Samuel Greene, a statistician and former deputy minister of economic affairs. Following a coup d'état, Greene had been charged with high treason and incarcerated without trial in the Belle Yella prison compound, notorious for its brutality. Three months following his appeal, Kaplan received a note from Greene. "Immediately after my release from prison," he wrote, "I read with sincere appreciation your letter. . . . It certainly gives me a sense of pride and joy to know that somewhere someone cares."

Back at Stanford, Kaplan challenged students and residents to think creatively; their ideas continued to energize him. And on Monday afternoons, he joined Saul Rosenberg in lymphoma clinic. His clinical acumen was as sharp as ever, his enjoyment of patients increasing with the years. Henry Kaplan had a full life. And then he started coughing.

⌒

In 1983, Kaplan had a busy travel schedule. In five months, he gave honorary lectures at the University of Wisconsin, Colorado State University, and the American Roentgen Ray Society in Atlanta; he served as a visiting professor at the NIH and at Harvard's Bicentennial Celebration. His booming voice occasionally faltered; it had taken on a raspy quality. He was coughing so much at the Wisconsin lecture that he had to stop and ask for a glass of water. At an Israeli symposium on the mechanisms of metastases, Michael Feldman and Zvi Fuks expressed concern over his cough. When Henry said he was having an allergic reaction to some plant blooming in the spring, Zvi pointed out that it was already summer.

In midsummer, Leah accompanied Henry to a meeting in Denmark. They joined Robert Gallo in Copenhagen and spent a day viewing a private art collection. While Henry was studying a modern Danish piece, Leah confided to Gallo that she worried about Hank's health. He assured her that Henry had more energy than both of them combined. A short time later, at a Cold Spring Harbor Laboratory symposium on Long Island, Gallo heard Henry repeatedly clear his throat. "Good Lord," he thought, "Henry has developed an affectation, like some proper Englishman." When the hacking continued, however, Gallo asked about his problem. Henry told him he just had a sore throat and was taking erythromycin.

Leah urged Henry to see his internist, but he always gave her an excuse. She enlisted friends to pressure him into getting a checkup. At dinner with Abe and Gita Braude, Leah said, "Abe, don't you think Henry should have an x-ray?" When he agreed, Henry changed the subject. Leah sensed something was wrong.

In August, Kaplan participated on a jury to select the next recipient of the General Motors Award for scientific achievement. Sitting beside him, Vince De-Vita noticed he was coughing almost continuously. "Henry," Vince whispered during the proceedings, "get a chest x-ray." Kaplan said he had found mold growing on the carpet in his office and was treating himself with a course of antifungal antibiotics. A month later, Michael Feldman and Kaplan attended a meeting together in Annapolis. Feldman observed that his friend could barely get through a sentence. "Why are you coughing more than one should?" he asked. When Henry had no answer, Michael implored him to get evaluated.

Back home, Leah had tired of Henry's explanations. For months he had made a series of self-diagnoses from pharyngitis to mold allergy. He had treated himself with cough syrup, erythromycin, and antifungal antibiotics, but he was getting worse. Fed up, she confronted him the night he got home from Annapolis. "Look," she said, "your cough hasn't gone away. I don't care if you're right or wrong; get a checkup tomorrow."

The next evening, Henry came home looking exhausted. Leah was waiting at the front door. "Well," she said as soon as he entered the house, "did you get an x-ray today?" He stood in the foyer, looking down at the floor. "Yes," he replied. After a prolonged silence, he spoke in a barely audible voice. "I have lung cancer."

44   Felled

Henry Kaplan had spent almost his entire life fighting cancer. Now it was stalking him. What had he thought when he put his own chest x-ray up on the view box and saw a mass the size of a baseball in his left lung? He must have known it was malignant. Was he shocked, or had he suspected cancer when his cough had persisted for months? Was he frightened—did images of his father, withering away in pain at the age of forty-five from the same disease, rise up before him? Perhaps he was angry. At sixteen, he had vowed to cure cancer; now almost fifty years later, the death rate from lung cancer was still rising. Or was he just terribly sad?

As Kaplan stood in the dark radiology viewing room staring at his chest x-ray, the usual daily activities were going on around him. Technicians loaded films onto alternators; physicians sat reading films, drinking coffee. For them, this was just another day. For Henry Kaplan, September 28, 1983, marked the time his life changed forever.

He went to his office and tried to reach Michael Feldman. They had just attended a meeting together in Annapolis, so he called the hotel where Michael was staying. The desk clerk told him that Dr. Feldman had checked out. He called Michael's home in Israel; his wife said she didn't expect to hear from him until the following day. Outside his office window, sunlight made the foothills look golden, but likely Kaplan didn't notice. He didn't sit at his desk for long. However unnerved he may have been, he somehow controlled his emotions and began the workup for a patient with suspected lung cancer. Kaplan the doctor stood apart from Kaplan the patient and took over the case.

He paged chest radiologist Norm Blank to look at his films. Blank concurred that he probably had a malignancy and set up a needle biopsy. Within an hour, the pathologist confirmed the diagnosis—poorly differentiated lung cancer. Blank was surprised that Kaplan showed no reaction, just moved on to the next step in his evaluation. Kaplan knew surgical resection provided his only chance for cure, so Blank arranged a CT scan to determine if the cancer remained confined to the chest or had spread to other organs. "A lasting impression of Henry for me," radiologist Les Zatz said, "was a view of him standing in the diagnostic reading room with several physicians, discussing his scans as though he were consulting on some other patient." The cancer appeared localized to the left upper lobe, so Kaplan called surgeon Jim Mark.

That afternoon when Mark entered the clinic room, Kaplan was sitting on the exam table. Mark marveled at how dispassionate he seemed. Kaplan proceeded to give him a complete history as if he were talking about someone else. After Mark examined him, they reviewed the scans together and went over the technical aspects of the operation. "Henry never questioned my professional expertise," Mark recalled, "but it was clear that he was going to make all the major decisions in his case. He wanted surgery, and that was that." Mark found their interaction a bit surreal. They talked about the operation as if they were discussing a case Kaplan had referred to him. The only time Mark saw any change in Kaplan's expression was when he asked if he anticipated any insurance problems. "I have Medicare," he replied, pulling his card out of his pocket. He smiled faintly as if acknowledging that yes, he was now a patient.

At the end of the day, Kaplan faced his most difficult task—he had to tell Leah. She met him at the door, and as they stood in the foyer, he simply related the facts. He had finally had a chest x-ray, which showed a mass. A biopsy had revealed lung cancer, and Jim Mark would remove it in a few days. He didn't tell her how stunned he had been when he looked at his own x-ray and saw a large tumor. He didn't complain about the discomfort from the needle stuck deep into his chest or the angst of waiting while the pathologist processed the specimen and reviewed the slides. And he didn't reveal the sickening feeling in his stomach when the pathologist confirmed the diagnosis. He wanted to spare her the pain.

Leah felt scared, but she, too, checked her emotions. She didn't gasp or cry or rush to embrace her husband. She had lots of questions, but she tightened her lips. "I just shut up," she recalled. "I didn't want to burden Hank." They stood in silence trying to protect each other from the ugly reality looming between them. Finally, Leah spoke: "What are we going to do?"

"We are going out to dinner with Gladie and Hadley," Henry replied. They had made plans with their longtime neighbors weeks before, and he saw no reason to cancel. So they met the Kirkmans at the Faculty Club. Perhaps Kaplan found something comforting about the familiar—the maitre d' who recognized him and indicated his usual table, the awkward student waiter, and Gladie and Hadley. A professor of anatomy, Hadley Kirkman had been a friend of Henry's since the 1950s when he offered to share their two-acre lot so the Kaplans could build on campus. For over twenty-five years, the two families had shared potluck dinners, pool parties, political discussions, and laughter. The Kirkmans had just returned from China, and that evening, they compared their impressions with Henry's from his earlier trips. All through dinner Henry seemed as cordial as ever. It wasn't until dessert that he casually mentioned that he had just been diagnosed with a tumor in his lung and would be having an operation in a few days. He acted nonchalantly, as if he were having a skin cancer removed, and quickly turned the conversation back to China.

The following morning, Kaplan went into work as usual. Nelson Teng recalled the day vividly. Between surgical cases, he had gone to the CBRL to check on an experiment when Kaplan asked if he could spare a moment for a lab meeting. Teng said he had to rush back to the operating room. "This won't take long," Kaplan replied. When Teng entered the conference room and saw the entire CBRL staff gathered, he expected an important announcement. In a matter-of-fact manner, Kaplan told them that he had just been diagnosed with lung cancer and would undergo surgery in a few days. The room remained silent. "What do you say to one of the world's greatest cancer doctors when he tells you he has cancer?" Teng later asked. Kaplan went on to say he would be out for a week and outlined what should be done in his absence. The meeting ended in a few minutes, and the staff returned to their work, dazed.

Finally, Henry needed to tell his children; he couldn't put it off any longer. When he called Paul and asked him to come home, Paul immediately sensed that something was seriously wrong. He knew his father had gotten a chest x-ray, and he sounded low on the phone. "I drove over there numb," Paul recalled. "I managed to stop at stop lights and go at green lights, but I don't have any memory of driving because all I was thinking was 'he has cancer.'" Paul had heard stories of his grandfather dying of lung cancer, and many dinner conversations had focused on the disease.

When Paul entered the house, everything seemed calm, a bit too calm. His mother's face, usually full of expression, looked flat. Paul asked what had happened, and when Henry confirmed his fears, Paul flinched. "I felt plunged into a totally primal experience," he said. He wanted to respond like a child—yell or cry or throw something—but he could see how hard his parents were trying to control themselves. So he subdued his own emotions in order to support them. "Life changed in that instant," he said.

Henry had tried to protect everyone from feeling the gravity of his situation by remaining objective and detached. But when Annie came in a few minutes later, he couldn't speak. He just put his arms around her. For the first time, Leah openly sobbed. "It broke my heart," she said. Soon they were all crying. Henry had handled his diagnosis well as a physician, colleague, neighbor and even husband. But as a father, he could no longer suppress his grief.

Slowly, in an ever-widening circle, people began to learn that Henry Kaplan had cancer. Michael Feldman's wife met him at the airport and said that Henry had been trying to reach him; it sounded urgent. Jim Mark called Saul Rosenberg. Saul didn't contact him right away; he knew that if Kaplan wanted his advice, he'd ask. Radiation oncologist Don Goffinet suddenly appeared at Sarah Donaldson's office door. His usually ruddy face looked blanched; Sarah thought he was sick. "You'll never guess what happened," he blurted out. Then he closed the door and told her about Kaplan. For a moment, Sarah couldn't breathe; she thought she was going to faint. When Maureen O'Hara came into work on Monday morning, she saw Henry Kaplan's name on the patient roster. Meredith Haws, the night nurse, reported that she had gotten a call the evening before asking if she had a single room for Dr. Kaplan. She had thought he was admitting a patient; then he and his wife arrived on the unit with a valise. Dr. Kaplan said that he had lung cancer, and instead of going to the surgical floor, he wanted to be cared for by the CRC nurses. "We have a single room," Meredith said. "But you know what happens if a protocol patient comes in and needs it," she teased. "I know," he replied. "I get bumped to the ward."

Norm Coleman ran into radiologist Stuart Young in the parking lot. "This is none of my business," Young told him, "but I know you are close to Dr. Kaplan, and he has a big lung cancer." "I almost vomited," Coleman said. He telephoned Eli Glatstein. "I was shocked," Glatstein said, "dumbfounded. HSK never smoked; he abhorred smoking." Glatstein called James Mark, then Rosenberg. "What the hell is going on?" he asked. Everyone was asking the same question—how did Henry Kaplan get lung cancer?

Kaplan knew; he felt certain. During his residency at Michael Reese Hospital forty years earlier, the chief of Radiology had assigned him the task of preparing radon paste, a popular treatment for several skin conditions. Kaplan had to take a container of radium, extract radon gas, one of its decay products, and mix it with Vaseline to make the paste. To perform the extraction, the chief had designed a homemade machine of glass with rubber tubing—"leaky as hell" Kaplan once told Bagshaw. "That goddamn son of a bitch made us make the radon paste," he said. "I'm sure I inhaled liters of radioactive gas."

An odorless, colorless gas, radon had long been implicated as a cause of lung cancer. In the Middle Ages, miners in the Erz mountains in Germany had frequently died from a lung disease called *Bergkrankheit*, or "mountain sickness." In the early 1900s, epidemiologists found that up to half of these deaths were from lung cancer, and in 1924, radon was detected in high concentrations in the mines. It wasn't until 1950, however, that the U.S. Public Health Service initiated a study of health hazards from uranium mining; and ten years later, results showed that U.S. miners exposed to low doses of radon had three times the expected number of lung cancers. In 1941, when Kaplan was beginning his residency, radiation therapists didn't appreciate the dangers of radon. Environmental protection and radiation safety were practically unknown concepts at the time. Kaplan hadn't used a hood to collect the fumes; he had had no badge to measure exposure. Radioactive particles had likely lodged in his lungs and emitted radiation over a prolonged period of time.

↞

On October 3, 1983, James Mark, assisted by his surgical residents, opened Henry Kaplan's chest. The first thing they found was a large cancer involving almost the entire left upper lobe of the lung, fixed to the first rib. Through dissection and electrocautery, they extricated the upper portion of the mass. To find the lower end, they followed it centrally toward the heart. There they ran into the first problem—tumor was attached to the pulmonary vein, the blood vessel that drains oxygenated blood from the lungs into the heart. The tumor proved more extensive than anticipated. A mass had invaded the pulmonary artery—the major vessel that pumps blood from the heart into the lungs. Cancer had spread to lymph nodes throughout the left chest. After they had resected all visible tumor, they closed him up. Mark left his senior resident, John Baldwin, to finish suturing and went out to talk to Henry's family.

No sooner had Mark left the surgical suite and taken off his gloves and mask than a nurse called him back urgently. As he entered the operating room, he heard the high-pitched alarm indicating a cardiac arrest. Baldwin already had Kaplan's chest open and was squeezing his heart with both hands. The heart wouldn't beat on its own, so they administered electric defibrillation. After several shocks, his heart responded; the alarm changed to a steady beep, and his blood pressure rose. Mark transferred Henry to the intensive care unit, intubated on a respirator, with an intravenous line stuck in his jugular vein, two large tubes draining his chest, and a catheter in his bladder.

Meanwhile, the Kaplan family paced. The anticipation was overwhelming, and Leah wanted to prepare herself. Instead, she had to chat politely with a number of well-wishers whose company she didn't enjoy even under the best of circumstances. "I wanted to yell, 'Go away and leave me alone,'" Leah said, "but I had to make nice." Leah, Paul, and Ann kept checking their watches, telling themselves that the longer the operation took, the better; that meant it wasn't an "open and close" case.

Finally, they spotted Dr. Mark coming around the corner in his scrub suit and white coat. Paul studied his expression as he walked toward them. "He didn't look downcast," Paul recalled. They interpreted that as a good sign. Mark took them to a quiet part of the waiting area and described the operation, saying they had been able to remove all apparent tumor. There had been a "little bump in the road," a cardiac arrest, but Henry had quickly recovered and was out of danger. Paul saw his mother turn white, and he steadied her. After a few more questions, and seemingly composed, Leah thanked Mark and asked: "Are you all right, Jim? It must have been a tough morning for you."

As Paul listened to Dr. Mark, the image of a 747 pilot in a storm came to mind. Despite simultaneous acute problems, he maintained a calm demeanor and radiated confidence, which comforted Leah and Annie. Paul could tell, however, that they were not processing the information. He felt that he had to put his own sorrow on hold and manage the family. He asked Dr. Mark to clarify several points: What were the chances? What were they facing? "Getting data was a way to anchor myself," Paul said. Besides, someone had to serve as family spokesperson for the large number of relatives and friends who would soon be calling. Ann lost all objectivity. She could only respond emotionally. "The hardest thing I remember," she said, "was seeing him in the hospital. The night before he had surgery, he was still the same person. After that, he was never the same; he never regained any peace."

When Leah, Ann, and Paul were allowed to visit Henry in the ICU, they were unprepared for what they saw. Henry lay flat on his back, motionless. His usually tense jaw hung slack, and wide strips of tape held an endotracheal tube in place. The constant beep of the EKG monitor was out of sync with the sucking of the respirator's bellows. Annoying as the sounds were, they reassured the family that Henry was still alive. Saline ran through an intravenous line into his neck, and blood-tinged fluid drained from the chest tubes. Nurses, anesthesiologists, and technicians bustled around adjusting, measuring, injecting. Henry's eyes were half open, yet he gave no sign of recognition. "There is no way to spare anybody that shock," Paul said; "to see someone like my father, who is so intense, just lying there without the presence of his mind."

Leah bent close to his ear. "Do you know that I'm here?" she whispered. The beeping of the EKG monitor increased. "He can't respond, but he knows you're here," the nurse assured her. "His pulse just went up." The family was allowed to stay only a few minutes. As they left, they noticed that Jim Mark had posted a sign on the ICU door: "Dr. Kaplan thanks you very much for your concern; however, no visitors at this time." They felt grateful for his thoughtfulness.

In a couple of days, Henry no longer needed the respirator, and he could talk. Chest tubes still in place, he began to take charge. He and Mark discussed the details of his operation, and he reviewed his own pathology report—poorly differentiated adenocarcinoma that extended to the chest wall, invaded blood vessels, and had spread to lymph nodes. Maureen O'Hara recalled how upset Dr. Kaplan looked when she came upon him reading that report. He knew the prognosis—

only one in ten patients with this stage of disease survived. He planned to be one of them, but he needed aggressive therapy. He asked Malcolm Bagshaw and Don Goffinet, both adept at treating lung cancer, to devise a radiation plan. They recommended 6,000 rads to the tumor bed and 5,500 rads to the mediastinum. He agreed. "He was just like he was when he talked about patients," Bagshaw said, "straightforward, scientific, and unemotional—at least in my presence."

Now Kaplan faced the decision of whether or not to take chemotherapy. DeVita felt adamant that he should. Whereas the physicians caring for him had been deferential to Henry, Vince confronted his friend. "I went after him," he said. "I told him the chances of being cured with radiotherapy alone were none; he had to come to the NIH and get chemotherapy." DeVita believed that he could cure his friend. "Vince felt patients only die of cancer because their doctors don't treat them hard enough or use the right drugs," Norm Coleman said. DeVita had already made arrangements for Kaplan at the Bethesda Naval Hospital. "I was going to be the heavy," DeVita said. "I told Henry if he complained chemotherapy made him sick and he didn't want anymore, I would nail him to the bed." Vince spoke with such vehemence that Kaplan started to laugh and grabbed his chest in pain. He begged him to stop.

Despite DeVita's conviction, Henry expressed doubts about the efficacy of chemotherapy. Trials were under way, but as yet, no data showed that drugs could reduce the rate of metastasis or increase the length of survival. To persuade him, DeVita took an unprecedented step—one only he as director of the NCI could take. He broke the code on a randomized national study of adjuvant chemotherapy for lung cancer before it reached completion. The two reviewed the results and concluded that the chemotherapy arm had a small, but definite, survival advantage. So Henry agreed to drug treatment after completion of radiation if tests indicated that his cancer had not yet spread.

Saul opposed chemotherapy. He considered it useless for lung cancer, just adding unnecessary toxicity and diminishing quality of life. This disagreement highlighted the chronic conflict between DeVita's and Rosenberg's approaches to cancer. For years they had argued about the intensity of chemotherapy required to cure Hodgkin's disease. Their individual stances carried over into every cancer they treated. This time the clash focused on Henry Kaplan. Rosenberg looked at the 90 percent death rate and asked, "Why add chemotherapy and make him miserable?" DeVita interpreted the same figures as a 10 percent cure rate and said, "Why not improve upon it with chemotherapy?" Rosenberg criticized DeVita for his insistence on what he considered ineffective, toxic therapy, and DeVita chided Rosenberg for trying to change Henry's mind about treatment. Rosenberg told DeVita that he was crazy to think anyone could ever change Kaplan's mind.

Seeking more objectivity, Kaplan turned to one of his prior students, John Minna, for advice. Minna had gone to the NCI, where he directed one of the largest lung cancer programs in the country. He had made significant scientific contributions, including detection of genetic abnormalities underlying lung cancer. He happened to be on his way to Stanford for his twentieth-year class reunion and had planned to call on his mentor, unaware of recent events. Checking into a hotel, he found an urgent message from Rosenberg. When they met outside the hospital, Rosenberg looked shaken. He took Minna to Kaplan's room and left. Kaplan wanted to speak with Minna alone.

Although Minna had cared for hundreds of patients with lung cancer, when he entered the hospital room, Kaplan's appearance startled him. "It was like seeing a wounded lion in a cage," he said. After inquiring about John's work, Kaplan asked his opinion about adjuvant chemotherapy for lung cancer. Minna could guess what his boss had advised: "Vince honestly believed that if he took Henry back to the NCI and treated him aggressively, he could cure him." Minna thought differently. Given the extent of tumor at surgery, he knew that it was highly likely that Kaplan already had undetected metastases, and in that case, chemotherapy would not extend his life. He sat at Kaplan's bedside and tried to refocus the conversation, asking what he wanted to get done over the next few months. The important question was how he could best be treated so that he could accomplish those things. For example, radiation could palliate his pain. This was not what Kaplan wanted to hear. He asked John to take some of his tumor back to the NIH and try to grow it so they could test its sensitivity to chemotherapy. "When I walked out of that room," Minna said, "it struck me that even if you're the greatest cancer specialist in the world, and you know all the facts, hope still springs eternal."

A week later, Henry Kaplan registered as a new patient in Radiation Oncology. Bagshaw arranged for him to be treated late in the afternoon to maintain his privacy. After the other patients were finished for the day, the doors to the treatment area were closed, and at 6:30 he walked in. A selected team delivered his therapy; other staff discreetly avoided eye contact. No matter how special his treatment, however, when Kaplan put on a gown, he became a patient. Tattoos marked his radiation field. And he followed the same routine as anyone else. He lay on the x-ray table and stared at the ceiling while a technician positioned the blocks. Pasted on it were pictures drawn by children with Hodgkin's disease, most of whom he had treated. The blocks in place, the door to the vault clicked shut. A soft buzz indicated that the machine had been turned on, and a sharp smell of ozone followed. In a few moments, the treatment ended, and the tech helped him off the table. Henry Kaplan had crossed over the imaginary line that separates well people from those with cancer. How poignant it was for this great man to be treated for a barely curable disease in the department he had built to cure cancer. The faculty he had trained were using the techniques and skills he had taught them. And he was depending on the linear accelerator he had invented three decades earlier, never imagining that it would one day provide his only hope.

Kaplan tolerated irradiation with minimal side effects. His appetite improved; his cough resolved. He considered himself in the recovery phase. After a month of therapy, he reached 4,000 rads—time to reassess the treatment plan. Bagshaw ordered a CT scan and brought it to the radiation therapy workroom to review. He had begun to examine the lung fields when he noticed a round spot in Kaplan's spine. He couldn't believe what he saw. It looked like a metastatic lesion in the bone. He called Norm Blank to take a look. For a long time, they stood staring at the film, trying to convince themselves that it wasn't true. On the prior scan, Kaplan's spine had been clear. The disease had progressed in just a few weeks. Bagshaw knew that lung cancer spread to bone, but he hadn't thought that would happen to Henry. He had considered him invincible. Kaplan had defied statistics when treating so many others, why not for himself? Blank shook his head; Bagshaw ran his fingers through his hair. They both knew that Henry would not survive.

That afternoon, when Leah saw Malcolm Bagshaw standing at the front door, she knew something was wrong. He usually appeared chipper. Today he gazed past her; his voice sounded weak. "He looked stricken," Leah recalled. She offered him coffee and cookies, but he declined. He got right to the point. Trying to lessen the blow, he told Henry that in reviewing the CT scan, he had seen a worrisome spot. Kaplan remained calm. "I knew it had to be something like this to bring you over to the house in the middle of the afternoon," he said. "So where do we go from here?" Bagshaw had arranged for a bone scan.

Later that day, when radiologist Ross McDougall came into the x-ray room to scan Kaplan's bones, he found Henry lying on the examination table with his eyes closed. "I'm a doomed man," he said, "and it's just terribly sad."

The scan looked dreadful—widespread bony disease. Henry and Leah were waiting in Bagshaw's office. Malcolm had difficulty composing himself when he gave Henry the results—essentially a death sentence. Then he left them alone so that they could pull themselves together before they had to walk through the Radiation Oncology Department and the Medical School on the way to their car. Henry took Leah's hands in his. "I'm just sorry I have to put you through this," he said.

45

Dying Adagio

Henry Kaplan began to prepare for the end. Throughout his life, he had never left an obligation untended, a task incomplete. A few years earlier, he had told Leah that he felt he was racing against time. He still had much he wanted to accomplish. Time had seemed limitless then; now it was finite. He knew that his life was marked in months, maybe weeks. He would not be able to finish what he had set out to do. He had not isolated the malignant cell in Hodgkin's disease; he had not found the human lymphoma virus; he had not seen mono-clonal antibodies come to fruition in treating cancer. He had to leave too many chapters unfinished.

Kaplan tried to reply to correspondence from fellow scientists; after all, he always had. "I have developed adenocarcinoma of the lung with spread to several bony sites," he wrote Karl Musshoff in Germany. "My health and strength are failing rapidly, and I do not think it will be possible for me to find the energy to look up the paper to which you referred." He began to cancel obligations. "Since the course of metastatic adenocarcinoma of the lung is usually quite rapid," he wrote Joseph Fortner, president of General Motors Cancer Research Foundation, "I doubt that I will be able to participate in . . . the Awards Assembly this coming year." He notified the Board of Governors at Ben Gurion University and the Weizmann Institute that he could no longer serve. He resigned as chairman of the Scientific Advisory Committee at Hadassah Medical Center. He would never see his beloved Israel again.

Then he turned his attention to the CBRL. "My cancer is no longer curable," he wrote them. "Large cell cancers of the lung . . . usually progress to a fatal outcome within a few months." Many had worked with him for most of their careers, and his departure put their positions in jeopardy. "The CBRL has always been my baby," he went on to say, "and I have felt very close to all of those who have worked along side me here. I am deeply distressed that I will not be able to continue to do so. . . . We have funding for approximately six months after my death, and this should provide everyone with a reasonable opportunity to look around for other suitable jobs. . . . Let me close by saying how proud I am of all of you and of all that we have been able to accomplish together." During the short time he had left, he tried to find jobs for as many of them as possible.

Finally, his patients had to be notified, their appointments rescheduled. Hundreds came yearly for follow-up visits; some were still on treatment. Kaplan didn't worry about their medical care: Rosenberg, Coleman, Donaldson, and Rich Hoppe would take over. But he didn't have the energy—physical or emotional—to say good-bye to them. He would never again put on his white coat, enter a clinic room, and examine a patient. He would never hear about a patient's trip or look at pictures of her children. He would no longer be a healer.

News that Henry Kaplan had metastatic cancer circulated quickly. Those who loved and revered him tried to let him know in whatever way they could. Many with whom he had sparred sought to resolve their differences, perhaps more for their own sakes than his. After years of estrangement, biochemist Arthur Kornberg, the Nobel laureate whom Kaplan had worked hard to recruit and then fought with over Robert Glazer's appointment as dean, stepped forward and tried to be a friend. His search for experimental biologic therapies touched Henry.

Relatives, friends, trainees, colleagues asked to visit, and although Henry was beginning to experience pain and fatigue, he turned no one away. People came in such numbers that Leah had to schedule visits so as not to exhaust Henry. After he had dressed, gone for radiation treatments, and chatted with his guests, he felt drained. Their home was starting to feel like a funeral parlor. She tried to steer the conversation toward the visitor—their work, family, travels. Invariably, however, the guest brought up remembrances—some good, some bad, all painful. Leah saw how uncomfortable many seemed, trying to express gratitude or make a confession. She had to change the scene. So she held open houses on Sundays and served wine and cheese. This gave people a chance to pay their respects while keeping the atmosphere festive.

Hundreds of people wrote to Kaplan. Among them were reminiscences from prior students and radiation therapy trainees, such as that from Joel Bookstein, a resident from the 1960s who had become a prominent vascular radiologist. After expressing his appreciation, he wrote: "Do you remember the time I approached . . . the back of the linear accelerator and got knocked flat by a 12-inch spark? I was also flattened once during a party at your home after walking into a glass wall." A postdoctoral fellow from Tehran, whose training Kaplan had funded himself, thanked his mentor one last time for his inspiration. "Most great achievements of man seem to originate from the greatness of spirit of their teachers," he wrote. "It is this which enables your followers to carry on your work and never let the torch fall." Notes from former staff evoked a myriad of memories, which together formed a collage of his life in the lab. Mary Brown Lawrence recalled the time they had gone to the San Francisco airport at 3 A.M. to pick up the colony of C-57 black mice. Others had a more serious tone. "You saved my life," wrote a research associate, recounting her bout with depression and how Kaplan had seemed to be the only person who cared.

Some spoke of his anti-war and human rights activism. Professor Merton Bernfield recalled Kaplan's speech on the Cambodian invasion when he had contrasted his "small victories" against Hodgkin's disease with the "wholesale slaughter" in Southeast Asia. "The message was clear to me," Bernfield wrote. "It is not enough to be content solely with pursuing scientific and medical 'truths'. One must speak out on other issues and make a commitment." Ginetta Sagan wrote to tell him that the new government of Argentina had just brought to trial several high-ranking officials responsible for the *desaparecidos*. This would not bring back the thousands who had been murdered, but, Sagan wrote, "it was efforts such as those you made at the International Cancer Congress in 1978 that generated the momentum on behalf of the victims that led to the indictment."

Prior Stanford presidents, Board members, and deans with whom Kaplan had clashed sent notes. They might have disputed his views, but they respected the man. Among them was Robert Glaser. "I have been distressed greatly by the problem that has confronted you," he wrote. "Despite the fact that I wasn't always able to respond to your requests when I was Dean, no one at Stanford . . . had greater regard for your skills as teacher, clinician and investigator than I."

Colleagues at Stanford rushed to honor Kaplan. He received the first Alvin Rambar Award honoring an outstanding, compassionate physician. His own department set up the Henry Seymour Kaplan Fund to support faculty and resident research. Dean Crowley announced the Henry Seymour Kaplan Professorship to be awarded to a senior scientist who would carry on his work in cancer biology. The finishing touch was to be an outdoor sculpture placed in front of the fountains at the medical center Kaplan had helped to build. In a letter to the faculty, Bagshaw called this sculpture "a tangible memorial which would serve as a constant reminder to those of us who will continue in the tradition he has established." Kaplan was asked to select the piece. He chose *Song of the Vowels* by Jacques Lipchitz, a preeminent cubist and one of the leading figures of twentieth-century sculpture. The seventeen-foot piece depicted twin harpists playing a song, composed only of vowels, which could subdue the forces of nature. With its theme of humanity's power to triumph over adversity, *Song of the Vowels* was a perfect piece to commemorate Henry Kaplan.

Asked in an interview a few weeks before his death how he would like to be remembered, Kaplan answered:

for my accomplishments that stand the test of time such as the work on Hodgkin's disease and malignant lymphomas . . . as the co-developer of the medical linear accelerator for cancer treatment . . . and for developing not just the machine but the standards for its use . . . as somebody who has been basically kind and deeply concerned about his patients, at the same time . . . as somebody who was tough enough to be willing to fight the battles. I'd also like to be remembered as somebody with a reasonably good sense of humor . . . and hopefully, as a good husband, a good father, and a loyal friend.

And then there were his patients. One by one, they learned of his illness. Chris Jenkins found out when he called to make his yearly appointment. Cured of his Hodgkin's disease, he had found his raison d'être—to help eliminate environmental causes of cancer. Chris felt heartsick; apparently there was no hope for this great man, who had never given up on him. Flying to Europe, Douglas Eads struck up a conversation with the man beside him to find he was a Stanford professor. When Eads told him that he had been treated at Stanford for Hodgkin's disease, the professor told him Henry Kaplan was gravely ill. Christine Pendleton had gone for her yearly checkup when she learned of Kaplan's situation. She was stunned and angry. "He had so much more to offer," she said. "I would have been willing to be in his place."

Henry Kaplan had given solace to so many patients, and now they were comforting him. John Korman of Saint Louis had just reached his fifth year in remission. "No other man on the face of this earth has personally touched my life as you have," he said. "I was a man on the brink of death's door. . . . I am now a living testimony . . . of your skilled art and true genius." Paul Kaufmann of San Francisco wrote, "The past 15 years have been a gift." He had lived to see his oldest daughter married and his youngest daughter enter Brown University. Dianne Kaufman-Darmady had recently given birth to a daughter, Ariel. She wrote that because of Dr. Kaplan, "I will be able to raise my baby, and God willing, watch her grow into a beautiful woman." Marty Tepper said his thoughts had turned to Dr. Kaplan as he listened to his oldest daughter chant from the Torah at her bat mitzvah. "You gave me hope when I had none," he wrote.

He received letters from parents whose children he had treated. Having just learned of Kaplan's situation, Leon Uris wrote: "I'm afraid I'm too shaken up to express myself. . . . What can a man say to a man who has given life to his son? My son and so many sons and daughters are indebted to you and will honor you by giving some of the things you have given. I say without shame that I love you very much. May God give you and your family comfort." And he received notes from people he hadn't treated himself but who had been cured by his therapies. "We've never met," Bob Jones wrote, "but you saved my life. . . . Your work allowed me to survive. . . . I never knew you, but I will always remember you." Ian Anderson of Palo Alto wrote: "You don't know me. I am one of the many thousands of Hodgkin's sufferers whose life has been spared due to your pioneering. . . . In this, your hour of need, I trust that you will take comfort in the realization that your research has meant so much for so many people."

In Kaplan's remaining weeks, those colleagues with whom he had worked closely came for the last time. From the day he learned of Henry's illness, Zvi Fuks called once or twice a week. He had difficulty sleeping; he kept remembering the time Henry had sought him out at the Art Institute of Chicago—the turning point in his life. He had returned to Jerusalem in the mid 1970s to head the Department of Oncology at Hebrew University–Hadassah Medical Center. Despite numerous obstacles, he had developed a first-rate program, lauded by Kaplan. When he flew from Israel to see his mentor, the change shocked him. Deep creases crossed Henry's face; the bones of his skull appeared more prominent. And he seemed to have shrunken. It was the only time in his life Fuks had seen Kaplan quiet. He kept saying, "It's sad." Fuks thought he knew what he meant: this was the end of the Henry Kaplan story at Stanford. He had not built a cancer center, and even the CBRL would probably be torn down some day to make room for another building. Henry didn't say these things outright; it hurt too much. He simply repeated, "It's very sad." Zvi said what he knew would be his last good-bye. "Then I went out," he said, "and I cried like a baby."

Eli Glatstein called often, but he sensed Henry wanted to see him. Kaplan had considered Glatstein his heir-apparent with regard to the lymphomas. He had the academic credentials: fifty-five publications, member of nine professional societies. An outstanding radiotherapist from a technical standpoint, Eli also cared deeply for patients. And he had Kaplan's daring. He had defended staging laparotomy and total lymphoid irradiation against tough critics. Kaplan felt comfortable entrusting his patients and the lymphoma trials to Eli.

Eli had seemed happy at Stanford. Then, in the spring of 1977, he had called Kaplan to say he had been offered two positions—chief of the Radiation Oncology Branch at the National Cancer Institute and chief of the Joint Center at Harvard. On a Friday evening, they had sat in Kaplan's living room reviewing the offers. After Kaplan had analyzed the pros and cons of these two prominent positions, he said, "I wish you wouldn't go. If it would help you to stay, I will step out of the clinic completely and let you handle all the lymphomas. Saul would probably like that." Eli couldn't reply; he had a catch in his throat. But he knew the time had come to leave Stanford, and eventually he accepted DeVita's offer. He always thought of himself as one of the Kaplan boys, however, and every year at Christmas, he sent Kaplan a large chocolate cheesecake.

Glatstein flew from Washington to Stanford, and the two spent an afternoon talking about their work and the people they had known. Only after Leah left the room did Henry reveal to Eli how bitter he felt about his fate. When Eli was leaving, Kaplan asked, "Have you got any advice, any words of wisdom?" Eli had asked Kaplan this same question on numerous occasions. He could only shake his head; he had none to give.

Robert Gallo found Kaplan's approaching death one of the toughest ordeals he had ever faced. Although he had the reputation of being brash and cocky, Gallo had depended on Kaplan for support. He felt lost. "Who would I talk to now?" he wondered. At first, all he could do was write: "I don't know how this will sound to you, but every time I look at one of my slides of a lymphocyte or a virus, I keep thinking about you. . . . I have probably been influenced by you as much as any scientist. I see your spirit, and I intuitively try to reach for it. . . . Henry, fight this with all of your might for the selfish reasons of people like me."

Eventually, Gallo came to California for a scientific meeting at which time he planned to visit Kaplan. But when he got there, he just couldn't face what he thought would be a deathbed scene. Tears came to his eyes thinking about it. "I just didn't have the courage to see him," he said. A few weeks later, Gallo forced himself to visit Kaplan. He prepared for the worst—this great scientist lying in bed, an uncomfortable few last words. Surprisingly, Gallo found the situation to be quite different. Henry was sitting in his den fully dressed. He talked matter-of-factly about what things would be like after his death—the medical school, the CBRL, cancer research. He asked Gallo if he would consider coming to Stanford as director of the CBRL. Gallo didn't know how to respond. In retrospect, he thought he should have said "possibly" or "I'm not sure," but he wanted to please Kaplan. So he said he said, "I'd be honored." Once he saw the relief on Kaplan's face, he couldn't retract his pledge. Gallo never did come to Stanford, and he struggled with his conscience for years.

Malcolm Bagshaw visited Kaplan regularly, but they didn't talk about the inevitable. For decades, they had met at four o'clock almost every afternoon with faculty and residents to discuss new cases. On Wednesday afternoons, they had conducted chart rounds, reviewing those undergoing treatment. Now they couldn't talk about Henry's fate, even though it stared them in the face. When Malcolm came to visit, he spoke about departmental affairs. He made pots of his famous spaghetti, always keeping the conversation light. Once, however, when Bagshaw was leaving, he could no longer control the feelings he had bottled up for weeks. Tears filled his eyes; he leaned over and kissed Henry on the forehead.

Saul Rosenberg, too, had great difficulty dealing with Kaplan's pending death. At fifty-five, Rosenberg had published two hundred articles and belonged to thirteen professional societies, including the prestigious Institute of Medicine. Awards and medals filled his bookshelves. Patients traveled hundreds of miles and sat in the waiting room for hours just to see him; many thought his very presence healing. A beloved mentor, he had instilled his exacting standards for research and insistence on clinical excellence into a generation of oncologists. Yet his melancholy eyes bespoke something missing. He had entered medicine seeking reverence and prestige, but as the years passed, the discordance between his accomplishments and unfulfilled needs had grown. And one need dominated all others—to be respected. Yes, his patients called him a prince, a saint. Yes, his trainees heaped adulation on him, dubbing him "SAR Superstar." Yes, he had garnered almost every honor bestowed upon an academic oncologist. But he needed more. He wanted respect and praise from Henry Kaplan—and that he never received.

Leah found Saul's visits uncomfortable because they were obviously painful for him. He didn't seem able to put his feelings into words. She knew Saul felt conflicted; his and Henry's had not been an easy relationship. For a while, they talked about a set of manuscripts on Hodgkin's disease that he and colleagues were writing in dedication to Kaplan. Other than that, there weren't many words between them. When Leah peeked into the room, she saw Saul sitting with a frozen half-smile on his face, as if he were waiting for Henry to say something. But he never said the things that Saul longed to hear—that he had enjoyed their years of working together, that he felt confident leaving the Hodgkin's trials in Saul's hands, that he was sorry for all the grief he had given Saul. Nothing. One day, about a week before her husband's death, Leah saw Saul take Henry's hand and kiss it. It was the first time she had ever seen them touch; it was the last time Saul saw Henry.

Most people, even Kaplan's colleagues, weren't comfortable acknowledging death and talked around the reality in front of them; DeVita didn't. Their relationship had always been foursquare, and Henry's approaching death didn't change it. Henry told him how sad he felt to be leaving the world at a time when things were going well scientifically. He spoke of his disappointments, of his bitterness toward certain people and events, especially over the cancer center failure. "To the end, he was Henry," DeVita said. Regarding his death, he told Vince he wanted to die quietly—no heroics, no hospitalizations with a medical team trying to keep him alive one more day. Eventually, DeVita had to return to Washington. Their parting was an emotional one. Their friendship, born of a mutual respect, had flourished with their zest for discovery, deepened with shared tragedy. These two men who had devoted their lives to the cure of cancer were being separated forever by the disease they had challenged.

And finally, Henry had to say goodbye to Michael Feldman. He had immediately written Michael when he developed metastases. His friend was grief-stricken. "I read your letter with profound sorrow and pain," he wrote back.

"How bitterly I will miss you ... you are literally irreplaceable." In January, Michael spent a week with Henry, helping him organize his papers and tie up the loose ends of his work. They sat by the pool and talked about science—how much they had done, yet how far they were from achieving what they'd set out to do. They talked of the sadness and irony that Henry was dying from the exact disease he had vowed to cure. Henry told Michael that he didn't fear death; he feared being alone. Most of the time, however, the two old friends reminisced about the things they had enjoyed together—a favorite restaurant, a painting that had driven them to a state of ecstasy, a barely known ruin they had explored. They both enjoyed life in a profound way. It was clear to Leah that in Michael, Henry found peace. Neither could imagine life without the other. Their final parting was heartbreaking.

One person who didn't visit or call was his brother Richard. Colleagues and friends flew from around the world to spend an hour with Henry. But his own brother, who lived only thirty miles away, didn't come, though he knew Hank was dying. The two hadn't spoken since their mother's death a year earlier. Richard was afraid to see Henry. Freed from the oppressive personalities of his mother and brother, he was proud to have created his own identity. But he still felt vulnerable, and he feared that facing his brother would destroy him. Instead, he wrote:

> Dear Hank:
>
> For several weeks, I have intended to write this letter. Procrastination, however soothing, can be its own form of decision, and that's not the decision I intended. ... Ours has been a complicated situation. I know that our rupture (a euphemism, I suppose) of some 22 years ago, has been a sore point for all. ... The break I made had to be made, indeed, should have been made sooner, and then perhaps it could have been done less violently and less totally. ... Because of my lifelong dependence on you, seeking your views and values, I was not able to have my own individuality. ... I had become too much like a satellite, and it took an explosion for me to leave that orbit.

Richard went on to express his conflicted feelings about Hank—"love and hate, admiration and envy, respect and contempt"—feelings that had haunted him throughout his life. In conclusion, he wrote:

> I could not have said this in person; it would have come out wrong. I do want you to know that I care a great deal for you. I also thank [you] for getting me out of my terrible situation as a kid in Chicago, for getting me out of the house, for helping me learn what my goals were and then helping me to follow them. ... You have always been strong. Be strong.
>
> My best wishes. And love,
> Dick

When Hank put the letter down, he wept. He knew he would never see his brother again.

Kaplan wanted to die at home. The process, however, was more difficult than he had anticipated. Each day he lost a little more of himself. He could measure his deterioration from the way his pants gathered at the waist and his sleeves hung loose at his wrists. His once booming voice faded to a whisper. He no longer enjoyed wine; he put aside his scientific journals. For weeks he had listened repeatedly to Mozart's Piano Concerto No. 21 in C Major. Now he wanted silence. And then there was the pain. Every day he faced the same choice—take enough narcotics to be pain-free, but barely able to think, or endure the pain and hope that for part of the day he would be free from it and have a lucid moment of enjoyment.

Leah tried to meet all her husband's needs. "Mother was a saint," Ann said. "She was everything—loving wife, nurse, confidante." When Henry was irritable and demanding, Leah handled him with grace. She had played the supporting role in his life, and she had played it well. She had never complained when he came home smelling of mice or announced that six Chinese scientists were joining them for dinner. She had never resented his travels or the hours holed up in his study, leaving her to deal with a caustic mother-in-law, a dyslexic child. She had met every challenge, given selflessly because she believed in her husband—and she loved him. But now she feared she couldn't hold on. The reality of her imminent loss hit her when Henry needed a hospital bed, and she had to move into Annie's old room. They would never sleep together again. Overwrought, Leah found herself in tears more than she wanted. Half of her was dying.

Ann spent more time at home. It had been easier for her to deal with her father's illness when she was working. She had briefs to prepare, court appearances, each day a set of tasks at which she was highly proficient. When she came home on weekends, she and her father talked about her cases. But after he developed metastases, all that changed. He started to withdraw. "I just sat and combed his hair," Ann said. She closed her eyes and tried to hold on to the image she had of her father prior to the cancer.

A few weeks before he died, Henry asked to speak with Annie alone. He told her how proud he was of her and expressed concern for Leah, not financially—he had seen to that—but emotionally. He said he didn't fear death; he had more concern about those left behind. And he had one final request: he wanted a grandchild. This puzzled Ann. Did her father want to be sure the Kaplan family didn't end with her and Paul? Or would the prospect of a grandchild give him a reason to keep living? She never asked.

Paul spent part of every day with his father. He had been planning to film a documentary in Israel when his father was diagnosed, but he put the project on hold. He did whatever his father asked with patience—adjusted the television, made calls, ran to the office for documents, or rushed to the pharmacy for more pain medication. "That period was one of crisis management," Paul recalled. "I lived a year in a minute."

Paul talked more with his father in the last weeks of his life than in all their years together. "He didn't talk about death," Paul said. "He talked about life." He told Paul that one could always wish for more time, yet he felt satisfied with what he had done. He warned Paul that he had identified too closely with him, comparing himself at thirty to his father at the end of a successful career. Henry said his beginnings had been humble. He was no genius, just persistent; he wasn't gifted, just lucky. And he knew his fame was fleeting; he would soon be just a footnote in some book. But he didn't feel cheated. On the contrary, he felt blessed because of Leah. He had been an intense, unpleasant young man, whom she had humanized. Without her, life would not have been worth living. He knew he was dying, yet, an inveterate atheist, he didn't wish to invoke a god now. "He believed life was for living," Paul said, "and if anything came after that, he was prepared to be puzzled and surprised."

But dying was more difficult than he thought; he didn't just close his eyes and drift away. This obstacle course called the terminal state wasn't so simple to maneuver. Hiccups plagued him, each jolt racking him with pain. He craved certain foods, then felt too nauseated to eat. Getting up to go to the bathroom or shower proved an ordeal. Though Leah had counseled grieving families, and Henry had cared for many dying patients, they were floundering. Leah, Paul, and Ann were almost at their wits' end when Norm Coleman and Maureen O'Hara joined the family circle.

Norm had called Leah to make an appointment, as had other faculty. At first, he and Henry talked about work—a grant that had just gotten funded, a complex case—but they easily slipped into topics no one else had broached with Kaplan—how one controls symptoms, such as pain and fatigue, and how people with cancer die. Norm spoke openly. Listening, Leah felt relieved. Everyone else had avoided these subjects, but they didn't fluster Norm. Leah invited him back.

Within a short time, Norm and Paul became close friends, like the brothers neither had. They both enjoyed jokes, especially puns. Although Henry rolled his eyes in mock disgust at their banter, their relationship pleased him and Leah. Norm appreciated Paul's sensitivity and intuition—how he wheeled his father around the house, showing him the art he loved, the sun glimmering on the pool, the row of olive trees he had planted around the perimeter of their property twenty years earlier. He anticipated his father's needs, knowing just how to massage his legs to break the cramps. "Paul Kaplan is one of the most magnificent people I have ever met," Coleman said years later. And the Kaplan family fell in love with Norm. He tackled problems with honesty and good humor.

Kaplan still received palliative radiation for his bone pain. As he shuffled into the treatment vault, silence prevailed, as if everyone was afraid to breathe. Once Norman got involved, however, things changed. He didn't hesitate to joke. "It wasn't a funeral yet," he said. Once when Kaplan was being positioned for treatment, the technician didn't get out of the way of the mobile table and got caught between the accelerator and Kaplan's head. She was obviously embarrassed. "I guess you're caught between a rock and a hard place," Coleman said. All three laughed. Leah was touched to see how gentle Norm was with Hank. He waited for Henry at the radiation department and walked or wheeled him out to the parking lot. Leah noticed how he always protected her husband's head with his hand as he helped him into the car.

Coleman rode his bike over to the Kaplans' home daily. He usually found Henry dressed and sitting out on the deck reading. Kaplan wanted to hear about Stanford activities. "He didn't talk much about himself," Norm said. He tried to optimize each day by giving Kaplan a goal. "Let's see if we can get you on your feet today," he said after he had changed the pain regimen. Henry was delighted he could take three steps. Other days weren't as good. He tried to talk about science but just couldn't. "It wasn't for lack of interest," Coleman said. "It's just that his sails were luffing a bit."

Maureen O'Hara knew she needed to get involved the day Rosenberg asked her how to order an eggshell mattress; Dr. Kaplan thought it might make him more comfortable. "He must mean an egg-crate mattress," she replied. "I'll get one." This request made two things clear to Maureen: First, Dr. Kaplan must be close to bedridden if he was asking for this mattress designed to prevent bedsores. Second, he was trying to direct his own care, and he wasn't doing a very good job of it. He needed a nurse. When she left the mattress for him, she attached a note offering her help. The next day Leah called.

Assessing the situation, Maureen realized Dr. Kaplan didn't get proper pain control because he took narcotics only when the pain became unbearable; he hadn't thought of preventing pain by taking medication around the clock. Next, she suggested ways to preserve his energy. He became exhausted just going to the bathroom, so she suggested a urinal. She arranged home nurses to relieve Leah, Paul, and Ann so that they could spend good time with him and let someone else do the nursing. She ordered a recliner so that he could sit in the den with his family. At one point, Kaplan told her how hard it had become to take a shower and how he longed to wash his hair. "No problem," Maureen said. "We have special trays so we can wash a patient's hair in bed."

"You nurses have everything," he said. "You've done more to make me comfortable in ten minutes than all my physician friends have in months."

"That's because this is nursing, not doctoring," she replied. "Nurses deal with symptom management. That's our bag."

"For the first time in my life," Kaplan said, "I understand the difference." Their relationship was an easy one with no sense of embarrassment. At times Maureen knew Kaplan was suffering, but he never complained. He did confide in her how difficult it was to watch himself deteriorate physically. Then he changed the subject.

Dying was the hardest thing Henry Kaplan had ever done. Intensely independent, starting at the age of sixteen, when he became the man of the family, he had spent his life doing for others. Now he had to ask others to do those things he had taken for granted, like bathing or cutting his food. He was slowly slipping away. "The weight loss became more and more dramatic," Paul said. "The only thing that didn't shrivel along with his body was his will. It would submerge quite often, then reemerge as an expression in his eyes, on his face, an occasional joke." Weakness eventually confined him to bed. Paul had to lift him from his bed to the recliner in the den. It was a poignant moment; Henry had done the same for his father. "Here was the strongest, most dynamic man I'd ever known," Paul said, "and I was carrying him around like a sack of groceries."

By the end of January, barely four months after his diagnosis, Henry had finished his arrangements and said good-bye to friends and colleagues. "He began closing doors," Coleman said, "so I knew he was near the end." Leah, Ann, Paul, Norman, and Maureen tended to him in his final days. His pain intensified; his respiration became labored. The family sat by, wishing for his sake that each breath was his last, hoping for theirs that it wasn't. The family worked hard to let this man who had been in control his entire life remain so until the end. He had seen many people die, and he knew how he wanted to go. "I lived my life with dignity," he told Leah. "I want to die with dignity."

February 4, 1984, was a beautiful day—sunny with the cloudless, azure sky Henry Kaplan loved. Leah and Paul took him outside to enjoy the morning. He said it was his day to die. He gathered his family about him for a last embrace. Then he wanted to be alone with Leah. Paul carried him back into the bedroom, and Leah closed the door. The end came quickly.

Epilogue

News of Henry Kaplan's death circulated worldwide. "Dr. Henry S. Kaplan Is Dead at 65: Aided in Cure of Hodgkin's Disease," read a headline in *International Herald Tribune*. "Dr. Kaplan, Cancer-Fighter, Is Dead," began an article in the *New York Times*. The *Washington Post, Jerusalem Post, Boston Globe*, and other newspapers around the world published similar announcements. His obituary appeared in *Time*. President Ronald Reagan sent a cable to be read at the Third International Summit on Leukemia and Lymphoma. "We are heartened and encouraged by the advances that can be made when the best scientists of great nations work together," he wrote. "It is also a fitting occasion to pay tribute to Henry S. Kaplan who gave so much of his life to the conquest of this disease."

Scientists, colleagues, patients, and friends mourned his death. Leah received hundreds of condolence notes and telegrams, including those from the Institut Pasteur in Paris, the Royal College of Radiologists in London, and almost every major international cancer institute. She opened mail with embossed letterheads of the United States Senate, the Consulat général de France, and the United Nations. The Church of Saint Bernadette in Omaha, Nebraska, wrote they had offered several masses for Dr. Kaplan.

For Leah, however, the most poignant letters came from patients. She considered them the living expression of her husband's work. She received cards signed "a grateful mother" or "a soon to be grandmother." She read the names of sons and daughters—Jeff, Christopher, Roberta, Dena, David—diagnosed as children—whose parents, once heartbroken and desperate, could now rejoice as they reached adulthood. Each letter related a special story: a family kept together because of Henry Kaplan; the Stanford undergraduate who went on to attend Harvard Medical School; the Claremont College student now a practicing oncologist; the teen who had become a law professor and served in the Carter administration. It wasn't just that Dr. Kaplan had cured them, they said; he had treated them with kindness and respect. Always honest about the cancer and its prognosis, he had instilled in them the will to survive.

~~

In the two decades since Kaplan's death, the management of Hodgkin's disease has continued to evolve. Although the Stanford lymphoma team remains a major voice, the endeavor to eradicate this disease has become even more global, just as Kaplan wished. Significant contributions have come from Milan, Amsterdam, Cologne, Vancouver. And the names of the key players have changed: Sandra Horning, Volker Diehl, Richard Hoppe, Peter Mauch, Joachim Yahalom, Patrice Carde, and Harald Stein now lead the conferences, conduct the signal trials.

Today almost 85 percent of those afflicted with Hodgkin's disease are cured. For children, the figure has reached over 90 percent. Before long, the goal of near universal cure with minimal long-term effects will likely be reached. Much of the credit belongs to Henry Kaplan for his seminal accomplishments: development of a linear accelerator, design of curative radiation fields, setting standards for clinical trials, and initiation of the multidisciplinary approach.

But Henry Kaplan's story doesn't end with Hodgkin's disease. His work has served as a model for the treatment of many other cancers. In the end, this is his legacy. As a result of his efforts, hundreds of thousands afflicted with cancer around the world will survive. They are his immortality.

Source Notes

Abbreviations

cv	curriculum vitae
HD	Henry S. Kaplan, *Hodgkin's Disease* 2nd ed
HSKP	Henry S. Kaplan papers (SC317) Stanford University Archives
LKP	Leah Kaplan personal files
LMA	Lane Medical Archives, Lane Medical Library, Stanford University School of Medicine
MR	Medical record, Department of Radiation Oncology, Stanford University Hospital
OCHD	"Obstacles to the Control of Hodgkin's Disease"
SA	Spyros Andreopoulos, "A Conversation with Henry Kaplan" (1984 interview)
SA2	"Reinventing the Stanford Medical School"
SSHD	Symposium: Staging in Hodgkin's Disease
SU	Stanford University School of Medicine, *The First Hundred Years*
VTD	Vince T. DeVita's personal files

Interviews

AD	Alain Declève		DN	Del Nord
AE	Alan Epstein		DR	David Rytand
AG	Avram Goldstein		DS	Donald Seldin
AK	Arthur Kornberg		EC	Eve Culberg
AKS	Ann Kaplan Spears		ED	Ernest DeVita
AR	Annunziata Radicchi		EF	Emil Frei III
CE	Claire Edes		EG	Edward Gilbert
CJ	Chris Jenkins		EJG	Eli J. Glatstein
CNC	C. Norman Coleman		EL	Edward Laden
CP	Christine Pendleton		ELG	Edward L. Ginzton
CR	Clayton Rich		ER	Ernest Rosenbaum
CSP	Carol S. Portlock		FD	Frederic de Peyster
CVE	Carl von Essen		GB	Gita Braude
DE	Douglas Eads		GC	George Canellos
DG	Don Goffinet		GK	Gladys Kirkman
DK	David Korn		GS	Ginetta Sagan

HA	Herb Abrams	MMV	Mary Murray Vidal
HH	Halsted Holman	MO	Maureen O'Hara
HI	Helen Issacs	MT	Maurice Tubiana
HJ	Henry Jones	MW	Mitchell Weissbluth
HL	Harry Lebeson	NC	Norman Crocker
HS	Herbert Schwartz	NS	Norman Shumway
HT	Herb Trace	NT	Nelson Teng
IL	Irwin Linn	PB	Paul Berg
ILW	Irving L. Weissman	PC	Paul Carbone
IW	Isabel Walker	PK	Paul Kaplan
JA	James Arseneau	PP	Philip Pizzo
JB	Joan Bull	RA	Robert Alway
JBM	James B. Mark	RC	Robert Chase
JD	Jan DiJulio	RCG	Robert C. Gallo
JE	John Earle	RD	Rose Dockterman
JFH	James F. Holland	RFK	Robert F. Kallman
JG	John Glick	RG	Robert Glaser
JH	Jacob Haimson	RJL	Robert J. Lukes
JHM	John H. Moxley	RK	Richard Kaplan
JI	Joseph Izenstark	RL	Ronald Levy
JK	Joseph Kriss	RLi	Robert Linn
JL	Joyce Lawson	RS	Robert Schimke
JM	John Minna	RTG	Ruth T. Gross
JMM	John M. Molendyk	SAR	Saul A. Rosenberg
JU	John Ultmann	SD	Sarah Donaldson
JW	John Wilson	SDS	Sir David Smithers*
KO	Kent Osborne	SMS	Samuel M. Strober
LC	Lawrence Crowley	SR	Steven Rosen
LK	Leah Kaplan	SS	Shirley Shanker
MAB	Malcolm A. Bagshaw	TT	Tran Tuyet
MB	Marsha Bieber	TW	Todd Wasserman
MBL	Mary B. Lawrence	VD	Vincent T. DeVita, Jr.
MC	Max Crocker	VP	Vera Peters
MD	Mary Kay DeVita	WC	William Creger
MF	Michael Feldman	WP	Wendy Podwalny
ML	Miriam Lieberman	ZF	Zvi Fuks
MLi	Muriel Linn		

Prologue

"Hodgkin's disease survivors": *San Jose Mercury News*, May 8, 1982. event: IW, JD, MO, SD, SAR. "Maureen, this is": MO. "The patients looked": JD. "I was treated": JD. "Remember me": JD. "You've got to come": JD. "Mr. Wonderful": EJG. "He didn't think": EJG. "There was such": MO. "Every cancer patient": Kennedy, "Welcome," May 8, 1982, HSKP. "I guess you": ibid. "Kaplan boys": CNC. "It was like": JD. "HSK had a":

*Interview conducted by Todd Wasserman

EJG. "Moby Dick": LK. "For all their": CNC. cocktail party talk: SA2. treatment of baby: SA2. "living autopsies": EJG. "Without the patients": *Friends of Radiology News Letter,* Summer 1982. "Radiologists had an almost": *Stanford MD,* Fall 1982. "burning bodies": author. "Today about 40%": *Stanford MD,* Fall 1982. "survivors of trench": DeVita, "On the Treatment of Hodgkin's Disease," May 8, 1982, HSKP. "He was different": Shapiro 2000, 143. "Twenty years ago": *Friends of Radiology News Letter,* Summer 1982. "awful": SAR. "It's a measure": *Stanford MD,* Fall 1982. "I am happy": Murray-Vidal, "A Patient's Perspective," May 8, 1982, HSKP. "From the very": ibid. "My first chemotherapy": ibid. "I'm not sure": *Friends of Radiology News Letter,* Summer 1982. "That reception was": SAR. "It was like": MO. "I'm a survivor": LK. "Do you know": MO. "Twenty-five years": *Peninsula Times Tribune,* May 1982. "It never left": LK.

1. Morbid Appearances

Hodgkin's life: Foxon 1966; Hale-White 1924; Hancock 1963; Hardwick 1966; Hill 1966; Kass 1966; Kass and Kass 1988; Wilks 1909. "sweetly docile" and "extremely volatile": Kass and Kass 1988, 4. "thou and thine": Hardwick 1966, 255. "At the beginning": Abel-Smith 1964, 1. Guy's: Abel-Smith 1964; Handler 1976; Kass and Kass 1988; Ober 1973. "Guy's alone of all": Ober 1973, ix. "King Harrison": Kass 1966, 276. "In the 1820's": Abel-Smith 1964, 1. "With the arrival": Foxon 1966, 251. "To connect accurate": ibid., 252. "I quickly perceived": Hill 1966, 284. description of Hodgkin's disease: Hodgkin 1937. "equalling in size": ibid., 742. "rose-red lump" and "testicle": ibid., 747. "an infinite number": ibid., 748. "from that of" and "semi-cartilaginous hardness": ibid., 751. "All these cases": ibid., 751–52. "The morbid alterations": ibid., 741. "A pathological paper": ibid., 759. "affection": ibid., 741. "To those who": Hill 1966, 300. "This resignation was": Wilks 1909, 532. "pitiful": Kass and Kass 1988, 432. Hodgkin's friendship with Montefiore: Kass and Kass 1988; Rosenbloom 1921. "To one so guileless": Hardwick 1966, 261.

2. Arrogant Ancestors

Russian Jews: Greenberg 1976; Sachar 1958. Brilliant family: AKS, LK, MC, PK, RK. "red-headed *frimayeh*": RK. "mental strain": MC. "Russian youngsters got": MC. "people torn in two": Sachar 1958, 248. "There was always": MC. "Throughout her life": LK.

3. Diagnosing Hodgkin's Disease

"extensive disease of": *HD,* 3. "One or two": Wilks 1856, 131–32. "It must take": ibid., 63. Reed's life: Conway 1992, 171–99; Zwitter et al. 2002. autopsy: Reed 1902, 157–66. "a chestnut to": ibid., 158. "It is seventy years": ibid., 133–34. Reed's work on Hodgkin's disease: Conway 1992, 171–99; *HD*; Rather 1972; Reed 1902; Zwitter et al. 2002. "During the first": Reed 1902, 144. "a peculiar type": Simonds 1926, 395. "The clinical histories": Reed 1902, 140–41. "little difficulty": ibid., 155. "No therapeutic measure": ibid., 144. "The large giant cells": ibid., 151–52. "a peculiarly characteristic": Rather 1972, 944. "great opposition": Conway 1992, 192. "May 30, the very": ibid., 193. "Virtually all of": *HD,* 12.

4. Growing Up Brilliant

Maxwell Street: Berkow 1977. "Life in Chicago": MC. "In my family": MC. "king of mushrooms": RK. Brilliant family: DN, EC, LK, MC, PK, RD. Kaplan family: CE, EC, RD, RK. "Nathan was a sweet": CE. "always a smile": CE. Nathan and Sarah: CE, EC, MC, RD, RK. "Everyone around us": RD. *Zinu*, "adorable son": LK, RD. young Henry: CE, EC, LK, RD, RK. "She ached so": DN. "mental strain": MC. "She was a self-centered": DN. portrait of Henry: RK. "She would be": RK. "Take that off": LK. "She always felt": CE. "Dirty boys": LK. "He didn't have": MC. Richard: LK, RC, RD, RK. "He's perfect": RK. "Why should you": RK. "Throw that kid": LK. "Brat": RK. "You're an idiot": RK. "such a sweet": RD. Sarah's love for son: CE, DN, LK, RK. "You can't understand": RK. "She pushed him": CE. Hawthorne Place, grade school: EC, JI, LK, RK. "Mrs. Hayes, our": HT. Kalom family: CE, EC, MC, RK. high school years: AKS, HT, JI, LK, MC, PK, RK. "Hymie Einstein": RK. "His favorite word": RK. "I think the gentleness": DN. "You could feel": Bird 1966, 22. "Everyone knew of someone": ibid., 23. fights: LK, RK. "He's such a nice": RK. "Even five or ten": RK. "I virtually can't": RK. Nathan's illness: ibid. Sarah bought pharmacy: EC, LK, MC, RD. "it was the thing": RK. letters from Nathan: personal files of Richard Kaplan. "In those days": RK. Nathan's death and funeral: EC, RD, RK. "It was one": RK. "Someday I'm going": RK.

5. Roentgen's Rays

"No therapeutic measure": Reed 1902, 144. "extirpate so thoroughly": Yates and Bunting 1917, 748. early treatment of Hodgkin's disease: *HD*; Utz and Keatinge 1931; 1932. Roentgen: Dewing 1962; Streller 1973. "Sensational discovery": Dewing 1962, 31. "the marvelous triumph": Bleich 1960, 4–5. "In all probability": ibid., 7–8. "According to the good": ibid., 10. history of radiation: Brecher 1969; Buschke 1970; Dewing 1962; *HD*. "a mass of glands": Pusey 1902, 168. "I prescribed": Senn 1903, 666. "The eminent success": ibid., 668. "The prescription of": Dewing 1962, 110. health hazards of x-rays: Bleich 1960.

6. A Spartan Existence

Chicago winter of 1934: *Chicago Tribune*, Dec. 2, 6, 12, 1934; Chandler 1970; Cromie 1984. "Hawk": Berkow 1977, 1. "dismal decade": Cromie 1984, 119. "1000 men eating in bread lines": Chandler 1970, 45. New York Life Insurance to Sarah Kaplan, Dec 24, 1934, Richard Kaplan personal files. Nathan's estate: RK. Sarah talked of suicide: RK. "childhood vanished overnight": PK. Sarah and pharmacy: CE, LK, NC, RD, RK. "She was a woman": MC. "He's my rock": IL. "I gave her": RD. "She was a sharp": MC. "She spoke of Walgreens": RK. "I remember people": RD. "Hey, that's a real gun": RK. "He must be": Murphy 1976, 163. Hank at University of Chicago: EL, IL, NC, RK. "ten brightest freshmen": *Chicago Daily News*, Nov. 3, 1934. Henry stood fourth: ibid. Hank with friends: IL, MLi, NC, RLi. "six-way elitist conversation": NC. "We'd listen to": MLi. "Of course if you": IL. "didn't know a lamb": MLi. "If you needed": RLi. "He didn't allow": IL. "Hank wasn't very": RK. "he was going": RK. "I brought him": NC. "Mercedes of the twenties": NC. "I liked Hank": RK. "Hank went out": NC. "Hi, Stinky": NC. University of Chicago Medical School: Harvey 1981, 343–57. "he knew the answers": FD. curriculum, classmates: EL, FD. "It was as": FD. "going into the district": FD. Abe Braude and Hank: EL, GB, LK, NC. "Those two or three": Kaplan to Braude, Gita Braude personal files. Leah: DN, LK, RK, RLi. "Hello, I'm Leah": LK.

7.   The Courtship of Leah Lebeson

Leah Lebeson's life: HL, LK, SS. "I don't love": Kaplan to Braude, Gita Braude personal files. "blood money": LK. "was like crossing": RK. "When I first": LK. "the bear that": LK. "Sisters Karamazov": LK. "They were two": NC. "Mr. Lebeson's got": RLi. "I told him": NC. Leah and Hank's relationship: NC, SS. "Hank and Leah": NC. internship: EL. "If you planned": EL. "local anesthesia": LK. "Leah, let's get": LK. "So, how are": RK. Sarah's reaction: LK, RK. Lebeson met Kaplan: DN, HL, SS. "I often thought": SS. "Dad, Hank and I": LK. Harry's reaction: HL, IL, MLi. "But I liked": HL. "Look, we've quite": HL. the wedding: DN, LK, SS. "the three wise men": LK. "He just loves": IL. "My mother understands": LK.

8.   Headway with Hodgkin's Disease

"These significant differences": Craft 1940, 405. types of Hodgkin's disease: Jackson and Parker 1944a, 1944b, 1947. progress in radiation therapy: Brecher 1969; Buschke 1970; Kaplan 1979. crossfiring: Brecher 1969, 294. Schreiner and Mattick study: Schreiner and Mattick 1924. total body irradiation: Medinger and Craver 1942. "all wandering malignant": ibid., 651. Gilbert's strategy: Gilbert 1939. "This is a question": ibid., 215. "It is impossible": Merner and Stenstrom 1947, 362.

9.   The Fledgling Investigator

life in Minnesota: LK, RK. "May I come": LK. Kaplan to his mother: letters dated Jan 14–Aug 10, 1943, LKP. "Eat hearty": LK. "It gave me": RK. "Sometimes I feel": LK. "It doesn't make": LK. mice experiments: Kirschbaum and Kaplan 1944. "We published some": Kaplan to Astin, Aug 2, 1972, HSKP. "I knew it": LK. Hugh Wilson: HJ, JK. "His manner in": Kaplan to Evens, Dec 10, 1970, HSKP. "education by scarification": ibid. "Jewish, but a": HJ. "Henry won more": ibid. L. C. Strong: Kaplan to Astin, Aug 2, 1972, HSKP. "L. C. Strong's mouse house": MAB. "When I arrived": SA. "He was so excited": LK. inbred mice, C57 blacks: MBL, SA. lymphomas arose in thymus: Kaplan 1947. spread of lymphomas in mice: Kaplan 1948. "These findings are": ibid., 196. social life: DS, HJ, LK. "If there's a revolution": HJ. "cultural binge": LK.

10.   The Unlikely Aftermath of Mustard Gas

Bari incident: DeVita and Chu 2008; Hersh 1968, 7–8; Krakoff 1994; Stockholm International Peace Research Institute 1970. toxicities of mustard gas: Hersh 1968, 47–8; Wachtel 1941, 228–32; U.S. Office of Civilian Defense, 1943, 8–14; Great Britain, War Office, 1941, 16–26. "so thickened that": Wachtel 1941, 230. story of *Bisteria*: Stockholm International Peace Research Institute 1970, 148–9. smell of garlic: Waitt 1942, 53. "Never take some": Waitt 1942, vi. sulfur mustard: Wachtel 1941, 221. irritant properties: Jacobs 1942, 31. "a drop the size": U.S. Office of Civilian Defense, 1943, 8. first mustard attack: Waitt 1942, 19–20. "run in the gutters": ibid., 21. 400,000 casualties: Stockholm International

Peace Research Institute 1970, 2–10. treaty outlawing use: Hersh 1968, 6. rationale for Gilman and Philips work: Gilman and Philips 1946. effects of mustard explosion at Bari on lymphoid tissue: ibid.; DeVita and Chu 2008. "These studies revealed: Gilman and Philips 1946, 409. anal and penile cancers: Adair and Bagg 1931. "We believe that": ibid., 199. case of L.W.: Goodman et al. 1946. "The face and neck": ibid., 127–28. meeting at Gibson Island: Moulton 1947. "After a few": ibid., 4. "The efficiency of": ibid., 314. "The use of these": ibid., 346.

11. The Stanford Wooing

"Henry had barely": LK. history of Stanford medical school: Harvey 1981; Lane 1862, 1870; Nagel 1970; Rixford 1913, 1932, 1933; SU; Whitfield 1949. "diploma mills": Whitfield 1949, 48. "We are glad": Whitfield 1949, 103–4. "a bit of ": HA. "elegant and modern": Pacific Art Company, 1905, 60. Lane Hospital ca. 1948: HJ, JK; SA. Henry Garland: HJ, JK, RFK; SA. "wooing": LK. "It could be": LK. "Not only is Hoover": LK. "If you want": LK. "It seems to": Garland to Kaplan, Feb 12, 1948, HSKP. "I have suggested": ibid. "We are confident": Chandler to Kaplan, Mar 26, 1948, HSKP. list of requirements: Kaplan to Chandler, Apr 3, 1948, HSKP. "It has been": ibid. "I am definitely": Wilson to Kaplan, Feb 11, 1948, HSKP. "a parochial, rather": AG. "I [am] excited": Kaplan to Wilson, Feb 20, 1951, HSKP. Garland's pledge: HJ, JK, RFK.

12. The Outsider

Stanford Hospital: DR, JK, WC; SU. "To X-ray and Zander": DR. original radiation department: HA, HJ, MBL, RFK; SA2. "bare wires, carrying": SA2, 14. "I had more": SA2, 14. "a disgrace": SA. "The only thing": SA. "major-domo": CVE. "You could only": CVE. Kaplan's lab: MBL, RFK; SA. "Work was his": MBL. request for cancer ward: Kaplan to Chandler Mar 26, 1948, HSKP. Bloomfield rounds: DR, HA, JK, WC; Rytand 1984. "the Professor": Nagel 1970, 87. "He was coldly": Rytand 1984, 51. "You could set": JK. "In freshly donned": Rytand 1984, 16. "Let us rather": Nagel 1970, 82. Kaplan at grand rounds: DR, HA, LK, WC. "deference was not": HA. "an outsider": DR. "Bless him": WC. "Gentlemen, radiology": LK. Henry Garland: CVE, HA, HJ, LK, RFK; SA. "his brain and": HA. "There was no": HA. "Go upstairs": HA. "tend to result": Garland to Kaplan June 2, 1953, HSKP. "Look what the": LK. "He was capable": HA. "mouse radiologist": JK. "malignant son-of-a-bitch": HJ. Kaplan ignored Garland: SA. "He was snide": LK. "the professor from Palestine": RFK. "It is well-known": JK. "There aren't enough": Leah to Sarah, undated, LKP. infertility problem: LK. radiation exposure: MBL. "The damn things": MAB. "Had it not": HJ. renovation: HA, HJ; SU. "The next time": Kaplan to Rigler June 27, 1949, HSKP. Henry Jones: CVE, DR, HA; SA; SU. "shortly after you": Kaplan to Jones Aug 4, 1953, HSKP. new faculty: HJ; SA; SU. "that a nurse": MBL. Kaplan's lab: CVE, HA, MBL; SA. "He was a": CVE. "He just couldn't": HA. "He was like": CVE. HSK: MBL. "there are 28,000": SA. "There wouldn't even": MBL. thymic lymphomas: Kaplan 1948; Kaplan 1952. shielded parts of body: Kaplan and Brown 1951. transplanted thymus glands: Kaplan, Hirsch and Brown 1956. systemic factor: Kaplan 1959. "I used to think": RFK. "He had that rare": MBL. first child: AKS, LK. "She's perfect": LK. "good-old-boy cronyism": AG. "A chummy family": AG. "an Eastern aggressiveness": DR. "a good citizen": DS. "He was a giver": CNC. "a man to be": HA.

13. Vera Peters: Daring to Cure Hodgkin's Disease

Peters's paper: Peters and Middlemiss 1958. life of Vera Peters: VP; Sutcliffe and Gospodarowicz 1994. "Quite apart from": www.caro-acro.ca. "Mom will never": VP. Gilbert's treatment plan: Gilbert 1939. "You can never": VP. "I enjoyed every": VP. survival data: Peters 1950. "I was fascinated": VP. staging system: Peters and Middlemiss 1958. "He sat in": VP. "In light of": Peters 1950. "The reasons for": Shimkin et al. 1955, 145. "The figures are": ibid., 150. "It has been": Peters and Middlemiss 1958, 114. "If indicated, segmental": ibid., 119. prophylactic radiation: Peters and Middlemiss 1958. "The former prevailing": Peters 1973, 119. "They all rushed": VP. "He was very": VP. "Clinically localized Hodgkin's": Brown and Kaplan 1975. "Although the staging": *HD*, 558. "Peters was the": ibid., 368. woman with large mass: HA. Kaplan heard of atom smasher: SA2.

14. The Cancer-Killing Cannon

three events: TW. radiation in early 1900s: Bleich 1960; *HD*; Henry S. Kaplan, "Experimental Frontiers in Radiation Therapy of Cancer," HSKP; Kaplan 1979. "The early x-ray": HD, 366. nuclear physics: JH; Ginzton, Mallory and Kaplan 1957. "a vestige of": Bleich 1960, 344. megavoltage radiation: JH; Bleich 1960; Brecher and Brecher 1969; Ginzton, Mallory and Kaplan 1957; *HD*; HS Kaplan and EL Ginzton, "Some Considerations of the Potential Usefulness and Design of Linear Electron Accelerators for Medical Applications," HSKP; Schulz 1975. "magnificent monster": Schulz 1975, 547. cost of radium: *San Francisco Examiner*, Oct 13, 1957. "shotgun": SA2, 21. history of radar: Boot and Randall 1976; Bowen 1987; Page 1962; Swords 1986. klystron: Ginzton and Nunan 1985; *Stanford University Campus Report*, Aug. 26, 1987. magnetron: Boot and Randall 1976. postwar development of linear accelerators: JH, MW. Ginzton's work: ELG; Ginzton and Nunan 1985. how linear accelerator works: JH; Ginzton and Nunan 1985; Kaplan and Bagshaw 1957. Kaplan heard of atom smasher: Ginzton and Nunan 1985; SA2. "You could accelerate": SA. Ginzton and Kaplan built accelerator: ELG; Ginzton and Nunan 1985; Ginzton speech at Kaplan memorial service, HSKP. funding problems: Kaplan and Ginzton, "Some Considerations of the Potential Usefulness and Design of Linear Electron Accelerators for Medical Applications," HSKP; SA2. "It took us": SA2, 20. British organization to build accelerator: Ginzton and Nunan 1985; Newbery and Bewley 1955. "I was interested": SA. "junior-sized": *San Jose Mercury News*, Jan 10, 1954. "Ed's passport": LK. design of Stanford accelerator: ELG; Ginzton speech at memorial service, HSKP; MAB; *Stanford University News*, July 15, 1952. "I wish I could": Kaplan to Wilson, Oct 22, 1952, HSKP. Stanford vs. British effort: JH. "This has never": Ginzton speech at memorial service. description of accelerator: *San Francisco Examiner*, Apr 27, 1956; *Stanford University Bulletin*, Aug 15, 1956; *Stanford University News*, Apr 27, 1956; Weissbluth et al., 1959. "Atom Cannon Will": *Los Angeles Examiner*, Jan 10, 1954. "Office-Size A-Smasher": *Los Angeles Times*, Jan 10, 1954. problems moving accelerator: SA2. "Our linear accelerator": Kaplan to Horecker, July 14, 1955, HSKP. "Something was being": JK. story of Gordon Issacs: HI; MR; SA. getting machine ready: MW; SA. "I don't think": SA2, 21. "When the doctors": ELG. "The lesion at": MR. "The mother states": MR. "We were deeply": ELG. "quiet little smile": HI. Kaplan opened champagne: HI. "New Cancer-Killing": *San Francisco Examiner*, Apr 27, 1956. "Stanford Researchers Have": *San Francisco Chronicle*, Apr 27, 1956. "It is not": Brecher 1969, 355. "There is a common":

ibid., 358. comparison with cobalt: JH; Meredith 1958. "Here's a black box": JH. Garland criticized Kaplan: HA, HJ, MAB; Garland 1961; SA. "This is the comparison": MAB. "the slop-through-it school": HJ. "I'd like to": SA. "That piece you": Smithers to Wasserman, Dec 10, 1986. Hammersmith Hospital accelerator: Newbery and Bewley 1955. Uhlmann accelerator: CVE; *Michael Reese News*, May 28, 1982; RFK. Kaplan's contribution: MT, MW. Varian: ELG. "His only compensation": Ginzton speech at memorial service, Feb 12, 1984, HSKP.

15. Moving to the Farm

second factor: TW. "We were used": LK. Kaplan home: AKS, LK, PK, RTG. "The view became": LK. "I would never": LK. "animal, mineral, vegetable": PK. "Dear, why don't": PK. "Henry and Leah": AG. Sausalito friends: AG, AKS, LK, PK. "I would have": PK. Paul in father's lab: LK, PK. Expanded department: MAB, RFK. "a deceptively quiet": Kaplan to Alway, Nov 20, 1958, HSKP. "I saw no": SA2, 14. "This school is": RFK. outcry against move: AG, DR, HJ, JK; SA2. "worst decision imaginable": SA. "He had a": Chaplin 1973, 27. "being a modest": WC. "Cutting wanted to": SA2, 15. "Perhaps it's not": SA. "I was hurt": SA. "Do you believe": SA. Packard episode: SA. "Henry, it's been": SA. "That's interesting": SA. "Would you mind": SA. "Hello, David.": SA. "What's all this?": SA. "It's very simple": SA. "You are the chairman": SA. Goldstein: SU. biochemistry: AG; SA. Harvard offer: Dean Berry to Kaplan, Mar 22,1957, HSKP. Terman meeting: RFK; SA. "I told him": SA2, 18. "I hope you'll": ibid. "This is the": Sidney Farber to Kaplan, Apr 8, 1957, HSKP. "a necessary evil": AG. "to move the": RA. "I said he": SA2, 15. "He played an": Goldstein, "Eulogy on Henry S. Kaplan," Feb 12,1984. Alway: JK, RA, WC; *Palo Alto Times*, Sept 15, 1959; Stanford University School of Medicine, *The Alway Years, 1957–1964*, 1966. "the unsettling effects": *Palo Alto Times*, Sept 15, 1959. "Kaplan said he": RFK. "Henry and Avram": RA. party at Berg's house: AK; SA. "It seemed like": SA2, 19. new curriculum: AG, JK, RTG, WC. "We perceived": AG. journal club: JM, RL. "We went mad": WC. new hospital: *Architectural Record* Oct, 1957. "This research mission": Goldstein, "Eulogy on Henry S. Kaplan," Feb 12,1984. Stanford accomplishments, early 1960s: *Palo Alto Times*, Sept 15, 1959. "He was the symbol": Goldstein, "Eulogy on Henry S. Kaplan," Feb 12,1984.

16. Saul Rosenberg: a Promising Young Oncologist

third factor: TW. Rosenberg's life: SAR; *ASCO News*, April–June, 2002. "Lymphosarcoma: a review": Rosenberg's cv. Kaplan-Rosenberg relationship: CNC, CSP, EJG, JG, LK, SAR, TW. "Saul was the complete": EJG. "His presence demanded": CSP. "a progressive condition": Kaplan 1962a, 553. "thus avoiding the": Easson 1966, 349. fragmented care: SAR. staging conference: CNC, CSP, JG, SAR, ZF. "Even if Kaplan": SAR. "A lot of people": CSP. Stanford's staging system: Kaplan 1962a. mantle and inverted Y techniques: ibid.; HD. segmental fields: *HD*; Peters 1966. "It is highly": *HD*, 375. "The onus of": Kaplan 1962a, 559. "HSK had the": SAR. "The selection of": *HD*, 370. "Saul was a": CSP. "friendly debates": SAR. "They enjoyed one": CSP. "Saul began to": ibid. "It was to": SAR.

17. The L-1 Protocol: Christine Pendleton and Douglas Eads

Christine Pendleton: CP, SAR; MR. "walking pneumonia": CP. "I felt as": CP. "That's where you": CP. "Dr. Kaplan": CP. L1 protocol: Bagshaw, Kaplan, and Rosenberg 1968; Kaplan and Rosenberg 1966a. "What was considered": SAR. Pendleton treatment: MR. mantle field: Kaplan 1966. "If other therapists": ZF. "Dr. Kaplan had": CP. "I was alone": CP. Lhermitte's syndrome: *HD*, 432. "I felt like": CP. Kaplan ascribed mass to scar tissue: *HD*, 423. "These pictures of": Pendleton to Kaplan, Oct 20, 1983, LKP. Douglas Eads: DE; MR; *Stanford MD*, Fall 1982; *Stanford University Medical News Bureau*, May 1982; *Peninsula Times Tribune* (Palo Alto), May 1982. "Dr. McCarroll walked": DE. "I imagined that": DE. "I've got nothing": DE. "He inspired confidence": DE. "He must have": DE. "Once a resident": DE. results of L1 protocol: Bagshaw, Kaplan, Rosenberg 1968; Kaplan and Rosenberg 1966a; Rosenberg and Kaplan 1985. "Kaplan was good": TW.

18. The L-2 Protocol: Petra Ekstrand and Joey Radicchi

Petra Ekstrand (K.M.): CNC, EJG, JE, MO, SAR; MR. L2 protocol: SAR; Rosenberg and Kaplan 1985. "When we first": *HD*, 414. toxicities of inverted Y, oophoropexy: *HD*. leukemia following radiation: Bleich 1960; *HD*. "A priori, the": *HD*, 414. Creger criticized Kaplan: SAR, WC. technicians uneasy: JL. "They'll never survive": JMM. "Kaplan was considered": EJG. "Kaplan was exceedingly": CSP. Joey Radicchi: AR, CNC, EJG, MO, SAR, SD; MR. "My husband find": AR. "He's going to die": AR. "He didn't say": AR. "I've got a": AR. "What happened to": AR. results of L2 protocol: SAR; Kaplan and Rosenberg 1966a; Rosenberg and Kaplan 1985. debate over closure of L2: LK. "When I can't": LK. "I'm the voice": *ASCO News* April–June, 2002. "What if it": LK. Kaplan-Rosenberg relationship: CNC, CSP, EJG, LK, SAR, ZF. "Saul was an": CNC. "Hank," "Dr. Kaplan": SAR. water polo: LK, PK, SAR. "I'm sure he": SAR. personal issues not at stake: CNC, LK.

19. International Cooperation

Paris meeting: MT, RJL, SAR, SDS, VP; "Radiothérapie de la maladie de Hodgkin" 1966. state of Hodgkin's disease: MT, SAR. "require immediate radical": Easson and Russell 1963, 1707. "Many of the earlier": Easson 1966, 349. "lymphocytic and/or histiocytic": RJL. lymphangiogram: Kinmonth 1952. Peters received less credit: MT, VP. accomplishments of Paris meeting: MT, SAR, RJL, VP. "age of resolution": Peters 1973, 117. Kaplan took lead: MT, SAR, VP. "He decided that": MT. Rye conference: JU, MT, PC, RJL, SAR, SDS, VP; OCHD. "silver-throated Sidney": RJL. "Most clinicians have": RJL. "Those with lots": RJL. committee on staging: MT, RJL, VP. "Henry came out": VP. Stanford's staging system: OCHD. "It is therefore hoped": OCHD, 1310. disagreement over staging system: Easson to Kaplan, Dec 1, 1965; Kaplan to Easson, Dec 17, 1965; Kaplan to Tubiana, Dec 17, 1965; Rosenberg to Karnofsky, Dec 13, 1965, HSKP. "I have sufficient": Kaplan to Tubiana, Dec 17, 1965, HSKP. "multifocal origin": Smithers 1970. "contiguous spread": Kaplan 1971. "road map for": *HD*, 339. "HSK promulgated the": VD. Kaplan needled Pack: JU. "When Kaplan was": JU. "If you are": SDS. "Where does aggressiveness": OCHD, 1265. "Five years ago": ibid. "The hazard of": OCHD, 1264. "During this phase": ibid. "It should be": OCHD, 1303. Kaplan skeptical about chemotherapy: SAR. symposium outstanding: RJL, VP.

20. A Famous Father

Kaplan's awards: curriculum vitae. Chevalier de la Légion d'honneur: Birdsall to Kaplan, Feb 14, 1966, HSKP. "His name is": Errera to Leah Kaplan, Feb 16, 1984, LKP. "missionary work": LK. red-eye: VD. "Drop that gun": LK. fish heads: LK. "the Messiah": ZF. "He couldn't even": LK. Fight with Richard: AKS, LK, PK. "I remember sitting": Kirkman to Kaplan, Dec 25, 1983, LKP. "I don't care": LK. "Our home was": PK. journal club: LK, JM. "Trying to learn": PK. "I saw a": AKS. "The cheese you": PK. "It was very hard": PK. Sarah: AKS, PK. "She had an intensity": PK. Richard stood up Paul: AKS. "No, that's nonsense": PK. Eagle River: PK. "I had a great": PK. "Just concentrate": PK. "When patients would": PK. "fear of success": PK. Owen diagnosed dyslexia: LK, PK. "much like a dancer": PK. Israel trip: MF, PK. "My father was": PK.

21. The Single-Minded Focus of Vince DeVita

DeVita at AACR: DeVita and Serpick 1967. audience astonished: JU. nitrogen mustard: Goodman et al. 1946. vincristine: Noble, Beer, and Cutts 1958. "The cancer worker": Noble, Beer, and Cutts 1958, 882. "This order of": Carbone and Brindley 1962, 309. procarbazine: Bollag and Grunberg 1963. procarbazine trial: Mathe et al. 1963. prednisone: Dougherty and White 1943. prednisone trial: Hall 1966. Skipper's work: DeVita 1971; Skipper, Schabel, and Wilcox 1964. Frei's leukemia work: Frei et al. 1965. DeVita's life: ED, MD, VD; DeVita to author, Feb 6, 1991. "I always knew": VD. "I spent a lot": VD. "don't embarrass me.": VD. "When I arrived": VD. "Mr. DeVita, I": VD. "kidney shed": VD. "My life might": VD. Emil Frei: GC, JHM, VD; www.stmargaret.shaw.org/school/alumni/ distinguished/frei. "idea generator": GC. "He took all": VD. four clinical associates: EF, GC, JHM, MD, VD. "Good morning, honey": GC. "For the first": VD. leukemia service: Frei et al. 1965. MOMP: EF, GC, JHM, PC, VD. "Frei was the": JHM. "What the hell": JHM. "I well remember": DeVita 1981. "Once you see": VD. MOMP data: DeVita et al. 1965. "My recollection is": Moxley to DeVita, June 2, 1979, VTD. "Intensive Combination Chemotherapy": DeVita et al., 1965. "You can't use": VD. "Vince was a treater": JHM. changes in protocol: PC, VD. fifty-eighth annual meeting of the AACR: *Proceedings of the American Association for Cancer Research* 1967. AACR presentation of MOPP: DeVita and Serpick 1967. "It appears that": ibid., 13. "Have any of": JHM. MOPP data published: DeVita, Serpick, and Carbone 1970. "In the wake": EF. credit for MOPP: CNC, EF, JHM, JM, GC, PC, SAR, VD; DeVita to author, Feb 6, 1991; DeVita to Fortner, Mar 9, 1981, VTD; DeVita to Hennemann, Jan 31, 1980, VTD; Frei to Carter, Mar 7, 1977, VTD; Frei to DeVita, Nov 11, 1979, VTD; Moxley to DeVita, June 2, 1979, VTD. "paving the way": JHM, VD. "Vince deserves": Frei to Carter, Mar 7, 1977, VTD. "Great outspoken characters": GC. "While I was away": VD. "Who actually designed": JM.

22. A Walking Textbook of Radiation Morbidity

"In my opinion": Kaplan 1968, 894. Radicchi's treatment: MR. complications of radiotherapy: AR; MR; *HD*; Kaplan and Stewart 1973. Kaplan paid hotel bill: AR. bony abnormalities: CNC. "skeletal stigmata": MR. herpes zoster: AR; *HD*. radiation pericarditis: Kaplan and Stewart 1973. "Joey was a walking": EJG. "What do we": AR. "Drug therapy should": Kaplan and Rosenberg 1966b. "At present, radiotherapy": Kaplan 1968,

894. Rosenberg's attitude toward MOPP: SAR. "I remember giving": JB. "I'll take it": AR. side effects: AR, MO. "Mom, you didn't": AR. April Fool's joke: AR, CNC, EJG, MO. "I feel terrible": MO. "April Fool!": MO. Joey's life after chemotherapy: AR.

23. Living Autopsies

Glatstein's life: EJG; curriculum vitae. "Mr. Wonderful": EJG, SD. "He knew absolutely": SD. Glatstein as a resident: CNC, EJG, SD. "toots": SD. events leading up to laparotomy: EJG, SAR. Glatstein's results: Glatstein et al. 1969. "It is disheartening": ibid., 718. "Laparotomy, splenectomy, liver": ibid. "That was a very": EJG. "Kaplan could probably": EJG. "What's the matter": EJG. "Kaplan was off": EJG. "There were a lot": SAR. criticism: EJG, SAR; Johnson 1971. "living autopsies": author. results of staging laparotomy: Kaplan et al. 1973. life of Mary Murray: MMV; MR; "A Patient's Perspective," May 8, 1982, HSKP. "The world was": MMV. "I wasn't really": "A Patient's Perspective," May 8, 1982, HSKP. "Mustard is for": SD. "The rest of": ZF. Rosenberg and Kaplan disagreed: SAR. Murray-Vidal's treatment: MMV; MR; "A Patient's Perspective," May 8, 1982, HSKP. "It was beyond": MMV. "It was a very": MMV. "When you're going": MMV. infertility: MMV; "A Patient's Perspective," May 8, 1982, HSKP. results of H-5 study: Kaplan and Rosenberg 1973b; Rosenberg et al. 1972; Rosenberg and Kaplan 1985. Kaplan wanted Saul's opinion: CNC. "As chemotherapy became": SAR.

24. Protégés

"Kaplan boys": EJG. "He made you": JG. "As residents we": SD. Kaplan's bedside manner: CNC, EJG, JG, SD, ZF. "The way he": JG. Kaplan called Danny Thomas: SD. "He didn't approach": ZF. "When I was": Nossal to Leah, Feb 27, 1984, LKP. "Henry came to town": Borson to Leah, Feb 21, 1984, LKP. Donaldson's trip to France: SD. "Bonjour, Mademoiselle": SD. "No thank you": SD. "Kaplan had a": CNC. "I have three": EG. HSK: CNC, EJG, SD. patient Roberto: SD; MR. "It was clear": SD. "Maybe we could": SD. "Some decreased growth": MR. patient Mark: SD; MR. "Don't let anyone": SD. pediatric trial results: *HD*. Donaldson's work: Donaldson cv. "When I first": SD. mycosis fungoides: Fuks and Bagshaw 1971. "It appears highly": ibid., 146. "I had a sense": ZF. "On that afternoon": ZF. "HSK loved his": CNC.

25. Intellectual Playmates

"Viewed from one": SA. "In truth, the": Avram Goldstein, "Eulogy on Henry S. Kaplan," Feb 12,1984. Alway and new chairmen: AG, HA, LK, RFK; Stanford University Medical Center: 25 years. "shared the vision": Walsh 1971a, 552. "When we were": SA. "There was tremendous": SA. "The Alway years": AG. social gatherings: AK, HH, LK. Kaplan-Kornberg friendship: AK, LK. esprit de corps eroded: LK, RFK. "intellectual playmates": SA. "One of our most": SA. Kaplan disappointed with Holman: HA, LK, RFK. "I had some memorable": SA. Kornberg's authoritarian stance: HA, LK, RFK; *Stanford Medicine*, Spring 1988. "Arthur, when it": LK. "The medical school": Alway to Leah, undated, LKP. Dean's Selection Committee: Minutes of the Executive Committee Meeting, Stanford University School of Medicine, July 1965–July 1970, LMA. Robert Glaser: HA, LK, RFK, RG; Glaser cv. history of Medical Service Plan: Wilson to Crowley, May 15, 1984, LMA.

Abrams and Medical Service Plan: HA, LK, RFK; Minutes of the Executive Committee, Oct 2, 16, 1964; By-Laws of the Medical Service Plan, Dec 7, 1964, LMA. Glaser meeting with Abrams: HA. Executive Committee accepted Glaser proposal: Minutes of the Meeting of the Executive Committee, Jan 28, 1965, LMA. "I have read": Abrams to Glaser, Feb 3, 1965, HSKP. "Where's Kaplan?": RFK. "The man has made": HA. Abrams meeting with the Dean's Selection Committee: HA, RFK. "The letter spoke": HA. "I will simply": HA. Hamburg meeting with Kaplan: LK. "You were so good": LK. Kaplan's reaction: HA, LK, RFK. "He expected them": HA. "He was utterly": AG. "The Executive Committee": AG. "Your memorandum": Glaser to Kaplan, May 20, 1968, HSKP. "My sincere congratulations": Kaplan to Glaser, June 11, 1968, HSKP. "The way Kaplan": RG. "Look, my father": RG. Kaplan took on the Executives: AK, HH, RFK, RG. "He'd come sailing": HH. "Henry seemed to": RG. "He always came": JW. Kaplan objected to Hamburg's plan: Minutes of Executive Committee, Dec 1965, LMA. "dean-run practice": SA. "It's time to blow": Walsh 1971b, 656. "Is that fair?": RFK. "He made it": SA. "Robert S. Glaser": Walsh 1971a, 551. "The main complaint": Walsh 1971b, 654. Glaser-Kaplan fights: AG, LK, RFK, RG. "I want to": SA. "Henry had a": AK. "the original three-dollar": LK. "There were shouting": AK. "I consider Kaplan": HH. "I never enjoyed": SA. Lederberg, Kretchmer and Kornberg tried to apologize: LK. "I don't understand": LK. "As much as Henry": RG.

26. Peace Now!

"University strikes against": *Stanford Daily,* May 4, 1970. protests: ibid.; *Palo Alto Weekly,* July 3, 1991. "We do not call": *Stanford Daily,* May 4, 1970. Stanford's strike rally: *Palo Alto Weekly,* July 3, 1991. "The wave of protest": Statement by President Kenneth S. Pitzer, Stanford University. medical student demonstrations: JW, LC. "He had a": LC. May 4 convocation: JW, LC, LK; news releases, May 5, 6, 12, 13, 1970, LMA; *The Goose,* June 4, 1970. "above politics": news release, May 5, 1970, LMA. "Genesis of a": *The Goose* June 4, 1970. Kaplan's social conscience: LK, RK. Kaplan at Kriss's hearing: JK, LK, RK; Record of Proceedings: Hearing in case of Dr. Joseph Kriss, U.S. Naval Station, Treasure Island, San Francisco, 1955, Kriss personal file. "It is basically": ibid. Kaplan refused to speak at Moscow Cancer Congress: ER, LK. Letter in *Science*: Kaplan 1962b, 998. Houston Cancer Congress: ER, JFH, LK; *Tenth International Cancer Congress,* 1970. "On behalf of the President": ibid., 6. "Peace now!": JFH. Kaplan's protest: ER, JFH, LK. Agnew blocked nomination: ER.

27. Mary Lasker's Moon Shot for Cancer

Cancer Act: Greenberg 1972; Rettig 1977; Spingarn 1976. "We are here": Rettig 1977, 277. Mary Lasker: Breo 1991; Culliton 1976; Moss 1989; Rettig 1977; www.laskerfoundation.org. "Her presence caused": Breo 1991, 1844. "a rare passion": ibid., 1843. "Medical research is": National Cancer Program 1991, S-15. "When I think": www.laskerfoundation.org. "benevolent plotters": Rettig 1977, 18. American Cancer Society: Moss 1989; Rettig 1977. "Have lunch with": Breo 1991, 1845. "I am opposed": www.laskerfoundation.org. conclusions from space program: Garb 1968. "moonshot" for cancer: Rettig 1977. "Mr. Nixon: You Can Cure Cancer": *New York Times,* Dec 9, 1969. Yarborough Committee: Rettig 1977. Schmidt: ibid.; Spingarn 1976. "There was hardly": Kaplan 1972, 277. "Why, if we": Culliton 1976, 60. "An effort to cure": ibid. "I virtually lived": Kaplan

1972, 277. "managed approach to": Kaplan 1972, 277. "The really good": Thomas 1977, 257. "What emerges unexpectedly": Amos 1977, 262. "Funding patterns of": Kaplan 1972, 274. scientific plan: Kaplan 1972; Rettig 1977. problems with NIH, NCI: Garb 1968; Rettig 1977. Kaplan's concerns with Yarborough report: Greenberg 1972; Kaplan 1972. "I found out": Greenberg 1972, 289. "My powers of": ibid. "a whole new": Kaplan 1972, 278. "The time has": Rettig 1977, 126. "The scientists and": ibid., 152. "Cancer claims the lives": ibid., 175–76. "a conclusion with": ibid., 243. "politics of compromise": ibid., 248. "Hope and comfort": ibid., 277–78. "Great Persuader": Breo 1991, 1844. name deleted from guest list: LK. "a serious sin": Blair to Kaplan, Jan 4, 1984, LKP. nominations blocked: LK, VD.

28. A Cancer-Causing Virus

Vianna's Albany study: Vianna, Greenwald, and Davies 1971. "This outbreak involving": ibid., 1210. Hodgkin's disease in two homes: Gilmore and Zelesnick 1962. cases among people living together: Abramson 1973. cases in married couples: Dworsky and Henderson 1974; Mazur and Straus 1951. Vianna found cases linked: Vianna et al., 1972. "Albany cluster": Smith and Pike 1976, 660. "Other studies have": ibid. "Hodgkin's disease": *BMJ* 4: 564–65, 1972. "The results support": Vianna and Polan 1973, 499. "The apparent impressiveness": Smith and Pike 1976, 661. virus may be implicated: *HD*. patient with concurrent diseases: Massey, Lane, and Imbriglia 1953. Smithers's four cases: Smithers 1967. Ronald F. and Gary T.: *HD*. Kaplan's patients with mono and Hodgkin's disease: *HD*. Connelly and Christine's investigation: Connelly and Christine 1974. "Our findings support": Rosdahl, Larsen, and Clemmesen 1974, 255. elevated EB levels: Carvalho et al., 1973; Levine et al., 1971. Kaplan's work on murine leukemia: Fuks and Feldman 1985; Kaplan 1967; Lieberman and Kaplan 1959. viruses and cancer: Phillips 1983; Stephenson 1980. Rous's work: Rous 1911; Stephenson 1980. "For many years": *World Book Encyclopedia* 1985, 452. Gross: Beiss 1976; Gross 1953; Kaplan 1967. "There were even": Beiss 1976, 295. "I did not wait": ibid. "Gross's early work:" Kaplan 1967, 1326. cartoon of Gross: MBL. "The discovery of": Stephenson 1980, 13. "Confronted by the": Kaplan 1967, 1326. Lieberman: AD, AE, ML. "Herr Professor": ML. "He was the brains": AD. Kaplan's leukemia work: Kaplan 1967; Kaplan 1978; Lieberman and Kaplan 1959. "The essence of": *Modern Medicine*, Apr 16, 1973.

29. The Ann Arbor Conference

"There was no": SDS. "The fragmentary, anecdotal": Kaplan 1977, 551. Carbone at Brown: PC. camaraderie: MT, SDS, VD, VP. "There was only": VD. "Ralph Johnson is": VD. Ann Arbor conference: SSHD. Rosenberg's anticipation: SAR. Peters's expectations: VP. Peters's keynote address: Peters 1971. Peters interrupted: VP. "Vera, you'll never": VP. Peters's data on laparotomy: Peters 1973. Smithers's concerns: SSHD. Rosenberg's rebuttal: SSHD. "It seems more": SSHD, 1751. "Unless information is": SSHD, 1752. Kaplan during meeting: SAR, VD. "But as so often": SAR. "That's rotten": VP. "It was a slap": VP. Rosenberg's report for Committee on Staging Procedures: Rosenberg 1971. "In view of": ibid., 1863. Carbone reported for Committee on Staging Classification: SSHD. "Henry was instrumental": PC. "The main business": SSHD, 1870. "I was one": SAR. "I think Kaplan": VP. "Vera, I think": VP. "It was the lowest": VP. "Kaplan credited a Toronto": *Toronto Star*, May 8, 1976. "HSK achieved his": TW.

30. Bookends

Kaplan's honors: cv. "The longer we're": Kaplan to his mother, May 21, 1943, LKP. "To my wife": LK. Annie's and Paul's activities: AKS, LK, PK; Kaplan to Feldman, Nov 4, 1970, June 14, 1972, HSKP; Kaplan to Dr. and Mrs. Leon Heppel, Apr 10, 1973, HSKP. Feldman-Kaplan friendship: LK, MF, PK. "The year Monet": Feldman to Kaplan, Sept 23, 1959, HSKP. "I was introduced": MF. "I am interested": Kaplan to Feldman, Apr 16, 1971, HSKP. "Looking back at": Feldman to Kaplan, Nov 14, 1965, HSKP. "Your office is": Kaplan to Feldman, Dec 22, 1976, HSKP. "I am due": Kaplan to Feldman, Apr 16, 1971, HSKP. "I look forward": Kaplan to Feldman, Sept 15, 1981, HSKP. "the Gauguin of": MF. "There have been": Kaplan to Feldman, Nov 12, 1973, HSKP. "You could have": PK. "Whatever he was": MF.

31. The Cancer Center Debacle

cancer centers: Rettig 1977. Roswell Park: "Information: History of Roswell Park Memorial Institute." MD Anderson: "Shining Past Brilliant Future": The University of Texas MD Anderson Cancer Center 1991. "Center of Tomorrow": "A Century of Commitment: A History of Memorial Sloan Kettering Cancer Center" 1993. total Stanford faculty: Walsh 1971a. "Stanford was already": SAR. $15,000,000 over three years: Rettig 1977, 253. Wilson's attitude toward Kaplan: JW. membership of CRC committee: memos to Executive Committee, March 7, 1969; Feb 17, 1971, LMA. "pseudoscientists": RS. Korn: Korn cv; DK. Kaplan presented proposal: Minutes of Executive Committee meeting, Feb 19, 1971, LMA. "to a lesser extent": memo to Executive Committee, Feb 17, 1971, LMA. "The plan was full": HA. Kaplan's plans: RFK. "The enterprise of academic": DK. problem of billets: DK, RS, PB. "A star system": Walsh 1971a, 552. "There was an anti-center": CR. Kaplan taped up cards: MAB. "Basically it got": MAB. "Rosenberg was extremely": RS. "The basic scientists": LC. CRC committee didn't want Kaplan to have control: DK, LC, MAB, RS, SAR. "My impression is": RG. "When Henry came": RS. control of gift funds: SAR. "Henry respected Saul's": RFK. Bagshaw proposal: MAB. "I know exactly": HH. Clayton Rich: Rich cv; CR, RC, RS. "Stanford was packed": CR. hospital protest: CR, HS, LC, RS; *Campus Report*, Apr 14, 21, 1971; *Modern Hospital*, May, 1971; *Stanford Daily*, Nov 19, 1991. "More than fifty": *Campus Report*, Apr 14, 1971. "It looked like": CR. "I wondered if": HS. Kaplan to represent Executive Committee: Minutes of Faculty Senate, Apr 12, 1971, LMA. Kaplan's attitude toward demonstrators: HS, JW, LC, LK. bullet holes: LK. construction costs doubled: CR. Rich's position on cancer center: CR. Kaplan's resignation as chair of Radiology: DK, EJG, MAB, SAR; Kaplan to Glatstein, Dec 27, 1971, HSKP. "The Executive Committee extends": Minutes of Executive Committee, July 21, 1972, LMA. Kaplan at CRC committee meetings: CR, DK, RC, RFK. "We wrangled with": DK. "Internal pressures building": Walsh 1971b, 657. Kaplan called for a vote: DK, MAB, RC, RS, SAR. "None of us failed": DK. CRC Committee policy statement: memo to Executive Committee, Jan 21, 1972, LMA; Minutes of Meeting of Executive Committee, Feb 18, 1972, LMA. Kaplan couldn't walk away: LK. Breach of loyalty, sadness: LK, MF, RFK, VD. "Why? What were": LK. "One day when": MAB. "The subject was": MAB. Kaplan's diminished involvement: CR, LC, MAB, RC, RFK. "Henry essentially seceded": NS. "He was bitter": LC. "Kaplan was on": MAB. relationship with Bagshaw: LK, MAB. resentment of Korn: DK, LK, RFK, RS. "I became the": DK. Saul and Henry: LK, RFK. disagreements at staging conference: CSP, MAB. "esteemed colleague": author. incident at Kaplan's home: CSP, DG, EG, EJG, SAR. "Why don't you": EG. "You could see": DG. "We loved both": EG. "You've never made": SAR.

32. Deadly Complications

"Winning a Battle with Cancer": *Burlingame [CA] Advance-Star*, Apr 22, 1972. "The first time": ibid. "Cancer Victim": *Nevada State Journal*, Dec 11, 1975. "The worst thing": *Nevada Appeal*, Jan 6, 1976. patients with second cancers: Arseneau et al. 1972. reaction of NCI group: GC, JA, VD. "It was clear": GC. "nasty and fast-growing": JA. other reports: Berg 1967. "the risk of late": *HD*, 439. acute leukemia in Hodgkin's patients: Crosby 1969. "My main concern": VD. "at least the": GC. "We had people": VD. "must be balanced": Arseneau et al. 1972, 1122. "Saul called us": GC. "There is now": Kaplan and Rosenberg 1973a, 370. "In my opinion": SAR. "We have been": Rosenberg 1973, 469. "Let me handle": JA. "We share Dr. Rosenberg's": DeVita et al. 1973, 470.

33. High-Dose DeVita

DeVita's accomplishments: DeVita cv. DeVita's reputation: CNC, GC, JG, KO, TW. "Italian boss": TW. "magnificent clinician": JG. "high-dose DeVita": KO. "He was a believer": JG. "Henry really kept": VD. "He was a": ibid. "I enjoyed seeing": DeVita to Kaplan, June 9, 1975, HSKP. Teddy's illness: CNC, TW, VD; Memorandum for the Record, Chief, Pediatric Oncology Branch, DeVita to Kaplan, Mar 9, 1976, HSKP. aplastic anemia: Erslev 1972. cause of Teddy's anemia: VD. laminar airflow room: CNC, TW. "The logistics and": Erslev 1972, 220. "I'll never forget": VD. "I was driving": VD.

34. The S-5 Protocol: Chris Jenkins

H studies: Rosenberg and Kaplan 1985. PAVe: Wolin, Rosenberg, and Kaplan 1979. "Kaplan thought PAVe": SAR. S studies: Rosenberg and Kaplan 1985. "I have no": DeVita to Rosenberg, Sept 17, 1981, SAR personal files. DeVita criticized PAVe: SAR. Chris Jenkins's life: CJ, TT. "My father was very": CJ. "I got caught": CJ. siege of Hué: Karnow 1983. "I suddenly found": CJ. "You ask about": CJ. "People were being": CJ. "You can't leave": CJ. "I looked like": CJ. Jenkins's medical history: MR. "nice narrow chest": CJ. "Did you eat": CJ. "We're going to": CJ. "You don't always": CJ. "Mrs. Jenkins, have": TT. "You felt like": CJ. "If you had": CJ. herpes zoster: Goffinet, Glatstein, and Kaplan 1973. Jenkins's hospitalization: MR. "How do you": CJ.

35. Inconsolable

Joey's life: AR. Joey's hospital course: AR, CNC, EJG, MO; MR. "I suspect the": MR. Kaplan kept names on index cards: SD. study of second cancers: Coleman et al. 1977. "You can't help": SAR. "He was overcome.": CSP. "There is currently": Coleman et al. 1977, 1252. "It wasn't the": CNC. "Norman, we have": CNC. "We found a tumor": AR. "I knew what": AR. "More often than": MO. "He is stable": MR. "He couldn't breathe": AR. "I don't know": CSP.

36. Without a Spleen

Chris Jenkins's life: CJ, TT; MR. "Come to the": TT. "emaciated, febrile, shaking": MR. infants' susceptibility to infection: King and Shumacker 1952. Melbourne series: Horan and Colebatch 1962. British report: Lowdon, Stewart, and Walker 1966. "[It] slays so quickly": Symington 1969, 175. Judith Hurt: SD. Australian report: Whitaker 1969. Donaldson study: Donaldson et al. 1972. "To the rest": SD. Jenkins's illness: CJ, TT; MR. "Among acute bacterial": MR. "This is a very": CJ. "The room seemed": CJ. "Who are you?": CJ. "Why don't the": CJ. "HSK felt responsible": EJG. "We weren't going": SD. "He felt terribly": EJG. Kaplan assessed approaches: HD. vaccine: Siber et al. 1978. "splenosis": Brewster 1973, 14. "born-again spleen": Pearson et al. 1978, 1389. *Kaplan* suggested splenosis: *HD*. "Until such time": Donaldson, Glatstein, and Vosti 1978, 1957. Petra Ekstrand (alias K.M.): CNC, EJG, MO; MR. "She has no": MR. Autopsy report: MR. "What happened to": author.

37. Kaplan's Moby Dick

family life: AKS, LK, PK. "In his heart": AKS. Leah's career: LK. sleeping with the enemy: LK. "She is known": *Campus Report*, 1982. "The pressure I": PK. Ann and Paul's education and careers: Kaplan to Professor and Mrs. Eric A. Wright, Jan 23, 1970; Kaplan to "Old Folks in Frozen Upstate New York," Apr 10, 1973; Kaplan to Dr. and Mrs. Leon Heppel, Dec 31, 1974; Kaplan to Feldman, Dec 22, 1976, Feb 17, 1977; Kaplan to Heller, Feb 16, 1977, HSKP. "My father had": AKS. "I didn't start": PK. "a smorgasbord of": PK. "Paul is deeply": Kaplan to Feldman, Jan 14, 1972, HSKP. "I started learning": PK. Paul's first show: LK, PK. "It was something": PK. "Paul seems seriously": Kaplan to van Putten, Jan 11, 1979, HSKP. "Paul is currently": Kaplan to Wright, July 8, 1980, HSKP. being the child of Kaplan: AKS, PK. "a particularly shameful": MF. "He was like": AD. "There is nothing": AD. "The dream is": AD. CBRL: *Stanford M.D.*, 15, 1976. "I guess you": *Modern Medicine*, Apr 16, 1973, 49. "This is my personal": *Campus Report*, Oct 8, 1975. "formidably difficult": ibid. "He told me": LK.

38. The Elusive Human Tumor Virus

Koch's postulates: Kaplan 1978; Phillips 1983. cell cultures: AE; Kaplan 1967; Kaplan 1978; *Stanford M.D.*, Winter, 1976. Alan Epstein: AE; *Stanford M.D.*, Winter, 1976. "The lymphoma cell": Kaplan to Feldman, June 4, 1974, HSKP. "An important laboratory": Stanford News Bureau, 1976. "If we really": *Stanford M.D.*, Winter, 1976, 7. CBRL: MBL; *Campus Report* Oct 8, 1975; *Stanford M.D.* Winter, 1976; Stanford University Medical Center News Bureau, Feb 14, 1973, Oct 1, 1975. "The most exciting": Kaplan to Feldman, Aug 22, 1975, HSKP. human tumor virus researchers: RCG. "Mr. D. P. Burkitt": Glemser 1970, 160. story of Burkitt: Glemser 1970; Burkitt and Wright 1970. "How long have": Glemser 1970, 71. "It was a milestone": ibid., 81. "Commonest Children's Cancer": ibid., 160. "After he had been talking": ibid., 160. "bombshell": ibid.,105. Epstein grew Burkitt's cells: Epstein, Achong, and Barr 1964. "After this remarkable": Phillips 1983, 126. Gallo: RCG; Albert Lasker Medical Research Award, 1982 Nomination; Shilts 1988; www.hiv. org; www.virusmyth.net. "First came God": www.virusmyth.net. reverse transcriptase: Kaplan 1978; Phillips 1983. Gallo discovered human leukemia virus: Gallagher and Gallo

1975; Stephenson 1980. "that was the lowest": RCG. "His career took": Shilts 1988, 201. Kaplan found C-type particles: Kaplan et al. 1977. "I am writing": Kaplan to Epstein, June 20,1974, HSKP. "There is no": Epstein to Kaplan, June 28, 1974, HSKP. "Any man or": Glemser 1970, 162. site visit: RCG. "His was intellectual": RCG. "Gallo had the courage": Albert Lasker Medical Research Award, 1982 Nomination. "When I got": RCG. Kaplan's lymphoma cell line: Kaplan et al. 1977; Kaplan et al. 1979; Stephenson 1980. "A team of": Stanford University Medical Center News Bureau June 27, 1977. "To our knowledge": Kaplan et al. 1977, 2568. Kaplan sloppy: AD. "He was like": AD. "Henry, why would": AD. "I thought my": AD.

39. The Quiet Conviction

Kaplan supported scientists: Niwa to Leah, Mar 22, 1984, LKP; Nossal to Leah, Feb 27, 1984, LKP; Ochan to Kaplan, Dec 10, 1983, LKP; Shin-Hwa Yeh to Kaplan, Jan 11, 1984, LKP; Hamelin to Kaplan, Jan 12, 1984, HSKP. advisory committees, boards: Berenblum to Kaplan, August 18, 1968, HSKP; Israel Cancer Association telegram to Leah, 1984, LKP; Sela telegram to Leah, Feb 6, 1984, LKP; Prywes telegram to Leah Kaplan, 1984, LKP; Mann to Kaplan, May 9, 1977, HSKP; Gayne to Leah Kaplan, Feb 23, 1984, LKP. delegation to China: *Palo Alto Times*, May 19, 1978. Cassidy: Sagan and Jonsen 1976. Neto: *Observer Weekend Review*, May 28, 1961. coup and torture in Chile: Anderson 1993; Sagan and Jonsen 1976. Kaplan's advice: GS. physician role in torture: Sagan and Jonsen 1976. "RESOLVED: That the": ibid., 1429. "Physicians must take": News release, May 5, 1970, LMA. "quiet conviction": LK. wrote to Kuchel: Kaplan to Senator Kuchel, Aug 25, 1966, HSKP. eight scientists disappeared: Wade 1976, 1977; Where is Federico Alvarez Rojas? 1977. Argentine history: Andersen 1993; Bethell 1993; Crawley 1984. "Dirty War": Andersen 1993, 1. prisons and torture: GS; Andersen 1993; Crawley 1984; Feitlowitz 1998. *Desaparecidos*: Andersen 1993, 2. repression of Argentine scientists and physicians: Andersen 1993; Berger 1978; Kates 1978; Wade 1976, 1977. "A reverence for": Kates 1978, 503. "For days I": Andersen 1993, 18. Amnesty got reports of physician torture: GS; notice Re: Dr. Alberto Samuel Falicoff from Amnesty International. Kaplan wrote Videla: Kaplan to Videla, Sept 17, 1980, HSKP. Boycott of Cancer Congress: ER, LK; Cancer meeting under boycott 1978; Duzgunes 1977; Kaplan to Rappaport, July 25, 1977, HSKP; *Medical World News*, Nov 13, 1978; Montoro 1978; Stanford University Medical Center News Bureau, Dec 4, 1978. UICC and boycott: Kaplan to Veronesi, Mar 2, 1979; van Bekkum to Veronesi, Feb 5, 1979; Veronesi to van Bekkum, Jan 18, 1979, HSKP. "It will be": Canonico to Musshoff, Nov 30, 1977, HSKP. "The undersigned physicians": Kaplan to editor, *Science*, Aug 9, 1977. Leon Schwartzenberg: Schwartzenberg 1979. mission to Argentina: ER, GS, LK; Kaplan to Aaronson, Oct 22, 1978; Kaplan to Mignone, Sept 14, 1978; Kaplan to Posner, Sept 11, 1979; Kaplan to Royston, Dec 4, 1978; Kaplan to Rutledge, Nov 14, 1978, HSKP; *Le Monde*, Feb 22, 1984; Low-Beer, GA: Report to the Royal College of Psychiatrists, Oct 24, 1978, HSKP. "My God, each": LK. "If their release": *Miami Herald,* Sept 29, 1978. "Buenos Aires is": Low-Beer, GA: Report to the Royal College of Psychiatrists, Oct 24, 1978, HSKP. Low-Beer briefed at British embassy: ibid. Kaplan and Tex Harris: LK; Andersen 1993; Kaplan to Harris, Sept 14, Oct 6, 1978, HSKP. "We observed that": Kaplan to Rutledge, Nov 14, 1978, HSKP. Kaplan saw Mothers of the Disappeared: LK. "a collective funeral": "Join the Mothers of Plaza De Mayo," HSKP. "some convenient political": Kaplan to Rutledge, Nov 14, 1978, HSKP. "The Paris conference": Low-Beer, GA: Report to the Royal College of Psychiatrists, Oct 24, 1978, HSKP. Kaplan met families: Kaplan to Rutledge, Nov 14, 1978, HSKP. "They were profoundly": Low-Beer, GA: Report to the Royal College of Psychiatrists, Oct 24, 1978, HSKP. "Let's look at": LK. "The horror we": Low-Beer, GA: Report to the Royal College of Psychiatrists, Oct 24, 1978, HSKP. "Bodies of decapitated": Kaplan to Rutledge, Nov 14, 1978, HSKP. "How could one": *Le Monde*, Feb 22, 1984. "makes people ignore": Low-Beer, GA: Report to the Royal College of Psychiatrists, Oct 24, 1978, HSKP. "He was a pig": LK. "It is impossible": *Le Monde*, Feb 22, 1984. group registered writ: Kaplan to Aaronson, Oct 22, 1978; Kaplan to Harris, Oct 6,1978; Kaplan to Posner, Sept 11, 1979; HSKP. escape: LK. "enemy of the people": *Le Monde*, Feb 22, 1984. "We didn't come": *Le Monde*, Feb 22, 1984. "Politics splits cancer": *Medical World News*, Nov 13, 1978. "The issue of": ibid. "Marcelo Parrilli told": Sagan to Kaplan, Jan 9, 1984, LKP. "I understand you went": Barreiro to Kaplan, Aug 28, 1980, HSKP.

40. The Boy in the Bubble

"We are growing": DeVita to Kaplan, Oct 30, 1978,HSKP. Teddy's case: CNC, SR, VD; Memorandum for the Record, Chief Pediatric Oncology Branch, DeVita to Kaplan, Mar 9, 1976, HSKP; Memorandum, Senior Investigator, Pediatric Oncology Branch, DeVita to Kaplan, Mar 16, 1976, HSKP. "There was a": PP. "the boy in": VD. description of Teddy: CNC, PP, SR, VD. DeVita's career: VD; DeVita cv. "Vince was a powerful": PP. letter to *New York Daily News*: PP, VD. "A somewhat distasteful": DeVita to Kaplan, Mar 9, 1976, HSKP. "Removal would now": Memorandum for the Record, Chief Pediatric Oncology Branch, DeVita to Kaplan, Mar 9, 1976, HSKP. transplant for aplastic anemia: Camitta et al. 1976. Kaplan and Strober studied transplant rejection: SS; *Campus Report*, Oct 21, 1981; *Palo Alto Times*, July 22, 1980. Rosa: SS; Kaplan to Pizzo, Jan 30, 1979; Mar 6, 1980, HSKP. Kaplan wrote DeVita of his work: Kaplan to DeVita Nov 13, 1978, HSKP. "While we have": Pizzo to Kaplan, Jan 12, 1979, HSKP. Ted as a teen: CNC, PP, SR, VD. "It was a": VD. Kaplan's plans for double transplant: CNC, VD. "What do you": CNC. "Kaplan would go": CNC. "Henry was driving": VD. Ted's death: PP, SR, VD. "I'm out of here.": PP.

41. The C-1 Protocol: Wendy Podwalny

"Before the Diagnosis": W. Podwalny, unpublished. Podwalny's life: WP; MR. "abnormal growth": WP. "I was so": WP. Stanford trials: Rosenberg and Kaplan 1985. "We're now looking": *Sacramento Bee*, Oct 19, 1981; *San Ramon Valley Herald*, Oct 19, 1981. "Doctors Work to": *Sacramento Bee*, Oct 19,1981. VBM: Horning et al. 1988. "At the time": WP. "I wanted to bang": WP. "Cure": W. Podwalny, *Surviving!* (a publication of the Dept of Radiation Oncology). "Stanford's choice of": *San Francisco Sunday Examiner & Chronicle*, Sept 13, 1981. "confidence in cure": Proceedings of the Symposium on Contemporary Issues in Hodgkin's Disease, 1045. "laced with both": ibid., 1045. DeVita invited press: Saltus to Rosenberg, Sept 21, 1981, HSKP. "keep forever": Proceedings of the Symposium on Contemporary Issues in Hodgkin's Disease, 1051. "the most elegant": ibid., 1053. "I was deeply": Kaplan to DeVita, Sept 14, 1981, HSKP. Kaplan upset: CNC, LK, SAR, VD. "Saul and I have": Kaplan to DeVita, Sept 14, 1981, HSKP. "Our choice of": Rosenberg to DeVita, Sept 14, 1981, HSKP. "My son, who": Stokes to Rosenberg, Sept

21, 1981, HSKP. "pulled the trigger": DeVita to Rosenberg, Sept 17, 1981, HSKP. "While Vince was": SAR. "our usual soul-searching": DeVita to Rosenberg, Sept 28, 1981, HSKP. "Though we did": Rosenberg to DeVita, Oct 14, 1981, HSKP. "shocked": DeVita to Kaplan, Sept 23, 1981, HSKP. "Kaplan never forgot": SAR. Vince and Henry reconciled: LK. VBM results: Horning et al. 1988. "Greater patient numbers": ibid., 1830. "I told my": WP. "Bringing another life": *Campus Report,* Oct 14, 1987.

42. The Quest for the Magic Bullet

"The Quest for": *Time,* Aug 11, 1980. first monoclonals: Köhler and Milstein 1975. mouse monoclonal antibodies: Lewin 1981. Kaplan made human monoclonal: MB, NT, RL; *Medical Tribune,* Oct 22, 1980; Olsson and Kaplan, 1980; *San Francisco Examiner,* July 30, 1980; Stanford University Medical Center News Bureau, July 28, Nov 7, 1980. "something of an art": Lewin 1981, 768. "The whole process": ibid. "The first cellular": *Medical World News,* Nov 10, 1980. "Artificial production of pure": "Artificial human antibody excites scientific world," Associated Press, July 31, 1980. "The Quest for": *Time,* Aug 11, 1980. samples available to scientific community: Lewin 1981; Reimers to Ferris, Sept 30, 1980, HSKP; *Blue Sheet* Aug 20, 1980. No measurable antibody: MB. contamination: MB, NT. "Lab distributed tainted": *Stanford Independent,* Feb 12, 1982. "Once they found": MB. treatment of mycoplasma: MB, NT. "We shared many": NT. experiment didn't work: MB, NT. "Many investigators have": Sikora and Neville 1982, 316. "It was logical": NT. "This was completely": MB. "He had a lot": RL. "There are only": NT. "Kaplan was my": RL. "He had a couple": RL. "I think he": MB. Kaplan's reaction: MB, NT. "He believed with": NT. Teng proposed heteromyeloma: MB, NT, RL. developed heteromyeloma: Teng et al. 1983. "Henry was visionary": NT. monoclonals against endotoxin, Rh factor: NT. potential uses of monoclonals: *Medical World News,* Nov 10: 61–73, 1980. "cruise missile": *Medical World News,* Nov 10, 1980. "The sky was": NT.

43. The Death of a Difficult Woman

Sarah stories: AKS, LK, PK, RK. "It was particularly": PK. "His feelings were": AKS. Sarah's medical problems: Kaplan to Vince DeVita, Jan 20, 1983; Kaplan to Mehlman, Feb 14, 1983, HSKP. "The past two": Kaplan to DeVita, Jan 20, 1983, HSKP. Sarah's memorial service: PK. "I didn't like": EC. "What I remember": PK. "One of the saddest": ibid. "the swellest mom": Kaplan to Sarah, undated, LKP. "the mom I adore": Kaplan to Sarah, June 20, 1943, LKP. Henry cried: EC. "Our report has": Fabrikant to Kaplan, Dec 31, 1980, HSKP. "harsh and inhumanitarian": Kaplan to Brezhnev, June 29, 1982, HSKP. appeals for Kovalev: ibid.; Kaplan to Rekunkov, June 29, 1982, HSKP. appeals for Sakharov: Kaplan to Dobrynin, May 16, 1980, HSKP; *New York Times,* Feb 4, 1980. "Simply deploring and": Kaplan to Stone, undated, HSKP. Kaplan to president of Liberia, Mar 2, 1981, HSKP. Samuel Green: Bers memo to Committee on Human Rights, Feb 20, 1981, HSKP. "Immediately after my": Greene to Kaplan, June 10, 1981, HSKP. travel schedule: Kaplan cv. cough: LK, MF, RCG, VD, ZF. "Good Lord": RCG. "Abe, don't you": LK. "Henry get a": VD. "Why are you": MF. "Look, your cough": LK. "Well, did you": LK. "I have lung": LK.

44. Felled

Kaplan tried to reach Feldman: MF. Blank looked at film: JBM. "A lasting impression": Zatz to Leah, Feb 8, 1984, LKP. "Henry never questioned": JBM. "I just shut": LK. "We are going": LK. dinner with Kirkmans: GK, LK. "This won't take": NT. "What do you": NT. "I drove over": PK. "I felt plunged": PK. "It broke my": LK. "You'll never guess": SD. "We have a": MO. "This is none of": CNC. "I almost vomited": CNC. "I was shocked": EJG. how Kaplan got cancer: CNC, MAB, RCG. "leaky as hell": MAB. "That goddamn son": MAB. radon as cause of lung cancer: Donaldson 1969. Kaplan's operation: JBM; MR. "I wanted to": LK. "He didn't look": PK. "Are you all": JBM. 747 pilot: PK. "Getting data was": PK. "The hardest thing": AKS. "There is no": PK. "Do you know": PK. "He can't respond": PK. "Dr. Kaplan thanks": PK. Kaplan took charge: JBM, MAB. pathology report: MR. "He was just": MAB. "I went after": VD. "Vince felt patients": CNC. "I was going": VD. Vince broke code: VD. Saul opposed chemotherapy: JM, SAR, VD. "Why add chemotherapy": SAR. "It was like": JM. Kaplan's therapy: MAB, SD. CT scan results: MAB. "He looked stricken.": LK. "I knew it": MAB. "I'm a doomed": CNC. "I'm just sorry": LK.

45. Dying Adagio

"I have developed": Kaplan to Musshoff, Nov. 29, 1983, HSKP. "Since the course": Kaplan to Fortner, Nov. 28, 1983, HSKP. "My cancer is": Kaplan to CBRL Staff, Nov 28, 1983, LKP. reactions to Kaplan's illness: LK, PK. Kornberg offered help: Arthur to Henry, Nov 29, 1983, LKP. Leah scheduled visits: LK. "Do you remember": Edith and Joel Bookstein to Kaplan, Jan 6, 1984, LKP. "Most great achievements": Rooholamini to Kaplan, Mar 1, 1984, LKP. "You saved my life.": anonymous to Kaplan, Sept 30, 1983, LKP. "small victories": Bernfield to Kaplan, Nov. 29, 1983, LKP. "it was efforts": Ginetta [Sagan] to Kaplan, Jan. 4, 1984, LKP. "I have been distressed": Bob [Robert Glaser] to Kaplan, Jan 20, 1984, LKP. Kaplan Professorship: LC; Bagshaw to colleagues, Jan 30, 1984, HSKP. "a tangible memorial": Bagshaw, ibid. "Song of the Vowels": LC, MAB; *Palo Alto Weekly*, July 11, 1984. "for my accomplishments": SA. Jenkins learned of illness: CJ. Eads learned of illness: DE. "He had so": CP. "No other man": Korman to Kaplan, Dec 5, 1983, LKP. "The past 15 years": Paul [Kaufmann] to Kaplan, Dec. 15,1983, LKP. "I will be": Kaufman-Darmady, to Kaplan, 1983, LKP. "You gave me": Tepper to Kaplan, 1983, LKP. "I'm afraid I'm": Uris to Kaplan, Dec 21, 1983, LKP. "We've never met": Jones to Kaplan, 1983, LKP. "You don't know": Anderson to Kaplan, Jan 13, 1984, LKP. "It's sad": ZF. "I wish you": EJG. cheesecake: Eli to Kaplan, Dec 20, 1982, HSKP. "Have you got": EJG. "Who would I": RCG. "I don't know": Gallo to Kaplan, 1983, LKP. "I just didn't": RCG. Bagshaw kissed Kaplan: MAB. Rosenberg's accomplishments: Rosenberg cv. "SAR Superstar": author. Saul's visits: LK. "To the end": VD. "I read your": Feldman to Kaplan, Dec. 23, 1983, HSKP. Michael's visit: MF. "Dear Hank: For": Dick to Hank, Dec. 25,1983, RK personal files. Hank cried: LK. Kaplan deteriorated: LK, MO, PK. "Mother was a": AKS. "I just sat": AKS. Kaplan wanted a grandchild: AKS. "That period was": PK. "He didn't talk": PK. O'Hara and Coleman's help: CNC, LK, MO, PK. "Paul Kaplan is": CNC. "It wasn't a funeral": CNC. "He didn't talk": CNC. "He must mean": MO. "No problem": MO. "You nurses have": MO. "That's because this": MO. "For the first": MO. "The weight loss": PK. "He began closing": CNC. "I lived my": LK. Kaplan's last day: CNC, LK, PK.

Epilogue

"Dr. Henry S. Kaplan": *International Herald-Tribune*, Feb 7, 1984. "Dr. Kaplan, Cancer-Fighter": *New York Times*, Feb 6, 1984. *Washington Post*, Feb 7, 1984; *Jerusalem Post*, Feb 1984; *Boston Globe*, Feb 7, 1984. Obituary in *Time*, Feb 20, 1984. "We are heartened": cable from Reagan in DeVita to Leah, Oct 30, 1984, LKP. progress in Hodgkin's disease: SAR; Rosenberg 1996.

Bibliography

Books

Abel-Smith, Brian. *The Hospitals, 1800–1948: A Study in Social Administration in England and Wales*. Cambridge, MA: Harvard University Press, 1964.

American Association for Cancer Research. *Proceedings of the American Association for Cancer Research: 58th Annual Meeting, April 13–15, 1967, Chicago, Illinois*. Baltimore: Published for Cancer Research, Inc., and the Association by Williams and Wilkins, 1967.

Andersen, Martin Edwin. *Dossier Secreto: Argentina's Desaparecidos and the Myth of the "Dirty War."* Boulder, CO: Westview Press, 1993.

Berkow, Ira. *Maxwell Street: Survival in a Bazaar*. Garden City, NY: Doubleday, 1977.

Bethell, Leslie. *Argentina Since Independence*. Cambridge: Cambridge University Press, 1993.

Bird, Caroline. *The Invisible Scar*. New York: David McKay, 1966.

Bleich, Alan Ralph. *The Story of X-Rays from Roentgen to Isotopes*. New York: Dover, 1960.

Bowen, E. G. *Radar Days*. Bristol: Adam Hilger, 1987.

Brecher, Ruth and Brecher, Edward. *The Rays: A History of Radiology in the United States and Canada*. Baltimore: Williams and Wilkins, 1969.

Burkitt, D. P., and Wright, D. H. *Burkitt's Lymphoma*. London: E. & S. Livingstone, 1970.

Chandler, Lester V. *America's Greatest Depression: 1929–1941*. New York: Harper & Row, 1970.

Conway, Jill Kerr, ed. *Written by Herself: An Anthology*. New York: Vintage Books, 1992.

Crawley, Eduardo. *A House Divided: Argentina, 1880–1980*. London: C. Hurst, 1984.

Cromie, Robert. *A Short History of Chicago*. New York: Lexikos, 1984.

Dewing, Stephen B. *Modern Radiology in Historical Perspective*. Springfield, IL: Charles C. Thomas, 1962.

Erslev, A. J. "Erythrocyte Disorders—Anemias Related to Disturbance of Stem Cell Proliferation or Differentiation." In *Hematology*, edited by William J. Williams, Ernest Beutler, Allan J. Erslev, and Wayne R. Rundles, pp. 207–27. New York: McGraw-Hill, 1972.

Feitlowitz, Marguerite. *A Lexicon of Terror*. Oxford: Oxford University Press, 1998.

Garb, Solomon. *Cure for Cancer: A National Goal*. New York: Springer, 1968.

Glemser, Bernard. *Mr. Burkitt and Africa*. Cleveland: World, 1970.

Great Britain. War Office. *Medical Manual of Chemical Warfare.* Reprint. Brooklyn: Chemical Publishing Co., 1941.

Greenberg, Louis. *The Jews in Russia: The struggle for Emancipation.* New York: Schocken Books, 1976.

Handler, Clive E. *Guy's Hospital: 250 Years.* London: Guy's Hospital Gazette, 1976.

Harvey, A. McGehee. *Science at the Bedside.* Baltimore: Johns Hopkins University Press, 1981.

Hersh, Seymour M. *Chemical and Biological Warfare: America's Hidden Arsenal.* New York: Bobbs-Merrill, 1968.

Jackson, H., Jr., and Parker, F., Jr. *Hodgkin's Disease and Allied Disorders.* New York: Oxford University Press, 1947.

Jacobs, Morris B. *War Gases: Their Identification and Decontamination.* New York: Interscience Publishers, 1942.

Kaplan, Henry S. *Hodgkin's Disease.* 1972. 2nd ed. Cambridge: Harvard University Press, 1980.

Karnow, Stanley. *Vietnam: A History.* New York: Penguin Books, 1983.

Kass, Amalie M., and Kass, Edward H. *Perfecting the World: The Life and Times of Dr. Thomas Hodgkin, 1798–1866.* Boston: Harcourt Brace Jovanovich, 1988.

Lane, L. Cooper. "Elias S. Cooper." In *Representative and Leading Men of the Pacific*, edited by Oscar T. Shuck, pp. 237–47. San Francisco: Bacon, 1870.

Moss, Ralph W. *The Cancer Industry: Unraveling the Politics.* New York: Paragon House, 1989.

Moulton, Forest Ray. *Approaches to Tumor Chemotherapy.* Washington, DC: American Association for the Advancement of Science, 1947.

Murphy, William M., and D. J. R. Bruckner, eds. *The Idea of the University of Chicago.* Chicago: University of Chicago Press, 1976.

Nagel, Gunther W. *A Stanford Heritage.* Stanford: Stanford Medical Alumni Association, 1970.

Ober, William. *Great Men of Guy's.* Metuchen, NJ: Scarecrow Reprint, 1973.

Pacific Art Company. *San Francisco, 1904–1905.* San Francisco: Pacific Art Company, 1905.

Page, Robert Morris. *The Origin of Radar.* Garden City, NY: Anchor Books, Doubleday, 1962.

Phillips, Leo A. *Viruses Associated with Human Cancers.* New York: Marcel Dekker, 1983.

Powell, Lawrie W., and Kurt J. Isselbacher. "Disorders of Metals and Metallo Proteins." In *Principles of Internal Medicine*, edited by Kurt J. Isselbacher, Raymond D. Adams, Eugene Braunwald, Robert G. Petersdorf, and Jean D. Wilson, pp. 488–91. New York: McGraw-Hill, 1980.

Rettig, Richard A. *Cancer Crusade: The Story of the National Cancer Act of 1971.* Princeton, NJ: Princeton University Press, 1977.

Rytand, David A. *Medicine and the Stanford University School of Medicine Circa 1932: The Way It Was.* Stanford: Department of Medicine and Alumni Association, 1984.

Sachar, Howard M. *The Course of Modern Jewish History.* Cleveland: World, 1958.

Shapiro, Dan. *Mom's Marijuana: Life, Love, & Beating the Odds.* New York: Harmony Books, 2000.

Shilts, Randy. *And the Band Played On: Politics, People and the Aids Epidemic.* New York: Penguin Books, 1988.

Stanford University School of Medicine. *The Alway Years, 1957–1964.* Stanford: Stanford University, 1966.

Stanford University School of Medicine. *The First Hundred Years.* San Francisco: Stanford University, 1959.

Stephenson, John R. *Molecular Biology of RNA Tumor Virus.* New York: Academic Press, 1980.

Stockholm International Peace Research Institute. *The Problem of Chemical and Biological Warfare.* Stockholm: SIPRI, 1970.

Streller, Ernst, et al. *Wilhelm Conrad Roentgen, 1845–1923.* Bonn–Bad Godesberg: Inter Nationes, 1973.

Swords, Séan S. *Technical History of the Beginnings of Radar.* London: Peter Peregrinus, 1986.

Symington, Thomas. *Fundamental Pathology of the Human Adrenal Gland.* Baltimore: Williams and Wilkins, 1969.

Tenth International Cancer Congress. Chicago: Year Book Medical Publishers, 1970.

U.S. Office of Civilian Defense. Medical Division. *First Aid in the Prevention of Chemical Casualties.* Washington, DC.: Government Printing Office, 1941, 1943.

Wachtel, Curt. *Chemical Warfare.* New York: Chemical Publishing Co., 1941.

Waitt, Brigadier-General Alden H. *Gas Warfare.* New York: Duell, Sloan, and Pearce, 1942.

Whitfield, Robert G. "Historical Development of the Stanford School of Medicine." Thesis, Stanford University School of Education, 1949.

Wolin, E. M., S. A. Rosenberg, and H. S. Kaplan. "A Randomized Comparison of PAVe and MOP(P) as Adjuvant Chemotherapy for Hodgkin's Disease." In *Adjuvant Therapy of Cancer II: Proceedings of the Second International Conference in the Adjuvant Therapy of Cancer, Tuscon, Arizona, March 28–31, 1979,* edited by Stephen E. Jones and S. E. Salmon, pp. 119–27. New York: Grune & Stratton, 1979.

The World Book Encyclopedia. Chicago: World Book, 1985.

Journal Articles

Abramson JH. Infective agents in the causation of Hodgkin's disease. *Isr J Med Sci* 9: 932–53, 1973.

Adair FE and Bagg HJ. Experimental and clinical studies on the treatment of cancer by dichlorethylsulphide (mustard gas). *Ann Surg* 93: 190–99, 1931.

Amos H. Basic science and public policy. *Yale J Biol Med* 50: 261–64, 1977.

Andreopoulos S. Reinventing the Stanford Medical School: a conversation with Henry S. Kaplan. *Sandstone & Tile* 32: 13–21, 2008.

Arseneau CJ, Sponzo RW, Levin DL, et al. Nonlymphomatous malignant tumors complicating Hodgkin's Disease. *N Engl J Med* 287: 1119–22, 1972.

Bagshaw MA, Kaplan HS, and Rosenberg SA. Extended-field radiation therapy in Hodgkin's disease: a progress report. *Radiol Clin North Am* 6: 63–69, 1968.

Beiss M. How the mouse leukemia virus was discovered: a talk with Ludwik Gross. *Nouv Rev Fr Hematol* 16: 287–304, 1976.

Berg JW. The incidence of multiple primary cancers: I. Development of further cancers in patients with lymphomas, leukemias, and myeloma. *J Nat Cancer Inst* 38: 741–52, 1967.

Berger PB. Amnesty International charges repression of physicians in Argentina. *N Engl J Med* 299: 1259, 1978.

Bollag W and Grunberg E. Tumor inhibitory effects of a new class of cytotoxic agents: methylhydrazine derivatives. *Experientia*: 15: 130–31, 1963.

Boot HAH and Randall JT. Historical notes on the cavity magnetron. *IEEE Trans Electron Devices* 23: 724–29, 1976.

Breo DL. The Lasker awards: honoring the spirit of medical science. *JAMA* 266: 1843–45, 1991.

Brewster DC. Splenosis: Report of two cases and review of the literature. *Amer J Surg* 126: 14–19, 1973.

Brown FA and Kaplan HS. Hodgkin's disease: a revised clinical classification and an approach to the treatment of its localized form. *Stanford Med Bull* 15: 183–90, 1975.

Buschke F. Radiation therapy: The past, the present, the future. *Amer J Roent Rad Ther Nucl Med* 108: 236–46, 1970.

Camitta BM et al. Severe aplastic anemia: a prospective study of the effect of early marrow transplantation on acute mortality. *Blood* 48: 63–66, 1976.

Cancer meeting under boycott. *Science* 199: 666, 1978.

Carbone P and Brindley CO. Clinical studies with leurocristine. *Proc Amer Assoc Cancer Res* 3: 309, 1962.

Carvalho RPS et al. EBV infections in Brazil. I. Occurrence in normal persons, in lymphomas and in leukemias. *Internat J Cancer* 11: 191–201, 1973.

Chaplin G. Windsor Cooper Cutting. *Pharmacologist* 15: 25–28, 1973.

Coleman NC et al. Hematologic neoplasia in patients treated for Hodgkin's disease. *N Engl J Med* 297: 1249–52, 1977.

Connelly RR and Christine BW. A cohort study of cancer following infectious mononucleosis. *Cancer Res* 34: 1172–78, 1974.

Craft CB. Results with roentgen ray therapy in Hodgkin's disease. *Bulletin of the Staff Meetings University of Minnesota Hospital* 11: 391-409, 1940.

Crosby WH. Acute granulocytic leukemia, a complication of therapy in Hodgkin's disease? *Clin Res* 17: 463, 1969.

Culliton BJ. Mrs. Lasker's war. *Harper's*, June, 1976.

DeVita VT. Cell kinetics and the chemotherapy of cancer. *Cancer Chemo Rep* 2: 23–32, 1971.

DeVita VT. The consequences of the chemotherapy of Hodgkin's disease: the 10th David A. Karnofsky Memorial Lecture. *Cancer* 47: 1–13, 1981.

DeVita VT and Chu E. A history of chemotherapy. *Cancer Res* 68: 8643–53, 2008.

DeVita VT and Serpick A. Combination chemotherapy in the treatment of advanced Hodgkin's disease (HD). *Proceed Amer Assoc Cancer Res* 8: 13, 1967.

DeVita VT, Serpick AA, and Carbone PP. Combination chemotherapy in the treatment of advanced Hodgkin's disease. *Ann Intern Med* 73: 881–95, 1970.

DeVita VT et al. Intensive combination chemotherapy and X-irradiation in the treatment of Hodgkin's disease. *Proc Amer Assoc Cancer Res* 6: 15, 1965.

DeVita VT et al. Letter to the editor. *N Engl J Med* 288: 470, 1973.

Donaldson AW. The epidemiology of lung cancer among uranium miners. *Health Physics* 16: 563–69, 1969.

Donaldson SS, Glatstein E, and Vosti KL. Bacterial infections in pediatric Hodgkin's disease. *Cancer* 41: 1949–58, 1978.

Donaldson SS et al. Characterization of postsplenectomy bacteremia among patients with and without lymphoma. *N Engl J Med* 287: 69–71, 1972.

Dougherty TF and White A. Effect of pituitary adrenotropic hormone on lymphoid tissue. *Proc Soc Exper Biol Med* 53: 132–33, 1943.

Duzgunes N. Cancer congress boycott. *Science* 198: 782, 1977.

Dworsky RL and Henderson BE. Hodgkin's disease clustering in families and communities. *Cancer Res* 34: 1161–63, 1974.

Easson EC. Possibilities for the cure of Hodgkin's disease. *Cancer* 19: 345–50, 1966.

Easson EC and Russell MH. The cure of Hodgkin's disease. *BMJ* 1: 1704–7, 1963.

Epstein MA, Achong BG, and Barr YM. Virus particles in cultured lymphoblasts from Burkitt's lymphoma. *Lancet* 283: 702–3, 1964.

Foxon GEH. Thomas Hodgkin: 1798–1866: A biographical note. *Guys Hosp Rep* 115: 243–54, 1966.

Frei E III et al. The effectiveness of combinations of antileukemic agents in inducing and maintaining remission in children with acute leukemia. *Blood* 26: 642–56, 1965.

Fuks Z and Bagshaw MA. Total-skin electron treatment of mycosis fungoides. *Radiology* 100: 145–50, 1971.

Fuks Z and Feldman M. Henry S. Kaplan, 1918–1984: A physician, a scientist, a friend. *Cancer Surveys* 4: 295–311, 1985.

Gallagher RE and Gallo RC. Type C RNA tumor virus isolated from cultured human acute myelogenous leukemia cells. *Science* 187: 350–53, 1975.

Garland LH. Optimum radiotherapy of cancer. *Current Medical Digest* 28: 58–59, 1961.

Gilbert R. Radiotherapy in Hodgkin's disease (malignant granulomatosis): anatomic and clinical foundations; governing principles; results. *Amer J Roent* 41: 198–241, 1939.

Gilman Maj A and Philips 1st Lieut FS. The biological actions and therapeutic applications of the B-chloroethyl amines and sulfides. *Science* 103: 409–15, 1946.

Gilmore HR and Zelesnick G. Environmental Hodgkin's disease and leukemia. *Pennsylvania Medical Journal* 65: 1047–49, 1962.

Ginzton EL and Nunan CS. History of microwave electron linear accelerators for radiotherapy. *Int J Radiation Oncology Biol Phys* 11: 205–16, 1985.

Ginzton EL, Mallory KB, and Kaplan HS. The Stanford medical linear accelerator: I. Design and development. *Stanford Med Bull* 15: 123–40, 1957.

Glatsetin E et al. The value of laparotomy and splenectomy in the staging of Hodgkin's disease. *Cancer* 24: 709–18, 1969.

Goffinet DR, Glatstein E, and Kaplan HS. Herpes zoster infections in lymphoma patients. *Natl Cancer Inst Monogr* 36: 463–64, 1973.

Goodman LS et al. Nitrogen mustard therapy: use of methyl-bis (beta-chloroethyl) amine hydrochloride and tris (beta-chloroethyl) amine hydrochloride for Hodgkin's disease, lymphosarcoma, leukemia and certain allied and miscellaneous disorders. *JAMA* 132: 126–32, 1946.

Greenberg D. Funding and decision-making in science. *Ann NY Acad of Sciences* 196: 279–91, 1972.

Gross L. A filterable agent, recovered from AK leukemic extracts, causing salivary gland carcinomas in C3H mice. *Proc Soc Exp Biol Med* 83: 414–21, 1953.

Hale-White W. Thomas Hodgkin. *Guys Hosp Rep* 74: 117–36, 1924.

Hall TC. New chemotherapeutic agents in Hodgkin's disease. *Cancer Res* 26, part I: 1297–1302, 1966.

Hancock PE. Thomas Hodgkin. *J Royal College of Physicians* 2: 404–21, 1963.

Hardwick C. Thomas Hodgkin 1798–1866. *Guys Hosp Rep* 115: 25–61, 1966.

Hill W. Thomas Hodgkin: a bibliography. *Guys Hosp Rep* 115: 281–303, 1966.

Hodgkin T. On some morbid appearances of the absorbant glands and spleen. *Medical Classics* 1: 741–70, 1937.

Hodgkin's disease: a clue or a fluke? *BMJ* 4: 564–65, 1972.

Horan M and Colebatch JH. Relation between splenectomy and subsequent infection. *Arch Dis Childh* 37: 398–410, 1962.

Horning SJ et al. Vinblastine, bleomycin, and methotrexate: an effective adjuvant in favorable Hodgkin's disease. *J Clin Oncol* 6: 1822–31, 1988.

Jackson H and Parker F. Hodgkin's disease: I. General considerations. *N Engl J Med* 230: 1–8, 1944a.

Jackson H and Parker F. Hodgkin's disease: II. Pathology. *N Engl J Med* 231: 35–44, 1944b.

Johnson RE. Is staging laparotomy routinely indicated in Hodgkin's disease? *Ann Intern Med* 75: 459–62, 1971.

Kaplan HS. Observations on radiation-induced lymphoid tumors of mice. *Cancer Res* 7: 141–47, 1947.

Kaplan HS. Comparative susceptibility of the lymphoid tissues of strain C57 black mice to the induction of lymphoid tumors by irradiation. *J Nat Cancer Inst* 8: 191–97, 1948.

Kaplan HS. Radiation-induced lymphoid tumors of mice. *Acta Union internat contre le cancer* 7: 849–59, 1952.

Kaplan HS. Some implications of indirect induction mechanisms in carcinogenesis: a review. *Cancer Res* 19: 791–803, 1959.

Kaplan HS. The radical radiotherapy of regionally localized Hodgkin's disease. *Radiology* 78: 553–61, 1962a.

Kaplan HS. Letter to Professor Zhdanov. *Science* 135: 997–98, 1962b.

Kaplan HS. Role of intensive radiotherapy in the management of Hodgkin's disease. *Cancer* 19: 356–67, 1966.

Kaplan HS. On the natural history of the murine leukemias: presidential address. *Cancer Res* 27: 1325–40, 1967.

Kaplan HS. Clinical evaluation and radiotherapeutic management of Hodgkin's disease and the malignant lymphomas. *N Engl J Med* 278: 892–99, 1968.

Kaplan HS. Contiguity and progression in Hodgkin's disease. *Cancer Res* 31: 1801–13, 1971.

Kaplan HS. Emotion versus objectivity in the funding of biomedical research. *Ann NY Acad Sci* 196: 274–78, 1972.

Kaplan HS. Hodgkin's disease: multidisciplinary contributions to the conquest of a neoplasm. *Radiology* 123: 551–58, 1977.

Kaplan HS. Etiology of lymphomas and leukemias: role of C-type RNA viruses. *Leukemia Research* 2: 253–71, 1978.

Kaplan HS. Historic milestones in radiobiology and radiation therapy. *Seminars in Oncology* 6: 479–89, 1979.

Kaplan HS and Bagshaw MA. The Stanford medical linear accelerator: III. Application to clinical problems of radiation therapy. *Stanford Med Bull* 15: 141–51, 1957.

Kaplan HS and Brown MB. Further observations on inhibition of lymphoid tumor development by shielding and partial body irradiation of mice. *J Nat Cancer Inst* 12: 327–36, 1951.

Kaplan HS and Rosenberg SA. Extended-field radical radiotherapy in advanced Hodgkin's disease: short-term results of 2 randomized clinical trials. *Cancer Res* 26: 1268–76, 1966a.

Kaplan HS and Rosenberg SA. The treatment of Hodgkin's disease. *Med Clinics of North America* 50: 1591–1610, 1966b.

Kaplan HS and Rosenberg SA. Current status of clinical trials: Stanford experience 1962–72. *Natl Cancer Inst Monogr* 36: 363–71, 1973a.

Kaplan HS and Rosenberg SA. New approaches to the treatment of advanced Hodgkin's disease. *Proc XIII Internat Cong Rad* 2: 109–11, 1973b.

Kaplan HS and Stewart JR. Complications of intensive megavoltage radiotherapy for Hodgkin's disease. *Natl Cancer Inst Monogr* 36: 439–44, 1973.

Kaplan HS, Hirsch BB, and Brown MB. Indirect induction of lymphomas in irradiated mice: IV. Genetic evidence of the origin of the tumor cells from the thymic grafts. *Cancer Res* 16: 434–36, 1956.

Kaplan HS et al. Staging laparotomy and splenectomy in Hodgkin's disease: analysis of indications and patterns of involvement in 285 consecutive, unselected patients. *Natl Cancer Inst Monogr* 36: 291–301, 1973.

Kaplan HS et al. Isolation of a type C RNA virus from an established human histiocytic lymphoma cell line. *Proc Natl Acad Sci USA* 74: 2564–68, 1977.

Kaplan HS et al. Biology and virology of the human malignant lymphomas. *Cancer* 43: 1–24, 1979.

Kass EH. Thomas Hodgkin, physician and social scientist. *Guys Hosp Rep* 115: 269–80, 1966.

Kates RW. Human issues in human rights. *Science* 201: 502–6, 1978.

King H and Shumacker HB. Splenic studies. *Ann Surg* 136: 239–42, 1952.

Kinmonth JB. Lymphangiography in man. *Clin Science* 11: 13–20, 1952.

Kirschbaum A and Kaplan HS. Induction of leukemia in mice. *Science* 100: 360–61, 1944.

Kohler G and Milstein C. Continuous cultures of fused cells secreting antibody of predefined specificity. *Nature* 256: 495–97, 1975.

Krakoff IH. Progress and prospects in cancer treatment: the Karnofsky legacy. *J Clin Oncol* 12: 432–38, 1994.

Lane LC. Editor's table. *San Francisco Medical Press* 3: 226–43, 1862.

Levine PH et al. Elevated antibody titers to Epstein-Barr virus in Hodgkin's disease. *Cancer* 27: 416–21, 1971.

Lewin R. An experiment that had to succeed. *Science* 212: 767–69, 1981.

Lieberman M and Kaplan HS. Leukemogenic activity of filtrates from radiation-induced lymphoid tumors of mice. *Science* 130: 387–88, 1959.

Lowdon AGR, Stewart RHM, and Walker W. Risk of serious infection following splenectomy. *BMJ* 1: 446–50, 1966.

Massey FC, Lane LL, and Imbriglia JE. Acute infectious mononucleosis and Hodgkin's disease occurring simultaneously in the same patient. *JAMA* 151: 994–95, 1953.

Mathe G et al. Methyl-hydrazine in treatment of Hodgkin's disease and various forms of haematosarcoma and leukaemia. *Lancet* 2: 1077–83, 1963.

Mazur SA and Straus B. Marital Hodgkin's disease. *Arch Internal Med* 88: 819–30, 1951.

Medinger FG and Craver LF. Total body irradiation (with review of cases). *Amer J Roent* 48: 651–71, 1942.

Meredith WJ. Some aspects of supervoltage radiation therapy. *Amer J Roent Rad Ther Nucl Med* 79: 3–12, 1958.

Merner TB and Stenstrom KW. Roentgen therapy in Hodgkin's disease. *Radiology* 48: 355–68, 1947.

Montoro AF. Cancer congress boycott and human rights. *Science* 199: 480, 1978.

National Cancer Program. The Impact of the National Cancer Act. *JNCI* 83: S-1–16, 1991.

Newbery GR and Bewley DK. The performance of the medical research council 8 MeV linear accelerator. *British J Radiology* 28: 241–51, 1955.

Noble RL, Beer CT, and Cutts, JH. Role of chance observations in chemotherapy: *Vinca rosea. Ann N Y Acad Sci* 76: 882–94, 1958.

Obstacles to the Control of Hodgkin's Disease. Symposium sponsored by the American Cancer Society and the National Cancer Institute. *Cancer Res* 26: 1015–312, 1966.

Olsson L and Kaplan HS. Human-human hybridomas producing monoclonal antibodies of predefined antigenic specificity. *Proc Natl Acad Sci USA* 77: 5429–31, 1980.

Pearson HA, Johnston D, Smith KA, and Touloukian RJ. The born-again spleen: Return of splenic function after splenectomy for trauma. *N Engl J Med* 298: 1389–92, 1978.

Peters MV. A study of survivals in Hodgkin's disease treated radiologically. *Amer J of Roentgenol* 63: 299–311, 1950.

Peters MV. Prophylactic treatment of adjacent areas in Hodgkin's disease. *Cancer Res* 26: 1232–43, 1966.

Peters MV. The need for a new clinical classification in Hodgkin's disease: keynote address. *Cancer Res* 31: 1713–22, 1971.

Peters MV. The evolution of the radiotherapeutic concept in Hodgkin's disease. *Series in Hematology* 6: 117–38, 1973.

Peters MV and Middlemiss KCH. A study of Hodgkin's disease treated by irradiation. *Amer J Roent Rad Therapy* 63: 114–21, 1958.

Proceedings of the Symposium on Contemporary Issues in Hodgkin's Disease: biology, staging, and treatment. *Cancer Treatment Reports* 66: 601–1067, 1982.

Pusey WA. Cases of sarcoma and of Hodgkin's disease treated by exposures to x-rays: a preliminary report. *JAMA* 38: 166–68, 1902.

La radiothérapie de la maladie de Hodgkin. *Journal de radiologie* 47: 1–176, 1966.

Rather LJ. Who discovered the pathognomonic giant cell of Hodgkin's Disease? *Bull NY Acad Med* 48: 943–49, 1972.

Reed DM. On the pathological changes in Hodgkin's Disease with especial reference to its relation to tuberculosis. *Johns Hopkins Hospital Report* 10: 133–96, 1902.

Rixford E. Early medical schools on the Pacific coast. *Pacific Medical Journal* 56: 154–65, 1913.

Rixford E. Levi Cooper Lane, M.D. *California and Western Medicine* 37: 382–84, 1932; 38: 37–39, 1933.

Rosdahl N, Larsen SO, and Clemmesen J. Hodgkin's disease in patients with previous infectious mononucleosis: 30 years' experience. *BMJ* 2: 253–56, 1974.

Rosenberg SA. A critique of the value of laparotomy and splenectomy in the evaluation of patients with Hodgkin's disease. *Cancer Res* 31: 1737–40, 1971.

Rosenberg SA. Other tumors complicating Hodgkin's disease. *N Engl J Med* 288: 469–70, 1973.

Rosenberg SA. The management of Hodgkin's disease: Half a century of change. *Annals of Oncology* 7: 555–60, 1996.

Rosenberg SA and Kaplan HS. The evolution and summary results of the Stanford randomized clinical trials of the management of Hodgkin's disease: 1962–1984. *J Rad Oncol Biol Phys* 11: 5–22, 1985.

Rosenberg SA et al. Combination chemotherapy and radiotherapy for Hodgkin's disease. *Cancer* 30: 1505–10, 1972.

Rosenbloom J. An interesting friendship: Thomas Hodgkin, M.D. and Sir Moses Montefiore, Bart. *Annals of Medical History* 3: 381–86, 1921.

Rous P. A sarcoma of the fowl transmissible by an agent separable from the tumor cells. *J Exp Med* 13: 397–411, 1911.

Sagan LA and Jonsen A. Medical ethics and torture. *N Engl J Med* 294: 1427–30, 1976.

Schreiner BF and Mattick WL. Radiation therapy in forty-six cases of lymphogranuloma (Hodgkin's disease). *Amer J Roent* 12: 133–37, 1924.

Schulz MD. The supervoltage story. *Amer J Roent Rad Ther Nucl Med* 124: 541–59, 1975.

Schwartzenberg L. Interview with Professor Schwartzenberg. *Rev Infirm* Mar (3): 8–11, 1979.

Senn N. The therapeutical value of the roentgen ray in the treatment of pseudoleucaemia. *NY Med J* 77: 665–68, 1903.

Shimkin MB et al. Hodgkin's disease: An analysis of frequency, distribution and mortality at the University of California Hospital, 1914–1951. *Ann Intern Med* 42: 136–53, 1955.

Siber GR et al. Impaired antibody response to pneumococcal vaccine after treatment for Hodgkin's disease. *N Engl J Med* 299: 442–48, 1978.

Sikora K and Neville AM. Human monoclonal antibodies. *Nature* 300: 316–17, 1982.

Simonds JP. Review: Hodgkin's Disease. *Arch Path Lab Med* 1: 394–430, 1926.

Skipper HE, Schabel FM Jr, and Wilcox WS. Experimental evaluation of potential anticancer agents: XIII. On the criteria and kinetics associated with "curability" of experimental leukemia. *Cancer Chemo Rep* 35: 1–111, 1964.

Smith PG and Pike MC. Current epidemiological evidence for transmission of Hodgkin's disease. *Cancer Res* 36: 660–62, 1976.

Smithers DW. Hodgkin's disease–I. *BMJ* Apr 29: 263–68, 1967.

Smithers DW: Spread of Hodgkin's disease. *Lancet* 295: 1262–67, 1970.

Sutcliffe SB and Gospodarowicz MK. In memoriam: Vera Peters. *J Clin Oncol* 12: 239–40, 1994.

Symposium: Staging in Hodgkin's disease. *Cancer Res* 31: 1707–1869, 1971.

Teng NNH et al. Construction and testing of mouse-human heteromyelomas for human monoclonal antibody production. *Proc Natl Acad Sci USA* 80: 7308–12, 1983.

Thomas L. On the planning of cancer science. *Yale J Biol Med* 50: 253–59, 1977.

Utz L and Keatinge L. Hodgkin's disease. *MJA* 1: 397–407, 1931.

Utz L and Keatinge L. Hodgkin's disease: a treatise. *MJA* 1: 521–25, 1932.

Vianna NJ and Polan AK. Epidemiologic evidence for transmission of Hodgkin's disease. *N Engl J Med* 289: 499–502, 1973.

Vianna NJ, Greenwald P, and Davies JNP. Extended epidemic of Hodgkin's disease in high-school students. *Lancet* 1: 1209–10, 1971.

Vianna NJ et al. Hodgkin's disease: cases with features of a community outbreak. *Ann Intern Med* 77: 169–80, 1972.

Wade N. Repression in Argentina: scientists caught up in tide of terror. *Science* 194: 1397–99, 1976.

Wade N. Academy to campaign publicly for oppressed scientists. *Science* 196: 741–43, 1977.

Walsh J. Stanford School of Medicine (I): problems over more than money. *Science* 171: 551–53, 1971a.

Walsh J. Stanford School of Medicine (II): clinicians make an issue. *Science* 171: 654–57, 1971b.

Weissbluth M, Karzmark CJ, Steele RE, and Shelby AH. The Stanford medical linear accelerator: II. Installation and physical measurements. *Radiology* 72: 242–53, 1959.

Where is Federico Alvarez Rojas? *Nature* 266: 395, 1977.

Whitaker AN. Infection and the spleen: association between hyposplenism, pneumococcal sepsis and disseminated intravascular coagulation. *MJA* 1: 1213–19, 1969.

Wilks S. Cases of lardaceous disease and some allied affections with remarks. *Guys Hosp Rep* 2: 103–32, 1856.

Wilks S. A short account of the life and works of Thomas Hodgkin, M.D. *Guy's Hospital Gazette* 23: 528–32, 1909.

Yates JL and Bunting CH. Results of treatment in Hodgkin's disease. *JAMA* 68: 747–51, 1917.

Zwittter M et al. Dorothy Reed and Hodgkin's disease: a reflection after a century. *Int J Radiat Oncol Biol* 53: 366–75, 2002.

Index

The initials HSK refer to Henry Kaplan.

AACR, *see* American Association for
   Cancer Research
Abrams, Herb, 98, 99, 141, 196, 214, 215–17
ABVD chemotherapy, 356–57
Adair, Frank, 83
Adams, Ansel, 309–10
Addison, Thomas, 14, 15
Adelman, Gladys, 52
Adriamycin, 356–57
Africa: lymphomas, 316–18; physicians, 327
Agnew, Spiro T., 226
Albany, New York, Hodgkin's disease in,
   238, 240
Alkeran, 285
Allied School of Mechanical Trade, 58, 64
Alway, Robert, 128–29, 212, 213, 214
American Association for Cancer
   Research (AACR), 187, 188–89, 331
American Cancer Society, 116, 163, 229,
   275, 331
American Medical Association, 327
Amnesty International, 327, 330, 338, 373,
   374
Anderson, Ian, 389
Ann Arbor Conference, 204, 248, 249–55
Ann Arbor staging system, 254–55, 256
Antidepressants, 181, 347–48
Antioch College West, 257, 309
Aplastic anemia, 106–7, 282–83, 349–51
Argentina: *desaparecidos*, 328–38, 387;
   Dirty War, 329–38; International
   Cancer Congress (1978), 330–37, 387

Armstrong, Alfred, 184
Arseneau, James, 276–77, 278
Atomic bomb survivors, 152–53, 276
Atomic Energy Commission, 138
Auger, Colette, 332–37

Bagg, Henry, 83
Bagshaw, Malcolm: Cancer Research
   Center Planning Committee, 262–67,
   269, 271; relationship with HSK, 263,
   270, 387, 390; at Stanford, 124, 209;
   treatment of HSK's cancer, 382, 383, 384
Baldwin, John, 380
Baltimore, David, 331
Bang, Oluf, 243
Barr, Yvonne, 319
Barreiro, Hipolito, 338
Berg, Paul, 129, 262, 263, 265
Bernard, Jean, 159
Bernfield, Merton, 387
Bieber, Marsha, 367, 368, 369
Black, Thomas, 15
Blank, Norm, 376–77, 384
Bloomfield, Arthur, 94–95, 101, 125
Bonadonna, Gianni, 356
Bone marrow: effects of radiation thera-
   py, 47, 152–53; transplants, 349–51
Bookstein, Joel, 386
"Boy in the bubble," *see* DeVita, Teddy
Braude, Abraham, 56, 58, 62, 258, 370, 375
Braude, Gita, 375
Breast cancer, 46, 104, 255
Brezhnev, Leonid, 373–74
Bridges, Sam, 268

Bright, Richard, 14, 15, 23
Brilliant, Abraham, 20, 21
Brilliant, Clara, 20, 22
Brilliant, Florence, 20, 22
Brilliant, Henry, 20–21, 29
Brilliant, Sarah, *see* Kaplan, Sarah
 Brilliant
Britain: Guy's Hospital, London, 12, 13–14,
 17, 23; Hodgkin's disease treatment by
 Easson, 160; medical linear accelerator
 development, 115–16, 121; radar, 113
Brown, Mary, 93, 99, 100–101. *See also*
 Lawrence, Mary Brown
Bull, Joan, 194
Bunting, C. H., 42
Burchenal, Joe, 231
Burkitt, Denis, 316–18, 319
Burkitt's lymphoma, 316–19

Calder, Alexander, 226
California Institute of Technology, 111–12
Cancer: caused by radiation, 276, 357;
 clusters, 238–41; in former Hodgkin's
 disease patients, 275–79, 295–98;
 skin, 47, 209–10, 275; treatments,
 82–83, 209, 382; virology, 243–47. *See
 also* Chemotherapy; Clinical trials;
 Hodgkin's disease; Leukemia; Lung
 cancer; Lymphomas; Radiation therapy
Cancer Biology Research Laboratory
 (CBRL), Stanford: building, 312, 315–16;
 human monoclonal antibody research,
 365–70, 373; opening, 312, 313; plans
 for, after HSK's death, 385–86, 389,
 390; safety risks, 315–16, 324; search for
 human lymphoma virus, 313, 314–16,
 321–22, 323–25; staff, 323, 385–86; virus
 research, 323–25
Cancer centers, 230, 261, 262–67, 268–72,
 274, 311, 368, 391
Cancer research: on breast cancer, 255;
 federal funding, 228, 232–33, 234, 236–
 37; National Panel of Consultants on
 the Conquest of Cancer, 230–33, 234,
 235–36, 262; virology, 243–47. *See also*
 Cancer Biology Research Laboratory;
 National Cancer Institute

Cancer Research Center (CRC) Planning
 Committee, 262–67, 268–72, 274, 311
Canellos, George, 185, 190, 276, 277–78
Canonico, Abel, 331
Carbone, Paul: chemotherapy research,
 180, 186, 187, 188, 190; at international
 conferences, 249, 253, 254, 255; relation-
 ship with HSK, 248
Carcinogenesis, 75–77, 78, 100, 242–43,
 246–47, 312
Cassidy, Sheila, 327
Castellino, Ronald, 141
Castro, Raul, 336
CAT chemotherapy, 297–98
CBRL, *see* Cancer Biology Research
 Laboratory
Champlin, John, 290, 291
Chandler, Loren: recruitment of HSK,
 88, 89–90, 92, 94; retirement, 101, 125;
 as Stanford Medical School dean, 87,
 88, 93
Chase, Robert, 219
Chemical warfare, 80–85, 179–80
Chemotherapy: ABVD, 356–57; cancer
 treatment, 82–85, 179–82, 185, 297,
 382; CAT regimen, 297–98; clinical
 trials, 186–90, 201–3; combination,
 186–90; doses and scheduling, 181–82;
 Hodgkin's disease treatment, 7, 8, 83–
 85, 140, 167, 180, 181, 186–90, 193; lymphoma treatment, 180, 297–98; MOMP,
 186–87, 190; nitrogen mustard, 83–85,
 167, 179–80, 187, 194; non-cross-resistance, 181; nonoverlapping toxicities,
 180; palliative use, 193; PAVe, 284–86,
 292; with radiation, 7, 8, 193, 201–3;
 research, 185–90, 280; Skipper's tumor
 models, 182, 186, 190; toxicity, 84–85,
 187, 194, 297, 358; VBM, 357–59, 360–63.
 See also MOPP chemotherapy
Chicago: Depression in, 37–38, 49; Jewish
 neighborhoods, 28; Michael Reese
 Hospital, 62, 97, 115, 121, 379
Chicago Art Institute, 210
Childhood leukemia, 182, 185–86, 320
Children: cancer treatments, 209; with
 Hodgkin's disease, 207–9, 398; of

Hodgkin's disease patients, 363; lymphomas in Africa, 316–18. *See also* DeVita, Teddy; Infertility; Kaplan, Ann; Kaplan, Paul
Chile, human rights violations, 327
Christine, Barbara, 242
Church, Thomas, 130
Clark, R. Lee, 226
Clinical trials: beginning, 5, 144; blind selection process, 144; chemotherapy, 186–90, 201–3; early closure, 156–57; number of patients, 156; protocols, 144, 162; radiotherapy and chemotherapy for children, 208–9; of total lymphoid irradiation, 6, 151–58, 162, 191, 201–3, 285–86, 357, 363; twenty-year celebration, 1–10, 371
—protocols, 144, 162; C series, 357–59, 360, 363; H series, 201–3, 274, 284; L-1, L-2 protocol, 146–50, 162; S series, 285–86, 292, 356
Cobalt 60, 113, 120
Coleman, Norman: analysis of second cancers in Hodgkin's disease patients, 295; on HSK, 207, 210, 297; HSK's cancer and, 379, 382, 394–95, 396; patients of, 194, 297, 353; photograph of, 345 (fig.); research, 207; at staging conferences, 272; at twenty-year celebration, 2, 3, 5
Colleagues: conflicts with faculty peers, 211–13, 216–17, 218–21, 262–63, 266–67, 269–72, 368; faculty peers, 95, 102, 124; fellow scientists, 168, 248–49, 255–56, 385; isolation from, 259–60, 368; relations with in last months of life, 389–91. *See also* Friends; Rosenberg, Saul
Collins, David, 274
Congress: House Un-American Activities Committee, 225; National Cancer Act, 228, 233–36, 237, 253, 261; National Panel of Consultants on the Conquest of Cancer, 230–33, 234–36, 262, 264; NIH funding, 230–31
Connally, John B., 226
Connelly, Roger, 242

Contiguous spread theory, 165–66, 199, 204, 250
Coolidge, W. D., 111
Coolidge tube, 47–48, 111
Cooper, Astley, 12, 13
Cooper, Elias Samuel, 86
Cooper Medical College, 87
Corbett, Mario, 122
Cortisone, 181
Coy, John, 138
Craft, Charles, 66, 70
Craver, Lloyd, 69, 139
CRC Committee, *see* Cancer Research Center Planning Committee
Creger, Bill, 95, 125, 153
Crocker, Max, 21, 22, 28, 32, 50–51, 53
Crocker, Norman, 53–54, 61–62
Crowley, Larry, 223, 262–67, 271, 387
Culberg, Eve, 373
Cutting, Windsor, 101, 125, 126, 127, 128
Cyclophosphamide, 186
Cyclosporin A, 350–51, 353

David, Vernon, 55
Declève, Alain, 246, 311–12, 323, 324–25
De Peyster, Frederic, 55
Depression, 37–38, 49
Desaparecidos, see Argentina
DeVita, Mary Kay Bush, 184, 283, 354
DeVita, Teddy, 282–83, 347–50, 351–53
DeVita, Vincent T., Jr.: chemotherapy research, 7, 179, 185–90, 193, 201, 280, 360; criticism of Rosenberg's chemotherapy regimens, 7, 285, 359, 360–63; at international conferences, 253, 360–63; life and family, 182–84; at National Cancer Institute, 275–79, 280, 296, 322, 348, 351, 362, 389; photographs of, 341 (fig.), 345 (fig.); relationship with HSK, 6, 248–49, 258, 270–71, 280–82, 283, 361, 362–63, 375, 382, 391; relationship with Rosenberg, 362; son, 282–83, 347–50, 351–53; at Stanford, 281
Dick, George, 55
DiJulio, Jan, 2, 7
Dirty War, *see* Argentina
Doggett, Scotte, 146, 147

Donaldson, Sarah: HSK's cancer and, 379; in Paris, 206–7; patients of, 2, 8, 9, 207–9, 301–2; photograph of, 341 (fig.); study of infections after splenectomy, 301–2, 306; training with Kaplan, 205, 206–7

Dorfman, Ronald, 141, 142

Dougherty, Thomas, 181

Dyslexia, 175–76, 309, 310

Eads, Douglas, 1, 8–9, 148–49, 388

Easson, Eric, 160, 161, 162, 166

Ebstein, Wilhelm, 24

EBV, *see* Epstein-Barr virus

Edes, Claire, 31–32, 34, 371–72, 373

Ekstrand, Petra, 151–52, 153, 154, 306–7

Ellerman, Vilhelm, 243

Epstein, Alan, 315, 323

Epstein, Michael Anthony, 316, 318–19, 322, 323

Epstein-Barr virus (EBV), 241–42, 319, 322

Ewing, James, 82–83

Farber, Sidney, 163, 164

Fein, Mirielle, 52, 53

Fein, Niecy, 52

Feldman, Michael: Glaser's visit and, 218; on HSK, 311; HSK's letters to, 310, 315; office at Stanford, 316; relationship with HSK, 177, 258–59, 271, 374, 375, 376, 379, 391–92

Fortner, Joseph, 385

Fowl sarcoma, 243–44

France: Institut Gustave Roussy, 159, 206–7; Legion of Honor, 168. *See also* Paris

Fredell, Bill, 145

Frei, Emil, III (Tom): chemotherapy research, 167, 187, 189, 190; human rights issues and, 331; leukemia research and treatment, 182, 185–86; life and career, 184–85, 188

Freireich, Emil J., 182, 185–86, 190

French language, learned from mystery novels, 169, 206–7

Friedell, Hymer, 138

Friends: Feldman, 258–59, 271, 374, 375, 376, 379, 391–92; fellow students, 36–37,

52–54, 56; Gallo, 323, 374–75, 390; of HSK and Leah, 74, 78, 123, 139, 158, 174, 212; in last months, 391–92; male, 53–54, 56, 258–59, 280–82; perceived betrayals by, 216, 220–21, 270–71. *See also* DeVita, Vincent T., Jr.

Fuks, Zvi, 206, 209–10, 374, 389

Gagliani, Oliver, 310

Gallo, Robert, 316, 319–21, 322–23, 343 (fig.), 374–75, 390

Gamma rays, 112–13

Garb, Solomon, 230

Garland, Leo Henry, 88, 89, 91, 95–97, 120

George Washington University School of Medicine, 184

Gilbert, Edward, 272–73

Gilbert, René, 69–70, 105, 107, 108, 165

Gilman, Alfred, 82, 179–80

Gilmore, Hugh R., 238–39, 241

Ginzton, Edward, 5, 114–15, 116–18, 119, 121, 124, 258

Glaisyer, John, 12

Glaser, Robert Joy, 213–21, 262, 266, 387

Glatstein, Eli: HSK's cancer and, 379; life, 196; at National Cancer Institute, 210, 389; patients of, 8, 193, 194–95, 297, 298, 305; personality, 196; photograph of, 341 (fig.); recommended staging laparotomy, 196–98; relationship with HSK, 389–90; training with HSK, 207; at twenty-year celebration, 2, 3

Glick, John, 205–6, 210

Godlee, Sarah, 12, 14, 18

Goffinet, Don, 273, 379, 382

Goldstein, Avram: on HSK, 217; relations with deans, 128, 129, 218; research, 127; at Stanford, 127, 130, 211, 212, 213

Gonda, Thomas, 268

Goodman, Benny, 53

Goodman, Louis, 84, 85

Granuloma, 67, 161

Greenbaum-Miller, Betty Ann, 363

Greene, Samuel, 374

Gross, Ludwik, 243, 244–46

Guy's Hospital, London, 12, 13–14, 17, 23

Haimson, Jacob, 120

Hall, Thomas, 181

Hamburg, David, 211, 212–13, 215–16, 219, 220

Hanks, Gerry, 198

Hansen, Bill, 114

Harris, Tex, 333, 336

Harrison, Benjamin, 12, 17

Harvard University Medical School, 127–28

Harvey, Mary, 274–75

Haws, Meredith, 379

Henle, Gertrude, 319

Henle, Werner, 319

Herpes zoster (shingles), 108, 192, 292, 299, 319

Heteromyelomas, 369–70

Heublein, Arthur, 69

Heublein therapy, 69

Hirsh, Barbara, 99

Hodgkin, Thomas: death, 19; description of Hodgkin's disease, 3, 15–16; at Guy's Hospital Museum of Pathology, 13–14, 17, 23; health problems, 18–19; interest in medicine, 11–13; life, 11–19; marriage, 18; medical career, 13–16, 17–18; physical appearance, 11; portrait, 131 (fig.); reform efforts, 14, 16–17; research, 13–14

Hodgkin's disease: clusters of cases, 238–41; constitutional symptoms and outcomes, 108, 146; contiguous spread theory, 165–66, 199, 204, 250; debate on causes, 25–26, 42, 68; description of, 3, 15–16; diagnostic criteria, 26–27; naming of, 23; pathologic classifications, 67, 161, 164; pediatric, 207–9, 398; subtypes, 67, 161. *See also* Staging

Hodgkin's Disease (Kaplan), 257, 276

Hodgkin's disease research: early, 23–27, 42; on infectious causes, 238–47; international collaboration, 159–67, 248–55; international conferences, 159–67, 249–55, 359–63; in 1940s, 66–68; since HSK's death, 398. *See also* Clinical trials

Hodgkin's disease treatment: in 1960s, 140, 159; chemotherapy, 83–85, 140, 167, 180, 181, 186–90, 193; drugs, 43; early,

24, 25, 26, 42–44, 46–47; importance of staging, 44; remission rates, 189, 398; surgery, 42, 141, 166; vaccines, 43–44

Hodgkin's disease treatment, at Stanford: chart rounds, 205, 390; chemotherapy and radiation, 7, 8, 193, 201–3; of children, 207–9, 388; criticism of, 153, 359–63; debates on, 143–44, 158, 193, 198, 272; factors in success, 111, 122, 137; high-dose radiation, 191–93; infections after splenectomy, 301–2, 303–5; multidisciplinary team, 3, 140–41; radiotherapy, 109–10, 142–43, 146; remission, 153, 163, 195, 203, 274–75, 388; Rosenberg-Kaplan collaboration, 140, 141–42, 143–44, 151, 157–58, 162, 198, 272; second cancers in patients, 295–98; staging conferences, 141–42, 143–44, 146, 158, 272, 374; surgery, 141; survival rates, 143, 161, 296; total lymphoid irradiation, 6, 151–58, 162. *See also* Clinical trials; Staging laparotomies

Hodgkin's disease treatment, radiotherapy: with chemotherapy, 186, 201–3, 208–9, 276, 278, 296; of children, 207–9; of contiguous nodes, 199; disease spread theories and, 165, 166–67; doses, 105, 109–10, 162, 166; early, 46, 66; in early 1960s, 6; extended field irradiation, 146, 149–50, 167; high-dose, 142–43; involved field radiation, 146, 149–50, 208, 357, 358, 363; mantle and inverted Y ports, 142, 143, 151, 152, 162; Peters's research, 103, 105–9, 160–61, 162; as primary treatment, 85, 161; prophylactic, 108, 142, 143, 146, 162, 165, 166–67; radical, 142–43; remission rates, 160, 161; second cancers in patients, 275–79, 295–98; survival rates, 66, 70, 106, 109, 143, 160; total lymphoid irradiation, 6, 151–58, 162, 166, 201–3; toxicity, 110, 143, 147, 151, 152–54, 156, 191–93, 296, 306

Hoffman-LaRoche Laboratories, 181

Hogben, C. Adrian, 184

Holland, James, 227

Holman, Emile, 95, 101, 125, 211

Holman, Halsted, 211, 212, 213, 215–16, 220, 267
Hoover, Herbert, 88
Hoppe, Richard, 355–56
Horning, Sandra, 358
Hospitals, 87–88, 92, 94–95. *See also* Stanford University Hospital
House Un-American Activities Committee, 225. *See also* Congress
Howard-Flanders, P., 121
Human Leukemia 23 virus (HL23V), 321
Human lymphoma virus, 313, 314–16. *See also* Human tumor virus
Human monoclonal antibodies, 365–70, 373
Human rights issues, 327, 328–38, 373–74, 387
Human tumor virus, 245, 257, 316–25
Hurt, Judith, 301–2
Hybridomas, 365, 367

Immune system: antibodies, 314, 319, 364–65, 370; bone marrow transplants and, 349; effects of Hodgkin's disease, 26; effects of radiation, 152, 192, 350, 353; graft rejection, 349, 350; human monoclonal antibodies, 365–70, 373
Infections: after splenectomy, 300–307; meningitis, 300, 304. *See also* Viruses
Infectious mononucleosis, 239, 241–42
Infertility: effects of chemotherapy, 201–2, 203; effects of radiation exposure, 97–98, 101, 152, 153, 357, 363
Institut Gustave Roussy, 159, 206–7
Interleukin-2, 322
International Cancer Congresses: alternate in Paris, 337; Buenos Aires (1978), 330–37, 387; Houston (1970), 226–27; Moscow (1962), 226
International Congress of Radiology (1956), 103, 108–9
International Union Against Cancer (UICC), 226, 330, 337
Irvine Foundation, 118
Israel: HSK's travel to, 176–77, 326, 374; Weizmann Institute, 169, 177, 178, 258, 385

Issacs, Gordon, 118–19, 121, 135 (fig.)
Issacs, Helen, 118–19
Izenstark, Joseph, 36–37

Jackson, Henry, 67–68
Jackson-Parker system, 161, 164
Jenkins, Chris, 2, 3, 8, 286–93, 299–300, 303–5, 343 (fig.), 388
Jenkins, Melinh, 2, 8, 290, 305, 343 (fig.)
Jews: anti-Semitism, 18; in Chicago, 28; history in Israel, 176–77; Holocaust, 74, 177; medical school quotas, 52, 138; in Palestine, 18–19; physicians in Chicago, 62; pogroms, 21–22, 58; in Russia, 20–22, 29, 58
Johns Hopkins Medical School, 24, 87
Johnson, George, 88
Johnson, Ralph, 186, 199, 249, 252, 253, 254
Jones, Bob, 388–89
Jones, Henry, 98, 120
Jordan, David Starr, 87

Kahn, Marvin, 37
Kallman, Robert, 98–99, 100, 125, 215, 266, 267, 271
Kalom, Anuta Brilliant, 20, 21, 22, 29, 31, 35, 36
Kalom, Arnold, 35
Kalom, Benjamin, 21, 29, 35, 36
Kalom, Henry, 35
Kalom, Lawrence, 35
Kalom, Lucille, 35–36
Kalom, Seymour, 35
Kaplan, Ann (daughter): birth, 101; career, 309, 372; childhood, 122–24, 170–73, 175, 259; education, 257, 309; HSK's cancer and, 378, 380–81, 393, 394, 396; marriage, 309; photograph of, 134 (fig.)
Kaplan, Henry: birth and childhood, 30–37, 174; dating, 53, 54; death, 396, 397; deformed fingers, 3, 31, 75, 94, 156, 225–26; education, 34–35, 36–37, 50, 51–52, 53; infertility due to radiation exposure, 97–98, 101; interest in science, 36–37, 55; last months of life, 385–96; letters to mother, 73–74, 75–76;

lung cancer of, 374–75, 376–85; medical education, 54–56, 61–63, 379; as patient, 376–77, 380–84; personality, 4, 140, 158, 211; photographs of, 133 (fig.), 134 (fig.), 135 (fig.), 340 (fig.), 344 (fig.), 346 (fig.); physical appearance, 3, 33, 313; political views and involvement, 37, 223–27, 268, 327–38, 373–74, 387; relationship with brother, 33–34, 53, 73–74, 169–70, 173, 372; relationship with father, 32, 40; relationship with mother, 31–32, 34, 40, 50, 53–54, 72–73, 169, 170, 371, 373; travel, 168–69, 171, 172, 258–59, 326, 332–37, 374–75; at twenty-year celebration, 3, 5–6, 9–10; work in family pharmacy, 51

Kaplan, Henry, career: accomplishments, 4, 398; assistance to scientists in other countries, 326–38, 373; awards and honors, 168, 257, 387; books written, 196, 257, 276; drive to cure cancer, 4, 41, 65, 109, 231, 255–56, 267, 313, 369; effects on family, 123–24, 169–78, 259, 308; international conferences, 159–67, 253–54, 255, 256, 359–60; legacy, 210, 387–88, 398; medical career plans, 35, 55; in Minnesota, 65, 75–77; organizational involvement, 168, 188–89, 231–33, 234–36, 373; reputation, 97, 101–2, 162–63, 166, 168, 172, 322; research goals, 75; sabbaticals, 172, 196, 296; teaching skills, 77; at Yale, 77–78. *See also* Cancer Biology Research Laboratory; Stanford University School of Medicine

Kaplan, Henry and Leah, marriage of: children, 97–98, 101, 122–24, 170–78, 257, 259, 309–11; courtship and engagement, 56–57, 58, 60–65; early years, 71–75, 76; friends, 74, 78, 123, 139, 158, 174, 212; homes in California, 122–23, 212; relationship, 72–73, 76, 171, 257, 308, 394; wedding, 64–65

Kaplan, Jeannette (grandmother), 29

Kaplan, Leah Lebeson (wife): childhood, 58–60; education, 60, 61, 71, 72, 78; family, 56, 58, 60; on Glaser, 213–14; HSK's cancer and, 377, 380–81, 384, 386, 393, 396; personality, 56–57, 61; photographs of, 133 (fig.), 134 (fig.), 344 (fig.); psychiatric social work career, 78, 88, 171, 225, 257, 308–9; relationship with mother-in-law, 63, 72–73, 173; travel, 88–89, 169, 374–75; at twenty-year celebration, 9. *See also* Kaplan, Henry and Leah, marriage of

Kaplan, Motell (grandfather), 29, 33

Kaplan, Nathan Morris (father): death, 40–41, 49; dental practice, 34; family, 29; health problems, 38–40, 376; marriage, 29–30, 37–38; personality, 29, 37; photograph of, 132 (fig.); relationship with HSK, 32, 40

Kaplan, Paul (son): birth, 101; childhood, 122–24, 170–78, 259; Coleman and, 394; dyslexia, 175–76, 309, 310; education, 309, 311; as film maker, 309; on grandmother, 371, 372, 373; HSK's cancer and, 378, 380–81, 393–94, 396; as photographer, 257, 309–11; photographs of, 134 (fig.), 136 (fig.); relationship with HSK, 310–11, 394

Kaplan, Richard (brother): birth, 32; career, 73–74, 170, 372; childhood, 32–33, 35, 38–39, 40–41, 49, 50, 51; education, 73, 170; Leah and, 63; on Lebeson family, 60; marriage and children, 372; in Minneapolis, 73–74, 169–70; photographs of, 133 (fig.), 340 (fig.); relationship with HSK, 33–34, 53, 73–74, 169–70, 173, 372, 392–93; relationship with mother, 74, 372, 373

Kaplan, Sarah Brilliant (mother): childhood in Ukraine, 20–21, 22, 30; death, 372–73; drugstore management, 50–51, 53–54, 224; family, 20–21, 35–36; grandchildren and, 173; life in Chicago, 28–34; marriage, 29–30, 37–38; in old age, 371–72; personality, 29–30, 31, 173; photographs of, 132 (fig.), 340 (fig.); physical appearance, 29; political views, 224; relationship with HSK, 31–32, 34, 40, 50, 53–54, 72–73, 169, 170, 371, 373; relationship with Leah, 63, 72–73, 173; relationship with Richard, 74, 372, 373;

stroke, 173; widowhood, 49–50; work in pharmacies, 30, 38–39
Kaplan Pharmacy, 50–51, 53–54, 63, 224
Karnofsky, David, 84, 85, 187, 188, 201, 258
Katz, Joe, 50
Katz, Rose, 33, 50, 51
Kaufman-Darmady, Dianne, 388
Kaufmann, Paul, 388
Keatinge, Leila, 44
Kennedy, Donald, 3, 308
Kennedy, Edward, 234
Kinmoth, J. B., 141
Kirkman, Gladie, 377–78
Kirkman, Hadley, 377–78
Kirschbaum, Arthur, 75–77
Klystron, 114, 116, 121
Koch, Robert, 314
Koch's postulates, 314
Köhler, Georges, 364–65
Korean War, 139
Korman, John, 388
Korn, David, 262, 263, 265, 269–70, 271–72
Kornberg, Arthur, 174; dean selection issue and, 213, 215–16; Nobel Prize, 213; recruitment by Stanford, 127–28, 129, 211, 265; relationship with HSK, 212, 213, 220, 221, 386; at Stanford, 129, 212, 220, 263
Kovalev, Sergey, 374
Kretchmer, Norman, 212, 213, 215–16, 221
Krikorian, John, 295
Kriss, Joseph, 215, 225

Laden, Ed, 62
Laennec, René, 13
Laminar airflow rooms, 282–83, 347–49, 351–52
Landers, Ann, 235
Lane, Levi Cooper, 86–87
Lane Hospital, 87–88, 92
Lasker, Albert, 228, 229, 230
Lasker, Mary, 228–34, 235, 236–37
Lasker Foundation, 229
Lauritsen, Charles, 111–12
Lawrence, Mary Brown, 387. *See also* Brown, Mary

Lebeson, Harry, 58, 59–60, 63–64, 65, 72, 173, 174
Lebeson, Leah, *see* Kaplan, Leah Lebeson
Lebeson, Sarah Greenberg, 58, 59
Lebeson, Shirley, 58, 61, 62, 64, 73, 133 (fig.), 173
Lederberg, Joshua, 211, 212, 213, 215–16, 220, 221, 262–67
Legion of Honor, 168
Leibler, Bob, 52
Leukemia: caused by radiation, 152–53, 246, 276; chemotherapy, 7, 180, 182; childhood, 182, 185–86, 320; in former Hodgkin's disease patients, 295–96; Gallo's research, 319–21; research on genesis of, in mice, 75–77, 78, 100, 242–43, 245–47, 312; spread, 78; viral causes in animals, 243, 245–47, 373
Levine, Arthur, 349
Levy, Ron, 368
Liberia, 374
Lieberman, Miriam, 246–47, 314, 323, 373
Linear accelerators: development, 111–14; electrons produced, 124; medical, 5, 114–21; at Stanford, 110, 114–15
Linn, Irwin, 52, 53
Linn, Mirielle Fein, 52, 53
Linn, Robert, 52, 53
Lipchitz, Jacques, *Song of the Vowels*, 346 (fig.), 387
Lister, Joseph, 14
Lithium, 347–48
Liwski, Norberto, 330
Lobe, Kenneth, 105
London: Guy's Hospital, 12, 13–14, 17, 23; St. Thomas's Hospital, 12
Lorenz, Egon, 79
Louis B. Mayer Foundation, 316
Low-Beer, Gerald, 332–37
Loyalty oaths, 225
Lukes, Robert, 160, 161, 164, 167
Lung cancer: causes, 379–80; of HSK, 374–75, 376–85; of Nathan Kaplan, 40, 376
Lungs, side effects of radiation, 192, 379–80

Lyman, Richard, 267, 268
Lymphangiography, 141, 161, 196–98, 250
Lymphomas: antibodies against, 370;
    Burkitt's, 316–19; cell lines, 315, 323;
    chemotherapy, 180, 297–98; in former
    Hodgkin's disease patients, 295; HSK's
    research on, 312–13; mycosis fungoi-
    des, 209–10; non-Hodgkin's, 280, 312,
    315; research in mice, 242–43, 312;
    Rosenberg's research on, 139; search for
    virus causing, 313, 314–16; viruses linked
    to, 316–18. *See also* Hodgkin's disease
Lymphoma staging conferences, 141–42,
    143–44, 146, 158, 272, 374
Lymphoma Task Force, 189

Madres de la Plaza de Mayo (Mothers of
    the Plaza de Mayo), 334, 337
Magnetrons, 114, 115, 121
Mark, James, 377, 379, 380–81
Marriage, *see* Kaplan, Henry and Leah,
    marriage of
Mathé, Gerald, 181
Mattick, Walter, 69
Mayer, Louis B., 316
Mayer Cancer Biology Research
    Laboratory, *see* Cancer Biology
    Research Laboratory
Mayo Clinic, 39
McBain, Earle, 118
McClosky, Herb, 170, 174, 225
McDougall, Ross, 384
MD Anderson Cancer Center, 188, 226,
    261, 262
Medical education: of HSK, 54–56, 61–63,
    379; Hodgkin's reform efforts, 14;
    quotas for Jewish students, 52, 138; at
    Stanford, 87–88, 129, 212
Medical linear accelerators: British, 115–
    16, 121; cautious views, 119–20; develop-
    ment, 5, 114–21; facilities, 117–18; first
    patient, 118–19, 121; maneuverability,
    116–17; production, 121; standards and
    training, 121. *See also* Linear accelera-
    tors
Medinger, Fred, 69

Memorial Center for Cancer and Allied
    Diseases, 139
Memorial Hospital, New York City, 69,
    82–83, 84, 106, 140, 201, 231
Memorial Sloan-Kettering Cancer Center,
    167, 187, 231, 261
Meningitis, 300, 301, 304
Meredith, W. J., 121
Methotrexate, 186
MF, *see* Mycosis fungoides
Mice: C57 blacks, 78, 94, 242–43, 246–47,
    387; cancer research using, 244–47, 312;
    monoclonal antibodies, 364–65; mu-
    rine leukemia virus, 245–47, 373; re-
    search at Stanford, 94, 100, 245–47, 373;
    research on genesis of leukemia, 75–77,
    78, 100, 242–43, 246–47, 312
Michael Reese Hospital, Chicago, 62, 97,
    115, 121, 379
Midler, Jack, 249
Mignone, Emilio, 334
Miller, C. W., 121
Miller, Daniel, 167
Milstein, César, 364–65
Minna, John, 383
Minneapolis, Kaplans in, 65, 71–77,
    169–70
Misetich, Antonio, 328
MOMP chemotherapy, 186–87, 190
Mononucleosis, infectious, 239, 241–42
Montefiore, Moses, 18–19
MOPP chemotherapy: for children,
    208–9; clinical trials, 8, 187–90, 201–3,
    274, 284, 285–86; compared to other
    treatments, 285–86, 356, 360; develop-
    ment, 7, 179, 189–90; drugs, 179–81, 187;
    nonoverlapping toxicities, 180; remis-
    sion rates, 179; toxicity, 194, 195, 201–2,
    284; use at Stanford, 193, 201–3, 208–9.
    See also Chemotherapy
Moxley, Jack, 186, 187, 188, 190
Murine leukemia virus (MuLV), 245–47,
    373
Murray-Vidal, Mary, 7–8, 199–203, 342
    (fig.)
Musshoff, Karl, 253, 385

Mustard gas, 80–85, 179–80
Mycosis fungoides (MF), 209–10

Narodick, Benjamin, 37
National Academy of Sciences Committee on Human Rights, 332, 373
National Cancer Act, 228, 233–36, 237, 253, 261
National Cancer Institute (NCI): bureaucracy, 230; cancer in former Hodgkin's disease patients, 275–79, 295; chemotherapy research, 167, 179, 180, 185–90; DeVita as director, 322, 351, 362, 389; HSK and, 79, 86, 90, 168, 227; Hodgkin's disease treatment, 254, 275–79; human tumor virus research, 316, 319–21, 322–23; laminar airflow room, 282–83, 347–49, 351–52; leukemia research, 185; lung cancer program, 383; relationship with other NIH branches, 233; research funding, 232, 236; Rye Conference funding, 163; structure, 236; support of International Cancer Congress, Buenos Aires, 331. *See also* Cancer centers
National Institutes of Health (NIH), 115, 116, 121, 184, 230–31, 236
National Panel of Consultants on the Conquest of Cancer, 230–33, 234, 235–36, 262, 264
National Research Council, 83
NCI, *see* National Cancer Institute
Nelsen, Thomas, 141, 198, 200
Neto, António Agostinho, 327
Nigarada, Susie, 99
NIH, *see* National Institutes of Health
Nitrogen mustard, 83–85, 167, 179–80, 187, 194
Nixon, Richard, 222–23, 228, 234–35, 236
Nobel Prize winners, 45, 129, 130, 213, 244
Noble, R. L., 180
Non-Hodgkin's lymphoma, 280, 312, 315. *See also* Lymphomas
Nossal, G. J., 206

O'Hara, Maureen: HSK's cancer and, 379, 381, 395–96; patients of, 194–95, 292, 297, 298; at twenty-year celebration, 1–3, 9
Oliphant, Mark, 114
Olsson, Lennart, 365–68, 369
Oncology, *see* Cancer; Rosenberg, Saul
Oncovin, *see* Vincristine
Ophuls, William, 87
Owen, Freda, 175–76

Pack, George, 166
Packard, David, 126
Palo Alto, California: City Council, 125–26; Stanford Medical School relocation to, 117, 122, 124–28, 130
Palo Alto-Stanford Hospital Center, 125–26, 128, 218
Panel of Consultants, *see* National Panel of Consultants
Paragranuloma, 67, 161
Paris, Hôpital Necker, 13
Paris conference, 159–63, 168
Parker, Frederic, 67–68
Parrilli, Marcelo, 338
Pathologic classifications, Hodgkin's disease, 67, 161, 164
Pathologists, 141, 160, 164, 197, 253, 263
Patients, HSK's relations with: assistance for, 172; bedside manner, 32, 55, 147, 148–49, 155–56, 200, 202, 205–6, 274, 291, 356; letters from, 397; reaction to deaths, 298, 307, 308; reaction to second cancers, 296. *See also* Clinical trials
PAVe chemotherapy, 284–86, 292
Pediatric Hodgkin's disease, 207–9, 398. *See also* Children
Pel, Pieter Klaases, 24
Pendleton, Christine, 3, 145–48, 339 (fig.), 388
Pendleton, Red, 3, 145
Peter Bent Brigham Hospital, 139
Peters, Vera: honors, 255; at international conferences, 160–61, 162, 165, 167, 253, 254; keynote address at Ann Arbor Conference, 249, 250, 251; life, 104–5; personality, 103–4; photograph of, 134 (fig.); relationship with HSK, 109, 248–49, 255; research, 103, 105–9, 144,

160–61, 162, 255; staging process, 252; staging systems, 106, 109, 164, 165, 250, 251, 253; treatment of Hodgkin's disease, 70, 105–6, 108, 162, 165; view of HSK, 163; view of Rosenberg, 165
Philips, Frederick, 82
Picket-fence fever, 24
Pitzer, Kenneth, 222–23
Pizzo, Phil, 347–48, 351, 352–53
Pneumococcus, 302, 303, 305, 307
Podwalny, Misha, 354, 355, 358, 359
Podwalny, Sergey (Gary), 354, 355, 363
Podwalny, Wendy, 344 (fig.), 354–56, 357–59, 363
Portlock, Carol, 272, 273, 296, 298
Prednisone, 181, 186, 187, 194
President's Commission on the Accident at Three Mile Island, 373
Procarbazine, 187, 194, 285
Pseudoleukemia, 24–25, 47. *See also* Hodgkin's disease
Pusey, William, 46

Quakers, 11, 18

Radar, 113–14
Radiation: atomic bomb survivors and, 152–53, 276; gamma rays, 112–13; infertility due to exposure, 97–98, 101, 152, 153, 357, 363; measurements of dose, 48, 68, 112; risks of exposure, 47, 97–98, 106–7, 152–53, 276, 315–16, 380; virus activation, 246, 247
Radiation leukemia virus (RadLV), 247
Radiation therapy: cancer treatment, 46, 48, 112, 118–19, 124, 218; development, 45–48, 68–70; dosimetry, 68, 112; effects on radiologists and researchers, 47, 97–98, 106–7, 152, 276; equipment, 47–48, 68, 92–94, 111, 112, 115; fields, 69; linear accelerators and, 114–21; for lung cancer, 382, 383–84; prophylactic, 69–70, 108, 142, 143, 146, 162, 165, 166–67; research, 68–70; rotational, 68; safety standards, 97–98; seed implantation, 218; total body irradiation, 69, 76; toxicity, 47, 48, 68, 70, 276. *See also*
Clinical trials; Hodgkin's disease treatment, radiotherapy
Radicchi, Annunziata, 154–56, 191, 193, 194, 294, 297, 298
Radicchi, Joey, 154–56, 191–93, 194–95, 294–95, 297–98, 340 (fig.)
Radicchi, Nello, 154, 191, 194
Radiology Department, Stanford, *see* Stanford University School of Medicine, HSK as Radiology Department head
Radiotherapy, *see* Radiation therapy
RadLV, *see* Radiation leukemia virus
Radon, 379–80
Rall, Dave, 184
Rappaport, Henry, 164, 249, 330–31
Rauscher, Frank, 348
Reagan, Ronald, 397
Reed, Dorothy, 24–27, 42, 67, 131 (fig.)
Reed-Sternberg cells, 26–27, 67
Regaud, Claude, 48
Research, *see* Cancer Biology Research Laboratory; Cancer research; Clinical trials; Hodgkin's disease research
Retinoblastoma, 118–19
Reverse transcriptase, 320, 321, 323
Rich, Clayton, 267, 268, 270
Richards, Gordon, 105–7, 108, 165
Rigler, Leo, 65, 88, 90, 98
Roberto (infant patient), 207–8
Robinson, J. Eugene, 99
Roentgen, Wilhelm, 44–45
Roentgen rays, *see* X-rays
Rogers, Paul, 235–36
Rooney, Vera, 53
Rosdahl, Nils, 242
Rose, Glen, 37
Rosenberg, Saul: arrival at Stanford, 137, 139–40; bedside manner, 139–40, 155; Cancer Research Center Planning Committee, 262–67; cancer treatment by, 203, 382; career, 138–39, 249–50, 390–91; chemotherapy treatments, 284–86, 292, 297–98, 357–59, 360–63; clinical trial designs, 284, 285–86, 357–59; contiguous spread theory, 165–66, 199, 204, 250; education, 137–38;

family, 137; HSK's cancer and, 379, 382, 390–91, 395; at international conferences, 161–62, 164–65, 167, 249–50, 252–55; marriage, 139; patients of, 193, 203, 294–95, 297–98; personality, 140; photographs of, 339 (fig.), 342 (fig.), 345 (fig.); physical appearance, 7, 140; relationship with DeVita, 362; relationship with HSK, 5, 6–7, 139–40, 143–44, 157–58, 193, 255, 262, 266–67, 270, 272–73, 391; relations with patients, 7, 154–55, 156, 157; research approach, 368; sabbaticals, 281; second cancers in patients, 277–79, 296; staging process, 142, 161–62, 197, 198, 250, 252–54; at twenty-year celebration, 3, 5, 6–7, 9
Rosenberg, Shirley Strahl, 139
Roswell Park Cancer Institute, 261
Rous, Francis Peyton, 243–44
Rush Medical College, 54–56, 61–62
Russia, Jews in, 20–22, 29, 58. *See also* Soviet Union
Rye Classification, 164
Rye Conference, 163–67, 248, 251

Sagan, Ginetta, 327, 338, 387
St Jude's Children's Hospital, 206
Sakharov, Andrei, 374
Salk, Jonas, 229
San Francisco: Kaplans' visit, 88–89; University of the Pacific, 86. *See also* Stanford University School of Medicine
Sarcoma, 67, 161
Sausalito, California, 122–23
Schimke, Robert, 262, 263, 266, 270
Schmidt, Benno, 231, 232, 233–34
Schreiner, Bernard, 69
Schwartzenberg, Leon, 332–37
Schweisguth, Odile, 206
Seldin, Don, 78
Senn, Nicholas, 46–47
Sepsis, 302
Shapiro, Dan, 7
Shingles, 108, 192, 292, 299, 319
Shumway, Norman, 271
Siebert, Dean, 185

Skin cancer, 47, 209–10, 275
Skipper, Howard, 182, 190
SMCP, *see* Stanford Medical Community for Peace
Smith, Homer, 184
Smith, Kendric, 99
Smithers, David: concerns about staging laparotomies, 252; debate on spread of Hodgkin's disease, 165; on HSK, 162–63, 166; at international conferences, 160, 248, 252, 253, 254; research, 121, 241
Society of Friends (Quakers), 11, 18
Soiland, Albert, 111–12
Song of the Vowels (Lipchitz), 346 (fig.), 387
Soviet Union, 226, 373–74
Spears, Ann Kaplan, *see* Kaplan, Ann
Spears, Robert, 309
Spleen: HSK's research on, 305–6, 365–66; infection prevention role, 302; involvement in Hodgkin's disease, 197; seen as nonessential, 197, 300
Splenectomies: increased risk of infection, 300–307; spleens used in research, 365–66; during staging laparotomies, 196, 197, 198–99, 200–201, 250, 252, 254, 300, 301
Splenosis, 305
SS *John Harvey*, 80–82
Staging, of Hodgkin's disease: Ann Arbor system, 254–55, 256; clinical assessment, 197, 198; exploratory laparotomies, 197; importance for treatment, 44; influence on survival, 66, 106, 108; international negotiations on system, 164–65, 249, 250–51, 253; Peters's system, 106, 109, 164, 165; procedures, 252–54; Rosenberg's role, 142, 161–62, 197, 198, 250, 252–54; Stanford system, 142, 164–65, 250; TNM system, 250, 251, 253
Staging conferences, 141–42, 143–44, 146, 158, 272, 374
Staging laparotomies: concerns about, 5–6, 302; debates on, 198–99, 252; routine use, 254, 302; splenectomies, 196, 197, 198–99, 200–201, 250, 252, 254, 300, 301; use at Stanford, 5–6, 196, 200–201, 305

Stanford Medical Community for Peace
(SMCP), 224
Stanford University: anti-war protests,
222–24, 287; board of trustees, 125–26;
Ann Kaplan as student, 257, 309; Leah
Kaplan as assistant dean, 308–9; linear
accelerators, 110, 114–21
Stanford University Hospital, 136 (fig.);
architecture, 129–30, 220, 268; joint
ownership with Palo Alto, 125–26,
128, 218; Lipchitz sculpture, 346 (fig.),
387; location, 130; protest by minority
employees, 267–68; research patients,
261–62
Stanford University School of Medicine:
anti-war protests, 223–24, 327–28;
cancer center issue, 262–67, 268–72,
274, 311; clinical care, 214–16, 261–62;
curriculum, 129, 212; deans, 87,
101, 125, 128–29, 217–21, 267; Dean's
Selection Committee, 213–17; Executive
Committee, 218–19, 220, 223, 269, 270;
facilities and equipment, 218; faculty,
87, 94–95, 101, 125, 126–28, 129, 130,
211–13, 219, 262; faculty recruiting,
127–28, 211–12, 263, 265; history, 86–87;
hospitals in San Francisco, 87–88, 92,
94–95; medical service plan, 214–16,
218; Nobel Prize winners, 129, 130, 213;
organizational structure, 264–65; relocation to Palo Alto, 117, 122, 124–28, 130;
research funding, 214; research orientation, 87, 129, 130, 211; rounds, 94–95,
205, 390. *See also* Cancer Biology
Research Laboratory; Hodgkin's disease treatment, at Stanford
Stanford University School of Medicine,
HSK as Radiology Department head:
cancer center goal, 262–67, 268–72, 273,
274; changes made, 89–90, 93, 98–100;
clinical service, 93, 98, 99, 261–62; conflicts with deans, 126, 127, 128, 217–21;
criticism, 120; dean selection issue and,
216–17; early years, 89–97, 98–102; facilities, 88, 92–94, 98, 99–100; focus on
work, 94, 100–101, 123–24; goals, 90–91,
98; grants, 93, 116, 118; laboratory,
93–94, 99–100, 124, 312–13; medical
linear accelerator, 5, 116–19, 124; move
to main university campus, 124–28;
recruitment, 86, 87–91; reputation as
dean killer, 128, 215, 308; research, 100,
305–6, 312–13, 368; resignation, 269;
second cancers in patients, 297; staff,
93, 98–100, 246–47; students and trainees, 2, 129, 171–72, 205–7, 210, 272–73,
326, 368, 386–87. *See also* Colleagues;
Hodgkin's disease treatment, at
Stanford; Patients
Sterling, Wallace, 124, 214
Sternberg, Carl, 25, 26–27
Stone, Edward, 129–30, 220
Strober, Sam, 350, 373
Strong, Lionel, 77
Students and trainees, 2, 129, 171–72,
205–7, 210, 272–73, 326, 368, 386–87
Surgery: exploratory laparotomies, 197;
Hodgkin's disease treatment, 42, 141,
166. *See also* Splenectomies; Staging
laparotomies

Temin, Howard, 320, 331
Teng, Nelson, 367–68, 369–70, 373, 378
Tepper, Marty, 388
Terman, Frederick, 127–28
Teschendorf, Werner, 69
Thomas, Danny, 206
Three Mile Island, 373
Thymus gland, 100, 243, 247
Thyroid, effects of neck irradiation, 108
Tissue culture techniques, 315
Tizard, Henry, 113
TLI, *see* Total lymphoid irradiation
Toronto General Hospital, 105
Total body irradiation, 69, 76
Total lymphoid irradiation (TLI): clinical
trials, 6, 151–58, 162, 191, 201–3, 285–86,
357, 363; combined with chemotherapy,
201–3, 285–86; concerns about, 6, 166;
effects on immune system, 152, 350, 352,
353; introduction, 6, 151–52, 162; low-
dose, 191
Trace, Herb, 34
Trainees, *see* Students and trainees

Tran Khanh Tuyet, 3, 287–88, 289–90, 291, 299, 300, 303, 304, 343 (fig.)
Tuberculosis, 25–26
Tubiana, Maurice: Donaldson and, 206–7; on HSK, 163, 255; at international conferences, 159–60, 161, 251, 252, 253; relationship with HSK, 248; staging systems and, 165
Tuftsin, 305–6
Tumor immunology, 364–70
Tumor virology, 243–47

Uhlmann, Eric, 115, 121
UICC, *see* International Union Against Cancer
Ultmann, John, 189
University of Chicago, 50, 51–52, 53, 61, 73, 84
University of Chicago High School, 37, 60
University of Edinburgh, 13
University of Michigan, *see* Ann Arbor Conference
University of Minnesota, 65, 66, 70, 71, 73, 75–77, 88, 106, 170
University of the Pacific, 86
University of Toronto, 104
Uranium mining, 379–80
Uris, Leon, 388
Utz, Leslie, 44

Vaccines, 43–44, 305, 370
Van Bekkum, Dirk, 332–37
Varian Associates, 121
VBM chemotherapy, 357–59, 360–63
Velban, 285, 356, 357, 358, 363
Vianna, Nicholas, 238, 240–41
Vidal, Elie, 199, 200, 201–2, 203
Videla, Jorge, 329, 334
Vietnam, volunteers in, 287–89
Vietnam War, 286–87; anti-war protests, 222–24, 227, 287, 327–28; Tet offensive, 288
Vincristine, 180, 186, 187, 194, 195
Viruses: Epstein-Barr, 241–42, 319, 322; Human Leukemia 23, 321; human tumor, 313, 314–16, 318–25; infections caused by, 243; linked to cancer, 243–46; linked to lymphoma, 316–18; murine leukemia, 245–47, 373; radiation leukemia, 247; woolly monkey, 321, 322–23
Von Essen, Carl, 115, 124

Wallhauser, Andrew, 43
Weissbluth, Mitchell, 118–19
Weizmann Institute, 169, 177, 178, 258, 385
Westcott, Thomas, 15
Western Reserve University, 137–39
Whitehead, J. M., 43
Wilbur, Ray Lyman, 87
Wilks, Samuel, 23–24
William and Mary, College of, 183–84
Williams, Mary, 60
Wilson, Hugh, 88, 90, 91
Wilson, John, 219, 223, 267
World War I, 81–82
World War II, 74–75, 80–81, 113–14, 137–38, 179–80

X-rays: discovery, 44–45; therapeutic potential, 45–48. *See also* Radiation

Yale University, 77–78, 82, 88
Yarborough, Ralph, 230–31, 234
Yard, Florence, 53
Yates, J. L., 42
Young, Stuart, 379

Zatz, Les, 377
Zelesnick, Gabriel, 238–39, 241